The Rand McNally Encyclopedia of
Transportation

The Rand McNally

Encyclopedia of Transportation

Rand McNally & Company
Chicago

Photo credits
Aerofilms; Aeronutronic Ford Corporation; Aldus Books;
Association of American Railroads; Bailey-Watson & Associates
Ltd; Barnaby's Picture Library; Bay Area Rapid Transit;
P. Brierley; British Aircraft Corporation; British Airport Authority;
British Airways; British Petroleum Company Ltd; British Railways
Board; Camera Press; Canadaire Ltd; Dallas Chamber of Com-
merce; Dunlop; English Electric Company Ltd; Mary Evans Picture
Library; FIAT; Ford Motor Company Ltd; Foster-Wheeler Power
Products; French Railways Ltd; General Motors Ltd; Grumman;
Hawker Siddeley Aviation Ltd; R. Hunt Library; Imperial War
Museum; Interfoto NTI; Keystone Press Agency Ltd; Lancia;
Leyland Motors Ltd; London Transport Authority; Marconi In-
ternational Marine Company Ltd; Mercedes-Benz (UK) Ltd; NASA;
National Maritime Museum; National Motor Museum; Novosti Press
Agency; Opel; R. Piaggio; P. Popper Ltd; Port Authority of NY & NJ;
Radio Times Hulton Picture Library; Bruce Robertson; Rolls-Royce;
Science Museum; Skyfotos; Rodney Steel; D.R. Stiess; Triborough
Bridge & Tunnel Authority; Union Pacific Railroad and Company;
US Army; USIS; US Navy; Westland Aircraft Ltd; D. Whiting;
Willerby Caravan Company Ltd.

First United States publication 1976 by Rand McNally & Company,
Chicago
Copyright © 1976 by Reference International Publishers Limited

Printed in the United States of America.

ISBN 0-528-81050-2

LCCN 76-3364

Foreword

Modern industrial society depends for its very existence on the rapid and efficient movement of people and goods. The transportation revolution which has made the development of this society possible has taken place in the span of just 150 years. The evolution of our present modes of travel has thus been rapid, but it has left vast areas still almost untouched. There are, for example, some 200 million automobiles in use thoughout the world, but over 90% of them are in the countries of North America, Western Europe and Japan. There are other curious features as well. Although transportation is one of the principal technologies of our civilization, it would be interesting to speculate on the percentage of passenger-miles still traveled on foot or on the simplest of man's transportation aids, animals and bicycles. It even remains true that in parts of the world a man may be born into the stone age and progress in his lifetime through thousands of years of transportation history to pilot a supersonic airplane.

The advance of transportation before the Industrial Revolution has owed something to the life style of various cultures as well as to their level of economic development and technical capability.

The invention of the wheel some 6,000 years ago, for example, represented a notable advance, but the Incas and other American Indian civilizations managed very successfully without it.

In ancient times the Romans developed land transportation to a peak of efficiency, largely by virtue of their remarkable network of roads. But with the decline of the Empire the roads decayed and were not replaced, and for some 1,500 years advances in transportation by land were limited to marginal improvements to such features as harnessing and wagon suspensions.

At sea, however, the situation was very different. Ancient peoples made some remarkable voyages in the interests of trade and exploration. The Phoenicians are reputed to have sailed around Africa in 600 BC, while some 1,500 years later Polynesians crossed the Pacific to New Zealand, and Vikings took their long boats across the Atlantic to North America. Remarkable as they were, these voyages were limited in their implications for society and the world in general. By contrast, the great voyages of discovery of the 15th and 16th centuries, made possible by the development of more effective rigs, stronger construction and greater size, vastly extended man's horizons, his knowledge of the world, and his contact with other cultures. The growth of sea transportation brought increased and wider trade and communication, and it brought long-distance sea warfare and colonization.

Technologically this revolution in transportation by sea was complete by about 1600. Thereafter there were no significant advances in shipping for nearly 200 years, when man's impatience and competitive instincts led to the creation of the clipper ships. Sailing over twice as fast as earlier freighters, clippers transported valuable cargoes across oceans, and they carried determined prospectors to the gold rushes in California and Australia. But their day was short, because by then the modern mechanical world had arrived. Steam power had been invented, and was to bring an uprecedented revolution in transportation at sea and on land.

At first sight it seems strange that developments on land had to wait so long. Wealthy people lived in style and comfort at home; they had ingenious and delicate machinery (in clocks and watches, for example), yet they accepted appalling roads and primitive methods of travel as a matter of course, despite the fact that increase in business and trade made improved transportation highly deisrable. Canals were improved and extended for carrying heavy bulk freight, and down the mines wagon-ways (simple railroads) were laid to simplify the movement of coal and ore through the mine, and to the canal. But the roads and road vehicles were in some respects worse than those of the Romans. The problem of course was a source of motive power, and a national policy of road building. The latter was first undertaken in France, leading to an improvement in the speed and comfort of animal-powered travel, and giving an incidental stimulus to the surprisingly late development of the bicycle. The driving chain was not invented until the mid-19th century, but complex systems of gears existed much earlier and might easily have led to an effective bicycle design. It may be that those who could have afforded them would not have appreciated having to power their own conveyances.

Steam power was first employed in driving pumps. Various attempts were made to adapt the Newcomen engine for transportation on water and land, with little success as the engine was excessively heavy, bulky and inefficient. Though by the end of the 18th century the steam engine had been sufficiently improved to power boats and road vehicles, the fact aroused astonishingly little interest or enthusiasm. People were either indifferent to limitations in existing modes of travel, or they were suspicious of the new invention, or indeed hostile towards it. Fortunately there were those who were more adventurous, or had more foresight, and by the 1830s steam power had led to the creation of freight and passenger railroads. These opened up the interior of North America, accelerated the pace of industrial growth, and ultimately revolutionized society. For the first time land transportation was capable of hauling considerable loads at what were then considered shattering speeds. By the same period steamboats and ships were gaining acceptance, while steam-powered road vehicles had been convincingly demonstrated, and equally convincingly rejected by the public (and by some governments).

Steam "automobiles" of the 1840s and 1850s were heavy and clumsy, but they worked and there was no technological disadvantage in steam power. Indeed during the first decade of the 20th century steam cars were in most respects superior to their gasoline-fueled rivals. In effect the automobile had been invented, and although it would later revolutionize society it was as yet unwanted. Curiously it was the sudden development and popularity of an unpowered and previously unpopular mode of transportation that prepared society for the 20th century revolution, namely the bicycle. By the time the internal combustion engine had been developed, and Benz and Daimler had constructed the first practical gasoline-engined automobiles, the bicycle craze of the 1870s and 1880s had created both interest and demand and the automobile era could commence. Thus while earlier inventors had given up through lack of incentive, Benz, Daimler and others established the automotive industry, Henry Ford began production of the Tin Lizzie, and for the first time in the world's history there was an effective means of powered personal transportation.

The development of the automobile engine led to a further revolutionary mode of travel, powered heavier-than-air flight. Leonardo da Vinci, among others, had suggested this idea. Sir George Cayley prepared the groundwork and convincingly demonstrated the possibility, and with the new gasoline engine the Wright Brothers turned the possibility into reality. Society was intrigued by this new invention, and enjoyed spectacular barnstorming shows, even if it failed to appreciate the airplane's potential. However, World War I served as a proving ground, by the start of World War II air transportation had grown from adventure to routine, and today is unrivaled for long distance travel. The great ocean liners have been forced to retire, and in the United States and elsewhere transcontinental trains are no longer commercially viable.

Statistics show remarkable differences in the use made of various modes of travel between one continent and another. On a world basis the percentages for automobile, bus, train, and air travel are 66.3, 16, 13.2, and 5.4 respectively. In North America the proportion of travel by automobile is over 85% (7.3% by air, 5.8% by bus, and less than 1% by train). In the Soviet Union automobile travel accounts for only 9.4%, with 44.4% by rail, 33.2% by bus, and a very high 13.1% by air. In Western Europe, where journeys are generally shorter, the proportion of travel by air is only 3.3%, whereas trains account for the high figure of 12.9%. At sea and on railroads the emphasis now is on bulk and specialization in freight transportation, and on speed for short or medium distance passenger routes: by 150 mph (240 km/h) gas turbine or electric trains on land, and by 40 to 80 mph (64 to 128 km/h) hydrofoils and air-cushion vehicles at sea. For the future, ram wing aircraft may combine the features and the advantages of air-cushion vehicles and airplanes for rapid bulk transport; giant airships may carry vast loads of freight across the oceans; nuclear-powered submarines may transport bulk cargoes under the Arctic, thus dramatically shortening certain sea routes; pipelines may be more widely used to transport non-liquid bulk; and magnetic levitation and the linear induction motor may transform urban and inter-urban mass transit systems.

In the air the jet age inaugurated in the 1950s by the de Havilland Comet and the Boeing 707 has been followed by the jumbo and now the supersonic age, and hypersonic flight is on the horizon. Space travel has been successfully pioneered, and the space shuttle promises to extend its potential. However the current preoccupation in air transportation, and on the highways, is with improved safety, adaptability, economy, automation, and freedom from pollution. Indeed it is arguable that mankind's headlong enthusiasm for ever greater size and speed has reached a peak, and it is certain that the startling rate at which the speed of travel has risen cannot continue. 150 years ago man's highest speed was that of a galloping horse. Today it has increased by a factor of over 1,500 to some 25,000 mph (40,230 km/h). Speed, then, seems to have reached a peak, while the popularity of air travel seems to have passed its peak. The value of earnings has dropped, and unless it rises again, or unless technology can lower the cost of flying (perhaps by the retrograde step of lowering speeds) ever fewer people will be able to benefit. Technology's concern over the next decades will be to make transportation cleaner, quieter, safer, less congested and less wasteful, to the extent that serious consideration is being given to a return to sailing ships for certain types of cargo.

This volume is unique in that for the first time it draws together under one cover a wealth of information on every important facet of transportation. As an encyclopedia, it provides the reader with a complete appreciation of all the technical complexities of the field; of the many and various and often indispensable roles that transportation plays in modern society; of the inventive genius behind the evolution of land, sea and air travel.

Included in the encyclopedia are details of the inner workings of almost every conceivable type of engine, from that of the smallest motorcycle to that of the most powerful jet aircraft. There are extensive articles on every mode of travel, and on associated topics such as bridges, tunnels, highways, and navigation. And there are accounts of their historical growth and possible future developments. A large number of biographical entries describe the people associated with the milestones of transportation: the inventors, pioneers, innovators, and record breakers. Other entries cover specific ships and airplanes, and the numerous topics and concepts involved in or connected with transportation, from the smallest components to broad areas such as associated industries and subjects (e.g. petrochemicals and oceanography).

Transportation is an extremely important and wide-ranging aspect of our total inventive achievement. An encyclopedic view of the subject is therefore long overdue. The reader interested in the technology of transportation will find the facts here in readily accessible form, while those interested in one particular aspect will be able to fit this knowledge into the field of transportation in its widest sense.

A1
A symbol denoting first class. It was used from 1775 in Lloyd's Register of Shipping to denote the highest class of wooden ships, well-built and in sound condition. For modern ships the Lloyd's symbol is 100A1.

A-4
The original designation given to the German rocket which became known as the V-2, *Vergeltungswaffe zwei* or vengeance weapon two (see V-2).

Accelerometer
An instrument which measures acceleration, an important component in INERTIAL GUIDANCE Systems. In its simplest form an accelerometer consists of a mass maintained in an equilibrium position by springs along an axis. The mass stays in this position if the body is at rest or in steady motion, but if the body experiences acceleration, the tension of the springs will alter, and this change can be detected electrically. A system of accelerometers measuring changes in velocity along three mutually perpendicular axes and mounted on a gyroscopically-stabilized frame is used to guide submarines and rockets.

Ackerman steering
The geometrically correct method of steering used in motor vehicles, in which the front wheels turn at slightly different angles while the axle itself remains fixed. They turn so that they follow a circular path around a common center, with the inner wheel turning at a somewhat sharper angle than the outer wheel, since it needs to describe a smaller circle. The system is named for the Anglo-German inventor Rudolph Ackermann, who patented the idea in 1818.

Additives
Compounds added to gasoline to improve combustion in the cylinders. The most common additive is tetraethyllead, which is added to improve the OCTANE rating of the gasoline and its antiknock characteristics (see KNOCKING). When leaded gasoline burns, lead oxide is formed, and to prevent this from being deposited inside the cylinder, other additives are included in the gasoline — ethylene dibromide and ethylene dichloride — which react with lead oxide and form volatile compounds that are swept away in the exhaust gases. These volatile lead compounds are some of the main pollutants emitted by the gasoline engine, and steps are being taken to reduce or eliminate the lead content in gasoline (see POLLUTION). A number of other additives are incorporated in small quantities, including antioxidant compounds to prevent the gasoline hydrocarbons from oxidizing or entering into combination with one another, and metal deactivators to reduce the susceptibility of the gasoline mixture to metallic contamination.

Advanced Passenger Train (APT)
An experimental high speed passenger train involving advanced technology which is currently undergoing extensive trials in Britain. The average speeds attained by ordinary express trains, no matter how powerful, is limited by curves and other track features. Consequently, any further increase would necessitate the re-laying of much of the track at considerable expense. The APT has a unique wheel mounting system that will enable it to negotiate the same curves at speeds 50% faster in complete safety and without the slightest discomfort to passengers.

These special wheel trucks respond to censors which continually monitor the lateral acceleration of the body of the train.

As the train passes over a curve they can give the body an extra tilt of up to 9° over that which is given by the normal cant of the track, thus counteracting the additional centrifugal force generated by the higher speeds. In addition, the APT concept embodies lightweight alloy stressed-skin construction to reduce axle loads and thus keep rail stresses and track maintenance costs to a minimum. Conventional friction brakes are replaced with hydrokinetic brakes mounted on each axle to provide additional braking power so that signaling distances can remain unchanged; power is derived from gas turbines or lightweight electric motors.

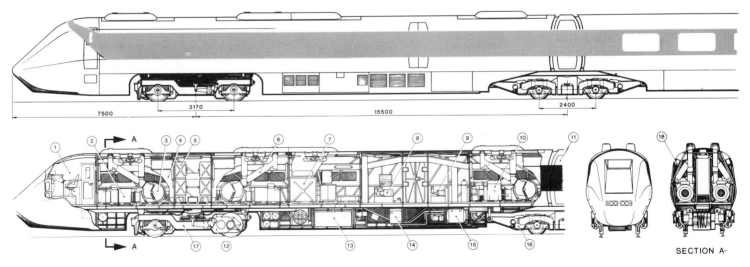

1. Driver's cab
2. Traction alternator & rectifier
3. Leyland gas turbine
4. Turbine air intake
5. Electrical control equipment
6. Exhaust silencer
7. Dynamic brake resistors
8. Body tilt system pack
9. Levelling system & brakes power pack
10. Auxiliary power alternator
11. Joint module
12. Traction motor
13. Fuel tank
14. Hydrokinetic brake radiator
15. Hydrokinetic brake reservoir
16. S.A. trailer bogie
17. E.I. power bogie
18. Combustion air filter

Cutaway diagrams of British Rail's Advanced Passenger Train (APT).

British Rail's Advanced Passenger Train (APT) is equipped with special tilting devices to enable it to negotiate curves at high speed without passenger discomfort. The APT can travel at up to 155 mph (250 km/h) on existing track, and will be used on British Rail's very successful Inter-City services.

The prototype experimental unit now undergoing trials has already sustained average speeds of over 150 mph (240 km/h). APTs will eventually replace conventional trains on all the main intercity routes throughout Britain, giving average speeds between city centers of at least 100 mph (160 km/h). The next generation of APTs, running on realigned tracks, will be capable of speeds up to 250 mph (400 km/h).
The U.S. Department of Transportation has expresed considerable interest in APT trains for the Northeast corridor route.

Aerobatics

The art or sport of executing rapid aerial maneuvers or assuming unorthodox flight attitudes, such as loops, rolls, and spins. Aerobatics has become an internationally organized sport, supervised by the Fédération Aéronautique Internationale.
In a loop the wings remain level throughout, control being exercised principally by the elevator. A slow roll is initiated

mainly with the ailerons, rotating the airplane around its longitudinal axis while the pilot keeps the nose aligned with a selected point on the horizon. Half-rolls and barrel rolls are variations on this. A stall turn is made by holding the nose up and using hard left or right rudder just before the stall to cartwheel the airplane into a steep dive. Spins occur when the wing drops at the stall and the aircraft yaws out of control (see STALLING). These basic aerobatics also underlie the maneuvers of aerial combat.

Aerodynamics

The behavior of air flowing around an airplane in flight is evaluated by the science of aerodynamics.
When an airplane moves through the air it generates pressure and friction. Pressure is greater below the machine than above it, providing LIFT through the medium of downwash. The total area of the AIRFRAME over which air passes (and thus produces friction) is known as the *wetted area.*
The corridor of disturbed air trailed along behind an airplane after its passage includes not only the lift-producing downwash, but also the SLIPSTREAM or jet efflux from the propulsive source, vortices emanating from the wing tips where air circulates from the high pressure area below the wing to the low pressure area above it, and a wake of air caught up by the airframe and dragged along by it causing drag. The latter may vary from perhaps one-thirtieth of the lift of a high-performance sailplane to one-fifth of the lift of a supersonic transport.
The aeronautical engineer seeks to ensure that every component part of an airframe is as aerodynamically efficient as possible without disrupting the airflow over adjacent parts of the machine. Hence fairings and fillets are employed at the junction of AIRFOIL surfaces with the fuselage to minimize the loss of lift that must inevitably take place at these points, although their presence increases the wetted area and hence skin friction drag.
The lift generated by a WING depends on the amount of air the airfoil displaces downwards. This is determined by the product of the distance flown and the span: a short-span wing has to travel further to generate a given amount of lift than a long-span wing.
In subsonic airplanes the fuselage in side elevation can be considered as a very low aspect ratio airfoil — its shape

The RAF Red Arrows team demonstrating high speed formation aerobatics. These maneuvers require a very high degree of precision, and include the famous "crossover" in which four planes cross at the center of the airfield at closing speeds of around 1,300 mph (2,092 km/h).

Setting up a scale model of an airplane in a wind tunnel for aerodynamic research on the behavior of air flowing past the plane.

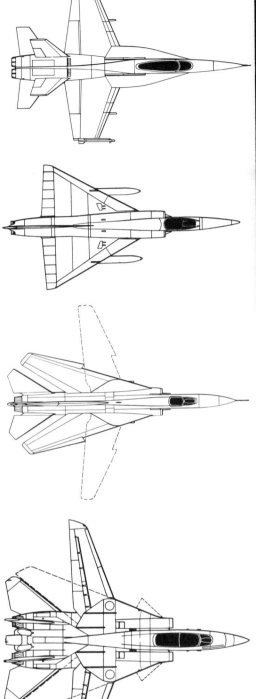

Four supersonic jet fighter airplanes, from top to bottom: the Northrop 600, with conventional fixed wings; the delta-wing Dassault Mirage; the variable geometry (swing wing) Mikoyan Flogger; and the swing wing Grumman Tomcat. Delta designs have proved very successful in overcoming the aerodynamic problems of supersonic flight, while swing wings combine the advantages of the delta at high speed with those of the conventional wing at low speeds. The Tomcat is unusual in having small retractable foreplanes (shown as dotted lines) which are extended as the main wing is swung back, thereby helping to balance the aerodynamic pressures on the plane.

is in fact comparable (on a much larger scale) to the wing sections used for subsonic flight. The wings do not usually form an integral aerodynamic entity with the fuselage and the resultant junctions between the components yield a large wetted area, but this configuration nonetheless provides efficient load-carrying characteristics providing the speed of sound is not approached.

For SUPERSONIC FLIGHT, however, the drag due to shock wave formation must be minimized. Fuselage shapes tend to resemble supersonic airfoil sections (long, thin and pointed) and may even incorporate camber to minimize loss of lift at the junctions with lifting surfaces. The amount of wetted area relative to the total wing area is reduced as much as possible. Since the circulation of air from below the wing to its upper surface is only influenced by the wing- and tail-tips in the disturbed air caused by *Mach cones* shed from these points, the inefficient portions of the airfoil surfaces are often cropped. In subsonic flight the flow of air around the tips influences the pressure distribution of the entire wing, and an elliptical planform is the most efficient layout for this performance envelope since it incurs minimum vortex drag and so gives a constant downwash across the span. Elliptical wings involve manufacturing complications, however.

The achievement of supersonic speed in level flight required a revised aerodynamic approach. Swept-wing aircraft that retained the orthodox relationship of wings and fuselage merely deferred the

onset of compressibility. To surpass the speed of sound and cruise at supersonic velocities it was necessary to evolve new design concepts (e.g. AREA RULE), and to re-proportion the airplane so that the entire airframe was kept within the Mach cone shed from the nose. As a result short-span, low aspect ratio wings were adopted, and the advantages of deltas became apparent: with sharply swept-back wings the lift can be maintained further forward in a delta than is possible on a more conventional machine, unless a special layout is used or the fuselage itself can be designed to provide lift. Swept wings of large span also encounter aero-elastic problems at high MACH NUMBERS, distortion by the disturbed airflow leading to instability.

At speeds of around Mach 3 the predominant feature of the airflow is shock wave propagation, and the designer seeks to make use of the relatively high-pressure regions that exist behind these waves (compression lift).

Providing a means of changing the characteristics of wings to suit different flight conditions offers many advantages at the expense of technical complexity (see SWING WING). Simple slats that open automatically at low speed can be incorporated in the leading edges: stalling speed is reduced, but there may also be a slight loss in maximum speed due to increased drag even when the slats are closed. Trailing edge FLAPS alter the camber of a wing and may be of considerable complexity. The Boeing 727, for example, uses triple trailing edge flaps allied with a spoiler (or lift dumper, to assist braking

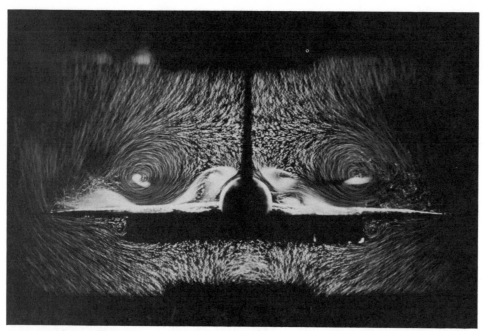

Schlieren photography in a wind tunnel records the aerodynamic configuration of high-speed airflow over a model of a supersonic plane.

after landing), and a leading-edge flap in combination with another spoiler. Control of the BOUNDARY LAYER can be achieved by employing suction over the surfaces of the airfoil or by generating supercirculation with compressed air discharged over the flaps, ailerons and tailplane.

Handling qualities are substantially improved (particularly at the onset of compressibility) if every section of a wing operates at the same lift coefficient. To achieve this, a negative camber may be adopted at the wing root. This causes the inboard part of the wing to stall at the same time as the tip. Other means of improving the local airflow over a wing by preventing span-wise drift of the boundary layer towards the tip and a tendency for it to separate include notched leading edges and boundary layer fences; a dogtooth or cambered leading edge reduces the peak pressure and again serves to inhibit boundary layer separation (see also AIRPLANE).

Aeronautics

The scientific knowledge upon which aeronautical engineering is based. It relates to the science of designing, building, operating, and testing aircraft of all classes. Interest in developing machines for flight began in earnest in the 16th and 17th centuries; successful flight first took place in balloons at the end of the 18th century; but the mechanical genius of the 19th century laid the groundwork for powered aviation as the main and expanding branch of aeronautics in our own times. As the range, operating height, and speed of aircraft have increased, so too have the problems of de-

sign, choice of materials, propulsion, involving other sciences, particularly AERODYNAMICS — a branch of fluid mechanics concerned with the motion of air and other gaseous fluids. Aeronautics deals with aircraft operating within the earth's atmosphere; the newer science of astronautics deals with space vehicles.

Aerospace

The realm embracing both the earth's envelope in which aircraft can fly, and outer space beyond, in which spacecraft travel.

Aerostatics

The science of the equilibrium of gases and of floating bodies in them, when influenced only by gravity. It is the science of lighter-than-air craft (*aerostats*), embracing the building and operation of AIRSHIPS and BALLOONS of all types. The main activity in the field of aerostatics is now the increasingly popular sport of hot-air ballooning, which originated with the MONTGOLFIER BROTHERS' ascents in France beginning in 1783. Recently, the practicability of designing and using lighter-than-air craft for heavy loads has been reappraised, creating a new interest in aerostatics.

Aerotrain

Tracked AIR-CUSHION VEHICLE developed by the Bertin Company of France. On January 22, 1969, a 6-seat half-scale test vehicle with rocket propulsion, reached 264 mph (425 km/h). A full-scale 80-seat version was built in 1969 for tests at up to 188 mph (302 km/h) on an 11-mi. (17.6 km) track near Orleans. Proposals to build an Aerotrain line in the Paris suburbs in the early 1970s were not carried out. Aerotrains have a metal or concrete track like an inverted letter "T." The center fin runs through a slot along the center line of the car and is used only for guidance purposes; the cars are supported by air cushions. The cars are driven along the track by turbine-powered propellers, but LINEAR INDUCTION MOTORS are being considered. Similar vehicles are being tested in other countries, including Britain and the United States.

The French Aérotrain, a tracked air-cushion vehicle. This experimental train attained a record speed of 231 mph (372 km/h).

Afterburner

Device in a JET ENGINE, located between the turbine and the nozzle, which provides greater thrust (an increase of as much as 40%) by burning additional fuel. Exhaust gases, at a temperature of about 1,500°F, may be insufficient to produce spontaneous combustion, and an additional ignition source may be needed in the afterburner itself. The augmented thrust results from an increase in the mass of the exhaust gases from the additional fuel and an increase in the exhaust velocity brought about by combustion. Afterburners are used only for brief periods during take-off and climbing, or by military aircraft in combat. Heavy fuel consumption makes extended use impractical.

Agricultural aircraft

Airplanes or helicopters built or adapted for special tasks to aid cultivation in any way. They date from 1921, following a test by the Ohio State Experimental Station in which lead arsenate was sprayed from an airplane over a catalpa grove to poison insects destroying the trees. During the 1930s the regular crop-dusting of cotton fields established the utility of agricultural aircraft. Their scope increased from pest-control to seeding and fertilization, and to combating weeds, fungus, and compaction.

In recent years over 2,000 Cessna AGwagon and some 5,000 Piper Pawnee agricultural airplanes have been built, and many helicopters have been adapted to specialized uses. Fittings include chemical tanks and spraying rigs, hoppers and dispensers for solids, and special ventilation for pilot and operators. The effectiveness of such aircraft can be gauged from an orange grower in Florida, whose 15-acre grove took three days to spray from the ground, but only 30 minutes by air and at less cost.

Ailerons

The outboard trailing edges of the wings include a pair of hinged surfaces called ailerons, which are operated to impart roll. When one aileron is depressed it increases the lift supplied by its parent wing and lifts the wing; the opposite aileron is interconnected and simultaneously comes up to reduce the lift from the other wing, which consequently drops. The ailerons are principally used to induce banking when turning.

Air bag

See AUTOMOBILE SAFETY.

Air brake

The type of braking system used on trains in America and in many other countries. It uses compressed air to operate the brakes, in contrast with vacuum braking, in which atmospheric pressure is used to apply the brakes (see VACUUM BRAKE). In some countries, including Britain, both systems are used. The American inventor George Westinghouse introduced his "automatic air brake" in 1871. It was of the direct-release type, like most modern air brakes. In this system a brake pipe runs the whole length of the train. This is charged with compressed air to a pressure of about 70 pounds a square inch. It feeds an auxiliary reservoir through a triple valve. Another connection from the triple valve leads to the brake cylinder which applies braking effort.

To apply the brakes the pressure in the brake pipe is reduced, which causes a piston to move in the valve. As the piston moves it isolates the auxiliary reservoir from the brake pipe and connects the reservoir to the brake cylinder. The compressed air in the reservoir forces the brake shoes against the wheels. This system is FAIL-SAFE. Should the compressor system fail or a car be uncoupled the brakes will be applied automatically.

To release the brakes compressed air is admitted into the brake pipe, moving the piston in the triple valve. This movement opens the connection to the auxiliary reservoir. It also allows the compressed air in the brake cylinder to exhaust to atmosphere, thus releasing the brakes. In the direct-release air brake the brakes are fully released straight away. On long gradients this can be a great disadvantage, for it would be better if the brakes could be released gradually. A modified type of air brake known as the graduated-release air brake was designed for use in such situations. It incorporates an additional control reservoir and a modified triple valve. Heavy trucks and buses also use a system of air brakes, in which compressed air takes the place of hydraulic fluid in carrying pressure to the brake shoes.

The European A 300 Airbus. In service since 1974, it is one of the modern generation of wide-bodied jets designed to carry large numbers of passengers over short and medium length routes. Others include the DC 10 and the Tristar.

Airbus

Large, wide-bodied aircraft with high passenger capacity generally used for short hauls. "Airbus" is also the name of Airbus Industrie's A300 design, a 260-281-seat airliner in service from May 1974. This is the first large airliner built by a European consortium consisting of France (Aérospatiale), Britain (Hawker-Siddeley), West Germany and Holland (VFW-Fokker) and Spain (CASA).

Using agricultural aircraft such as the highly successful Cessna AGwagon shown in the photograph, crop spraying and other operations can be performed quickly and at less cost than by traditional methods.

(Above) *The* USS Constellation, *a modern aircraft carrier. In sharp contrast the photograph (below) shows an early British carrier,* HMS Furious.

Air-cooled engine

An engine that relies on a flow of air to remove the heat developed in the cylinders by combustion (see COOLING SYSTEMS).

Aircraft

Airborne vehicles for operation within the earth's envelope. The term covers a range of aerial devices, from the kites flown by the Chinese in ancient times, to the most modern supersonic transports. All aircraft can be divided into two classes, the heavier-than-air *aerodynes* and the lighter-than-air *aerostats*. Development of the aerostat was limited to the balloon and the airship, while the development of the internal combustion engine, applied to the aerodyne, gave birth to the airplane, soon diversifying into land plane, FLOATPLANE, FLYING BOAT and AMPHIBIAN. This new field of progress in aerodynes became known as aviation (see AVIATION HISTORY). Aerodynamic progress with the airplane opened up another field, for the use of unpowered aircraft, GLIDERS or SAILPLANES. Rotating wings brought a new range of aircraft with AUTOGIROS in the 1920s and HELICOPTERS in the 1940s, although the giroplane theory went back centuries. Some missiles, aerial targets self-powered or towed, and unmanned aerial reconnaissance systems, are all classed as aircraft. However, as man started his exploration of outer space from the 1950s, the building of craft for probing and stationing beyond the earth's atmosphere, led to a new departure. For the first time, devices designed to leave the earth's surface came outside the aircraft category, forming a new class of their own, aptly named spacecraft. In the new realm of aero-space, aircraft are craft confined to the air.

Aircraft carriers

These are the largest ships of today's navies. Among them are the greatest WARSHIPS ever built. Aircraft carriers are in effect floating airfields with hangar space beneath a flat-topped flying deck for up to 200 aircraft. A superstructure on the starboard side of the deck, called the island, houses the flying and navigational controls. The true aircraft carrier, as distinguished from the early seaplane carriers and present-day helicopter carriers, operates fixed-wing aircraft in attack, fleet defense, reconnaissance, and antisubmarine roles. The aircraft may take off under their own power, or with the aid of a catapult; when returning landing speed can be retarded by ARRESTING MECHANISMS. On modern carriers the deck is angled to port away from the island and a crash barrier can be quickly brought into action in an emergency.

from the static system is fed to the airtight case and causes the absolute capsule to expand with altitude, while air from the pitot system enters the differential capsule and expands it as the speed increases. The two capsules are both connected to the needle which records the MACH NUMBER.

Vertical speed indicators (VSIs) contain a capsule connected to the static pressure system with a capillary leak to the inside of the airtight instrument case. As the aircraft climbs (or descends), the pressure in the capsule becomes less (or more) than the pressure in the instrument's case and the indicator needle moves. When level flight is resumed the pressure equalizes by means of the capillary leak. The turn and slip indicator has a gyroscope aligned across the aircraft which indicates rate of turn, together with a slightly curved fluid-filled tube containing a ball to show slip. Formerly an important instrument, the turn and slip indicator now usually occupies a subordinate position on the panel.

AUTOMATIC PILOTS, AVIONICS, the automatic landing system and engine instrumentation require their own separate data recording displays and controls in the cockpit.

Aircraft propulsion

Aircraft may be powered by PISTON ENGINES, turbojets (see JET ENGINE), RAMJETS, PULSE JETS, or rocket motors (see ROCKETS).

Piston engines drive propellers and are either in-line (frequently of V configuration) or radial (with the cylinders arranged in one or more rows around a central crankcase). Large in-line engines are normally liquid-cooled, while radials are air-cooled.

Turbojet engines embody an axial or centrifugal compressor to suck air into combustion chambers. THRUST is created by the exit of exhaust gases. Turbofans are equipped with a fan which enables some of the air to bypass the combustion chambers, and their efficiency equals that of the best piston engines. Turbojets can also be used to drive propellers (TURBOPROP engines).

Ramjets rely on the forward movement of the aircraft to force air into the engine, while pulse jets function through the creation of reduced air pressure in the combustion chamber during the exhaust phase, which sucks air in.

Rocket motors can operate in a vacuum because they carry their own oxygen, either in liquid form or as a component of the combustible constituents used in solid-fuel engines. They are therefore the sole practical means of propulsion for space flight.

The flight deck of a modern airliner. Each pilot has his own set of flight instruments and controls, while the central display and other instruments in the cockpit show the performance and condition of engines and other systems.

PAUL B. CORS

Naval aviation was born in 1911, when a Curtiss biplane landed on a wooden platform on the U.S. cruiser *Pennsylvania* and then took off again. But the first true carrier with an unobstructed flight deck joined the British Navy at the end of World War I. During World War II the United States, Britain, and Japan were the world's carrier powers. At present the United States has overwhelming superiority in carriers with the nuclear-powered *Nimitz* and *Enterprise* (ships of over 85,000 tons and some 1,100 ft. — 336 m — long) and 19 fleet carriers of the Forrestal, Midway, Hancock and Essex classes. In comparison, Russia has only the two new Kuril Class carriers; France two, and a nuclear-powered one building; Britain the *Ark Royal* for fixed-wing aircraft; with four countries, Argentina, Australia, Brazil, and India, each having an ex-British carrier.

Aircraft instruments

The principal flying instruments, which include an ALTIMETER and an ARTIFICIAL HORIZON, are arranged in a T-shaped layout on the pilot's instrument panel, with the artificial horizon in the center.

To the left of the T is the air-speed indicator (ASI), which is graduated in knots and may have two needles (indicating tens and hundreds of knots). Inside the airtight case is an expanding metal capsule to which the needle(s) are attached. A tube leads into the capsule from the PITOT TUBE, which records the air pressure created by the aircraft's forward movement. A second tube connects the instrument case to the static vent, which measures the external atmospheric pressure. The differential between these two pressures expands and contracts the capsule, moving the needles.

The horizontal situation indicator (HSI, direction indicator) is at the bottom of the T-shaped instrument panel. It comprises a rotating compass card attached to a gyroscope with a horizontal spin axis. Once calibrated with the magnetic compass, the HSI will give a steady reading uninfluenced by irregularities in the earth's magnetic field or by magnetism in the aircraft itself, and is not swung about by the aircraft's motion.

The machmeter measures aircraft speed in relation to the local SPEED OF SOUND at any altitude. It contains two capsules: air

The British SR.N6 flexible skirt air-cushion vehicle, with a capacity of 38 passengers and a speed of about 60 knots. The photograph (left), shows the ACV's unique ability to travel over any reasonable flat surface. The photograph (right), shows the SR.N6 in closeup.

A diagram showing the main parts of a flexible skirt ACV, the SR.N6

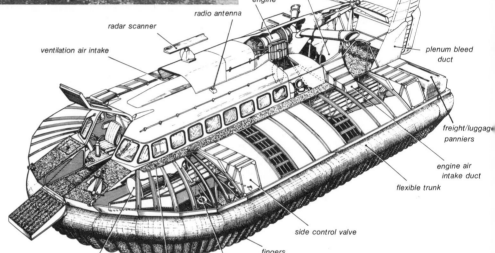

lifting fan air intake
gnome engine
radio antenna
radar scanner
ventilation air intake
plenum bleed duct
freight/luggage panniers
engine air intake duct
flexible trunk
side control valve
fingers
side buoyancy tank
forward fuel ballast tank
walkway

Air-cushion vehicle (ACV)

Machine that when in motion is supported by a layer, or "cushion," of air in contact with the ground. Another name for it is ground-effect machine (GEM). In Britain ACVs are known as hovercraft, and it was in that country that pioneering development of ACVs took place. Christopher S. Cockerell patented an air-cushion craft in 1955, and the first flight by a full-scale ACV (the SR-N1) was made four years later.

Many kinds of ACVs are now in operation throughout the world, and their use is increasing. The most highly developed form of ACV is that designed for water transport. This kind of craft is extremely versatile and is completely amphibious. It can travel equally well over the land as over the water, with a smooth transition from one to the other. It can negotiate all kinds of terrain — prepared surfaces, unmade roads, ploughed fields, potholes, swamps, stony ground and mud. ACVs have widespread military as well as civilian uses. One great military advantage is that ACVs can operate from small coves and beaches and require no deep-water ports or anchorages. They are extremely fast and maneuverable and, equipped with missiles, they can take on larger vessels. They are immune from torpedoes and undetectable by sonar, since they move above the surface of the water. Many ACVs are in service with the U.S. armed forces, and they proved extremely valuable in patrolling the river delta regions in Vietnam. The U.S. has well advanced plans for ship-size vessels employing the air-cushion principle. They include the 2,000-ton surface-effect ship (SES) and the more ambitious 10,000-ton air-capable ship (ACS) for service in the late 1970s. The ACS is planned to carry vertical takeoff and landing aircraft of the Harrier type (see VTOL).

The most successful large ACV to date has been the British SR-N4, a fleet of which now operates a car-ferry service across the English Channel (see SR-N4).

Compared with other forms of transportation, travel by water in conventional ships is very slow. Only comparatively few are able to exceed 30 knots, which is less than half the speed the SR-N4 is capable of. The only craft able to match the speed of ACVs on water are hydrofoil boats (see HYDROFOIL). Both ACVs and hydrofoils achieve high speeds because their body or hull is out of contact with the water. In the ACV the body is lifted by an air cushion, in the hydrofoil by underwater "wings." Once the body is clear of the surface it is no longer subject to the enormous drag of the water. Wave formation is also avoided. Both drag and wave formation absorb a great deal of energy, and in conventional vessels most engine power is expended in overcoming these effects. Once the hull is clear of the water, however, engine power can be applied primarily to propulsion, and hence high speeds are attainable.

ACV principles and practice. In an ACV an air cushion must be established and maintained beneath the craft to raise it above the surface. In the simplest design the underside takes the form of a concave chamber called a plenum. Air is blown into the chamber and causes it to lift slightly above the surface. Naturally, air leaks away from beneath the lower edge and has to be continually replenished. In practical ACVs a box-like structure is incorporated inside the plenum chamber, and air is directed around it downwards and inwards. It forms a "curtain" of flowing air that establishes and helps to contain the air cushion beneath the craft. The air is directed through slots or orifices in the lower edge of the plenum chamber. With such a momentum curtain, air leakage is reduced, and a deeper cushion can be maintained for lower power consumption. Stability is also achieved.

In seagoing ACVs the box structure within the plenum chamber is made watertight and serves as a buoyancy tank so that the craft can float on the water when it is at rest. Seagoing craft are also fitted

is not acceptable commercially because it is deafeningly noisy, and subsequently experimenters turned to the newly developed LINEAR INDUCTION MOTOR. This is a kind of "opened-out" electric motor invented by Britain's Eric Laithwaite which offers a silent, pollutionless and reliable means of propulsion with high efficiency and a high power/weight ratio.

Most tracked ACVs are designed to run on a single track rather like a conventional MONORAIL of the "saddle" type. It sits astride the rail, and air pressure raises it up a fraction and also maintains clearance at the sides of the rail.

An experimental tracked air-cushion vehicle. Propelled by linear induction motors, and with design speeds of around 300 mph (480 km/h), such vehicles may be the trains of the future.

with a flexible skirt. This is a tough plastic membrane fitted around the lower edges of the plenum chamber. It allows a much deeper cushion to be created and enables the craft to negotiate high waves, sandbars, and the like. Craft designed for calm-water operation, however, may have rigid side walls.

The main kind of propulsion used in ACVs at present is air PROPELLERS, and usually propellers that push rather than pull (in contrast to airplanes). A small ACV might be propelled by a single propeller about 8 ft. ($2\frac{1}{2}$ m) in diameter, powered by an automobile gasoline engine. A large seagoing ACV on the other hand has four variable- and reverse-pitch propellers

The futuristic Bell Hydroskimmer air-cushion vehicle, a high speed flexible skirt craft with four lifting fans and propulsion by twin airscrews.

measuring 20 ft. (6 m) across and powered by gas turbines.

Massive lift fans, or blowers, are required to provide the air flow to maintain the air cushion. Most ACVs have an integrated lift/propulsion system, in which a gas turbine drives both fan and propeller through gearing. The engine speed is

adjusted to give the required lift, which is the critical factor, and the speed of propulsion is regulated by varying the pitch of the propellers.

Since an ACV effectively flies, it is provided with airplane-type control and stabilizing surfaces. Most ACVs have vertical tail fins with hinged rudders at the rear. Some have in addition horizontal tailplanes which move bodily. Further control may be achieved by swiveling the propellers on their pylons. To aid steering at low speeds, some large ACVs have jet thrusters at each corner, working off air bled from the plenum chamber.

A somewhat different kind of ACV is more akin to a boat, and is often called an air-lubricated boat. It generally has rigid-sidewall construction. It may be powered by a marine propeller, which extends down into the water on a shaft, rather like that in a hydrofoil, or by water-jet propulsion. Steering is usually effected by means of a conventional rudder.

Tracked ACVs. Many researchers have seen the possibilities of applying the air-cushion principle to land transport on a specially prepared track. The idea is simply to propel a train on a thin cushion of air, thereby eliminating friction between wheels and rails. Unlike its sea-going counterpart, the tracked ACV needs only to be supported by a thin film of air about half an inch thick. Early experiments with tracked ACVs demonstrated that speeds of 250-300 mph (400-480 km/h) were attainable. Such speeds are impossible on rails, for the wheels lose their grip at about 200 mph (320 km/h).

In France M. Bertin built experimental craft which he called Aérotrains (see AÉROTRAIN). These were propelled by a turbine-driven propeller, but the system

Other ACV applications. A variety of other air-cushion devices are in use. In industry air-cushion transporters, or hoverpallets, are coming into widespread use for moving heavy machinery around the factory. Using such a device two men can move and guide a multi-ton load with ease. A typical transporter consists of a steel frame beneath which is fitted a flexible plastic membrane. The membrane is inflated, and controlled leakage of air from beneath the membrane creates an air cushion often less than a millimeter — a 25th of an inch — thick. This cushion acts as a lubricating layer between the load and the floor.

In the field, towed hovertrailers are often used to transport heavy loads such as pipes over terrain that would not otherwise support their weight. Air-cushion platforms have also been used to support excavators working on soft mud during reclamation operations. Some heavy road transporters have been designed with air-cushion capability to reduce the bearing load on the axles.

One of the most unusual applications of the air-cushion principle is in aircraft landing gear. Some airplanes have been fitted with air-cushion devices in addition to, or even instead of, the conventional undercarriage. The air cushion permits the planes to operate on soft terrain.

Airfield

Facility designed for the operation of land planes. It may range from a rough strip in a jungle clearing to a sophisticated military or commercial base with long concrete runways (see AIRPORT).

Airfoil

The special shape of an airplane wing section which has a rounded upper surface and a relatively flat under surface. The front, or leading edge, is broad while the rear, or trailing edge, is sharply tapered. Airplane propellers and helicopter rotors also have an airfoil cross section (see AERODYNAMICS).

Airframe

The body-shell of an aircraft, including the WINGS, FUSELAGE and TAIL surfaces of an aircraft, which carries the engine(s), fuel tanks, and payload.

Originally airframes were made of wood or metal girders, covered with fabric and sometimes wire-braced. This system was largely replaced by metal stressed-skin riveted to a substructure of longerons (carrying end loads), stringers, bulkheads, and frames, with cantilever wings usually based upon a main spar, a rear spar, and internal ribs (to form the airfoil section).

The construction of the airframe and the choice of materials depend on the proposed function of the aircraft. The stresses and strains to which it will be subjected have to be calculated and the gauge of metal used has to be one above that indicated by stress analysis. Cutting windows or other openings weakens the structure and this has to be taken into account.

Metal fatigue is an important factor, and milling skins and stabilizing members from solid billets can reduce the number of weakening joints.

Air freight

Usually considered to include all types of cargo other than mail and baggage. The development of large long-range transport aircraft during World War II made possible the establishment of the modern air cargo industry during the late 1940s; prior to this aircraft had lacked the size and performance to carry really bulky freight. A striking example of the new freight-carrying capabilities of aircraft was during the Russian blockade of Berlin from July 1948 to May 1949, when over 2 million tons of freight were flown into the German capital. Air freight nonetheless contributed only a small proportion of the growing commercial aviation industry: between 1927 and 1941 PAN AMERICAN's air cargo business never represented more than about 5% of the airline's total revenue, and in 1947 the figure was only just over 10%. Today it is 15% ($226 million) of a far larger total.

The advantage of speed in air freighting perishable goods, medical supplies, livestock, or urgently needed tools was evident, but there was never more than a limited market for freighter aircraft such as the Douglas DC-6 Liftmaster, Boeing Stratofreighter or modified Sykmasters, Constellations or DC-3s. Several commercial operators became specialist freight carriers, however, notably Seaboard World and the Flying Tiger Line.

The jetliners that began operating in the late 1950s offered substantial below-deck freight accommodation, and when the even larger BOEING 747 and DC-10 types appeared a decade later they offered more below-deck freight accommodation than most routes required: over the North Atlantic they operated with cargo load factors as low as 35%. Boeing 747s with main-deck cargo capability

began to appear early in the 1970s and Lufthansa's nose-loading 747F started to operate in 1972. By 1975 air cargo (which includes mail and baggage) was contributing 17% of British Airways' total revenue and 25% of Lufthansa's. Wide-bodied freighters take standard 8 ft. by 8 ft. (2.4 m × 2.4 m) containers in lengths of 10, 20 and 40 ft. (3.05 m, 6.1 m, 12.2 m), together with various pallets of

Air freight planes have various special features to facilitate loading. The giant Super Guppy (right), with the largest cargo compartment of any plane, has a hinged nose, as does the Boeing 747 (left).

similar width and height, or "igloos" of 88 by 125 in. (223 cm × 317 cm) or 88 by 108 in. (223 cm × 274 cm). As air-freight traffic increases, assembly of loads away from the airport, probably using inter-modal containers that can be transferred directly to and from trucks, will become increasingly common, although the use of pallets and "igloos" is likely to be favored by some operators.

Despite mechanization at cargo ports and computerized documentation, handling costs reached $120 per metric ton in 1975, double the 1968 rate, and the average international shipment took six days in transit, only 8% of this time being actually spent in the air.

Large freight aircraft can carry bulky engineering equipment to remote localities where oil or mineral prospecting is taking place — for example, the Russian An-22s that airlift oil drilling machinery to Siberia. Boeing 747Fs on the New York - London route have carried complete loads weighing nearly 245,000 lb. (111,130 kg), and items as large as a pipe-laying machine measuring 22 ft. by 9 ft. 9 in. by 10 ft. high (6.7 m × 3.0 m × 3.05 m).

The largest air freight operator is the Russian airline Aeroflot, which in 1972 carried over 2 million tons of cargo. In 1974 Pan American was the second-biggest, followed by the Flying Tiger Line and United Airlines.

The airframe of a DC 10 under construction. The center segment of the fuselage with wings attached is in position for joining to the forward section, while the rear section is ready to be moved up for joining.

The "scissors" platform shown in the 747 photograph can be adjusted to the correct height so that freight can be easily rolled in. Other possibilities include the swinging tail (as on the Canadair CL-44), and the special undercarriage of the Galaxy. This permits the plane to "kneel" so that vehicles and so on can run straight into the hold up a loading ramp.

Airlines

Airlines operate aircraft commercially on scheduled or chartered service for the conveyance of passengers or freight. While any organization may use the title airline, it is usually considered that the word applies to operators of aircraft carrying 30 or more passengers. Other operators are called feeder lines or air-taxi services. The first known scheduled service was run by the Benoist Company, January to April 1914, using one of their own-design flying boats from St. Petersburg to Tampa, Florida. The first international route was a service mainly for military use from Vienna (Austria) to Kiev (Russia) from March 11, 1918 until the collapse of the German Army the following November. To Germany goes the credit of inaugurating the first sustained air service, Berlin-Weimar, from February 1919. The first properly constituted international airline, using specially built aircraft, was Air Transport and Travel Ltd, which started on August 25, 1919 with a London-Paris service using De Havilland 16 single-engined cabin biplanes. That year also saw the formation of the first of the international airlines, KLM — Royal Dutch Airlines, jointly owned by the Netherlands government and private interests. From 1919 the U.S. government airmail routes paved the way for airlines operating across America. The major American airlines Pan Am,

TWA and United, all have a lineage going back to the 1920s, when they extended networks by amalgamating small companies. The production of successful large flying boats brought transoceanic travel in the 1930s, with Britain reaching out to the extremities of her empire, South Africa and Australia, while from 1935 Pan American started transpacific flights.

In the 1940s there was a swing back to land planes for transoceanic flying. Surplus military transports after 1945 led to many new airlines forming, while the established lines ordered larger aircraft and regular transatlantic services resulted.

Currently there are some 650 airlines at all levels, of which over 200 operate internationally. The largest airline is Aeroflot, the Soviet international and domestic airline, responsible for almost the whole of Russian civil aviation which, it is estimated, handles some 87 million passengers annually.

Of the major American lines, United has the largest air fleet in the world under private ownership and carries the largest number of passengers, while Pan American World Airways (Pan Am) is the largest of the purely international route lines, and Trans World Airlines (TWA), with both world and domestic interests, has the largest fleet of Boeing airliners. Recently higher fuel charges, bringing

higher fares, have caused a slump in traffic, and airline staffs have been cut to effect savings.

The trend in Europe is for airlines to group together to avoid route duplication, standardize equipment and use common servicing bases. The two major groupings are *Atlas* embracing the national airlines of Italy (Alitalia), Germany (Lufthansa), Belgium (Sabena), France (Air France), and Spain (Iberia); and *KSSU* standing for KLM (Royal Dutch Airline), Scandinavian Airlines System (SAS), Swissair, and Union de Transports Aériens (UTA). The last-named serves most of the African nations and extends to the Pacific through a network built up among territories of the former French colonial empire. One of the world's biggest airlines, claiming the largest and most comprehensive international network, is British Airways, a state corporation reformed in 1971 by combining its European (BEA) and overseas (BOAC) interests under one organization.

Airliners. Airliners are strictly large passenger carrying aircraft, but the word is also applied to all aircraft operated by airlines, whether airplanes or helicopters. The early airliners dating from 1919 were chiefly converted bombers, but by the end of the 1920s specially built airliners were being produced by Boeing, Fokker, Handley Page and others to serve the expanding air routes. However, with transoceanic travel in the 1930s there was a swing to the flying boat, with Sikorsky designs leading in the United States, and Short Brothers paving the way in Britain. After World War II the Douglas DC-3 used as a utility airliner, was followed by the DC-4, DC-6, and DC-7 in the 1950s with passenger capacities rising from 36 to 100. Simultaneously Lockheed was producing the CONSTELLATION, used by airlines worldwide. On May 2, 1952 came great change when the De Havilland COMET, the world's first jet-engined airliner, went into service with British Overseas Airways. Then, in May 1959, France showed the recovery of her industry from the ravages of war by putting the world's first rear-jet airliner, the CARAVELLE, in service. In the 1960s Boeing airliners predominated with the 707 design followed closely by the Douglas DC-8 of very similar configuration, bringing passenger capacities over 200. The 1970s have brought seating close to the 350 mark with the Lockheed TriStar and McDonnell Douglas DC-10, and new BOEING 747 versions can raise seating to 498. Meanwhile, Britain and France are producing the CONCORDE and Russia the TU-144 for supersonic air travel.

Airplane

Powered aircraft with fixed wings are referred to as airplanes. The basic requirements of an airplane are an engine to move it through the air, airfoils that will generate LIFT, accommodation for a pilot, and a system of control surfaces. Other considerations depend on the purpose for which the machine is to be used.

Wings and fuselage. The airfoils for supplying lift are the WINGS, usually of MONOPLANE configuration, although BIPLANES still have a limited application. Wings are constructed on a framework of transverse ribs and longitudinal spars, with stringers to support the skin. High aspect-ratio (about 14:1) wings have a wide span and narrow chord: they tend to be heavy because of the need for a strong

A modern airbus, the Lockheed L-1011 Tristar can carry over 300 passengers at a cruising speed of 560 mph (900 km/h). Its unusually quiet Rolls-Royce RB-211 turbofan engines have earned it the title of "whisperliner," and presage a new era of quieter airliners.

A typical modern light airplane, the Cessna 177.

structure, but very efficient at subsonic speeds. Low aspect-ratio wings have a short span and wide chord: an aircraft with this type of wing can assume a large angle of attack during landings and has a relatively low stalling speed, but aerodynamic efficiency at subsonic speeds is reduced. Tapered wings are structurally lighter than wings of a rectangular plan, and the taper shifts weight to the stronger inboard area of the wing. Sweptback wings facilitate SUPERSONIC FLIGHT, and variable geometry wings (see SWING WING DESIGN) combine the low-speed handling qualities of straight wings with the transonic efficiency of the sweepback.

Airplanes may be low-wing, high-wing or mid-wing, depending on where the wings join the fuselage (shoulder wing is intermediate between mid and high). Fillets smooth the airflow at this junction and also at engine nacelle attachment points. The wings of large aircraft with tail-mounted engines have to be very strong since they lack the strengthening provided by engine nacelle mountings.

The FUSELAGE provides accommodation for the crew and usually for the payload (any load carried that is not essential to the operation of the airplane). The framework consists of transverse frames, formers and bulkheads, with longitudinal

longerons and stringers. In two-seat aircraft the occupants may be in tandem or side-by-side; large aircraft have the crew assembled together on a flight deck.

Care is required when preparing an airplane for flight to ensure that the disposition of the load does not upset the designed center of gravity. The control systems allow minor inequalities of weight distribution to be trimmed out.

Controls. The stabilizer (see ELEVATORS) provides control in the climbing and diving attitudes and enables level flight to be maintained. It is normally at the aft end of the fuselage (and known as the tailplane) but in DELTA WING aircraft it is generally dispensed with and sometimes it is fitted at the nose (canards). The tailplane usually is located clear of turbulent air flowing back from the wings. Placing it on top of the fin will make a high angle of attack for landing impossible, for it will then drop into the

The Lockheed Jetstar, introduced in 1960 as the first "executive jet," its four turbojet engines give it a maximum cruising speed of 550 mph (885 km/h). I carries up to 10 passengers and has a range of some 2,000 mi. (3,220 km).

slipstream from the wings, but on the other hand, in this position it acts as an endplate across the top of the fin and increases the fin's stabilizing effect (see TAIL).

Yawing is controlled by the RUDDER, which is attached to a fin located at the tail end of the fuselage; twin fins and rudders are not uncommon, sometimes with an additional median fin. High-performance aircraft often have all-moving fins and stabilizers to control the aerodynamic forces of transonic flight.

Undercarriages are now usually retractable, folding up into the wings or fuselage, or (in some multi-engined aircraft) into the engine nacelles. Tail-wheel undercarriages have become rare, and the nose-wheel tricycle-type is now normal. Heavy aircraft often have multi-wheel assemblies (frequently retracting into housings at the sides of the fuselage), bicycle undercarriages likewise folding into the fuselage but requiring small stabilizing wheels along the wing. Disk brakes are customarily employed, the springing medium ranging from bungee rubber cord (in light planes) to oleo-pneumatic struts.

Propulsion. Power units may be PISTON ENGINES, JET ENGINES, TURBOPROPS or ROCKETS.

Jet engines may be buried within the structure of the wing or fuselage (aerodynamically clean, but it makes maintenance difficult and could result in extensive structural damage if, for example, a turbine blade failed), or housed in pods attached to the wings or tail. In twin-engined airplanes the engines cannot be placed too far out along the wing, or an engine failure will result in severe asymmetric handling problems. Many jets therefore have the engines at the tail, which also reduces cabin noise levels. The disadvantage of this layout is a rearward movement of the airplane's center of gravity.

The thrust obtained from a propeller is opposed by the drag which acts on the blades as they revolve. This drag causes torque that tends to twist the airplane in the opposite direction to the rotation of the propeller, and twin-engined aircraft therefore have propellers rotating in opposite directions to eliminate this phenomenon, while powerful single-engined machines have contra-rotating propellers

Design. The first consideration in the design of an airplane is its intended function: what it must carry, how far it will fly and at what speed and altitude, where it will be used, who will pilot it, and how much it is going to cost to buy and to operate. Airliners, for example, require high cruising speeds, economical altitude performance, and safe low-speed flying characteristics. They must be very stable, while a military machine should be highly sensitive to the controls.

From these considerations the designer decides if he should employ a conventional fuselage-and-wing layout or a delta type. He chooses his engines, and specifies what type of wing to use; this involves working out the wing loading (the

A general purpose STOL (short takeoff and landing) utility airplane, the Short Skyvan. Known as "the van that flies" it is robust and unpretentious, and can be put to a multitude of uses.

"stretching" the fuselage to accommodate more passengers, or extending the range by providing additional fuel tank space in the wings.

Short-range airliners (feeder liners, because they feed passengers to the international terminals) have a range of less than 1,500 mi. (2,400 km) and accommodate about 100 passengers. Medium-range jet liners fly internal continental services, linking the European capitals, or operating American domestic routes. They generally accommodate up to about 200 passengers over 3,000 mi. (4,800 km) ranges. The biggest airliners can fly 4,000 mi. (6,400 km) and carry 400 or more passengers; they have three or four turbofan engines and gross weights exceeding 500,000 lb. (225,000 kg). The AIRBUS concept of large 300-passenger jetliners operating over short-haul routes has already been successfully realized by a European consortium of manufacturers.

STOL (Short Take-Off and Landing) machines embody various means of diverting the engine thrust downwards and/or augmenting the lifting capacity of the wing by special flaps through which the engines force the airflow (see STOL).

WARPLANES still fall broadly into two categories: fighters and bombers. However, long-range missiles have reduced the deterrent value of the heavy bomber, and small nuclear devices of great destructive power can now be carried by strike aircraft of the fighter-bomber type. Military transports include some of the largest airplanes flying, since they may be required to carry armored fighting vehicles or missiles: examples of such giant airplanes are the Russian Antonov An-22, with a wingspan of 211 ft. (64.3 m) and the American C-5A GALAXY, whose wings span 223 ft. (67.9 m) and has a fuselage measuring 248 ft. (75.6 m).

Miscellaneous categories of fixed-wing airplanes include LIGHT AIRCRAFT, AGRICULTURAL AIRCRAFT, racing planes, aerobatic biplanes, FLOATPLANES, FLYING BOATS, and various experimental high-speed or high-altitude types.

Among the many specialist roles assigned to airplanes today, one of the most spectacular is the use of water bombing to control forest fires. The planes scoop water into the massive floats by simply taxiing along a suitable stretch of water. The STOL (short takeoff and landing) de Havilland Twin Otter illustrated can also be fitted with special "wheel-skis" to permit normal runway landings (with the skis retracted), and ski landings on small snowbound mountain landing strips.

(a pair of opposite-turning propellers on a single hub).

From the cockpit the pilot uses a control column to operate the flying controls (ailerons, elevators, rudder), with separate controls for FLAPS; aircraft INSTRUMENTS tell him what the attitude and performance of his airplane is, and whether all the systems are functioning correctly.

Electronic flight aids (AVIONICS), including radio and radar, facilitate navigation and are an integral part of INSTRUMENT LANDING SYSTEMS and GROUND-CONTROLLED APPROACH techniques.

expected weight of the airplane per unit of wing area), because a high wing loading means that the handling requirements are more demanding, with a higher stalling speed.

Performance depends on the amount of lift and propulsive force that is left after overcoming weight and drag. If an airplane is to operate off short runways it will need more powerful (hence less economical) engines and larger wings (which will tend to reduce cruising performance).

Commercial airliner designs should be capable of further development, usually

Air pocket

An obsolete term once used to account for the uncomfortable sensation experienced when an aircraft abruptly lost height after encountering a downdraft or gusty winds. Uneven heating of the ground by the sun also leads to "bumpy" conditions, with rising convection currents becoming more active over towns or rocky areas than over wooded regions or water.

Airports

The structure, form and facilities of modern international airports are dictated to a large extent by the operating characteristics of the largest jets, which may require up to 12,000-ft. runways and carry 400 or more passengers. Airports usually serve large cities, and transportation for passengers to and from the adjacent metropolis is a major problem. Road and rail systems are sometimes combined in efforts to solve this difficulty, but the use of helicopters has not provided a solution owing to lack of capacity (very large helicopters cannot operate into city centers). With expansion in air travel many big cities built a second or third airport to meet their requirements. These second-generation airports were designed to be modern first-class facilities from the start, instead of gradually growing up from primitive airfields like many first-generation terminals.

Runways. The main runways are aligned to provide takeoffs and landings into the prevailing wind, the first two digits of their magnetic heading being marked on the threshold (04 corresponds to 040 degrees, 34 to 340 degrees). Often parallel runways are used to increase traffic capacity (04 left/22 right and 04 right/ 22 left at New York's Kennedy, for instance). Additional runways are frequently provided (e.g. 31/13 at Kennedy), but crosswind landings in powerful modern jets are not difficult and Frankfurt, for example, has only a single pair of long runways (07/25). Runway lengths have to be increased at high-altitude airports because of the longer takeoff runs needed in the thin air: Nairobi (5,000 ft., 1,525 m) has a runway of 13,507 ft. (4,115 m); Mexico City (7,347 ft., 2,240 m) has a 10,824-ft. (3,300 m) runway (see RUNWAY).
Construction is usually of concrete about 2-ft. (0.7 m) thick to withstand the 775,000-lb. (350,000 kg) weight of a BOEING 747. Not all runways are absolutely level, and the surface sometimes has transverse grooves to facilitate braking in rainy conditions.
For night use there are white lights along the edge of a runway, with a row of

An aerial view of Dallas Love Field airport, Texas.

green lights across the near threshold and red lights across the far end. Airports certificated for instrument landings with a cloudbase down to 100 ft. (30 m) and quarter-mile (0.4 km) visibility must have runway center-line lights, and for operations with still lower levels of visibility it is necessary to have lights demarcating a narrow touchdown zone on the runway. Calvert system approach lights are in three sections, the outer section being of triple lighting units, the middle section of double units, and the final section of single lights; six illuminated crossbars of decreasing length provide an artificial horizon, the widest being the furthest out and the narrowest the nearest to the runway. Sequenced flashing lights are also used on the approach, and Visual Approach Slope Indicators (VASI) are based on the use of a color code to keep the pilot on the correct glide slope.
Taxiways are carefully laid out so that aircraft can clear runways as quickly as possible after landing and reach the apron where the terminal facilities are located without having to encroach on any other runways.

Buildings and facilities. Terminal buildings may be located between a pair of parallel runways (which can be either staggered or exactly aligned), in the angle between two convergent but non-intersecting runways, or (especially at very large airports) in the center of a complex of parallel pairs of runways that intersect. Arrival and departure facilities are usually on different levels to speed up passenger processing, and all the buildings need to be well grouped to facilitate transfers of passengers from one airline to another. This is particularly important because some of the larger airports handle millions of passengers annually (e.g. in 1974, Heathrow, London: 20,424,000 and O'Hare, Chicago: 37,893,000). Each airline has administrative accommodation and there may be facilities for government services (customs, immigration) as well as shops and restaurants. Piers (fingers) incorporating lounges and boarding gates now often extend out onto the apron, and access for passengers is by covered walkways leading right out to the aircraft doors. A circular pattern terminal has been adopted by some operators (e.g. Pan American at Kennedy), with aircraft pulling into positions around the perimeter. Moving sidewalks for passengers are sometimes incorporated, and baggage handling is facilitated by conveyer belts. At some airports magnetic baggage tags are used in conjunction with automatic sorting systems, but generally baggage passes to a central sorting post where it is reassigned to the appropriate loading bay.
The focal point of the terminal area is the CONTROL TOWER, but with modern radar installations many air traffic control

centers have been moved away from the airport.

Servicing and emergency facilities must also be readily available. Fuel is dispensed from 12,000-gallon tankers or a built-in hydrant system, and hangars big enough to accommodate the largest jets have to be built for undertaking major servicing and overhauls.

Growth and development. The planning of modern airports must take into consideration the need for future expansion: it should not be necessary to demolish existing buildings or runways to make way for new facilities. Choice of sites should also take into account the surrounding terrain and the location of nearby towns or other human habitations. Approach and takeoff routes at many existing airports leave a great deal to be desired: on Hong Kong's landward approach for example the landing lights follow a curve instead of a straight line because of the proximity of the surrounding mountains, with airliners coming in low over Kowloon just before touchdown. At most major airports, however, there are restrictions which regulate throttle-settings and rates of climb to mimimize aircraft noise nuisance. Night operations are often limited.

Airports opened in the 1970s included Charles de Gaulle at Paris and the Dallas-Fort Worth Regional Airport. The Texas terminus measures 9 mi. (14.4 km) from north to south and 8 mi. (12.8 km) from east to west. There are two pairs of main north-south runways; the two outer ones will be lengthened if necessary from an initial 13,400 ft. (4,080 m) to 20,000 ft. (6,000 m). Crosswind runways are located at either end of the row of 13 terminal buildings, and separate additional run-

ways will be provided for executive and STOL (Short Take-Off and Landing) aircraft. The control tower is 200 ft. (60 m) high. This complex will be able to operate 266 aircraft movements an hour in visual meteorological conditions, and by the end of the century will probably handle 40 million passengers and 3½ million tons of cargo a year, with 234 gates capable of accepting jumbo jets.

As the range of airliners has increased, a number of island airports that were once important as refueling stops have declined in significance. On the North Atlantic route, Goose Bay in Labrador, Gander in Newfoundland, Søndrestrømfjord (Bluie West 8) in Greenland, and Prestwick in Scotland have all lost business, while across the Pacific the airports on Guam, Wake Island and Midway are no longer obligatory refueling stops. In the Mediterranean, long-distance services now over-fly Malta and Cyprus, and the expensive runway built on the Cocos Islands for airliners on the South Africa-Australia route is now largely derelict.

Smaller fields. In addition to the big international airports serving major cities, there are numerous smaller fields, some (in the United States and Canada, for example) well equipped, others (like many in South America and the Australian Outback) with only unpaved dirt runways. Heliports have been built in a number of cities such as New York, Brussels, and Melbourne but the limited scale of helicopter operations means they are only of small size. Special STOL runways are being incorporated in some airport layouts (e.g. New York's La Guardia), so that STOL aircraft need not use the long runways required by conventional airliners.

Airship

A lighter-than-air aircraft which has its own engines and which can be steered. An alternative name for it is *dirigible*, which comes from the Latin meaning "able to be steered." The first successful airships were built in the early 1900s and came into widespread use in the 1920s and 1930s. They pioneered long-distance air travel when the airplane was in its infancy, and they were also the first effective bombers. However, by the late 1930s a number of airships had suffered spectacular accidents in various countries, and interest in them waned. By then, also, long-distance airplane travel had become more reliable.

A pre World War I British army airship; the Beta (1910).

Today only a few airships are flying, including blimps built by Goodyear. One of their principal uses is to provide a stable platform for aerial television cameras. It has been suggested that airships would make excellent, large-capacity cargo carriers or be valuable for specialist uses such as transporting large industrial equipment or rockets between the factory and site of use. Semirigid airships had a metal keel along the length of the envelope which tended to keep the airship in shape length-wise. The flying shape of the craft was maintained by the gas pressure.

Nonrigid airships, or blimps, the only types still flying today, have no supporting framework whatsoever. They have an envelope of rubberized fabric to retain the lifting gas within them. Its front end is stiffened by battens to withstand wind pressure. In the front and rear of the blimp are air bags, or ballonets, used to control lift. They are vented to lighten the craft and make it rise and filled to make the craft heavier and cause it to descend.

Airships are powered by engines that drive propellers, usually rearward-facing "pushing" propellers. Directional control of the airship is provided by rudder and elevators, much as it is in an airplane.

Design and construction. An airship is essentially a streamlined bag filled with

The aircraft control centre at Heathrow, London. Airport traffic zones have an Approach Control for craft landing or taking off and an Airport Control Unit to regulate movement on the field.

Rigid airships under construction, showing how the circular crosswise members are linked by longitudinal struts and a mass of cables.

or not. Control of lift was provided by venting the gas (to go down) or releasing water ballast (to go up).

Development of the airship. Henri GIFFARD is considered to have built the first airship, when he fitted a steam engine to a cigar-shaped balloon and traveled 20 mi. (32 km) in it in 1852. Charles Renard and A.C. Krebs designed a quite successful craft, *La France*, in 1884, which was powered by an electric motor. In 1897 David Schwarz built the first rigid airship, and his work influenced the greatest airship designer of all, Count Ferdinand von ZEPPELIN. Zeppelin launched his first airship, 420-ft. (128 m) long, in 1900. Many of the airships built in other countries in succeeding years were based on Zeppelin's designs, including Britain's *R-34* (1919) and the American ship *Shenandoah* (1923). (See also GRAF ZEPPELIN; HINDENBURG; R-34; R-101; SHENANDOAH.)

The British R-34 rigid airship which made the first airship crossing of the Atlantic in July 1919.

a gas that is lighter than air. Beneath the bag is slung a car, or gondola, for cargo and passengers, and engines to provide propulsion. Control surfaces at the rear allow the airship to be steered.

When a bag is filled with a gas that is lighter than air, it experiences a net upthrust, or lift, that causes it to rise. This follows from the principle of buoyancy which applies to fluids in general — gases as well as liquids. The best gas for airships is the lightest of all, hydrogen, which has a weight of only 0.09 g/liter (air weighs 1.2 g/liter). The great disadvantage of hydrogen is that it is highly flammable and many airship disasters were caused by the hydrogen gas exploding. The alternative to hydrogen is the next-lightest gas, helium, which has a weight of 0.18 g/liter. Helium does not provide as much lift, and it is very expensive to produce on a large scale. However, it has the great advantage of being nonflammable.

There are, or rather were, three types of airships — rigid, semirigid, and nonrigid. The largest airships built — the famous zeppelins — were of rigid construction. The main body or hull of the ship consisted of a rigid framework of

The British R-100 rigid airship. Designed by Sir Barnes Wallis, it made its first flight in December 1929, flew to Canada and back in the following year, and was dismantled after the disastrous crash of the R-101 in October 1930.

light metal (usually aluminum alloys) made up of circular crosswise members linked by longitudinal struts and cables. Fabric was stretched over the framework, forming the envelope, or skin. The lifting gas was contained in a number of gas bags inside the frame. Because of their structure rigid airships kept their shape whether they were filled with gas

Airspace

The space above the territorial limits of each state, over which it has sovereignty. The precise height to which this authority extends has not been internationally agreed. For practical purposes the word is taken literally to mean space containing air, and does not include control of outer space beyond.

Air traffic control

The volume of modern air traffic makes it essential to operate an orderly system of regulating flights. This function is exercised by air traffic control, which directs the movement of airplanes within the congested areas of the sky adjacent to busy airports or along the *Airways* linking important places (controlled air space). Air traffic control also provides a general information service for pilots. All transmissions are in English, the international air traffic control language. The Airways provide controlled routes for flights between specific places. They extend for a distance of five nautical mi. on either side of a straight line joining the point of origin and their destination, with upper and lower limits specified so that other traffic may cross above or below. Identification is by means of a color combined with a number (e.g. Amber 2).

Where the Airways converge on an airport they enter a Terminal Control Area (with an Area Control Center) which also has specified upper and lower limits, although it is irregularly shaped according to requirements. Immediately surrounding an airport is a Control Zone, extending upwards from ground level to a specified height and supervised by a Zone Control Unit. Airport traffic zones begin about 9,000 ft. (2,700 m) from the boundary of the field and normally extend up to 2,000 ft. (609 m); they have an Approach Control for aircraft coming in to land or taking off, together with an Airport Control Unit to regulate movements on the field itself.

The nerve center of the Airport Control Unit is the control tower, where the controllers sit at their desks and consoles. Equipment will include radar, telephone links with all of the airport services (meteorological office, emergency services, apron supervisor, customs etc.), and tape recorders to maintain a record of radio conversations with pilots. All aircraft movements and other significant occurrences are noted down in the "watch log book." In case an aircraft suffers total radio failure a Verey pistol and an Aldis lamp are available, and there is a code of colored light signals to direct landing aircraft and planes on the maneuvering area.

Circuits are normally left-handed, since the 1st pilot sits in the aircraft's left-hand seat and thus has the best view. If large numbers of airplanes are waiting to land they may be subject to STACKING above a demarcated holding point until they are cleared by the Approach Controller to come in over the radio beacon (which is usually located about four nautical miles downwind of the runway).

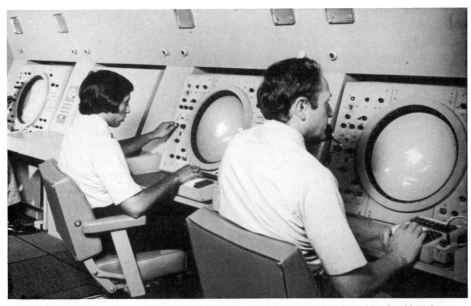

The first minicomputer-based automated air traffic control system, developed by Lockheed Electronics Company, and already in use at a number of airports. The system can process data from up to 256 aircraft simultaneously, and displays the information on the air traffic controllers' screens.

If visibility permits, VFR (Visual Flight Rules) will operate. Outside controlled airspace a pilot flying at or below 3,000 ft. (900 m) may use VFR providing he remains clear of cloud and in visual contact with the ground; above this height he has to be able to see at least five nautical mi. and he must keep one nautical mi. horizontally and 1,000 ft. (300 m) vertically away from cloud. Within controlled airspace (an area where pilots are under the jurisdiction of air traffic control), the visibility criteria applicable above 3,000 ft. (900 m) in uncontrolled airspace apply at any height.

Once visibility deteriorates to less than these values by day, IFR (Instrument Flight Rules) apply, and at night they are always mandatory. Under this system, pilots in controlled airspace will follow the instructions of the air traffic controller. Outside controlled airspace, aircraft are required to fly according to quadrantal and semicircular rules, which stipulate that below 25,000 ft. (7,620 m) pilots on a magnetic track of less than 90° will cruise at a level corresponding to an odd number of thousands of ft., between 90° and 180° at odd thousands plus 500 ft. (152 m), between 180° and 270° at an even number of thousands of ft., and between 270° and 360° at even thousands plus 500 ft. (152 m). For greater heights, magnetic tracks up to 180° are allocated a different series of cruising levels from tracks between 180° and 360°.

Altimeters are calibrated before flight by setting the atmospheric pressure (in millibars) in a special window contained within the dial. The pilot may request from air traffic control either a QNH setting (which will give him altitude above sea level), or QFE (height above a reference datum — usually the airfield). QFE is normally used only for takeoffs, landings and flying in the circuit. Once above 3,000 ft. (900 m) (the transition altitude), the international standard atmosphere of 1013.2 mb can be set, which will enable the pilot to use flight levels (flight level 30 is 3,000 ft. (900 m), flight level 200 is 20,000 ft. (6,100 m) etc.).

All pilots proposing to make a flight must notify the airport air traffic controller of their intention (booking out) and request permission to taxi. Filing a flight plan is recommended if the pilot is going to fly more than 10 mi. (16 km) from the coast or over sparsely populated areas. In the event of a forced landing, the rescue services will then know where to look for him as soon as he is reported overdue at his destination. For flights in controlled airspace, flight plans are obligatory.

Flight over certain areas is expressly prohibited or subject to special restrictions, their nature and locality being notified to pilots in the information bulletins of national aviation authorities (e.g. the Federal Aviation Agency in the United States, the Civil Aviation Authority in Britain). Examples are atomic energy establishments and military firing ranges (particularly those which operate target drones).

Modern airliners can operate even in very poor weather conditions, using GROUND CONTROLLED APPROACH techniques and INSTRUMENT LANDING SYSTEMS, together with RADAR aids (see also AIRPORT).

Alaska Highway

Link between the road system of Alaska and the highway networks of Canada and the United States. It runs for 1,523 mi. (2,450 km) from Dawson Creek, British Columbia, to Fairbanks, Alaska. It was built by U.S. Army engineers as a military route during World War II. Much of the highway is hard-surfaced, and the route is kept open throughout the year.

Albert Canal

Waterway crossing Belgium to link the port of Antwerp with the industrial city of Liège. It is 80 mi. (128 km) long, 180 ft. (55 m) wide, and 16 ft. 6 in. (5 m) deep, and can take 2,000-ton ships. It was completed in 1939.

Alcock and Brown

Two British aviators who made the first nonstop flight across the Atlantic, from Newfoundland to Ireland. Their aircraft was a converted twin-engined Vickers Vimy bomber, with Captain John William Alcock as the pilot and Lieutenant Arthur Whitten Brown as his navigator. They took off from St. John's, Newfoundland, on June 14, 1919 flying into a 40 mph gale. Their radio failed almost at once. When night came they ran into fog, and the aircraft went into a spin. Alcock brought the plane out of the spin a few feet above the water, and upside-down. Brown had to crawl out on the wings six times during the flight to chip off ice. Alcock put the plane down in a bog at Clifden, in Galway. Total flying time was 16 hours 12 minutes, with a coast-to-coast time of 15 hours 57 minutes. Both men were knighted for their exploit, and shared a £10,000 prize offered by the *Daily Mail* newspaper of London. Alcock (1892-1919) had served in the Royal Naval Air Service in World War I, and was Vickers' chief test pilot. He died in a crash in December 1919. Brown (1886-1948), born in Glasgow of American parents, was an engineer who served

in the British army and air force in World War I.

Alternator

An electricity generator used in many automobiles which produces alternating current (see GENERATOR).

Altimeter

An airplane's flying height is registered by the altimeter. The airtight instrument case is connected to the static system, that is, to the air outside, and contains a capsule (or series of capsules) from which the air has been evacuated. As the aircraft climbs, the air pressure in the instrument case falls, so the capsule expands and moves a needle on the dial.

The Vickers Vimy biplane bomber in which Alcock and Brown made the first nonstop flight across the Atlantic in June 1919. The crossing took 15 hours 57 minutes from the coast of Newfoundland to the coast of Ireland.

There may be up to three needles (hundreds, thousands and tens of thousands of feet), and a digital display. A small panel set into the dial enables the pilot to calibrate the instrument by setting the ambient air pressure in millibars: QNH is the code for height above sea level, QFE for height above the airfield.

Radio altimeters measure the time radio pulses take to return from the ground below. They are very accurate near the ground but have an upper limit of about 25,000 ft. (7,620 m). Their principal use is in automatic landing systems.

Alweg system

System of monorail transportation conceived by Dr. Axel L. Wenner-Gren after whom it is named. It was first demonstrated in 1952 at Fühlingen, Germany. Alweg trains run on top of a concrete "beamway" at ground level or supported on pylons. The trains have rubber-tired driving and supporting wheels running on the top surface of the beam and guiding and supporting wheels running on the sides (see MONORAIL).

Ambulance

See PUBLIC-SERVICE VEHICLES.

American-type locomotive

A classic early American design which was developed in the 1840s and dominated the locomotive scene until the 1890s. It had a 4-4-0 wheel arrangement, featuring two pairs of driving wheels. By 1900, American manufacturers had produced 25,000 4-4-0s: three to one of any other kind.

A classic American-type locomotive on the Meadville, Conneaut Lake and Linesville Railroad in 1890.

Ammann, Othmar (1879-1965)

Swiss-born American civil engineer, one of the world's most noted bridge designers. While working for the Port of New York Authority, he was involved in the design and construction of the GEORGE WASHINGTON BRIDGE (1931), the longest suspension bridge of its day. He was later consultant on the building of the GOLDEN GATE BRIDGE (1937) in San Francisco, and designer of the VERRAZANO-NARROWS BRIDGE (1965), now the world's longest-span suspension bridge.

Ammeter

An instrument that measures the amount of current, generally in amperes, flowing through a circuit. It can also be a simple center-needle instrument that indicates which way the current is flowing in the circuit. An automobile ammeter will show a discharge (−) when the vehicle is being started, indicating that current is flowing from the battery. When the engine fires, the ammeter needle should register charge (+), indicating that current is flowing from the generator to the battery.

Amphibian

An aircraft equipped to operate off either land or water. Such aircraft are usually FLOATPLANES or FLYING BOATS to which wheels have been added; attaching a water-planing surface to a land plane while retaining the normal undercarriage would be extremely difficult. Wheeled beaching gear is available for flying boats, but its use does not make them true amphibians. Some helicopters are also amphibians.

An amphibious truck, the Stalwart, demonstrating its abilities.

Amphibious vehicles

Vehicles designed for use on land and in water. Their main role has been in warfare. Even before the end of World War I an amphibious tank was under development in Britain, and in 1918 an amphibious car (the *Hydrometer*) was made in Seattle. World War II amphibians included small modified jeeps, and larger craft such as the American tracked DUKW (the "Duck") and the British Terrapin, which moved on rubber tires on land and was propeller-driven in the water. Modern armies have fully amphibious tracked assault vehicles and guns, and AIR-CUSHION VEHICLES. Although the latter are the only vehicles which can travel easily and at speed over any reasonably flat surface, they are not normally considered true amphibians since they "fly" rather than travel *on* the land or *in* the water.

In recent times a number of small "go anywhere" vehicles have been developed for general sale. These include the four-seater German Amphicar and the little Amphicat. With six-wheel drive, this and others like it have proved to be excellent for rescue (or farm) work in difficult terrain.

AMTRAK

The National Railroad Passenger Corporation set up by Act of Congress in 1970, a public corporation with authority to use federal funds to maintain intercity railroad passenger services in the United States. It began operations on May 1, 1971 with 16 railroads participating. Railroads can contribute to AMTRAK funds and be represented on the board, but most funds are voted by Congress which ultimately determines where services are to be run. AMTRAK was set up at a time when many railroads were reducing unprofitable passenger services and concentrating on freight. Today AMTRAK runs some 225 long-distance passenger trains a day. (Twenty thousand ran daily in 1929.) It is currently introducing new cars and raising standards.

Anchor

Device for securing a ship or boat to the sea-bottom. It is thrown overboard on the end of a long cable or chain, whose weight also helps to moor the boat. Several types are in use.

Early anchors consisted of a main shaft, the shank, which ended in a double hook called the crown. At the opposite end of the shaft to the crown, and at right angles to it, was a fixed crosspiece, the stock, often made of wood. The purpose of the stock was to tilt the anchor so that one of the hooks caught in the sea-bottom.

Admiralty pattern anchors, introduced in the early 1800s in the British Royal Navy, have removable metal stocks which enable them to be stowed more easily. *Stockless anchors*, now generally used in large ships, have tilting crowns shaped so that the hooks, or flukes, will engage on the sea-bottom when the anchors lie flat. The absence of a stock means this type of anchor can be drawn up into a ship's hawsehole — the opening for the anchor cable. *Mushroom anchors*, so named because of their shape, are used for lightships and other vessels needing permanent moorings. *Grapnels* have four or more flukes, and are used by small boats. *Sea anchors* are floating devices of wood and canvas used to keep a ship pointing into the direction of the waves.

Angle of attack

The angle at which an airfoil strikes the air flow (see WINGS).

An amphibian, an airplane equipped with wheels and floats for operating off land or water. It is essentially a flying boat to which wheels have been added.

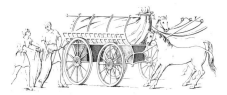  

A horse wagon used for carrying water in ancient Pompeii.

Animal transport in ancient times.

Animal transport

First used before the invention of the SLED or the WHEEL for carrying packs, animal transport was later developed for drawing vehicles and carrying people. Although domestication of animals may have taken place as early as 9000 B.C., harnessing of animal tractive power probably did not occur until just prior to 5000 B.C., when sleds pulled by reindeer or dogs are thought to have been used in Northern Europe. Oxen, too, were used with land sledges in Ancient Mesopotamia by 3500 B.C. The first pack animal was the ass, represented in Egyptian art around 3500 B.C., and in common use well before 3000 B.C. Its relative, the onager,

Yaks are still valuable pack and draft animals in parts of Tibet and China, and on the southern slopes of the Himalayan mountains.

was harnessed to a vehicle in Mesopotamia at this time. It is not known when the camel was first used as a beast of burden, but the two-hump Bactrian variety is depicted on an Egyptian tomb of about 3000 B.C., and the one-hump Arabian type was used in Mesopotamia as a pack animal around 1000 B.C. Other early transport animals were the dog, elephant, yak, water buffalo, llama, and goat. The horse was a comparative latecomer; it was introduced into Egypt by invading Hyksos around 1675 B.C., and subsequently the horse and chariot spread over the whole of the ancient world.

Technology and scientific animal husbandry have assisted animal transport by devising more efficient types of vehicle, harness, and riding equipment, and ultimately by specialized breeding, the potential of which the Romans saw but failed to realize. Until about the 15th century, the English draft ox and horse

were small and ill-fitted for their work, but by the 17th century the modern heavy horse breeds were beginning to appear.

Early vehicles included sleds and probably some sort of travois, but effective use of animal tractive power awaited the invention of the wheel. The earliest evidence of a wheeled vehicle has been found in Lower Mesopotamia, and dates from soon after 3500 B.C. Animal-drawn wheeled vehicles reached the Indus valley by 2500 B.C., Europe by 2000 B.C., Egypt by 1600 B.C., China by 1500 B.C., and Britain by about 500 B.C. All the earliest vehicles had solid wheels and were hauled by a pair of animals. The first

evidence of the spoked wheel, which gave greater speed and maneuverability to vehicles, comes in about 2000 B.C., again in Northern Mesopotamia. It appears in China in 1300 B.C., and was adopted in Egypt soon after 1600 B.C.

Harness and shoes. The ancient method of horse harness, using throat and girth bands, prevented the animal from exerting its full strength by constricting its breathing and limiting its blood circulation. The Chinese had produced an efficient breast-strap type of harness by the second century A.D., but the Romans never achieved this. The invention of the horse collar in China, in the first century B.C., and its introduction to Europe around the 10th century A.D., was of enormous importance; pressure now fell on the front of the animal's shoulders, multiplying the effective pulling strength of the horse four or five times.

Tandem harnessing was a further im-

provement. The Romans usually harnessed draft animals side by side, which was bad for team discipline, and could result in tangential pulling if the number of animals was wider than the load. Shafts became widely used in the western world in the Middle Ages, as did traces. With shafts, a horse was able to back a load, and it could exert a braking effect by leaning against the shafts when traveling downhill. Modern draft horse harness has changed little since 1800; it is still based on the collar, usually with the addition of a saddle to support the shafts.

Ox harness has changed little, and the ancient method whereby a yoke rests on the animal's back is still seen today. Alternatively, the yoke can be fixed to the head or horns, as seen in present-day southern Europe, and occasionally the breastband or collar is used. Horseshoes greatly increase efficiency by enabling the animal to point its toes, dig into the ground, and exert more strength. They probably date from pre-Roman times: the Celts are said to have used them as early as 300 B.C. Iron was not the only material used, nor horses the only animals to receive protective shoes. Esparto grass, for example, was used in classical times, and the Japanese made straw sandals for horses until the 19th century. Leather has also been used until relatively modern times to muffle the sound of horses' hooves. After the ninth century A.D. iron horseshoes became widely used in western Europe.

The principle of controlling a horse by reins attached to a bit through its mouth was already well developed in the ancient world. The bit and bridle system dates from at least 1500 B.C. The nomadic peoples of the steppe lands of Asia were largely responsible for developing the use of the horse as a riding animal, during the last millennium B.C. They rode bareback, but in the fourth century B.C., the Scythians were riding with a type of horse-cloth which was an intermediate step towards the saddle. The Chinese had padded saddles as early as the first century A.D., although they did not reach Rome until the fourth century A.D. Achievement of a really secure seat came with the introduction of the stirrup. Looped leather straps date from the fourth century B.C., but these may simply have been a mounting aid. The first rigid metal rings in the Far East date from the sixth century A.D., but they were not common in western Europe until the eighth or ninth centuries. Stirrups permitted more effective control of the animal and easier use of spurs. They also facilitated the extension of horseback riding to a larger group of people by reducing the amount of strength needed.

Road transportation. The more rational system of horse-harnessing caused the horse to replace the ox on western European roads. However, in the New World, to which both draft ox and horse were taken in the 16th century (the indigenous horse had become extinct), oxen continued to be used for heavy draft work until the end of the 19th century. Horses could now pull heavier loads, and four-wheeled wagons gradually came into commercial use during the 16th century. At this time too, comfort for passenger traffic arrived in England in the shape of the coach; its body was suspended by straps from the chassis, and it had a pivoting front axle. Springs date from the 17th century, and the development of Macadamized roads in the 18th century, with the introduction of staging posts, led to an increase in the speed of travel; an average of up to 10 mph (16 km/h) could be achieved. Horses also worked on the early railroads, and pulled barges. A horse could pull 50 tons on a canal (30 on a river) compared with only 1 to 8 tons in a wagon, depending on the nature of the road; a packhorse carried 278 lb. (126 kg).

The second half of the 19th century saw the application of power-driven machinery to transport on a large scale. But although the spread of the railroad network had a great effect on long-distance road transport, contrary to popular belief, it did not immediately bring about a fall in demand for horses. The increased volume of traffic on the railroads caused the number of cab and dray horses to rise more than the number of coaching horses declined. Indeed, horse-drawn transport was indispensable until the arrival of the automobile in the 20th century, the peak year for horse traffic in Britain being 1902, when there were 3,500,000 of them. At the same time there were 30,000,000 horses in the United States. In the western world the horse has now returned to its original role as a sport animal.

Animal transport today. Animal transport is essentially a feature of an agricultural rather than an industrial economy. Thus, while animal tractive power has virtually disappeared from the western world, in Asia and the Far East agricultural use remains high. In eastern Europe, horses still pull the farm wagon, and in Egypt bovines do the farm work while horses provide road transport. In Asia, oxen carts are ubiquitous, and horses are used for passenger transport.

In addition, where there are extreme climatic conditions or difficult terrain, specialized forms of animal transport still exist: the snow sled drawn by dogs, reindeer, or horses remains in use wherever wheels slip, get stuck, or break the ice; a light wooden sled drawn by water buffalo is used in the forests of Thailand and Borneo; reindeer are ridden and used as draft animals in Lapland and Siberia; and large breeds of sheep and goats are beasts of burden at high altitudes in Tibet, and over the Himalayan passes between Tibet and India. Water buffaloes are still important work animals in southern Asia and Egypt; the camel as a beast of burden in desert areas is as yet irreplaceable (the dromedary continues to be important in the semi-desert areas of north Africa and southwest Asia, and the two-humped Bactrian camel is a pack animal in central Asia, northern China and Mongolia). Even elephants still serve as baggage animals and for transporting logs in India, Burma and Sri Lanka.

A comparison of present-day loads reveals that a single reindeer can draw a weight of up to 330 lb. (150 kg) on a sled at a fairly slow pace, and a load of 165 lb. (75 kg) at an average pace. Eight husky dogs harnessed in double file may

A team of dogs being used as draft animals in Belgium just one hundred years ago.

pull loads of 1,490 lb. (675 kg) or more; in Russia teams of four to six dogs pull up to 350 lb. (158 kg). As pack animals, reindeer commonly carry 143 lb. (65 kg) for 50 mi. (80 km) per day; in China, Bactrian camels can bear an average load of 275 lb. (135 kg) at 1.9 mph (3 km/h) for 25 mi. (40 km) per day; in India a dromedary can carry up to 550 lb. (295 kg) at up to 2.8 mph (4.5 km/h) over a distance of 20 mi. (32 km) per day; elephants can bear a load of up to 795 lb. (360 kg) depending on their size; llamas usually carry only 60 lb. (27 kg) for not more than 18 mi. (30 km) per day; and large breeds of sheep and goats can carry at most 40 lb. (18 kg) for 9 mi. (15 km) per day.

It seems likely that the need for specialized forms of animal transport, and for a multipurpose draft animal in underdeveloped countries will ensure the survival of animal tractive power in the foreseeable future. (See also CARRIAGES AND CARTS.)

Camels being used as pack animals by Bedouin tribesmen in Morocco. Camels are also ridden, and despite modern technology, have not yet been supplanted for desert transportation.

Antifreeze

A compound incorporated in the cooling
water of a water-cooled engine to prevent
it from freezing. Antifreeze mixtures
usually incorporate the compound ethylene glycol, which acts by lowering the
freezing point of the water. They are very
penetrating and will seep through poorly
tightened joints. A dye is often incorporated in the mixture to show if leakage
occurs. An inhibitor is also sometimes
included to prevent internal corrosion.

Appian Way

In Latin the *Via Appia*, the most famous
Roman military road and the route to
ports for the eastern Mediterranean.
It extended from Rome south and east to
Brundisium (modern Brindisi). It was
named for a censor, Appius Claudius
Caecus, who began it in 312 B.C. At first
it ran only as far as Capua, 132 mi. (212
km) southeast of Rome, but reached
Brundisium about 80 years later. It was
at least 18 ft. (5.5 m) wide, and a section
of it was paved with carefully fitted slabs
of lava. Modern roads still follow part of
its course (see ROMAN ROADS).

Aquaplaning

A condition in which a vehicle's tires
begin sliding on a wet road. Tires have a
variety of tread patterns which ensure
that they will grip the road well in most
weather conditions. In wet weather the
tread pushes the water on the road surface aside or forces it through zig-zag
grooves to the rear. This leaves a relatively dry area for the tire to grip.
As the amount of water on the road increases, or as the speed of the vehicle
rises, the water-ridding action of the
tread becomes less efficient, and a wedge
of water will eventually build up in front
of and beneath the tires. Then the vehicle
is aquaplaning — sliding on water out of
control. With relatively "bald" tires,
aquaplaning can occur at speeds as low
as 35 mph (55 km/h). With good tires in
moderate rain, aquaplaning should not
occur below about 65 mph (105 km/h). On
modern grooved concrete highways
aquaplaning is less likely to occur.

Aqueduct

In modern terms an artificial channel or
pipeline in which for domestic, power, or
other use water flows from its source to
a primary distribution point, generally
by gravity. In earlier times, aqueducts
were bridgelike structures built to carry
water across valleys. The greatest builders of aqueducts in the ancient world
were the Romans, many of whose structures still stand. One of the most notable
is the Pont du Gard at Nîmes, France,

The famous Pont du Gard aqueduct at Nîmes, France, built by the Romans in 19 BC.

*A 19th century open-channel aqueduct carrying a
canal across a valley.*

built in 19 B.C. and 155 ft. (47 m) high to
span a valley.
Modern aqueduct building began in the
19th century. Open-channel aqueducts
are used to carry water for irrigation or
hydroelectric schemes, but most domestic
water supplies are enclosed. The water
is generally carried under rivers and
other obstructions in pressure-tunnels
or pipes by siphoning or pumping. The
state of California has the world's largest
water conveyance system. The State
Water Project begun in 1960 and expected to take 25-30 years, is designed to
transport 4,230,000 acre-ft. of water
per year

Arch bridge

One of the main kinds of bridges, capable
of spanning gaps of over 1,600 ft. (485 m).
The load on an arch bridge is transmitted

along the arch and exerts a sideways as
well as a downward thrust on its supports, or abutments. The arch is in a
state of compression throughout, which
means that materials such as stone and
concrete can be used, for they are strong
in compression. Today reinforced concrete and steel are the materials most
widely used in arch-bridge construction.
The prime examples of stone arch bridges were those built by the Romans, including their famous AQUEDUCTS. Abraham
Darby III pioneered metal arch-bridge
building in 1779 with his cast-iron bridge
at Coalbrookdale in Shropshire, England
(see IRONBRIDGE).
One of several methods may be used to
construct arch bridges. Where possible,
concrete arches are built on falsework
supported from the ground. The GLADES-
VILLE BRIDGE in Sydney, the world's
longest-span concrete arch, was erected
on falsework. It was constructed from
precast ribs winched into position from
barges. In other arch bridges the concrete for the arch is poured on the
site.
Occasionally, steel-arch bridges
are erected over falsework. The BAYONNE
BRIDGE, in its time the world's longest-
span steel arch, was erected in this way.
However, it is not always practicable to
use falsework in the gap or channel to be
spanned. Often the channel is too deep,
as it is at the harbor of Sydney, Australia. The SYDNEY HARBOUR BRIDGE was erected, like many other steel arches, by a
cantilever method. Construction proceeded from each end. The growing
halves were attached to wire stays anchored to the bank. Sections of the
bridge were placed in position by creeper
cranes and when the final sections had
been placed on either side, the retaining
stays were gradually relaxed until the
two halves met.

A typical rural masonry arch bridge, on the Isle of Skye, Scotland. Modern arch bridges are usually made of steel or reinforced concrete.

Area rule

When difficulty was experienced in breaking the sound barrier in the 1950s, it was found it was necessary to contour the fuselage of an aircraft to achieve the lowest possible transonic wave drag. The increase in cross-sectional area where the wings and tail join the fuselage can be compensated by waisting the fuselage (see COKE-BOTTLE DESIGN). The expansion and compression shock waves from the waisted section of the fuselage are canceled out by compressions and expansions generated by the wings. (See SUPERSONIC FLIGHT.)

Armored personnel carrier

See MILITARY VEHICLES.

Arresting mechanism

The device on an aircraft carrier that catches and slows down a landing plane. It is designed to slow down the plane progressively, thus avoiding undue stresses on airframe and pilot. When a plane comes in to land on a carrier, it extends an arrester hook from its tail. The hook catches a cable raised slightly above the landing deck. The cable is attached to an energy-absorbing mechanism.

In one type widely used on American carriers the arresting cable is linked to a piston or ram which absorbs energy as it forces fluid through a control valve. The expelled liquid compresses gas in a chamber, which acts as an energy reservoir. The compressed gas is then used to return the arresting cable to its original position.

Arthur Kill Bridge

A VERTICAL-LIFT BRIDGE between Elizabeth, N.J., and Staten Island. With a length between towers of 558 ft. (167 m), it has the longest span of any movable bridge. It was opened in 1959 and carries rail traffic.

Articulated vehicle

See TRAILER TRUCK.

Artificial horizon

The attitude director or artificial horizon tells the pilot if he is rolling, climbing or diving. It is based on a gravity-oriented gyroscope maintained in position by torque motors governed by mercury-level switches. The *flight director* consists of two moving lines at right angles to each other superimposed on the face of the artificial horizon. They are controlled by a computer receiving information from the other flight instruments; the pilot maintains his course by aligning the aircraft symbol on the instrument's glass with the intersection of the moving lines.

Asphalt

A black sticky substance like tar that is mainly used for surfacing roads. Depending on its source it may contain some mineral matter. Asphalt may be simply sprayed on the road surface or mixed with gravel or stone chips and then rolled. Roads made in this way are often termed black-top roads. Among its other applications, asphalt is added to canal and other waterwork linings to protect them.

Asphalt is usually distilled from petroleum though it is sometimes found naturally in great pools, being the heavy residue remaining after the more volatile hydrocarbons have evaporated.

Assembly line

Method of industrial mass production pioneered by Henry FORD. The manufacturing process is subdivided into a sequence of short operations, each workman on the line performing the same operation over and over again. In the case of an automobile the line generally begins with the basic chassis. This moves slowly along a conveyer, beside which stand the workmen, and the necessary tools and parts, so that as the growing automobile travels along the line, each operation can be performed without interrupting the flow. Complex units such as the engine or carburetor are constructed on sub-assembly lines and conveyed to the main line at the appropriate point.

When Ford entered the automotive industry in 1903 the automobile was regarded as a luxury plaything rather than as a utility vehicle, and many of Ford's associates and stockholders opposed his beliefs. However, once the famous Model T (see TIN LIZZIE) had proved its popularity, Ford was able to implement his ideas, and by 1913 the Model T was being mass-produced on a moving assembly line. This process enabled Ford to build automobiles with much greater speed and less expense, and each year the price of the Tin Lizzie was lowered. Its 1909 price of $950 had dropped to just $290 by 1926, and annual production figures rose from 300,000 in 1914 to over 2,000,000 in the peak year of 1923.

The development of the assembly line by Ford spread quickly through the automotive industry and to other fields, and represented a major contribution to modern industrial technology.

A section of an automobile assembly line, with the engine and rear axle assembly being positioned by hydraulic lifts.

The astrolabe was one of the earliest instruments used for determining the position and altitude of stars and planets. Although effective on land, its value as a navigational aid at sea was restricted as accurate readings from a rolling or pitching ship were virtually impossible.

Astrolabe

An ancient astronomical instrument employed by navigators from the 15th century until the appearance of the SEXTANT. It was used to determine the positions of the stars on the celestial sphere or simply to measure the height of the sun or stars above the horizon (from which the observer's latitude could be derived). In its simplest form it consisted of a graduated circular disk with a movable sighting device (see NAVIGATION).

Atlantic intracoastal waterway

Shipping route along the eastern coast of the United States, comprising river segments, canals, bays, sounds, and open sea. It extends from the Boston area 1,600 mi. (2,600 km) southward to Key West off the southern tip of Forida. Key links along its length include the CAPE COD and the CHESAPEAKE AND DELAWARE Canals. Originally it was planned as part of a 3,000-mi. (4,800 km) intracoastal waterway including what is now the GULF INTRACOASTAL WATERWAY, but the necessary link through northern Florida has not been made.

Atmospheric railroad

Railroad on which the trains are propelled by air pressure. The idea of an atmospheric railroad dates to the 1820s, the time when the steam railroad was beginning to establish itself. But practical schemes did not appear until the 1840s. Railroad-builder Isambard Kingdom BRUNEL was among those who saw the atmospheric railroad as a clean, silent and efficient alternative to the filthy, noisy and inefficient locomotives of the day. The idea was also taken up in the United States, Ireland, France and Italy.

In one relatively successful atmospheric scheme motive power was provided by means of a piston moving in an ingeniously sealed pipe running along the middle of the track. The locomotive that hauled the carriages was connected to the piston by a plate which passed through a slot in the top of the pipe. The slot was covered by a greased leather flap. By means of a stationary steam-driven pump, air was evacuated from the tube in front of the piston. Rollers fitted behind the piston lifted up the flap and allowed air into the pipe. With a partial vacuum in front and normal air pressure behind, the piston was forced to move.

Atomic power

Power that is derived from the splitting or fission of atoms, usually of uranium; alternatively called nuclear power, since it is the nucleus of the atoms that splits. Controlled nuclear power is used to propel some ships and submarines (see NUCLEAR PROPULSION).

Austin 7

One of the most successful early baby automobiles, produced in Britain between 1922 and 1938. Designed by Herbert Austin, it had a 747 cc engine that produced 13 brake horsepower. Its top speed was about 50 mph, and it could travel up to 50 miles per gallon. Several racing variants were produced, including a supercharged version developing 32 bhp.

Autobahn

Germany's high-speed highways. The autobahns were conceived as a national major highway system in the late 1920s, at first mainly for their potential military value, rather as the Roman roads were. The first autobahn, on the Cologne-Bonn route, was opened in 1932. By the early 1940s Germany had built 1,300 mi. (2,000 km) of autobahns. Now, with already more than 3,000 mi. (4,800 km) of autobahns, Germany plans to triple this figure by the mid-1980s. The Hafraba autobahn is one of the longest autobahns, stretching for more than 500 mi. (800 km) from Hamburg to Basel.

Autogiro

An aircraft supported in the air by freely revolving rotors turned by the airflow, not by direct engine drive as with a helicopter. These aircraft have a conventional propeller, fuselage, and undercarriage, but no wings. The rotors, mounted above the fuselage, could be clutched into the engine initially to be brought gradually to lift approach at about 180 rpm. The wheel brakes would then be released, the rotors disengaged

and the engine revved up. The autogiro would taxi a few yards and then lift as passage through the air and propeller slipstream drove the rotors faster. Horizontal and vertical stabilizers were also conventional, but they lacked a rudder or elevators since control was effected by alterations to the axis of the rotor shaft.

The first successful autogiro flight was at Gatafe, near Madrid, on January 9, 1923 by Juan de la CIERVA, whose designs were built in Britain, France and Germany. The first military autogiros, Avro Cierva C30s, entered RAF service in 1934. The U.S. Army Air Corps ordered a few Kellett autogiros in 1937 and others were used in World War II. Speeds were from about 30 to 125 mph (50-190 km/h). The autogiro could not hover motionlessly like the helicopter, which has now all but totally supplanted it.

The photograph (above) shows one of de la Cierva's autogiros being prepared for a demonstration flight in 1925. Today the autogiro has been almost entirely supplanted by the helicopter, although a few small machines are in production, including the lightweight single seater Beagle-Miles-Wallis Wa 116 shown in the photograph (below).

Automatic flying control systems

The simplest types of automatic flying control systems are of a purely mechanical nature. Leading edge slats, for example, are held shut by the airflow during normal flight, but if the speed declines they open automatically. The airflow over the wing is artificially speeded up and the stalling speed reduced. Aircraft may incorporate fly-by-wire controls in which the control surfaces are operated by electrical circuits connected to servo motors. This system enables automatic limitations to be built into the circuitry, thus ensuring that the airframe is not inadvertently over-stressed (see AUTOMATIC PILOT).

Automatic pilot

Fatigue and monotony in long distance flying is relieved by the automatic pilot. The instrument consists basically of three gyroscopes oriented to detect variations in pitch, roll, and yaw. If the aircraft deviates from its flight path in any of these planes, the gyroscope concerned will move and electrically activate the control surfaces to rectify the error, either by means of electric motors or by operating selector valves on hydraulic jacks.

Autopilots will also automatically trim an aircraft so that the flight attitude is maintained when the autopilot is switched off and does not abruptly change as the loads on the control surfaces imposed by the gyroscopes are removed. Trim indicators in the cockpit tell the pilot whether the system is functioning correctly.

The rate at which an aircraft is deviating from its required flight path can also be measured by autopilots, so that if necessary, a correction is applied before the aircraft has moved far from its normal course or attitude.

Automatic train control

A system by which a locomotive engineer is given instructions from a central control while his train is in motion. One aspect of this control is the automatic braking system which operates if the driver ignores a restrictive signal. Train speed may also be subject to automatic control. London's Victoria Line is run automatically with the exception that the engineer starts the train in the station, stops it, and opens the doors. The New Tokaido Line in Japan is completely computerized over 320 mi. (510 km), and a similar system is in operation on the BAY AREA RAPID TRANSIT.

Automatic transmission

A transmission system in which the gears are selected and changed automatically to suit different speeds and road con-

Although fully automatic landing systems have been developed, as shown in this photograph in which a Hawker Siddeley Trident makes such a landing, their use is not yet widespread. However, as more airliners and airports are equipped with the necessary technology, delays and rerouting due to fog should become things of the past.

ditions. With this transmission an automobile is fitted with only two pedals — brake and accelerator. The clutch pedal necessary with a manual gearbox is absent. A form of fluid drive called a TORQUE CONVERTER transmits power from the engine to the automatic gearbox. The automatic gearbox is a very complex assembly of EPICYCLIC-GEAR trains, clutches and brake bands. Different speed ratios can be had by locking either the planets, the sun wheel, the planet carrier, or the annulus of the epicyclic gear and letting the other parts rotate. An automatic gearbox has several sets of epicyclic gears compounded together. The different parts of the gear trains are locked by brake bands or connected by clutches which are operated by hydraulic valves. The operation of the valves is controlled by the gear selector or by the throttle opening and road speed.

One novel type of automatic transmission is the VARIOMATIC system fitted to the Dutch DAF auto.

Automatic warning system

A method of calling the attention of the locomotive engineer and crew to the state of trackside signals. The information is usually given to the train by induction coils mounted on the ties. As early as 1922, 49 railroads in the United States were ordered to install such systems. A distinctive, audible indication is given when the signal immediately ahead shows "clear." If the signal is at "caution" or "danger" a different sound, such as a horn, is activated, and if the driver takes no steps to slow the train the brakes are applied automatically after a pre-set interval. Detectors on the tracks also set the signals to "danger" if equipment is dragging, and can warn of rock slides, floods, shifted freight loads, damaged wheels, and other dangers.

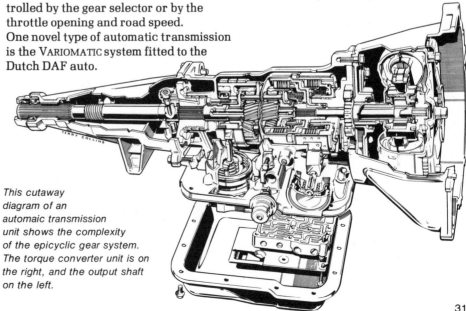

This cutaway diagram of an automaic transmission unit shows the complexity of the epicyclic gear system. The torque converter unit is on the right, and the output shaft on the left.

A 1914 version of the Model T Ford, probably the most famous automobile of all time, and certainly the first rugged "go anywhere" inexpensive automobile for everyman.

Automobile

In 1900, 15 years after BENZ constructed the first practical gasoline-engined automobile, there were some 10,000 cars in the world. Today there are around 200 million, with nearly half of them in the world's most automobile-centered nation, the United States. The automobile has revolutionized man's way of life and is considered by many to be one of the most beneficial inventions ever made.

In most industrialized countries, and for most people, the automobile provides by far the principal means of transportation. Although in Asia and the Soviet Union public transport still accounts for the majority of passenger travel, overall world figures show that three out of four journeys are made by automobile. In the United States, with just 1% of travel being by rail and 6% by bus, the figure is considerably higher, and there are half as many automobiles as there are people.

The automobile's popularity, and its flexibility as a means of personal transport, has brought its own problems. Most city centers are dominated by automobiles and are chronically overcrowded. People are not willing to give up the great convenience of cars, despite the expense and the traffic jams, and even, it seems, where efficient public transportation is available. Thus San Francisco's new Bay Area Rapid Transit (BART) system has been notably unsuccessful in persuading people to switch to public transport. It seems increasingly probable that large cities everywhere will soon be forced to impose restrictions on automobile traffic. Nevertheless, the modern automobile is

not only a triumph of technology and engineering, it is also a vital part of economic life.

Body and chassis. In many American automobiles the body is made of pressed steel sheet attached to a rigid CHASSIS, while some European and Japanese manufacturers employ UNITIZED BODY CONSTRUCTION, in which the body and chassis are combined in a single structure. A few firms make car bodies from glass-reinforced plastic (GRP), which is lighter than steel, and corrosion-free. It is however more expensive, and more brittle.

The passenger compartment has reinforcing beams so that it retains its shape in the event of a crash. On the latest models the doors are similarly reinforced, and are fitted with burst-proof locks. The front and rear ends, on the other hand,

are designed to collapse progressively in a crash, and thus to protect occupants from the worst of the impact.

The basic body styles are the enclosed SEDAN, with two or four doors and a separate luggage compartment; the CONVERTIBLE, with a folding roof; the STATION WAGON, with an extended body and a rear door, offering a large loading space; the "five door sedan" which, with a fifth door at the rear, combines features of the sedan and station wagon; and the low-slung highly-tuned SPORTS CAR. Other body styles include rugged jeep-type vehicles (often with four-wheel drive), and "campers," providing mobile homes in miniature.

The roof of an enclosed automobile was once supported on three pillars at either side, but today the central pillars are often omitted to produce a more open design known as the "hard top."

The "fastback," a recent innovation with a sloping back which reduces aerodynamic DRAG, heralded the present concern with STREAMLINING. This improves performance and reduces fuel consumption significantly. Three streamlined designs now gaining favor are the low slung "shark" (sloping down at front and rear), the "wedge" (with a sloping front like the shark, but cut off straight at the rear), and the roomy "streamlined box" (a blunt-nosed wedge).

Engines and cooling systems. The great majority of automobiles are powered by reciprocating GASOLINE ENGINES working on the FOUR-STROKE CYCLE. Most have four, six or eight cylinders, with power outputs ranging from less than 40 brake horsepower (bhp) to over 350, and most are water-cooled (see COOLING SYSTEMS). This allows a more consistent control of engine temperature than does air cooling, and better sound insulation, but the engine is subject to freezing, boiling, and corrosion problems. Because of these

A typical large American automobile of the 1950s, the 225 hp Lincoln Capri coupe. After several years' further increase in size, automobiles have at last begun to get smaller.

drawbacks, and because air-cooled engines run at more efficient higher temperatures, air cooling is used in many engine designs.

Alternatives to the reciprocating gasoline engine include DIESEL ENGINES, which are more efficient and use cheaper fuel, but are generally heavier, more costly and less smooth in operation; and the revolutionary rotary WANKEL ENGINE, which has gained more acceptance in Europe and Japan than in the United States. Various manufacturers continue to experiment with ELECTRIC CARS, the ultimate success of which depends on the development of a long-lasting storage battery or FUEL CELL, and with combined gasoline and electric systems in which electric motors are used in town and the gasoline engine elsewhere (and for charging the batteries). Another interesting idea is the gasoline-electric, in which a gasoline engine running at a constant speed (that at which it is most efficient and pollution-free) generates electricity for traction motors.

STEAM CARS, very popular in the automobile's early days, are being reconsidered, as is the STIRLING ENGINE (which can run on, for example, peanut oil). Recent research on all types of engines has concentrated on increased efficiency (and therefore fuel economy), and on emission control and alternative fuels.

Engine position and transmission. Most automobiles have the engine at the front driving the rear wheels through a DRIVE SHAFT which runs under the floor. Alternatives are front-engine/FRONT-WHEEL DRIVE; mid-engine/rear-wheel drive, rarely used except in high-performance sporting models since a centrally positioned engine limits passenger accommodation; and rear-engine/rear-wheel drive, notably in the Volkswagen Beetle.

Each combination has its advantages. An automobile is generally most stable if the loads on front and rear axles are relatively balanced, a condition which is more likely to be achieved with the engine at the front or in the middle. However, the use of light aluminum and magnesium alloys has reduced engine weight and made it possible to place the engine at the rear without sacrificing stability.

The conventional front-engine/rear-wheel drive design is usually considered the best compromise, taking into account simplicity of engineering and maintenance, handling qualities, and sound insulation. However, placing the engine and gearbox close to the wheels they drive is obviously a neat and logical arrangement. Front-wheel drive was pioneered by CITROEN in

Automobile manufacture in 1914 (above) *and today* (below). *The development by the automotive industry of mass production and automation (the modern photograph shows automatic welding equipment) was a major contribution to industrial technology.*

the 1930s, and since the problems associated with using the front wheels for both steering and driving have been overcome (by improved suspension systems and UNIVERSAL JOINTS), it has become increasingly popular, particularly in Europe. A transversely mounted front-engine driving the front wheels removes the need for a long drive shaft and its projecting tunnel along the floor, allows the fuel tank to be mounted between the rear wheels, and thus frees significantly more space for passengers and luggage. It also provides better traction, if slightly less balanced braking.

Rear engines are less common, and bring problems in cooling, and in the provision of adequate luggage space.

A gasoline engine, unlike a steam engine or an electric motor, has very little torque (turning power) at low speeds, and thus a CLUTCH is needed to couple engine and wheels gradually when moving off from rest. The engine in fact develops maximum power when turning over at around 5,000 rpm. In most circumstances (as when cruising at steady speed along a level road) maximum power is not needed, and a lower engine speed is sufficient and more economical on fuel. Hence the need for a GEARBOX to adjust engine speed and power to a wide variety of road speeds and loadings, and of course to allow the direction of rotation of the drive shaft to be reversed for backing up. Manual TRANSMISSIONS incorporate a pedal-operated clutch and a manual gear shift, the clutch being used to disengage the engine from the remainder of the transmission while the driver changes gear. However, most American automobiles have automatic transmission with a fluid coupling or TORQUE CONVERTER and an automatic gearbox. This is not only simpler to operate but it gives better performance since power is not disconnected from the wheels during gear changing.

The FINAL DRIVE is through a DIFFERENTIAL gear and two half-shafts (one to each

The American tradition of big automobiles is today being challenged on the grounds of economy and space. The photograph shows a prototype three-wheeler commuter car.

A Rolls-Royce Silver Ghost of 1909. Introduced in 1906 the Silver Ghost quickly earned a reputation as the best car in the world, and was the first automobile to combine high performance with comfort, quietness and reliability.

driving wheel), to ensure that when cornering, the outer wheel, which has further to go, is turned faster than the inner one.

Steering, suspension, and brakes. Steering is always on the front wheels, and normally employs a rack-and-pinion or worm-and-nut mechanism to transform the rotation of the steering wheel into the push and pull movements of the track rods which swivel the wheels. When turning, the inner wheel follows a smaller circle than the outer one, and for this reason the STEERING SYSTEM is so arranged that the inner wheel swivels to a sharper angle than the outer. Power steering is normal on larger automobiles.

As an automobile travels over an uneven surface its wheels jerk up and down. The SUSPENSION SYSTEM insulates the vehicle and its systems from shocks transmitted from the road, and is as important to road-holding and safety as it is to passenger comfort. Independent coil springs

are usual on the front wheels, and leaf springs on the rear, with shock absorbers on all four wheels to damp out the tendency of the springs to make the vehicle bounce. However, hydraulic and pneumatic suspension systems are increasingly employed, some of which have automatic self-leveling features (see HYDROPNEUMATIC SUSPENSION, and HYDROLASTIC SUSPENSION).

The TIRES also provide a cushioning effect, but their main function is to provide a safe grip on the road in all conditions, and particularly during braking, cornering, and acceleration.

All automobiles have two independent BRAKING SYSTEMS. A HYDRAULIC SYSTEM operated by foot pedal acts on all four wheels, while a mechanical system operated by a hand lever acts only on the rear wheels and is known as the emergency brake. DRUM BRAKES are usual on the rear wheels, while more efficient but more costly DISK BRAKES are now normal at the front. Dual-circuit hydraulic sys-

tems are becoming increasingly common as an aid to safety (if one circuit fails, the other still provides reasonable braking power), as are special mechanisms to prevent the wheels from locking when braking hard or on slippery surfaces. Larger automobiles are normally fitted with power brakes.

Fuel and lubrication systems. The main elements of the FUEL SYSTEM are the fuel tank and pump, and the CARBURETOR, where air and gasoline are mixed into an explosive vapor which is taken to each cylinder in turn and ignited by the spark plugs. In some automobiles the carburetor is replaced by a FUEL INJECTION device to improve efficiency and economy. The LUBRICATION SYSTEM reduces friction and wear on moving parts, it helps to prevent overheating, and it provides a seal between piston and cylinder. The system consists essentially of a sump to hold the oil and a pump to circulate it under pressure to all moving parts.

Electrical system. The most important part of the electrical system, and the only part in early automobiles, is the IGNITION SYSTEM. This provides accurately timed sparks to ignite the fuel-air mixture in each cylinder in turn. In addition, a modern automobile needs electricity to power the STARTER MOTOR, the headlights, signals, and horn, and such extra items as radio, windshield heater, air conditioning unit, motor to open and close windows, and other accessories.

A 12-volt storage BATTERY provides power for starting, and a reserve of electricity for use when the primary energy source, a GENERATOR driven by the engine, is inactive. The traditional dynamo has been largely supplanted by a more powerful alternator which maintains its output even at low engine speeds.

1932 Duesenberg. The classic American car was so handsomely finished and solidly built that the name became a byword for luxury.

A 3½ hp Renault of 1899. Rejecting belt and chain drive mechanisms Renault pioneered the use of propeller shaft drive.

Many automobiles have four headlights, although with modern advanced photometrics it is now possible to provide excellent illumination and intensity with a two-light system.

Automobile history

During the 17th and 18th centuries many attempts were made to supersede the horse by sail, kite, windmill and even clockwork power, but nothing significant was achieved until the development of the steam engine. In 1769 a French artillery officer, Nicolas Cugnot, built a massive steam tractor with boiler and engine mounted on the single front wheel. Designed to haul guns, it was too cumbersome to have any practical value, but it worked, and was the world's first full-scale powered vehicle (see CUGNOT'S CARRIAGE).

Other inventors followed, including William Murdock in England, and in America Nathan Read, Apollo Kinsley and Oliver EVANS, whose steam dredge trundled through the streets of Philadelphia in 1805 on its way to the docks. But the first reasonably efficient and practical road vehicles were probably those built by Richard TREVITHICK in England in 1801 and 1803. His 1803 steam carriage conveyed eight people at a steady 12 mph (19 km/h). However, it frightened horses, alarmed pedestrians, and aroused no interest.

A few years later a Swiss engineer Isaac de Rivaz removed the steam engine from his "horseless carriage" and fitted a primitive gas internal-combustion engine, in which the single cylinder was forced up by exploding gas and down by gravity. His vehicle moved, but only just. Then, around 1825, an Englishman Samuel Brown constructed the first working internal-combustion engined vehicle. But its large gas engine was less efficient than a steam engine.

Early steam cars. The 1830s saw the peak in popularity of steam coaches, and by 1860 a number of two- or three-seater steam cars had been made, at least one of which (the Rickett) was in limited series production. They required the services of a "chauffeur" to stoke the fire, but they could travel at around 20 mph (32 km/h) and were comparatively quiet and reliable. However, opposition from horse-drawn coach operators and competition from the railroads killed the steam coach, while in Britain the notorious RED FLAG LAW of 1865 restricting powered road vehicles to a maximum of 4 mph (6.4 km/h) was one factor preventing the spread of steam cars. Another was that the vast majority of people simply were not interested, and would not be until the bicycle craze of the late-19th century had given them a taste of the enjoyment to be had from a mechanical means of transport.

The first gasoline-engined automobiles. In 1860 Étienne LENOIR fitted one of his successful gas engines to a vehicle, and two years later he devised a carburetor to vaporize gasoline and constructed the world's first gasoline-engined automobile. With a top speed of about 4 mph (6.4 km/h) it made a journey of 6 miles (9.6 km). One was ordered by Alexander II of Russia, but Lenoir did not develop his invention. The next step was taken by the Austrian Siegfried MARCUS who built a crude clutchless four-wheeler in 1864 and followed with an improved version in 1875. This made several successful runs (it was overhauled and driven in Vienna in 1950), and Marcus made two further models before being forced off the streets by the police. In any event nobody (Marcus included) was particularly impressed by the invention, and as late as 1898 Marcus called the automobile "a senseless waste of time and effort."

In 1862 the French engineer Alphonse de Roches worked out the four-stroke principle; in 1876 a German, Nikolaus OTTO, assisted by Gottlieb DAIMLER and Wilhelm Maybach, designed a four-stroke engine; and in 1882 Daimler and Maybach set up their own workshop to develop it as a power unit for the horseless carriage (Daimler believed that the automobile era would begin with motorized horse carriages). Meanwhile Carl BENZ, risking security and reputation (many of his colleagues thought that he was wasting his talents) devoted himself to developing what he conceived to be an entirely new type of road vehicle, the automobile. In 1885 he completed the world's first practical and successful gasoline-engined automobile, a light three-wheeler with a single-cylinder engine developing ¾ hp, capable of 10 mph (16 km/h). The follow-

An impressive and dignified Chevrolet sedan of 1929. One of the most popular American automobiles of the period, and one which was progressively improved and developed up to 1953, it is seen in this photograph as an export model with right hand drive.

ing year he demonstrated it in public, while Daimler produced his first automobile, a four-wheeled horseless carriage.

In 1888 Benz's improved 1½-hp three-wheeler was on sale as the first production internal-combustion engined automobile, and in 1890 Daimler set up his factory. The automobile era had begun, and the style for the following 50 years was set by the French PANHARD-LEVASSOR of 1891. The first "modern" automobile, it had the engine at the front under a hood, a gearbox, foot-controlled clutch, and rear-wheel drive.

Pioneers in the United States. Claimants for the creation of the first gasoline-powered automobile in the United States include John W. Lambert of Ohio City (1890), Gottfried Schloemer of Milwaukee (1890), and Charles Black of Indianapolis (1891). But the best known, and the first to open an automobile factory (in 1895) were the DURYEA Brothers. Their first car, a converted carriage, ran in September 1893, and in 1895 a later model won America's first automobile race. By 1898 there were over 50 automobile manufacturers in the United States, including Oldsmobile, Winton, and Packard, and in 1901 Oldsmobile introduced their famous Curved Dash Runabout, the world's first mass-produced automobile.

Henry Ford founded the Ford Motor Corporation in 1903, and in 1906 the United States overtook France as the world's largest automobile manufacturer.

Steam and electric. Early gasoline-powered automobiles were generally noisy, difficult to start, and unreliable. Once Léon Serpollet of France had perfected the multi-tube kerosene-fired flash boiler, the STEAM CAR was in most respects superior to its gasoline-powered rival, and in 1900 40% of the 8,000 automobiles in the United States were steamers (22% gasoline, 38% electric). Their popularity continued until the invention of the electric self-starter, first fitted as standard equipment by Cadillac in 1912. The most famous make was the STANLEY STEAMER, and later (1914-1931) Dobel, the finest of them all and one of the most expensive luxury cars on the market during the 1920s.

As with steam, ELECTRIC CARS had significant attractions in the early years, and reached a peak of popularity in 1912 when there were nearly 34,000 in the United States. Their overriding disadvantage was lack of range, and as gasoline automobiles became more reliable and easier to drive electrics suffered the same fate as steamers.

A mass market. Until about 1908 in the

United States, and 10 or 15 years later in Europe, automobiles were generally regarded as playthings for the wealthy. They provided little or no weather protection; spares and service were hard to obtain; the first roadside gasoline pump was not set up until 1906. However, with the astounding success of the Model T Ford (see TIN LIZZIE); with improved design and engineering (a 1907 Rolls-Royce was virtually as new after a 15,000-mi. — 24,000-km — test run); and with new safety and comfort features such as pneumatic tires, four-wheel brakes, windshield wipers and electric starters and lights; the automobile had by 1920 become a part of everyday life, a necessity. In that year there were 8,000,000 automobiles registered in the United States.

The post-World War I years saw the introduction to Europe of Ford's mass-production methods by manufacturers such as CITROEN (France), FIAT (Italy), and Austin and Morris in Britain. Following the example set by Ettore BUGATTI's Bébé Peugeot of 1911, these companies built true large cars in miniature to replace the often dangerous cycle cars that had enjoyed a vogue in the immediate pre- and postwar years. They also produced inexpensive and reliable family automobiles, and on both sides of the Atlantic more practical sedans replaced the open models of earlier years.

During the 1920s and 1930s, particularly in America, automobiles became ever larger and more comfortable. An increasing number of refinements such as heaters, synchromesh (and later automatic transmission), and power steering became standard. And many of the most finely engineered high performance luxury automobiles of all time were built; by DUESENBERG, Pierce-Arrow, Packard and CADILLAC in the United States; by ROLLS-ROYCE and BENTLEY in Britain; and by BUGATTI, HISPANO-SUIZA and others on the continent of Europe.

The modern period. Since World War II several European manufacturers have followed Citroen's example by adopting front-wheel drive. The emphasis in Europe and in Japan (which became a large-scale producer in the 1960s) has in general been on efficiency and economy, rather than on size and luxury as until recently in the United States. STREAMLINING, FUEL INJECTION and other fuel saving techniques are no longer unusual. The trend towards smaller automobiles has become more marked since the recent energy crisis, and has reached the United States, where imports of European models rose, as did sales of American-built compact automobiles. During the 1950s experiments were made with gas turbines, and the revolutionary rotary WANKEL ENGINE, now available on several European and Japanese models, appeared. More recently, increasing concern about air pollution has led to renewed interest in steam and electric power, and to the development of efficient EMISSION-CONTROL SYSTEMS for gasoline engines. The two other major preoccupations of today are AUTOMOBILE SAFETY, and the possibility of automated cars on electronic highways.

Automobile Racing

Since the earliest days of the automobile, racing has been a popular sport, a stimulus to designers and a proving ground for their work. Most races are organized and supervised by national clubs, and at an international level by the Fédération Internationale de l'Automobile (FIA). Races are generally between cars of a specific formula or group, with engine size and fuel consumption, weight, and various other factors delimited so that in theory all competitors have an equal chance of winning. Designers, manu-

ance add the element of endurance and vary the theme in that the winner is the car that covers the greatest distance in the alloted time. Drag racing is a test of acceleration, rather than speed, while in events such as the Canadian-American Challenge Cup (the Can-Am series) points alloted to the finishers in each of the ten races of the series are added up at the end of the season to determine the overall winner.

Races are held on a number of types of courses, or venues. Many are road races, which may take place on a circuit of public roads (closed to other traffic for the occasion), or on special race tracks laid out like normal roads with bends, curves, hills and so on. For important events the alternative is the speedway, a symmetrical (usually oval) track, often with banked corners. One of the best known, the 2½-mi. (4 km) INDIANAPOLIS SPEEDWAY, is the scene of one of the main events in the annual racing calendar, the Indianapolis 500. Many lesser and often local events are held on cross-country courses, especi-

Paris to Rouen in France in 1894, in which the winners averaged just over 11 mph (176 km/h) — to the "Race of Death," the Paris-Madrid race of 1903. With an estimated 3 million spectators and 216 entries, with insufficient supervisors, and with blinding dust thrown up from the road making it difficult for drivers to see, there were so many accidents and deaths that the race was halted at Bordeaux. Since then most races have been held on closed circuits, with the notable exception on the Italian Mille Miglia ("thousand mile") which between 1927 and 1957 was a major annual event. Finally it too had to be banned. There was, and is, no way of ensuring safety over a long inter-city course. Even on closed circuits, with safety barriers, fireproof fuel tanks, automatic fire extinguishers, and other safety precautions demanded by today's racing organizations, accidents are inevitable. Of the many types of automobile racing, the Grand Prix events are the most famous, particularly the Formula 1 races, for which there are only about 30 qualified drivers in the world. (To qualify a driver must have won or finished in the first three in several important races.) Formulas 2 and 3, among others, were introduced to provide a training ground for would-be Formula 1 drivers. Grand Prix cars are all single-seater open-wheeled racers with built-in AIRFOILS front and back. These work on the same principle as an airplane's wing, but being inverted they provide downward pressure and thus help the car "stick" to the road.

Cars in the Manufacturers International Championship races include special production GRAND TOURING cars, production SPORTS CARS, and prototype sports cars. Competitors in the Can-Am series, two-seater racing cars with unlimited engine displacement, are among the fastest and most powerful of all, with top speeds around the 200 mph (320 km/h) mark. Many events are organized for production sports and touring cars, and for so-called stock cars. These look like normal passenger cars, but in some classes there are virtually no restrictions on modifications, and many "stock" cars are in reality specialized racers.

Other forms of automobile racing include midget car and kart events; hill climbs, in which only one car races at a time; and, with the strangest cars of all, drag races. These are accelerating races from a standing start over a ¼-mile (0.4 km) straight track, the contestants racing in pairs (the loser of each pair being eliminated). There are drag races for most kinds of cars; the fastest are the "slingshots." Burning special fuels, these reach speeds of 200 mph (320 km/h) or more in their ¼-mile sprint.

A modern Formula 1 racing automobile, the Ferrari 312 B 2. Airfoils at front and rear help to hold the car down, thereby improving maneuverability.

facturers, mechanics, and engine tuners combine their skills to get as much as possible out of a given formula, not only in speed but also in reliability, maneuverability, and safety. Some race formulas are for standard production cars (e.g. Formula V for Volkswagens), some for prototype models, and others for highly specialized racing cars which bear little or no resemblance to ordinary automobiles. The majority of races are straightforward speed events. The competitors start together and the one to complete the course first wins. Events such as the famous LE MANS 24-hour Grand Prix d'Endur-

ally in Britain (Rally-Cross) and France (Rallye Infernal and Rallye des Cimes). In America the National Off-Road Racing Association stages two annual off-road races, the Baja 500 and the Mexican 1000. The courses include rough trails, open desert, dunes, and rock and boulder strewn terrain. At the other extreme, drag races are held on straight and level tracks.

There is one further venue which was once popular, but is no longer used, the inter-city course. Most early automobile races were town to town events, from the first of all — the reliability trial from

Automobile safety

With the ever increasing death toll on the roads accounting for almost half of all accidental deaths and representing a major hazard in modern life, automobile designers are becoming more safety conscious, and governments are enacting increasingly stringent safety legislation.

There are two main aspects of automobile safety: features built into a car to minimize the chance of accidents (active safety); and features designed to minimize danger and injury in the event of a crash (passive safety). Of the greatest importance for active safety are road-holding qualities. Weight must be distributed so that the car is well balanced, thus reducing the danger of skidding when cornering or braking at speed. Recent experiments have been made in which the fuel is distributed among several tanks by an automatic pumping system to maintain trim. Efficient suspension and shock-absorber systems damp out the effects of rough roads not only on the occupants, but also on road-holding and steering, while torsion bars prevent outward tilt on corners.

Steering must be smooth, precise, and responsive, and modern braking systems are designed to prevent the wheels from locking, so that the driver is in full control even when braking hard. Drum brakes, prone to overheating and fade, are increasingly being supplanted by the more costly but much safer disks, and many automobiles are now fitted with dual-circuit braking systems.

With improved adhesion, steering response and general handling qualities, the radial-ply tire represented a major advance in automobile safety, and the new tires take this a stage further by virtually eliminating danger after a blow-out.

Automobile manufacturers are paying increasing attention to providing an unrestricted view of other traffic, non-dazzle fittings, efficient lights, properly designed seats and air conditioning to reduce driver fatigue, and controls that can be operated without removing the hands from the steering wheel.

Other new ideas being tested include adjustable airfoils to hold the car down, thus reducing the possibility of loss of adhesion, and radar collision avoidance systems. These consist of a radar eye measuring the distance from the vehicle ahead, and linked to a computer which calculates the safe distance and if necessary slows the car.

Passive safety. The main structure of a "safe" automobile is such that in the event of a crash the passenger compartment is strong enough to retain its shape, or "integrity," while the front and rear sections collapse or deform progressively to absorb much of the energy of the impact and reduce the rate of deceleration. Passenger compartment integrity is achieved with reinforcing beams in the main structure and in the doors, and with burst-proof door locks.

Various types of energy-absorbing bumpers are in production. One works on the conventional shock-absorber principle, and like several other types, regains its original shape after the impact. Others are designed to crush progressively and must be renewed after "use."

Inside the automobile, SEAT BELTS are compulsory, but not often used, and inconclusive tests have been made with air bags which inflate rapidly in the event of an impact, to provide a cushion between

The Australian Lawrence Hargrave flying a boxkite in 1894. His experiments helped to establish the form and success of early biplanes.

occupants and interior fittings. The steering wheel is a major source of danger, now eliminated on many automobiles by collapsible steering columns. Any other interior projections are now kept to a minimum, are padded, and may be designed to collapse progressively. Laminated windshield glass, compulsory in the United States, has greater flexibility than tempered safety glass and is designed to prevent broken glass fragments from causing serious injuries.

Exterior safety. Exterior safety features, for the protection of pedestrians and bicyclists, include rounded or recessed door handles, foam-padded bumpers, smooth lines and an absence of projections. In addition it has been found that positioning the bumpers lower than usual considerably reduces danger by knocking a pedestrian's feet from under him, thus

landing him on the hood, rather than pushing him onto the road.

All these safety features are tested on special ESVs (experimental safety vehicles). To incorporate them all on production automobiles would at least for the present be prohibitively expensive, but in time more safety features are likely to be made compulsory.

Autostrada

Italy's high-speed highways. Italy was the first country to build a superhighway or expressway especially for high-speed motor vehicles. This was the Venice-Turin autostrada, begun in 1934. One of the most impressive routes is the nearly 500-mi. (800 km) Autostrada del Sole, which extends from Milan in the north to Reggio in the south, via Florence and Rome. Like the other autostrada, it is a toll road.

Aviation history

The WRIGHT BROTHERS' first successful powered flight at Kitty Hawk, North Carolina, on December 17, 1903 marked the beginning of aviation history. The Wrights' pusher aircraft were deliberately designed to lack stability, so that they would be inherently maneuverable. Banking was achieved by warping the wings, pitch was controlled by a forward-mounted elevator, and a rudder counteracted warp drag and enabled turns to be made.

In Europe, stability was sought by most of the pioneer pilots (Ferber, Archdeacon, Esnault-Pelterie), who consequently achieved only limited success. Wing warping was little understood and control in the rolling plane was generally neglected.

However, in 1909 Louis Blériot, the French protagonist of the MONOPLANE, made the first flight across the English Channel (July 25) and the following month an international flying meeting was held at Rheims which established the BIPLANES of Henri Farman as outstandingly successful designs.

By 1910 the military implications of the airplane were being appreciated, although largely in terms of reconnaissance. A twin-engined machine was flown in 1911 (Short Triple-Twin) and 1913 witnessed the first aerobatics (Adolphe Pégoud flying a Blériot).

When World War I began in 1914, the biplane in both tractor and pusher forms was the most widely used type. Single-seater scouts (e.g. the Sopwith Tabloid) could achieve 100 mph (160 km/h), two-seater aircraft (such as the BE2C) about 75 mph (120 km/h) with a ceiling of 10,000 ft. (3,050 m). Monoplanes had

Charles Lindbergh taking off in his Ryan monoplane Spirit of St Louis on his historic flight from New York to Paris in 1927. The achievements of pioneering airmen such as Lindbergh aroused enormous enthusiasm and encouraged the development of civil aviation.

One of the many weird experimental airplanes of the early days, this curiosity by the Frenchman Dorunt crashed.

A successful all metal monoplane airliner of the 1930s, the Ford Trimotor. Air passenger transport had by then become safer and more reliable, but it was still considered something of an adventure. Affectionately known as Tin Goose, and so robust that many examples remained in service for over 40 years, the Trimotor carried 12 passengers at a maximum speed of 132 mph (212 km/h).

acquired an unjustified reputation for structural weakness, but by 1915 the Fokker Eindecker had become the most formidable fighter on the Western Front.

As the war progressed the demands of air fighting placed a premium on maneuverability, and fighters were almost all biplanes (Sopwith Camel, Fokker D.VII), speeds having risen to 125 mph (200 km/h) and service ceilings to over 20,000 ft.

A successful early biplane with pusher propeller, the de Havilland 2 of World War 1.

(6,100 m). Multi-engined long-range bombers were widely used by Russia (the Ilia Mourometz of SIKORSKY) and Germany. Conventional wood, wire, and fabric construction was being superseded by metal airframes, with a metal-skinned Junkers cantilever monoplane appearing in 1915 (J.I). Engines developed over 200 hp and included 8- and 12-cylinder in-line power units as well as rotaries.

After the Armistice in November 1918, many war-surplus aircraft passed into civilian use, particularly bombers which could carry mail or passengers (DH4, DH9, Farman Goliath).

In 1919 a Vickers Vimy bomber piloted by ALCOCK AND BROWN became the first aircraft to fly the Atlantic nonstop, although a Curtiss NC-4 flying boat had made the crossing in stages a month earlier. Successful three-engined airliners were introduced by Fokker (the F-VII) and Junkers (the G-31) which could cruise at 90-110 mph (145-175 km/h) carrying 15-20 passengers over 500-mi. (800 km) stages.

In America the Ford Trimotor made its debut in 1926, followed a year later by the Lockheed Vega, a single-engined machine with a stressed skin that could carry 6 passengers at cruising speeds of 135 mph (215 km/h) and had a range of up to 900 mi. (1,450 km).

The flying boat was widely favored for long-range operations, particularly in Britain and Germany (where the Dornier company evolved the 12-engined Do X).

Flying competitions (e.g. the Pulitzer Trophy) and record-breaking flights became increasingly important to the aircraft industry. At the end of 1919 Ross Smith and his crew flew a Vimy from London to Australia (taking four weeks), and in 1923 the first nonstop North American coast-to-coast flight was made by Lieutenants Kelly and Macready in a single-engined Fokker (26 hours 50 minutes). The first round-the-world flight (27,500 mi; 44,000 km) was achieved in 1924 by two U.S. Army Douglas biplanes, and before the decade was out Lieu-tenant-Commander Richard Byrd's three-engined Fokker had become the first plane to fly over both the North Pole (in 1926) and the South Pole (1929).

One of the outstanding aviation events of the 1920s was Charles LINDBERGH's solo flight from New York to Paris in the single-engined Ryan monoplane *Spirit of St Louis* (May 20-21, 1927 in 33 hours 39 minutes), while a Junkers monoplane made the first westbound crossing of the Atlantic in April 1928 (H. Koehl).

High-speed design was influenced by the Schneider Trophy seaplane competitions, which were concluded when Britain won three consecutive events (1927, 1929, 1931). The victorious Supermarine low-wing monoplanes with V-12 Rolls-Royce liquid-cooled engines were capable of 400 mph (640 km/h).

In the 1930s a new generation of mono-plane fighters (Messerschmitt 109, Spit-fire) appeared with retractable under-carriages and enclosed cockpits, features that were also adopted for high-speed bombers, especially in Germany (Heinkel 111, Junkers 86).

Modern airliners originated with the twin-engined BOEING 247 of 1933 and Douglas DC-2 of 1934. The four-engined Boeing Stratoliner of 1938, with a pressurized fuselage, was the next important step forward in commercial airplane design. During World War II the heavy bomber was extensively developed in Britain (Lancaster) and the United States (B-17, B-24, B-29). American long-range military transport aircraft (DC-4, CONSTELLATION, STRATOCRUISER) became mainstays of post-war civil aviation, and in competition with these efficient land

Presaging the era of large airliners, the Bristol Brabazon was a prototype 80-100 seater first flown in 1949 and finally scrapped for political reasons in 1953. With eight 2,500 hp engines, the Brabazon had a span of 230 ft. (70 m) and a length of 177 ft. (54 m).

planes the flying boats of the 1930s (Boeing 314, Short C-class) proved to be among the last of their line.

The first jet-propelled aircraft had been flown in Germany during 1939 (He 178), and by 1945 both the RAF and the Luft-waffe had jets in action. Wartime piston-engined fighters (P-47, P-51) eventually achieved almost 500 mph (800 km/h), but they were supplanted by jets (F-86, MiG-15) that were flying as fast as sound. Turboprops found an application for large aircraft, but during the 1950s jet-engined bombers (Canberra, B-47, Il-28) and civil transports (COMET, BOEING 707) came into service.

By 1956 jet fighters were attaining almost three times the speed of sound (F-104) but accident rates were high; later mach-ines (F-4, MiG-21) were endowed with more amenable handling qualities and in the 1970s fighter design tended to favor greater maneuverability rather than pure speed (F-16).

The bomber's role was reduced by the advent of intercontinental ballistic mis-siles, although the eight-jet B-52 served with the USAF for over 20 years. In the

early 1970s wide-bodied airliners seating 400 passengers were in service (BOEING 747, Douglas DC-10), and Russian and Anglo-French manufacturers were dev-eloping supersonic commercial aircraft (TU-144, CONCORDE).

See also AIRLINE; JET ENGINE; LIGHT AIRCRAFT; SUPERSONIC FLIGHT; WARPLANE.

Aviation medicine

Aviation medicine studies the effects of flight on human physiology. The most immediate medical problem likely to face a flier is the progressive rarefication of the atmosphere with height. Lack of oxy-gen as the atmospheric pressure falls leads to anoxia. Above 4,000 ft. (1,200 m) night vision becomes impaired due to this factor, at 10,000 ft. (3,000 m) anoxia begins to appear if heavy work is under-taken, and from 14,000-18,000 ft. (4,200-5,400 m) efficiency is seriously affected. Between 18,000 and 34,000 ft. (5,400-9,300 m) oxygen equipment will maintain sea-level capability, but above 34,000 ft. (9,300 m) even 100% oxygen will not prevent some degree of anoxia. To com-bat this, cockpits are pressurized to an altitude corresponding to 25,000 ft. (7,500 m).

Air pressure variation can cause injury to the ear structure and air passages if the subject does not mitigate the effect (e.g. by yawning); flying with a cold in an atmospheric pressure less than that cor-responding to about 8,000 ft. (2,400 m) can cause sinus barotrauma.

Accelerative and decelerative forces are measured in terms of g (1g equals an acceleration of 32.2 ft./sec./sec.). Sub-stantial positive g (which drains blood away from the head) is experienced in high-speed pullouts and tight turns, and also during the lift-off phase of space missions. Individual tolerances to g vary considerably, but at +4g most subjects suffer impaired vision (grayout) due to reduced retinal blood supply, followed by blackout at +5g and unconsciousness at +6g. Blackout thresholds as low as +2.5g or as high as +9g do occur, how-ever. Unconsciousness due to negative g

In long distance air transport the 1930s were the years of the flying boat. Able to land on any calm stretch of water, they were the largest and most luxurious airliners of the period and included the famous PanAm Clippers. Shown in the photograph is the British Short Empire Class flying boat, with a smaller seaplane riding piggyback. Requiring no fuel for takeoff, the smaller plane was able to fly nonstop from Scotland to South Africa, an all-time record distance of 5,998 mi. (9,653 km).

(which forces blood into the head) occurs at −4 or −5g if this value is maintained for about 5 seconds, the cause being critical and prolonged reduction of the arterio-venous pressure differential. Research has also been undertaken into the very high g forces experienced momentarily during the use of ejection seats. These can be as high as +25g for a fraction of a second, the pilot's tolerance being dictated by the strength of his spine.

Aviation medicine is also concerned with more fundamental physiological and psychological aspects of flying, such as the cause of motion sickness, the selection of trainees for aircrew training, the effect of noise and vibration on a pilot's capability, spacial disorientation, decompression sickness, and the layout of controls and instruments.

The photograph shows the mass of electronic equipment fitted in a modern supersonic military airplane to handle such jobs as navigation, bombing and fire control, radar search, and automatic identification of aircraft (see Avionics).

Avionics

A term derived from *aviation* and electronics, to describe the adapting of electronic systems to aircraft and the associated field of applied research. Until the 1940s, the systems involved in operating aircraft were purely mechanical, electric or magnetic, with radio apparatus the most sophisticated instrumentation. The advent of radar and the great advance made in airborne detection during World War II led to the general adoption of electronic distance-measuring and navigational aids. In military aircraft such devices improve weapon delivery

accuracy and in commercial aircraft give greater safety in operation.

A basic aircraft instrument, such as the ALTIMETER for giving an indication of height, provides a typical example of the application of avionics. Earlier altimeters were, in effect, aneroid barometers graduated to read off on a height scale by atmospheric pressure, giving a guide to height above sea level. The radar altimeter, by sending and measuring a radio pulse from the aircraft to the ground and back, gives a true reading of the aircraft's actual height over the terrain below.

Avionics play an important part in navigation, where previously magnetism — in the form of the ordinary compass — was used to indicate direction. The radio compass can identify the direction of a ground station and home an aircraft accordingly. Certain avionic equipment is now mandatory on civil aircraft to comply with international safety regulations.

A military aircraft, such as the Grumman A-6 Intruder, fitted with an intricate electronic device like the Norden multi-mode AN/APQ-148 radar, can simultaneously perform ground-mapping, identification, tracking, and ranging of moving targets.

A modern "instant bridge" constructed of aluminum alloy girders and designed to replace the Bailey Bridges of World War II. A 100 ft. (30 m) bridge can be assembled by 24 men in one hour, and can carry a 60 ton load.

Many avionic devices are based on television transmission and reception principles with similar cathode-ray tube displays; alternatively there may be a digital display, or linking to bring other systems, including weapon delivery, into action.

B

Backfire

An explosion in the exhaust system of an internal combustion engine sounding like a gun shot. It generally occurs when the

engine is throttled back while the vehicle continues at speed, going downhill for example. There are several reasons why an engine backfires: the ignition timing may be retarded; the fuel mixture may be too weak; or there may be a leak in the exhaust system.

Bailey bridge

A temporary steel-lattice bridge, named for its designer, Sir Donald Bailey, who introduced it in 1941. Bailey bridges were widely used by the Allied Forces in World War II to replace blown-up bridges, or to effect river crossings where there were no bridges. In peacetime Bailey bridges have shown their value as emergency structures where bridges have been damaged or swept away by floods.

The Bailey bridge is made by bolting a number of standard-size bays, or sections, together. Each bay consists of steel-girder side pieces, or trusses, and a sheet-steel deck supported by cross members.

To span a wide river, intermediate lattice piers may be built up from the river bed and the bridge constructed span by span. Alternatively, the river can be spanned by floating the Bailey bridge on buoyant floats, or pontoons. The sections of the floating bridge are connected flexibly to allow for movement up and down as a heavy vehicle passes across.

Baker, Sir Benjamin (1840-1907)

A British civil engineer, designer of the FORTH RAIL BRIDGE in Scotland (built 1882-1890) for which he was knighted. He was responsible for the construction of some of London's earliest underground railways, (see SUBWAYS), including the first deep-level "tubes." He also served as a consultant on the construction of the bridge over the Mississippi River at St. Louis, built by James Eads in 1867-74, and the first Aswan Dam in Egypt, completed in 1902.

Ballast

In ballooning, ballast is the material such as sand, which is released by the pilot when he wishes to ascend. In shipping, ballast is material carried to make a ship more stable when empty. Oil tankers, for example, use sea water as ballast. Submarines have ballast tanks, which are flooded with sea water to make them descend. In railroad engineering, ballast is the stone chippings laid beneath the track to allow rapid drainage of water.

Balloon

The simplest form of aircraft, in which lift is provided by a gas that is lighter than air. It was in balloons that man made his first flights, and balloons and their powered successors, the AIRSHIPS, have played a significant role throughout the history of aviation. The first balloon flights took place in France in 1783 when the MONTGOLFIER BROTHERS Joseph and Etienne invented the hot-air balloon. A few days after the successful flight of the *Montgolfière* another Frenchman, Jacques A.C. Charles, launched the first hydrogen balloon. For a while there was great rivalry between the supporters of the *Montgolfière* and the *Charlière*. But soon the hydrogen balloon established its supremacy, and hot-air balloons went out of use.

Today ballooning is becoming an increasingly popular sport: international meetings are held regularly and attract a large attendance. A significant feature of recent years has been the resurgence of the hot-air balloon.

Apart from sporting and military uses, the balloon has been valuable in scientific research and meteorology. Balloons are used to carry a variety of instruments high into the atmosphere to monitor conditions. Radiosondes are sounding balloons that collect data and then relay it back to the ground.

The theory of ballooning. The Greek scientist Archimedes (3rd century B.C.) established the simple principle of buoyancy on which balloon flight depends. The principle states that when a body is immersed in a fluid, it experiences an upward force-lift or upthrust — equal to the weight of fluid it displaces. This applies to a gas such as air as well as to any liquid, and so to make a balloon experience a net upthrust, it must be filled with a light gas. The balloon will then displace a sufficiently large volume of air, whose weight will exceed that of the balloon. Obviously hydrogen, the lightest of all gases, would be the first choice for ballooning, because it will provide the greatest lift. The drawback is that hydrogen is highly flammable. It is also very

Traditional Thames barges from the days of sail. Their masts could be lowered for passing under bridges.

penetrating, so that the bag, or envelope, needed to contain it must be relatively thick and heavy. Helium, the next lightest gas, provides about 90% of the lift of hydrogen but is nonflammable. It is, however, very expensive, and the most practical alternative for amateur balloonists is hot air, though it provides only about 25% the lift of hydrogen.

The gas balloon. The gas balloon consists of a spherical skin, or envelope, over which is slung a net. The net is attached to a load ring from which a light wicker basket, occupied by the crew, is suspended. The net distributes the weight of the payload — the basket and passengers — evenly over the envelope. The envelope itself is made of fabric impregnated with rubber to make it airtight.

At the bottom of the envelope is a narrow open-ended tube called the appendix, which acts as a kind of safety valve. As the balloon rises, the surrounding air pressure falls and the gas in the balloon expands. If the envelope were sealed, pressure would build up inside and would eventually cause it to rupture. But the appendix allows the gas to escape.

A balloon will continue to rise until the density of the surrounding atmosphere, which decreases regularly with height, equals the overall density of the balloon. At this point the balloon is in equilibrium. To rise higher, the balloon pilot must throw the ballast, usually sand, overboard. When all the ballast has been used up, the balloon can go no higher. To descend, the pilot releases gas from the top of the envelope through a valve. When the pilot has reached the ground, he rips open a ripping panel near the top of the envelope. This lets the gas inside escape and allows the envelope to deflate quickly before it is carried away by the wind.

The hot-air balloon. The original Montgolfier hot-air balloon consisted of an envelope of fabric and paper with a wide

opening at the bottom. Below the opening was a furnace burning straw. Since all the materials were highly combustible, it was not surprising that many of the early hot-air balloons caught fire. The modern hot-air balloon has an open lower end into which hot air is directed from a burner slung beneath it. The burner is fueled by bottled propane gas.

The envelope is usually made of light nylon, treated to make it more airtight. Unlike gas balloons, hot-air balloons require no ballast and have no need of a release valve to make them go up or down. To make the hot-air balloon ascend, the pilot switches on the burner to heat up the air inside. To make the balloon descend, the pilot allows the air inside to cool. Like the gas balloon, the hot-air balloon is fitted with a ripping panel for quick deflation on landing.

The hot-air balloon can lift less than the gas balloon and stay in the air for a much shorter period. But it can be more readily inflated, and is simpler and cheaper to run and inherently safer.

Baltimore and Ohio Railroad

The first American railroad to act as a common carrier of passengers and freight. It was incorporated in 1827, and backed by the merchants of Baltimore as their answer to the ERIE CANAL as a means of tapping the trade of the West. It opened for regular passenger and freight traffic on May 24, 1830, between Baltimore and Ellicott's Mills, a distance of 13 mi. The first trains were drawn by horses, after experiments with sail power and treadmill locomotives, but the performance of the tiny one-ton engine, the "Tom Thumb," persuaded the directors to decide on steam locomotives. The railroad finally reached the Ohio River in 1852; it now has over 5,500 mi. (8,800 km) of route extending as far west as St. Louis and Chicago, and is under the control of its former rival the Chesapeake and Ohio.

Barges

At one time the term barge was used to describe any small cargo-carrying sailing vessel, but the modern barge is a flat-bottomed boat designed to carry cargo on inland waterways. Those carrying heavy goods on the great European rivers such as the Rhine and Volga are very large and have their own engines, covered holds, and accommodation for the crew. Barges used on many American rivers and lakes are also large, but they have neither engine nor accommodation. These straight-sided craft may be lashed together in a compact mass and pushed from behind by specially developed pusher tugs. Or they may be joined end to end in line and towed or pushed. Over 20 barges with a combined load of 60,000 tons or more may be linked in a single "tow."

Barges like these with no engine are known as dumb barges. They may be pushed, towed, or simply allowed to drift with the current. Dumb barges used to take cargo from large ships to the shore — or to another part of a dock or harbor — are an essential part of the equipment of any port, and are usually called lighters.

The size of barges depends to a great extent on the depth and width of the waterway, the sharpness of its bends, and the speed of the current. Draft is normally between 5 and 10 ft. (1½ and 3 m), and average dimensions are about 175 ft. (53 m) long by 25 ft. (7.5 m) wide. However 300-ft. (90 m) barges carrying over 3,000 tons of cargo are not uncommon.

Some large dumb barges are fitted with an auxiliary sail, but the days of the true sailing barge are past. These workhorses of inland and coastal waters usually

A gigantic "push tow" of about 40 barges lashed together and pushed by a single tug, typical of American inland waterways.

carried a huge mainsail held taut by a diagonal spar or sprit. The mast was counterbalanced for easy lowering when negotiating bridges.

Bark and barkentine

Sailing vessels with three or more masts and a combination of square and fore-and-aft sails. On the bark, the after (mizzen) mast carried fore-and-aft sails, while the other masts were square-rigged. On the barkentine only the foremast was square-rigged. These rigs were introduced when competition from steam forced cuts in costs. Fore-and-aft sails are easier to handle and require smaller crews.

A typical powered barge of European inland waterways.

Bascule bridge

A kind of movable bridge in which the bridge deck pivots upward to allow traffic to pass through. It is the modern equivalent of the drawbridge, and is used in locations where substantial headroom is required for passing cross traffic, as for example in ship canals or port approaches. The simplest kind is the single-leaf bascule, which consists of a counterweighted cantilever, pivoting horizontally, whose overhang spans the gap to be bridged. More common is the double-leaf bascule, employing twin cantilever arms. London's TOWER BRIDGE is an outstanding example of the double-leaf bascule. But

A Norwegian Bark, with square sails on the fore and main masts, and fore-and-aft sails on the mizzen (unlike the full-rigged ship which has square sails on every mast, and therefore required a larger crew).

the largest-span bascule is the railway bridge at Sault Sainte Marie, Michigan, whose span is 336 ft. (100 m). More than 20 bascule bridges were built to span the Chicago River (see BRIDGES).

Bathyscaph

A navigable diving vessel designed by the Swiss scientist August PICCARD for observation and research in the deepest parts of the ocean. Driven by electrically operated propellers, the bathyscaph has, like an airship, two closely linked components: a small steel observer's cabin, strong enough to withstand the enormous pressures at the sea bed; and a large float filled with gasoline (which is lighter than water) to provide buoyancy. Air-filled ballast tanks give enough lift to keep the bathyscaph afloat on the surface. To submerge, these tanks are filled with water. To decrease the speed of descent, or to ascend, ballast in the form of metal pellets is released.

In 1960 the bathyscaph *Trieste* descended to the bed of the Marianas Trench in the Pacific — the deepest part of any ocean — reaching a depth of 35,800 ft. (10,912 m). This is over twice the depth of the deepest dive by any other submersible. In 1972 *Trieste II* carried out the deepest ever salvage operation, at a depth of 16,500 ft. (5,029 m).

The bathyscaph Trieste, showing clearly the small spherical observer's cabin and the massive gasoline-filled float. This vessel descended 35,800 ft. (10,912 m) to the deepest part of the ocean in 1960.

Bathysphere

A development of the diving bell, designed by the Americans William BEEBE and Otis Barton. A steel sphere about 5 ft. (1.5 m) in diameter, with portholes and searchlights, and carrying supplies of compressed air for the occupants to breathe,

the bathysphere was the first diving vessel to reach great depths. The culmination of a series of dives off Bermuda in the early 1930s was a descent to 3,028 ft. (923 m).

In spite of this spectacular success, the bathysphere had obvious drawbacks. It was suspended by cable from a support ship on the surface. It was therefore unmaneuverable, and any damage to the cable — caused, for example, by surface waves — would mean certain death for the occupants (see BATHYSCAPH).

Battery

Batteries are used in motor vehicles and other forms of transportation to provide electrical power to start the engines and run the electrical systems. They are also sometimes used as a source of motive power, driving electric motors.

A battery is made up of a number of cells, in which electricity is produced by electro-chemical reactions. Essentially a cell consists of two plates (electrodes) immersed in a chemical solution that conducts electricity (an electrolyte). Chemical changes take place at the electrodes which result in each acquiring an electric charge. When the electrodes are connected to an external circuit, electrons flow from the cathode, or negatively charged electrode, to the anode, or positively charged electrode. This flow of electrons constitutes an electric current. (By convention, we always say that the current flows from positive to negative, but in fact, the electron flow is in the opposite direction.)

The cells used in vehicle batteries are

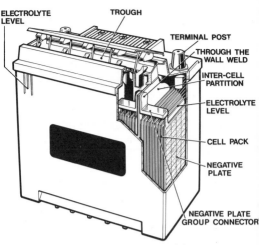

A cutaway view of a typical automobile storage battery.

known as secondary, or storage cells because they can store an electric charge. When connected to an external circuit they discharge and eventually lose all their charge, but can then be recharged with electricity from another source, such as a generator.

The most widely used storage battery is the lead-acid type. This is made up of either three or, more usually, six cells connected in series, each producing a little over 2 volts and thus giving a 6-volt or 12-volt battery. There are two sets of plates in each cell, one set forming the cathode, the other the anode. They are kept apart by separators. The anode is made of lead peroxide, the cathode of porous, spongy lead. The electrolyte is dilute sulfuric acid.

When an external circuit is connected to the battery, the acid reacts with the electrodes, and electric current flows. The lead peroxide and lead electrodes are both converted to lead sulfate, and water is produced, thereby diluting the acid further. The battery is recharged by connecting it to an external source of electricity, done automatically in motor vehicles by the generator-dynamo or alternator. When the battery is being charged, the lead sulfate on the anode and cathode changes back to lead peroxide and lead respectively. During the charging sequence, oxygen is given off at the anode and hydrogen at the cathode. The gases come from the breakdown of water in the cells, and thus the cells must be topped up with distilled water from time to time. The "health" of a battery can be tested with a HYDROMETER. A fully charged battery should show a specific gravity reading of about 1.28, while a flat battery will show a specific gravity of only about 1.11. Batteries usually fail to hold their charge when they get old. This is due to the plates buckling, becoming encrusted with sulfate, or short-circuiting.

Other types of secondary cells, or accumulators, are in use including alkaline cells, which use an alkali as the electrolyte rather than an acid. The two commonest kinds are nickel-iron and nickel-cadmium, both of which use potassium hydroxide as electrolyte. They have positive plates of nickel hydroxide packed in a steel grid, and negative plates of finely divided iron and cadmium respectively. Nickel-cadmium batteries are widely used in airplanes for ground power-supply functions and as in-flight back-up units.

The silver oxide-zinc battery with potassium hydroxide electrolyte is another alkaline type. This could have widespread application in electric propulsion for automobiles since it has an unusually high capacity. Silver oxide-zinc batteries are used for providing power in spacecraft and space stations such as Skylab. Another promising battery for electric automobiles is the sodium-sulfur type, which could give the automobile a cruising range of up to 200 mi. (320 km), a considerable improvement upon existing vehicles (see ELECTRIC CAR).

Bay Area Rapid Transit (BART)

One of the most modern and advanced rapid transit systems in the world. It grew from the work of the San Francisco Bay Area Rapid Transit Commission, a study and planning group formed in 1951 and including representatives of all nine Bay Area counties. The Commission recommended a 385-mi. (616 km) system of which 123 mi. (196 km) would be built in the first stage, consisting of the 75-mi. (120 km) system now open plus planned links to Marin and San Mateo counties, which withdrew from the scheme in 1962. The double-track system was authorized the same year by Alameda, Contra Costa, and San Francisco counties and includes 19 mi. (30 km) in subway and tunnel, 27 mi. (43 km) on the surface, 4 mi. (6.4 km) in the immersed twin-tube running under the Bay and 25 mi. (40 km) of ele-

The Bayonne Bridge between Bayonne, N.J., and Staten Island, N.Y. Completed in 1931, it was for 45 years the world's longest steel arch bridge.

vated construction. There are 33 stations, 22 of which have car parking facilities. The trains are automatically driven under instruction from a central computer at Lake Merritt which controls their speed, their spacing on the track, and stops as well as train announcements at stations. The trains are electrically driven, picking up current from a third rail at 1,000 volts DC. They are air-conditioned, carpeted, and have 72 seats in the 70-ft (21 m) long aluminum alloy bodies. The average service speed is 42 mph (67 km/h) but the cars can attain 80 mph (128 km/h) with only 90 seconds separation between trains at peak hours. The first section opened on September 11, 1972 and the final section, the Trans-Bay tube, opened for public service on September 16, 1974.

Bayonne Bridge

One of the longest steel-arch bridges in the world, with a span of 1,652 ft. (504 m). It crosses the Kill van Kull between Bayonne, N.J., and Staten Island, N.Y. De-

signed by Othmar H. AMMANN and completed in 1931, the Bayonne bridge carries automobile and truck traffic. It was built with the aid of temporary trestle falsework, which is unusual in a steel-arch bridge of such a size (see ARCH BRIDGE).

BB 9004

This SNCF (French Railways) electric locomotive holds, jointly with CC 7107, the world rail speed record of 205.6 mph (330.8 km/h). BB 9004 achieved this speed pulling three cars weighing 100 tons from Facture to Morcenx on the Bordeaux-to-Dax line on March 28, 1955. Weighing 108 tons, BB 9004 normally develops 4,300 hp at 1,500 volts DC, but for its record run developed a peak 12,000 hp.

Beach buggy

An open-bodied vehicle designed primarily for traveling on sandy beaches. Californian enthusiast Bruce Meyers conceived the beach buggy in 1966 by fitting a simple lightweight open body onto the chassis of a Volkswagen and creating what came to be called the Meyers Manx.

Beam bridge

The simplest kind of bridge, which consists of a straight beam of timber, reinforced concrete, or steel supported at or near each end. The beam is horizontally self-supporting and exerts only a downward thrust on its supports. The beam cannot span too great a gap because it tends to sag under its own weight, and will eventually collapse in the middle. The simple beam can be strengthened by building a metal TRUSS on it either above or below. Railroad bridges are often strengthened in this way.

A four-car train on the Southern Alameda elevated section of San Francisco's Bay Area Rapid Transit (BART) system. The automatically driven trains reach speeds of 80 mph (128 km/h), and average 42 mph (67 km/h).

The beam experiences different forces in its upper and lower parts, or chords — compression in the upper chord and tension in the lower chord. The materials used for a beam bridge must be capable of withstanding both compression and tension, which is a basic design disadvantage. In practice the simple beam is usually the most economical form of bridge where the gap to be spanned is small — up to about 130 ft. (40 m). Greater gaps can, of course, be spanned if intermediate supporting piers can readily be built. The 23.87-mi. (38.4 km) long PONTCHARTRAIN CAUSEWAY in Louisiana is an impressive example of a multispan beam bridge, with 2,170 short spans.

The cantilever is a beam that is supported at one end and near the middle so that the upper chord is in tension and the lower chord in compression — the reverse of the simple beam. Cantilevers are able to span greater gaps than simple beams (see CANTILEVER BRIDGE). Many modern bridges incorporate both beams and cantilevers in a composite design. The 2¾-mi. (4.5 km) Tappan Zee Bridge across the Hudson River above New York consists mainly of short-span beams, but has a 1,325-ft. (404 m) cantilever span over the navigation channel (see BRIDGES).

Bearings

Bearings are fitted to machines to support rotating parts and to minimize friction between the surfaces in contact. The two main types of bearings are plain or journal bearings and rolling bearings.

One major type of plain bearing is the shell bearing. This is the kind used to support the crankshaft and the ends of the connecting rods in an automobile engine. A shell bearing is split into two halves for easy assembly. It has a steel backing and inner shells of softer bearing metal. When the crankshaft is rotating, oil is fed to the main bearings through a hole in each shell. From there it passes to a groove around the inner surface of the shell. Rotation of the shaft distributes the oil around the bearing. It creates an oil wedge which separates the shaft and bearing. A plain bearing that is not split in two halves is often called a bush bearing. The camshaft in an automobile engine usually rotates in bush bearings.

A variety of materials are used for the inner lining of bearings, including white-metal alloys, or babbits, copper-lead alloys, aluminum-tin alloys, and bronzes. The babbits may be lead base or tin base. The lead-base alloy consists of a soft matrix of lead containing hard crystallites of tin and antimony. The tin-base alloys consist of hard cuboids of tin-antimony alloy and needles of copper-tin alloy in a soft matrix of tin-rich solid solution. In

Tapered four-row cone assembly.

Spherical roller bearing.

Spherical plain bearing.

each case the soft matrix smears out under load to form a thin lubricating film. Any abrasive dirt that finds its way into the bearing should embed itself in the soft matrix rather than scratch the shaft. Since babbits are relatively weak they require an intermediate layer of bearing alloy between them and the steel backing. This layer is often made of copper-lead alloy or leaded bronze. Often bronze bearing alloys are used by themselves, and are strong enough not to need a steel backing. Sometimes porous materials are used for bearings. They are made from metallic powders by sintering and pressing — a technique called powder metallurgy. These materials, which include bronzes containing 90% copper and 10% tin, can absorb as much as 35% lubricating oil by volume.

Roller bearings support rotating parts on a set of very hard rolling elements, such as balls, rollers or needles. The idea behind these bearings is to replace the sliding motion of one surface against another by rolling motion. Since rolling friction is much less than sliding friction, these bearings are also called antifrictional bearings. The balls or rollers usually roll between smooth, hardened steel rings called raceways. They are generally held in position by a so-called cage. The inner part of the bearing is called the inner race, the outer part, the outer race. In a typical application — say, a wheel bearing — the inner race fits over the axle, and is stationary, while the outer race rotates with the wheel. Rolling bearing materials are made from the highest quality steel, usually a hardened high-

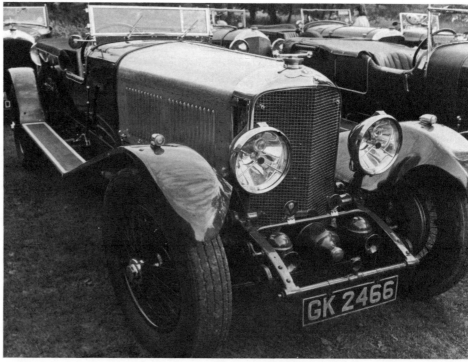
Bentley's luxurious 8-liter limousine, expensive and beautifully engineered.

carbon steel containing about 1% carbon and 1-1.5% chromium.

Beebe, (Charles) William (1877-1962)

An American biologist, made the first deep-ocean descent of more than half a mile (0.8 km). Beebe pioneered the design of the craft in which he made the descent, the bathysphere, in collaboration with the American engineer Otis Barton (see BATHYSPHERE).

The world's first practical gasoline engined automobile, Carl Benz's three-wheeler of 1885. Unlike Daimler's first machine of 1886, it was designed as an entity, and the improved model of 1888 was the first automobile in series production.

Belt drive

Transmission of power by means of a belt. In some automobile engines, for example, it is used instead of the usual chain to drive the camshaft. Teeth on the inner surface of the belt mesh with teeth of the pulleys on the crankshaft and camshaft. The radiator fan and water pump in car engines are driven from the crankshaft by belt — the fan belt. Also, belts are used in the unique variomatic automatic transmission used in DAF automobiles.

Bentley

British car manufacturer, Captain W.O. Bentley had been in the automobile business before World War I, and during the war he designed aircraft engines, playing a pioneering role in the use of aluminum pistons. His first car, a 3-liter, 4-cylinder model of 80 bhp, was shown at the 1919 Motor Show. One of the great vintage sports cars, the 3-liter was Bentley's greatest success. It was produced in

three models and won the coveted 24-hour Le Mans race in 1924 and 1927; later and larger Bentleys won the event in 1928, 1929, and 1930. Other famous models include the Big Six, the Speed Six, a popular 4½-liter sports car, and the luxurious 8-liter limousine.

Bentley cars were superbly engineered — and very expensive. By 1930 Bentley was in serious financial trouble, and in 1933 the model name was taken over by Rolls-Royce.

Benz, Carl (1844-1929)

German mechanical engineer, a pioneer of the internal combustion engine and a founder of the automobile industry. Carl Benz built the world's first successful gasoline-engined car, his "Motor-wagen," in 1885. A three-wheeler, it was powered by a ¾-hp single cylinder four-stroke engine, had electrical ignition, belt drive, and an advanced differential gear. Unlike most early experimenters, who built engines and fitted them to existing vehicles (i.e. a coach or cart designed to be pulled by a horse), Benz designed his car as a complete entity. His design was patented the following year, and he gave the first public demonstration on July 3, 1886, when he reached a speed of 9 mph (15 km/h). Benz went on to manufacture the world's first standard production model. This was his 1½-hp three-wheeler, which was advertised as "an agreeable vehicle as well as a mountain climbing apparatus." Few sales were actually made, but the 3-hp Viktoria of 1893 (his

first four-wheeler), and the smaller Vélo of 1894 became the first production models to be built and sold in significant numbers. In 1895, Benz's factory turned out 62 Vélos and 36 Viktorias. By 1898 annual production had risen to well over 400; and before the end of the following year the 2,000th Benz left the works. After a period of decline between 1901 and 1904, when the firm lagged behind others in design, Benz went on to produce many successful cars, including the gigantic 22-liter 200-hp "Blitzen Benz" racing car.

Benz and DAIMLER are reputed to have spent their lives vying for recognition as inventor of the automobile. However in 1926 the two firms merged, and their products carried the name Mercedes-Benz.

Bernoulli's principle

The 18th-century Swiss mathematician Daniel Bernoulli first expressed the principle that the pressure of a moving fluid varies inversely with its velocity. In simpler terms, if the speed of a fluid increases, then its pressure decreases, and vice versa. This principle has widespread applications in fluid mechanics and aerodynamics. It explains the operation of the VENTURI in a carburetor and the action of an airfoil (see AERODYNAMICS).

Best Friend of Charleston

The first commercial steam locomotive built in the Western Hemisphere, and the first to run in regular service pulling a train of passenger cars. It was built at the West Point Foundry in New York City and made its first run from Charleston, on what was then the South Caroline Railroad, on December 25, 1830. Six months later, a crewman, annoyed by the noise of the escaping steam, tied down the safety valve and the "Best Friend" exploded. It was rebuilt as the "Pheonix," and a "barrier car," loaded with six bales of cotton, was placed between the engine and the passenger coaches.

Best Friend of Charleston, the first American-built steam locomotive.

Bicycle

Variously considered a toy, or an ideal vehicle for mass urban transit, or a pleasant means of recreation, the bicycle was the first form of mechanical transportation to enable man to travel under his own power faster and further than his feet could carry him. Probably the most efficient method of using human energy for propulsion, the bicycle increases man's speed and range by a factor of four or five.

There are today two main types of bicycles: those with a traditional triangular frame, and those with the cross-framed model invented by the English engineer Alexander Moulton in 1958. The former

open frame is not as strong as the complete triangle.

The frame is usually made of steel tubing, or (for lightweight racing models) of aluminum alloy. The various members are welded together or joined by brazed lugs.

Transmission and gears. Although shaft and belt transmissions have been tried, bicycle drive is almost invariably by a chain which transmits the drive from a large sprocket turned by the pedals to a small one which rotates the rear wheel. Altering the relative sizes of the two sprockets alters the gearing — the greater the difference between them,

ated by back-pedaling, which expands a split-sleeve against the inside of the rear wheel hub, coaster brakes have the great advantage of being unaffected by wet weather and being almost maintenance-free. DRUM BRAKES, similar to those on automobiles, are sometimes used, while in Europe most cycles have CALIPER BRAKES. Cable-operated by handlebar levers, these force brake pads against the sides of the wheel rim. Many older bicycles have rod brakes, in which rods (again operated by handlebar levers) pull the brake pads against the rim. Despite the use of high-friction materials, drum, caliper, and rod brakes are all prone to slip when wet.

A Draisienne or dandy horse of 1819. Although "walked" along like its predecessors, it represented a notable advance in that it was the first steerable type of bicycle.

A boneshaker bicycle of 1869, the year before the first use by Starley of wire spoked wheels.

A "high bicycle" (or penny farthing) of the 1870s. The enormous front wheel improved the speed potential at the expense of stability and ease of riding.

has a pair of subsidiary triangles at the back to hold the rear wheel, and a pivoting steering column at the front to which are attached curved front-wheel "forks." The forks are curved to create slight springiness; this type of cycle has no other form of suspension beyond that given by the seat springs and the pneumatic tires. Triangular-framed cycles normally have wheels with a diameter of 26 or 27 in. (66 or 68.6 cm), while the cross-framed Moulton type has small 16-in. (40 cm) wheels.

The Moulton cycle frame consists of one main tube of oval cross section with two parallel rising tubes attached to this at right angles, one for the seat and one for the steering column and front forks. Front- and rear-wheel forks are attached to the frame by rubber suspension units, giving a significantly smoother ride than conventional machines.

Another advantage of the small-wheeled design is the increased baggage space and the lower and therefore more stable positioning of the baggage carrier. Also, since there is no high horizontal crossbar, the cycle is equally suitable for both sexes; the woman's version of the triangular framed cycle omits the crossbar, and although reinforced, the resultant

the greater the speed potential. The highest speed reached on a bicycle is just over 140 mph (225 km/h). It was achieved by riding in the slipstream of a specially adapted automobile, and by using a pedal sprocket almost as large as the wheels. Some racing cycles have a "fixed wheel," in which the rear sprocket is fixed to the wheel, but normally the rear sprocket has a ratchet mechanism to permit coasting. Two types of gears are used: the dérailleur, in which the chain is "derailed" from one to another of a series of sprockets (with up to six sprockets on the wheel and three on the crank, a combination which gives 18 possible gear ratios); and the epicyclic hub gear, which alters the ratio between the wheel sprocket and the driving axle, normally providing from two to five ratios.

Bicycle safety. Recent safety rulings in the United States require all cycles to have reflectors on the front, back, sides, and pedals; protective coverings on metal edges(fenders, projecting bolts, etc.); locking devices to secure wheels, seat, handlebars and stem; and efficient brakes.

The most usual type of brake in the United States is the coaster brake. Oper-

Lights at front and rear may either be clip-on battery-powered types, or be wired up to a dynamo or generator (fitted in the front wheel hub, or acting by friction on the side of the tire).

History. It was only after man had been using the wheel for some 5,000 years that an inventor first thought of placing two wheels in line and sitting on the bar that joined them. Various hand-driven three- and four-wheelers appeared in 18th-century France and England, but the first

A typical modern bicycle with triangular frame, epicyclic hub gears, and cable operated caliper brakes on both wheels.

two-wheeler was probably invented in 1790 by a Frenchman, de Sivrac. He called his machine a *célérifère*. It had heavy cart-type wheels, no provision for steering, and no propulsion mechanism (the rider simply "walked" it along with his feet on the road).

In 1817 the *célérifère*, or "horse on wheels" (it often had a carved horse's head), was superseded by the *Draisienne* or dandy horse. Invented by Baron Karl von Drais, this was as heavy as its predecessor, and was propelled in the same way, but it was steerable.

The first mechanically driven bicycle was invented in 1839 by a Scottish blacksmith, Kirkpatric Macmillan. It weighed 57 lb. (26 kg), including its carved horse's head, had iron-tired wheels, and was pro-

on the front wheel would improve the machine's usefulness and efficiency. Thus the velocipede or "boneshaker" was born, and the following year series production began. The bicycle had arrived and was promptly labeled by the London *Times* newspaper "a new terror to the streets." By 1865 the Michaux factory was producing 400 cycles a year, and in 1866 an American company was set up by one of Michaux's mechanics.

In 1870 James Starley patented the first lightweight all-metal bicycle, with (a vital advance) wire-spoked wheels. Starley's machines had a large driving wheel (the larger the wheel the greater the speed possible), and a small rear wheel. Further

hub and dérailleur gears, lightweight metals, and so on. But the cycle remained essentially unchanged until 1958, when Alex Moulton designed his small-wheeled machine, which with its rubber suspension units rapidly became popular.

The bicycle today. In recent years more bicycles have been sold annually in the United States than automobiles, and the total number in the country exceeds 80 million (out of a world total of around 135 million). However, although widely used by students and children, the cycle is not generally a popular means of transportation. The situation is very different in Europe and Asia, especially in the two

A tricycle of the 1880s, with steering by "remote control."

The Coventry rotary tricycle of 1880, an attempt to combine the speed potential of the high bicycle with greater stability and ease of riding.

A safety bicycle of 1885, the immediate precursor of the modern cycle, with chain drive to a sprocket on the rear wheel.

pelled by swinging the feet backwards and forwards to move long levers attached to cranks on the axles of the rear wheel. Macmillan used his machine over a period of several years, but it aroused little interest and was soon forgotten.

It was not until 1861 that the idea was taken up again, this time in France. A Parisian coachbuilder, Pierre Michaux, was asked to repair a *Draisienne*. Realizing its limitations, his son casually suggested that fitting cranks and pedals

The frame of this modern child's bicycle is a variant on the Moulton design. The cycle has dérailleur gears, and "feature" saddle and handlebars (the latter are generally considered less safe than the conventional type).

improved by the addition of gears, these "penny farthings," as they were called (after two coins of the period), dictated the design of the bicycle for the next decade. Also known as the High Bicycle, or the Ordinary, it enjoyed a widespread vogue despite its instability and the high risk of being thrown over the handlebars when braking.

Then came the invention of the endless chain and the brilliant idea of placing the pedals between the wheels, and driving the rear wheel with a chain. The wheels could now be the same size, since speed depended on the size of the sprockets. Known as the "safety bicycle," and invented by H.J. Lawson in 1874, the design was much improved by James Starley, who began production of the Rover Safety bicycle in Coventry, England, in 1885. With the addition of the pneumatic tire in 1888, the modern bicycle was complete. During the 1890s, the cycle industry boomed both in Europe and America. For the first time ordinary people were able to get out and about and enjoy the countryside with very little expense. This popularity paved the way for the success of the autombile.

Minor improvements followed: rim brakes, ball bearings, curved front forks,

traditionally cycle-oriented nations of Denmark and the Netherlands. The two European countries have the advantage of being relatively flat, but on the other hand winters in all three areas are cold, a factor which does not deter the millions of people who ride to work every day. In the Netherlands 76% of the population own cycles, and special cycle tracks are provided in towns and beside many interurban highways. Experiments along similar lines have been and are being tried in other countries, including Britain.

The advantages of bicycles for urban transit are many. They are quiet, cheap, healthy, and pollution-free; in crowded conditions they are often faster than automobiles or buses; they require far less road space — a 12-ft. (4 m) wide cycle track can carry five times more people than a 24-ft. (8 m) automobile road — and the pavement is very much cheaper to construct. On the other hand they are, unless provided with separate paths or tracks, relatively dangerous; and in adverse weather they are uncomfortable. However, it seems probable that the energy crisis, the growing use for recreation and other factors will make them more rather than less popular in the coming years.

Big Boy

The largest conventional steam locomotives ever built, designed to take Union Pacific freight trains over the Wasatch Range in Utah without help from other engines. Twenty-five were built in 1941 and 1944. They were articulated on the Mallet principle with a 4-8-8-4 wheel arrangement. They weighed 604 tons and developed over 6,000 hp at 75 mph (120 km/h). At full throttle they used 50 tons of water and 22 tons of coal an hour. They were built by Alco (American Locomotive Company), and the name "Big Boy" was given by an Alco workman who chalked it on one of the huge locomotives while it was still being built.

Giant Big Boy steam locomotive, built to negotiate the Rocky Mountains.

Biplane

Airplane with two sets of mainplanes (wings) placed one above the other. As the first successful airplane, built by the Wright Brothers, was a biplane, this design had a headstart over the early single-winged airplanes, such as the Blériot monoplanes. The two wings of a biplane, however, with their interconnecting struts, experienced more drag than a single wing of equivalent area. Design trends swung to the monoplane in the 1930s and the few biplane types still built today are mainly for sport flying and aerobatic display, where control and handling are more important than speed.

Bireme

A WARSHIP of the ancient world, propelled by two banks of oarsmen, and often carrying a square sail on a mast stepped amidships. At the bow a massive pointed ram provided the main armament.

Black box

An apparatus such as a bombsight, automatic pilot, control box, or electronic device that can be removed as a complete package. In recent years it has meant particularly the flight recorder. These instruments were first used to record the verbal reports of test pilots while trying out new designs and their use was extended to monitor instruments and record readings. Test pilots previously had to scribble their findings on knee pads at a time when their utmost concentration was needed. Since such recordings of crew conversation during flight might throw light upon accident causes and so contribute to future flight safety, airliners are also fitted with these recorders. Made in specially strengthened cases to withstand impact, they are anything but black to render them conspicuous to those searching wreckage to recover them.

Black-top road

A road paved with tar or bitumen. (See HIGHWAYS, ROADS, and STREETS.)

Blériot, Louis (1872-1936)

French pioneer aircraft constructor and pilot, best known for accomplishing the first flight across the English Channel (July 25, 1909). Blériot studied engineering at the École Centrale des Arts et Métiers, and began to study aeronautics in 1896. Ten years later he established the first French airplane factory, at Issy-

Louis Blériot standing in front of his famous monoplane in which he made the first airplane crossing of the English Channel in 1909.

les-Moulineaux, where he concentrated on the development of monoplanes. He was awarded the Prix de Voyage in 1907 for a flight from Étaples to Orleans, and completed another successful cross-country flight between Tours and Arthenay. His historic flight across the English Channel from Les Baraques, near Calais, to Northfall Meadow, near Dover castle, took $36\frac{1}{2}$ minutes (from 4.41 until $5.17\frac{1}{2}$ a.m.), and earned him a prize of £1,000 presented by the London *Daily Mail*. At the end of 1909, Louis Blériot also held the world air speed record of 47.85 mph (77.03 km/h) in a type XII monoplane (established during the Rheims aviation meeting of August 1909).

Blimp

A non-rigid AIRSHIP, which has no skeletal structure to support its gas bag.

Block system

A method of separating trains by a distance sufficient to ensure that they cannot collide. In early days, a man at important stations held a train until the one ahead had been gone for a certain time. This "time-interval" system could not take into account emergency stops, and so it was never certain that the line was really clear. When the electric telegraph was invented, it became possible to use the "block" system, in which the line is divided into sections or "blocks," and a train not allowed into a block section until it is certain that the previous train has left it. The automatic block system (1872) provided the basis for general improvements in railroad signaling. This system incorporates electrical circuits on the tracks, which are short-circuited by the train's wheels. The current activates the danger signals. Despite these advances, some railroads still use a manual block system.

Blue Riband

A silver trophy presented to the passenger ship making the fastest crossing of the North Atlantic, from the early days of steam until the 1950s. The list of famous Blue Riband liners includes the *Mauretania* (she held it for over 20 years, her best average speed for the crossing being 27.4 knots), *Normandie* (31.3 knots), *Queen Mary* (31.69 knots), and *United States* (35.59 knots) — the fastest liner ever.

Boat lift

A means of transporting a vessel through a change of water level on a canal, eliminating the need for a deep lock or "staircase" of locks. The vessel floats into a steel chamber or caisson, which is then sealed at each end and lifted or lowered between the two levels. One of the first lifts was built at Anderton, England, in 1875, to negotiate a 50-ft. (15 m) level change. One of the deepest boat lifts is at Niederfinow, Germany, whose 117-ft. (35 m) lift can accommodate 1,000-ton vessels.

Boats

Small and often open watercraft. The term SHIP is used for large vessels, while a YACHT is usually between a boat and a ship in size, and is enclosed (it has a deck, and a cabin to provide shelter and accommodation for crew and passengers). In fact, many powered pleasure and ferry boats are partly or completely enclosed, and some naval vessels commonly known as boats (patrol boat or torpedo boat, for example) are fully enclosed.

Coracle fishermen in Wales in the mid 19th century. Among the earliest framed boats, coracles are similar to the American Indian bullboat and corita, and are still used in parts of Wales and Ireland.

Boats may be paddled, rowed, or (in shallow waters) poled; or they may have an engine or sails (see SAILBOATS). They range from small ROWBOATS through MOTORBOATS and large cabin cruisers, to speedboats which can skim along at over 100 mph (160 km/h). The traditional boat has a rounded bottom. Sitting as it does fairly deep in the water, this gives a steady ride, and it passes through the water with a minimum of resistance. To improve stability the bottom of the curve is often somewhat flattened. The two other basic hull forms are the flat bottom, which is easy to build and very stable in calm water, but inefficient; and the V-

The traditional method of boat construction, with a framework (keel, stem and stern posts, and ribs) and a cladding of timber planks. The planks may be laid edge to edge (carvel built) as in the photograph, or they may be overlapped (clinker built).

bottom, which represents a compromise between round and flat. With the advent of modern materials such as fiberglass, almost any shape is possible, and a great many sections have been tried. But for most purposes, rounded or deep V-shaped hulls are still usual. They are roomy and stable. They slip through the water easily, and yet have a good grip in the water which makes them responsive when maneuvering and helps prevent their being blown sideways by crosswinds (a flat-bottomed boat, like an AIR-CUSHION VEHICLE or a car on ice, is inclined to skid when cornering).

Boats with flat, round or V-shaped hulls are displacement craft. That is, they are designed to travel in the water, displacing an amount of water equal to their own weight. Because they have to force their way through the water, which is over 800 times as dense as air, very high speeds are not practicable. Boats de-

signed to travel at more than about 40 knots are normally planing craft. At rest and at low speeds, they sit in the water like displacement boats, but at speed their bow rises up out of the water and the craft skims on the surface (or planes). For this, an entirely different hull shape is required. The forward half or two-thirds of the hull is usually conventional in form, for travel at slow speeds. But towards the stern there is a distinct step (sometimes two) up. The stern is thus shallower, and often almost rectangular in cross section. As the boat speeds up, the forward part of the hull lifts clear of the water, and the craft skims along the surface on the flat stern "step." Speedboats thus designed are often called hydroplanes. Speeds of over 100 mph (160 km/h) are not unusual, while the official record for a propeller-driven hydroplane stands at 202.42 mph (325.76 km/h). With jet propulsion much higher speeds are possible. The official record, held by Lee Taylor, Jr., of California in *Hustler* is 285.213 mph (459.005 km/h), and on his fatal last run Donald Campbell reached 328 mph (527.8 km/h) in *Bluebird K7*.

At high speed, hydroplanes can be extremely dangerous except on dead calm water, and even then, with no grip on the water, they are difficult to maneuver. On choppy or rough waters they skim into the air off one wave, and crash down on the surface, only to bounce off the next wave. The result is exciting and spectacular, but if the "landing" is uneven it may be disastrous. And while a powerful displacement boat with a top speed of 35 knots can maintain 20 knots in rough weather, a fast planing boat may be forced to reduce speed to less than 10 knots.

Other kinds of motorboats include inflatable craft fitted with outboard motors, and houseboats. Originally broad-beamed box-like boats with no engine, modern houseboats are powered and normally have a pointed bow and a shallow V-shaped bottom. They range from medium-sized weekend or "camper" types, to luxury floating homes 60 ft. (18 m) or more in

A typical small boat of far eastern waters, the sampan, Much larger sampans are also made, often with one or more lug sails.

The popular and adaptable outboard motor is used on a wide variety of boats, large and small. The photograph shows an outboard motor powered inflatable rubber dinghy.

length and capable of speeds of about 30 mph (50 km/h) in sheltered waters. With their shallow draft and their high house-like sides, they are not suitable for offshore cruising.

Most parts of the world have their own typical boat designs. The sampans of the Far East, usually propelled by a single oar at the stern, are one example. The graceful gondolas which convey people along the canals of Venice are another. Some 30 ft. (9 m) long, with their prow and stern sweeping high out of the water and tapering to a point, they are rowed from a standing position by one or two gondoliers. But there as elsewhere the traditional craft are suffering from competition from powered ferryboats. Flat-bottomed punts are still used in many places. With no stempost, sternpost or keel these square-ended floating boxes are propelled along shallow waterways with a pole. At the other extreme are lightweight racing boats on which the rowlocks project well out beyond the side to give the rowers extra leverage and therefore greater power and speed.

Materials and construction. Until quite recent times boats were normally made

of wood. A strong frame is constructed first. This consists of the stempost, stern-post and keel (which together form the backbone), and a series of curved ribs. A watertight skin of wooden planks is then fitted onto the skeleton. The planks may be laid edge to edge (CARVEL CONSTRUCTION) or they may be overlapped (CLINKER CONSTRUCTION). A great many boats are still made by this traditional method. For some time plywood was a popular alternative to planks. Strong, smooth, pliable and inexpensive, its use led to the development of flat or V-bottomed boats with straight sides. Plywood is, however, limited by the fact that it cannot be curved in two planes (if it is curved lengthwise along the boat it cannot be "pinched" in to form a pointed or sloping bow or stern), and today fiberglass, aluminum and plastics have largely supplanted it, and sleek curves have replaced the angular look of plywood boats. These modern materials are virtually maintenance-free, but they are not buoyant, and a double hull or bottom (or air tanks) are normally fitted for safety.

Engines and propulsion. Engines may be inboard (built-in and with propeller and propeller shaft fixed in place), outboard (slotted over the stern and detachable), or inboard-outboard (with fixed inboard motor, but with propeller and shaft removable so that the boat can be dragged up the beach or poled through very shallow water). Boats fitted with outboard or inboard-outboard engines are steered by turning the whole engine, or only the propeller unit, to alter the angle of thrust; while the inboard-engined boat is normally steered with a rudder. An alternative is to fit two propellers side by side, changing direction by altering their relative speeds or varying their pitches. Water-jet propulsion, in which a stream of water is simply pumped out through a nozzle in the stern, is occasionally used, especially in very shallow or weed-choked waters, and for towing water-

skiers who otherwise risk being injured by the propeller.

Gasoline engines and diesels essentially the same as those used in road vehicles are both common. There may be a gearbox with a series of forward speeds and reverse. Or a variable pitch propeller may be fitted. In this case the engine turns over at a more or less constant speed (that at which it is most efficient). To alter speed, or to reverse, the pitch of the propeller blades (the angle at which they cut into the water) is altered: the coarser the angle the greater the thrust. Fast naval boats are often powered by gas turbines.

Naval boats. These are warships in miniature, and scarcely fall within the normal definition of a boat. Their main features are their small size, by naval standards (up to about 100 tons), and their great speed. Powered by gas turbine or combined diesel and gas turbine engines, some achieve speeds greater than 50 knots. The three main types are the gunboat, the guided missile boat, and the torpedo boat. Similar craft are used by coastal police and coast guard services.

History. The first "boats" were probably floating logs, or bundles of reeds. An unusually buoyant hollow log may have led to the idea of the dugout, a craft made by hollowing out a solid tree trunk. And once early man had discovered the art of lashing objects together with skin thongs or strands of vine or other plant stems, he would no doubt have improved on the bundle of reeds and constructed a primitive raft.

There is no way of knowing how long ago these first man-made boats appeared. The earliest known pictures of boats date from about 6,000 years ago, in Egypt; and remains from earlier times have been found in the Middle East and northern Europe. These include a dugout canoe of about 6300 B.C. and a paddle nearly 1,000 years older than that.

Gradually came new developments to improve the strength, stability, and capacity of early boats. The Brigg boat, a Stone Age dugout unearthed in Lincolnshire, England, in 1886 was 48 ft. (15 m) long and 4 ft. 6 in. (1.5 m) wide. To increase the lateral strength of this unusually large shell, the builders wedged timber struts at intervals across the boat, bored a series of holes along each side, and lashed thongs of hide through them across the boat. The lashing held the sides firmly against the struts, so that between them thongs and struts would stop

thick rope fixed at bow and stern and passing along the length of the boat on high forked supports. It helped to keep the craft from bending in the middle when riding over a wave. Strengthening devices like this were essential because the dugout and the much larger Egyptian boats were basically simple shells. The latter were in fact built up of short, thick, almost brick-like planks, simply pinned or pegged together. The revolutionary idea of first constructing a strong skeleton, and then cladding it with a timber or other "skin" had not yet dawned. Among

magnificent Viking LONGSHIPS. One of these, the Gokstad ship, was excavated near the entrance to the Oslo fiord in Norway, and an exact replica was successfully sailed across the Atlantic in 1893. Measuring 76 ft. (23 m) long and 17 ft. (5 m) wide, it had 16 oar holes in each side and a single mast. Viking and northern European boats were normally clinker built and double-ended. Those of the Mediterranean countries were carvel built and pointed only at the bow. The basic methods of boat construction embodied in the Viking longships and their

A displacement-type motorboat for pleasure cruising on inland waters.

Elegant houseboats moored on the Thames, England, in the late 19th century. Modern houseboats are often powered and luxuriously equipped.

the sides collapsing inwards or outwards. This was an ingenious solution to the problems of lateral strength in a frameless craft. Another method of strengthening (and enlarging) the dugout was first to soften it by soaking in special liquids containing animal fats or mineral salts, and then to stretch it and insert bracing ribs.

The dugout was further improved by the addition of stabilizing OUTRIGGERS, and of planks fitted onto the sides of the bottom shell to increase the boat's capacity. Although the dugout is historically a deadend design (major advances were only possible with built-up boats), many primitive peoples still use dugouts and have in the past achieved astonishing voyages in them. A little over 1,000 years ago Polynesians made the voyage between Oahu in the Hawaiian Islands and New Zealand, a distance of some 3,500 mi. (5,600 km) across open ocean, in dugouts.

The ancient Egyptians devised a simple yet effective way of increasing longitudinal strength. This was the truss, a

the earliest framed boats were the CORACLES and similar craft. These have a frame of some pliant wood such as willow, hazel or bamboo, to which a covering of animal skin or woven plant stems was attached. The coracle itself is a tublike vessel, but other craft constructed in the same way such as the Eskimo KAYAK are boat-like in shape.

Other primitive boats include the inflated animal skin, of which the rubber dinghy is the modern version; the bark canoe used by for example the American Indians; and the curious ceramic boats of the Ganges Delta in India. In use until quite recent times, these were turned on a potter's wheel. Hemispherical in shape, they measured about 3 ft. (1 m) in diameter.

Most of these primitive boats are still in use in various parts of the world. All are practical craft within their limits. But because of those limits (in size, strength, and seaworthiness) the framed plank-covered boat was developed by the great seafaring peoples of the ancient world. It reached a peak of design in the

Mediterranean counterparts remained essentially unchanged until the appearance in modern times of plywood and other man-made materials.

Bobsled

A long racing sled fitted with two sets of runners in tandem and equipped with steering gear (see SLED).

Boeing 247

Frequently cited as the first "modern" airliner, the Boeing 247 first flew in 1933. This low-wing, all-metal aircraft was powered by two Pratt and Whitney Wasp radial engines and featured a retractable undercarriage. It had a cruising speed of 155 mph (250 km/h), 50 mph (80 km/h) faster than most other existing airliners, and 60 Model 247s, each with accommodation for ten passengers, were ordered by United Airlines.

The 13 Model 247Ds of 1934 (also built for United Airlines) had fabric-covered tail control surfaces and variable-pitch propellers — innovations that were retrospectively incorporated in the earlier aircraft.

Boeing 707

The first American commercial jet transport. A prototype flew in 1954, and the first 707-120 airliner entered service on the North Atlantic route in 1958. The

707-320 Intercontinental appeared in 1959. The 707-320B of 1962, seating 189, had improved takeoff performance and better payload/range characteristics. The 707-320C was fitted with side-loading freight doors and could be used for air cargo; with a gross weight of 333,600 lb. (151,300 kg) it cruises at 550 mph (885 km/h) for 4,300 mi. (7,000 km) and carries up to 219 passengers. The 720 is a smaller variant of the 707 that carries up to 167 passengers; the 720B has turbofan engines that improve its performance. Military versions of the 707 serve as transports, flight refueling tankers, and airborne early-warning radar stations.

A Boeing 707, the first American commercial jet transport. The photograph shows the 336-B version of this very successful airliner.

Boeing 747

A giant airliner (the "jumbo jet") powered by four Pratt and Whitney turbofan engines that made its first flight in February 1969. With a wingspan of 195 ft. 8 in. (59.6 m) and a length of 231 ft. 4 in. (70.5 m) the 747 was designed to carry 490 passengers in a double-deck fuselage that accommodated 10 seats across its 20-ft. (6.1 m) width; the 57 first-class passengers have an 8-seat lounge on the upper deck.

Equipped with 43,500-lb. thrust engines, the 747 entered service with Pan American across the North Atlantic in January 1970. The 747B is powered by up-rated engines of 45,500-lb. thrust. It has a range of 4,330 mi. (6.930 km) and a maximum speed of 608 mph (970 km/h) at 30,000 ft. (9,000 m).

A convertible freight/passenger variant is known as the 747C; both this aircraft and the 747F freighter have nose-loading doors. A short range model, the 747SR, carries 498 passengers and has been specially stressed for a high frequency of takeoffs and landings, while the 747SP is a short-fuselaged variant intended for long-haul, low-density routes.

Because of its great size the 747 needs 18 undercarriage wheels (four 4-wheeled main assemblies and a twin nose-wheel). The fuel capacity is over 50,000 gallons, and engines of 52,500-lb. thrust can be fitted.

Boiler

A vessel in which water is converted into steam. It is an essential feature of any steam-generating plant, except those deriving their heat from nuclear power. A steam locomotive has a boiler, as does a steamship and a steam automobile. In a boiler, fuel — commonly oil — is burned in an integral furnace or combustion chamber to provide the necessary heat. The way in which this heat is utilized provides a means of classifying the boiler.

In the so-called fire-tube type, the hot gases produced by combustion are directed through a multitude of tubes passing through the water in the boiler. The gases give up their heat to the surrounding water as they pass through. Often the tubes are arranged so that the gases go three or four times through the boiler before escaping up the flue. This type of boiler is often termed a Scotch boiler. It contrasts with the water-tube boiler, in which the hot combustion gases flow over water-filled tubes. Banks of tubes are set around the walls and across the flue, and the water inside absorbs the heat of the gases and circulates to a steam drum where steam is produced.

In general, the fire-tube boiler is used for smaller installations and is used for example in steam locomotives. It is simpler to make, and easier to install and operate. The water-tube boiler is used for larger installations when it can be run with high efficiency at high pressures and temperatures. The higher the operating pressure and steam temperature, the greater the efficiency.

The water-tube boiler is invariably used

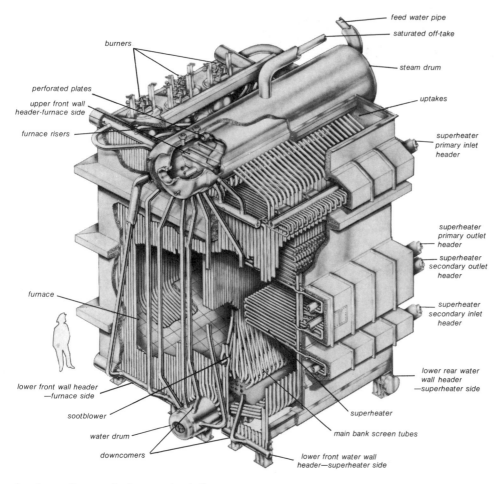

A cutaway diagram of a large marine boiler.

burners
feed water pipe
saturated off-take
steam drum
perforated plates
upper front wall header-furnace side
uptakes
furnace risers
superheater primary inlet header
superheater primary outlet header
superheater secondary outlet header
superheater secondary inlet header
furnace
lower rear water wall header —superheater side
lower front wall header —furnace side
sootblower
superheater
water drum
main bank screen tubes
downcomers
lower front water wall header—superheater side

for marine steam-turbine installations, where operating pressures are commonly up to 800 lb. per sq. in. and temperatures up to 450°C. Superheaters and economizers are incorporated in the boiler to increase efficiency. In the superheater section, steam from the steam drum circulates through tubes across the boiler flue and extracts more heat from the flue gases, thereby becoming superheated. The flue gases then circulate through the economizer, which is a heat exchanger, and give up their heat to feed water going to the boiler. In this way the maximum heat is extracted from the gas before it escapes through the funnel (see STEAM ENGINES).

Bosporus Bridge
A SUSPENSION BRIDGE across the Bosporus at Istanbul, Turkey. The bridge, whose span is 3,523 ft. (1,074 m), links Europe and Asia. It was opened in 1973.

Boundary layer
When the wing of an aircraft in flight moves through the air, the particles of air are pushed aside to let it through. Those particles that are in contact with the surface of the wing retain their position relative to the wing's surface owing to skin friction and do not move. Particles in the next layer are restrained from moving by the air particles below them and have a very small relative movement. The next layer moves more quickly, and so on until the full relative velocity of air is reached.

The region in which this velocity transition from zero to normal takes place is called the boundary layer. It may be only .01 in. (2.5 mm) deep, but if it can be kept free of TURBULENCE the power-consuming drag generated as the aircraft moves through the air will be substantially reduced. To achieve this smooth flow, holes may be made in the wings to exert a suction effect, or air may be blown out from inside the wing to help the flow. At very low speeds the boundary layer becomes increasingly turbulent and eventually breaks away from the wing surface, causing a stall. Leading-edge slats opening at low speed increase the air flow and delay the onset of STALLING.

Box kite
See KITE.

Brabazon
A huge experimental aircraft built in the years 1945-49 as an attempt to solve the problems associated with large-scale, high-speed air transport. With eight 2,500-hp radial engines, 230 ft. (70 m) wingspan, 177 ft. (53.95 m) length, a cruising speed of 250 mph km/h) and a range of 5,500 mi. (8,850 km), the Mark 1 Brabazon was designed to carry up to 80 passengers.

One of the most ambitious projects that had ever been attempted by the British aircraft industry, the Brabazon was technologically ahead of its time. However, as more and more money was ploughed into its development, the Brabazon became an embarrassment until the end of its eight-year career. Finally the one and only completed aircraft was broken up, having amassed less than 400 hours flying time in its four-year life.

Brake fade
When the brakes of an automobile are applied for a long period, braking becomes progressively less effective. The braking surfaces become very hot, and the frictional properties of the brake linings deteriorate. The brakes return to normal when they cool. Drum brakes are particularly prone to fading, because the heat produced by braking cannot readily be dissipated. Disk brakes are much less prone to fading because most of the disk is exposed to cooling air.

Brake horsepower
The effective horsepower of an engine. Brake horsepower (bhp) is less than the theoretical, or indicated horsepower developed because of energy loss due to friction within the mechanical parts. It is so termed because it is measured by means of a brake attached to the engine drive shaft and recorded by DYNAMOMETER.

Braking distance
The distance it takes a vehicle to stop after the brakes have been applied. For a vehicle traveling at 30 mph (48 km/h) the braking distance is about 50 ft (15 m), assuming an 80% braking efficiency, good tires, and a good road surface. At 70 mph (113 km/h) the braking distance is

A large water-tube boiler for a marine steam turbine installation.

some 275 ft. (84 m). In wet or icy conditions the distances are very considerably increased. To find the overall stopping distance between when a driver sees a hazard and stops his vehicle, a "thinking distance" must be added to the braking distance. This is the distance the vehicle travels in the time it takes the driver to react. The thinking distance is about 1 ft. per 1 mph of speed.

Braking systems

All vehicles used in transportation need some form of braking system for slowing their speed and for stopping. On most land vehicles, the brakes consist essentially of a brake shoe which is forced against the wheel or some part that rotates with the wheel. At its simplest, as on a bicycle, the shoe is simply forced against the rim of the wheel by a cable or levers.

The frictional resistance between shoe and wheel slows the wheel, and the vehicle; the greater the pressure, the larger the surfaces in contact, and the greater the frictional resistance between the surfaces, the stronger the braking effect. In the process a great deal of heat is generated. In fact, in mechanical braking of this type the vehicle's kinetic energy is dissipated in the form of heat. If the brakes are to be effective the shoe must be lined with some heat-resistant material (usually asbestos), and as far as possible the heat must be dissipated (into the air) as it is generated.

Road vehicles. Two types of brakes are used on automobiles, and two methods of applying them. For the rear wheels DRUM BRAKES, in which the shoes expand against the inside of a drum that turns with the wheel, are usual. However, efficient dissipation of heat is impossible with the shoes inside the drum, and such brakes tend to get very hot and temporarily lose their power (see BRAKE FADE). For this reason the more efficient DISK BRAKES are normally fitted to the front wheels. Here a pad or ring-shaped "shoe" is forced against a disk which rotates with the wheel and is open to the air (and thus has less tendency to overheat).

The hand or emergency brake is operated mechanically by cable, and only brakes the rear wheels. It would be virtually impossible to achieve consistent equal braking on all four wheels (an essential for safe, controlled braking) with a mechanical system, and the main braking system is therefore hydraulic. Depressing the foot pedal forces fluid from a master cylinder equally into the four slave cylinders that actually operate the brakes (see HYDRAULIC SYSTEMS). Some auto-

mobiles have dual-circuit hydraulic systems, so that should a leak develop in one, the other will still function. In addition, the latest systems include a mechanism to prevent the brakes from locking the wheels, something which can otherwise occur when braking sharply, especially when the road is slippery.

On some large road vehicles the brakes are operated by compressed air instead of hydraulic pressure, giving greater power with less effort from the driver. Power brakes (used in most large automobiles) can also be fitted.

A totally different braking method, often used on trucks operating in mountainous terrain, is the hydrodynamic system. This comprises a fixed element, or stator, and a rotating element, or rotor. Between the two is a fluid (usually water). Braking is effected by fluid friction, which slows the rotor. With an efficient cooling system for the liquid, hydrodynamic brakes can dissipate heat quickly and are therefore

becomes a generator), a process that absorbs considerable energy and therefore slows the train. The electricity generated may be fed back into the supply system, or used to produce additional braking power by operating brake shoes electromagnetically.

Airplanes and spacecraft. Airplanes have wheel brakes similar to those used in land vehicles, and in addition employ aerodynamic braking to reduce speed before landing. This relies on friction between the plane and the air. Numerous hinged surfaces (spoilers) on the wing's upper surface are angled up to spoil the airflow over the wing, thereby increasing drag (and reducing lift); while flaps at the wing's trailing edge are rolled out and down to increase drag further (and lift). Many supersonic planes also deploy one or more parachutes to slow their movement after touch down, while others simply reverse the thrust of their engines.

A Lockheed F-104 Starfighter using parachute braking after touchdown. The downward angle of the flaps produces additional aerodynamic braking, while conventional friction brakes in the wheels also help to reduce speed (see Braking systems).

valuable when great braking power is needed. They cannot, however, bring a vehicle to a halt, and are thus always auxiliary to a conventional system.

Railroad braking systems. The high speed and enormous weight of a train necessitates very powerful brakes. These must operate on all the cars and be applied automatically in the event of part of the train being accidentally uncoupled. The brakes, which are applied by compressed air or vacuum (see AIR BRAKE and VACUUM BRAKE), consist of external metal shoes that act directly on the circumference of the wheels.

Electric trains also use a braking system which absorbs energy electrically. Instead of the motor turning the wheels, the wheels turn the motor (which thus

Except during and after reentry into the earth's atmosphere, when air friction exerts a braking effect, spacecraft rely entirely on rocket retro-braking, a process of firing the rocket against the direction of the vehicle.

Watercraft. Most ships can only brake by reversing the thrust of the propellers. The procedure is inefficient and slow: a 250,000-ton ship traveling at 16 knots will take 20 minutes to stop, during which time it travels 3 mi. (4.8 km). Surface-skimming craft (see HYDROFOILS and AIR-CUSHION VEHICLES) travel at speed just above the water and can stop very quickly by reversing thrust and leaving the water to do the rest (the craft rapidly settles in the water as speed begins to drop, and is rapidly slowed down by it).

Breakwater

An offshore barrier against the waves constructed to produce calm water within a harbor. It also intercepts longshore currents, thereby reducing shore erosion. There are three main types of breakwaters: vertical-sided structures made of cemented masonry; sloping-sided structures formed by dropping stones, rubble, and concrete blocks into the sea; and composite breakwaters, in which both principles are utilized. Breakwaters extend along thousands of miles of coastline all over the world.

Breeches buoy

A traveling lifebuoy long used for getting people off ships in rough seas when it is impossible to send a rescue boat alongside. The "breeches," in which the person being rescued sits, consist of a canvas sling with leg holes. This is attached to a lifebuoy and suspended from a cable. The breeches buoy is hauled

The bridge of a large modern freighter, with in the foreground the "engine room telegraph" and beyond radar and navigational equipment.

An engraving from the 1890s showing a breeches buoy being used for rescue work in rough seas.

back and forth, carrying one person at a time. A "high chair line," employing similar principles, has largely replaced the breeches buoy in many situations, and helicopters are also now increasingly used in rescue work.

Bridge

Raised deck extending from side to side across a ship, from which the vessel is navigated and commanded. The bridge is usually amidships or at the stern. The most important part of the bridge is the wheelhouse, which in a large modern ship resembles a scientist's laboratory, with its mass of electronic equipment. The three essential items, however, are the wheel, with which the ship is steered; the compass; and the engine room telegraph, through which the officer in

charge relays instructions as to the speed and direction of thrust of the engines. The electronics, often contained in one large console, include radar, automatic pilot, navigation equipment, radio and telephone communications systems, and a range of instruments to monitor "ship condition." Also on the bridge are the chartroom, where the course is plotted and recorded, and the captain's quarters. The radio room is usually just behind the bridge.

Bridges

Structures built across ravines, waterways, roads, or valleys to provide a path for pedestrian, motor or rail traffic. As

speed of transportation becomes ever more important, bridges are increasingly used to replace ferries, or to open new or more direct routes. Provided that the water is neither too deep nor too fast flowing, multispan bridges of almost any length can be constructed. To date, the longest, the 1969 PONTCHARTRAIN CAUSEWAY linking Lewisburg and Metairie, Louisiana, measures 23.87 mi. (38.4 km).

Types of bridges. The earliest bridges were simple stone or timber beams placed across natural supports. Today bridge builders have a choice of several main types: ARCH, BEAM (including girder and CANTILEVER), SUSPENSION and cable-

This multiple span masonry arch bridge over the River Tweed in Scotland is a direct descendant of similar bridges built by the Romans in ancient times.

stayed. The choice depends on the site, the kind of traffic to be carried, the overall width and the length of the longest span, the materials available, and on aesthetic considerations.

A beam or cable-stayed bridge rests on the ground and on supporting piers where used, the weight being directly downward. An arch, on the other hand, thrusts both down and outward, while a suspension bridge thrusts down and pulls inward on its anchoring cables. Thus arch and suspension bridges need very solid foundations to resist the thrust or pull, and are most often built in rocky areas. Where the ground is soft it is usually simpler and safer to construct a beam bridge.

For very long spans the suspension bridge is the only possibility. This consists of a deck hung from steel rods. These are fixed to steel cables which loop from shore to shore, are run over massive towers at each end and are anchored in

The George Washington Bridge crossing the Hudson River at New York. The span of 3,500 ft. (1,067 m) was the world's longest when it was completed in 1931, and was almost double that of the previous longest bridge (the Ambassador Bridge, Detroit).

Early history. To cross very long stretches a bridge must be made up of several spans supported on intermediate piers. The Romans, the great bridge-builders of antiquity, constructed many impressive bridges in this way, combining two of their most notable inventions: the semi-circular masonry arch, in which each stone was so accurately shaped that no mortar was needed; and the cofferdam, a temporary enclosure in the water within which the pier foundations are built. In fact the Romans rarely made deep enough foundations for permanency, and most Roman bridges still in existence are on solid rock.

In medieval times bridge builders evolved pointed and later flattened elliptical arches, and they learned to spread the weight of piers on more extensive foundations. Then, during the 1740s, a Swiss engineer Charles Labelye, devised a new type of pier foundation for London's first Westminster Bridge, using CAISSONS. Today both cofferdams and caissons are employed, although they are of course sunk to much greater depths than in earlier times. A more recent technique is the use of large diameter piles to support the piers. These may be driven 250 ft. (76 m) or more into the bed, and are often hollow. They are reinforced and filled with concrete after being driven to the required depth.

The railroad age. With the appearance of a new form of transportation, which was not only faster and vastly heavier than its predecessors, but which in addition was incapable of surmounting anything be-

An early British suspension bridge across the Menai Strait, Wales. Built between 1818-26 by Thomas Telford, it was the first major modern suspension bridge. Spanning 580 ft. (177 m), the deck was suspended from 16 wrought iron chains, and with the later addition of strengthening railings and transverse bracing it survived for 115 years before being substantially rebuilt in 1939.

the ground beyond the towers. The center span of a suspension bridge (i.e. the distance between the towers) can exceed 4,000 ft. The longest (4,260 ft., 1,298 m) is the VERRAZANO-NARROWS BRIDGE across the entrance to New York Harbor, and still longer spans are planned. By comparison, the longest span of a cantilever bridge is 1,800 ft. (549 m), on the QUEBEC BRIDGE over the St. Lawrence River in Canada; the longest steel arch is 1,700 ft. (578 m), the New River Gorge Bridge near Fayettesville, West Virginia; the longest steel truss, the Astoria Bridge, Oregon, measures 1,232 ft. (375 m); and the longest stone arch is a mere 295 ft. (90 m), at Plauen in East Germany.

Cable-stayed bridges. The longest span on a conventional box girder bridge is 984 ft. (300 m) on the Rio-Niterói bridge across Guanabara Bay, Brazil (opened

to traffic in 1974), but in recent years cable-stayed bridges have been developed to allow much wider spans. On these, prestressed steel cables run over the top of tall pylons built up on the main piers, and fan out and down onto the spans on either side, which they thus support. The weight, as with normal girder bridges, is directly down through pylon and pier.

The longest cable-stayed bridge yet built crosses the Loire estuary in France, and has a central 1,325-ft. (403 m) span flanked by two 518-ft. (157 m) outer spans. Cable-stayed spans of 2,500 ft. (762 m) have been proposed, and it is likely that this method of construction will supersede the suspension bridge for all but the widest spans. Since no cable anchorages are required, it is both simpler and cheaper. Cable-staying is also increasingly used on concrete bridges.

Cable spinning operations during the construction of the Verrazano-Narrows suspension bridge, which has the world record span of 4,260 ft. (1,298 m). Each of the four main cables is 3 ft. (0.9 m) in diameter, and a total of 142,500 mi. (229,300 km) of wire was used.

yond a very gentle gradient, the mid-19th century was a period of rapid advances in bridge building. More, longer, and stronger bridges were needed.

The timber truss bridge, developed for large scale use in 18th-century Switzerland, was widely adopted in North America, later to be strengthened with iron verticals, while the first iron truss bridge in the United States was constructed in 1851. The world's first iron bridge, a 100-ft. (30 m) arch in Shropshire, England, was built in 1779, but the most famous of the iron bridges were those across the Menai Strait in North Wales, and the Tay River in Scotland. The former, known as the Britannia

The southern cantilever of the world's first important cantilever bridge, the Forth Rail Bidge in Scotland.

An early cast iron bridge, this 236 ft. (72 m) span arch at Sunderland in northeast England was built in 1798.

The Europa Bridge in Austria, a modern rectangular box girder bridge. With a maximum height of 624 ft. (190 m) it is Europe's highest bridge.

Bridge, was designed by Robert STEPHENSON and completed in 1850. The prototype of the modern box-girder bridge, except that traffic ran through the girder instead of on top of it, the Britannia Bridge survived until 1970 when it was badly damaged by fire. The TAY BRIDGE, a wrought-iron truss structure opened in 1878, belatedly brought attention to the importance of wind pressure when it was blown down in a gale in 1879 with the loss of 75 lives.

Many early suspension bridges suffered the same fate, and since they were generally considered inadequate for rail traffic, most long-span railroad bridges were arched or cantilevered. During the latter part of the 19th century steel replaced iron; the first major steel bridge was the triple-arch Eads Bridge across the Mississippi at St. Louis (1867-74). Another famous early steel arch was that below the Niagara Falls, with an 840 ft. (256 m) span (completed in 1898, it was destroyed by an ice jam 40 years later), while the first large cantilever bridge was the FORTH RAIL BRIDGE in Scotland (opened in 1890, and still in use today). The first suspension bridges incorporating stiffening trusses to give the necessary strength and rigidity to survive rail traffic and wind action were those

designed by John ROEBLING, and include the Grand Trunk Bridge below Niagara (which survived for 42 years, from 1855) and the famous BROOKLYN BRIDGE which was opened in 1883.

Concrete bridges. Concrete was first employed in bridge building late in the 19th century, and today it is one of the most common materials. Early concrete bridges were of reinforced concrete, but today prestressed concrete is more common. Because it is so strong, significantly less material is needed, and the structures can be very much lighter and slimmer. The great majority of reinforced concrete bridges are arches, but prestressed designs include girders, arches, cantilevers, beams, and cable-stayed structures.

Aerodynamics. Many early suspension bridges were broken up by winds, as was the iron-truss Tay Bridge of 1878, and in modern times the TACOMA-NARROWS BRIDGE at Puget Sound. This notorious suspension bridge had a span of 2,800 ft. (853 m), and collapsed a few months after completion in a 40 mph (64 km/h) wind. Following this, bridge engineers incorporated greater rigidity, width, and weight in their designs to resist wind,

and it later became standard practice to test all designs in wind tunnels. Aerodynamic efficiency was taken a stage further in the suspension bridge opened across the Severn River in England in 1966. Here the deck was given a streamlined airfoil shape to eliminate dangerous wind eddies, making possible an overall saving in weight of about 30%.

Movable and pontoon bridges. Where a bridge crosses a waterway used by ships, it must either be high enough for vessels to pass under, or an opening bridge must be built. A BASCULE BRIDGE has counterweighted pivoted arms which can be swung up, or leaves which can be rolled back along tracks, while on the vertical lift type the entire span is raised bodily up the end towers. SWING BRIDGES are sometimes used, in which the span swings horizontally.

PONTOON BRIDGES, resting on floating pontoons, are most useful as a temporary expedient, especially for military purposes, but they are expensive to maintain, and they obstruct shipping. The world's longest floating bridge (7,131 ft., 2,139 m) is over the Hood Canal near Seattle, while two others cross Lake Washington. All three have opening spans for navigation.

A 19th century French brig. This type of rig takes its name from the large fore-and-aft "brig" sail on the after mast.

Bridgewater Canal

Artificial waterway which pioneered the great age of industrial canals in England. It runs from Worsley, now a suburb of Manchester, through Manchester to Runcorn on the Mersey River, a distance of 42 mi. (68 km). The canal was built by James BRINDLEY between 1761 and 1776 at the sole expense of the 3rd Duke of Bridgewater, to transport coal from his estates at Worsley. A great aqueduct carries the gravity flow canal over the Irwell River, and another swing-aqueduct now takes it across the Manchester Ship Canal. With the completion of the first section of the canal to Manchester in 1761 the price of coal dropped by half; the Bridgewater Canal and its successors helped make the first stages of the Industrial Revolution possible.

Brig and brigantine

Sailing vessels with two masts and a combination of square and fore-and-aft sails. The brig carries a full complement of square sails on each mast, and in addition has a fore-and-aft "brig" sail (which later became known as a gaff sail) on the aftermast. The brigantine has a fully square-rigged foremast, the mainmast carrying only fore-and-aft sails. Both have fore-and-aft staysails and jibs. Brigs and brigantines were used by coastal and short sea traders carrying such cargoes as coal or fish. Both types are still afloat, serving as training ships for naval cadets.

Brindley, James (1716-1772)

English engineer, builder of Britain's first industrial canals. He was a millwright by trade and virtually illiterate, but his skill in other civil-engineering work led the 3rd Duke of Bridgewater to engage him to construct a canal from his estates to carry coal to Manchester (see BRIDGEWATER CANAL). Brindley later designed and built a further 360 mi. (580 km) of canals.

British Rail

The opening of the Liverpool and Manchester Railway in 1830, with all trains hauled by steam, marked the beginning of the Railway Age in Britain and, indeed, in the world. The expansion of railroad transportation in Britain created a need for centralized management, which led to amalgamations. Government control of railroads during World War I ended with most railroads merged into four large geographical groups, and in 1948 the entire system was nationalized under the British Transport Commission (B.T.C.). Subsequent changes abolished the B.T.C. and the British Railways Board was created to control all but a few railroads in Britain from January 1, 1963. At the end of 1973 British Rail had nearly 11,400 mi. (18,350 km) of track, over 3,600 diesel and 330 electric locomotives, as well as 3,500 diesel and 7,173 electric multiple-unit passenger vehicles. There were over 7,000 locomotive-hauled passenger cars and 5,500 other passenger train vehicles and some 250,000 freight cars.

Brooklyn-Battery Tunnel

Longest underwater vehicular tunnel in the United States, linking Brooklyn and lower Manhattan, completed in 1950. Its twin parallel tubes descend to a maximum of 115 ft. (35 m) beneath New York Harbor. Its overall length is some 9,120 ft. (2,780 m). Over 16 million vehicles use the tunnel each year.

Brooklyn Bridge

Southernmost of the suspension bridges connecting Manhattan and Brooklyn over the East River in New York City. It was designed by John A. ROEBLING, who died from injuries sustained while surveying the site, and built by his son Washington, who was permanently crippled by caisson disease. The Brooklyn Bridge has a central span of 1,595 ft. (486 m), and when it was completed in 1883, it had the longest suspended span in the world. The four 16-in. (40-cm) thick steel suspension cables hanging from 275-ft. (83-m) high towers, were a major innovation in bridge building.

Brougham

A closed four-wheeled one-horse carriage with the driver's seat outside. Certain early automobiles were called broughams.

Brunel

Name of two Anglo-French engineers, father and son.

Sir Marc Isambard Brunel (1769-1849) is chiefly remembered as the builder of the modern world's first underwater tunnel. He was born in France, but left to settle briefly in New York, where he became the city's chief engineer, before arriving in England in 1799. Brunel was a prolific inventor, but his great work was the construction of the Thames Tunnel, between Rotherhithe and Wapping, just below the City of London. For this project he designed the first tunneling shield, devised to hold back the water and mud, while the tunnel lining was put in place. Work was begun in 1825, but the 1,506-ft. (460 m) tunnel was not completed until 1842. A million people walked through it in the first 3½ months.

Isambard Kingdom Brunel (1806-1859) was the son of Marc Brunel. He was a visionary of supreme genius and probably the greatest figure in the heroic age of civil and mechanical engineering. Brunel joined his father's business in 1823 and took charge of the work on the Thames Tunnel, during which he was injured. In

The Brooklyn Bridge, designed by John Roebling and completed in 1883 with the then record span of 1,595 ft. (486 m).

1833 the newly-formed Great Western Railway Company appointed him their chief engineer. He persuaded the company to adopt the 7-ft (2.1 m) broad gauge, a brilliant technical solution which, however, had to be abandoned in the 1890s to conform with other railroads. Brunel not only surveyed the course of the railroad, but designed all its bridges and tunnels, many of them engineering feats still unequaled today. Among other bridges he designed were the Tamar Bridge in Cornwall, and the Clifton Suspension Bridge, Bristol.

As a marine engineer Brunel designed three great ships. The *Great Western* (1837) was a pioneering transatlantic paddle steamer; the GREAT BRITAIN (1843) was the first iron screw-propelled liner; and the legendary GREAT EASTERN (1858) was the largest ship built until the 1890s.

Buckboard

An open, four-wheeled carriage whose seats rested on boards that lay directly on the carriage's axles.

Bugatti, Ettore (1881-1947)

Italian automobile engineer. After working for other manufacturers, Bugatti established his own factory in 1909 at Molsheim in Alsace. One of the great "artist engineers" of his time, Bugatti designed a series of beautifully engineered and highly successful sport and luxury cars. At the other end of the scale,

Isambard Kingdom Brunel, 19th century British engineer famous for his broad gauge Great Western Railway, and for his three revolutionary ships, the Great Western, Great Britain, and Great Eastern.

he sold a light car design to Peugeot which became the Bébé Peugeot of 1911. His straight-eight Type 35, a classic racing car of the late 1920s, with a top speed of 125 mph (190 km/h) was the most successful Grand Prix racing car of all time; while his 13-liter Type 41 (the Royale) of 1927 was the largest (2½ tons) and one of the most meticulously built and expensive production cars ever made.

Bulk carrier

Large cargo ship designed to transport a specific cargo. There are specialized bulk carriers for sugar, grain, timber, ores, chemicals, liquefied natural gas (which has to be maintained at a temperature of −161°C), bitumen (which must be kept at 221°C), and of course oil (see TANKERS). A bulk ship loads and unloads at a berth equipped with specialized handling gear and storage facilities, thus saving time and money. The great disadvantage of such ships is that they normally make the return journey "in ballast" — i.e., carrying ballast, usually water, for stability, but no cargo. To eliminate this waste, multipurpose bulk carriers have been developed such as the OBO (Oil Bulk Ore) carrier and the LASH (Lighter Aboard Ship) vessel. Though far more costly to build, these are ultimately more profitable ships.

Bulldozer

Caterpillar-tracked tractor fitted with a large shovel-like blade in front. It has been used extensively since about 1945 in all kinds of construction work for ground clearance, demolition, and earth-moving generally. The bulldozer blade slices off a layer of soil as it goes forward and rolls it up. It can be raised and lowered and tipped backwards and forwards by means of cables or by hydraulic power. A small bulldozer is sometimes called a calfdozer. A bulldozer with its blade angled so that it pushes the earth it excavates to one side is called an angle-dozer.

Buoy

A floating object fixed by anchor in a particular spot to indicate the presence of submerged hazards, to direct the course of shipping, or to provide a mooring for vessels. In daylight, buoys can be distinguished by their different colours and shapes, while at night or in fog each buoy is recognizable by devices such as whistles, bells, fixed or flashing lights, and radar reflectors. All buoys are marked on charts.

Navigation buoys are most frequently used in coastal waters and estuaries, where they mark the approaches to ports and harbors, isolated wrecks, sandbanks and other hazards, and the limits of deep water channels. Wreck buoys are green, while those marking a quarantine ground are yellow. In the usual Lateral system of buoyage, conical buoys mark one side of the channel, can-shaped ones the other side, and spherical buoys mark the middle ground. In some places the Cardinal system is followed, in which the shape of the buoy shows the bearing of the feature it marks.

A recent development is the large automatic navigation buoy, or LANBY. About 40 ft. (12 m) in diameter with tall superstructures, carrying their own power plant and powerful light and fog signals, LANBYs can survive the worst seas. They are employed to keep shipping in "lanes" in very busy seaways such as the Straits of Dover between England and France, and to mark deep-water channels for supertankers and other bulk carriers with a very deep draft.

Buoyancy

The upward force that makes an object float, equal to the weight of water that it displaces. A lump of iron sinks because the water it displaces equals its own volume, but not its weight (since water is less dense than iron). The same lump of iron molded onto a boat-shape displaces far more water, so that the force of buoyancy (the weight of the water displaced) now equals the weight of the object, and it floats.

Burma Road

A 717-mi. (1,154 km) supply route running from Lashio, in eastern Burma, to Kunming, in southern China. It was built in 1937-39 to serve as a back-door supply route for Chinese forces, then engaged in fighting Japanese invaders. It remained the main link until early 1942 when the Japanese captured Lashio and the rest of Burma. In January 1945, the STILWELL ROAD from India was opened to link up with the Chinese section of the route.

Bus

A self-powered public service road vehicle carrying fare-paying passengers on specified routes. The bus is generally considered to be the most practical form of public transport in small cities and rural areas, because of its adaptability and cheapness. Streetcars and trolleybuses must follow their rails or cables, but a bus route can be altered at a moment's notice to meet temporary emergencies, new traffic schemes, or the changing needs of the community. In a large city subways and commuter rail lines may be necessary to cope with the vast numbers of travelers; they are much faster and can carry far more passengers than can buses. But their expense can only be justified in a large urban area. And even where such systems exist, buses still provide an essential additional service, particularly for short journeys. With closely spaced bus stops, and a much denser network of local routes, they meet a specific need. Their main problem is other traffic. Some cities have considered banning private vehicles from

A horsedrawn bus of 1847. Carrying 13 passengers inside, and about 14 on top, this "improved" model featured a higher roof for ease of access, a sprung "buffer" at the rear in case of collision, and a strong brake "to supersede the necessity of stopping to put on a drag on descending a hill."

the city center to free the roads of traffic jams, and enable the bus to provide a much faster and more efficient service. A few small-scale experiments have been made along these lines, but it is far from certain that such a ban would be acceptable on a large scale.

The world's first buses entered service in Paris in 1662. The eight-seater horse drawn vehicles ran a scheduled service at roughly eight minute intervals, with a flat-rate fare. They were a popular novelty for a few months, but the craze soon died. Horse-drawn buses reappeared in Paris in 1819, and in Nantes (France) in

1823 where the word "omnibus" was coined — "bus" is an abbreviation of "omnibus," a Latin word meaning "for all." The first self-propelled buses were steam powered. They enjoyed a brief period of success during the 1830s. In England harsh restrictions forced them out of business, while in France they soon lost popularity, and the remainder of the 19th century was the era of the horse-drawn bus.

Just as the railroad preceded the motor car, the steam (and later electric) tram or streetcar preceded the motor bus. A number of experimental steam, gasoline,

An early London double-decker motor bus, around 1910. In that year motor buses outnumbered horsedrawn types for the first time, although the last horsedrawn buses were not withdrawn until 1916. During the 1920s low chassis buses appeared, removing the need for several steps up to the platform, and the top deck acquired a roof.

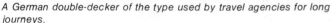

A German double-decker of the type used by travel agencies for long journeys.

A modern single-deck city bus in New York.

and electric buses were tried during the last decade of the 19th century, but their power and carrying capacity were very limited, and only after World War I did the motor bus seriously challenge the streetcar. On the first gasoline-engined bus service, in Germany during 1895, the average speed of the 5-hp Benz vehicle was 9 mph (14 km/h), and the passengers had on occasion to help push the bus uphill. But by 1905 the motor bus had been much improved, and during the years that followed its use spread rapidly. By 1914 London had over 3,500 motor buses, compared to only 20 in 1904, and the trend was the same throughout Europe and America. After 1918, bus routes were extended, and comfort and design improved. Until 1922 buses were built on conventional truck chassis, but in that year the Fageol Safety Coach Company of Oakland, California, produced the first specially built bus chassis. Its lower frame removed the need for a flight of steps up to the platform and lowered the center of gravity. Safety was further enhanced by the vehicle's long wheelbase and wide tires.

Four years later Fageol followed with another revolutionary innovation by placing twin engines between the axles, under the floor. The bus also had an integral frame in which roof, floor, and sides were all structural members. This was essentially the modern bus, to be improved in detail over the years. Pneumatic tires became normal during the late 1920s. The diesel engine was introduced in 1938, and is still standard, although experiments have been made with gas turbines and with silent and pollution-free electrically-driven buses. Britain's urban double-decker buses reflect a striking difference in approach from the standard practice in, for example, continental Europe and the USSR, where single-deckers may carry more passengers than a British double-decker by the simple expedient of providing few

seats, and packing in large numbers of standing passengers. London has succumbed to this approach with its Red Arrow single-deckers (with seating for 25 and standing room for 48), and as roads become ever more crowded the trend is likely to become widespread on suburban buses. Twin-car articulated buses have been tried in some countries, carrying up to 200 passengers. Those in service in Johannesburg, South Africa, have the distinction of being the world's longest buses (65 ft. or 20 m). Lack of maneuverability and a large turning circle restrict their general value.

In the United States the use of buses has declined drastically since the peak year of 1945. Between 1950-71 the annual number of bus and subway rides dropped from 17 billion to 7 billion. However in the early 1970s the federal government was considering spending large sums on improving bus and other public transport systems, and both the Federal Highway Administration and the Secretary of Transportation decided to encourage the use of buses in preference to individual automobiles. On urban and suburban commuter routes the effect could be dramatic; it has been estimated that a single expressway lane can handle about 2,400 car passengers an hour, whereas a fleet of high-speed buses on the same lane could carry up to 50,000.

Bushnell, David (1742-1824)

American inventor and pioneer of the SUBMARINE. Earlier experimental submarines had been built, but Bushnell's one-man *Turtle* of 1776 was the first to attack an enemy ship. Propelled by hand-cranked screws, *Turtle* carried a mine designed to be attached to the enemy vessel by a boring tool. The attempt to sink a British warship in New York Harbor failed because of the ship's copper sheathing, but the *Turtle* is still considered the earliest effective submarine (see SUBMARINE).

C

Cab
The name given in the 19th century to a HACKNEY CARRIAGE, that is, a carriage for hire, and still surviving in the name taxi-cab. "Cab" is derived from *cabriolet*, a hooded gig used in continental Europe in the late 1600s. The first cabs for hire were light, two-wheeled covered vehicles, drawn by a single horse and carrying two passengers. The driver sat beside the passengers. In 1834 Joseph Aloysius Hansom, an English architect, introduced an improved version, the HANSOM CAB.

Cabin cruiser
See MOTOR BOAT.

Cable brake
The handbrakes of most bicycles are operated by a lever acting through a cable, as are the front brakes of a motorcycle. Also cable-operated is a car's emergency or hand brake, which controls an independent braking system applied to the rear wheels. The cable works the brakes directly by pressing the brake shoes (in DRUM BRAKES) against the inside of the drum, bypassing the vehicle's hydraulic system (see BRAKING SYSTEMS). Bicycle cable brakes work on the caliper principle (see CALIPER BRAKES).

Cable cars
Cars or carriages drawn by cables. They may run either on rails along the ground, or on overhead cableways, or ropeways. They are used for transporting passengers and freight up and down steep gradients or over rivers or valleys. Aerial cable cars are used in most mountainous parts of the world. They may run on monocable ropeways, which have only a single continuous cable which

serves both to support the cable cars and to draw them along. But for safety and strength most run on ropeways that have separate carrier and hauling ropes. The longest and highest aerial ropeway, or *téléphérique,* is in Venezuela. It runs 8 mi. (13 km) in four sections from Merida City to the summit of Pico Espejo, climbing more than 10,000 ft. (3,050 m). The ropeway with the longest single span is in California. It extends more than 13,500 ft. (4,115 m) from the Coachella Valley to Mount San Jacinto. Probably the most famous rail cable cars run in San Francisco. Each car is attached to, and hauled by, an endless steel cable that runs beneath the pavement. Railroads are also sometimes operated by cable. A notable example is the Santos Jundai Railway of Brazil, which was opened in 1867. It works on the funicular system, in which the descending car is linked with the ascending car (see FUNICULAR). The modern subway at Haifa, Israel, is also cable-hauled because of the gradient.

Cable ship
Oceangoing vessel used for laying, inspecting and repairing submarine telephone cables. Up to 1,800 miles (2,880 km) of cable is carried in giant drum-like holds, and is paid out or (during maintenance or repair work) hauled in over guides and rollers (sheaves) at stern and bow respectively.
Maneuverability and accurate positioning are vital, and cable ships are therefore normally equipped with bow thrusters (see SHIPS), variable pitch propellers, and with diesel-electric propulsion.

Cable stayed bridge
The cable stayed bridge is a recent application of the SUSPENSION BRIDGE principle to strengthen steel and concrete girder bridges, and to allow them to be built with much greater spans (see BRIDGES).

Cableway
Method of transporting loads by a system of overhead cables. It is widely used in bridge and dam construction, for example, where a large site area has to be served. Because it is an aerial system, it does not interfere with work in progress beneath it.
A typical fixed cableway consists of two high masts — head and tail masts — supported by guy ropes. A main track cable is strung between the masts, and a load car travels along it. A traverse rope driven by a winch moves the car back and forth. The winch also operates a hoist rope which can raise or lower the load. Traveling cableways are also used. In these the track cable is held by self-supporting towers, suitably ballasted for

Cable cars in the Austrian Tyrol. The steepest gradient used on rack railroads is 1 in 2, but cable cars have been built with a gradient of 1 in 1.25.

stability and mounted on wheeled trolleys that run on rails.

Cadence braking
Braking intermittently in conjunction with suspension movement. It is a technique useful in bad weather conditions to prevent the rear wheels from locking and skidding.

Cadillac
Famous trade name used by General Motors Corporation for its most prestigious car. The original Cadillac Automobile Company was founded in 1902 by Henry M. Leland. The Cadillac Company was absorbed by General Motors in 1908, along with 10 other automobile manufacturing concerns.

Caique
Rowboat or a sailboat found in the eastern Mediterranean and on the Bosporus.

Caisson
Structure, usually made of reinforced concrete, constructed on shore and then sunk onto a riverbed or seabed to form the foundation of a bridge, pier, breakwater, or other underwater structure. The simplest form of caisson is a hollow cylinder with a cutting edge at the bottom. Material is excavated from within, so that the cutting edge bites deeper into the bed. Excavation proceeds until bedrock or firm strata are found. A floor is placed on the bottom to seal it and it is then filled with concrete.

The pneumatic caisson is equipped with an air lock and has a working chamber at the bottom in which men can dig. Air pressure keeps out the water. Like divers, the workers must decompress gradually when they leave the pressurized chamber, or else they may succumb to a very painful condition called the bends, or caisson disease. It is caused by nitrogen bubbling out of the blood when the pressure drops too quickly (see also DIVING).

Caledonian Canal
Waterway cutting Scotland in two, about a third of its length man-made. It consists of a series of natural lochs and artificial connecting channels. With a total length of nearly 60 mi. (100 km), the Caledonian canal runs from Loch Linnhe in the southwest, through Loch Locky, Loch Oich, and Loch Ness, to the Moray Firth in the northeast. The canal was planned by Thomas Telford and opened in 1882. It is now too small for large modern ship traffic.

Caliper brake
A kind of brake in which the braking effort is applied to the sides of a wheel rim or disk in a pincer-like movement. Bicycle handbrakes are the simplest examples. When the brakes are applied, the brake cable pulls the arms of the scissor-like caliper, and the brake shoes on the other ends are forced against the wheel rims. The disk brakes on automobiles also work by pincer action. Two pads are

Reindeer-hauled sleds in Finland. The traditional mode of transportation in snowbound regions, sleds have in most areas been replaced by snowmobiles and larger tracked vehicles.

A camel caravan in the Uzbek region of the Soviet Union. Technology has as yet produced no satisfactory rival to camels for desert travel.

▽ *The proposed French airship Obelix looks unwieldy, but it is based entirely on existing technology and will require very little maintenance or ground facilities. The ship will land on its own four legs and lift huge loads into its cargo area with a minimum of difficulty.*

△ *Airship port of the future. The landing strips are for ships which are partly aerodynamic and partly aerostatic. Long-bodied giants are moored into the wind at their masts with the help of skytugs, while below them the great saucer-shaped ships can land unaided on concrete aprons.*

Loading and unloading are achieved by helicopter as well as powerful winches carried by the airships and elevators housed in the mooring masts. In the distance a barge carrying liquid cargo is being towed to the port.

▽ Skyship's revolutionary shape allows it to land on a relatively small concrete apron and to ignore wind direction. Powered by giant helicopter-type engines, it can move at 90 mph. and may help solve the heavy transport problems of less industrialized countries.

A Boeing 747 "jumbo jet," created to meet a now non-existent boom in cheap air travel, passenger models of this giant transport often fly half-empty. But increased interest is being shown in all-freight versions.

The Anglo-French SST (supersonic transport), Concorde. Carrying around 100 passengers at just over twice the speed of sound, supersonic travel makes the executive's "day return trip" across the Atlantic a reality, and brings Tokyo within a working day's flight from Los Angeles.

forced against the sides of the disk, which rotates with the wheel. Operation is by means of hydraulic pistons (see DISK BRAKE).

Cam

An eccentric projection of a shaft that moves another component when the shaft rotates. The CAMSHAFT in a gasoline engine operates linkages that open the valves to the cylinders. A cam on the distributor shaft opens and closes the contact-breaker points.

Cam and peg

A type of STEERING SYSTEM in which a worm gear (cam) at the base of the steering column moves a tapered peg attached to the drop arm.

Camber

In highway engineering the camber is the slight convex curvature in the cross section of a road to allow water to drain off. The Romans introduced camber into road building more than 2,000 years ago.

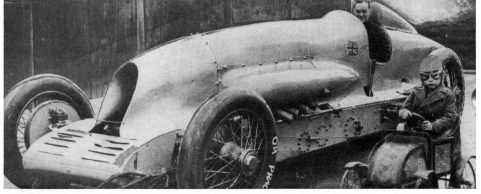

Sir Malcolm Campbell and his son Donald photographed in 1926. Sir Malcolm is seated in his record breaking Bluebird.

In automobile engineering the camber is the sideways tilt given to the front wheels of an automobile. The angle of camber must be the same for both wheels. The camber may be positive, with the wheels leaning slightly outwards, or negative with the wheels leaning slightly inwards. Most cars are designed with positive camber. This keeps the steering joints under positive load and tends to reduce rattle and wear as well as allowing light-

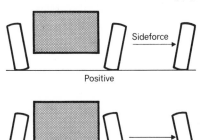

er steering. The camber angle must be periodically checked because incorrect camber can result in poor handling and excessive tire wear.

In aerodynamics camber is the curvature of an airfoil (see AERODYNAMICS).

Camelback

A type of locomotive with a raised cab in the center resembling a camel's hump. This positioning provides increased visibility for an engineer on a locomotive designed to run equally well in both directions. The first "camelbacks" were steam locomotives, usually switchers, but subsequently many electric and diesel locomotives had cabs of this type, with the equipment compartments sloping down from the cab to each end.

Campbell

The name of a British father and son who both held world speed records on land and water.

Sir Malcolm Campbell (1885-1948) began automobile racing in 1910. He achieved his first world land-speed record in 1924 with 146.16 mph (235.22 km/h) over a "flying mile." He was to break this record eight times from 1927 onwards, driving a succession of automobiles named "Bluebird." In 1935 he became the first man to drive at more than 300 mph, attaining an average speed of 301.13 mph (484.62 km/h) in two runs on the Bonneville Salt Flats in Utah. He then turned to high speeds on water, breaking the record in 1937, 1938, and 1939. The record he set in 1939, 141.74 mph (228.06 km/h), still stood when he died in 1948.

Donald Malcolm Campbell (1921-1967) continued in his father's footsteps. In 1955 he finally broke his father's record on water. By 1964 he had raised the record to 276.3 mph (444.7 km/h). In the same year he also broke the world land-speed record with 403.01 mph (648.58 km/h), driving a gas-turbine "Bluebird"

on the Lake Eyre Salt Flats in South Australia. He was killed three years later on Coniston Water, in England's Lake District, while trying to break the water-speed record once again.

Camshaft

A shaft in a gasoline engine that operates the VALVE GEAR in the cylinder head. Cams — projections on the shaft — are set at various angles around the shaft to match the firing order in the cylinders. The camshaft, which is machined precisely and hardened to withstand wear, is supported by three or five bearings. It is usually driven by chain from the engine crankshaft, though a toothed belt is occasionally used.

In many engines the camshaft is housed within the crankcase and operates the valves via tappets, push rods, and rockers. In others, termed overhead-cam engines, the camshaft is mounted on the cylinder head. Often twin overhead camshafts are required. Overhead cams operate more directly than conventional camshafts and are particularly suited to high-speed operation.

Canadian National Railways

Publicly-owned rail network created by act of Parliament in 1923 to amalgamate a number of government-owned railroads. Its 25,300 mi. (40,480 km) of track reach into 13 states as well as all the Canadian provinces. It has an important transcontinental line between Montreal and Vancouver, in addition to routes in the East. It also operates the 3ft.-6in. Newfoundland Line. The CNR has over 2,000 diesel-electric locomotives, 1,500 passenger cars, and over 100,000 freight cars.

Canadian Northern Railroad

With the Grand Trunk Pacific Railroad with which it eventually amalgamated, one of the pioneer railroads which opened up Western Canada to settlers. It began with only 100 mi. (160 km) of track, three locomotives, and 18 coaches but at the time of amalgamation it covered over 5,000 mi. (8,000 km).

Canadian Pacific Railway

A transcontinental railroad spanning Canada from Vancouver, British Columbia on the Pacific Coast, to Halifax, Nova Scotia, on the Atlantic. The original 2,881-mi. (4,636 km) railroad was begun in 1881, and the last "golden spike" was driven on November 7, 1885. The first passenger train left Montreal in June 1886, taking 5½ days to reach the Pacific. The railway now has 21,500 mi. (34,400 km) of track in Canada and (through a subsidiary) in the United States.

A contemporary engraving showing a convoy of boats steaming through the Suez Canal at its opening in 1869.

Canals and inland waterways

Most nations make some use of inland waterways for transportation, usually for freight but occasionally for passengers as well. Waterways are of various types: canals, canalized rivers, unimproved rivers (tidal or otherwise), lakes, and estuaries. The technology required varies with waterway type, but the principles are generally the same.

The first canals were probably built for irrigation or drainage purposes, only later becoming important for navigation. Today, many canals still serve both purposes, and may also be used for the generation of hydro-electric power. Most of the ancient civilizations of the middle east, Europe and China had remarkably advanced canal systems. A canal was built across the Isthmus of Suez between 616 and 521 B.C., while the famous GRAND CANAL of ancient China was opened in 610 A.D. The main limitation of the ancient canals was the absence of locks. Canals can not often be built on one level, and are usually constructed as a series of level reaches or pounds. Where one reach meets the next there is a step, the water in the upper level being held in by some form of watertight gate. In the early days a vessel could only move from one reach to another either by opening the gate and thus temporarily leveling the water in two reaches or by hauling the vessel

out of the water along a slipway. Such primitive methods made it impractical to construct canals over anything but a very gentle gradient, and it severely restricted the size of craft.

Until the arrival of railroads in the first half of the 19th century, canals provided the only means of transporting large quantities of heavy goods inland. During the 14th and 15th centuries the use of locks became widespread and canal systems were developed to meet the growing needs of commerce. But it was in the 18th century that the canal era really began. England's BRIDGEWATER CANAL was opened in 1761, and before long a network of some 3,000 mi. (4,828 km) had been built, on which the country's prosperity depended.

In the United States the pace of growth was at first slow. In 1800 there were just 100 mi. (160 km) of canals. However, it was soon realized that inland waterways provided the key to the development of the interior, and by the end of the century over 4,000 mi. (6,437 km) had been opened. The only ways of transporting heavy freight from the towns of the Atlantic seaboard to the midwest prairies were by land (a difficult and expensive journey), or by long sea routes. The Alleghany Mountains ruled out a direct canal link with the interior, and the state of New York decided to build a canal from

Albany on the Hudson to Buffalo on Lake Erie. Begun in 1817 and completed in 1825, the 363 mi. (584 km) ERIE CANAL was a brilliant success, and it assured New York's position as the major city on the Atlantic. It was followed by the Champlain (1823) and Chambly (1843) canals which provided a link to the St. Lawrence, and by a number of others which made navigation possible between the Great Lakes.

In 1834 a 394 mi. (630 km) canal between Philadelphia and Pittsburgh linked the Susquehanna and Ohio rivers, with the assistance of a central railroad section to carry passengers and freight 1,399 ft. (425 m) to the summit. In the following years further canals were constructed to join this system to the Erie Canal, and in 1848 the Illinois-Michigan Canal was opened, linking the Philadelphia—Erie—Great Lakes system to the United States' greatest natural inland waterway, the Mississippi, and triggering the meteoric rise of Chicago.

With the arrival of the railroads, half the canals in the United States closed in the mid-19th century, and today almost all the old network has been abandoned. However, a new inland waterway transport system has replaced the old, based primarily on the Mississippi, the Great Lakes, the intracoastal waterways, and various linking stretches of modern canals.

Inland waterways today. Now that the towing of vessels from the bank by draft animal, electric locomotive or diesel tractor is virtually obsolete, nearly all vessels using canals and waterways are either self-propelled, towed by a tug or towboat, or assembled into a rigid raft (called a "push-tow") and pushed from the rear by a single pusher tug. The capacity of the vessels used is governed by the channel cross-section or by navigation works such as bridges and locks. A great range of sizes may therefore be found, the largest single vessels being the Great Lakes freighters of up to 33,000 tons, though big push-tows with over 30 barges may carry twice as much. The tug in such a case would typically provide 6,000 to 10,000 hp, and would be equipped with radar.

Although inland waterway networks are relatively limited in extent compared to road or rail, and although travel is very slow, inland waterway transportation retains a vital role for certain types of bulk freight carriage. The lack of speed is offset by the enormous size of the load, while the low manpower necessary and the low resistance to motion reduce the cost of wages and fuel to give significantly lower rates per ton-mile than either road or rail transportation. In addition the physical connection between waterways and oceans reduces the need for transshipment at maritime ports, and the size of waterways and barges enables cargoes of unusual size to be carried.

Thus the commodities carried by inland waterway tend to be low-value materials which are required in large quantities and can be easily handled in bulk. Typically these are building materials, ores, coal, oil, chemicals, and grains. Manufactured goods and machinery are not carried to a great extent, though there are notable exceptions such as the use of multi-decked car-carriers in both Europe and the United States. Although the classic barge is a simple open-topped rectangular steel vessel, specialist craft such as refrigerated barges, wine tankers, and bulk cement carriers are in operation in many countries.

The rapid growth in the use of road-rail-sea containers (see CONTAINERIZATION) has its waterway counterpart. Not only are container-carrying barges operated, but also the barge itself can be treated as a container which can be packed at an inland center, sealed by customs, and pushed to a maritime terminal for direct loading onto a "mother ship" for ocean transit. The most successful system so far in use, LASH (lighter aboard ship; see FREIGHTERS) comprises two dozen mother ships and over 3,000 barges, giving a worldwide service linking the inland waterways of many nations. The attractions of this development are that it adds, to the many desirable features of containerization, a large unit size (410 tons, nearly 20 times the size of the largest ISO container), and the ability to by-pass conventional port facilities, as all mother ships are equipped to lift loaded barges on and off their decks. Other systems under development in the United States and the Soviet Union, include BACAT (barge aboard catamaran) and Seabee, which are respectively smaller and larger versions of the LASH idea.

Waterway structure. Civil engineering works associated with waterways can be divided into four categories. Firstly, an adequate channel must be provided either as a totally artificial canal, or through improvements to an existing watercourse by dredging, piling, and elimination of sharp bends. On canals, the provision of a level channel may involve the construction of tunnels, aqueducts, embankments, and cuttings. Ground conditions may demand waterproofing of the canal bed. Secondly, level-changing services may be required at intervals; these are almost invariably LOCKS, though a few barge-elevating structures exist in Europe and the Soviet Union (see ELEVATORS; INCLINED PLANE). Thirdly, provision must be made for the supply or passage of water. Many canals require reservoirs to feed their higher reaches, and many canalized rivers exhibit massive weir or dam structures, often with associated hydro-power plant. Fourthly, terminal facilities are needed, in the form of basins, harbors, or inland ports, equipped with quays, cranes, and other bulk-handling devices. The extent of all these works varies with the nature of the waterway, but even lakes and estuaries require terminals, and frequently channel dredgings and marking as well.

Waterways in the United States. Since the early years of this century all waterways (except the NEW YORK STATE BARGE CANAL) have been a federal responsibility, resulting in massive development on a national scale. Between 1960 and 1970 alone, about $5 billion was spent on navigation works, the Ohio, Arkansas, and Trinity Rivers each receiving about $1 billion. Recent projects include the opening of the Kaskasia River to navigation

The Grand Union Canal, England, with a typical "narrow boat" of the canal era. The boat's small size was specifically designed for Britain's narrow canals, but after the arrival of the railroad it made them uneconomic. Today little commercial use is made of most of Britain's canals, although they, and the narrow boats, are popular for vacation cruising.

after 50 years of disuse, and the start in 1974 on a new 258-mi. (415 km) link between the Tennessee and Tombigbee Rivers, requiring, besides river improvement, 10 new locks and 46 mi. (74 km) of artificial waterway connecting a series of lakes.

The United States now has over 25,000 mi. (40,000 km) of commercial waterway (excluding the Great Lakes), of which about 15,000 mi. (24,000 km) offer a depth of 9 ft. (2.7 m) or greater. The waterways contribute about 10% of the nation's freight transportation, and the Great Lakes an almost equal share. The Mississippi system forms a network of 2,500 mi. (4,000 km), stretching from the Gulf of Mexico to Minneapolis, Pittsburgh, and Tulsa. The ATLANTIC INTRACOASTAL WATERWAY runs along the east coast from Delaware to Miami and provides a partly-protected waterway route at sealevel, connecting with a number of river navigations. The GULF INTRACOASTAL WATERWAY performs similar service between Florida and the Mexican border. A connection between these waterways, the Cross-Florida Barge Canal, was started in 1964. The ST. LAWRENCE SEAWAY, a joint United States/Canadian project, was opened in 1959, giving 2,300 mi. (3,700 km) of navigation to vessels up to 715 ft. (218 m) long. It supplemented and improved existing navigation works and now includes the St. Lawrence River, WELLAND SHIP CANAL, the Great Lakes and other short canals and locks. Connections to the Mississippi system are via Chicago, and to the 522-mi. (840 km) long New York State Barge Canal system via Buffalo or Oswego. There are plans to increase its capacity by lock rebuilding or even new canal sections between lakes. On the west coast, the generally steeper terrain is less favorable for inland navigation. Apart from a few short estuarial waterways, use is made of the Sacramento River and the Columbia River system. The Sacramento Deepwater Ship Canal and Columbia River projects will extend the network to provide over 500 mi. (805 km) of navigable waterways from the Pacific to Lewiston, Idaho. Some Alaskan rivers also offer navigation to shallow craft.

Without doubt the most striking waterway structures in the United States are the huge locks and dams astride the larger rivers. A number exceed 100 ft. (30 m) in height (e.g. the 103-ft. (31.4 m) Ice Harbor Lock on the Snake River, and the 113-ft. (34.4 m) John Day Lock on the Columbia River). Despite their great height, sophisticated design allows emptying or filling in under 15 minutes without undue disturbance to barges.

European waterways. In Europe, rivers have long been used for transportation and the first totally artificial waterway connecting two river basins, the Stecknitz Canal in Germany, dates from the late-14th century. Since then, many other canals have been built and rivers improved, but today's waterway network is a 20th-century creation, still undergoing major extension. The great rivers, the Seine, Rhine, Rhône, Elbe and Danube and their major tributaries, were the starting point for many imaginative canal schemes linking the river basins to provide an extensive system covering much of central and northern Europe. Compared with North American rivers, those of Europe are generally steeper and smaller; hence Europe's waterways reveal a more highly developed infrastructure technology, even though the vessels and channels are considerably smaller. Towed and self-propelled vessels predominate, but push-towing is increasing. National frontiers also present problems, but since World War II, significant cooperation has been evident; an example is the adoption of a standard for new waterway construction, the "Europa Ship" of 1490-ton capacity. The central European network connects Austria, Belgium, Bulgaria, Czechoslovakia, East Germany, France, Hungary, Luxembourg, the Netherlands, Poland, Romania, Switzerland, the Soviet Union, West Germany, and Yugoslavia, though not all connections can yet accommodate Europa Ships. Additionally, Finland, Italy, Portugal, Spain, Sweden, and the United Kingdom have separate waterway systems. Belgium has a 950-mi. (1,540 km) network of which nearly half is of Europa standard. Much of the 110 million tons of traffic is international, moving between Belgian ports and France, Germany, the Netherlands, and Switzerland. Since 1954 many routes have been considerably modernized, the most notable of the new works being the Ronquières inclined plane. Its two steel tanks running on a concrete slope can lift or lower Europa ships 220 ft. (67 m) in 20 minutes.

In France, the 4,500-mi. (7,200 km) system is currently not so well developed, but even so transports over 110 million tons annually. Much was built a century ago for 380-ton craft, but important routes are being enlarged for Europa Ships or even larger push-tows. A series of dams and locks has recently been completed to control the hitherto treacherous Rhône, resulting in greatly increased traffic. One of the most interesting French developments is the waterslope on the Garonne Lateral Canal at Montech. It uses a sloping concrete channel to connect the upper and lower sections

Items of freight too large for any truck or railroad car can be easily transported on inland waterways.

Ships negotiating the flight of locks into Gatun Lake at the Atlantic end of the Panama Canal.

of the canal. The upper end is sealed by a steel gate. A second tightly-fitting gate can be moved along this channel by diesel-electric locomotives. This gate retains a pool of water above it and thus a barge in the pool may travel up or down the slope. The upper gate is removed temporarily to allow the barge to enter or leave the pool. The slope bypasses five locks previously used to overcome the 43-ft. (13 m) level change.

Germany's 2,700-mi. (4,370 km) network has recently been increased by the opening in 1975 of the Elbe Lateral Canal, whose 71 mi. (114 km) connect the River Elbe to the Mittelland Canal. This is an excellent example of modern waterway construction with bitumen or PVC lining, and the use of only two structures to raise barges 200 ft. (61 m). The Lüneburg elevator is the world's highest at 125 ft. (38 m), and each of its two independent steel tanks can hold a Europa Ship. At Uelzen, the world's highest canal lock raises barges 75 ft. (23 m). 60% of the

lock water can be stored for reuse in reservoirs alongside.

Internationally, the most important current project in Germany is the construction of a canal joining the Main to the Danube, thus completing a route for craft from the North Sea to the Black Sea. The canal, whose highest point is 1,330 ft. (406 m) above sealevel, will also transport water from the Danube to the Main. The Danube itself and its tributaries have also been improved by Austria, Bulgaria, Romania, and Yugoslavia. One of its greatest hazards, the rapids at the Iron Gate, has been eliminated by the recent construction of a dam and lock. In the Netherlands about 40% of freight is moved by waterway, an exceptionally high figure which owes much to the flat terrain traversed by the Rhine and its distributaries. The NORTH SEA CANAL boasts one of the largest canal locks in the world, 1,320 ft. (402 m) long by 165 ft. (50 m) wide.

In the Soviet Union, many major cross-

watershed canals have been built in recent years, examples including the Dneiper-Bug and Volga-Don Canals. Inland waterways account for about 5% of freight and 1% of passenger transportation. The world's highest lock is in Russia, at Ust-Kamenogorskiy. 138 ft. (42 m) high, it lifts 1,760-ton barges past a hydroelectric dam on the River Irtish.

Ship canals. Besides freight transportation, waterways can also provide shortened routes for ships, both freighters and others. Some of the most famous canals, including the PANAMA CANAL and SUEZ CANAL, are of this type, for although freight travels along them, it is rarely for canalside destinations. Many transits are made by ships in ballast, naval vessels, passenger liners, fishing boats, and so on. A recent example is the 200-mi. (320 km) canal between the Baltic and White Seas opened by Russia in 1975 to allow naval vessels access to the main naval repair yards at Leningrad.

Canoes

Light, shallow draft boats pointed at both ends. Normally propelled by paddles, but sometimes carrying a single mast and one or two sails, most canoes are narrow and easily capsized. To improve stability an outrigger may be fitted, or the canoe may have two hulls.

The canoe is one of the oldest types of boat. In its most primitive forms it is constructed either by burning or cutting out the inside of a log to make a dugout, or by covering a wooden framework with skin or bark. Early canoes were used for local transportation, fishing and the like, as they still are in some parts of the world, while large twin-hulled canoes were sailed far out on the Pacific Ocean by the Polynesians over 1,000 years ago.

North American Indian birchbark covered canoes are so light that they can easily be carried on the back, and of such shallow draft and efficiency that they provide an ideal form of transportation over shallow rocky rivers and rapids. They were extensively used for carrying people and goods by early pioneers in Canada.

Canoes do not usually exceed about 20 to 30 ft. (6 to 9 m) in length, but the Polynesian craft were up to 150 ft. (45 m) long. Ancient British dugouts were typically about 35 ft. (10 m) long, and 5 ft. (1.5 m) wide, although one with a length of 48 ft. (14.5 m) has been found, while Maori war canoes were over 60 ft. (18 m) long. Large canoes were often constructed by building planked sides onto a dugout, a line of development that led eventually to the framed and planked boat and ship.

Today canoes are used primarily for pleasure, sport, and fishing, although in modern times they have also been employed in survey work, and in warfare (for reconnaissance and commando raids). In addition to planked timber construction, canoes are made of molded plywood, canvas (on a wooden frame), plastic or glass, magnesium, and aluminum (see also BOAT; KAYAK).

Cantilever bridge

A kind of BEAM BRIDGE incorporating twin cantilever arms. A cantilever is a beam fixed at one end and supported underneath at a point usually about halfway along. The other end therefore overhangs the support. This arrangement produces compression in the lower edge, or chord, and tension in the upper chord. This is the reverse of the forces in a simple beam supported at the ends. A cantilever bridge with twin cantilever arms, with the overhanging ends meeting in the middle, can span much larger gaps than

One of the oldest types of boat, the canoe is still widely used in many areas. These carved and painted fishing canoes are in Ghana.

can a simple beam bridge. Often a suspended span is added between the overhanging cantilevers to increase the total span still further.

The QUEBEC BRIDGE over the St. Lawrence River in Canada, and the FORTH RAIL BRIDGE across the Firth of Forth in Scotland are the largest steel cantilever bridges ever built. In their day they were the longest span bridges in the world. Today, however, long-span cantilever designs are not economical — arch and suspension bridges are much less expensive. Cantilever design is still widely used for smaller spans, however, and is usually executed in prestressed concrete rather than steel girders (see BRIDGES).

Capacity

Or cubic capacity, of an engine, a measurement of the volume swept by the pistons from top to bottom of their stroke. It is usually expressed in liters, cubic centimeters (cc), or cubic inches.

Cape Cod Canal

Sea-level waterway cutting $17\frac{1}{2}$ mi. (28 km) across the base of Cape Cod, at the southeastern corner of Massachusetts. It was built 1909-14 (later improved) and shortens the sea route between New York and Boston by more than 68 mi. (110 km). Some 475 ft. (145 m) across, it is one of the world's widest canals.

Capital ship

A WARSHIP of the largest class. The term was first applied in the 1600s to the SHIPS OF THE LINE — those large enough to take their place in the line of battle. Until the 1950s the term capital ship included battleships, battle-cruisers, cruisers, and aircraft carriers. It now applies almost solely to aircraft carriers, which are the only really large warships in active service (see AIRCRAFT CARRIER).

Capstan

A mechanical appliance used mainly on ships and piers to move heavy weights such as anchors by winding in a cable or chain. The capstan consists of a cast-iron drum on a vertical spindle. The drum is narrower in the middle than at the top and bottom and rotates on the spindle. It may be driven by steam or electricity, or, with the aid of capstan bars inserted in holes at the head of the drum, by hand. The cable is wound several turns round the drum and grips it by friction. A ratchet mechanism keeps the drum from unwinding.

Caravan

A group of travelers who journey together for mutual protection, particularly in the wild desert country of North Africa and the Middle East. Traditionally, the camel is the main animal used because of its ability to cover long distances without

A caravan crossing the desert. Despite modern technology, camels are still unrivaled for desert transportation.

Aérospatiale Caravelle airliners. The Caravelle entered service in 1959, and was the first rear-engined jet airliner.

need for water. The word comes from the Persian *Karvan*.

Caravans generally follow well-defined routes in the deserts between oases or smaller water-holes. They are strictly organized, with regular halts for food and rest. Caravanserais are buildings erected for accommodating caravan travelers.

Caravel

A small ship of the 15th and 16th centuries, which had a narrow, high stern and broad bows, and typically three masts, though some larger oceangoing caravels had four masts. Caravels ranged in size from 10 tons for coastal work to 50 tons for long ocean voyages. The sail plan varied; smaller vessels were lateen-rigged, with triangular sails, but some of the larger ones carried square sails on all but the aftermast. Two of Christopher Columbus' ships, the *Niña* and the *Pinta*, were caravels. The name caravel comes from the Latin *carabus*, a light boat.

Caravelle

One of the most successful short-to-medium range airliners ever built. Designed by the French Sud-Aviation, now part of Aérospatiale, the prototype of the twin rear-jet Caravelle flew in 1955. The latest version, the Caravelle 12, has a wing span of 112 ft. (34 m) and an overall length of 119 ft. (36 m). It can seat a maximum of 139 passengers. Its two turbofan engines give it a cruising speed of 512 mph (825 km/h). In January 1968, a Caravelle made the first-ever fully automatic landing in poor visibility on a scheduled flight from Lyons to Paris.

Carbon monoxide

One of the most deadly of the exhaust gases given out by internal combustion engines. It is formed by the incomplete combustion of hydrocarbon fuel. It is

particularly dangerous because, having no color or smell, it cannot readily be detected. Inhaling as little as one part of carbon monoxide in 750 parts of air can cause death within half an hour. To reduce the risk of carbon-monoxide poisoning, a car engine should never be run in a closed garage. Exhaust-system leakages should be repaired immediately to minimize the chance of gases filtering into and building up in the passenger compartment.

Carbon monoxide causes death by depriving the body of oxygen. It enters lungs and combines much more readily than oxygen with the hemoglobin in the blood. The hemoglobin is thereby prevented from carrying out its essential function of carrying oxygen to the cells.

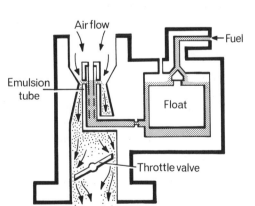

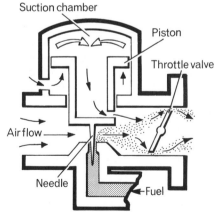

Cutaway diagrams of fixed jet (left) and movable jet (right) carburetors.

Carburetor

In a gasoline engine the carburetor is the device that mixes together gasoline and air in the correct amounts and in a suitable condition to be burned in the engine cylinders. Some engines have a single carburetor, which supplies the fuel needs of all the engine cylinders through a common intake manifold. Others have

twin or multiple carburetors, in which one carburetor serves a pair of cylinders through short forked manifolds. Twin carburetors are commonly fitted to high-performance cars to improve the carburation.

Not all gasoline engines have a carburetor. Some have a fuel-injection system which delivers a precise metered amount of gasoline into the inlet duct to each cylinder just before the inlet valve (see FUEL INJECTION).

There are many kinds of carburetors, but the principles of operation are basically similar. Gasoline is piped from a reservoir, the FLOAT CHAMBER, to a jet in the narrowest part of a narrow-throated passage called a VENTURI, or choke tube. Filtered air is drawn through the venturi by the piston suction produced in the engine cylinders. As it enters the narrow throat, its speed increases but its pressure drops (see BERNOULLI'S PRINCIPLE), and gasoline is sucked from the jet. The gasoline emerges as a fine spray of droplets which mix with, and start to evaporate, in the rushing air stream, a process called "vaporization." A "butterfly" throttle valve, operated by the driver's accelerator pedal, controls the degree of suction, and therefore the amount of mixture entering the cylinders.

For efficient combustion, air and gasoline must be mixed together in proportions of about 15:1. As the air speed through the carburetor increases, the air density falls. The gasoline density remains constant, however. Thus with increasing air speed, the resulting mixture becomes richer and richer, making combustion

progressively more difficult. Practical carburetors are designed to compensate for this effect.

Carburetors may be described as updraft, downdraft or sidedraft according to the direction in which the air stream flows through them. Basically there are two main carburetor-types — fixed-jet and variable-jet. The fixed-jet carburetor

A covered stage wagon of the early 19th century. The concave wheels were considerably lighter than conventional types.

compensates for the increased richness at higher speeds by means of an emulsifying tube. This is a perforated tube in a cell leading to the main jet. As the engine speed increases, air is drawn through the emulsifying tube and mixes with gasoline before it is sprayed through the main jet. The mixture is thereby weakened. The amount of air entering the tube increases as the engine speed increases. An accelerator pump sprays more fuel into the airstream for rapid acceleration. A separate jet provides a dribble of fuel for idling.

Variable-jet carburetors, such as the SU and the Stromberg, have a single jet, in which a tapered needle is located. The needle is held by a sliding piston, which rises in proportion to the engine suction. As it rises it causes the size of the venturi throat to vary so as to provide an almost constant pressure. This keeps the mixture strength constant. The needle is tapered so that as it rises (when the engine speed increases) it allows more gasoline through the jet.

Some carburetors fitted to high-performance engines have two venturis to improve the fuel flow. They are fed by a common float chamber and may lead to a common manifold or to separate manifolds to single cylinders. In twin-barrel, or twin-choke carburetors such as the Weber, both venturis operate simultaneously. In compound carburetors, a smaller primary venturi provides smooth-running at low speeds. A larger secondary venturi opens only when maximum power is required.

A somewhat different carburetor is used on airplane piston engines. It is an injection type, in which the whole system is maintained under pressure. This is es-sential when the pressure outside changes with altitude. Fuel is pumped into the carburetor and through a fuel-pressure valve to a rotating spinner ring, which discharges through the inner air duct to the cylinders. The pressure of the fuel is regulated by means of a multiple-valve arrangement in the main air intake. The change in mixture strength required as the altitude changes is brought about by means of a pressure valve operated by the bellows-like aneroid capsule.

The aneroid capsule is a flexible bellows filled with inert gas. As the atmospheric pressure varies, the bellows expands or contracts to allow more or less air through a valve into a diaphragm chamber which regulates the fuel pressure.

Cargo ship
See FREIGHTER.

Carnot cycle
A principle of thermodynamics originated by Sadi Carnot in the early 19th century. The cycle consists of a sequence of operations of an ideal heat engine working at maximum efficiency: isentropic compression, isothermal heat addition, isothermal expansion, and isentropic heat rejection process. The Carnot cycle establishes that the greater the temperature difference between the high-temperature source and the low-temperature sink, the greater the efficiency of the heat engine. It shows, however, that even under ideal conditions, not all of the heat energy can be converted into mechanical energy.

Carrack
A large merchant ship, which also carried some guns, similar to a GALLEON.

Carriages and carts
The first simple carts were evolved over 5,000 years ago, probably by the Sumerians, from the sled-like devices that early human communities used to haul goods. These were wheeled chariots drawn by teams of four wild asses harnessed on either side of a pole with a yoke resting on their shoulders.

Early wheels were either of one piece or comprised several planks joined together and trimmed to a circular shape with copper nails in the rim, but by 2000 B.C. the spoked wheel had appeared, together with linchpins and axle trees. These were now drawn by horses controlled by bridles equipped with snaffle bits.

Early wheeled vehicles. Wheeled vehicles reached the Indus Valley and the central steppes of Asia by 2500 B.C., Syria by 2200 B.C., China by 1500 B.C. and Sweden by 1300 B.C. The best known of these early vehicles are the war chariots, but by the second millennium B.C. there were examples of wagons in Sweden which had iron tires and (probably) a swivelling front axle.

To carry light baggage the Romans used various heavy carts and a few wagons known as *carpentas*, in which seats were sometimes installed. These vehicles probably incorporated steerable axles and owed their origin (at least in part) to the Greek agricultural wagons and the Hungarian *reda*.

By 70 A.D. the Romans were apparently using paired shafts so that only one animal (with a collar) was needed to pull a vehicle. In China, traces attached to the wither strap were introduced about 200 B.C., together with a lowered front strap that relieved the pressure on a horse's windpipe. The Chinese also used lighter concave wheels.

The Middle Ages. European roads deteriorated after the fall of the Roman Empire. War chariots disappeared, but some carts and carriages were still made. "Carriage" originally probably meant just the "undercarriage" (the running gear), while "coach" (a vehicle suspended by braces or straps) is derived from Kotze, a town in Hungary where this type of conveyance originated.

In the 10th century the Slavs suspended the bodies of vehicles on chains and by the 14th century longitudinal straps were employed in Germany to cushion the ride, but medieval carts still had solid wheels and wagons employed front and back wheels of equal size.

During the 16th century there were stage wagons — massive timber vehicles hauled by up to 10 horses guided by drovers walking alongside. Canvas tops

A landau. Widespread in Britain from the 18th century, and also popular in the United States, this type of carriage had two folding hoods which when raised met in the middle to form a fully protected passenger compartment. Heavier models were drawn by four horses.

(294 km) between London and Manchester, while London to Edinburgh (400 mi.) took up to 12 days with 18 hours a day on the road.

Meanwhile in London there were, by 1650, over 300 Hackney coaches (from the French haquenée, meaning a horse for hire). They were originally small, narrow vehicles drawn by two horses, but after the Great Fire of London (1666) the streets were widened and discarded gentlemen's town coaches were pressed into use.

During the 17th century small front wheels were adopted so that sharp turns could be made without the wheels scraping the carriage, and more attention was devoted to suspension systems. About 1660 Filippo de Chièse's Berlin coach appeared in the city of that name. This light, fast vehicle had two perches, C-springs and leather braces. Initially it carried only two people, but later models accommodated four passengers.

The cost of running a stage route in England made it an uneconomic proposition without either exorbitant fares or a subsidy from carrying mail. As a result the British post office arranged to hire and operate mail coaches that could also carry eight passengers (four inside, four outside). The first of these was introduced by John Palmer of Bath in 1784, and subsequently they were built, maintained and hired out to the post office. Mail coaches were driven fast and required a change of horses every 7-10 miles.

Stage coaches modeled on the mail coach pattern also appeared in 1784. Initially fairly light but high-built, they gradually became heavier until eventually they were accommodating 14 people on top as well as the inside passengers.

Phaetons became popular at the end of the 18th century. These four-wheeled vehicles were owner-driven with two, four or six horses and a postillion. Very high and lightly built, they had up to 5-ft. (1.5 m) diameter front wheels and 6-ft. (1.8 m) back wheels, using a perch or crane-neck undercarriage. Known as "highflyers," they were sporting but dangerous.

People of means would at this time use in town a two-wheeled curricle, a four-wheeled landau (which originated in Germany about 1790 and seated four, with a hood that opened from the middle), a landaulet (drawn by a single horse instead of a pair and accommodating two people), or a flat-bottomed two- or four-horse Austrian Britchka in which the passenger could recline at full length. The landaulet was later used as a Hackney carriage and known as a fly.

were fitted to protect goods and passengers, while the wheels became so wide that they eventually resembled rollers (it was thought they would improve the atrocious rutted "roads").

It was soon found advantageous for vehicles to have a separate undercarriage that embodied the primitive suspension and steering systems. The two axles were joined by long wooden poles (the perch), which inserted into a transom located above the front axle and was secured at the back to the rear axle. Steering was effected by a swivel pin driven through both the transom and the front axle. To form a floor, crosspieces were mounted above the transom and the back axle to support longitudinal poles and planks; uprights at the extremities of the crosspieces formed a basis for the body panels.

European vehicles, 16th-18th centuries.

The first English stage coaches appeared during the 16th century, but they were initially heavy, square-shaped vehicles adapted from town coaches (two-, four- or six-horse carriages used by the nobility). By 1662 there were six coaches operating throughout the summer months, from London to York, Chester, Exeter, Oxford, Dover and Plymouth. Nearly a century later, in 1754, the express coach still took 4½ days to cover the 184 mi.

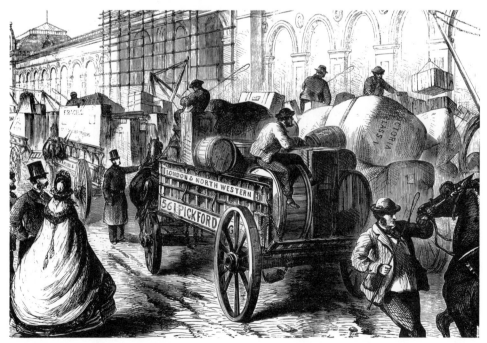

Horsedrawn dray carts such as these were used for transporting heavy goods well into the 20th century.

A hansom cab. The driver sits on a raised seat at the rear, and can communicate with his passenger through a trapdoor in the roof. Hansom cabs were very popular in Boston and New York before the arrival of the automobile.

The two-wheeled gig was exceedingly common and simple versions of this open, high-built cart were widely used by even the less well-off. The heavy Tilbury gig became popular in Italy and Portugal, and buggies (hooded gigs) were introduced in America, although the term "buggy" was also used for light, fast four-wheeled vehicles. A sulky accommodated only one person (hence the name) and a refined version is still used for trotting racing. Dog carts were also derived from gigs and originally had a deep, slatted boot for carrying sporting dogs, but later this feature disappeared, four wheels were fitted, and this type of vehicle became a popular conveyance for shopping and country pursuits until the beginning of the 20th century. The Collinge axle, carrying three months' supply of grease instead of one day's, appeared in 1792, and elliptic springs had been developed by Obadiah Elliott of Lambeth, in London, by 1804.

American vehicles. In America the English stage coach proved unsuitable for the rutted tracks that usually served as roads. During the 1820s Lewis Downing of Concord, New Hampshire, and his partner J. Stephen Abbot, produced the first of the famous Concord stages that by mid-century were being supplied to Europe, South America, Africa, and Australia. Constructed of specially seasoned timber with a minimum of ironwork, Concord stages had curved body panels for

strength, a high driving seat, and leather thoroughbraces for suspension.

In the 1840s a 2,500-lb. (1,125 kg) Concord stage cost about $1,200. Downing and Abbot also built rugged mud wagons (for very rough or muddy conditions) and light celerity wagons (for mail or express lines where passengers were only a small part of the business). These vehicles had a lower center of gravity and enhanced stability at the expense of some reduction in comfort, but cost only

around $800 each.

The settlers who headed for the Western frontier during this pioneering period carried their goods in covered wagons — also known as Conestoga wagons or prairie schooners. The beds of these massive vehicles were sometimes 16 ft. (4.8 m) long, with back wheels 6 ft. (1.8 m) in diameter and hoops for the canvas tops arching 11 ft. (3.3 m) above the ground. To pull them, teams of six horses or mules were necessary.

Regular overloading of stage coaches in California during the gold rush years of the 1850s and 60s led to development of the Wells Fargo type, with the coupling beams suspended below the rear axle instead of mortised through it, strengthened running gear, stronger thoroughbraces, and more powerful brakes.

19th century Europe. As the English road system improved, carriages for out-of-town use appeared in greater numbers. The Dormeuse (1820) was a Britchka with a hard top that could be used for winter travel, while phaetons became lower and ranged in size from the massive mail phaeton (1828) suitable only for men drivers, to the light, elegant spider phaeton and park phaeton. For summer family outings there were wagonettes (1842; two-, three- or four-horses), their rather larger derivative, the brake (1860) being used mostly for transporting staff or carrying parties to sporting functions. The char-a-banc (1844) was also of wagonette origin; it was capable of carrying more people, however, and eventually became a gaudily painted conveyance for public sightseeing although originally only used privately by

An unusual French goat cart of the late 19th century. Such vehicles were more often drawn by dogs.

large wealthy families.

In London two-wheeled cabriolets introduced from France in 1815 were licensed for hire from 1823 (hence "cab"), and the first clumsy Hansom cab with 7 ft. 6 in. (2.3 m) wheels appeared in 1834, but this type of vehicle was not successful until a revised design was produced by John Chapman in 1836. Four-wheel cabs seating four (clarences, later growlers because of the noise they made) appeared soon after. Rubber-tired Hansoms were introduced in 1880.

Formal carriages included the barouche (or German wagon) for two to six horses (a large, clumsy low-built vehicle of canoe-like shape with a hood at the back only), the milord (a cab-like vehicle on

but later on landaus and barouches. Small vehicles of the late 19th century included the two-wheeled governess cart (c. 1900) for carrying children (usually in the country), the float, which resembled a governess cart but required a large horse to pull it and was used by dairies because its low build facilitated the loading of churns, and such curiosities as the Ralli car (1898), and the cocking cart, drawn by a pair, with slatted venetian blinds each side so that fighting cocks could be transported. The carriage shape and form was conserved for a time in the first automobiles — the "horseless carriages" — and even to the present in the seating arrangement of European railroad cars (see also ANIMAL TRANSPORT).

smooth and streamlined, but less strong than with CLINKER CONSTRUCTION.

Cascade Tunnel
The longest railroad tunnel in North America. It carries the Great Northern Railway for 7.8 mi. (12.5 km) under the Cascade Range in Washington, about 60 mi. (100 km) east of Seattle. It was driven through solid rock, and was completed in 1929. It is 16 ft. (4.9 m) wide and 23 ft. (7 m) high. It serves as one of the principal routes crossing the Cascade Range, replacing an earlier tunnel dating from 1897.

Caster angle
For safety, automobile must have an inbuilt tendency to "steer straight" and to straighten up after a turn. One of the main design features affecting directional stability is the caster angle — the angle at which the steering pivots are inclined back from the vertical. Because of this angle, the wheels tend to trail, inducing directional stability.

Catalytic converter
A unit fitted to some automobile exhaust systems to reduce pollution (see EMISSION-CONTROL SYSTEM).

Catamaran
The word means "tied logs," and strictly speaking it refers to a primitive Indian fishing boat made by lashing logs together. However, in modern usage, a catamaran is a twin-hulled SAILBOAT, usually capable of very high speeds.

A monohull sailboat obtains its stability from its weight and its depth in the water. A catamaran has a very broad effective beam and can therefore be very light and of very shallow draft, and can carry more sail than a monohull (hence its superior speed). The one disadvantage is that should it capsize it does not, like a conventional boat, right itself.

A two-wheeled ostrich carriage in Paris in the 1870s. Two-wheeled passenger carts or chariots were widely used in Roman times, but did not become popular in Europe until the 18th century.

four elliptic springs favored in England and on the Continent until the 1850s when it was reintroduced into England as the Victoria for private use in about 1870), and the sociable (1870) drawn by a pair of horses and seating four people in facing pairs. The Brougham (1839), designed for Lord Brougham, was a widely used one-horse two-seat conveyance later enlarged to provide cramped accommodation for four occupants, and the Droitska was a Russian four-seat open carriage built on a perch with C-springs. For formal state occasions there were elaborate dress chariots and state coaches.

In 1846 the London coachbuilding firm of Hoopers had introduced suspension incorporating a single wrought iron perch supported by horizontal undersprings, initially on Broughams and sociables,

Carrier Pigeons
Carrier pigeons have been used to carry messages since at least the days of ancient Greece and Rome. The homing pigeon possesses an uncanny ability to find its way back to its loft. Scientific tests suggest that the pigeon navigates by calculating the sun's position in relation to the horizon; the mechanism involved is still unknown. Carrier pigeons have been used in warfare as recently as the Korean War.

Cartography
The art of making MAPS and CHARTS.

Carvel construction
A method of fitting the planks of a ship or boat's hull together edge-to-edge to provide a flush finish. The result is

Cat-and-mouse engine
A rotary gasoline engine, developed by T. Tschudi in 1927. It contains pairs of pistons that move away from and then catch up with each other, rather like a cat playing with a mouse. The two pairs of pistons rotate in opposite directions inside a cylinder, which has an inlet port and an exhaust (outlet) port. They move closer together or farther apart at different points in the engine cycle in a way that duplicates the volume changes that occur in a conventional piston-engine cycle.

The four stages in the standard FOUR-STROKE CYCLE take place simultaneously in different parts of the cat-and-mouse engine. Each space between the four pistons undergoes the stages in turn. As a pair of pistons nears the inlet port, they are closest together. The trailing piston then stops while the other continues, and the mixture is sucked in. Then the leading piston stops and the trailing piston swings round, compressing the mixture, which then ignites. The expanding gases force the leading piston around on its power stroke, while the trailing piston remains stationary. The leading piston completes its circle, uncovering the outlet port. The trailing piston then swings round and expels the exhaust gases. The pistons return to their original positions and the cycle begins again.

Catboat

The simplest kind of sailing boat, with a single mast located well forward in the bow. On this mast is a single large sail, an arrangement called a catrig. A catboat generally has a CENTERBOARD.

Catch Me Who Can

A locomotive built by railroad pioneer Richard TREVITHICK in 1808. Trevithick ran the locomotive and cars around a circular track in Euston Square, London, and charged one shilling for passengers to ride in it.

Caterpillar track

An endless track of jointed steel plates fitted to some tractors and other vehicles, enabling them to travel over rough and muddy ground (see CRAWLER TRACK).

Cathode-ray-tube display

In all sections of transportation cathode-ray-tube (CRT) devices are widely used. They form the essential part of the closed-circuit television receivers used, for example, to monitor traffic conditions on roads, display flight information at airports, and read freight-car numbers at railroad classification yards. They also form the display screens of radar sets at airports and on board ships and aircraft (see RADAR).
The cathode-ray tube is an evacuated glass tube. It is narrow at one end and widens out to form the screen at the other. An electric gun at the narrow end "shoots" narrow beams of electrons towards the screen. The beam is accelerated down the tube by anodes, which also serve to focus the beam. A control grid located in front of the anodes controls the beam's brightness. Before the beam widens out two coils or plates produce a magnetic field to deflect the electron beam horizontally and vertically. The screen end of the tube is coated internally with phosphors that glow momentarily when struck by the electron beam. Information is displayed on the screen by feeding appropriate signals to the grid and to the two deflecting coils.

Cathodic protection

A means of protecting underground steel pipelines (and occasionally ships' hulls) from corrosion. Corrosion is an electro-chemical process, and in an unprotected steel pipe, tiny electrolytic cells form over the surface, with the iron in the steel forming the anode in the circuits. When current flows in the cells, the iron gradually corrodes.
In cathodic protection, current from an external circuit is applied to the steel in the opposite direction to the corrosion current to turn the steel into the cathode in the circuit. Being cathodic, the steel is no longer subject to corrosion. The anode in the circuit is designed to be worn away and can be readily and cheaply replaced.

Cat's-eye

A reflecting stud used to mark the boundary, central point or lane in a road. Cat's-eyes are invaluable for night driving. British inventor Percy Shaw devised the cat's-eye in 1934 after noticing how brilliantly the eyes of cats reflected the headlights of his automobile. The stud has a rubber pad set in a metal base. A pair of glass reflectors is set in each side of the rubber pad so that the stud shows up from either direction. The pads are depressed when a vehicle runs over them, which helps rub dirt from the reflectors.

Caulking

An essential stage in wooden-boat building, in which materials are wedged into cracks and seams to make them watertight. Traditional caulking materials include oakum — coarse hemp rope fibers; tow — coarse linen fibers; cotton; and bitumen.

Causeway

A raised road across marshy ground or across an arm of a sea or lake. A famous example is the causeway linking Mont St. Michel, off northwestern France, with the mainland. A modern example is the John Ringling Causeway linking Sarasota, Fla. with four offshore islands between Sarasota Bay and the Gulf of Mexico.

Cavitation

A condition in which bubbles form in the wake of a ship's propeller, or screw, turning rapidly through the water. Bubble formation absorbs a great deal of energy and reduces a propeller's efficiency. Reduced pressure behind a swift-moving propeller allows the air dissolved in the water to come out as bubbles, which can

A catboat, with its single lateen type sail inherited from the traditional Arab dhow.

also wear down the propeller itself. Cavitation can be delayed by using specially designed supercavitating propellers, which are more screw-like than ordinary propellers.

Cayley, Sir George (1773-1857)

British landowner and scientist, a pioneer of aeronautics. Inspired as a boy by the balloon flights of the MONTGOLFIER BROTHERS, Cayley devoted his main interest to the problems of aerial navigation. He was the first scientist to point out that controlled flight would be impossible until a sufficiently light power source could be invented.
Discarding the then popular idea of imitating bird flight by flapping wings, Cayley designed a theoretical flying machine which closely resembled today's airplane, with a fixed wing and a tail unit. By 1804 he had designed a model glider, the first of several. Towards the end of his life, in 1853, he produced a glider large enough to carry a person. The first manned glider flight was made by a boy, probably the son of one of his servants. Cayley had a team of men run down a slope towing the glider until it became airborne. He repeated the experiment with his coachman, John Appleby.
Cayley also devoted a great deal of time to the problems of lighter-than-air flight, and was a pioneer of airship theory. His notebooks are full of diagrams and calculations related to flight and aerodynamics, including the lift required for an airship of given weight, and the power of the motor that would be needed to propel it. Cayley carried out experiments by whirling a flat plate around on the end of an arm to find its resistance and lift, and from this he evolved the idea of curved wing sections.

CC 7107
The twin of BB 9004, a French electric locomotive. They jointly hold the world railway speed record of 205.6 mph (330.9 km/h).

Ceiling
The maximum height to which a given aircraft can climb. The ceiling is primarily determined by the ability of the wings to provide lift in the rarefied upper air, by the deterioration in engine power at height, and by the amount of bite that a propeller can obtain from the thin atmosphere at high altitude.

The limitations of the propeller do not apply to aircraft with JET ENGINES or ROCKET motors. Jet aircraft can operate at up to 80,000 ft. (24,000 m) if they are designed for high-performance flight. Piston-engined aircraft will reach about 50,000 ft. (15,000 m) with the use of a supercharger (either mechanically or exhaust driven). Unlike jets and PISTON ENGINES, rocket motors do not require atmospheric oxygen, and rocket-powered craft can operate in the near-vacuum of space. The service ceiling is the greatest altitude at which a rate of climb of 100 ft. (30.5 m) per minute can be maintained.

Celestial navigation
Navigating by the stars (see NAVIGATION).

Centerboard
In a boat, a flat piece of wood or metal that extends like a KEEL. However, a centerboard can be raised and lowered through a slot in the center of the hull. Boats with a centerboard can thus sail in shallower waters than those with a fixed keel. Some boats have twin centerboards, called bilgeboards.

The computerized control room of a modern classification yard. Automation reduces delays to a minimum, but whenever possible rail freight is carried on unit trains which avoid classification yards altogether.

Centralized traffic control (CTC)
A system in which the flow of traffic on a railroad is remotely controlled from a central point. CTC is gradually replacing the traditional block-signaling techniques (see BLOCK SYSTEM) whereby signals control the traffic over a small section of track. The adoption of the CTC system enables more effective use to be made of existing track, because an operator can see at a glance the traffic situation over a large area.

A CTC system operator sits in front of a large illuminated board showing in miniature the track layout of the system under his control. The location of all trains in the system is shown by lights. He controls the progress of the trains by setting the switches and signals along the track. Information about the location of each train on the system is provided by means of track circuiting (see TRACK CIRCUIT).

Central Pacific Railroad
Now part of the Southern Pacific, formed, with the UNION PACIFIC, part of the first transcontinental route across the United States. It opened on May 10, 1869, and was extended to Alameda, on the coast, on September 6, 1869. It was one of the three great routes — the Southern, Central, and Northern Pacifics — put before Congress in 1855 but not agreed at the time. On July 1, 1862, however, a bill was passed authorizing a transcontinental line, in which the Union Pacific built westwards and the Central Pacific built eastwards from the Pacific. Land and part of the money were provided by the federal government.

Centrifugal clutch
A kind of friction CLUTCH found in some cars with automatic transmission. Weights within the clutch assembly are rotated by the engine. As the engine speeds up, the weights are flung outward by centrifugal force. They press against levers that move a pressure plate into contact with the driven plate that transmits motion to the driving wheels. This kind of system may be used in conjunction with coil springs. The variomatic transmission of the Dutch DAF automobile incorporates a centrifugal clutch.

Cermets
Temperature-resistant materials used in jet-engine and rocket construction which possess the ductility of metals and the high-

A model of Sir George Cayley's design of 1843 for a VTOL (vertical takeoff and landing) "aerial carriage." Cayley, rightly known as the father of aviation, constructed the world's first successful man-carrying airplane (a glider) in 1853.

temperature characteristics of ceramic materials. They are made by powder-metallurgy techniques — an intimate mixture of powdered metal and ceramic material is compacted and then sintered in an inert atmosphere. In a cermet the metal acts as a binder for the ceramic particles. Most cermets contain about 80% ceramic material and 20% metal. All highly refractory carbides, borides, and oxides are suitable for cermets. Among the metals used are zirconium, iron, chromium, tungsten, aluminum, nickel, molybdenum, and titanium.

Cetane number

A number used for assessing the ignition qualities of a diesel FUEL. It is equivalent to the OCTANE NUMBER of a gasoline. The number represents the percentage of cetane (which has good ignition characteristics) needed to be added to alpha-methyl napthalene (which has poor ignition characteristics) to create a mixture having the same combustion qualities as the fuel under test. Using diesel fuel with a low cetane rating may give rise to "diesel knock," caused by uneven combustion. Using fuel with too high a cetane number will result in unnecessarily high fuel consumption. In general, higher-revving engines require fuel with a higher cetane rating. An engine revving at 100 rpm would require a cetane rating of only about 15-30, but one revving at over 1,500 rpm would require a cetane rating of up to 60.

Chain drive

Chains are used in bicycles and in most motorcycles to transmit power to the driving wheels. The earliest automobiles also had chain drive, but their function is now performed by the DRIVE SHAFT. Chains are used, however, to drive the camshaft from the crankshaft. The most common form of chain drive uses a roller chain and toothed sprocket wheels. The chain consists of a series of flexibly pivoting pin links and roller links. The rollers are free to rotate. Another type of chain sometimes used in camshaft drives is the inverted-tooth chain. This consists of toothed links which together form a kind of flexible rack. Inverted-tooth chains are able to transmit greater power and operate at higher speeds than roller chains.

Channel Tunnel

A proposed undersea link between England and France beneath the Straits of Dover. As long ago as 1876, the governments of Britain and France agreed to preliminary excavations. The scheme was abandoned in 1882, revived in 1914, and dropped again with the outbreak of World War I.

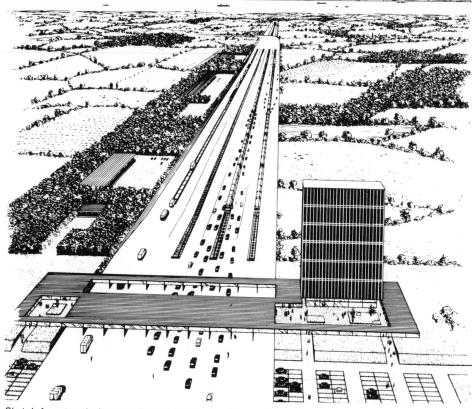

Sketch for a terminal on the French side of the Channel Tunnel as proposed in 1964. Special flatcar trains were to carry the cars and their occupants. Restaurants, hotels and customs facilities cluster around the disembarkation area.

Work began once more in 1973, and preliminary borings were completed on both sides of the English Channel by mid-1975. Work then came to a halt as economic difficulties brought about the scheme's indefinite postponement.

As planned in the 1970s, the tunnel was to consist of three bores each 32 mi. (51 km) long, of which 23 mi. (37 km) would be under the sea. Two of the tunnels would carry a main rail line, one in each direction, with a number of crossovers. The third tunnel would provide service facilities, with links to the other tunnels every 750 ft. (228 m). The service tunnel would have a diameter of 15 ft. (4.5 m), and the main tunnels would be 22 ft. 6 in. (6.85 m) in diameter. Trains would be electrically powered, with current supplied from overhead lines.

Chanute, Octave (1832-1910)

French-born American engineer and pioneer aviator. He was trained as a civil engineer, becoming chief engineer first to the Chicago-Alton Railroad (1867-73), and then to the Erie Railroad (1873-83). At the age of 64, inspired by the work of Otto LILIENTHAL, Chanute took up the study of aviation, and from 1896 onward he constructed and flew a series of gliders, making more than 1,000 flights without accident. His book, *Progress in Flying Machines*, led the Wright Brothers to begin their experiments.

Charles, Jacques Alexandre César (1746-1823)

French chemist and balloonist. Inspired by the balloon experiments of the MONT-GOLFIER BROTHERS in 1783, he joined with the Robert Brothers in similar experiments but using hydrogen in place of hot air. They sent up the first hydrogen balloon on August 27, 1783, and made their first manned flight on December 1 of the same year.

Charlotte Dundas

The first practical steamboat, built in 1801. Her designer, Scottish engineer William Symington, adapted James WATT's new steam engine to drive the boat's stern paddle wheel. The *Charlotte Dundas* successfully towed barges along Scotland's Forth and Clyde Canal in 1801-02, but was withdrawn from service because of fears that her wash would damage the canal banks.

Charts

Specialized maps used in air and sea navigation. Since the safety of air and sea transport depends on them, they must convey the latest information accurately and clearly. Both hydrographic and aeronautical charts are updated constantly through weekly bulletins. The International Hydrographic Organization and the International Civil Aviation Organization coordinate the production of charts and ensure standardization. *Hydrographic charts* are produced by hydrographic bureaus in 42 countries, including the U.S. Naval Oceanographic Office. At present over 20,000 charts are published. Since the oceans comprise over 70% of the earth's surface the compilation of hydrographic charts is an immense task. They are usually constructed on the Mercator projection and include ocean charts, coastal charts, and harbor plans. Unlike topographic maps, charts are not issued in series dependent on scale but in series dependent on function. Also, they employ much less use of color than topographic maps. The choice of colors is restricted by the operational conditions which require the use of amber or red lights in the chart room at night. The charts are characterized by pictorial symbols which depict all underwater features including sandbanks, wrecks, and reefs, as well as navigational aids. Water depths are noted by spot values or isobaths. Sketches of coastal features are often included to aid navigation.

The rapid growth in aviation in the last fifty years has prompted the evolution of *aeronautical charts*. Aeronautical charts are produced by various government agencies throughout the world, many by the U.S. Air Force. These charts are essential tools for air navigation and air traffic control. With almost every new aircraft design, new charts are required to allow for increased flying speeds. Aeronautical charts are usually constructed on the Lambert conformal conic projection. They include both air navigation charts and air- and ground-traffic-control charts. The charts show topographical features that are readily observable from the air as well as selected spot

heights with aeronautical information overprinted. Various traffic-control charts are also produced showing controlled airspace, flight information regions, airport obstructions as well as radar and radio aids (see also MAP).

Chassis

The strong steel frame of a vehicle which carries the engine and body. All automobiles were once built with a chassis giving the vehicle its inherent strength and rigidity. Now many cars are of UNITIZED BODY CONSTRUCTION, with no separate chassis and with the body shell itself forming the skeletal stress-bearing structure. Cars of chassis construction are generally heavier than those of unitized construction, but their body style can be changed without extensive redesigning, and repairs are easier.

Chassis frames are built in several configurations. One classic design consists of side pieces of channel section with an X-shaped stiffening structure between them. Many American cars have a rectangular box-section chassis, while the Volkswagen has a reinforced platform type.

Chesapeake and Delaware Canal

Waterway built 1824-29, later transformed into a modernized tidal canal, linking the head of Chesapeake Bay with the

Delaware River. It is 14 mi. (22.5 km) long and 27 ft. (8 m) deep, carrying some 10 million tons of cargo annually as an important link in the Atlantic Intracoastal Waterway.

Chesapeake Bay Bridge-Tunnel

A highway scheme across the mouth of Chesapeake Bay, completed in 1964. It comprises about 12½ mi. (20 km) of low-level concrete-trestle causeway, interrupted by four navigation channels. Two are spanned by bridges; the others are crossed by tunnels, each about 1¼ mi. (2 km) long.

The tunnel sections were formed of double-skinned steel tubes some 300 ft. (90 m) long, and 33 ft. (10 m) internal diameter. They were floated out into position, and concrete was poured into the hollow walls until they sank. Divers then locked the sections together. These sections incorporated roadway slabs, water and drainage pipelines, ventilation ducts, cable conduits, and the like. Steel bulkheads sealed the ends of the tunnel sections until they were joined. Concrete was poured around the joints to seal them, then a heavy blanket of sand was poured over the whole tube. Finally, the bulkheads were cut through to form a continuous tunnel.

Chicago Sanitary and Ship Canal

Waterway linking Lake Michigan with the Des Plaines River, for which engineers reversed the flow of the Chicago River which had previously carried Chicago's sewage into Lake Michigan. The canal is 30 mi. (48 km) long and was opened in 1900. It now forms a link in the ILLINOIS WATERWAY, connecting the Great Lakes with the Mississippi.

Choke

A mechanism in the fuel system of a gasoline engine for enriching the fuel mixture for cold starting. A warm engine runs on an air/fuel mixture of about 15:1, but a cold engine requires a mixture of about 3:1. In some engines, operating the choke control closes a butterfly valve in the air intake to the carburetor and opens the throttle slightly. With the airflow restricted, the mixture is enriched. Most automobile engines now have an automatic choke. When the engine is cold, the choke valve is held closed by a spring — a coiled bimetallic strip sensitive to temperature. As the engine gets hot, the spring expands and causes the choke valve to open.

In some carburetors, including the SU type choking is brought about in another way. Operating the choke control lowers the carburetor jet unit bodily, allowing more fuel to pass (see CARBURETOR).

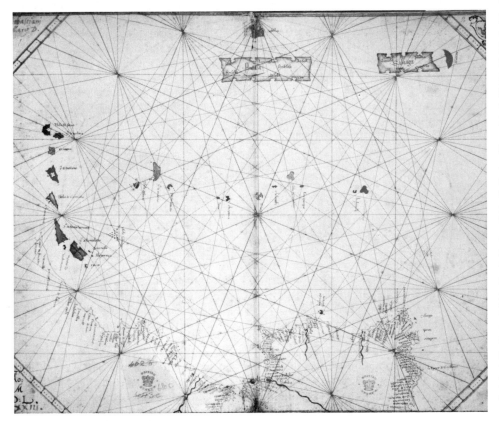

A portolan chart of 1463 showing the west coast of Spain and Portugal (bottom right) *the Straits of Gibraltar; and northwest Africa. The Atlantic Islands shown are* (from left to right); *the Canaries, the Madeira Islands, and the Azores. With the central compass rose radiating to the 16 roses around the perimeter the navigator could plot his course between any two ports on the chart.*

Chronometer

A highly accurate clock or watch, particularly one used for determining longitude at sea. Until the first successful marine chronometer was built in the mid-18th century, seafarers could pinpoint their latitude accurately by measuring the altitude of stars, but could only estimate longitude by "dead reckoning" (see NAVIGATION). With the chronometer set to the time at zero meridian (Greenwich, England), and local time calculated with a sextant, the navigator can determine how far ahead of or behind Greenwich Mean Time he is. It is then a simple matter to calculate distance east or west of Greenwich, i.e. longitude.

Chrysler

American automobile company, founded in 1925 by Walter Percy Chrysler (1875-1940). The first car, designed by Chrysler himself, was a very successful vehicle with a six-cylinder high-compression engine (a feature pioneered by Chrysler).

In 1928 Chrysler acquired the Dodge company, and taking advantage of Ford's temporary absence from the market (caused by the changeover from Model T to Model A) introduced the low-priced Plymouth. This was an immediate success, and Chrysler became one of the "Big Three" (the others were General Motors and Ford). Sales of the Plymouth, advertised as a "low priced car without that low priced look" continued to rise despite the Depression. During the early 1930s Chrysler introduced all-steel welded construction, and his remarkable "Floating Power," which gave his four-cylinder cars "the smoothness of an eight." Live rubber engine mounts and a flexible cantilever spring at the rear cradled the engine and reduced vibration to a minimum.

Then, in 1934, Chrysler introduced the "Airflow." Orville Wright had suggested testing automobile designs in a wind tunnel, and the streamlined "Airflow" was the result, a startling revelation in an era of high box-shaped cars. Beautifully engineered, it cruised effortlessly and almost silently at 80 mph (130 km/h). But it was ahead of its time. The public did not take to its new shape, and the car sold badly until it was re-styled as the more conventional "Airstream." In the 1960s Chrysler acquired Simca of France and the Rootes Group of Britain, and today the firm holds its place as one of the world's leading automobile manufacturers.

Cierva, Juan de la (1896-1936)

Spanish engineer, inventor of the AUTIGIRO. At the age of 16, Cierva began building a powered airplane, which flew successfully. By 1918 he had constructed a three-engined bomber; but its crash as a result of stalling the following year led him to start research on the deficiencies of fixed-wing airplanes, and he began working on the theory of rotating-wing craft. His early models proved unstable, but Cierva solved this problem by making each blade articulated. After a long series of tests he flew the first successful autogiro in 1923.

Citroën

Leading French automobile manufacturer founded by André-Gustave Citroën. Citroën studied Henry Ford's mass-production methods at first hand, and introduced them to Europe in his new automobile factory which began production in 1919. At first he concentrated on one model, a low-priced 10-hp car, which, by 1922, was being produced at the rate of 100 a day, but he soon abandoned Ford's single-model system and introduced a range of cars. One of the best known was the cloverleaf-shaped 1.4-liter three-seater, whose bright yellow color earned it the nickname "Citron pressé" (lemonade).

In 1934 Citroën introduced the revolutionary 7A model. The pioneer of front-wheel drive and of UNITIZED BODY CONSTRUCTION, the so-called "Traction Avant" was one of the most successful cars of its time and continued in various models until the 1950s, when Citroën introduced the advanced DS/ID range (see DS-19). With streamlined bodywork and HYDRO-PNEUMATIC SUSPENSION, these cars, and the CX of 1974, exemplify Citroën's continuing policy of keeping in the forefront of technological advance.

Clapper bridge

Name given to bridges built of unhewn granite slabs, spanning many small streams on Dartmoor, England. The slabs rest on stone piers. Clapper bridges were built by tin miners and others in the Middle Ages.

Classification yard

A classification yard is used to sort freight cars into trains going to the same destination. A car picked up from its loading point by a local freight is taken to the nearest classification yard. There it is sorted, with other cars, to make up a train going as near to its destination as possible. A single car may pass through several yards until it reaches a yard where a local freight or switching locomotive can take it to its final destination. Train *consists* — lists of cars with their destinations — are telephoned, teletyped, or sent by radio to the next yard so that operators there can sort the cars as soon as they arrive. Most yards are arranged with a hump at one end, up which the arriving train is pushed. The cars are uncoupled and run by gravity down the other side of the hump on to a grid of switches worked from a central tower. The cars are then switched to one of many parallel tracks so that cars for the same destination can be assembled into a new train.

Clermont

The first commercially successful steamboat, designed by Robert Fulton and built in New York by Charles Browne in 1807. Her engine, constructed in England by Boulton and Watt, drove two side paddle wheels. On her maiden voyage she averaged 5 mph (8 km/h) for 150 mi. (241 km) up the Hudson River to Albany. She carried passengers on the Hudson until withdrawn in 1814. Her full name was the *North River Steamboat of Clermont.*

Clinker construction

Method of building the planked skin of a ship or boat's hull in which the planks overlap each other. Clinker construction is stronger but less streamlined than CARVEL CONSTRUCTION.

Clipper

Very fast square-rigged sailing ship of the 19th century. The hull, five or six times as long as it was broad, had a steeply raked and pointed bow and a rounded sloping stern. The three tall, angled masts carried a mass of huge sails on wide spars. Unlike all previous sailing ships whose tubby rounded bows lifted them over the waves, the concave hull section at bow and stern allowed the clipper to slice through waves like a wedge. The first revolutionary advance in ship design for hundreds of years, the clippers were developed for maximum speed (20 knots was not uncommon) at the expense of capacity, and often at the expense also of strength and long life. Their history is linked with several enterprises requiring the greatest possible speed. These include the opium-smuggling trade, the California and Australian gold-rushes of 1848 and 1854, and the China tea trade for which the clippers were most famous. This was opened to American ships by the repeal of the British Navigation Laws in 1849, and developed into a race to get the new season's tea back first.

Donald McKay of Boston was the most famous of all the clipper builders. His clipper *Lightning* set a record of 436 nautical miles in a day, which was unsurpassed for many years, while his *Flying Cloud,* probably the fastest American clipper, twice sailed from New York to San Francisco around Cape Horn in 89 days, a record that was never beaten.

A traditional square-rigged Portuguese wine boat, with its long steering "sweep" (oar), on the River Douro. In the background is a modern steel arch bridge.

A sampan, the general purpose boat of Oriental waters, is here seen carrying coal on a canal in Thailand.

▷ Vehicle ferries on the cross-channel run between England and France. The truck trailers are "rolled-in" at one port and off at the other to provide a rapid and flexible method (known as Ro-Ro) of transporting goods from door to door.

British tea clippers were smaller than their American rivals, but often sturdier and faster. Two of the most famous, CUTTY SARK and *Thermopylae*, had unequaled records for sustained high speeds.

With the opening in 1869 of both the first railroad across America and the Suez Canal, the clippers' brief era of glory was over. They continued to operate under reduced sail in, for example, the Australian wool trade, but before long their place was taken by larger and more economical windjammers, and by steamships.

A mid 19th century American clipper, the Racer. *These graceful ships frequently attained 20 knots, compared to a maximum of about 9 knots of the tubbier sailing ships of the 18th century.*

Closed-circuit television (CCTV)
See CATHODE-RAY-TUBE DISPLAY.

Clutch
Part of the TRANSMISSION system of a vehicle, which disconnects the engine from the rest of the system while the driver is changing gear. Vehicles with automatic transmission have no clutch. Instead, most have a fluid-coupling device called a TORQUE CONVERTER.

In essence an automobile clutch consists of a driven plate and a pressure plate enclosed in a housing bolted to the engine flywheel. The driven plate is attached to the shaft leading to the GEARBOX. When the automobile is moving, the pressure plate sandwiches the driven plate against the flywheel and the whole assembly, including the housing, rotates with it. When the clutch pedal is depressed, the pressure plate is forced away from the driven plate, which loses its grip on the flywheel, and the engine is disengaged.

The driven plate is surfaced with a tough frictional lining that grips the surface of the flywheel without slipping. Since the clutch grips by friction it is called a friction clutch.

Two common types of clutches are used. In the diaphragm type a steel diaphragm spring presses the pressure plate against the driven plate. It flexes back to release the pressure plate when the clutch pedal is depressed. In the coil-spring type, thrust springs around the circumference press the pressure plate against the driven plate. The pressure plate is released by means of levers, the springs being compressed. The diaphragm clutch requires much less pedal effort than the coil-spring type. A third type of clutch is occasionally used — the CENTRIFUGAL CLUTCH — so called because it utilizes centrifugal force to exert pressure against the pressure plate. Some clutches work mechanically, with the pedal connected to the clutch by levers and rods. Others work hydraulically, with pedal pressure transmitted from a master cylinder to a slave cylinder at the clutch. The gearbox, as well, contains a clutch — the DOG CLUTCH, which connects the various gearwheels and shafts as re-quired to give different gear ratios. The essential part of the SYNCHROMESH mechanism is a kind of cone clutch which comes into play before two gearwheels mesh. An automatic gearbox also contains a number of plate clutches which automatically connect and disconnect the EPICYCLIC GEAR trains as the engine speed changes.

Coaches
Horse-drawn or steam-powered road vehicles for commercial passenger and mail transportation, with an enclosed passenger compartment, a suspension system between coach and chassis, and a pivoting front axle.

Hauled by teams of as many as 12 horses, and weighing up to eight tons, the 18th and 19th century STAGECOACHES could average up to 10 mph (16 km/h).

With the construction of CUGNOT'S CARRIAGE in 1769, and of Richard TREVITHICK'S experimental steam carriages of 1801 and 1803, the necessary technology for the steam coach had been developed. But despite the opening of a service in Paris, France, in 1800, little interest was shown in the new invention for many years. However, during the 1830s the steam coach enjoyed a brief period of commercial success in Britain and Europe. Experiments were also made in the United States, but the absence of paved roads limited their potential. In England Goldsworthy Gurney's steam coaches ran scheduled services between Gloucester and Cheltenham in 1831, while those of Walter Hancock pioneered regular services in London. Hancock's finest coach, *Automation* (1835) carried 30 men at 21 mph, (34 km/h) in a demonstration run, while usual averages were in the region of 12 mph (19 km/h) and running costs were well below those of horse-drawn coaches. But hostility from horse-coach operators, competition from the railroads (which were cheaper and faster), and in Britain the notorious RED FLAG LAW, had forced the steam coach off the roads by the early 1840s.

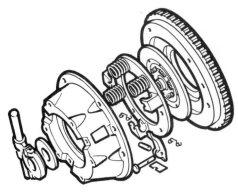

Diaphragm spring (left) and coil spring (right) clutch mechanisms.

Coaster

A ship which trades from one port to another along the coast. Coasters also load from oceangoing ships and deliver to coastal ports unable to accommodate larger vessels (see FREIGHTERS).

Coast Guard

Government service assigned to enforce maritime and customs regulations in coastal waters, to promote safety, and to assist any vessels wrecked or in distress. The United States Coast Guard has its origins in a group of 10 armed boats provided by Congress in 1790 to enforce customs laws and prevent smuggling. This became known as the Revenue Cutter Service. It joined forces with the Life Saving Service in 1915 to become the U.S. Coast Guard. Later the Lighthouse Service (1939) and the Bureau of Marine Inspection and Navigation (1942) were also absorbed to provide a single force dealing with maritime affairs. Today the Coast Guard is the federal government's main maritime law enforcement force. Its duties include the enforcement of laws relating to customs, immigration, the movement of vessels in territorial waters, and the security of ports. Its operations also extend well beyond the coast, with ocean patrols in the North Pacific and North Atlantic providing search and rescue services as well as communications and navigational aids, and participation in the International Ice Patrol, which warns shipping of icebergs in the North Atlantic. In wartime its expertise takes it to the scene of action for rescue work. During World War II the U.S. Coast Guard also played an important part in escort duty and in manning assault landing craft.

The U.S. Coast Guard is organized on a regional basis, with 12 district commanders. Overall coordination comes from the headquarters in Washington, D.C. Each district is fully equipped with lifeboats and larger rescue vessels, and aircraft for search and rescue work, and is linked to a chain of rescue coordination centers by radio.

The U.S. Coast Guard is not only concerned with enforcing law and rescuing vessels in distress, but also plays a vital role in prevention. Measures include the placing of lighthouses, lightships, buoys, radio beacons and radio direction-finding equipment for the guidance of shipping; the inspection of ships, their equipment, and their loading; and the education of ship operators in matters of safety at sea. Special duties include overseeing vessels carrying dangerous cargo, enforcing antipollution regulations, and protecting fisheries and marine life.

In Britain many of the duties performed by the coast guard in the United States are dealt with by other agencies (police, navy, etc.), the coastguard being a non-military organization concerned solely with safety and the relief of distress in coastal waters. Officially known as Her Majesty's Coastguard, the service is in fact administered by the Ministry of Transport. By means of a series of over 300 lookout posts placed strategically around the coast, and working in association with various search and rescue agencies (including the Royal Air Force and the voluntary Royal National Lifeboat Institution), its duty is to watch for vessels in distress (or in imminent danger) and to initiate action by the various agencies.

Other duties assigned to some coast guard forces include meteorological information services, the relief of flood and storm victims, and icebreaking on inland waterways.

Cockpit

The accommodation provided for the pilot(s) of an aircraft. The essential controls comprise a CONTROL-COLUMN (for the AILERONS and ELEVATORS), a rudder pedal, engine controls, AVIONICS, the AUTOMATIC PILOT, and the AIRCRAFT INSTRUMENTS (including ALTIMETER and ARTIFICIAL HORIZON). Military aircraft cockpits also incorporate the weapon-aiming systems.

The pilot sits on the left, with the copilot facing a duplicate set of controls in the right-hand seat. The center of the panel is usually reserved for engine instrumentation, throttle handles, and radar displays; the autopilot may also be located on the center console, or extended across the cockpit just below the windshield.

Coil

A transformer in the IGNITION SYSTEM of a gasoline engine that boosts the low voltage (generally 12 volts) of the lead-acid battery to as high as 30,000 volts. When this voltage is applied to the spark plugs, sparks are produced in the cylinders to burn the fuel mixture.

The coil is made up of two windings of copper wire around a soft iron core. The primary winding, of several hundred turns, forms a circuit with the battery and the contact-breaker in the distributor. Around the primary winding are several thousand turns of the secondary winding, which connects with the rotor arm in the distributor.

The contact-breaker alternately opens and closes, interrupting the battery current flowing through the primary winding, giving rise to a changing magnetic field. By electromagnetic induction the changing field in the primary winding sets up an electric current in the secondary winding which is at much higher voltage because the secondary coil has many more turns of wire.

Coke-bottle design

The fuselage of an airplane that has been designed in accordance with Area Rule for supersonic flight bears some resemblance to a coke bottle: it tapers down in the mid-section, where the wings are attached (see AREA RULE).

Collier

A ship used for carrying coal. Sailing ships were used in the coal trade until the mid-19th century, when the first steam colliers were introduced.

Combustion chamber

The part of an INTERNAL-COMBUSTION ENGINE in which combustion actually takes place. Gasoline, diesel, jet, and rocket engines have combustion chambers of various designs to suit the varied nature of the combustion taking place.

In a liquid-propellant rocket engine the combustion chamber is open-ended, becoming narrower at the open end, which connects with the exhaust nozzle. Fuel and oxidizer are sprayed into the chamber through atomizing injector nozzles so that they mix intimately before igniting. The temperature developed in a rocket's combustion chamber is of the order of 3,000°C. To keep the chamber cool and prevent it from melting, incoming fuel is passed through its walls — a process known as regenerative cooling.

In a JET ENGINE several kinds of combustion chambers are used. One common arrangement is the *cannular* type, which consists of as many as 10 cylindrical combustion "cans" arranged around the axis of the engine. Each can consists of an outer shell and a perforated inner shell. Air from the compressor enters the can and goes into the inner shell, where fuel is sprayed into it through a nozzle. Combustion takes place, and the can outlet delivers the exhaust gases to the turbine blades. An *annular* arrangement is also common. Fuel is sprayed into an inner perforated shell within the outer annules.

In a GASOLINE ENGINE combustion takes place in a hollow in the cylinder head, when the top of the piston is more or less flush with the top of the cylinder block. Various types of combustion chambers are used. One of the most common and efficient chamber shapes is the hemispherical; with the spark plug at the top and the inlet and exhaust valves on opposite sides. The symmetrical design gives short flame travel and thus efficient burning. It also allows large valves to be used, aiding engine "breathing." Many high-performance engines have this design. Another design is the wedge-shaped chamber. This has a sloping roof in which the valves are set. The spark plug is projected at an angle from the short side of the wedge. Another design is the so-called "bath tub," with a cross-section similar to that of a bath tub. The spark plug is set at an angle to the side and the valves are set vertically above the piston. The wedge and bath-tub designs are not quite as effective as the symmetrical hemispherical head, but they have the advantage that a simple single camshaft can be used to operate them.

Some gasoline engines have a combustion chamber within the crown of the piston. Many DIESEL ENGINES have a similar chamber design, though others have a separate chamber in the cylinder head. In the WANKEL ENGINE there is no combustion chamber as such. Inset in each side of the triangular rotor is a hollow which acts as a combustion chamber when it moves into the ignition position in the rotary cycle.

ber of Comet 1s were modified and subsequently used by the military.

The Comet 2, with 7,300-lb. (3,335 kg) thrust Avons and a slightly longer fuselage, never entered commercial service because of the Comet 1 accidents but was used by the British Royal Air Force as a transport.

The Comet 3 was a prototype only, but the Comet 4 series with four 10,500-lb. (4,700 kg) thrust Avons saw widespread service and inaugurated the first jet passenger service between London and New York (October 1958). The basic Comet 4, with leading-edge pannier fuel tanks, accommodated up to 81 passengers, but the 4B and 4C had lengthened fuselages that would seat 102. Short-range clipped wings without pannier fuel tanks were employed on the 4B.

Communications in transport

Communication plays a vital part in the efficient operation of all transport services. Advances in communications are often associated with advances in transportation, and, in fact, many improvements in telecommunications techniques have come about as a direct result of the demand for improved transport. At the

continue to have a limited use today, though mostly on naval vessels.

In 1912, when the *Titanic* sank in the Atlantic, a nearby ship passed without being aware of the SOS signal because it was not fitted with a radio. This highlighted the fact that radio (then in its infancy) could help to make the seas safer. Nowadays any ship exceeding 500 tons must be equipped with either a radio telephony or radio telegraphy facility. The minimum requirement for the majority of ships is for two transmitters — the *main* transmitter, powered from the ship's generator and capable of transmitting on several wavebands, also the *emergency* transmitter powered from an emergency battery and designed to transmit on the distress frequency of 500 KHz. Similarly, most ships are required to have at least three receivers:— the *main* receiver operating on several bands, corresponding to those of the transmitter, the *emergency* receiver for use even when the ship's generator is not working and the *loudspeaker-watch* receiver. This last provides a continuous monitor of the emergency frequency so that an SOS signal will be heard instantly. Where the ship does not have a radio officer at the radio continuously, an automatic alarm system will ring an alarm bell when the International Alarm Signal is received. Very specialized radios have been developed for lifeboats, these need to be rugged and capable of being worked by unskilled people, consequently, an automatic keying device switches the signal according to the distress code. Marine radios are also used for transmitting information about the weather, or near busy harbors a control center on the shore controls the movement of ships and pilots by radio on standard frequencies. All these facilities have been shown to improve safety at sea but perhaps the biggest impact has been from the introduction of radar.

Radar was developed during World War II to detect airplanes, but one important civil use today is for the detection of vessels at sea during poor visibility. A high power, short wavelength burst of radio energy is sent out along a rotating beam and reflections of the burst are received on the same antenna. These are displayed on a circular cathode ray tube (the plan position indicator or PPI) and objects show up as sources of light on the screen. Thus in conditions of poor visibility the coastline and other ships may be detected, making navigation far less hazardous. The sources of light move across the screen as the ship or neighboring ships change position. If the screen is designed to have a long persistance the source of light becomes a

A de Havilland Comet. Comets inaugurated the world's first jet airliner services in 1952, but were withdrawn in 1954 after a series of disastrous crashes due to fatigue failure. They were later reintroduced, and have continued in use in both civil and military roles.

Comet

The first pure-jet airliner to enter commercial service was the de Havilland Comet. The prototype made its first flight on July 27, 1949; and a scheduled BOAC service using Comet 1s with four 5,050-lb. thrust Ghost engines opened between London and Johannesburg in May 1952, with a Far Eastern route inaugurated in August of the same year.

Following the loss of three Comets between May 1953 and April 1954, all the aircraft were grounded and evidence of metal fatigue was found. A limited num-

heart of all transport communication systems are radio, telephone and radar, with an increasing role being played by television and computers.

Ships. Communication at sea before radio was available, consisted of transmitting messages by flags, each flag corresponding to a letter or digit and certain flags with special meanings. Alternatively a lamp could be used intermittently, using Morse code to form a message. The International Code of Signalling was drawn up in 1931 to standardize these codes, which line which represents the heading and relative speed of the other ships. Certain parameters describing the movements of the ship may be fed into a data computer as well as the information from the screen. This can be analyzed to produce actual figures for the relevant speed, range or heading of other ships, and this information can be displayed on the screen.

Radar is used at ports for the observation of ships entering or leaving the harbor. One of the busiest waterways in the world, the Straits of Dover has, by International Agreement, been divided into two halves, one for ships sailing Northwards and one for those sailing Southwards. The whole area is observed from radar stations on the coast who report any infringment of the rules and warn other ships by radio.

Trains. The railroad is a complex form of transport and requires an intensive communication network where reliability and safety are important features. Messages to the engineman on a train, particularly those concerning safety, generally take the form of signals displaying standard symbols for certain messages (see SIGNALING IN TRANSPORT). From the middle of the 19th century the telegraph was used for communications between one signal tower and the next to check that the section was clear. This is still in use today but has now often been replaced by automatic systems. With the invention of the telephone more information could be passed between points and this has a large application in railroad operation. All important points on a modern railroad system are connected to the company's own telephone system, and the efficiency of this is essential. In the United

States, where long distances are involved, the morse telegraph was used a great deal, but today some of the long lines are replaced by microwave links carrying speech circuits.

On many trains, the communication wires are carried through the cars, but on some long freight trains with locomotives at each end communication is achieved between each by VHF radio, which ensures that both locomotives start and brake uniformly, and avoids the expense of cable.

Throughout the railroad system staff use personal radios to stay in touch. Maintenance staff are called to equipment failures and men working in yards and depots are given instructions by radio. A useful development is direct two-way communication with the train operator. On London's newest underground line and on the Paris Metro the train driver can talk to the operating department using a radio frequency system via the D.C. traction current collection system. Similar systems operate in most of the world's subway systems. On Tokyo's Teito Line communication is made via trackside wires and an aerial mounted on the train.

Television has several applications on the railroad. Cameras on platforms or station areas allow observation of a relatively large area. Announcements can then be made to passengers where control of their movements is required. On rapid transit systems some trains are operated by one man who controls the train and opens the doors at stations, television monitors are provided to give him a satisfactory view of the platform. On some railroads certain grade crossings carrying considerable traffic are operated from remote sites and these are observed

on television screens to make certain that all vehicles are clear before trains are allowed onto the section. In Switzerland supervision of freight trains is carried out by closed-circuit television. Staff scan a train as it enters the yard for insecure doors or freight.

Computers are now being introduced to railroad operation. Data links connecting all yards and depots with a central computer process all information regarding the movement of freight wagons and by making more efficient use of these, their number has been reduced while carrying the same amount of freight. Additionally large freight yards are now automated, with the braking, accelerating and sorting of cars achieved by computer control.

Airplanes. Communication with airplanes is perhaps the most advanced of all transport communication systems. Motion in the air is in all three dimensions and any instructions need to be based on reliable information and passed by a good communications link. Area air traffic control centers are normally situated at airports. The controller is in radio contact with all airplanes in the area, and pilots must contact the controller of any area being traversed. Radio equipment fitted to airplanes must be capable of operating on several channels, generally in the VHF band. At large airports three different air traffic controllers may pass instructions — one for initial approach, one for final approach and one for movement on the airfield itself. The intensive service now operated at major airports would not be possible without the radio links now in use (see AIR TRAFFIC CONTROL).

A radio system is also employed to assist a pilot to position his airplane correctly for the final approach. A radio wave transmitted from the airfield activates avionic instruments on board the airplane to indicate whether the approach is being made at the correct angle. The pilot can correct his flightpath accordingly and bring the airplane to the runway safely in all but the worst weather. Fully automated landings are now achieved by combining a similar radio instrument landing system with a very accurate radio ALTIMETER to give the correct trim for a landing (see AVIONICS). Navigation between airports is achieved with the use of VOR (VHF omnidirectional range) radio transmitters, two of which, detected by the equipment on the airplane can be used to locate its precise position.

Radar, as already described in connection with shipping, is used a great deal to assist airplane flight operation. Two types of radar are used by air traf-

The radio room of a new cargo vessel showing, on the left, a Marconi Marine Conqueror transmitter and the Company's latest console unit carrying two receivers and a range of reserve equipments.

fic controllers at airports. The Airport Surveillance Radar (ASR) has a range of 30 miles or more and will cover the area over which the controller is required to direct approaches to the airport. This radar is specially designed to cope with the long distance and picks up reflections from nearby buildings that make resolution on the PPI impractical for planes less than five miles distant. For this closer range a Precision Approach Radar (PAR) is used, which will operate over a limited angle on the approach to a runway. In addition an Airfield Surface Movement Radar may be employed to monitor movements of airplanes and other vehicles on the airfield itself. Any radar will show up permanent objects such as buildings in addition to the airplanes and this can confuse the image on the PPI. If a continuous wave, rather than a pulsed radar is used then the frequency of the reflected wave from moving objects will be different from the original wave. By using special electronic circuits any reflected wave that has the originally transmitted frequency can be eliminated from the screen and only moving objects will be displayed.

Thus with this equipment the air traffic controller can locate moving aircraft in his area on the screen and in bad weather, or at night may "talk" the pilots down in safety.

The controller's task is also made simpler by Secondary Surveillance Radar. In this case the radar signal is detected on the airplane and this triggers a transmitter to return a signal of greater intensity than any reflection. This produces a better image on the controller's PPI, but also the transmitted pulse from the airplane is used to convey information about its identity and altitude. A data computer on the ground can detect this and display it on the PPI.

Radar instruments are carried on board airplanes for pinpointing ground features for navigational purposes, and for detecting storm clouds.

Road transportation. Less sophisticated, but increasingly important, are the two-way radio communication systems used by road vehicles such as trucks, buses and taxis. Advances in electronics have made such networks relatively inexpensive to maintain, and the benefits in efficient control over pickup and delivery of both freight and passengers can be readily seen. If the system is large enough to justify it, the position of vehicles on the road can be fed into a computer, which will produce the best options for routeing or the nearest available vehicle for a pickup. By being linked with a central controller, not only taxis,

Increasing use is being made of helicopters in traffic control operations. Using radio communications the airborne crew can quickly pass on information about potential or actual trouble spots to ground patrols.

but even small buses, are able to respond to telephone requests for service. An additional benefit is that feedback from the vehicles on the road produces an overall picture of traffic conditions that helps the controller select the most efficient options.

As a means of monitoring and controlling traffic flow on the roads and streets, both closed-circuit television and automatic electronic recording devices are now in use. These can also be linked to a computer which controls traffic signals and road signs to speed up or divert the flow of traffic. The eventual use of such electronic monitoring systems to change the speed and direction of road vehicles through built-in devices in the vehicles themselves may not be very far off.

Compass
An instrument for finding direction in navigation. The two main types are the magnetic compass, and the GYROCOMPASS. A magnetic compass as used at sea consists essentially of a magnetized needle attached to a round compass card on which are marked the points of the compass, the needle itself being fixed along the card's north-south line. Needle and card pivot as one on a jeweled pin, and the needle aligns itself on a north-south line with the earth's magnetic field. The compass is normally bowl shaped and filled with liquid to damp out vibrations and shocks. The bowl is mounted on pivots in such a way that it always remains level.

The magnetic compass was in use on ships of the Western world by the 11th century. Before its invention seafarers estimated their course with the help of the sun or stars, or (in areas where they were predictable or constant) the wind and current.

As Columbus found to his bewilderment

during his first voyage of discovery to America, the magnetic compass is subject to variation — it points not due north but to magnetic north. The degree of variation is not constant, being affected by position, by daily and seasonal changes, and by electrical storms and other factors. The magnetic compass must therefore be used in conjunction with detailed correction tables and meteorological information.

It is also deflected by magnetism in the ship's hull and fittings. Known as deviation, this is normally corrected by suitable weak magnets fixed in the compass mounting. Today the magnetic compass has been largely superseded by the GYROCOMPASS.

Compound engine
An engine in which steam from the boiler is used in two or more sets of cylinders. The steam may be allowed to expand once in a high-pressure cylinder and then, since it still retains considerable temperature and work potential, again in one or more low-pressure cylinders. A "chain" of double, triple, or even quadruple expansion is possible. The earliest compound locomotives had been in use in England, but it was a Frenchman, Anatole Mallet, who produced a compound locomotive in 1876 and revived interest. The compound locomotive did not reach the United States in quantity until the ideas of Samuel Vauclain and Albert Pitkin had been patented, separately, in 1889, and many Vauclain compounds were built around the turn of the century. Mallet articulated compound locomotives, with two sets of driving wheels, subsequently became popular in the United States, especially on routes involving steep gradients, and some 2,000 were built between 1904 and 1948.

Compression-ignition
The means used in a DIESEL ENGINE to burn the fuel. The fuel is injected under pressure into air that has been compressed to as little as a twentieth its original volume. Compression raises the temperature of the air to such a point that the diesel fuel ignites as soon as it enters the combustion chamber.

Compression ratio
One of the essential stages in the operating cycle of an internal combustion engine is that of compression. In the GASOLINE ENGINE it is compression of gasoline/air mixture. In the DIESEL ENGINE it is simply compression of air. In general, the higher the degree of compression, the more efficient is the combustion process. The degree of compression is measured in terms of the *compression ratio* — the

ratio of the volume of gas inside the cylinder before and after compression. In early automobile engines a compression ratio of about 6:1 was common. At present, most car engines are high-compression engines, with a compression ratio of about 9:1. Others have lower compression ratios — 7:1 and 8:1. Ideally, combustion should be a smooth, rapid burning rather than an explosion. But if too high a grade of gasoline is used in a low-compression engine, some of the fuel mixture will explode violently, causing a characteristic knocking noise (see KNOCKING).

In a diesel engine, the air needs to be compressed much more in order to raise its temperature above the flash-point of the fuel to be injected. Compression ratios of 15:1 are common, and they may be as high as 20:1. Diesel engines must be more sturdily built than gasoline engines to withstand the greater pressure.

Concorde

Supersonic jet transport (SST) plane, a joint venture by Aerospatiale of France and the British Aircraft Corporation. The first prototype flew at Toulouse, France, on March 2, 1969, followed closely by the second flying from Filton, England, and both achieved Mach 2 by late 1970. Two further pre-production examples, incorporating design improvements, lengthened fuselage and revised nose shape, set the style for the initial production order of 16. The first production Concorde flew on December 6, 1973.

With a crew of three or four, and carrying up to 144 passengers, Concorde is 204 ft. (62.2 m) long and has a wing span of 84 ft. (25.6 m). Four Rolls-Royce SNECMA Olympus turbojets give a cruising speed of 1,350 mph (2,170 km/h), and with maximum payload Concorde has a range of 4,000 mi. (6,440 km) at Mach 2. The high speed and operating level of SSTs create environmental problems. Early concern about pollution from exhaust emission was overcome on production models, but Condorde's noise levels are considered unacceptable by many countries. In November 1975 the U.S. Federal Aviation Administration stated that Concorde was at least twice as loud as the relatively noisy Boeing 707, and four times as loud as the more modern 747. As the development of quieter engines would require vast funds and take several years, prospects were not encouraging.

Concorde is designed to operate at altitudes of up to about 11 mi. (18 km). Problems of radiation and ozone at high altitude have been overcome by using solar-flare metering to advise pilots on safe height levels, and the pressurized cabin

A containership discharging at the dock. The giant gantry cranes normally load and unload simultaneously, and computers are increasingly used to automate the process.

air system caters for the heat decomposition of ozone, with filters for dealing with any residue.

Airlines, including TWA and Pan Am, had purchasing options which were later declined, but both China and Iran have shown interest.

After over 5,000 flying hours, visiting over 40 countries and landing at 70 international airports Concorde was given a certificate of air-worthiness and started airline operations with British Airways and Air France in 1976, initially with a twice weekly service London to Bahrein by British Airways and Paris to Rio de Janeiro by Air France.

Connecting rod

Part of the mechanism in a reciprocating engine that converts reciprocating (up-and-down or back-and-forth) motion into rotary motion. In a gasoline or diesel engine, for example, the connecting rod links the PISTON and CRANKSHAFT. One end is attached to the piston by a gudgeon pin; the other to the crankshaft by a crankpin. In a steam locomotive a connecting rod connects the piston rod through a sliding block to a crank on one of the locomotive's driving wheels.

Constant-mesh gearbox

The gear wheels in a modern automobile GEARBOX are meshed together at all times. Drive through two gear wheels is achieved by fixing one gear to its shaft and connecting the other to another shaft by a DOG CLUTCH.

Constant-velocity joint

A type of UNIVERSAL JOINT used on front-wheel drive automobiles to allow for steering movement. There is a constant-velocity joint at the road-wheel end of each half-shaft. In one design, the Birfield, power is transmitted from half-shaft to hub by means of steel balls engaging with grooves in a ball-and-socket arrangement.

Constellation

A four-engined pressurized transport aircraft built by Lockheed, which began service in World War II with the U.S. Air Force. The Constellation, together with the DC-3 and DC-4, was an important factor in the postwar recovery of civil aviation.

The first version weighed 86,250 lb. (39,205 kg), had a 2,200-hp engine, and could carry 43 passengers. After the war the plane was "stretched," and the final model, with seating for 109, was a leading long-range airliner.

Contact breaker

A simple mechanism in the DISTRIBUTOR of a GASOLINE ENGINE that allows the current to the primary winding of the ignition coil to be interrupted (see COIL). There are two contacts, or points, on the contact breaker; one remains fixed, while the other can move apart from it. An arm attached to the movable point is moved back and forth by a CAM on the distributor shaft (which also carries the ROTOR ARM). The point is forced back to its closed position by a spring. A condenser (capacitor) is fitted across the points to prevent excessive arcing when the current is interrupted.

Containerization

Important new technique developed in the 1960s for carrying cargo in large sealed standard-sized boxes (containers). Goods are loaded into the container at the factory and remain in it until they reach their destination. Containers are transported on or in specially designed trucks, railroad cars, and ships, with specialized handling equipment at each stage. Containerization is thus a complete cargo transport system in which road,

A containership. Freighters are only earning money while at sea, and the rapid turn round made possible by containerization reduces the time spent in port from about 75% for conventional freighters to around 20% for containerships.

rail, and sea are closely integrated. It is based on the fact that the fewer the number of units, and the fewer times they are handled, the greater the saving in time and expense, and the smaller the risk of damage. To a great extent containerization brings the benefits of the bulk carrier to the transport of general cargo.

The traditional method of handling general freight involves loading and unloading numerous items at each stage in the journey: from factory onto truck; from truck into dock warehouse; from there onto the dockside; from dockside into ship; and so on. The process is slow (turning round a general cargo ship may take two weeks), inefficient, and expensive. A containership, subdivided into standard container-sized "cells," is loaded and unloaded simultaneously. Straddle carriers on the dockside move the containers into position for giant gantry cranes which lower one container into its cell and then lift out another. The exact sequence of operations is usually decided by a computer. A large modern containership can be turned round in 36 hours or less. A ship is only earning money while at sea, so that the shipping company benefits as much as the manufacturer, whose transport and packaging costs may be reduced by as much as 50%.

On the North Atlantic route a conventional general cargo ship may spend as much as 75% of its life in port. With a containership the figure drops to around 20%, enabling the vessel to make three times as many voyages in a given period, and thus allowing the shipping company to carry three times as much cargo, or reduce its fleet by two thirds. Similar figures apply to railroads, where on suitable routes container trains can run fully loaded between city and port with none of the delays and handling charges associated with freight yards. Britain's Freightliner container trains, and continental Europe's TEEM (Trans-Europ Express Merchandise) are both successful links in container transport, while in the United States the PIGGYBACK idea is highly developed. Here the container remains on the trailer truck throughout its journey. Roll-on and roll-off (RoRo) is similar except that the wheeled container rolls straight from the road onto a ship. Both systems have the advantage over normal container transport of greater flexibility, and are valuable where this and speed are critical. But a roll-on roll-off container occupies considerably more ship space than a container, and is therefore only used on short routes.

To streamline transfers from one mode of transport to another, sophisticated systems are being developed to handle containers at terminals and intermediate stations. One suggestion is for overhead double rail structures which would enable containers to be transferred to and from moving trains or trucks.

The containers are 8 ft. (2.4 m) square in cross section, and while lengths of 20 and 40 ft. (6.1 and 12.2 m) are the most common, some lines use 35-ft. (10.6 m) containers. Made of steel, aluminum or FRP (fiberglass-reinforced plastic laminated plywood), they are waterproof, strong enough to survive repeated use and stacking over a period of years. On some, the end opens for loading and discharge, on others the top, or the side (or any combination of all three). There are specialized containers for a wide variety of goods. These include tank containers, in which the cylindrical tank is enclosed in a standard container-sized open framework; airtight insulated refrigerated containers (known as "reefers") for perishable goods; heated containers; ventilated containers; open-top containers; automobile transporters; cattle carriers; and so on. All have special lifting pads and fittings with which they can be fastened down. There are even floating containers for use in conjunction with the revolutionary new LASH (Lighter Aboard Ship) vessels. Here the ship carries its own traveling gantry crane which lifts and stows floating containers (lighters) while dockside cranes load in the usual way. LASH ships are particularly flexible, being equipped to carry bulk and other non-containerized cargo as well.

Many airlines are interested in containerization, and the process may in time reduce the costs of AIR FREIGHT. Modern jumbo jets are equal to the task. The all-cargo 747F can carry a payload of over 200,000 lb. (90,000 kg). But the problem remains of ensuring a sufficient flow of containers to justify the provision of regular container-aircraft. To wait until a container load has built up defeats the purpose of sending the cargo by air in the first place. And at the moment air transport is too expensive for most of the goods normally carried in containers.

Containerization provides a transportation system in which road, rail and sea are closely integrated. The photograph shows giant traveling gantry cranes in use at a road-rail container terminal.

Control column

The control column of an AIRPLANE operates both the AILERONS and the ELEVATORS. The column may be freely movable in all directions to provide interconnected operation of the ailerons and elevators, or it may be restricted to fore-and-aft movement for elevator operation with a wheel or pivoting hand-grip for the ailerons. Large aircraft or high-performance machines have their control surfaces operated through jacks governed by selector valves which the control column activates. To give the pilot an appropriate "feel" of control forces, speed sensors impose artificial loads on the control column by means of heavy springs.

In HELICOPTERS the control column tilts the rotor blades to alter the direction of flight and incorporates a collective pitch lever for climbing and descending.

Control tower

The nerve center of the airport control unit. See AIRPORT; AIR TRAFFIC CONTROL; GROUND CONTROLLED APPROACH.

Control unit

An essential part of the electrical system of an automobile containing a voltage regulator, current regulator and cut-out. The voltage regulator limits the output of the generator, which charges the battery to about 15 volts. This prevents damage to the battery and other electrical components in the system. The current regulator restricts the amount of current generated, protecting the generator. The cut-out is a switch that prevents the battery from discharging through the dynamo.

Convertible

An automobile with a roof that can be folded down or removed. Convertibles were once much more popular than they are today. This may be because driving is now regarded much more as a simple utilitarian means of getting from place to place, but safety in an accident, and protection from exhaust fumes on crowded roads, are obviously practical reasons for the decline of the convertible.

Convertiplane

Aircraft which combine the capabilities of an airplane and helicopter and can convert their functioning from one to the other. This concept had joint U.S. Army and Air Force support leading to the McDonnell XV-1, with a propeller driven by a piston engine and rotors powered by tip-mounted jets. The first vertical flight of the XV-1 in April 1955 was followed that August by vertical flights by the Bell XV-3, which had wingtip-mounted rotors that could tilt to act as propellers in level flight. The concept was pursued by several firms, notably Hiller and Vertol, during 1957-58, and successful transition from vertical to level flight was achieved. A more ambitious scheme sponsored by NASA led to the LTV-Hiller-Ryan XC-142 transport with wings tilting through 90°. It thus converted from an airplane to a helicopter by transforming its propellers into rotors. More recently the Canadian Government sponsored the Canadair CL-84 tilt-wing transport, but so far no convertiplane has advanced beyond an experimental stage.

Conveyors

One of the most useful materials-handling devices, conveyors can operate continuously and have a high load-carrying potential. Among the most common types are belt, chain, roller and screw conveyors. Conveyor belts are used for transporting all kinds of materials in mines and quarries, in factories, at the dock, at airports, and so on.

Essentially a conveyor belt is an endless moving belt looped at each end over pulleys, one of which drives the belt. In between, the belt is supported by idler rollers, often on both the carry and return sides. A device is incorporated to maintain belt tension. The belt may be made of plastic, rubber, leather or canvas.

For many applications the belt is run flat. For transporting powders, ores, and similar bulk materials it is troughed to increase capacity and prevent spillage. This is done by angling the outer idler rollers. Material may be loaded onto the belt by hand, chute or mechanical feeder. It may discharge over the end pulley, or it may be removed by means of a deflecting device. Often a belt forms part of a larger system of belts which allows a change of direction. Belts will operate up slopes, as long as the gradient is not too steep.

Chain conveyors can operate up quite steep gradients. In the scraper chain conveyor materials in bulk are pushed along a trough; in the push-plate, or push-bar, type this is done by means of a scraper attached to the chain; in the drag-link type it is done by the chain itself.

Particularly versatile is the overhead chain conveyor. This is used widely in the automobile industry, for example, to carry auto bodies through the assembly plant. The path of motion of the conveyor can be any irregular combination of horizontal runs, steep, shallow or vertical grades, bends and curves, as required. Since the system is usually mounted to roof members, valuable floor space is not taken up. In a typical overhead conveyor arrangement the load hangs from a wheeled trolley that runs along or inside

In an attempt to combine the advantages of helicopter and fixed-wing airplanes, several experimental convertiplanes have been built, including the Canadair CL-84 tilt-wing plane shown in the photograph. Once airborne, the wing is gradually tilted to the normal position for forward flight.

an overhead track. The trolleys are connected together by an endless chain. Various kinds of carrier hook, basket, tray or sling may be attached to the trolleys to carry the load.

Roller conveyors are also widely used. They consist of tubular rollers mounted on ball rails on a supporting frame. In the gravity type the rollers are freely rotating, and the flight of rollers is slightly inclined so that the load can move along it by gravity. In the powered type some or all of the rollers are driven by chain or belt and positively move the load along. Often both types are used in combination.

Screw conveyors, also called helix, scroll, spiral and worm conveyors, have wide application for moving bulk solids. The Greek scientist Archimedes is credited with the invention of this device, which is sometimes called the Archimedian screw. But the modern screw conveyor has its origins in the 18th century when it came into use in American flour mills. The conveyor consists of a large, wide-pitch screw rotating in a trough. Usually the pitch is the same as the screw diameter. Material is fed in at one end and is transported forwards as the screw turns.

Convoy

A fleet of merchant vessels sailing with a warship escort. Towards the end of World War I and throughout World War II convoys were used extensively by the Allied countries as a protection against enemy submarines. In World War II the United States and Britain combined forces to develop the convoy system, thereby saving thousands of ships and keeping essential supplies flowing to Britain and Russia.

Cooling system

Internal combustion engines such as the GASOLINE ENGINE burn their fuel in enclosed cylinders at temperatures of 750°C or more. Were this heat not removed, the engine would rapidly overheat and eventually fail. About half the heat produced passes out with the exhaust gases and some is lost heating the lubricating oil; but a great deal remains, and must be removed by an efficient cooling system.

The most usual form of cooling is by water. Most gasoline and diesel engines in automobiles, trucks, locomotives, and boats are water-cooled. But some automobile engines, most motorcycle engines, and many airplane piston engines are air-cooled. Rocket engines are generally cooled by circulating incoming fuel inside the double wall of the combustion chamber and exhaust nozzle in a process

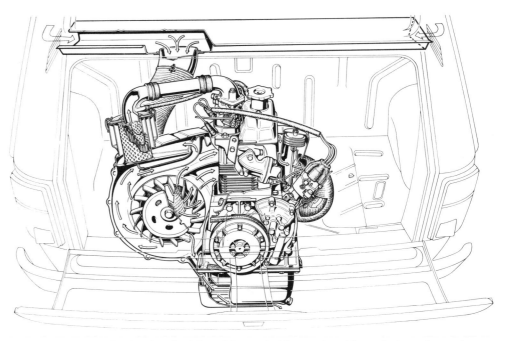

A cutaway diagram showing the circulation of the coolant in an automobile engine's cooling system.

called regenerative cooling (see ROCKETS). In a typical water-cooled gasoline engine, water is circulated through passages (jackets) around the engine cylinders and combustion spaces in the CYLINDER BLOCK AND HEAD. It absorbs heat and flows upwards through a THERMOSTAT into a RADIATOR. The hot water from the header tank of the radiator flows downwards through the thin-finned tubes of the radiator core. Air is drawn by a fan through the core over the finned tubes, and the water inside is thereby cooled. The cold water, sinking to the bottom of the radiator, is circulated back into the engine. The radiator is fitted with a pressure cap set at about 7 lb. per sq. in. This effectively raises the temperature at which the water boils, and helps prevent localized boiling at hot spots around the combustion spaces.

There is natural convectional circulation in a water-cooling system, but this is not fast enough to provide efficient cooling, and circulation is therefore aided by a water pump. This consists of an impeller mounted on the same shaft as the cooling fan, which is driven by a belt from a pulley on the end of the crankshaft.

In an air-cooled engine fans are used to force air over the engine cylinders. The cylinders are relatively exposed and the cylinder walls and cylinder head are fitted with fins, which give a greater cooling surface. The fins are longest at the top of the cylinders where the greatest heat is developed. Radial fans are often used, and direct air over the cylinder fins through ducting. Air cooling results in a much noisier engine; in water-cooled systems the water jacket deadens much of the noise. But air-cooled engines need little protection from temp-

erature extremes. Water-cooled engines must have ANTIFREEZE added to the water to prevent the system from icing up.

Coracle

Primitive Celtic fishing boat made of a wicker or lath frame covered by leather or undressed skins. A few modern examples are used by Welsh fishermen, and are covered with tarred canvas. A coracle is circular and lacks stability, but is light to carry. The kufas of Iraq is similar in construction.

Corinth Canal

Sea-level waterway in Greece, linking the Gulf of Corinth and the Saronic Gulf, cutting through the Isthmus of Corinth. It is 4 mi. (6.4 km) long, 70 ft. (21 m) wide, and has a minimum depth of 26 ft. (8 m). It was completed in 1893.

Corrosion

The destruction of a metal by chemical or electrochemical action. Its effect may be localized, to cause pitting, or it may affect the entire surface. The most common construction material, mild steel, is subject to corrosion by damp air, sulfurous fumes, salt water, and the like. These agents cause the steel to rust, or form a reddish-brown oxide film. The iron in effect is reverting to a lower energy state. In nature it is too reactive to remain in metallic form, and the same is true of most other metals.

One form of corrosion may be termed dry corrosion. It occurs through the chemical action of gases, particularly oxygen, on an exposed metal surface where a solid film of oxide forms on the metal surface. Usually the oxide film occupies more or less space than the metal it replaces. It is therefore porous and will crack or flake off. This allows the corroding agent to continue its attack. In some metals, however, the oxide film occupies the same volume as the metal it replaces. It adheres tightly to the metal beneath and acts as a barrier to further corrosion. It is this mechanism that gives aluminum and its alloys their corrosion resistance. For some applications the oxide film on aluminum is deliberately thickened to increase corrosion resistance, a process termed anodizing.

Most corrosion phenomena, however, are electrochemical in nature and involve the presence of an electrolyte in contact with the metal. Rusting is a typical example of this wet corrosion. Being electrochemical in origin, it involves the flow of electrons between regions of different electric potential, that is anodic (positively charged) and cathodic (negatively charged) regions of the metal. The whole forms a kind of electrolytic cell or series of cells. In such a cell electrons flow through the metal from anode to cathode. The metal at the anode passes into solution, or in other words, wears away. An electrolytic corrosion cell forms when two different metals are in contact with one another. This is called galvanic corrosion, and is sometimes turned to advantage and used to protect buried metal structures such as pipelines from corrosion (see CATHODIC PROTECTION). Cells also arise when a metal surface is exposed to varying concentrations of electrolyte or oxygen. This is often termed concentration-cell corrosion. Extensive corrosion can seriously weaken metal structures (bridges, automobiles, ships, boilers, etc.), and various methods are employed to prevent it. These include the use of coatings of paint, plastic, zinc, or aluminum. Alternatively the structure may be made of a corrosion-resistant alloy such as chromium-nickel steel or one of the many aluminum alloys.

Corvette

A three-masted, square-rigged WARSHIP, smaller than a FRIGATE. Corvettes were the first warships to be screw-propelled, though they retained their sails and wooden hull. True corvettes were no longer used after the early 1900s, but the term was revived during World War II to describe small antisubmarine escort vessels, and is used today for small, fast patrol ships.

Coupe

A closed, two-door automobile with a body smaller than that of a sedan. In the United States it is pronounced "koop," but in Europe it is spelled "coupé" and pronounced "koopay." The name comes from the French word meaning "cut," and originally referred to a closed two-seater carriage, which had a seat outside for the driver.

Cracking

An important oil-refinery process that breaks down heavier, or higher-boiling crude-oil fractions into lighter, or lower-boiling and more valuable products, particularly GASOLINE. Formerly, cracking was done by thermal treatment alone. Now a catalyst is used as well, leading to an improved yield of gasoline. Chemically, the use of a catalyst promotes carbon-bond rupture, polymerization of unsaturated hydrocarbons, and produces isoparaffins of high knock rating (see HYDROCARBONS). The gasoline produced has a much higher OCTANE NUMBER than "straight-run" gasoline produced by initial fractionation.

Catalytic cracking was first employed in the early 1930s, using a fixed bed of bentonite clay as a catalyst. Modern plants now use synthetic alumina-silica granules in a fluidized form, in which the particles flow like liquid. In the catalytic cracker a stream of heavy oil vapor picks up the finely divided heated catalyst and carries it into the cracking chamber, or reactor. There, at a temperature of about 500°C, cracking takes place. The cracked vapor is led off to a fractionating tower. Because the catalyst granules in the reactor gradually become covered with carbon, they are withdrawn continuously from the base of the reactor and circulated to a regenerator, where the carbon is burned off. The regenerated catalyst is then recycled (see REFINING).

Crankshaft

The part of a gasoline or diesel engine which converts the reciprocating motion of the piston into rotary motion to turn the wheels. It is invariably cast or forged in one piece and has to be machined accurately and balanced finely.

The crankshaft is made up of a number of cranks, or webs, and crank pins, which rotate in the bearings of the connecting rods that link with the PISTONS. The crank pins are set at different angles around the crankshaft to give uniform spacing of the power strokes of the pistons.

Typically, the crankshaft is supported in three or five main bearings. The front end of the crankshaft carries a pulley to drive the cooling fan and water pump. The rear carries a flange to connect with the FLYWHEEL. The flywheel is a heavy disk that conserves momentum and helps to keep the crankshaft turning steadily.

Crash gearbox

A GEARBOX fitted to early automobiles which did not have a SYNCHROMESH mechanism to equalize gear-wheel speeds before they meshed. The gear wheels had to be allowed to reach the same speed before the gearshift was moved. This was done on shifting into a higher gear by pausing slightly in neutral, and on shifting down by double declutching — engaging the clutch again while the gearbox was in neutral and revving the engine before selecting the lower gear. Crash gearboxes are still used on many racing automobiles because they consume less power.

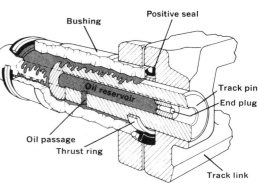

A cutaway cross-section showing the lubricating mechanism in the track pin of a crawler track. Each of the links which make up the crawler tracks rotates around a track pin.

Crawler tracks

Also called caterpillar tracks, broad, flat endless belts formed of interlinking hinged steel plates fitted instead of wheels to a variety of vehicles including bulldozers, excavators, mobile cranes, and tanks. Crawler-tracked vehicles can travel over much softer and rougher ground than can wheeled vehicles. Instead of concentrating the weight at one spot on each wheel, a tracked vehicle distributes the weight evenly over the whole bottom surface of the tracks.

The tracks circle around front and rear wheels. The rear wheels have teeth that engage with the tracks and drive them. Power can be applied to each track independently. A crawler vehicle is steered by braking or disengaging one of the tracks while the other is still being driven.

The most familiar tracked vehicle is the BULLDOZER, or its smaller relative the calfdozer. The largest land vehicle ever constructed has caterpillar tracks. It is the Marion crawler used to convey the giant Saturn V moon rockets to the launch pad at Cape Canaveral. Its four twin-caterpillar trucks, one on each corner, support a laden weight of 8,036 tons.

Crow's nest

A barrel or box-shaped structure at the masthead of a ship, providing a shelter for the lookout.

Cruiser

One of a class of fast WARSHIPS, smaller than a battleship but larger than a DESTROYER, with a great cruising range. Fast enough to run from a battleship's guns, cruisers in the two world wars hunted enemy battleships and convoys. A battle cruiser is equal to a battleship in armament, but possesses thinner armor and greater speed. Heavy, light, and antiaircraft cruisers all were important in World War II, and after the war the United States developed the nuclear-powered cruiser (with virtually unlimited range) and the guided-missile cruiser. Today the role of the cruiser is being supplanted by large, heavily-armed destroyers.

Cubic capacity

See CAPACITY.

Cugnot's carriage

Built in 1769, and often called the first automobile, a massive steam tractor designed to haul guns. It was slow, clumsy, and difficult to control (the single front wheel was used for both driving and steering), and had to stop every 15 minutes to build up steam, but Cugnot's carriage was nonetheless the world's first full-sized self-propelled vehicle.

Currents, ocean

Caused mainly by winds and influenced by the shapes of land masses, by different temperatures and densities of the sea water, and by the rotation of the earth, these currents affect all but the deepest parts of the ocean. Currents interact with the atmosphere to provide a major influence on climate and weather. Their study is therefore important to meteorology, and to navigation.

In the Northern Hemisphere giant current systems circulate in a clockwise direction; in the Southern Hemisphere the

A notable early aviator, Glenn Curtiss is also famous for his pioneer work on marine planes. He flew the first practical flying boat in 1912, and later developed the Curtiss NC-4 flying boat shown in this photograph, which in 1919 made the first air crossing of the Atlantic.

direction is reversed. West- or east-flowing boundary currents are "spun off" these rotating systems, forming currents such as the Gulf Stream.

Curtiss, Glenn Hammond (1878-1930)

Pioneer American pilot and airplane designer. He began his career building motorcycles, and was invited to construct engines for early U.S. AIRSHIPS. In 1907 he joined Alexander Graham Bell's Aerial Experimental Association. For this organization he built an airplane engine and then designed an airplane, the *June Bug*, in which in 1908 he won the *Scien-*

tific American trophy for flying over a measured course of 1 km (0.6 mi.) in 1 min. 42 sec. In January 1911 he made the first successful seaplane flight, and built his first flying-boat the following year. Curtiss won the first contract to supply planes to the U.S. Navy, and built up a large aircraft manufacturing business during World War I.

Cut-and-cover

A method of constructing shallow tunnels. Most of the New York subway system and London's Circle and District underground lines were built in this way. Excavation to the tunnel's formation level is done from the surface with mechanical diggers to create a deep trench. Then the tunnel itself is built in the trench from brick or concrete ribs and sections, and then covered over again to restore the original soil or road level (see TUNNELS).

Cutter

A single-masted fore-and-aft rigged vessel with a mainsail and two or more headsails. In the 19th century these fast, maneuverable craft were popular with smugglers and revenue forces alike. More recently they have been developed in Britain and the United States as racing craft.

Cugnot's carriage, 1769. Although too cumbersome to have any practical value, it was the world's first full-scale powered road vehicle.

A naval cutter is a small utility boat carried aboard a larger ship. Modern coast-guard vessels, performing the functions of the old revenue cutters, are still sometimes called cutters.

Cutty Sark

Famous three-masted British tea clipper, built in 1869 in Scotland. Measuring 212 ft. 5 in. (64.7 m) long with a 36-ft. (11 m) beam, the *Cutty Sark* carried a mainmast over 145 ft. (43.9 m) high. Calculations show that her sail plan could produce a drive of some 3,000 hp. Unlike American clippers, the *Cutty Sark* was a composite ship, with timber planking but an iron frame.

Cutty Sark served in the China tea trade until 1878, and then in the Australian wool trade, in which she made incredibly fast passages between Sydney and London averaging 80 to 82 days, despite her reduced sail plan and crew.

In 1895 she was sold to the Portuguese and traded as a tramp ship until 1922 when she returned to England and was

A Daimler 2¼ hp automobile engine of 1892.

restored and used as a training ship. *Cutty Sark* is now a museum, preserved in dry dock at Greenwich, England (see CLIPPER).

Cylinder block and head

The main parts of the body of a GASOLINE ENGINE. They are bolted together with a GASKET between them which acts as a seal to prevent water or gases from escaping from inside the engine. The cylinder block is generally made of cast iron, although some, particularly in air-cooled engines, are of aluminum alloys. The cylinder block contains the cylinders in which the PISTONS move. The cylinder bores are highly polished so that the pistons slide easily in them. If an alloy cylinder head is used, the bores must be lined with iron sleeves to withstand piston action. The cylinder head contains channels through which cooling water flows to carry away the heat developed during combustion. It contains holes to accommodate the push rods that operate the VALVE GEAR, oilways for the LUBRICATION SYSTEM and other openings where components such as the water pump and DISTRIBUTOR are mounted. At the base of the cylinder block, and usually an integral part of it, is the crankcase, which houses the CRANKSHAFT.

The cylinder head usually carries the valves and valve gear such as rocker arms and shaft. It contains holes for the push rods and channels for cooling water that marry with those in the cylinder block. Hollows in the underside of the cylinder head form the combustion chambers for the cylinders. The inlet manifold fits onto the side of the cylinder head, as does the exhaust manifold. The SPARK PLUGS screw into the side of the head. The cylinder head is also normally made of cast iron, though many car engines now have aluminum heads, which are not only lighter, but also conduct heat better. An aluminum head must also have inserts fitted to strengthen certain parts, such as the valve seats and guides.

D

Daimler, Gottlieb (1843-1900)

German engineer and inventor, pioneer of the internal-combustion engine and the automobile. Eager to find an alternative to steam power for a horseless carriage, he visited leading firms in France and England to gain experience. Then, in the 1870s, he worked with Nikolaus Otto (inventor of the FOUR-STROKE CYCLE) on the development of the gas engine, and then on the four-stroke. Otto worked out

a slide valve ignition system, and Daimler, seeing that Otto's still clumsy invention could be developed into a light high-speed power unit, decided to set up in business himself. Joining forces with Wilhelm Maybach, he devised a carburetor which enabled him to use gasoline instead of gas as a fuel, and in 1885 he patented an internal-combustion gasoline engine which ran at the then unprecedented rate of 700 rpm. He tried his new engine first on a two-wheeler (the world's first motorcycle), and then in 1886 on a four-wheeled carriage. This was the world's second successful gasoline-engined "automobile," and although more cart-like than the first (made by Carl BENZ the year before) Daimler's had the better engine. He set up the Daimler automobile factory in 1890. After his death the firm produced the first Mercedes, and in 1926 it merged with Benz to produce the MERCEDEZ-BENZ.

Dakota

Military version of Douglas' famous airplane, the DC-3 (see DC-3).

Daytona Beach

City on the Atlantic coast of Florida, famous in the history of automobile racing. Its 23-mi. (37 km) beach of hard white sand has been the scene of automobile speed trials since 1903 and the site of numerous world land-speed record attempts. The Daytona Beach International Speedway, a 2½-mi. (4 km) race-track, is the venue for America's most important motorcycle race, the Daytona 200, and for an annual 24-hour sports car race.

DC-3

Originally known both as the DST (Douglas sleeper transport), with accommodation for 16 passengers, and as the DC-3 seating 24, this aircraft was based on the 12-passenger DC-1 of 1933 and the 14-passenger DC-2 which took second place in the 1934 England–Australia race at an average speed of 156 mph (250 km/h) for the 11,300 mi. (18,000 km). It first flew in December 1935 and the following year entered service with American Airlines, initially between Chicago and New York. By 1940 a total of 430 had been delivered to various airlines, 100 of them to operators outside the United States. During World War II the military version (C-47 Dakota) saw service all over the world, and after the end of hostilities the DC-3 remained for many years a mainstay of commercial operators.

Early aircraft had 850-hp Wright Cyclone engines, but the use of 1,200-hp Pratt and Whitney power units raised the cruising speed from 192 mph (307 km/h) to about 207 mph (331 km/h), the range being extended from the original 1,400 mi. (2,240 km) to 2,100 mi. (3,360 km). DC-3 production continued until 1946. A total of 10,929 machines were built, of which 10,123 were originally military aircraft. The DC-3 was still in service with smaller airlines and some air forces in the mid-1970s.

Dead man's handle

A device to stop an electric train should the engineer become ill or otherwise unfit to drive. In order to drive the train he must keep the controller handle pressed down against a light spring. If he releases the handle for any reason, the power is cut off and the brakes are automatically applied.

Deadweight tonnage

The maximum weight a ship can carry in cargo and fuel. Deadweight tonnage is normally used to describe bulk cargo ships such as oil tankers (thus a supertanker with a dwt of 400,000 tons can actually carry that amount of oil) (see also DISPLACEMENT; TONNAGE).

Decarbonization

Removing carbon deposits from an engine, sometimes also known as "decoking." In a gasoline engine, for example, small amounts of carbon are produced during the combustion process. In time deposits can build up on the piston head, on the valves and valve seats and on the walls of the cylinder head. This buildup gradually reduces combustion efficiency. Fortunately, with modern fuels, decarbonization is seldom necessary for several tens of thousands of miles.

When decarbonizing, the cylinder head is removed from the cylinder block, and the valve gear on it is dismantled. Carbon deposits are scraped from all the exposed surfaces, and the valves are reground into their seats prior to reassembly. If the exhaust valves are badly pitted, they may have to be replaced, and it may often be worth fitting new valve return springs at the same time.

Decca navigator

A radio navigation aid widely used by both ships and aircraft. Low-frequency radio signals are generated by chains of transmitting stations consisting of a master station and two or three slave stations situated 50-80 mi. (80-130 km) distant from the master. The unmodulated radio waves create a pattern of hyperbolic position lines along which the phase difference between the outputs of the master and the slave station is con-

A Douglas Super DC-3. First flown in 1935, carrying 90% of the world's airline traffic in 1939. and still in service around the world, the DC-3 is probably the most successful airliner of all time.

stant. Instruments on the ship or aircraft identify these position lines by phase comparison carried out at a common frequency. In aircraft a flight log is an integral part of the system, which can also augment other navigational aids by connection to a computer.

De Havilland, Sir Geoffrey (1882-1965)

British aviation pioneer and designer. Though beginning his career as an automobile engineer, De Havilland built his first airplane in 1908, and taught himself to fly. From 1910 to 1911 he was chief designer and test pilot at the Royal Aircraft Factory, a British government enterprise. During World War I he was one of Britain's chief military airplane designers, and created the famous DH series.

In 1920 De Havilland formed his own company, producing the famous Moth series of light planes, the Mosquito fighter-bomber of World War II, and the COMET jetliner of 1949.

Deicing

Deicing measures to prevent the dangerous effects of ice forming on aircraft surfaces take several forms. On leading edges which are particularly prone to ice formation a pneumatically pulsating rubber envelope covering, known as a deicer boot or shoe, can be installed. Heating elements may also be used, or hot air from the engines channeled through porous material to the surface. Another preventative is the application of an alcoholic paste to surfaces. To prevent windshields in particular from icing, a liquid with a low freezing point can be sprayed as necessary.

Delta-wing

When an airplane's wings and tail are merged into one large flying surface with a swept-back leading edge, the design is

known as a delta-wing (from the shape of the Greek letter delta, Δ).

Because of its wide chord (see WING), a delta-wing can have an aerodynamically thin wing section while retaining sufficient depth for the incorporation of strong spars and room for fuel, engines, and equipment. In addition, the control surfaces are located well behind the aircraft's center of gravity where they can exert the most force.

The strength of a delta-wing, due to its thickness, resists distortion caused by the stresses and strains of flight. Drag is reduced by burying the engines within the wing and by eliminating the tailplane, while the large wing area gives a low wing loading that reduces takeoff and landing speeds without the need for FLAPS. Disadvantages of the delta layout are the nose-high takeoff and landing attitude necessary to obtain lift from a high angle of attack, maintenance problems incurred by burying the engines within the wing, an excessive increase in wing area if a long span is needed for high altitude flying, and inferior spin recovery characteristics.

The delta layout is particularly advantageous for large long-range aircraft (see CONCORDE).

Deltic engine

A type of DIESEL ENGINE whose cylinders are arranged in the shape of a Greek letter delta, Δ. It is used in diesel locomotives.

Derricks

Lifting devices used on board ship and on the dockside for handling cargo. The simplest is a guyed (cable-supported) pole, which has a pulley at the top. The guy derrick has a central pole or mast, from from which is suspended a lifting jib or boom, pivoted at the foot of the mast. Many freighters have derricks of this type (see MATERIALS HANDLING).

Destroyer

A fast warship, smaller than a CRUISER and generally displacing 2,000-4,000 tons. Originally armed only with light guns and designed to destroy the new fast torpedo boats of the late-19th century (and known in full as Torpedo Boat Destroyers), they were soon themselves equipped with torpedoes. The smallest of the big warships, and, with speeds of nearly 40 knots, the greyhounds of the fleet, their duties included providing escorts for merchant vessels and larger warships, scouting, minelaying and sweeping, and even attacking much larger ships. Today the era of the giant warship is past, and in most modern navies destroyers, sometimes now armed with guided missiles, are among the largest vessels (see WARSHIPS).

Detonator

An emergency warning device sometimes used on railroads, a small explosive fitted with soft metal straps so that it can be fastened to the head of a rail. It is of particular use in fog, when ordinary signals cannot be seen, to let engineers know whether track is clear, or in emergencies, to warn other trains of the presence of an obstruction. Detonators explode when trains pass over them.

Dhow

Fore-and-aft rigged traditional Arab trading vessel with one or two masts. Normally fitted with triangular lateen sails, the dhow is of ancient origin but is still common in the Indian Ocean and the Red Sea. The word is in fact actually used to describe a variety of Arab vessels including the *baghla*, the *zaruk*, and the *sambuk*.

Dial-a-ride

A special kind of bus system suitable for very low density residential areas where normal bus services would not be economically justifiable. Small 10-20 seat buses are used and the schedules and routes are flexible to a certain degree so that the buses can respond to the phoned-in requests for service on a door-to-door basis. A limited number of such systems have become quite popular in North America and in Britain, though few are profitable in the normal sense. Prospective passengers register their travel requests with a central control unit. Each individual request is analyzed, along with all others received, in terms of desired travel time, origin and destination. The best-placed bus of those deployed in the area is then instructed to divert and pick up the passenger. In the smaller schemes, such as that at Bay Ridges in Ontario or Harlow New Town in Britain,

where only four or five buses are in circulation, the number of destinations to which the buses will take people is strictly limited — usually to the local shopping center or railroad station. In these cases the routing and pick-up schedules are worked out manually at the control center. In a few larger scale systems, such as at Haddonfield, New Jersey, computers are used to optimize the bus operations, minimize the delay to people already on the buses, and ensuring that the buses arrive at the pick-up points on time.

Diesel, Rudolf (1858-1913)

German engineer, inventor of the form of internal-combustion engine that bears his name. Diesel spent years of experiment in an effort to produce an engine that would be more efficient than the wasteful steam engine, and decided that maximum efficiency would be gained with an internal-combustion system in which the fuel was compressed to ignition temperature. He was awarded his first patent in 1892, and produced his first successful full-sized engine in 1897. It was an immediate success.

Diesel engine

An internal-combustion engine that burns a light oil by means of compression-ignition. Diesels are widely used to power trucks, ships, and locomotives. A few automobiles are powered by diesel as well. For trucks, diesels developing a few hundred horsepower are used; for locomotives diesels of several thousand horsepower; and for motor ships diesels of tens of thousands of horsepower. Marine diesels are massive — as big as a two-story house.

Compared with a gasoline engine, the diesel is more efficient, more sturdily constructed, longer lasting, and uses cheaper fuel. But it is heavier, more expensive to build, and noisier, and has poorer acceleration. For marine, locomotive, and truck applications, these drawbacks are far outweighed by the advantages, in particular, the engine's efficiency. Whereas a gasoline engine can realize less than 25% of the energy in its fuel, the diesel engine can utilize as much as 40%.

The diesel engine has many features in common with the gasoline engine. It burns its fuel in enclosed cylinders to produce hot gases to drive a piston. Reciprocating piston movement is converted to rotary motion by means of a crankshaft, which connects through gears with the transmission system of the vehicle or vessel. Also, the diesel engine has cooling and lubrication systems similar to those in a gasoline engine, and similar valve gear. But there are significant differences. There is, for example, no carburetor, and there are no

A traditional Arab dhow, one of the earliest vessels with a fore-and-aft sail.

A typical 12 cylinder marine diesel engine on the testbed. Diesels power the great majority of modern ships; this particular engine provides, together with two 9 cylinder units, a total output of 75,000 bhp, and powers a large containership.

spark plugs. And a diesel engine has a very much higher COMPRESSION RATIO. The cylinders in the engine may be arranged in several ways, often in-line or in a V-form. Some locomotives utilize a deltic arrangement, named for the Greek letter delta, Δ. The cylinders are situated in a triangular configuration, with two pistons working in opposite directions in each cylinder.

The diesel engine may work on either a four-stroke or a two-stroke engine cycle. Most automobile and locomotive diesel engines work on a four-stroke cycle. On the first stroke (induction), air is drawn into the cylinder through the inlet valve as the piston moves down; the exhaust valve is closed. Then the inlet valve closes and the piston begins to move upward, compressing the air. As the air is compressed, it gets very hot. Near the top of the compression stroke, diesel fuel is sprayed into the combustion

chamber at the top of the cylinder. The fuel is chosen so that its flash-point (the temperature at which it will self-ignite) is below the temperature of the compressed air. Thus, when it is injected, the fuel burns spontaneously. After ignition, the gases produced force the piston down on its power stroke. As the piston begins the next upstroke, the exhaust valve opens, and the spent gases are forced out. The exhaust valve then closes, the inlet valve opens, and the cycle begins again.

In the two-stroke diesel cycle, common in marine engines, power is produced every downward stroke, rather than every other as in the four-stroke cycle. The two-stroke engine is also simpler in construction, having no valves. Instead, there are inlet and exhaust ports in the cylinder walls, and the piston itself acts as a kind of valve, covering and uncovering the ports in turn. With the piston

ready to commence its upward stroke, both the inlet and exhaust ports are open. Air rushes in the inlet port and swirls in such a way that it helps to expel the spent gases through the exhaust port. This is called scavenging. The piston rises, covering both ports, and compresses the air. Fuel is then injected and burns, and the piston is forced down. Near the end of its stroke, it first uncovers the outlet port, and the spent gases start to rush out. As it goes lower still, it uncovers the inlet port. The air enters, and the cycle begins again.

The combustion chamber is carefully designed to promote rapid mixing of the fuel with the air. In one design the chamber is formed by a curved depression in the crown of the piston which swirls the air as it is being compressed. Fuel is then sprayed directly into it. In an alternative arrangement the compressed air is forced into a separate swirl chamber in the cylinder head, into which the fuel is injected. Greater efficiency of combustion is achieved by forcing the air into the cylinders under pressure. This is called supercharging. Most large marine diesels and locomotive diesels are supercharged. The air is forced into the engine by means of a turbocharger — a rotary blower driven by a turbine spun by the exhaust gases.

Diesel locomotive
See LOCOMOTIVE.

Differential
A mechanism in the FINAL DRIVE of a motor vehicle that allows the wheels to move at different speeds while maintaining positive drive. This is necessary when the vehicle is cornering. The differential consists of four bevel gears and pinions at right angles to each other contained within a cage attached to the crown wheel.

When the vehicle is traveling in a straight line, the bevel pinions lock the bevel gears on the half-shafts together, and the whole unit rotates with the crown wheel. When the vehicle is cornering, one half-shaft slows down. This causes the bevel pinions to rotate, driving the other half-shaft faster.

Dihedral
Wings that incline upwards from their roots at the fuselage are described as dihedral. This configuration helps impart stability to the aircraft. If an aircraft with dihedral wings starts to sideslip, the wing on the side to which the machine is slipping immediately drops; because of the dihedral angle, the dropped wing then has a greater angle of attack (see WING) than the opposite wing

and generates more lift, thus leveling the aircraft. Swept-back wings require little or no dihedral.

Dinghy

A small boat with no deck. It may be a rowboat or a single-masted sailboat.

Dirigible

An AIRSHIP; literally a balloon that can be steered. (Dirigible means "able to be directed.")

Disk brake

The kind of brake used on the front wheels of many automobiles and other vehicles, and also on airplane wheels. It is essentially a caliper-type brake that works by pincer action. A cast-iron disk with polished flat surfaces is attached to the wheel and rotates with it. Applying the brake pedal forces brake pads against both sides of a portion of the disk, thereby slowing it, and the wheel.

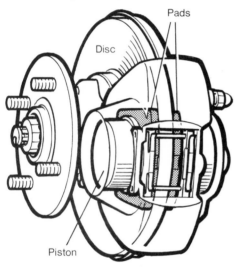

A cutaway diagram of a disk brake. The road wheel is fixed to the four bolts at the left. The disk rotates with the wheel.

The pads are forced against the disk by pistons which work by hydraulic pressure in the brake system. Generally two pistons are used, one on each side, though some cars have twin pistons on each side.

Disk brakes are generally fitted to the front wheels of modern cars since they take most of the braking effort, but are sometimes also fitted to the rear wheels. They are more effective than drum brakes and are self-adjusting. They are less susceptible to BRAKE FADE because they do not readily overheat.

A variation of the basic disk brake is the swinging-caliper type. This contains only one piston which acts directly on one pad only. Hydraulic pressure in the system causes the caliper to swing about a fixed pivot and push the other brake pad against the disk. Another variation

is the sliding caliper. Hydraulic pressure forces two pistons apart. One acts directly on one of the pads. The other pushes the caliper sideways to apply the other pad (see BRAKING SYSTEMS).

Displacement

A floating object displaces a volume of water equal to the volume of the object below the waterline. The weight of the water displaced (the displacement) equals the weight of the object (see BUOYANCY). The displacement tonnage of a ship thus equals the weight of the ship plus everything on board (see TONNAGE).

Distributor

Part of the IGNITION SYSTEM of a gasoline engine which distributes high-voltage electricity to the spark plugs at the appropriate point in the engine cycle. It also incorporates the breaker points that interrupt the battery current to the coil, and a condenser (capacitor) to reduce arcing between the contacts as they open. Through the center of the distributor base is a shaft driven from the engine camshaft. Cams on the shaft open and close the contacts as it rotates.
At the top of the shaft is the rotor arm. The high-voltage lead from the coil makes contact with the rotor arm through a spring-loaded carbon brush in the distributor cap. As the rotor arm rotates, its tip passes the terminals of cables connected with the spark plugs. The high-voltage current from the coil passes via the rotor arm to the terminals and thence to the spark plugs.
In the base of the distributor is a system of pivoted weights that move outwards progressively through centrifugal force

as the engine speed increases. This has the effect of advancing the point of ignition, a feature necessary at increased engine speeds. A vacuum advance may also be employed, working by the suction in the inlet manifold.

Docks

The working areas of ports and harbors, where ships are loaded and unloaded. A dock at its most elaborate is a basin-like enclosure with QUAYS, WHARVES, and piers on which cargo can be stored and moved during the processes of loading and discharge. Where the rise and fall of the tide is less than about 10 ft. (3 m) the dock is normally tidal: it is open to the river or sea, as in New York. But where the rise and fall is greater, an enclosed dock is used, in which the water level remains unchanging. Vessels enter and leave through locks, although at the point in the tide when the water levels outside and inside are equal both lock gates can be opened. Space within the dock basin is usually restricted, and ships are maneuvered into position in their berths by tugs (see PORTS AND HARBORS).
The emphasis in a modern dock is on speed and efficiency, and therefore on specialization. A ship is only earning money while at sea and so it must be turned round (discharged and loaded) as quickly as possible. A great many cargo ships carry only a specific cargo, and they dock at a berth equipped with specialized handling gear and (where necessary) storage facilities. There are, for example, specialized berths for grain ships (the grain is sucked straight from the hold into giant silos); for container

Docks at Le Havre, France, one of Europe's main oil ports. The quays in the foreground are for oil tankers, while those beyond are for passenger and freight liners and are equipped with a variety of handling gear and storage facilities.

ships; for ships carrying forest products, sugar, and other cargoes. To speed up the inevitably lengthy process of turning round a general cargo ship, the dock may provide facilities for loading and discharging over the ship's side into barges.

Some goods can be taken straight from the ship to waiting trucks or freight cars, but many items must be stored, and warehouses and transit sheds are an essential feature of docks.

As freight ships become ever larger, so must docks be enlarged and deepened. But few can accommodate today's supertankers; they usually berth at special terminals (see also DRY DOCK; FLOATING DOCKS).

Dodge Brothers

One-time American automobile manufacturer. The brothers John and Horace Dodge, who had previously built engines for the Ford Motor Company, produced their first car in 1914, a conventional 3.5-liter. The sturdy Dodge 4 was widely used during World War I as a staff car and ambulance, and provided the basis of the firm's success for many years. By 1916 Dodge was in terms of American sales the fourth-largest automobile company in the country, and in 1920 had risen to second place. Then, in 1928, the company was acquired by Chrysler at a price of $175 million. The make retained its individuality, however, until 1935, when Dodges appeared with the Chrysler Airstream styling. Today Dodge remains an important division of the Chrysler Corporation, with a wide range of automobiles and trucks.

Dog clutch

A mechanism in a GEARBOX which locks the selector collar to the gear wheels. The mating faces of the collar and gear wheels have projections, or dogs, at intervals around them. When meshed together, the dogs interlock and allow collar and gear wheel to turn together.

Doldrums

Regions at sea with calms or only very light winds, thunderstorms and heavy rains, dreaded in the days of sail because ships were often becalmed there. The doldrums occur in the equatorial belts of the Indian and western Pacific oceans where the northeast and southeast trade winds meet.

Dory

A small flat-bottomed fishing boat with high, curved sides (see BOATS).

Drag

See AERODYNAMICS.

Dredger

Vessel designed for underwater excavation, particularly for deepening canals, docks, harbors, deep-water approach channels, and the like, and for constructing dams, breakwaters, and similar structures. There are several types. The suction dredger trails a large bore pipe along the seabed through which a mixture of solids and water is sucked. The spoil, most often a mixture of sand and mud, may be pumped into hoppers in the dredger and either taken out to sea and dumped, or pumped ashore for land reclamation. Alternatively, the dredger may carry a long horizontal boom along which the spoil is pumped as it is produced, to be ejected well clear of the channel being excavated.

The bucket or ladder dredger has an endless chain of buckets on an angled frame (the ladder). With the ladder lowered to the bottom, the buckets descend on the ladder's underside, dig into the mud, and return on its upper side to dump their contents either into the dredger itself, or into a barge.

The grab dredger, useful for work at considerable depths, is essentially a water-borne derrick carrying a single bucket or grab; the dipper dredger is a barge-mounted power shovel. Both are necessarily much slower in action than the suction and bucket varieties. They are often anchored to the bottom by stakes called spuds.

Drifter

A kind of fishing boat that drops its nets and then drifts with the current.

Drive shaft

A tube that transmits power from the gearbox to the FINAL DRIVE in a conventional automobile transmission system. It is sometimes also known as a propeller shaft. It consists of a strong metal tube with a UNIVERSAL JOINT at each end where it connects with gearbox and final drive. The use of these flexible joints allows the shaft to move independently of the units at each end as is necessary when the vehicle travels over uneven surfaces. The universal joint coupling on the gearbox output shaft can slide on splines to accommodate differences in distances between the gearbox and final drive as the rear axle moves up and down.

Droshky

A low-slung, open four-wheel carriage used in Russia (see CARRIAGES AND CARTS).

A large modern suction dredger. The machinery between bridge and forecastle includes suction pipe hoisting equipment, and gear for discharging the spoil.

Drum brake

Brake fitted to many automobiles, now increasingly restricted to the rear wheels only. A cast-iron brake drum is attached to the wheel hub. Braking effort is applied by forcing a pair of nearly semicircular brake shoes covered with tough lining against the inner circumference of the drum. Because drum brakes are enclosed, they are more liable to overheat and suffer from fading (see BRAKE FADE).

Drum brakes may be operated by hydraulic pressure from the brake pedal, or mechanically from the hand, or emergency brake. When operated hydraulically, pressure in the braking system forces apart pistons in a slave cylinder mounted on a non-rotating back-plate.

The pistons force the pivoted brake shoes against the drum. Springs return the shoes to their original position when the brakes are taken off (see BRAKING SYSTEMS).

Dry dock

Enclosed basin which can be pumped dry, used for major repair work on ships. A dry dock is dug out of the land at the water's edge, and enclosed by a massive floating gate (held in position by gravity when the dry dock is empty, but easily floated out of the way when the dock is full of water), or by leaf gates similar to those used in a lock. With the dry dock flooded to the level of the water outside, the gate is opened or removed, and the vessel is maneuvered into position by tugs. The gate is then closed, and the water is pumped out, leaving the ship high and dry.

DS-19

Revolutionary automobile introduced by CITROEN of France in 1955. The first radically altered large Citroën since before World War II, it retained the front-wheel drive, self-leveling HYDROPNEUMATIC SUSPENSION, and (in an improved version) long-stroke four-cylinder engine of its predecessors. New features included power brakes and steering, the now standard Citroen single-spoke steering wheel, and the streamlined "dolphin" styling. Highly successful, but complicated and expensive, it was followed a year later by the cheaper ID-19, a similar car but without the power brakes and steering.

Duesenberg SJ

Famous American sports car. Introduced in 1932, it was a supercharged version of the Duesenberg J, a 6.9-liter straight-eight designed to be the fastest and finest luxury car in the world. With a top speed of 129 mph (206 km/h), the SJ could accelerate from rest to 100 mph (160 km/h) in 17 seconds. A symbol of elegance and speed, it is a prized collector's automobile.

Dugout

A primitive CANOE formed by hacking out the inside of a wooden log until it is hollow.

Dump truck

Type of truck used for carrying bulk loads of materials such as sand, earth, and ballast. The load-carrying section, which has sides but no top, can be raised hydraulically from the front or, on some models, from one side, to dump the load. The hydraulic jacking system is powered by the truck's engine.

One of the last East Indiamen to be built, the Dunbar. Constructed in northern England, and launched in 1853, she had luxuriously equipped passenger facilities, but was primarily a freighter.

Dunlop, John Boyd (1840-1921)

Scottish-born inventor of the first practical pneumatic tire. While working as a veterinarian in Belfast, Northern Ireland, Dunlop devised a pneumatic tire in order to make his son's tricycle ride more comfortably, taking out a patent in 1888 and forming a company to manufacture and market the tires in 1890. They were spectacularly and immediately successful in popularizing the modern "safety" bicycle and established the tire industry at the moment the first automobiles were about to appear. Dunlop's work was actually a re-invention, for a form of pneumatic tire was patented in 1845 by Robert William Thompson but not proceeded with.

Duryea

The Duryea Motor Wagon Company of Springfield, Mass., was the United States' first automobile manufacturer. The brothers Charles (1862-1938) and Frank (1870-1967) ran their earliest model, generally considered the first car built in the United States, in 1893. It was a powered horse buggy with a single-cylinder 4-hp engine. They entered their second car in America's first automobile race (in Chicago in 1895) and won, covering the 50-mi. (89 km) course in nine hours. The firm continued production until 1917, but the brothers soon parted company.

Dynamo

An electricity generator that produces direct current (see GENERATORS).

Dynamometer

An instrument that measures the power of an engine. The rope brake is an example. It consists of a rope extended over the flywheel or brake drum of the engine, with one end weighted down and the other attached to a balance. Another widely used type is the electric dyna-

mometer, which employs an electric generator. The engine output shaft is connected to the generator armature, and the generator stator tends to rotate with it. This torque is counterbalanced and measured by means of weights.

E

Earhart, Amelia (1898-1937)

Pioneer American aviator. While a nurse and social worker she learned to fly, and in 1928 became the first woman to fly across the Atlantic, traveling as a passenger. On May 20-21, 1932, she became the first woman pilot to make a solo crossing of the Atlantic, flying a Lockheed Vega from Newfoundland to Northern Ireland. Amelia Earhart's other achievements included the first solo flight by a woman from Hawaii to the American mainland and the first solo flights by a woman across the United States in both directions. She disappeared in the Pacific Ocean during an attempt to fly around the world; her copilot was Fred Noonan.

East Indiaman

Three-masted square-rigged merchant sailing ship engaged in trade between Europe and India and the East Indies from the 17th to the early 19th centuries, during which period it remained essentially unchanged. Sometimes called Tea Wagons, they were broad, round bowed, and with a top speed of about 10 knots, slow. Most were heavily armed, a necessary protection against rivals and pirates.

Echo sounder

Also known as a sonic depth finder, a device which transmits pulses of ultrasonic sound to the seabed, and by measuring the time taken for the reflected pulses to return, calculates the depth of the water. The idea is similar to RADAR, which measures electromagnetic (radio wave) echoes.

The sonic pulses can as easily be reflected off submerged objects as off the seabed, and echo sounders were originally developed during World War I to detect submarines. Today they are used on a wide range of ships. They are, for example, a valuable aid to fishing vessels, enabling shoals of fish to be located, and to deep-draft superships, giving warning of projections on the sea bottom.

The basic elements of an echo sounder are a transmitter to produce powerful electrical pulses; a transducer to convey these into ultrasonic pressure waves in the water, and to convert the reflected pulses back into electrical energy; and a device to measure the elapsed time and calculate and indicate the depth (or the distance and bearing) (see also SONAR).

Eddystone Lighthouse

Lighthouse situated in the English Channel 14 mi. (22 km) from Plymouth to mark a dangerous group of rocks visible only at low tide. The first lighthouse on the site, a timber structure, was built in 1696, and destroyed in a storm seven years later. The present lighthouse (the fourth) was completed in 1882. Standing 133 ft. (40 m) above the water, its light is visible for $17\frac{1}{2}$ mi. (28 km).

Efficiency

The thermal efficiency of a heat engine describes how effective the engine is in converting the energy put into it into useful work. Most common heat engines are lamentably inefficient. The steam engine can utilize only about 12% of the latent heat in its fuel, and the gasoline engine about 25%. The steam turbine and diesel engine are somewhat better, with efficiencies of up to 40%.

Mechanical efficiency indicates how effective a machine behaves as a machine. An efficiency of 100% is impossible because of friction, vibration, noise, and other losses within the mechanical components. The efficiency of an engine is defined as the ratio of the effective, or brake, horsepower, to the horsepower developed in the cylinders, known as indicated horsepower. Mechanical efficiencies of modern engines often exceed 95%.

Ejection seat

A seat which can, in an emergency, be catapulted (normally by an explosive charge) to take its occupant clear of the aircraft and enable a safe descent by

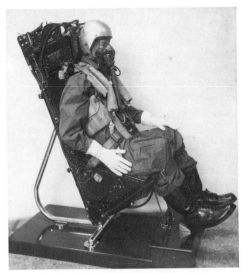

Safe escape from an airplane flying at high speed is only possible with an ejection seat. The photograph shows a mock up of the Martin Patent type.

parachute, either by the individual or as a complete seat unit. To facilitate exit the cockpit cover is either pre-ejected or the seat forces its way through the cockpit canopy. For certain naval aircraft there is a special system designed to eject underwater if necessary.

The first live ejection was made from an R.A.F. Gloster Meteor jet fighter in 1946; the first ejection at supersonic speed was made from a U.S.A.F. F-100 Super Sabre off the California coast in 1955. Pioneers and main producers of ejection seats are the Martin Baker Company of England, whose seats up to June 20, 1975 have

saved 3,849 lives. Research is proceeding on crew module ejection, which would enable a complete compartment to be ejected clear; a system incorporated in the prototype Rockwell B-1.

Electric car

In 1898 a Jeantaud electric car created a sensation when it reached the record speed of 39.3 mph (63 km/h), and in the following year Jenatzy's streamlined electric sprint car reached 65.75 mph (105 km/h). There is nothing new in the electric car, and in the early days of the automobile they were popular in the United States, and to a lesser extent in Europe. In 1900 38% of the automobiles in America were electric (with 40% steam and only 22% gasoline). At the peak of their success, in 1912, nearly 34,000 electric cars manufactured by over 20 companies were registered in America. Their advantages over gasoline cars were in those days considerable: they were quiet, easy to start and to drive, and being relatively simple they were reliable. Electric cars were, however, expensive. Well-known American makes included Baker, Milburn, Rauch and Land, and Detroit.

As the gasoline-engined automobile was improved, the disadvantages of electrics became more apparent, and by the mid-1920s they had almost disappeared from the scene. Those disadvantages are basically lack of speed and range due to total dependence on storage batteries. In the early 1900s Thomas Edison claimed to

An experimental city electric car in the Netherlands. Although silent and pollution free, electric cars still suffer from lack of speed and range due to their dependence on storage batteries.

have invented a "wonder battery" that would put gasoline cars out of business. In fact his invention was little better than the lead-acid battery, and scientists are still searching for Edison's dream. In recent years electric cars have been the subject of much research. They have the notable advantages already mentioned, plus excellent acceleration, needing neither clutch nor gears. They require minimal maintenance, use very little oil, and produce no exhaust fumes. Many prototypes have been made, the emphasis being on the small city car. British Ford's Comuta was one example, But its top speed of 35 mph (56 km/h) and range in town traffic of little more than 15 mi. (23 km) showed no advance on the "electromobiles" of the 1900s. The overriding problem remains the battery. Apart from its weight and expense, the greatest range possible before recharging is still around 40 to 50 mi. (64 to 88 km). A limited solution would be the provision of "battery banks" where the driver could exchange his flat battery for a fully charged one. Experiments have been made with silver-peroxide-zinc, cobalt, and ceramic storage batteries. But the greatest hope for the future seems to be the FUEL CELL, in which fuel is converted directly into electricity. The combined gasoline and electric car is another interesting possibility. The experimental General Motors XP-883 had an electric motor for pollution-free city driving and a gasoline engine for use on the open road (when the storage batteries would be recharged). The Japanese Mazda EX-5, an incredibly maneuverable runabout "bubble" car, had a small rotary engine generating electricity for four electric motors, one to each wheel. The great advantage of this system is that the gasoline engine is small and runs at a constant speed (at which it is most efficient).

Electric drive

A form of transmission in which rotary motion from a turbine or engine is used to power an electric generator. The electricity produced is conducted to electric motors that turn driving wheels or spin a shaft. Some locomotives have diesel-electric drive, in which the power comes from a large diesel engine. Many ships have turboelectric drive, the power in this case coming from a steam turbine.

Elevator

A device for raising and lowering freight and passengers, an essential invention for the development of the modern skyscraper. Early — and dangerous — freight elevators were in use in the first part of the 19th century, but the modern passenger, or safety elevators were built by Elisha Graves Otis in the 1850s. These were generally hydraulic-powered; the first electric elevator was installed in the Demarest Building in New York in 1889. Almost all modern elevators are electric.

In a modern automatic elevator the freight or passenger car runs between guide rails; it is suspended from multiple hoist ropes, on the other end of which is a counterweight. The hoist ropes pass over a winch which is driven by an electric motor. Automatic doors close the lift car and the entrances to it on each floor; safety circuits prevent the car from moving unless all doors are shut. Additional safety circuits immobilize the car if it is overloaded, or apply brakes if it exceeds its determined speed. Automatic control systems vary; the most popular is the collective selective system, in which all calls for the elevator, whether made from the car or any floor, are obeyed in the order in which the floors occur, regardless of the order in which they are given. This makes for economy of movement. Elevator speeds vary from 20 in. (50 cm)/sec. to 280 in. (710 cm)/sec. or more.

Elevators

Hinged control surfaces which impart pitch (nose-up or nose-down attitudes) to an aircraft. They are normally part of the tailplane or stabilizer. Moving the CONTROL COLUMN forward hinges the elevator downwards, increasing the lift imparted by the stabilizer and raising the tail so that the aircraft dives. Pulling the control column back raises the elevator, reduces the lift of the stabilizer and causes the tail to drop, enabling the aircraft to climb.

Elevon

Aircraft such as DELTA-WINGS which have no tailplane have instead control surfaces that combine the functions of ELEVATORS and AILERONS. Such control surfaces are called elevons, and are linked to the CONTROL COLUMN so that they act in unison (as elevators) when the controls are moved longitudinally and operate in opposition (as ailerons) if lateral movements of the column are made.

Emission-control systems

Emission-control systems are designed to reduce the discharge of pollutant gases and particles from automobile engines. The result of unburned fuel, these include hydrocarbons, nitrogen oxides, and carbon monoxide. Evaporation of gasoline from the fuel tank and carburetor is controlled by fitting a liquid-vapor separator and a canister of activated char-coal (which absorbs the vapor) between the fuel and the air.

Slight leakage between piston and cylinder is inevitable and allows unburned gases to escape into the crankcase. To prevent these "blow-by" gases from reaching the air, emission-control systems take them back to the engine intake for recycling. This source of pollution is now totally controlled, but control of exhaust gases presents a more difficult and more serious problem. The air-injection system pumps air into the exhaust ports to burn a high proportion of the noxious gases that would otherwise be discharged. The efficiency of this method can be increased by using a special thermal reactor exhaust manifold in which the gases continue to burn until they lose many of their harmful elements. In addition, the gases can to a considerable extent be prevented at the source by improving engine efficiency using various methods including more precise control of the fuel-air mixture with improved carburetors or fuel injection systems.

The catalytic converter is a further method of emission control. The exhaust gases pass through an insulated chamber where catalysts convert the carbon monoxide and hydrocarbons into carbon dioxide and water. But at low temperatures (during warm-up, for example) the catalysts are inactive, and they are adversely affected by leaded fuels, and by overheating (see also POLLUTION).

Engines

Strictly speaking an engine is a device which converts the chemical energy of a fuel into mechanical work, but this entry includes engines or motors used in transportation. Apart from clockwork motors, and from primitive reaction steam-turbine models, all early engines were reciprocating. They employed a force (compressed air, atmospheric pressure, steam, or an explosion) to push a piston up and down in a cylinder, and a mechanism to convert this into the rotary motion needed to turn wheels, paddles, or propellers. In 1799 a compressed air engine was patented in England, the theory being that vehicles could "recharge" at roadside compressor stations. Compressed air is today widely used to drive many pneumatic devices, but its principal application in transportation is to lift AIR-CUSHION VEHICLES off the ground,

The first successful piston engines were in fact atmospheric engines. Steam was used merely as a means of creating a vacuum. James WATT turned the atmospheric engine into a true steam engine by closing the top of the cylinder and

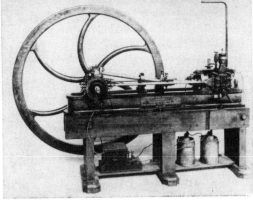

Jean Lenoir's gas engine of 1860, the first commercially successful internal combustion engine. Essentially a converted double acting steam engine with electric ignition (the coil and electric cells can be seen underneath the engine) it was widely used for pumping and other work. The large flywheel made the engine smooth-running, but with an efficiency of only 4% it was not suitable for automobiles.

A Rolls-Royce automobile engine of 1925. A symbol of superb engineering, these engines had a working life of up to a million miles (1.6 million km). Parts of the engine are cutaway to show the overhead valve gear, pistons, crankshaft, and sump.

using steam, instead of atmospheric pressure, to force the piston down; one of his assistants devised a crank, flywheel, and connecting-rod mechanism, and by 1810 working steamboats, road vehicles, and locomotives had appeared.

Meanwhile progress had been made with the "explosion engine," in which combustion takes place inside the cylinder. The first internal-combustion engines ran on coal gas, and were less efficient than steam engines, but with the invention of the FOUR-STROKE CYCLE and the development of the CARBURETOR, the gasoline engine was adopted for automobiles late in the 19th century, and then for airplanes.

A steam engine converts at most 12% of the latent heat of its fuel into power, a gasoline engine converts up to 28%, while the compression-ignition DIESEL ENGINE converts about 35%. Yet the reciprocating steam engine continued to be used in locomotives until the 1950s, and in many automobiles until the 1920s, It has the great advantage that it develops enormous power even when moving very slowly, and can therefore start a heavy load from rest with no clutch. An internal-combustion engine, with many small cylinders, only develops considerable power when turning over at speed.

The diesel uses relatively cheap unrefined fuel, but it is noisier than a gasoline engine and produces unpleasant exhaust fumes. It is today the normal engine for most large road vehicles, and for most ships, for many locomotives (in which the diesel normally generates current for electric traction motors), and is increasingly used for automobiles.

Rotary engines. Nineteenth-century marine reciprocating engines were sturdy and reliable, but they could not produce high speeds. Early in the 20th century they were replaced by STEAM TURBINES, in which steam is used to turn a rotor. This type of engine is much simpler and

smoother (all moving parts rotate) and is still used for very large ships, although on most vessels more efficient, though more complex and costly, diesels are normal. However, the steam turbine is enjoying a renaissance on nuclear ships, in which the nuclear reactor simply generates heat to produce steam.

The GAS TURBINE, similar in principle to the steam turbine except that the rotor is turned by hot gases produced by internal combustion, has been used experimentally in automobiles and is increasingly employed to power high-speed ships and locomotives. It is simple, light, and can produce very high speeds, but is expensive on fuel. It is, of course, an essential part of the JET ENGINE, in which the hot gases are thrust out at speed to drive an aircraft forward by reaction (instead of driving a rotor to turn a propeller). There is a limit to the speed at which a piston engine can turn, and to the altitude at which a propeller is effective, hence the adoption of the jet engine for high-speed aircraft.

If it can be made as efficient and reliable, a rotary engine is obviously more satisfactory than a reciprocating one. With the development of the revolutionary WANKEL ENGINE, which replaces the 150 or so moving parts of the normal automobile engine with two moving parts (both of which rotate), reciprocating engines may soon be obsolete.

Conventional electric motors are rotary. They are quiet, pollution-free, give excellent acceleration, and require no clutch. But they need electricity. With an onboard diesel to generate electricity, or with a track-side supply, electric traction is used for many modern trains. In the future, with an onboard FUEL CELL or solar cell, it may be more widely used in automobiles.

Linear engines. A rocket, like a jet engine, propels itself by reaction. But unlike the jet it carries its own oxygen and is thus the only form of propulsion that can as yet be used in space. It is at its most efficient at very high speeds, and although it has been tried experimentally on automobiles and aircraft, its real value is in space. Essentially the rocket has no moving parts, and its action is linear (in a straight line). Another "engine" with these features is the remarkable LINEAR INDUCTION MOTOR being developed for trains, in which opposed magnets provide propulsion. In conjunction with magnetic levitation (the use of opposed magnets to hold a vehicle just clear of the track), friction is nonexistent, and there are no moving parts. Very high speeds will be possible, with no wear, and no noise.

External combustion. The steam engine is one type of external-combustion engine. Another, the STIRLING ENGINE, was invented in 1816, and is today a possible pollution-free alternative to the internal-combustion engine for ships, road vehicles, and propeller-driven airplanes. One other form of less general application is that proposed for hypersonic aircraft. For flight at around 5,000 mph (8,000 km/h) fuel would be burned on the outside of the aircraft.

Engine tuning
Modifying the standard production engine of an automobile to achieve improved performance, particularly better acceleration and a higher top speed. Practically every mass-produced engine can benefit from tuning, but if engine power is to be increased substantially it may be necessary to carry out other modifications of the automobile, particu-

larly to the brakes to improve stopping power, and to the suspension to improve road-holding. Modifying an engine may result in shortening its life, since every component will be subjected to extra stress.

The most dramatic improvements in engine performance are brought about by modifying the cylinder head. First the surface of the combustion chambers and inlet and exhaust ports is polished. This allows a smoother flow of gases; they can also be reshaped to assist the flow and the inlet ports widened to allow more fuel mixture into the combustion space. Different-sized inlet valves may thus be required, and to cope with a higher-revving engine, the valve return springs may need to be strengthened. A layer of metal can be removed from the base of the cylinder head where it mates with the cylinder block. This reduces the volume of the combustion space and increases the compression ratio, making for greater combustion efficiency.

The inlet and exhaust manifolds need to be carefully aligned and mated so that there are no steps at the joints to create turbulence in the gas flow which could hinder engine "breathing." Ideally the exhaust manifold should have a large bore and have a branch leading from each cylinder. Including straight-through mufflers instead of those of the baffle type also improves breathing by reducing back pressure in the system. To benefit from a modified cylinder head the carburation must be improved. This is usually done by fitting larger-capacity or extra carburetors — replacing, for example, a single carburetor serving four cylinders with two twin-barrel carburetors, so that each cylinder is served by one barrel. Such improvements bring about an appreciable increase in engine power. More extensive modifications will increase performance still further. They include accurately balancing the crankshaft by grinding; fitting a new camshaft; overboring, or increasing the cylinder bore; and increasing the cylinder stroke, which will require a modified crankshaft.

Epicyclic gear

An essential part of an automatic gearbox. An epicyclic-gear train consists of a large central gear — the sun wheel — around which circle two smaller gears — the planets. The planet gears revolve around spindles on a U-shaped planet carrier. They mesh with the sun wheel and also with teeth on the inside of a ring or annulus. By holding still one of the components, the others can be made to rotate at different speeds and different directions, giving a variety of gear ratios.

For example, when the planets are locked the planet carrier turns the whole unit bodily in the same direction. With the planet carrier locked and the sun wheel rotating in one direction, the planets rotate and drive the annulus in the opposite direction.

Ericsson, John (1803-1889)

Swedish-born American engineer, best known as one of the earliest developers of the marine screw propeller and the builder of the *Monitor*, the first warship with an armored revolving turret. While living in England in 1836 Ericsson patented a screw propeller and built several ships of revolutionary design. Commissioned by the U.S. Navy to design the *Princeton*, the world's first screw-propelled warship, he came to the United States in 1839. During the Civil War Ericsson built a totally novel warship for the Union Navy, the famous *Monitor*. Jokingly called a "cheesebox on a raft," it opened the age of modern warships.

Erie Canal

Now part of the NEW YORK STATE BARGE CANAL SYSTEM, links Lake Erie with the Hudson River. When the canal was opened in 1825 it was 363 mi. (584 km) long, 40 ft. (12 m) wide, and 4 ft. (1.2 m) deep. It ran from Buffalo on Lake Erie, through Lake Oneida to Rome, N.Y.; from Rome it ran parallel to the Mohawk River to enter the Hudson just north of Troy. A total of 82 locks raised the level 500 ft. (152 m) from the Hudson to Lake Erie. The canal was later enlarged several times.

As a result of reconstruction in 1915-18 as part of the New York State Barge Canal System, the Erie Canal now has 34 locks and can take vessels with a 10-ft. (3 m) draft.

Escalator

Moving staircase designed to transport pedestrians from one level to another. Escalators were first introduced in the 1890s; they are extensively used in stores and public places.

An escalator consists of an endless series of steps independently fixed to chains which run around sprockets at the top and bottom. Each step is mounted on two two-wheeled assemblies, the forward pair running on separate rails from the rear pair. The rails are so positioned that the steps form a normal-shaped staircase; but at the top and bottom the configuration of the rails brings two or three treads level to make walking on or off easy. The risers of each step are curved so that they always keep close to one another.

Each step is covered with horizontal cleats; at top and bottom the cleats mesh with a tapered comb-plate which prevents any danger of tripping. A handrail moving at the same speed is provided at each side of the escalator. Safety precautions include emergency stop buttons; automatic stopping if anything jams the escalator; and a device which locks the steps in position if the escalator is stopped.

Escape velocity

The minimum speed at which an object must travel to escape the gravitational pull of a heavenly body. The earth's escape velocity is about 25,000 mph (40,000 km/h), while that of the moon, a much less massive body, is only about 5,300 mph (8,500 km/h).

Evans, Oliver (1755-1819)

American inventor and pioneer of steam locomotion. In 1805 he built a steam dredger grandly called *Oruktur Amphibolos* for the Philadelphia waterfront; to transport it from his workshop he mounted it on wheels driven by the dredger's steam engine, and drove it through the streets. The vehicle is regarded as America's first powered road vehicle. Evans developed the high-pressure steam engine that made America's great age of steamboats possible and pioneered a production line, complete with conveyers, elevators, and fully automatic operation, that was a century ahead of its time.

Exhaust system

The system in a motor vehicle that removes the spent gases from the engine cylinders after combustion and delivers them to the atmosphere away from the occupants. The system also has the function of silencing the gases, which are emitted by the engine at great speeds and are therefore potentially extremely noisy. The hot exhaust gases leave the cylinders through the exhaust valves and are collected by the exhaust manifold, which channels them to the exhaust pipe. They expand and lose speed as they travel along the pipe into one or more mufflers, which allow further expansion and silencing. Because of the pollutant effects of exhaust fumes, automobile manufacturers are now being required to take various steps often involving modifications to the exhaust system, including, for example, the addition of a catalytic converter (see EMISSION-CONTROL SYSTEMS).

Expressway

A multi-lane divided highway built specially for high-speed motor vehicle traffic. The expressway concept was born in Italy and Germany in the 1920s and was soon adopted in the United States. Expressway design aims at eliminating any contact between opposing traffic streams. Thus the traffic moves in each direction on lanes separated by a median strip or barrier. Access is limited and takes place at multi-level intersections. Cross-traffic passes under or over the expressway (see HIGHWAYS, ROADS, AND STREETS; TRAFFIC ENGINEERING).

External-combustion engine

A heat engine in which fuel is burned outside the engine to provide the heat necessary to run it, in contrast to the INTERNAL-COMBUSTION ENGINE. The STEAM ENGINE is an external-combustion engine. Fuel is burned in a separate furnace to provide heat to boil water into steam, which then powers the engine. The STIRLING ENGINE is another external-combustion engine, which works on hot gas.

The Kennedy expressway in Chicago's northwest side carries a very high volume of traffic and includes a twin track subway line, thus making good use of the central area between the roadways.

Fail-safe

A system which is designed to be safe if part of it fails. A well-known example of this in the field of transportation is the railroad AIR BRAKE. In order to release the brakes on his train, the driver has to apply a vacuum, that is, release air from the brake pipe. If for some reason this pipe is ruptured, atmospheric pressure rushes in, and the brakes are automatically applied. If the brakes worked on a pressurized system, rupture of the pipe would mean that the brakes could no longer be applied. Some automobiles have fail-safe braking systems in which a secondary circuit is activated if the main

brakes fail. A fail-safe system also works on nuclear reactors and prevents the chain reaction getting out of control. If the temperature in the core (a measure of the rate of reaction) rises unduly, neutron-absorbing control rods are inserted further in the core and reduce the number of neutrons available for reaction, and the reaction rate and temperature are lowered.

Fairlie locomotive

Unique locomotive design, patented in 1864, in effect two locomotives built back-to-back with a single footplate in the center. The frame is rigid but the wheel assemblies, or trucks, which in-

clude the driving wheels, are free to swivel. Fairlie locomotives can have two boilers with two fireboxes, two boilers with one firebox, or a single boiler only. These locomotives found particular application on sharply-curved, steep lines where a comparatively light locomotive was needed, especially on narrow-gauge railroads. Some of the biggest and fastest Fairlies, weighing 138 tons and having two six-coupled trucks, worked in Mexico.

Farman, Henri (1874-1958)

French aviator and airplane manufacturer, born in Paris of an English father. Farman took up flying in 1907, and the following year made the first flight of 0.61 mi. (1 km) in a closed circuit. In 1909 he made the first flight of more than 100 mi. (160 km). Farman founded a factory and a school of aviation, and in 1912 joined forces with his brother Maurice, who was also building airplanes. Farman bi-planes played a leading role in World War I, and the Farman factory became world-famous after the war.

Fathom

Traditional unit for measuring the depth of water, equal to 6 ft. (1.8 m).

Fatigue failure

Metal failure caused by repeated stress. At low stresses a ductile metal such as steel or aluminum stretches, but when the stress is removed, the metal returns to its original state. Beyond a certain stress, however, the deformation is permanent, and eventually a point is reached when the metal will fracture. Mild steel, for example, will fail when a stress of

A Fairlie locomotive on the early narrow gauge Festiniog railroad in Wales. Consisting essentially of two locomotives fixed back-to-back Fairlies were widely used in South America.

A crowded passenger and vehicle ferry on the Battery Park to Staten Island run, New York. Despite the shortness of the run radar equipment is vital in such a busy and occasionally fogbound waterway.

some 56.000 lb/sq. in. (386,106 kilopascals) is applied to it.

But mild steel may fail under much lower stress, if that stress is applied first in one direction, then in another, repeatedly. This is fatigue failure, and it produces a brittle fracture.

Fatigue failure may appear in all kinds of machinery and structures subjected to fluctuating stress or vibration. Airframes, for example, are subject to cyclic stresses, and this is a source of considerable danger in aviation practice (see COMET). Today test airframes are vibrated to destruction to ensure that fatigue failure will not occur during the anticipated lifetime of a plane.

Ferrous metals have a so-called endurance limit, which is the maximum stress that can be applied repeatedly without causing fatigue failure. Aluminum and magnesium alloys do not have an endurance limit. They will always fail after a certain number of stress cycles, however low the stress. So their behavior is defined in terms of fatigue strength, which is the maximum stress that can be repeatedly applied over a certain number of cycles without failure occurring. Fatigue failure almost invariably begins at irregularities on the surface of the metal. These points act as stress raisers. Under constantly repeated stress the metal crystals start to break up, and submicroscopic cracks form and spread. They eventually link together and visible cracks appear, weakening the metal so much that it eventually fails. Fatigue strength decreases as the temperature

increases. It is also adversely affected by corrosion and erosion, which provide potential sites for stress concentration.

Feeler gauge
A thin metal strip used for measuring the clearance between two parts — for example, the gap between the electrodes of a spark plug. Several strips of various thicknesses from about .002 to .025 in. are usually incorporated together in a swash.

Ferguson formula
A system of FOUR-WHEEL DRIVE.

Ferries
Boats or ships which carry people, goods, and vehicles across rivers, straits, bays, and other relatively short stretches of water. Most ferries are self-powered, although on very short crossings cable-hauled craft are sometimes used. Ferries range from flat-bottomed rafts or barges to sophisticated high-speed AIR-CUSHION VEHICLES and HYDROFOILS.

Early ferryboats were rowed, or towed by men or horses on the banks, later by tugs. Modern ferries are usually some 100 to 200 ft. (30 to 60 m) in length, and are often fitted with propellers and rudders at both ends to save turning around on a short crossing. Vehicle ferries are designed to dock end-on to a slipway, and if not double-ended are sometimes fitted with a turntable which rotates the entire load through 180° so that vehicles do not have to reverse off the ship.

Train ferries, with railroad tracks along the decks and often also equipped to carry road vehicles, are normally considerably larger. They are widely used, for example, across the English Channel to link the rail networks of Britain and continental Europe, and across the many stretches of water separating Denmark's principal islands from the mainland. Some Danish train ferries are well over 400 ft. (120 m) long, and one has four tracks across its breadth, giving a total track length of 1,350 ft. (510 m).

In North America train ferries were once common, especially on the Great Lakes. One of the earliest, operated by the Buffalo and Lake Huron Railroad, was opened in 1835, and as late as 1962 there were still 10 train ferries on Lake Michigan. But today the emphasis is on roll-on-roll-off (RoRo) road-vehicle ferries, which are more flexible in operation, and (wherever possible and economic) on the construction of bridges which avoid delays so often associated with ferries.

In recent years the British have pioneered the use of air-cushion vehicles operating high-speed ferry services. Most notable is the giant SRN 4, which crosses the English Channel at speeds of up to 77 knots, carrying 34 cars and 174 passengers. And on sheltered waters in Scandinavia, Russia, and elsewhere, hydrofoils have proved their value in providing smooth and rapid passenger and vehicle ferry services.

Festiniog Railway
Narrow-gauge Welsh railroad built between 1833 and 1836 to carry slate from the quarries of Blaenau Festiniog down to the sea at Portmadoc, 700 ft. (210 m) below. The gauge was 1 ft. 11½ in. and the length just over 13½ mi. (22 km). At first it carried only slate, but passengers were transported from 1865. It is claimed to be the first narrow-gauge railroad in the world, and it is preserved, with 9½ mi. (15 km) open and still worked by steam trains.

Fiat
Giant Italian industrial company best known for its automobiles, but also a producer of trucks and other commercial vehicles, aircraft engines and airplanes, marine engines and ships, and railroad cars. The company was founded in 1899, first made its name in the automobile racing world, and entered the mass market after World War I. Today it dominates the Italian automobile market with about 80% of all sales, and has factories or assembly plants in some 25 countries. The main foreign companies are Fiat-Concord (Argentina), Polski-Fiat (Poland), SEAT (Spain), Steyr-Puch (Austria) and

VAZ (Soviet Union — Fiat was the first major European automobile company with a factory in Russia).
The firm also owns Lancia, and has substantial holdings in Ferrari and Citroën.

Filters

Devices incorporated in the air, fuel, and lubrication systems of an engine to remove dirt which might otherwise penetrate inside the engine and cause wear or reduce efficiency.
Several types of filters may be used in air cleaners. Probably the commonest employs a paper element, consisting of a ring of corrugated paper treated with resin. It needs replacing when it is dirty, usually after about 12,000 mi. (19,200 km) in average conditions. In the metal-mesh type, the air is filtered as it passes through a metal mesh wetted by an oil film. It needs cleaning periodically and re-oiling. In the oil-bath type, useful in dust-laden atmospheres, the incoming air picks up oil from an oil bath, while shedding some of its dust, and is then rid of the oil and residual dust as it passes through a wire-mesh ring.
Two or more filters are generally fitted in the fuel system. In the fuel tank itself is a fairly coarse wire-mesh filter, and there is usually a similar filter in the fuel pump, and sometimes also one in the fuel line between pump and carburetor. Two filters are generally incorporated in the lubrication system, a fairly coarse gauze in the sump itself, which eliminates large particles, and a resin-impregnated paper element filter, which eliminates fine particles. This is usually located in a replaceable canister outside the crankcase.

Final drive

The part of a vehicle's transmission system which applies engine power to the road wheels. In a conventional automobile, with the front engine driving the rear wheels, the final drive consists of crown wheel and pinion, DIFFERENTIAL, and half-shafts leading to the driving wheels.
Power into the final drive comes from the drive shaft. A small bevel pinion on the end of the shaft meshes at right angles with the large crown wheel and turns it, effecting a necessary reduction in speed of about 4:1. The differential gear arrangement meshing the crown wheel with the half-shafts permits the individual half-shafts to move at different speeds when the vehicle is cornering. The final drive in a front-wheel drive design is incorporated in the gearbox-transmission unit. The short drive shafts between the final drive and wheel axles have rubber-mounted universal joints at each end to cushion transmission shock, as might occur when starting from rest.

Firing order

The order in which the cylinders in an engine fire. In a simple four-cylinder gasoline engine, the order is usually 1, 3, 4, 2, the numbers indicating the positions of the cylinders counting from the front of the engine. The firing order is arranged in this way in order to minimize stress on the crankshaft and bearings, and allows smoother running than would be obtained with a straightforward 1, 2, 3, 4 firing sequence.

Fitch, John (1743-1798)

American brassworker and gunsmith, builder of one of the earliest steamboats. It was 45 ft. (13.7 m) long, and first operated on the Delaware River in 1787. With his next vessel, 60 ft. (18 m) long, Fitch operated a regular service between Philadelphia and Burlington, N.J., but could not make it pay. Fitch went to France in search of backing, but returned disappointed and died destitute a few years later.

Flag codes

Means used for signaling since ancient times, and still used particularly at sea. In *semaphore signaling*, a man holds a flag in each hand; the position of the flags indicates a letter of the alphabet or a numeral. A single flag can be waved to indicate the dots and dashes of the Morse code.
The *International Flag Code* is used for signaling between ships at sea. It consists of 40 flags and pennants representing the letters of the alphabet, numerals, and repeaters. With these flags some 400,000 different signals can be made, using hoists of many flags. Messages can be spelled out, but if a ship flies the "code and answering" pennant it is sending and receiving messages according to the international code, which covers most eventualities at sea. A code book is published in seven languages.

Flag of convenience

A system of ship operation whereby a shipping company registers its vessels under a foreign flag (the "flag of convenience") to avoid tax and safety regulations of the home government. Most maritime nations only allow properly qualified and experienced personnel to command and crew ships sailing under the national flag, and government and classification inspectors ensure that all vessels are built, equipped and maintained to comply with high national and international standards.
Flag of convenience nations permit foreign ownership or control of "their" ships, and enforce few if any standards of quality or training. The leading flag of convenience countries include Liberia (with by far the largest merchant fleet in the world), Panama, Cyprus, Singapore, Somalia, and Lebanon (see MERCHANT MARINE).
Before World War II Britain, the United States, Japan, and the maritime nations of Western Europe between them owned some 90% of the world's merchant fleet. Today flag of convenience fleets account for over one-fifth of world shipping, and for a much higher proportion of accidents and losses at sea (in 1973, for example, they accounted for over 50% of the tonnage lost).

U.S. Air Force transport and fighter planes demonstrate flight refueling, an operation which demands very accurate maneuvering.

A large passenger carrying flying boat of the 1930s, the Short Empire class Canopus.

Flaps

To improve the handling qualities of an airplane at low speeds, flaps are fitted to the inboard section of the wing trailing edges. Lowering or extending the flaps increases the camber of the wing and thus the lift it is able to provide (see WINGS). As a result, the STALLING speed of the aircraft becomes lower and the landing speed is reduced. The use of flaps also increases the drag exerted on the airplane by the SLIPSTREAM, so that the landing approach follows a steeper angle of descent to the runway. The use of flaps on takeoff again augments the lift, and permits a steep climb out.

Simple flaps are merely hinged surfaces at the back edge of a wing. To preserve smooth airflow over the upper part of the wing, split flaps fitted only to the lower surface may be used. A variation of this pattern is the Fowler flap that extends backwards and has the additional advantage of increasing the actual wing area.

Slotted flaps have a gap at the hinge line between the wing and the flap through which the airflow is speeded up, thus delaying the onset of the TURBULENCE that leads to stalling. Leading-edge slats perform a similar function but are located at the front of the wing. At low speeds they open automatically and the airflow is speeded up through the gap between the slat and the wing to delay the onset of a stall. At high speed they are held shut by the air pressure.

Flight refueling

The passing of fuel from one aircraft to another in flight has not been adopted commercially, but it is a technique that greatly increases the range of military aircraft. The first pipeline refueling was made by two U.S. Army DH-4B biplanes in 1923. By 1939 the British pioneer, Sir Alan Cobham, was conducting trans-atlantic trials. In the late 1940s the U.S.A.F. introduced inflight refueling on a large scale. Boeing developed the "flying boom" method for the Strategic Air Command, whose current tanker-transport is the KC-135 — a basic Boeing 707. The Russian "looped hose" transfer was jointly developed by the U.S. and U.K. Other commands and the U.S. Navy adopted the British "probe and drogue" system, in which the receiver's probe connects into a drogue at the end of a hose trailing from the tanker. Certain helicopters are also fitted for inflight refueling.

Floating axle

A type of rear-axle arrangement in motor vehicles. In a semi-floating axle the half-shafts that carry the driving wheels are supported by bearings inside the axle housing. In a three-fourths floating axle the outer bearing is fitted between the axle housing and the wheel hub. In a semi-floating axle the half-shafts must bear the weight of the vehicle as well as transmit torque. In the three-fourths floating axle the half-shafts are subject only to bending on cornering. A fully-floating axle has two bearings between axle and hub, which support the weight of the car and withstand cornering forces.

Floating dock

A floating enclosed basin used for inspection and repair work on ships when there is no DRY DOCK available. The floating dock is cradle-shaped, and built up as a series of watertight ballast tanks. When a ship is to be docked, sufficient water is let into the ballast tanks to submerge the dock, so that the vessel can be floated in. Water is then pumped out until the ship is high and dry, after which inspection and repairs can be carried out exactly as in a dry dock. When work is complete, the floating dock is again submerged, and the ship floated out. Although usually constructed, like a ship, of steel, floating docks have also been made of reinforced concrete or timber. Floating docks are equipped with the traveling cranes and other equipment needed for ship repairs, and they can if necessary be towed from place to place.

Float plane

Aircraft intended for operation off water which are equipped with planing surfaces not an integral part of the fuselage. Normally there are two long floats, or pontoons, mounted below the fuselage. Subsidiary stabilizing floats towards the wing tip are unnecessary. Some single-engined float planes have only a single central float, however, and are equipped with auxiliary stabilizing floats.

Fluid flywheel

A form of fluid coupling often used in vehicles with AUTOMATIC TRANSMISSION. It consists of two basic parts — an impeller driven by the engine, and a turbine connected to the shaft leading to the gearbox. It thus differs from the TORQUE CONVERTOR, which has a reactor between impeller and turbine. The two parts of the fluid flywheel are roughly bowl-shaped and have vanes on their inside faces. They are housed in an oil-filled casing. When the engine is running, the impeller turns, imparting its centrifugal motion to the oil, which is directed against the vanes of the turbine. If the engine speed is sufficiently high, the oil will force the turbine to rotate, thus driving the automobile. The higher the engine speed, the greater will be the turning effect. The slip between impeller and turbine is significant only at low engine speeds.

Fluid mechanics

The science concerned with the study of fluids, gases as well as liquids. It plays an essential part in the design of planes and vehicles traveling through the air, of ships and submarines traveling through water, of hydraulic systems, and of pipelines. Fluid mechanics comprises fluid statics, the study of fluids at rest, and fluid dynamics, the study of fluids in motion. Fluid mechanics incorporates aerostatics, which deales with air and other gases at rest, and HYDROSTATICS, which deals with water and other liquids at rest, and the forces acting on bodies within these fluids. Fluid dynamics is subdivided into AERODYNAMICS, the study of air and other gases in motion and of bodies traveling through them; and hydrodynamics, or hydraulics, the study of liquids, particularly water, in motion and of bodies traveling through them (see also BERNOULLI'S PRINCIPLE; HYDRAULIC SYSTEMS; LAMINAR FLOW; REYNOLD'S NUMBER).

Flyer

Name given by the WRIGHT BROTHERS to their first powered airplane. On December 17, 1903, *Flyer* reached a speed of 8 mph (13 km/h) traveling into a 21-mph (34 km/h) headwind, and took off. This flight lasted just 12 seconds, but a later flight on the same day was 59 seconds long and covered 852 ft. (260 m). They were the world's first sustained man-carrying powered flights.

Flyer, a biplane with a wing span of 40 ft. 4 in. (12.2 m), a wing area of 510 sq. ft. (47 m²), and a length of 19 ft. 9 in. (6 m), had two pusher-propellers driven by bicycle chains and powered by a gasoline engine designed and built by the Wrights. Control was by double rudder and elevator structures, and by wing warping (a system of twisting the wing tips to achieve controlled banked turns). The pilot lay on the lower wing beside the engine.

Later designated *Flyer I*, this historic airplane was followed by *Flyer II* and in 1905 by *Flyer III*, generally considered the world's first fully practical airplane.

Flying Bedstead

Name given to two experimental Rolls-Royce aircraft engine thrust measuring rigs, looking somewhat like four-poster beds. Powered by two Nene jet engines, the first rig made tethered flights in July 1953, followed by free flights from August 1954. These constituted the first VTOL aircraft flights that did not use rotating wings.

Flying boat

When the principal planing surface of a large aircraft designed for operation off water is an integral part of the fuselage, the aircraft is known as a flying boat. Subsidiary stabilizing floats are usually fitted towards the wing tips, or alternatively there may be sponsons attached to the fuselage sides.

Since flying boats do not require expensive runways and enjoy a safety factor in the event of an emergency over the ocean, they were at one time favored for intercontinental flights. In the 1930s American flying boats pioneered commercial transpacific air routes and shared commercial proving flights across the North Atlantic with British Short C-class flying boats. Landplanes have now proved to be substantially faster because of the high airflow drag experienced with a bulky flying boat hull, and the reliability of modern aircraft engines largely discounts the safety factor.

Flying platform

A jet-propelled machine with helicopter-like mobility. One type under development is the WASP (Williams Aerial Systems Platform), which is essentially a small turbofan engine with a platform and handle-bars attached. Moving the handle-bars operates ducts that direct the exhaust in the appropriate direction to control lift, propulsion, and trim. Potentially the WASP has a top speed of 75 mph (120 km/h). STAMP (Small Tactical Aerial Mobility Platform) is a two-man vehicle being developed on similar lines for the U.S. Marine Corps.

Flying Scotsman

Famous British train which has left King's Cross Station, London, at 10 a.m. daily since June 1862 to run the 393 mi. (630 km) to Edinburgh, Scotland. The name has also been given to one of the 155-ton 4-6-2 "Pacific" locomotives built by Sir Nigel Gresley in the 1920s to haul this and other long-distance high-speed trains. This impressive locomotive is preserved and has toured the United States.

Fokker, Anthony (1890-1939)

Pioneer Dutch airplane manufacturer. He offered his services unsuccessfully to the Dutch, British, French, and Belgian governments, and finally set up a factory in Germany in 1912 which built warplanes, and developed a device to permit firing a machine gun through the propeller arc. After the war Fokker set up factories in the United States and the Netherlands, Fokker planes making the first non-stop crossing of the United States (1923), the first flight over the North Pole (1926), and the first crossing of the Pacific (1928). Fokker himself earned the nickname "the flying Dutchman." The Dutch *Fokker Friendship* and *Fellowship* have been among the most successful small airliners of modern times.

Ford, Henry (1863-1947)

American automobile engineer and manufacturer, founder of the Ford Motor Company. He is renowned as pioneer of the modern moving assembly-line method of mass-producing automobiles.

Ford was born at Greenfield, Michigan, and started work as a machinist in

A freighter high and dry for repairs in a floating dock. When work is complete the dock will be submerged and the ship floated out.

Flywheel

A heavy wheel attached to a shaft to reduce speed fluctuations and maintain even running. Flywheels are incorporated in reciprocating engines to keep the engine running smoothly between the power strokes of the pistons. Without the flywheel the rotation of the output shaft would be uneven and jerky.

In the gasoline engine the flywheel is located at the end of the crankshaft and connects with the transmission system. It has a toothed ring around its edge, called the starter ring. This engages with a pinion on the STARTER MOTOR for starting the engine.

Detroit. In about 1890 he began to experiment with engines and three years later built his first gasoline engine. He constructed his first automobile in 1896. Three years later he launched a company producing cars of his own design and in 1903 organized the Ford Motor Company. For a while Ford produced cars in the traditional manner with the work of construction and assembly being done by skilled engineers and craftsmen. The resulting vehicle was therefore relatively expensive and could be produced only in small numbers.

Ford's great contribution to the automobile industry was to design a means of

Henry Ford driving his first automobile. Built in 1896, the vehicle created such a sensation in the streets of Detroit that Ford had to chain it to a lamppost when he left it unattended.

Four-stroke cycle

The operating cycle of most gasoline and diesel engines, also called the Otto cycle, after Nikolaus August Otto, who introduced it (in a gas engine) in 1876. Power is produced on only one of the four strokes, in contrast to the TWO-STROKE CYCLE, in which power is produced every other stroke.

The four stages in the cycle are induction, compression, power, and exhaust. In a conventional reciprocating gasoline engine induction of fuel-air mixture through the open inlet valve occurs on the downstroke of the piston; the exhaust valve is closed. Then the inlet valve closes, and compression of the mixture begins as the piston rises on its upward compression stroke. When the piston has almost reached the top of its stroke, the spark plug ignites the fuel. The piston is forced down by the expanding gases on its power stroke, driving round the engine crankshaft via connecting rod and crank. As the piston begins to travel upward on its final exhaust stroke, the exhaust valve opens and the spent gases are expelled through it. The exhaust valve then closes, and the inlet valve begins to open as the piston moves down on the first stroke (induction) of the next cycle.

The operating cycle of the DIESEL ENGINE is

producing cars for a mass market which his own innovations created. First he decided to concentrate on a single model. He kept the design simple, but used high-quality materials throughout. Eventually he introduced the moving conveyor into assembly-line production, a radical improvement on Ransom Olds's static assembly line. In October 1908 the result of his revolutionary thinking began production — the Model T Ford. No major modifications were ever made to the design of the Model T, which enjoyed a total production run of more than 15 million vehicles over a span of 19 years. The disparaging nickname for the Model T — the "TIN LIZZIE" — referred to its flimsy appearance compared to the heavily built cars of the day. This was, in fact, due to the use of high-grade alloy steel in construction.

The "Tin Lizzie" established Ford's reputation, made his company prosperous and Ford a millionaire. He introduced a minimum wage of $5 a day, extended his factory, and bought out other shareholders in the company when they opposed his ideas. The Ford family retained sole control of the Ford empire until 1956. In 1919 Ford handed over nominal control to his son Edsel Bryant Ford (1893-1943), but resumed the presidency of the company after Edsel's death until his

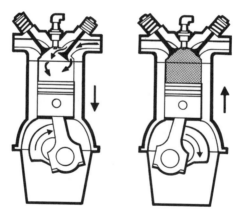
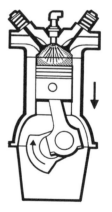
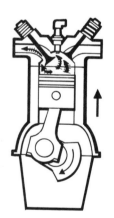

grandson, Henry Ford II (1917-   ), succeeded him.

Formula racing
See AUTOMOBILE RACING.

Forth Rail Bridge
A famous cantilever bridge over the Firth of Forth in Scotland. It is of triple-trussed steel cantilever design with twin main spans of 1,710 ft. (521 m). Designed by Sir John Fowler and Sir Benjamin Baker, it was completed in 1890 after eight years' work. It carries twin railroad tracks 150 ft. (45 m) above the water. The QUEBEC BRIDGE is the only cantilever bridge with a longer span.

The four-stroke cycle. From left to right: induction, compression, power, and exhaust.

basically similar, but with important differences. On the induction stroke only air is taken in. And at the top of the compression stroke diesel oil is injected into the combustion space. Ignition comes about because the temperature produced as a result of compression is greater than the flash point of the fuel, which thus burns spontaneously. In the rotary WANKEL ENGINE, which has no pistons, the four stages of induction, compression, power, and exhaust, occur simultaneously within different segments of the figure-of-eight casing.

The France, *the world's longest ever passenger liner. Like all other large liners, with the exception of the QE 2, the* France *has been withdrawn from service.*

Four-wheel drive

A vehicle transmission system in which the engine drives all four wheels instead of the normal two wheels. Cross-country vehicles such as Jeeps generally have this capability, enabling them to negotiate difficult terrain that would be impassable to conventional vehicles. Four-wheel drive vehicles usually operate on two-wheel drive on good road surfaces; the driver can engage four-wheel drive when he encounters bad surfaces.

A few high-performance sedans have a continuously operative four-wheel drive. One system, known as the Ferguson formula, incorporates a master differential that regulates the torque transmitted to front and rear wheels, which must travel at slightly different speeds when turning.

France

The longest passenger liner ever built, and the third largest in terms of tonnage (only exceeded by the original *Queen Elizabeth* and the *Queen Mary*). Some 1,035 ft. (315.5 m) long, 110 ft. (33.5 m) wide, with a gross tonnage of 66,300, a speed of 31 knots, and accommodation for 2,044 passengers, the prestigious *France* was from her maiden voyage in 1962 until her withdrawal from service in 1974 flagship of the Compagnie Générale Transatlantique.

Like the American *United States*, the

Italian *Michelangelo*, and other great transatlantic liners of recent years, the *France* ran at an enormous loss and had to be retired long before the end of her useful life.

Free-piston engine

A composite engine incorporating free-moving pistons and having a gas turbine as its power producer. Free-piston engines are used to power some ships and show a relatively high efficiency (35% or more). A typical free-piston engine has a pair of opposing pistons in a cylinder. Burning diesel fuel in the space between the pistons forces them apart. As they move they compress air at the ends of the cylinder. This pushes the pistons back towards the center, compressing air in the combustion space between them. Diesel fuel is injected into the hot compressed air and burns. The hot gases produced go to drive the turbine.

Freeway

A toll-free controlled-access divided highway. California's freeway system of 3,600 mi. (5,960 km) is the densest in the world, and is being further extended to meet the demands of the state's 14 million registered vehicles. It is possible to drive for over 500 mi. (800 km) at a stretch without meeting a single intersection or traffic light.

Freighters

Ships designed to carry freight, whether locally along the coast, or internationally across the oceans. They range from small coasters through general cargo liners and specialized bulk freighters, to giant tankers, the largest mobile objects ever built.

Since very early times water transportation has played an important role in the life of civilizations, and that role has become ever more vital with the continuing growth of industry and technology over the centuries. Even today no other form of transport can match it in the promotion of international trade, and its importance in the modern world is shown by the fact that during the 1960s the amount of freight carried by ships doubled to reach the figure of 2,570,000,000 tons at the end of the decade.

The ancient civilizations of the Mediterranean traded as far as Britain, East Africa and India in "round ships," tubby sailing vessels very different from the long pointed warships of the time. But from the Middle Ages until the mid-19th century, freighters differed little from warships, and were often (see EAST INDIAMEN) almost as well armed.

Then, the development of steam propulsion and of iron and later steel ships, and the opening of the SUEZ CANAL in 1869, led to a great expansion of trade

A cutaway view of a large tanker, showing how the steam turbine propulsion machinery, and the bridge and crew facilities are aft of and isolated from the cargo tanks.

and to rapid developments in freighters. Their main job was to carry raw materials (coal, oil, minerals, etc.) to centers of industry, and foodstuffs such as grain, sugar, fruit, and meat to centers of population.

The refrigerated ship made its appearance in the 1870s with the French *Frigorifique*. The first true oil TANKER appeared in the 1880s. Until then, oil had been carried in barrels aboard ordinary general freighters. It has only been since World War II, and especially during the last 15 or 20 years, that the modern freighter has come into being. Before the war the big ships were all passenger liners, and the typical freighter (bulk carriers included) was around 400 ft. (120 m) in length, was usually powered by steam turbines, and had a speed of less than 15 knots. Then, during the 1960s, came rapid rises in labor costs, and an enormous increase in international trade. These two factors brought about a revolution in freighters, with an emphasis on speed, automation, specialization, and improved methods of cargo handling.

The vast majority of freighters today are powered by diesel engines, with the notable exception of supertankers which normally have steam turbines, and are capable of speeds of over 20 knots. Russia has experimented with gas turbines (usually reserved for high-speed naval craft), and the United States with nuclear propulsion (see SAVANNAH). All large ships have highly automated engine rooms which require minimum maintenance and a relatively small crew (an important factor in keeping costs down). Coasters have changed least of all, since

A bulk ore/coal freighter. Bulk ships which can carry a variety of cargoes are increasingly popular as they do not have to make the return voyage "in ballast."

the nature of their work keeps them small. Trading from port to port along the coast, their role is to extend a country's internal transportation system, and to relieve the pressure on docks by taking cargoes directly off oceangoing vessels for distribution to small ports unable to take large ships. Coasters are in effect small brothers of the big freighters, and like them them appear in many forms, from general cargo ships to bulk carriers.

New methods have been evolved to speed up the inevitably slow process of loading and discharging general cargo liners. Increasing use is made of pallets (standard wooden platforms on which goods are stacked), and some of the latest ships have side hatches and elevator systems which enable the maximum use to be made of fork lift trucks. The roll-on-roll-off ship is a recent development of the

general cargo liner. With large openings at bow, stern and in the side, vehicles simply drive on at one port, and off at their destination. Such vessels may have as many as seven vehicle decks, and can be adapted to take automobiles or fully loaded trucks (or trailers). Much space is inevitably wasted in roll-on-roll-off ships, but this disadvantage is compensated for by speed and flexibility of handling, and the system is especially valuable on short routes.

Container ships bring the advantages of BULK CARRIERS (size, speed, and economy) to all forms of general cargo that can be pre-packed in standard sized containers (see CONTAINERIZATION). Instead of the usual holds, a container ship is subdivided into cells, each of which takes one container. Once loaded to deck level, the hatches are closed, and one or two further layers are stowed on deck. Carrying

700 or 800 standard 20-ft. (6 m) containers, cruising at about 20 knots, and with a turn-round time of 36 hours or less, container ships can in a given period carry three times as much freight as a conventional general cargo ship.

The LASH (lighter-aboard-ship) vessel is a recent variant on the container ship. Equipped with a large traveling gantry crane to lift the lighters (very large floating steel containers) from the water, turn round is very rapid, and a wide variety of commodities can be carried in the lighters.

Liquid bulk cargo and "liquid" dry bulk such as grain are easily and rapidly handled by automated pumps which measure the flow and direct it from or to the various holds or tanks to maintain the ship's stability. A recent development brings the same advantages to dry bulk such as iron ore, which is now mixed with water into a pumpable slurry.

A Great Lakes bulk freighter, with engines aft and bridge at the bow.

Liner and charter. In terms of method of operation there are two main types of freighters: the liner and the chartered "tramp" ship. A freight liner operates a scheduled service on a specified route, and usually carries a wide assortment of general cargo from possibly hundreds of different companies. The system is expensive since loading and discharge are slow, and extensive handling and storage facilities must be provided at every port en route. But for small consignments freight liners provide an essential service. Whenever possible, however, freight is carried in bulk in more or less specialized bulk carriers, and these are the basis of tramp-charter operations. Tramp-ship owners looking for cargoes, and shipping companies with freight looking for ships conduct their business through brokers. The most important center for such negotiations is the so-called Baltic Exchange in London. Rates vary from day to day according to supply and demand. The system, which is not unlike buying and selling on the stock exchange, ensures maximum competition and minimum prices, and demands great skill and judgment from all concerned. Shipowners must look ahead and try and have their ships in the right place at the right time, while shippers must find the best ship at the lowest price. Ships are normally chartered to carry a specified cargo between two ports, although they may be hired for a specified period of time.

There is in fact a third method of operation, in a sense a cross between the liner and tramp-charter systems. Here large companies (importers of oil, ore, sugar, and other bulk commodities) operate their own fleets of bulk carriers exclusively on company business. If work is slack they may charter their vessels as tramps, while in the reverse situation they may charter additional ships.

Friction clutch

A device for connecting or disconnecting two co-axial shafts, which grips on account of the friction between the two plates in contact (see CLUTCH).

Frigate

A fast naval ship. Originally used to describe a GALLEY-like craft with oars and sail, the term was adopted in the 18th century for a three-masted warship carrying up to 50 guns (one class below a SHIP O' THE LINE). The term went out of use during the late 19th century, but was revived in World War II to describe antisubmarine convoy escort ships. Today the term has no generally agreed meaning. In the U.S. Navy a frigate is larger than a destroyer and is often armed with guided missiles. In the British Navy frigates are smaller than destroyers.

A typical coaster in rough seas.

Front-wheel drive

A type of transmission used in many automobiles, in which an engine mounted at the front of the vehicle drives the front wheels. This is in contrast with the orthodox system of rear-wheel drive, in which a front engine drives the rear wheels. In general, front-wheel drive vehicles exhibit better road-holding than conventional rear-wheel drive vehicles, because the wheels pull the vehicle along rather than push it, and also because the greatest weight is over the driving wheels.

With front-wheel design, there is no need for a DRIVE SHAFT, and the FINAL DRIVE is incorporated with the gearbox. Because the engine must move in relation to the wheels, universal joints are fitted each side of the final drive, connecting with short half-shafts. At their other ends the half-shafts are linked by a special kind of universal joint, the constant-velocity joint, which allows drive to the wheels at any angle.

Fuel cell

A power source that produces electricity by means of a chemical reaction. British engineer Francis Bacon developed the most successful kind of fuel cell in 1959. It works by making hydrogen and oxygen combine to make water. The gases are fed to porous electrodes in an electrolyte. Such fuel cells were developed for the Apollo spacecraft where they provided not only electricity, but also drinking water for the astronauts. Fuel cells are a possible power source for terrestrial vehicles as well. A few experimental electric vehicles powered by fuel cells have already been tested. They possess the great advantage of producing no pollution.

Fuel gauge

In an automobile, a float-operated instrument indicating the amount of gasoline remaining in the tank. An arm attached to the float is connected to a rheostat (variable resistor). As the level changes, the resistance changes, causing the current through the gauge to alter. The current moves a gauge needle on the dashboard.

Fuel injection

In most GASOLINE ENGINES carburation provides a suitable fuel mixture for burning in the cylinders. Air is mixed with gasoline in a CARBURETOR, and the mixture is delivered to the cylinders by the inlet manifolds. In some engines, however, gasoline is squirted directly into the inlet duct of each cylinder — this is called fuel injection. Compared with carburation, fuel injection is expensive and requires expert maintenance. But it results in better acceleration, better response, and more power.

In a fuel-injection system a precisely metered amount of gasoline is sprayed under pressure through an injector in front of the inlet valve in each cylinder. Supply to the injectors may be controlled mechanically or electronically. The mechanical system uses a metering distributor containing a rotor driven by the engine, and a shuttle. The shuttle moves back and forth under fuel pressure, allowing fuel to flow to the injectors, which adjusts the flow. Information about engine conditions is constantly fed to the control unit by numerous sensors. The injectors themselves are opened by a solenoid directed by the control unit.

A fuel-injection method is also used in the DIESEL ENGINE, but in this case fuel is sprayed directly into the engine cylinders, where it immediately vaporizes and burns in the heat developed by compression.

Fuels

The engines that power vehicles, ships, planes, and rockets are generally heat engines — engines in which some kind of fuel is burned to produce heat, and hot steam or gases push pistons up and down or rotate turbines to produce motive power. In machines with electric propulsion, the electricity as a rule is ultimately produced by power stations burning fuel. In the past, solid fuels, notably wood and coal, were of prime importance, but in this century liquid fuels derived from petroleum and natural gas have become preeminent. The development of rocketry has led to the production of more exotic chemical fuels (see PROPELLANTS) and NUCLEAR PROPULSION, of course, requires nuclear fuels. In addition, FUEL CELLS have been developed which produce electricity directly from chemical reactions.

The heating value of a conventional fuel is expressed in terms of calorific value. This is the number of British Thermal Units (Btu) released per pound of fuel when it is burned. Wood has the low calorific value (CV) of about 7,000 Btu/lb.; coal has a CV of nearly double that; gasoline has a CV of more than 20,000 Btu/lb. The calorific value of gases is expressed in terms of Btu per cubic foot. Manufactured coal gas has a CV of about 550 Btu/cu. ft., while natural gas has a CV of more than 1,000 Btu/cu. ft.

Wood has long since been superseded as a significant fuel, but coal is still of enormous importance for generating electricity. In coal-burning generating plants today coal is generally burned in finely-divided, pulverized form to increase combustion efficiency. Like the other major fuels, coal consists mainly of hydrocarbons — compounds of hydrogen and carbon. Heat is released when the hydrogen and carbon combine with the oxygen of the air to form water and carbon dioxide respectively — if combustion is complete. There are several grades of coal, varying in carbon content, impurities, and calorific value. The lowest grade is lignite. Then come the common bituminous coals, which include the so-called "steam coals" used in locomotives and ships' furnaces. The highest grade of coal, which contains more than 93% carbon, leaves little ash, and is virtually smokeless, is anthracite.

The most important liquid fuels are those derived from petroleum. They are separated by distillation as fractions boiling within a certain temperature range. The straight-run fractions may be supplemented by others that have undergone further refining. The main fractions are gasoline (boiling between about 40° and 200°C), kerosene (140°-250°C), gas oils and diesel oils (250°-340°C), and residual fuel oils (200° upwards). The specific gravity of the fractions increases from about 0.7 for gasoline (water = 1) to over 1 for heavy fuel oils.

Gasoline is used in automobile engines and aircraft piston engines; kerosene in aircraft jet engines and rockets; gas oil in making oil gas; diesel oil in compression-ignition engines or diesels; and fuel oils in industrial furnaces, ships' boilers, and generating stations. A typical petroleum sample would yield about 45% gasoline, 5% kerosene, 16% gas/diesel oils, 25% fuel oils, and 9% lubricating oil, greases, wax, tar, and the like.

As fuels, the petroleum fractions have many advantages. They are high in calorific value; they produce little or no ash when they burn; combustion is easy to control; and they are easy and clean to handle. Similar advantages are associated with natural gas. It contains mainly methane, propane, and butane. It can readily be liquefied, and in this form has been used to power modified gasoline engines. Alcohol has also been used occasionally as a fuel, usually as an additive to gasoline. It is included, for example, in gasoline used in automobile racing engines and in aviation gasoline. It is valuable in having a very high anti-knock rating. Both methyl alcohol (methanol) and ethyl alcohol (ethanol) are employed.

Fuel system

The fuel system of a GASOLINE ENGINE, comprises the fuel tank, pipeline, pump, carburetor or injector, and inlet manifold. The fuel tank is mounted at a distance from the engine to reduce the fire

The modern general cargo freighter is equipped with a variety of handling gear to facilitate loading and discharge. Here one of the derricks on the American freighter Panama is being used to unload a small truck.

Bulk freighters force their way through ice on the Great Lakes. Various possibilities are being researched to keep the Lakes navigable through the winter.

A massive piece of equipment is loaded into the cargo hold of a large freight airplane. As with many freight planes, the entire tail (or nose) can be swung out to one side to facilitate loading and discharge.

Helicopters are invaluable for transporting heavy materials to inaccessible areas, and for lighter agricultural duties such as crop spraying. This small machine is carrying hay in the Blue Mountain region of New South Wales, Australia.

and mizzen; each is divided into three parts (mast, topmast, and topgallant mast), and most sails take their name from their mast and their position on it. Thus, in ascending order, the square sails on the mainmast are mainsail, main lower topsail, main upper topsail, main topgallant sail, main royal, and main skysail (with the occasional addition of cloudscraper, moonraker and stargazer). Stun'sails (studding sails) were often added on either side of the principal sails on fore and main masts to give added speed.

The largest full-rigged ship ever built was the steel five-masted *Preussen*, with a displacement of 11,400 tons.

Fulton, Robert (1765-1815)

American inventor whose steamboat CLERMONT (1807) was the world's first commercially successful steam-powered vessel. Born in Lancaster County, Pennsylvania, Fulton began work as an artist. He was not a success, and turned to

Robert Fulton, American inventor and pioneer of steamboats and submarines.

A full-rigged ship, with five square sails on each mast. Such vessels continued in service as freighters until the 1930s but are today used as training ships and for sport.

hazard. Baffles within the tank prevent the fuel from surging back and forth when the vehicle changes speed or direction abruptly.

The fuel is pumped from the tank to the engine by an electrical or mechanical pump. A diaphragm in the pump draws fuel in through one one-way valve as it moves back and expels it through another one-way valve as it moves forward. In an electrical pump the diaphragm is operated by a solenoid, and in the mechanical pump by means of a lever moved up and down by a cam on the engine camshaft. Filters are incorporated within the pumps to eliminate dirt.

In an engine with carburation the fuel is pumped into the FLOAT CHAMBER, which acts as a reservoir, and then enters the CARBURETOR or carburetors. Inside the

carburetor it mixes with filtered air and vaporizes. The vapor is then sucked into the combustion chamber via the inlet manifold. In the alternative FUEL-INJECTION system, fuel is pumped from the tank and injected in carefully metered amounts into the inlet ports to the cylinders.

Full-rigged ship

Sailing ship with three or more masts, each carrying a full complement of square sails, and with a number of fore-and-aft sails which may include staysails (set on lines called stays running forward and down between the masts), jibs (set between foremast and bowsprit), and gaff sails (set on booms pivoting from the foot of the main and mizzen masts).

On the normal three-masted full-rigger, the masts are known as the fore, main,

canal engineering, publishing a treatise on the subject in 1796. This too was a failure, and in 1797 Fulton traveled to France and proposed building a submarine for the French government. This, and a later version offered to the British, was a limited if impractical success (see SUBMARINES).

Meanwhile he had begun work on a steamboat, and shipped the parts from France to America in 1806. The craft was ready in 1807, and completed its 150 mi. (240 km) trial run from New York to Albany in 32 hours (compared to the four days taken by sailing vessels). Following the *Clermont*'s success, Fulton built several other steamboats for service on the Hudson and Raritan rivers, and as ferries for river crossings. Then in 1814, he constructed the world's first steam-powered warship, *Demologos*, a twin-hulled craft with the paddle wheel between the hulls, and a top speed of 6.35 knots.

Funicular

A railroad on which trains are hauled by a cable instead of a locomotive. Cables were used on some of the earliest English railroads, including the Canterbury and Whitstable Railway, opened in May 1830, and on the London and Blackwall Railway, authorized in 1836. Later, the use of cables became limited to railroads going up steep slopes where a locomotive could not grip the rails. In the United States, the Mauch Chunk Switch-Back, opened in 1844, was a famous example. On shorter slopes, two cars linked by cable to balance each other, one going up and the other down, are used. The Montmartre Line in Paris is a well-known example and there are many such funiculars in mountainous countries. The steepest Swiss funicular, between Piotta and Piora, has a gradient of 88%, that is, it climbs one foot for every 1 ft. 1½ in. it travels forward.

Fuselage

The main body of an airplane excluding the wings, tailplane and undercarriage; the hull of a flying boat; or the main body of a helicopter. The word is derived from the French for a slim, streamlined form. Fuselages may be constructed in two main ways: a braced box framework as a basis for *formers* and *stringers* over which a covering is placed, or a *monocoque* in which the fuselage is built like a shell (see MONOCOQUE CONSTRUCTION). The two methods can be likened respectively to two airplane models: one built of a balsa wood frame with a thin fabric covering, and the other a standard plastic model kit in which the fuselage is completed by joining two halves. Early aircraft like the Wright biplane did not have a fuselage, but since sustained flight necessitated protection for the pilot from the slipstream, the fuselage evolved, and it eventually became the basic component to which wings for lift and tail surfaces for control were fixed. The conventional fuselage of the early days of aviation is exemplified in the Curtiss JN ("Jenny") biplanes built in quantity during World War I, but monocoque construction was shown to America as early as 1912, when a French Deperdussin monoplane, with a fuselage built on these lines, won the Gordon Bennett Cup at Chicago. Up to 1915 construction was almost wholly in wood, but from that time the German firm of Junkers was in the forefront of metal construction. Duralumin, an aluminum alloy combining strength

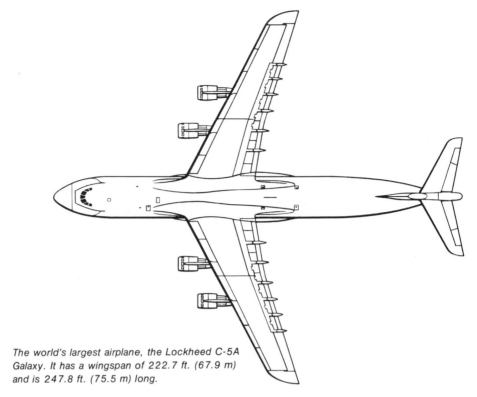

The world's largest airplane, the Lockheed C-5A Galaxy. It has a wingspan of 222.7 ft. (67.9 m) and is 247.8 ft. (75.5 m) long.

with lightness, became the prime material in the 1930s, and the 1960s have seen plastics used for light aircraft and special metals for high-speed aircraft. While normally an aircraft has only one fuselage, some aircraft of the past have had two. Examples are the British Blackburn TB of 1915 and the American P-82 Twin Mustang of 1945. In new "flying wing" concepts the fuselage may disappear.

G

Galaxy

The Lockheed C-5A, exclusive to Military Airlift Command of United States Air Force and the world's largest airplane. The first of 81 flew on June 30, 1968. Powered by four 41,000-lb. thrust General Electric TF-39 turbojets, the C-5A has a 581 mph (913 km/h) maximum speed and a 6,500 mi. (10,400 km) range. There are four crewmen, provision for relief crews, and room for 345 troops. As a cargo carrier, with nose and tail loading of its 248-ft. (75 m) fuselage, it can take two M60 tanks or five M113 armored carriers in addition to 75 men on an upper troop deck.

Galleon

Large sailing ship of the 16th and 17th centuries with three or four masts carrying both square and fore-and-aft sails. Probably developed in Spain and Portugal from the carrack, the galleon was by the standards of the time slender. Typical dimensions were around 160 ft.

(48 m) in length and 45 ft. (14 m) in breadth. With decks rising up in steps towards bow and stern, and with a long, low projecting beak in place of the overhanging forecastle of earlier ships, galleons served equally as warships (carrying up to three broadside tiers of guns) and commercial vessels.

Galley

Long, low seagoing vessel, usually with a pointed bow, and often fitted with one or two sails to supplement its oars. The galley, sometimes equipped with several banks of rowers (see BIREME), was fast and maneuverable, and retained its position as the principal ship of war from ancient times until supplanted by sailing ships in the 16th century (see WARSHIPS).

Gas engine

An internal-combustion engine using gas as fuel. Before the development of the gasoline engine, many experiments were made with gas. The first practical gas engine, made by Etienne LENOIR in 1860, had a single cylinder. Gas was injected and exploded in each end in turn. The first practical four-stroke constructed by the German inventor Nikolaus Otto, ran on coal gas and was a commercial success. Although gas is a satisfactory fuel for internal-combustion engines, it is less easily transported than gasoline or diesel oil, and is rarely used except in times of fuel shortages.

Gasket

A sheet of material placed between mating surfaces to act as a seal making them water-, gas-, or oil-tight. A cork gasket is used to make the rocker-box cover on a gasoline engine oil-tight. The gasket between the cylinder head and cylinder block, which must withstand engine heat, is made of asbestos covered with a thin copper sheet.

Gasoline

The most important fuel for providing motive power, derived mainly from petroleum. It is not a pure substance but consists of a blend of hydrocarbons of varying volatility, which boil in the approximate range 40°-200°C. Grades of commercial gasoline vary slightly in composition, depending on the type of GASOLINE ENGINE in which they are used — high- or low-compression automobile engine or aircraft PISTON ENGINE.

To be suitable for combustion any gasoline must contain a fair amount of low-boiling constituents to achieve good engine-starting from cold, but not so high a proportion that it will lead to VAPOR LOCK in warm weather or result in undue loss through evaporation. This is particularly critical for aviation gasoline used

is compressed by the upstroke of a piston and ignited by a spark from a spark plug. In normal combustion the flame front advances at an even rate from the vicinity of the spark plug through the gasoline mixture leading to a progressive expansion of gases that thrusts the piston down on its power stroke. If the gasoline is unsuited to the engine, some of the gasoline mixture detonates spontaneously before the flame front reaches it. The result is a series of small explosions that give rise to a characteristic "knocking" noise. These explosions result in loss of power and, if persistent, lead to the engine overheating. The tendency for knocking to occur increases as the engine's COMPRESSION RATIO increases. The antiknock qualities of a gasoline are assessed in terms of an OCTANE NUMBER.

To achieve the desired properties requires careful blending of hydrocarbons in the petroleum refinery. The hydrocarbons are produced by the simple distillation of crude petroleum; from subsequent REFINING processes; and also from natural gas. So-called natural gasoline is

50%. In these processes heavier, higher-boiling petroleum fractions are cracked, or broken down; or lighter, lower-boiling fractions are polymerized, in both cases to give hydrocarbons boiling within the gasoline range. These refinery processes yield a high proportion of hydrocarbons that are more resistant to knocking, including aromatics, cycloparaffins and isoparaffins such as isooctane.

The branched-chain paraffin, isooctane, is particularly resistant to knocking, in total contrast to the straight-chain paraffin normal heptane which is particularly prone to knocking. These two hydrocarbons form the basis of grading the antiknock characteristics of gasoline. Isooctane is assigned an octane rating of 100, normal heptane one of 0. A gasoline is given an octane number which represents the percentage of isooctane in a mixture of isooctane and normal heptane having the same knocking tendency as gasoline. Low-compression engines require a gasoline with an octane rating of about 90, while high-compression engines require a rating of 97 or 98. Aircraft piston engines need gasoline with an octane rating of 100 or more.

The octane rating of straight-run gasoline may vary from only 20 to about 70, and it must therefore be blended with higher-octane refined gasoline. But even this does not usually make the octane rating high enough for commercial gasolines, and a compound called tetraethyllead is added, which effectively raises the octane-rating by inhibiting knocking. It is present in automobile gasolines to the extent of up to 3 milliliters per gallon, though this proportion is being progressively reduced because of the pollution hazards associated with leaded gasoline. Aviation gasolines are more heavily leaded. Tetraethyllead is one of several ADDITIVES incorporated in gasoline.

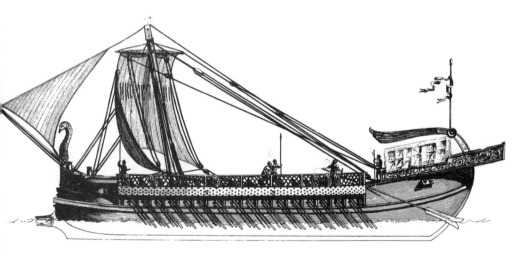

A Roman galley. Rowed galleys were fast and maneuverable, and retained their position as the principal ship of war until the 16th century.

in aircraft which operate at high altitudes where air pressure is low. Neither must there be too great a proportion of the high-boiling constituents, or else they will not be completely burned, resulting in buildup of carbon deposits within the engine and dirty exhaust. The gasoline should also be reasonably free from constituents that tend to break down and form gummy deposits in carburetors, on valves, or on spark plugs. Unsaturated hydrocarbons such as olefins cause gum formation when they oxidize. Inhibitors are often added to gasoline to prevent such oxidation.

One of the most important requirements of a gasoline is that it should burn smoothly in the engine cylinders. In the gasoline engine, the gasoline/air mixture

obtained from natural gas by compression or by absorption in oil. It contains straight-chain and branched-chain paraffin hydrocarbons with from three to eight carbon atoms in each molecule such as butane (C_4H_{10}) and octane (C_8H_{18}). The "straight-run" gasoline produced by fractionation of petroleum contains up to 30 paraffin hydrocarbons and up to 20 naphthenes or cycloparaffins (paraffins with their carbon atoms joined in a ring structure). In addition, aromatic hydrocarbons — those containing the benzene ring — are present in varying amounts, including benzene itself (C_6H_6) and toluene ($C_6H_5CH_3$). The straight distillation of petroleum yields only about 10-12% gasoline. Subsequent refinery processes increase this yield to between 40 and

Gasoline engine

The most common form of INTERNAL COMBUSTION ENGINE, used for powering most automobiles, motor boats, and light aircraft. German engineers Gottlieb DAIMLER and Carl BENZ developed the first successful gasoline engines in 1885-86 for use in their pioneer automobiles. They were not, however, the first to try replacing coal gas fuel with gasoline. Siegfried MARCUS in Austria constructed a simple gasoline engine in 1864 and fitted it in a crude automobile. Today the gasoline engine is under attack. It is not very efficient, converting only about 20% of the fuel's energy into power, and its toxic combustion products reach the atmosphere through the exhaust and cause POLLUTION. In certain cities pollution from vehicle exhausts has reached intolerable levels, and legislation has been enacted to force auto manufacturers to curb the noxious emissions. The United States, and the State of California in particular, has led the world in this respect (see EMISSION CONTROL SYSTEMS).

Many modified and alternative kinds of engine are under advanced development throughout the world (see for example ELECTRIC CAR, STEAM CAR, and STIRLING ENGINE), but it will be many years before acceptable alternatives to the gasoline engine are found.

Reciprocating engines. The commonest form of gasoline engine is the reciprocating engine, consisting of several cylinders in which PISTONS travel up and down. Gasoline vapor is burned in the cylinder, producing hot gases which expand and drive the piston. Valves regulate the entry of the mixture into each cylinder, and the ejection of exhaust gases. Most auto engines work on the FOUR-STROKE CYCLE, in which power is produced in each cylinder on every fourth piston stroke.

On the first stroke gasoline/air mixture is drawn into the cylinder through a valve. On the second the mixture is compressed, and then ignited by a spark. The third is the power stroke, while in the fourth (exhaust) stroke the spent gases are expelled from the cylinder and passed through a MUFFLER. A few auto engines work on a TWO-STROKE CYCLE, power being produced on alternate piston strokes. The more the fuel mixture is compressed the greater is the power output. In a medium-power engine the pistons compress the mixture into about one-ninth of its original volume (the COMPRESSION RATIO is about 9:1). High-compression engines may have a ratio of up to 12:1, and require higher-octane gasoline than low-compression (6:1 to 8:1) engines (see OCTANE NUMBER).

The reciprocating motion of the pistons is converted to rotary motion by means of CONNECTING RODS and a CRANKSHAFT. A heavy FLYWHEEL on one end of the crankshaft helps to keep the engine running smoothly between piston strokes.

Cylinder arrangement. The cylinders may be arranged in several ways, but usually they are in-line. Six-cylinder in-line engines are widely used, and four-cylinder are common in Europe. The six-cylinder engine is smoother because successive power strokes overlap. Cylinders may also be arranged in a V-formation, two lines of cylinders forming the top arms of the V and the crankshaft the base. V-4, V-6 and V-8 engines are produced. Compared with their in-line equivalent they are much shorter, permitting

a shorter and more rigid crankshaft. The V-4 arrangement is the least satisfactory because the power strokes do not overlap. The balance is poor, and an additional weighted balancing shaft has to be incorporated for smooth running. The V-6 design has a crankshaft with six crankpins, and with a V angle of 60° it is quite smooth running and well balanced. The V-8 requires a crankshaft with only four crankpins, spaced at 90° intervals, and the V angle also is 90°, giving smooth running and excellent balance.

A third variant is the flat horizontally opposed engine, which has its cylinders arranged in two flat banks with the crankshaft between them. This arrangement is compact and very well balanced. However, the engine is less accessible than the equivalent in-line type. Many piston aero engines have their cylinders arranged radially (see RADIAL ENGINES). The cylinders are located in the main body of the engine, the cylinder block (see CYLINDER BLOCK AND HEAD). To the top of this is bolted the cylinder head, which carries the valve-operating gear. At the base of the cylinder block is the crankcase, which houses the crankshaft. A sump at the bottom of the crankcase contains a reservoir of lubricating oil. The CAMSHAFT, which operates the VALVE GEAR, is driven from the crankshaft and may be located in the cylinder block, or, in an overhead-cam engine, in the cylinder head.

Fuel, ignition, cooling, and lubrication. In most FUEL SYSTEMS fuel is fed to the engine via a carburetor, where it mixes with air to form a vapor. Alternatively, fuel is injected directly into the airstream entering the cylinders (see FUEL INJECTION). The IGNITION SYSTEM provides the electric spark to ignite the fuel in the cylinders. Electric current from a battery is boosted to high-voltage by an induction coil and distributed by a DISTRIBUTOR to each spark plug in turn. A MAGNETO, which also works by electro-magnetic induction, provides the spark in piston aero engines. When gasoline burns in the engine cylinders, it produces a great deal of heat, which must be dissipated by a COOLING SYSTEM. Most engines are cooled by water circulating through channels around the cylinders in the cylinder block and head. The hot water leaving the engine is cooled as it passes through a radiator through which air is sucked by a fan driven by belt from the crankshaft. Some engines, however, are cooled by air blown by fan over the cylinders, to which are attached COOLING FINS.

Some heat is removed by the engine's LUBRICATION SYSTEM, but its main function is to lubricate the moving parts. Oil is

pumped from the sump through channels to the crankshaft connecting rod, and camshaft bearings, etc., and is sprayed up into the cylinders to lubricate the pistons and to provide an efficient gas seal between piston rings and cylinder.

Rotary engines. As well as reciprocating gasoline engines with pistons, there are ROTARY ENGINES without pistons. The best known of these is the WANKEL ENGINE. It has one or more rotors which are driven round directly by explosion of the gasoline mixture. There is thus no need of crankshaft, connecting rods, and complicated valve gear. Like most conventional gasoline engines, the Wankel engine works on the four-stroke cycle (see also PISTON ENGINE (AERO)).

Gas turbine

An engine in which the motive power is provided by a turbine spun by the expanding gases produced by combustion of a fuel. The aircraft JET ENGINE is a form of gas turbine that derives its thrust directly from a high-speed jet of gases. In the TURBOPROP engine the turbine is coupled to a propeller. Britain's Frank WHITTLE and Germany's Hans von OHAIN pioneered aircraft gas turbines in the 1930s. Gas turbines are being increasingly used to power ships, locomotives, long distance buses, and large trucks, and gas-turbine automobiles have also been developed, though not as yet with any great success. Britain's Rover Car Company designed a "turbo car" as early as 1950. Compared with conventional internal combustion engines, gas turbines are smooth running (producing rotary motion directly), simple, light, compact, and very powerful. In addition, they need no cooling system, produce fewer noxious gases, and can use cheap fuel (even powdered coal). However, they are expensive to manufacture, and burn a lot of fuel.

The main parts of a gas turbine are the compressor, combustion chamber, and turbine. Air is drawn in and compressed by a multi-stage compressor before it enters the combustion chamber or chambers. There, it mixes with fuel sprayed in through a fine nozzle, and the mixture burns. The hot, expanding gases rush from the combustion chambers and spin the blades of the turbine, which is mounted on the same shaft as the compressor and is also coupled to the output shaft of the engine (except in the case of the jet engine). The output shaft is connected to the propeller or driving wheels through suitable reduction gearing.

The efficiency of the simple gas turbine described is increased in the so-called two-shaft design, in which compression, combustion, and expansion take place in

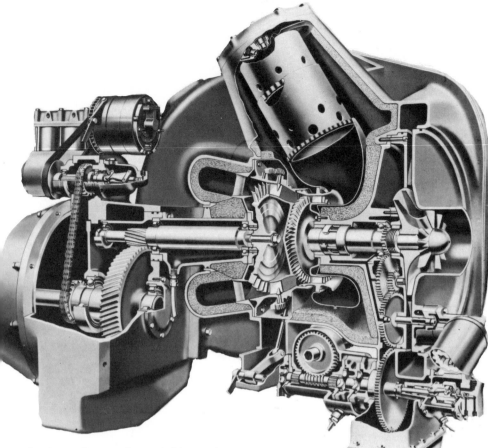

A cutaway diagram of a gas turbine engine.

two stages (low and high pressure) rather than one. One shaft carries the low-pressure compressor and turbine, while the other carries the high-pressure set. The air is cooled between the two compression stages (intercooling) and is heated in a heat exchanger by the hot outgoing exhaust gases (regeneration), before entering the high-pressure combustion chamber.

Gauge, railroad

The distance between the inside faces of the running rails. The "standard gauge," first used in England and later adopted by most other countries, is 4 ft. 8.5 in. (1.435 m). Today about 60% of the world's railroads are standard gauge, notable exceptions being the Soviet Union (5 ft., 1.5 m), Spain (5ft. 6 in., 1.7 m), and most of Japan (3 ft. 6 in., 1.07 m). There is no particular advantage of the standard gauge except that it is standard. Where several different gauges are current in one country, as was the case in the early days in the United States, Britain, and elsewhere, long journeys often involved gauge, and therefore train, changes.

Although more expensive, a broad gauge permits more spacious cars, greater stability, and higher speeds; in its day England's Great Western Railway, running on a 7 ft. (2.1 m) gauge, provided the fastest and most comfortable trains in the world.

Narrow gauges permit greater curvature, a particular virtue in mountainous terrain, and cheapness (not only of the track, but also of locomotives, cars, bridges, and so on). Thus despite limitations in stability and speed, they are widely used in sparsely populated and underdeveloped areas, with in some places gauges as narrow as 2 ft. 6 in. (0.76 m).

Loading gauge. This specifies the greatest width and height of locomotives and cars possible on a railroad, and depends on the dimensions of bridges and tunnels. The world's largest loading gauge (17 ft. 4 in., 5.3 m, high; 11 ft. 2 in., 4 m, wide) is that of the Soviet Union. The United States has the largest on standard gauge tracks (15 ft. 6 in., 4.7 m, high; 10 ft. 9 in., 3.3 m, wide).

Gearbox

As essential component in the transmission system of an internal combustion engined vehicle, the gearbox enables engine speed and power to be matched to a wide variety of road speeds and loadings. The ordinary gasoline engine, for example, can operate efficiently only over a relatively narrow range of speeds, developing optimum power at about 4,000 rpm. Yet the road wheels of an automobile need to turn at all speeds from almost zero to about 1,000 rpm at 70 mph, and beyond. To accommodate this basic discrepancy, a reduction gear of 4:1 is incorporated in the final drive. Further gear reductions are necessary to allow the engine to run fast and provide sufficient torque at lower road speeds;

this is the function of the gearbox. An infinitely variable gearbox would be the ideal, but in practice a multispeed gearbox with three or more forward gears and a reverse is used. The gears may be changed manually or automatically. Automatic gearboxes, coupled to the engine by a fluid drive, such as a TORQUE CONVERTER, are the rule in the United States (see AUTOMATIC TRANSMISSION). Elsewhere manual stick-shift gearboxes are more common, the driver having to disengage the engine from the gearbox by means of a CLUTCH whenever he changes gear. A semi-automatic system widely used on commercial vehicles is a modification of the PRE-SELECTOR GEARBOX. No clutch is required. To change gear, the driver simply moves the gear lever into a new position, after which the gear changes automatically.

The manual auto gearbox generally has four forward gears and one reverse. Heavy commercial vehicles may have as many as 16 forward gears and four reverse. This large number is obtained usually by the use of an auxiliary, or "splitter," gearbox in series with the main one. A five-speed, one-reverse main box, coupled with a two-speed auxiliary, is a common arrangement giving 10 forward and two reverse ratios. A four-speed, one-reverse main box coupled with a three-speed auxiliary, gives 12 forward and three reverse ratios. An auxiliary OVERDRIVE gearbox is sometimes fitted to automobiles to improve economy at cruising speeds.

In a typical four-speed gearbox the gears are in constant mesh, and are carried on three shafts (input, layshaft and output). The usual drive is from the input shaft to the layshaft, and then to the output shaft. The gears on the input shaft and layshaft are fixed, but those on the output shaft are free to revolve around it. Splined to the output shaft are collars with a DOG-CLUTCH on either side. In selecting a gear, the lever moves a collar back or forth along the output shaft to lock with a gear in mesh with and being driven by a gear on the layshaft, which in turn is driven by the input shaft. The collar and gear have a built-in synchronizing device (SYNCHROMESH) which ensures that they are rotating at the same speed before they lock.

In low-gear, speed reduction is greatest, the gear wheel on the layshaft being small and that on the output shaft being large. The layshaft gears get larger and those on the output shaft smaller as higher gears are selected. In top gear it is usual for input and output shafts to be locked together so that they turn at the same speed, this being known as direct drive. In reverse another collar slides a small idler gear into mesh between gears on the layshaft and output shaft, thus reversing the latter's direction of rotation.

The gear ratios in the various gears between input and output shafts are typically 3.5:1 in low gear; 2:1 in second; 1.4:1 in third and 1:1 in top. Assuming reduction gearing of 4:1 in the final drive, this gives overall gearing reduction from engine to road wheels of 14:1, 8:1, 5.6:1 and 4:1.

Gears

Toothed wheels used to transmit rotary motion from one shaft to another. By meshing together gear wheels with different numbers of teeth, speed or turning effort (torque) may be increased or decreased. The ratio between the number of teeth on each wheel is known as the "gear ratio." In a reduction gear the number of teeth on the input shaft is less than that on the output shaft. The speed transmitted is thus reduced, though the torque is increased. In a multiplying gear the input shaft gear is larger than that on the output shaft and thus drives it faster, but with reduced torque. The smaller gear of a pair is usually called the pinion; the larger one the wheel.

Gears vary in the way in which their teeth are cut. The simplest are spur gears, which connect parallel shafts. Their teeth are cut parallel to the shaft axis. A spur pinion can mesh externally with a wheel, or internally. In the former case input and output shafts move in opposite directions and in the latter in the same direction. Helical gears are quieter than spur gears at high speeds of rotation. Their teeth are cut at an angle, like a screw thread. The gears in a GEAR-BOX are of the helical type, except for the reverse gears, which are of the spur type. Helical gears produce some end thrust which can be avoided by cutting the teeth in a double-helix. The teeth of helical gears can be cut so that they mesh with their shafts at an angle. They are then called spiral or skew gears. In a gasoline engine the distributor shaft is driven from the camshaft by a spiral gear.

Worm gears are designed to connect non-intersecting shafts, usually at rightangles. The small worm pinion often takes the form of an endless screw, while the wheel may be a spur gear. Bevel gears connect shafts whose axles intersect, commonly at rightangles. The gears have teeth cut straight or spirally. Bevel gears are found, for example, in a DIFFERENTIAL. The crown-wheel and pinion in the final drive are also bevel gears. A set of gears meshed together are known as a gear train. A familiar example is the

EPICYCLIC-GEAR train used in automatic transmission.

General

One of America's most famous LOCOMOTIVES. The *General*, a 4-4-0 of the Western & Atlanta Railroad, was captured on April 12, 1862, during the Civil War, by Captain James J. Andrews, heading a Union raiding party. Andrews set off down the line, intending to burn bridges and destroy the telegraph behind him and so isolate Chattanooga from the South. He was hotly pursued by the conductor of the train the *General* left behind, William A. Fuller, at first by hand-car and then on the locomotive *Texas*, so that Andrews did not have time to carry out any sabotage. The *General* ran out of steam after 100 mi (160 km) and Andrews and his 20 men were captured. Later, the *General* was restored and preserved.

General Motors

Giant American automobile company founded in 1908 by William C. Durant and today the world's largest motor vehicle manufacturer. Durant, who headed the Buick Motor Car Company, established GM in 1908, rapidly acquiring Cadillac, Oldsmobile, and a number of smaller firms. His aim, unlike that of his principal rival Ford, was to produce a wide range of models, and in its early years GM was little more than a collection of individual operating units. After financial difficulties in 1910 Durant lost control, only to return in 1916, bringing the Chevrolet Motor Company with him. By the end of World War I General Motors was Ford's only serious competitor, and during the mid-1920s, now under the direction of Alfred P. Sloan, the corporation took the lead from Ford. During the following years General Motors strengthened its position as world leader by acquiring Pontiac, Vauxhall of Britain, Opel of Germany, and Holden of Australia.

The hundred-millionth automobile came off the production line in 1967, and during the corporation's peak year of 1972 worldwide sales amounted to a staggering $30,435,231,414 and net profits totaled $2,162,806,765 (an all-time record for any company in any industry). Today General Motors is responsible for approximately a quarter of the world's annual automobile production, and in addition manufactures aircraft engines, diesel engines and locomotives, refrigerators, and earth-moving equipment.

Generator

A device that produces electric current when it is rotated, also known as a dy-

namo. Generators are used in vehicles to run the various electrical systems and accessories and to charge the battery (which provides electric power when the engine, therefore the generator, is not running). In diesel-electric locomotives the diesel engine drives a generator which produces electricity for the traction motors. One type of generator produces direct current; another, known as an alternator, produces alternating current.

An automobile generator may be of either type, and is driven by the fan belt from the crankshaft. The alternator has the advantage that it can rotate much faster and generate a higher current; also it charges the battery even when the engine is idling.

In the alternator the armature, or rotor, is relatively small and has only one coil of wire wound round it. Its function is to provide a magnetic field, which it does when electric current is passed through it via carbon brushes and slip rings. The output current is generated in the stator coils which surround the armature. The current alternates every time the rotor rotates, and is fed to rectifiers which convert it to usable direct current.

In a d.c. generator the armature has many windings, and is surrounded by the field windings, which produce a magnetic field when electric current is passed through them. Rotation of the armature in this magnetic field induces electric current in its coils. The current surges back and forth in each armature coil at each revolution, but by the use of a many-segment commutator, one-way, direct current can be tapped off by carbon brushes.

George Washington Bridge

The world's strongest SUSPENSION BRIDGE, with four 36-in. (90 cm) diameter cables, it crosses the Hudson River in New York City. Its 3,500 ft. (1,067 m) span makes it the world's fifth longest-span suspension bridge. Designed by Othmar AMMAN, it was completed in 1931, and had one deck carrying an eight-lane roadway, and no stiffening trusses. A second deck was added beneath the original one in 1962, with stiffening trusses between the two. The suspension towers are 595 ft. (181 m) high, and are unusual in having no masonry facing.

Giffard, Henri (1825-1882)

French dirigible pioneer. Manufactured the first full-size airship, using steam power for propulsion, and flew it from Paris to Trappes on September 24, 1852, at an average speed of 6 mph (9.6 km). A second dirigible, completed in 1865, had a capacity of 109,550 cu. ft. but escaped from its holding net at takeoff.

Gladesville Bridge

Crossing the Parramatta River in Sydney, Australia, it is the world's longest-span (1,000 ft., 305 m) concrete ARCH BRIDGE. Completed in 1964, the Gladesville Bridge carries eight traffic lanes. The arch was constructed of four ribs, which were built of precast concrete units assembled on movable falsework (supporting structure).

Globtik Tokyo, *a super tanker, and at the time of writing the largest mobile object ever built.*

Globtik Tokyo

Giant Japanese-built oil tanker or VLCC (very large crude carrier), the largest vessel — in fact the largest mobile object — ever built. Completed in 1973, *Globtik Tokyo* is 1,243 ft. 5 in. (379 m) long, 203 ft. 5 in. (62 m) wide, has a draft of 92 ft. (28 m) and a deadweight tonnage of 483,664 tons. She is manned by a crew of 38, and powered by a steam turbine rated at 44,385 shaft horsepower. Her sister ship *Globtik London*, completed in 1974, is the same size.

Goddard, Robert Hutchings (1882-1945)

An American rocket pioneer, he launched the first successful liquid-propellant ROCKET on March 16, 1926. Fueled by gasoline and liquid oxygen, the 10-ft. (3 m) long rocket traveled a distance of 184 ft. (56 m). Goddard began experimenting with rockets in 1909, and in 1919 he published *A Method of Reaching High Altitudes* in which he outlined fundamental rocket principles. He also suggested reaching the moon and planets by rocket, an idea that was ridiculed at the time.

After his successful 1926 launch, Goddard continued with his experiments until his death. By 1937 his rockets could reach altitudes of more than 1.5 mi. (2.5 km) and travel at speeds exceeding 700 mph (1,130 km/h). They were equipped

with gyrostabilization and numerous instruments. His work was financed by the Smithsonian Institution and the Guggenheim Foundation.

Goddard also proposed a system of land transportation using a steel vacuum tube with cars suspended and propelled by magnetic forces, thus anticipating the idea of the LINEAR INDUCTION MOTOR and magnetic levitation.

Go-kart

Miniature rear-engined automobile with a low skeleton frame and no bodywork, used for sport and racing. First developed in the United States in the 1950s, the go-kart later gained popularity in Europe as well, and today karting (go-kart racing) is an international sport. The races are short (usually about 1,000 yards or meters), and yet despite a maximum engine displacement of only 200 cc, speeds of well over 100 mph (160 km/h) are achieved.

Golden Gate Bridge

Completed in 1937, this famous SUSPENSION BRIDGE spans the entrance to San Francisco Bay. Its 4,200 ft. (1,280 m) span was the world's longest for 27 years, until eclipsed by a mere 60 ft. (18 m) by the VERRAZANO-NARROWS BRIDGE in New York. Its suspension towers are 746 ft. (227 m) high, and two 36-in. (90 cm) cables support the bridge deck. This carries six traffic lanes about 220 ft. (67 m) above the water. Between cable anchorages its length is 6,450 ft. (1,965 m).

Governor

A device for automatically controlling the speed of an engine within certain limits by regulating the intake of fuel. The Scottish engineer James WATT developed the first successful governor in the

1780s, the centrifugal steam engine governor. This consists of two balls on the end of rods hanging from the top of a shaft driven by the engine. As engine speed rises, centrifugal force raises the balls up and out; as speed decreases, the balls move in and down. These movements are made to actuate a lever controlling the steam supply to the engine, restricting steam as the balls move up and increasing it as they move down, thereby helping to maintain a steady speed.

The centrifugal governor was one of the first devices to utilize the principle of feedback. Oil and gasoline engines are sometimes governed mechanically by weights and springs, pneumatically from the engine intake manifold, or hydraulically from the fuel pump (for example to prevent over-revving). Governors are also incorporated in epicyclic automatic gearboxes.

Graf Zeppelin

Highly successful rigid airship completed in 1928. After its initial commercial flight across the Atlantic, the *Graf Zeppelin* went on to fly round the world, completing nearly 22,000 mi. (35,000 km) in 21 days. It continued in service for nine years, making 590 flights, but was retired in 1937 after the disastrous explosion of the HINDENBURG.

Grand Canal

Name now given to China's Imperial Canal. Extending some 1,000 mi. (1,600 km) from Hangchow to Peking, it is the world's longest artificial inland waterway. The first section was opened around 500 B.C., but the full length was not completed until 1,800 years later. Originally built for the transportation of grain and other supplies, it was one of ancient China's most important transport links.

The canal gradually silted up, but was dredged in the 15th century and remained in use until the 19th century, when large sections were destroyed by floods and the canal was abandoned. In recent years it has been widened and deepened and is again navigable throughout its length.

The principal canal in the Italian city of Venice is also called the Grand Canal. It separates the two main groups of islands on which the city is built, and is some 2 mi. (3 km) long.

Grand Central Terminal

New York City's main railroad station. The first station under this name was built by Commodore Vanderbilt in 1869-71 after the style of St. Pancras Station in London. Although smaller than the present structure, it covered the largest interior space on the American continent. The present Grand Central Terminal, built 1903-12, is the world's largest station. It has 67 tracks on two levels, and can take 600 trains a day. An average of 180,000 people per day use the station. The concourse is 125 ft. (38 m) wide, 375 ft. (114 m) long, and 120 ft. (36.5 m) high. The use of multiple levels for express and suburban trains, with separate concourses, was an architectural and engineering triumph of its day.

Grand prix
The title given to major automobile races (see AUTOMOBILE RACING).

Grand Touring (GT)
Fast closed automobile, usually with only two doors and two seats, but sometimes accommodating two additional passengers in the rear. Midway between the family sedan and the high-performance sports car, the GT appeared after World War II as a luxury automobile for those who wanted speed, comfort, and flair. First introduced by Ferrari, GT models were soon built by other makers, including Aston Martin, Jaguar, and Jensen in in Britain, and Maserati and Lamborghini in Italy. Today the initials GT are often used to designate high performance two-door versions of conventional four-door sedans.

Granite Railway
A 5 ft. (1.5 m) gauge railroad, 3 mi. (4.8 km) long, built by Gridley Bryant to carry granite blocks for the Bunker Hill Monument from the Quincy Hills to the Neponset River at Milton, Mass. The Granite Railway Company, incorporated on March 4, 1826, was the first company to build and operate a railroad in the United States. It later became part of the New York, New Haven, and Hartford Railroad.

Great Britain
Large steamship designed by the famous British engineer Isambard Kingdom BRUNEL and launched in 1843. The first all-metal oceangoing liner, the first large ship with screw propulsion, and the first propeller-driven ship to cross the Atlantic, the *Great Britain* has been described as "the forefather of all modern ships." She was 322 ft. (98 m) long and 51 ft. (15.5 m) wide, by far the largest ship of her time. Abandoned and scuttled in the Falkland Islands, the *Great Britain* has been raised and towed back to Bristol, her place of launching, for restoration.

Great circle route
The shortest possible route between two points on the globe. A great circle is any circle on the surface of the globe (or any sphere) with its center at the center of the globe. Each meridian of longitude is thus half of a great circle. The Equator is a great circle, but all other parallels of latitude are not. In planning air and sea routes, a section of a great circle is followed wherever possible. An airplane traveling from New York to Tokyo, for example, flies over Alaska rather than following a parallel of latitude across the Pacific.

Great Eastern
Giant steamship designed by Isambard Kingdom BRUNEL and launched in 1858. A "floating city" for 4,000 passengers and 6,000 tons of cargo, the 692-ft. (210 m) long Great Eastern was five times the size of anything else afloat and remained for over 40 years the world's largest ship, with a displacement of 18,914 tons.

The only vessel with paddles, screws, and sails, she was a magnificent ship in conception but was dogged by ill-luck. Her launching took three months and bankrupted her owners, and instead of making the voyages to India, Australia, and the Orient for which she had been intended, she was put into service on the North Atlantic. She ran at a loss and was sold in 1864 to spend the remainder of her short working life as a cable layer, and was responsible for the first successful transatlantic cable.

Greathead shield
A tunneling shield designed by the British engineer James Greathead in 1879 providing the first practical method of tunneling under rivers. It affords protection for workmen tunneling in soft ground, and consists essentially of a cylinder with a cutting edge which is forced through the ground by hydraulic jacks. Excavation of the ground within the cylinder can then take place without fear of collapse. New sections of tunnel lining are put in place behind the shield, and the jacks push against them to drive the cutting edge further forward. Where water seepage may be a problem, the shield operates under compressed air.

Ground controlled approach (GCA)
A method of guiding an airplane's landing approach from the airport CONTROL TOWER. Radar displays in the control tower give air traffic controllers precise information about a plane's position and height. The controller tells the pilot what headings to fly and what height to main-

Brunel's famous Great Eastern *(1858), for over 40 years the world's largest ship, and the only one ever to have sails, paddles, and propellers.*

A Hawker Siddeley Harrier, the world's first operational VTOL airplane, demonstrates its ability to hover before vectoring the angle of jet thrust to the rear for the transition to forward flight.

tain to position himself correctly for his landing approach. The pilot confirms his instructions by repeating them back. About 8 mi. (11 km) from the runway a precision controller takes over. The pilot no longer has to repeat his instructions because any deviation from the required flight path is apparent on the radar display and the controller will issue corrections. When the runway comes into sight the pilot takes over. GCA may be used at busy airports to position aircraft for landing even in good visibility. However, it has at most airports been superseded by the INSTRUMENT LANDING SYSTEM, which is more accurate, and simpler to use.

Ground-effect machine (GEM)
An alternative name for AIR-CUSHION VEHICLE.

Gulf Intracoastal Waterway
The Gulf Intracoastal Waterway is a partly protected shipping route serving ports between Apalachee Bay, Florida, and Brownsville, Texas (a distance of well over 1,000 mi.; 1,600 km). It crosses many river estuaries, which provide access to inland river ports, and is sheltered for the most part by barrier beaches. 150 ft. (45.7 m) wide and 12 ft. (3.6 m) deep, it links the commercial regions around New Orleans, Mobile Bay, and the important ports of Texas to each other and to the United States' great natural inland waterway, the Mississippi. Access to the Mississippi itself is through the Harvey Lock at New Orleans, while the Plaquemine-Morgan City Waterway links the Gulf Intracoastal to the Mississippi River Valley network of waterways.

The Gulf Intracoastal was planned to link with the ATLANTIC INTRACOASTAL WATERWAY to provide a continuous route from New York to Brownsville, Texas. Construction of the linking Cross-Florida Barge Canal was started in 1964 but has encountered environmental objections.

Guppy
Giant American transport airplane designed for carrying outsize loads. The original "Pregnant Guppy" flew from September 1962, and consisted, like later versions, of a Boeing 337 Stratocruiser modified by Aero Spacelines. A massive lobe joined above the normal fuselage gave a 20 ft. (6.1 m) inside height. This plane was powered by piston engines, but turboprops were used on the later Super Guppy, which transported components in the Saturn rocket program. The nose of the Guppy swings to one side for easy loading.
Two Mini Guppies were followed by the Guppy 101, while the latest version is the 201. This entered service in 1971, and has the largest freight compartment of any transport; over 25 ft. (7.6 m) in diameter, it has a capacity of 39,000 ft.[3] (1,104 m³). Cruising speed is 288 mph (463 km/h).

Gyrocompass
A navigational instrument used for determining true north, and standard equipment on all large ships. It relies on the rotation of the earth and the properties of the gyroscope rather than on magnetism, and is therefore unaffected by variation and deviation (see COMPASS). A gyroscope consists of a heavy spinning wheel pivoted in such a way that it can

turn around any of three axes. With the wheel rotating rapidly its spin axis maintains a fixed position in space. In a gyrocompass the gyroscope is set up with the aid of pendulum and damping devices so that its spin axis aligns with that of the earth. In normal circumstances it will remain in this position, thus providing an accurate means of determing true north. However, it is affected by rapid turns and cannot, therefore, be used in aircraft or high-speed ships without special monitoring devices. These maintain the gyroscope on its north-south axis by compensating for the effects of rapid alterations in direction.

H

Hackney carriage
Originally a 4-wheeled carriage drawn by 2 horses and carrying 6 passengers, the term is now used for any passenger vehicle plying for hire. The first Hackney carriages appeared in England early in the 1600s, and their use reached a peak in the 1830s when there were 1,200 in London alone. They were run by the Hackney Coach Commissioners, who enjoyed a complete monopoly, but were later replaced by HANSOM CABS and Broughams (see CARRIAGES AND CARTS) and then by the first omnibuses (see BUS). The term comes from the French word *Haquénee*, a breed of horse used for riding and driving.

Hansom cab
Two-wheeled, one-horse vehicle plying for hire. It was invented in 1834 by Joseph Aloysius Hansom of Yorkshire, England, quickly becoming popular in London (and, later in New York and Boston). Its main feature was that it would not tip forward if the horse fell, or backward if it overbalanced. Passengers entered through two doors in front; the driver sat at the back above them, and spoke to them through a trapdoor in the roof.

Harrier
The world's first operational VTOL (vertical takeoff and landing) airplane, built by the British firm of Hawker Siddeley. The Rolls-Royce Pegasus vectored thrust turbofan engine has nozzles which swivel to direct (vector) thrust down or to the rear, giving VTOL and a maximum forward speed of over 737 mph (1,186 km/h). With reaction jet nozzles at nose, tail, and wing tips, the Harrier can maneuver while hovering, and can even fly back-

wards. A relatively small plane, the Harrier has a span of 25.25 ft. (7.7 m), and is some 49.5 ft. (13.87 m) long.

The aircraft was preceded by the Kestrel which first hovered in 1960 and went into limited production for evaluation by Britain, West Germany, and the United States. Developed as the Harrier in 1966 and in production from late 1967, it was built in single-seat strike and reconnaissance and two-seat trainer versions to equip four Royal Air Force and three U.S. Marine Corps squadrons; the two versions being designated AV-8A and TAV-8A respectively in United States service. Other versions have been developed, including the more powerful AV-16A, and the Sea Harrier.

Heat barrier

When an aircraft is flying at speeds of Mach 2 (see MACH NUMBER) and above, the friction between the surrounding air and the aircraft's metal skin generates heat. There is no specific "heat barrier" which can be broken and overcome. The faster the aircraft travels within the earth's atmosphere, the greater the heat produced; at speeds of Mach 6 skin temperatures of over 1,000 F (542° C) are found on the nose and wing leading edges. At these temperatures aluminum alloys are significantly weakened, and other metals such as titanium have to be used.

Heat engine

One in which the heat energy obtained by burning a fuel is changed into mechanical work. Gasoline, diesel, gas turbine, steam and Stirling engines are all heat engines. Gasoline and diesel engines are examples of internal combustion engines; fuel is burned inside the cylinders. The steam engine is an external combustion engine; fuel is burned outside the engine to produce steam. In internal combustion engines the gaseous products of combustion form the working fluid, developing power by pushing against the pistons or spinning turbines. In the external combustion engine a different working fluid is employed. In the steam engine it is steam. In the Stirling engine it is air or another gas in a sealed circuit. (See GASOLINE ENGINE, STEAM ENGINES, DIESEL ENGINE, GAS TURBINE, and STIRLING ENGINE.)

Heinkel He 178

The world's first jet-propelled aircraft, flown in Germany in 1939. A test bed for Pabst von Ohain's He S 3-B centrifugal-flow turbojet engine, the He 178 was strictly experimental. Although the aircraft was underpowered, it was a notable milestone in aviation history. The first jets to go into action (in July 1944) were the Me 262 (Germany) and the Gloster Meteor 1 (Britain).

The Fairey Rotodyne. With fixed wings and conventional propellers for forward flight, and a rotor for VTOL (vertical takeoff and landing), this craft was one of many experiments which attempted to combine the advantages of helicopters and conventional planes.

Helicopter

A wingless aircraft that obtains lift and propulsion from overhead horizontally turning rotors. Helicopters can take off and land vertically, they can hover, and they can move in any direction. All heavier-than-air aircraft depend on AIRFOILS to provide LIFT. The rotors of a helicopter fulfil the same function in this respect as the wings of an airplane, but the helicopter's engine rotates the rotors (which generate lift as the blades cut through the air), while the plane's power unit has to move the whole airframe to obtain lift from the wings.

With their VTOL capability, and their maneuverability, helicopters have obvious advantages over conventional airplanes in many applications. They are widely used for short range passenger transport (up to about 100 mi., 160 km), such as between cities, or from city center to airport. They are valuable for spraying and other agricultural operations; for observation, survey, police, ambulance, and rescue work; for carrying supplies for example to offshore oil rigs; for transporting heavy mining or other gear to remote areas that cannot be reached by road; and in warfare. However their value is restricted by the fact that they cannot carry such heavy loads as fixed-wing planes, and their speed is limited to a maximum of little more than 200 mph (322 km/h). (The world record stands at 220.885 mph, 355.485 km/h, achieved by a Sikorsky S-67 Blackhawk in 1970.) The tips of the advancing rotor blades achieve supersonic velocities at quite low aircraft speeds, while at quite modest forward speeds the roots

of the retreating blades are moving through the air relatively more slowly than the helicopter itself and generate no lift. Higher speeds (up to 316 mph, 508.5 km/h) have been reached by "compound helicopters," which have a supplementary means of propulsion (usually a jet engine). Numerous experiments have been made in an attempt to build a fixed-wing plane with a helicoper's versatility (see STOL and VTOL).

Most helicopters are powered by gas turbine engines, and they range in size from miniature unenclosed one-man craft, through the usual three or four seaters, up to transports carrying 25 or more passengers, and giant "sky cranes." These include the American Sikorsky S-64, which with a 72 ft. (21.9 m) diameter rotor can lift over 22,000 lb. (14,515 kg), and the Soviet Mil Mi-12. The latter, with 220 ft. (67 m) rotors, set a world record in 1969 when it raised a payload of 88,636 lb. (40,200 kg) to a height of 7,398 ft. (2,255 m). The greatest altitude achieved by a helicopter, a French Aérospatiale SA 315B Lama, is 40,820 ft. (12,442 m).

Rotors. There are a number of possible rotor layouts, the simplest being a single rotor system. A tandem has two rotors, one at each end of the machine; side-by-side rotors are displaced laterally; triple rotors usually have two set side-by-side and one carried forward. Multiple rotors may be designed to intermesh, or can be co-axial and counter-rotating. The blades themselves may be of metal, wood or composite construction, with up to six in each rotor.

The mounting of the rotor on the drive

shaft from the engine may be rigid (with only a facility for changing the pitch); set on a gimbal enabling the blades additionally to move (flap) as a unit; or provided with complex hinges so that each individual blade has a certain amount of movement both up-and-down and in the horizontal plane, together with a pitch changing facility.

For the rotor to generate lift, the pitch of the blades must be altered to give an ANGLE OF ATTACK (see WING) that will produce sufficient lift to raise the machine off the ground. The available pitch variation ranges from about 3 to 14 degrees, movement being effected via the collective pitch lever in the cockpit ("collective" because the pitch of all the blades is altered simultaneously).

There is a throttle control on the top of the collective pitch lever, but the inertia of the rotor blades makes it difficult to slow them down or speed them up quickly, so height is normally gained or lost by chang-

The Boeing-Vertol 107 transport helicopter seats 25 passengers, and can operate off land or water. The stub wing provides lift during cruising flight, thus reducing the load on the rotors.

A giant Russian "skycrane" helicopter, the gas turbine powered Mi-10. Heavy loads can be held firmly against the flat under-surface.

ing the pitch of the blades and hence the amount of lift they generate.

Flight technique. To move a helicopter forwards the rotors must be tilted forwards so that the airflow is directed slightly to the rear. This is achieved by cyclic pitch: the pitch of individual blades is increased as they pass to the rear (producing more lift) and decreased as they rotate to the front (reducing their lift). The blades are hinged at the rotor hub, either individually or on a gimbal, so that they can rise and fall (flap) under the influence of this increasing and decreasing lift. Inclination of the rotors is governed

by the pilot's control column: moving this forwards, backwards or sideways will tilt the rotors and move the helicopter in the desired direction.

The torque reaction from the spinning rotor tends to make a helicopter rotate in the opposite direction. A vertically oriented tail rotor, driven off the main rotor gearbox, will counteract this torque. The rudder pedals change the pitch of the tail rotor blades, increasing or decreasing their thrust and enabling the helicopter to be turned. In twin rotor helicopters the rotors turn in opposite directions and the torque is therefore canceled out, directional control being achieved by differ-

ential collective pitch changes (which alter the torque and hence turn the fuselage), or (in side-by-side rotor systems) by tilting the rotors in opposite directions. Maintaining a helicopter in position by balancing the torque of the main rotor by the thrust of the tail rotor leads in practice to a small amount of drift. This is combated by slightly inclining the main rotor, either through the medium of the cyclic pitch system or by tilting the drive shaft.

When changing from hovering to, for example, forward flight, some of the power previously used to maintain the hover is used to supply the forward movement. Unless the thrust from the rotor is increased by using more pitch there is therefore a tendency to sink. Conversely, when a helicopter comes to the hover there is a tendency to rise, combated by decreasing the main rotor's pitch.

The blades of the main rotor become inclined upwards (coning angle) during rotation, due to the influence of the lift they generate. However, centrifugal force and gravity prevent this angle from becoming excessive. Should the engine fail, the rotor blades (if in high pitch) will slow down, centrifugal force can no longer hold them out, and they will cone right up. If the pilot reduces the pitch, drag is reduced and the rotor blades will accelerate. The helicopter will now descend with the blades "gliding" in autorotation, inertia being built up in the rotor so that the pilot can coarsen the pitch during the last few moments of descent to cushion the landing.

History. Leonardo da Vinci made a drawing dated 1483 of a helicopter-like device intended to be lifted by a rotating screw. In 1784 Launoy and Bienvenu flew a model with a pair of rotors made of feathers and turned by a torsion wire spring (the first heavier-than-air machine to fly freely), and during the 19th century attempts were made to use steam power for helicopter-type aircraft.

The gasoline engine made powered flight a practical proposition, although a helicopter requires between two and three times the power of a fixed-wing aircraft to lift the same weight. Louis Breguet flew a helicopter with quadruple biplane-type blades in 1907; Renard pioneered the use of hinged rotor blades; and Igor SIKORSKY built two unsuccessful rotating wing aircraft in Russia during 1909-10. None of these early experiments solved the problem of torque, despite the use of counter-rotating rotors.

Between the wars interest in helicopters declined, partly because the AUTOGIRO was being developed with some success, but the appearance of the twin-rotor Focke-Achgelis Fa 61 helicopter in Germany in 1937 revived enthusiasm in the powered rotating wing. The Fa 61, with a 160 hp power unit, was fully controllable and could descend under autorotation if an engine failure occurred.

Towards the end of World War II Igor Sikorsky, now in the United States, produced the R-4, the first helicopter to enter extensive military service (over 100 were built). This 180 hp machine carried only one passenger and could not normally maintain the hover with a full load.

The Sikorsky R-5 carried two passengers in addition to its two-man crew and became the highly successful S-51 commercial helicopter. The S-55 and S-58 were larger, more powerful machines that carried 10 and 18 passengers respectively, their Russian equivalent being the Mil Mi-4. Using S-55s, New York Airways began passenger operations in July 1953 and SABENA became the first international helicopter passenger carrier in August 1953.

Hell Gate Bridge

A steel-arch bridge in New York City with a span of 977 ft. (297.8 m). It was completed in 1917 and for 14 years had the world's longest arch span. It carries four railroad tracks, links Long Island with the Bronx, and is by far the world's strongest steel arch.

Highway Patrol

Special branch of the police responsible for law enforcement, safety, and traffic regulation of the open highways. As well as ensuring that drivers comply with speed and other traffic regulations, highway patrols investigate accidents, help in the event of breakdown, regulate traffic when necessary (for example after an accident or other emergency), provide information, and chase criminals. Additional duties may include making spot checks on vehicles to test their roadworthiness, and administering breath-analysis tests on drivers suspected of drunken driving.

One of the most important aspects of the highway patrol's work is the enforcement of speed limits. Speeds are checked either with radar devices, or simply by pacing the suspect; but the known presence of patrol cars on a stretch of highway may be sufficient to keep most drivers from speeding.

In recent years airborne highway patrols in helicopters or light airplanes have proved invaluable, especially in locating traffic jams and potential sources of congestion and reporting the information to patrol cars near the scene.

Highways, roads, and streets

Traveled ways for foot traffic and wheeled vehicles. The term road is normally used for minor routes in rural areas; highways are broader and more important rural ways; while the term street is reserved for urban use. A major divided highway with controlled and limited access is often known in the United States as an EXPRESSWAY or FREEWAY. Elsewhere other terms are used, as for example motorway (Britain), AUTOBAHN (Germany), and AUTOSTRADA (Italy).

The ancient Romans appreciated the significance of a planned network of good roads throughout their empire, for military, commercial, and administrative purposes (see ROMAN ROADS). By 200 A.D. their road system radiated from Rome as far as the borders of Scotland in the north, to the Sudan in the south, and east and west as far as the Euphrates and Morocco. And at the same time the famous Silk Road extended from the edge of the empire to China.

A thousand years earlier, the Chinese had a highways commissioner, a system of traffic regulations, and five grades of roads, which ranged from pathways for foot traffic to three-lane highways. In South America during the 15th and 16th centuries, the Incas constructed a remarkable road system consisting of two main routes, one along the coast and one following the Andes, with linking roads between the two.

All these great networks of the past fell into disrepair with the decline of the empires that built them, and except in France, which has been called the cradle of modern road technology, planned highway systems were not developed until well into the automobile era. As early as 1716 France created a state department of roads and bridges, following this in 1747 with Europe's first school of road engineering. By the end of the 18th century France had an extensive network of state-built and maintained roads, divided into three classes: highways from Paris to the frontiers; highways between frontiers; and local roads linking towns. Meanwhile in Britain, roads were largely in the ineffectual hands of local parishes and were for the most part unplanned and badly maintained. Then, at the beginning of the 19th century, the British government appointed Thomas TELFORD to survey and build a major new highway from London to North Wales, and a network of roads in the Highlands of Scotland. Both were brilliant successes in terms of sound engineering and good planning. Unfortunately the invention of the railroad diverted the state's attentions from highways, and although great improvements were made to many existing routes by the work of Telford and McAdam (see MACADAM), a planned national network was not developed. A Road Board was at last set up in 1909, but it was not until the 1930s that the British government fully appreciated the need for a national system of highways.

Development in the United States. America's first "roads" were trails blazed across the country by the Indians. These included the Mohawk trail along the valley of the Mohawk River, traveled by countless settlers in their westward trek from New York and New England, and in use until the Erie Canal and the railroads supplanted it; the Old Connecticut path, which ran from the upper valley of the Hudson River to the Atlantic coast near Boston; and the famous Natchez Trace. Primitive though these trails were, they often followed the best possible route through local terrain and were therefore invaluable in opening up the country. The Natchez Trace, a 450-mi. (725 km) trail from Natchez, Mississippi to Nashville, Tennessee, became a vital highway in the Old Southwest, and today the Natchez Trace Parkway follows the same route.

The colonial governments did little about highways, and during the first century of independence Congress followed the same example, with the exception of the Cumberland (or National) Road. Financed by the federal government, and constructed between 1811 and 1837, this originally ran from Cumberland, Maryland, to Wheeling, West Virginia, and today forms part of U.S. Route 40. Otherwise, the first half of the 19th century was the age of wagon trails like the Santa Fé, and of turnpikes. These toll roads provided vital links until the invention of the railroads which, as in Britain, dominated transportation development during the latter half of the century. By the turn of the century several states had established highway commissions, and were providing aid for highway construction, while the Good Roads Movement was lobbying for a planned national network. At this stage the federal government had done no more than set up a Bureau of Public Roads to look into the question in 1893, but spurred on by the arrival of the automobile, Congress approved a Federal-Aid Road Act in 1916. This established the principle of federal aid for highways, but it left the actual routeing of those highways to the individual states. This however was altered by the Federal-Aid Highway Act of 1921 which formulated a national highway policy with balanced systems of interstate and intercounty highways. Between 1921 and 1960 the mileage of paved roads rose from 387,000 to 2,557,000 (619,200 to 4,091,200 km), and that of multi-lane highways rose from virtually nil to 34,190 (54,700 km). In the same period the United States' total road mileage increased by 21% from 2,925,000 to 3,546,000 (4,680,000 to 5,673,000 km). This increase was partly accounted for by the construction of new arterial divided highways, and partly by the development of parkways, but new urban streets constituted the largest factor. The parkways were originally designed to provide pleasure routes through scenic country rather than to relieve traffic congestion on overcrowded arterial routes, but today there is in most cases little real distinction between them and other expressways, except that generally commercial traffic is prohibited from parkways.

In 1956 new Federal-Aid Highway and Highway Revenue acts accelerated the pace of construction, and led to the completion during the first half of the 1970s of the INTERSTATE HIGHWAY SYSTEM. The total of 41,000 mi. (66,000 km), mostly of four-lane highway, represents only a small fraction of the United States' road mileage, but it is designed to take about 20% of the nation's road traffic, and is by far the largest expressway network in the world.

Today America's network of roads and streets covers 3,700,000 mi. (5,920,000 km) and sets an example to the world in range and efficiency. Yet in many places it is still inadequate, and will probably remain so until some revolutionary new mode of personal transport appears.

Design and location. In planning a new highway the traffic engineer is first

Flyover interchanges on a modern expressway at Detroit.

called in to predict the volume and speed of traffic the highway will carry, and to decide on such matters as width and number of lanes, height of bridges, gradients, maximum radii, and super-elevations of curves (see TRAFFIC ENGINEERING). Next the route is surveyed to see how the highway can be fitted into the terrain, with the minimum of expense and the minimum disturbance to existing roads and other features. One of the most costly aspects of highway construction is earth moving, and so the designer tries to balance excavations with "fills" (stretches where the road must be built up on an embankment).

The ancient Romans, and to a lesser extent the road engineers of 18th- and 19th-century France, laid out their highways as far as possible in straight lines. While this may seem an obvious approach,

providing the shortest route and in theory minimum strain on vehicles and their drivers, it is in modern crowded conditions highly unsafe. On a straight road, the driver has very little to do, very little to occupy his attention, and the dominance of parallel lines is liable to have a powerful hypnotic effect. It is also aesthetically unappealing in most circumstances; a broad and perfectly straight superhighway does not blend with natural scenery. Great care is now taken to landscape highways so that they not only fit as unobtrusively as possible into the countryside, but also give the motorist an opportunity to appreciate the scenery. Efforts are also made to reduce the apparent scale of the highway to the benefit of drivers and the landscape. Traveling along a six- or eight-lane divided highway it is easy to become disoriented and to lose all sense of speed, a danger that can be avoided by separating the two roadways visually if not physically.

Modern divided highways have done much to improve traffic speed and flow, and to increase the pleasure of driving. Also, despite the universal problem of multi-vehicle crashes caused usually by drivers who are careless and in too much of a hurry, the accident rate on expressways and freeways is only a fifth that on rural highways and urban streets.

Construction. Roman roads were built on the principle that the structure of the road should support the load, and they were accordingly up to 5 ft. (1.5 m) thick. Modern highways take enormously higher loads and strains, and yet are frequently only about 1 ft. (0.3 m) thick. Based on the principle that the subsoil should provide the support, the modern type of road was first developed in France and Britain during the second half of the 18th century. Most famous of the early road engineers were Thomas Telford and J.L. McAdam, both Scotsmen. Their roads were admirable for the wheeled traffic of the time, but proved totally inadequate for automobiles and trucks, whose tires loosened the stone surface instead of compacting it (hence the many stories from the early days of the automobile of motorists blinded by dust). This problem was eventually overcome by binding the surface with a bituminous material such as asphalt, a procedure that is still used.

The first step in constructing a highway is to remove all topsoil and vegetation, and then to cut, shape, and compact the ground in readiness for base layers (where needed) and the actual pavement. Wherever possible the subsoil itself is used to provide the foundation for the pavement, suitably stabilized by the addition of cement or bituminous materials to produce a kind of soil-cement. When the subsoil is unsuitable, a foundation (often in two layers known as subbase and base courses) of crushed rocks or coarse concrete is laid first. Essential features of the foundation are that it should be firm, well drained, and stable (not subject to swell and shrinkage).

The pavement may be either flexible or rigid. Flexible pavements are constructed from sand, gravel, and stone mixed with a bituminous material such as asphalt. There are various methods. In one, sometimes called tar macadam (tarmac), hot asphalt or tar is sprayed onto the compacted stone surface, after which a final layer of small stones is spread over and rolled in. A stronger type of flexible pavement is made by mixing the aggre-

This complex arrangement of flyovers and underpasses promotes safety and a steady flow of traffic on busy highways in New York.

gates with asphalt or tar before laying. Two or more layers of this "Plant Mix" compound, each 1-4 in. (2.5-10 cm) thick, produce a smooth pavement with excellent frictional qualities. It is suitable for very heavy traffic, and (an important factor in the design of a busy highway) easily repaired.

Rigid pavements are made of concrete, laid by enormous machines which form premixed concrete into complete slabs in one operation. Each slab is from 6 to 12 in. (15-30 cm) thick, about 24 ft. (7 m) wide, and up to 120 ft. (36 m) in length. The main problem of this type of pavement is in forming and maintaining the joints between slabs that are necessary to allow for shrinkage of the concrete as it sets, and for expansion and contraction caused by changes in temperature. An improved form of concrete pavement incorporates a reinforcing steel mesh. The steel effectively prevents the cracks from opening, so the surface remains watertight. With this method jointless slabs several miles long can be laid.

Many other types of pavement have been tried in the past, including stone and wooden blocks, both of which become slippery when wet, and rubber, which is still occasionally used outside hospitals to reduce noise.

Urban streets. Roughly one third of all automobile trips are on city streets, many of which are today hopelessly crowded. This is not a new problem. There were restrictions on wheeled traffic in ancient Rome, and the streets of many Italian cities during the Renaissance were so congested that Leonardo da Vinci proposed a two-level network, with vehicles and pedestrians separated.

Ideally an urban street should provide a means of access to the buildings along it, and in its vicinity, with all other traffic carried on through highways. Streets are often classified by the amount of through traffic they carry, those in the "highest" category carrying nearly 100% at certain times of day.

The problem for city planners of today is

how to relieve congestion in order to make urban streets reasonably pleasant and safe. One answer is to keep vehicles out of the city center (to a greater or lesser extent), or at least out of certain areas at certain times of day. In this way the city remains essentially a place for people. An alternative is to build elevated expressways into and across urban areas, a process which if carefully planned does much to relieve congestion on the streets, but which is very expensive. It can also dislodge thousands of people from their homes and disturb countless others, and radically alter the appearance of the city. In the United States, possibly the nation which gives the highest priority to the automobile, the second solution has been the usual one, and has been taken furthest in Los Angeles. It has been estimated that one third of this sprawling city is covered by streets and highways, another third by parking lots, leaving only the remaining third for people.

With a new city, planners can create a proper balance between streets and highways, people and traffic, but most cities were laid out before the automobile age, all too often with a rectangular block or gridiron pattern. In the United States, Philadelphia was the first city laid out in this way, but many others followed suit. The system is logical and simple, but the closely spaced intersections and the absence of through routes independent of the grid make it very difficult to achieve a reasonable flow of traffic, despite any number of one-way systems and computer-controlled traffic lights. Another typical layout inherited from the past resembles a spider's web (e.g. Paris). Many of the main streets, and therefore the traffic, converge at a central point (in Paris the Arch of Triumph). The streets radiating from the center are themselves congested with through traffic, while at the focus chaos ensues. To ease the situation in Paris, an expressway round the perimeter of the spider's web has been built, with highway links inside the web; while an underpass below the 12-way intersection at the Arch of Triumph reduces congestion at the center.

Like all solutions to congestion on urban streets, the result is only a partial success. But it seems likely that in the future more and more cities will be forced to take the advice of Julius Caesar and Leonardo da Vinci by restricting traffic, and by separating people and vehicles.

Electronic highways. There is no technological reason why development and construction of electronic highways cannot begin almost immediately. The principle is straightforward. The motorist drives his vehicle in the normal way on minor roads and streets. As he approaches an electronic highway (or "guideway") he slots a coded card into the vehicle's computer detailing his route and exit point. Computer-controlled traffic signals control entry to the guideway, and the vehicle is then locked into a guidance system provided by electronic impulses from cables buried in the pavement. This holds it on course, at a safe distance from others, and at the maximum safe speed. The driver can then read, work or sleep until an alarm signal informs him that he is approaching his exit. But however simple in theory these proposals for automated highways may be, their enormous cost stands in the way of their adoption for some years to come.

Hijacking

The unlawful seizure of airplanes, ships or vehicles is known as hijacking. Taking over airliners to secure political or criminal ends is often referred to as skyjacking, and has become the most notorious manifestation of this crime.

The first aerial hijack took place in 1933, when a Pan American airliner piloted by Byron D. Richards was captured by Peruvian bandits. The crime remained a rare occurrence until the late 1960s, with 1 case in 1947, 7 in 1948, 3 in both 1949 and 1950, but only 2 in the next seven years. There were 10 occurrences in 1962, however, 25 in the ensuing six years, and then no fewer than 33 during 1968, including 21 United States airliners that were forced to divert to Cuba.

In 1969 there were 82 attempted hijackings, in 70 of which the perpetrators either reached their desired destination or were paid a ransom. Among them was the flight of Raffaele Minichiello, who on October 31st seized a TWA airliner en route from Los Angeles to San Francisco and took it to Rome via Denver, New York, Bangor (Maine), and Shannon — one of the longest distances ever covered by a hijacked plane.

The seizure in September 1970 of three airliners by the Popular Front for the Liberation of Palestine was designed to secure the release of terrorists held in Europe and Israel. Their demands in Europe were largely met and the 300 hostages went free, but the aircraft were destroyed on a Jordanian desert air strip. Hijacking was made an extraditable offence by the Hague Convention for the Suppression of Unlawful Seizure of Aircraft (ICAO, December 1970), and during 1971 increased security reduced the incidence of hijackings. Airports and airlines introduced X-ray screening and physical searches of passengers and their baggage, although there were still instances of inadequate checks.

The improvement continued during 1972, but a one-day pilots' strike was called to emphasize the continuing seriousness of the situation, and Southern Airways paid $2,000,000 for a DC-9 ordered to Havana by three hijackers.

A six-week ICAO conference on hijacking took place in Rome in 1973, but there was disagreement on the granting of asylum to political refugees since there had been several instances of escapers from the eastern bloc seizing airliners.

Hindenburg

Hydrogen-filled German airship completed in 1936 following the success of the smaller GRAF ZEPPELIN. It was 804 ft. (245 m) long, and flew a scheduled service between Friedrichshafen, Germany, and Lakehurst, New Jersey, carrying a total of a thousand passengers safely across the Atlantic before disaster struck on May 6, 1937. While approaching her mooring mast at Lakehurst she burst into flames. This disaster, which has never been explained, followed several other airship accidents during the preceding years, and effectively marked the end of the airship experiment on a large scale.

Hispano-Suiza

Famous automobile and aircraft engine manufacturer during the years 1940-44. The original Spanish factory produced magnificent "motor carriages" as well as successful racers, but the make is most noted for its postwar models made by the French branch in Paris. The 150-hp V-8 Hispano-Suiza engine powered many World War I fighter planes, and from it was developed the 6.6-liter 135-hp engine of the 1919 HS-B automobile. It was designed as the ultimate in luxury and performance, and a sporting version, known as the Boulogne, appeared in 1924 with a top speed of 110 mph (176 km/h). In 1931 Hispano-Suiza introduced the HS-68, an equally famous luxury V-12 of 9½ liters, and followed it with the 11,300-cc 68 bis.

Holland, John Philip (1840-1914)

Designer of the world's first practical SUBMARINE, Holland was born in Ireland and emigrated to the United States in 1873. He tested his first submarine in 1875, and built another in 1879 called the *Fenian Ram*. These early models pioneered the use of horizontal fins for diving under power. In 1895 the U.S. Navy ordered a submarine from Holland's Torpedo Boat Company, but the resulting *Plunger* was a failure. Holland returned the navy's money and financed his next submarine himself. Launched in 1897, the *Holland* was ordered by the navies of the United States, Britain, Japan, and Russia.

Horn

A device used for sounding a warning signal. Noise is produced in a horn by a vibrating diaphragm. In a simple automobile horn the diaphragm is attached to a plunger which is attracted into a solenoid when the horn button is pressed. As it moves, it causes two contact points to separate, temporarily cutting off the current to the solenoid. The plunger and thus the diaphragm therefore oscillate back and forth causing the noise. In the so-called wind-tone horn, the diaphragm vibrates the air in a chamber giving a more pleasant sound. In the air horn the diaphragm is vibrated by compressed air supplied by an electric pump.

Horsepower

A unit of power in the English system, equal to 33, 000 foot-pounds of work per minute. Scottish engineer James Watt calculated that this was a good rate of working for a strong horse. The so-called metric horsepower is a rate of working of 4,500 kilogram-meters per minute (32,549 ft.-lb. per minute or 0.99 hp). The electrical equivalent of 1 hp is 746 watts, and the heat equivalent is 2,545 British thermal units per hour. The effective work output of an engine is called the brake horsepower (bhp) and is always somewhat less than the power developed in, for example, the cylinders, which is termed the indicated horsepower. The difference between them is accounted for by frictional losses.

Houston Ship Channel

A lockless waterway which allows ships to sail from the Gulf of Mexico to Houston, Texas. A little over 50 mi. (80 km) long, it was opened in its present form in 1914 and subsequently deepened to 36 ft. (11 m).

Howrah Bridge

In Calcutta, India, it has the world's fifth longest cantilever span (1,500 ft., 457 m). It was completed in 1943, and replaced an old floating bridge. The anchor arms were erected first, after which the cantilever arms were built using creeper cranes working over the top of the bridge. The bridge has central tramways and outer lanes reserved for bullock carts. Two footways are provided outside the main trusses.

Humber Bridge

A suspension bridge across the Humber River estuary on the east coast of England, due for completion in 1978. Its span of 4,625 ft. (1,410 m) will make it the world's longest-span suspension bridge, eclipsing New York's VERRAZANO-NARROWS BRIDGE by 365 ft. (111 m).
It will carry dual two-lane highways, cycle tracks and footways, is expected to cost £52 million, and is designed to encourage industrial developments in the area.

Huskisson, William (1770-1830)

British politician with the unfortunate distinction of being the first man to be killed by a locomotive (at the opening of the world's first all steam public railroad, the Liverpool and Manchester). He played a significant part in the reform of the Navigation Acts which later opened British trade to foreign ships and thus encouraged the development of fast-sailing merchant ships .

Hydraulic systems

Systems that work by liquid pressure. Liquids are virtually incompressible, and pressure applied at one point in a hydraulic system is transmitted without appreciable loss to other parts .Hydraulic systems are therefore a very effective way of transmitting power and are widely used in all kinds of vehicles and craft.
In automobiles they are used in the transmission, braking and steering mechanisms. An auto brake pedal is connected to the piston of a master cylinder. This is linked by pipelines to a slave cylinder on each brake. A piston in the slave cylinder applies the brake. The whole system is filled with hydraulic fluid (a synthetic liquid that does not affect rubber seals in the cylinders). Pressing down the brake pedal forces the piston down the master cylinder, and this transmits pressure equally and simultaneously through the fluid to the pistons in the four slave cylinders. The slave piston's diameter is usually greater than that of the master piston and it thus exerts greater force (though it travels proportionally less).
In an automatic gearbox a hydraulic pump supplies oil under pressure through valves to operate the brake bands and clutches that control the operation of the EPICYCLIC-GEAR train. The automatic gearbox is used in conjunction with a TORQUE CONVERTER which uses fluid to transmit motion between flywheel and gearbox. In power steering a hydraulic pump driven by the engine supplies fluid under pressure to the system. Movement of the steering wheel in one direction allows the pressurized fluid to press against one side of a ram that connects with the steering system.
Aircraft employ hydraulic systems to actuate the control surfaces (rudder, elevators, ailerons, flaps, etc.) and retractable landing gear. These systems are often duplicated or triplicated to prevent loss of control should one system fail. The hydraulic installation includes pumps for supplying oil under pressure; pipelines for distributing the oil; hydraulic rams or motors to move the control surfaces or landing gear; and a variety of pressure-limiting and non-return valves. Movement of the controls cuts in the appropriate pump and allows pressure through to the actuating motors or rams. Displacement pumps are used, and may be rotary vane, gear, or reciprocating plunger types. The latter are common because they can generate high pressure; they are driven by an angled swash-plate. The hydraulic motors are of similar type to the pumps already mentioned. Hydraulic rams convert hydraulic power into linear motion by admitting oil to either side of a piston.

A high-speed naval gunboat hydrofoil, the Grumman Flagstaff. This craft has three fully-submerged foils providing maximum smoothness, high maneuverability, and a stable gun platform.

Hydrocarbons

Organic compounds containing hydrogen and carbon only. Important as fuels and lubricants, they are also used in the production of a wide variety of substances including plastics and rubber. Petroleum and natural gas are made up almost entirely of hydrocarbons and are usually termed hydrocarbon fuels. One of the simplest hydrocarbons, found in natural gas, is methane, which has the chemical formula CH_4 (one carbon to four hydrogen atoms).

Hydrodynamics

The science of fluids, particularly water, in motion (see FLUID MECHANICS).

A hydrofoil ferry with V shaped surface-piercing foils. At rest and slow speeds the vessel sits in the water like a conventional boat.

Hydrofoil

Strictly speaking a hydrofoil is an underwater fin designed to provide LIFT in water exactly as the airfoil shape of an airplane wing provides lift in air. A vessel fitted with such fins is a hydrofoil craft, commonly known simply as a hydrofoil.

At rest and at slow speeds a hydrofoil remains in the water like a boat, but as it gathers speed the fins provide lift and raise the hull clear of the surface. Since their frictional resistance is so low, hydrofoils travel faster than normal watercraft. Speeds of around 40 knots are common, while experimental hydrofoils have reached 80 knots. Hydrofoils need great power in relation to their weight, and the stresses on the foils and their struts are considerable. This makes it unlikely that very large hydrofoils will ever be built. Ranging from small pleasure craft to naval patrol boats and passenger-automobile ferries, the largest hydrofoils are about 200 ft. (60 m) in length.

The foils are shaped like airplane wings, but are relatively small (the greater density of water creates a proportionately greater lift). Two types are used: surface-piercing foils, so-called because their tips project above the water; and fully submerged foils. Most early hydrofoils had ladder-like surface-piercing foils, each step on the ladder providing a separate lifting surface. Most famous of these was Alexander Graham Bell's world water-speed record-breaker of 1918, the HD 4. Propelled by aircraft propellers, the HD 4 reached 60 knots. The ladder foil is expensive and heavy, and modern surface-piercing foils are V-shaped.

Surface-piercing foils are fixed, relying on their geometry for control and stability. At low speeds the maximum amount of foil is underwater, giving maximum lift. At full speed, minimum foil-surface is needed to hold the craft up. If the craft heels over, the foil on one side becomes more submerged (and provides greater lift) than that on the other, and the hydrofoil automatically rights itself. This inherent stability is the prime advantage of surface-piercing foils. Their drawback is that the foil is affected by waves; in choppy or rough water they give an uncomfortable ride.

The fastest, smoothest, and most sophisticated hydrofoils have three fully submerged foils. These are comparatively uninfluenced by waves, and when properly controlled give a perfectly smooth ride over choppy water provided that the height of the waves does not exceed the length of the struts. However, such foils need adjustable control surfaces that resemble the AILERONS on an airplane wing. The control surface on each foil must be adjusted to balance the craft, a complex process that is performed by an electronic sensor which measures the height of oncoming waves, a computer which calculates the necessary settings for the foils, and a control mechanism which actually adjusts the foils.

Propelled by conventional marine propellers, or by water jets, and powered by diesel or lightweight gas-turbine engines, hydrofoils are fast and highly maneuverable (their stopping distance is roughly twice their length), and are admirable as fast patrol boats, and as ferries on sheltered waters.

Hydrography

Scientific study and description of the waters of the world. Using modern navigational aids for accurately fixing position, hydrographic research ships employ various techniques to survey and chart the contours of the ocean bed. These range from the traditional sounding pole in shallow waters to advanced ECHO SOUNDERS and include a technique known as wire-dragging, in which two vessels tow a submerged horizontal cable (at a known depth) to locate high spots that may have been missed by echo sounding.

Accurate and up-to-date hydrographic charts are of great importance to all shipping, but especially to modern superships, some of which have drafts of nearly 100 ft. (30 m). Detailed maps of the contours of the ocean bottom are also used in cable and pipeline laying operations.

Other data gathered by hydrographic research include details of tides, magnetic declination, and general facts about shipping routes (see OCEANOGRAPHY).

Hydrolastic suspension

An automobile suspension system linking front and rear suspensions and designed to give a more level ride by reducing the tendency of an automobile to pitch when the wheels hit an obstacle. It was introduced by British Motor Corporation (now British Leyland) on their 1100 range in 1962. A displacer unit is located at each wheel and incorporates a rubber spring, two-way valve, diaphragm, and piston. The displacer units at front and rear on each side are linked by fluid pipelines. When the front wheel goes over a bump, the piston and connecting diaphragm travel upward, displacing fluid along the connecting pipe to the rear unit. This displaces the rear diaphragm and connected piston, thereby raising the rear end. When the bump is passed, fluid returns to the front unit.

Hydroplane

A fast motor-boat that skims or planes over the surface of the water when it is traveling at high speed. The hull is shaped so that it lifts out of the water as speed increases (see MOTOR BOAT).

Hydropneumatic suspension

A combination hydraulic-pneumatic suspension system introduced by Citroën on their famous DS 19 model in 1955. An independent suspension unit is fitted to each wheel. A piston on the suspension arm attached to the wheel can move up and down in a hydraulic cylinder. The cylinder connects with a sphere in which nitrogen gas is trapped by a diaphragm. Upward movement of the piston forces fluid against the diaphragm, thus compressing the gas, which acts as a damper.

The piston and suspension arm also form part of a self-leveling system. Movement of the piston and suspension arm downward under load opens a slide valve, which allows more fluid (under pressure from an engine-operated pump) into the system until the original level is regained. When the load is removed, the suspension arm rises and fluid flows back until the normal level is reached.

Hydrostatics

The science concerned with the behavior and properties of a fluid at rest, and of bodies immersed in a fluid. It is con-

The U.S. icebreaker Glacier *forcing a passage through pack ice in the Ross Sea, Antarctica.*

cerned for example with liquid and gas pressure, buoyancy and flotation. One of the most famous laws of hydrostatics was discovered by the Greek scientist Archimedes in the 200s B.C. He found that when a body is placed in a fluid it apparently loses weight, and the weight of fluid displaced is equal to the apparent loss in weight of the body. The immersed body experiences an upward force (see BUOYANCY).

Another basic hydrostatic principle is that pressure in a liquid increases regularly with depth, and is equal to the product of depth and density. In sea water for example pressure increases by about 4½ lb./sq. in. for every 10 ft. of depth (31 kilopascals for every 3 m). At 300 ft. (91.44 m) the pressure is about 10 times that at sea level (see DIVING).

A third important hydrostatic principle is that liquids are virtually incompressible and pressure applied to them is transmitted evenly through them in all directions without significant loss. This forms the basis of the science of hydraulics (see HYDRAULIC SYSTEMS).

I

Icebreaker

A ship designed to maintain a channel through ice to keep ports and important shipping routes open. Icebreakers are unusually broad, since the path cleared must be wide enough for normal ships, have a thickened and strengthened hull to withstand constant battering from the ice, specially protected propellers, and gently sloping underwater lines at bow and stern. The ship rides up on the ice as it steams forward, and breaks it from above (rather than crashing into it). A modern icebreaker can steam steadily through ice up to about 3 ft. (1 m) thick (see also LENIN).

Ignition system

The system which provides the means of igniting the fuel in a HEAT ENGINE. In gasoline engines the fuel is ignited by an electric spark. In an automobile the battery supplies a low-voltage current to the primary windings of the induction COIL via the contact-breaker in the DISTRIBUTOR. The current flow is interrupted periodically as the contact-breaker points open, thus inducing a very high voltage (up to about 30,000 volts) in the secondary windings of the coil. This high voltage is led by the distributor to each spark plug in turn at the appropriate moment in the engine cycle, causing a spark which ignites the fuel in the combustion chamber. In airplane and motorcycle gasoline engines the high voltage is usually supplied by a MAGNETO instead of by battery and coil.

An advanced capacitor discharge ignition system is used in some automobiles. Here a 250-300 volt charge is stored in a capacitor, and is discharged to the primary windings of the coil by an electronic switching device. The system produces a more intense spark, giving improved starting and firing (even with flooded, dirty, or eroded points), and longer plug life.

In jet and rocket engines, ignition may also be electric, but it is usually required only when starting. Thereafter the incoming fuel will be ignited automatically as it is sprayed into the hot combustion chamber, which contains burning fuel.

In diesel engines, which burn light oil, ignition of the fuel takes place when it is injected into hot air. The air is heated by being compressed in the engine cylinder into one-fifteenth or less of the space it originally occupied. This is called COMPRESSION-IGNITION.

Illinois Waterway

Waterway connecting Lake Michigan (at Chicago) with the Mississippi River, allowing barges to travel from the Great Lakes to the Gulf of Mexico. Some 330 mi. (530 km) long, it incorporates seven locks and was completed in 1933. For part of its course it is paralleled by the now defunct Illinois and Michigan Canal, completed in 1848 (see also CHICAGO SANITARY AND SHIP CANAL).

Inclined plane

A sloping surface used on canals and inland waterways in place of a series of locks, to raise or lower vessels from one level to another, when the difference in levels is great. The vessel is floated into a tank or CAISSON which is hauled bodily up the inclined plane on rails. A typical modern example is the one at Ronquières, Belgium; with a vertical rise of 220 ft. (66 m), it replaces 17 locks, and thus saves a great deal of time.

Independent suspension

A vehicle suspension system in which each wheel is connected to the body independently. Thus, if the wheels on one side ride over a bump, the body does not tilt sideways appreciably, as it would if the wheels were linked by a rigid axle. Front-wheel independent suspension was pioneered in 1922 by Lancia on its Lamda model, and is today universal in automobiles. One of the commonest types is the double-wishbone (see SUSPENSION SYSTEM). Independent suspension of the rear wheels is becoming more common, though most vehicles still have a rigid rear axle.

Indianapolis Speedway

First opened as a dirt track on August 19, 1909, and soon afterwards paved with bricks, the 2½-mi. (4 km) race track is the scene of one of the world's most spectacular automobile races, the "Indy 500." First run on May 30, 1911, the race is today the peak of a month of events which include four-lap qualifying trials. The 33 drivers with the highest speeds in these trials compete in the actual Indy 500, a 500-mi. (804 km) race with prize money totaling over $1,000,000, and one of the events in the annual drivers' championship. Average speeds were around 75 mph (121 km/h) in the early days, but in recent years have exceeded 160 mph (257 km/h). In 1935 part of the speedway track was surfaced with asphalt, and in 1962 the entire track was asphalted except for a 3-ft. (91 cm) strip at the starting line where the traditional bricks have been retained. Sometimes called the "Hoosier Bowl" or "brickyard," the Indianapolis Speedway is oval-shaped.

Inertial Guidance

A method of navigation or guidance used in rockets, missiles, and submarines, and consisting essentially of ACCELEROMETERS, gyroscopes, and a computer. There are three accelerometers set up with their axes mutually perpendicular. They sense and measure changes of speed in any direction, and are coupled to gyroscopes, which provide an independent frame of reference.

The measurements of the accelerometers are fed into the computer, which works out the actual path of the body from a known starting point, and records it. Alternatively, the computer may have been programed with the desired course, in which case it acts as an automatic pilot. If the actual course coincides with the programed one, the computer takes no action; if they differ, it sends appropriate signals to the controls to correct deviations.

Inertial guidance is thus a sophisticated form of dead reckoning, the traditional procedure of estimating position from speed and direction (see NAVIGATION). It is an entirely self-contained system, and as such is invaluable to submarines, which are isolated from radio or celestial navigation. It produces errors of less than 1 mi. (1.6 km) after a week's continuous cruising. However a submarine on prolonged submerged missions normally ascends to periscope depth from time to time to check position by radio or celestial navigation.

Inland Waterways

See CANALS.

Instrument Landing System (ILS)

A radio aid that enables a pilot to make his final approach to the runway in adverse weather, and is in fact often used as a matter of routine even in good visibility. A meter in the flight deck registers signals from "localizer" and "glide path" transmitters. The localizer antenna is in line with but beyond the far end of the runway, and transmits a narrow beam extending 2½ degrees each side of the runway center line. If the plane is within this beam, the meter's localizer beam pointer hangs vertically; the pilot knows that he is on course. If the plane flies to the right of the beam, the needle swings to the left; the pilot must "fly left" to get back on course (and vice versa).

The glide path antenna is positioned near the touchdown end of the runway and in effect transmits a beam angled up at about three degrees to the horizontal. When a plane is on the glide path beam, the second meter pointer is horizontal. If the pilot deviates above the beam the pointer swings down, indicating "fly down" (and vice versa). Two additional antennae transmit vertical beacons at distances of about 5 mi. (8 km) and ¾ mi. (1 km) from the touchdown point as a position check. ILS provides an accurate and reliable guide for the approach, but not for the actual landing, which is performed visually (see AIR TRAFFIC CONTROL).

Internal Combustion Engine (ICE)

An engine which derives its power by burning fuel in an enclosed chamber. The gaseous products of combustion act directly on a piston or rotor, driving it down or around and thereby developing mechanical power. Most engines used in transportation are of the internal combustion type, including the GASOLINE ENGINE, the DIESEL ENGINE, the GAS ENGINE, the GAS TURBINE and the JET ENGINE. The ICE contrasts with the external combustion engine such as the steam engine, in which fuel is burned outside the engine to provide heat for power. Internal combustion engines may be classified in many ways. These include: heat cycle (constant volume or constant pressure), mechanical cycle (two-stroke, four-stroke); single-acting, double-acting; method of cooling (air, water); reciprocating, rotary; cylinder arrangement (in-line, horizontally-opposed, V); valve arrangement (side-valve, overhead-valve); method of firing (spark-ignition, compression-ignition); supercharged or unsupercharged (naturally aspirated); carburated or fuel-injected; type of fuel (gas, gasoline, diesel, oil); high-compression, low-compression; application (automobile, aircraft, marine).

International Air Transport Association (IATA)

The majority of the world's scheduled airlines are members of IATA, which helps operators to correlate their routes, collectively negotiate fare structures, and reciprocally complement each other's services. International airlines are full members, domestic operators are associates.

There is a Financial Committee (currency exchange, insurance, taxation, inter-line transactions), a Legal Committee, and a Technical Committee. Traffic Conferences are normally held every two years and decide policy for passenger fares and freight rates, other matters being referred to special conference committees.

IATA itself was founded in 1945, but owes its origins to the International Air Traffic Association which was established at The Hague in 1919. It has main offices in Montreal and Geneva.

Intersection

An area where two or more highways join or cross, an intersection includes the roadway and the roadside facilities for traffic movement. The design of intersections forms one of the most important parts of traffic engineering. The ideal is to ensure a rapid and smooth flow of traffic with optimum safety.

On a grade intersection the highways join or cross at the same level. Direct conflict between the intersecting traffic streams is further complicated by diverging and merging movements of turning vehicles, particularly by left-turning traffic which must cut across oncoming traffic (with right-hand rule of the road). Conflict can be minimized by the use of carefully sited small islands, widely curving curbs and clear traffic-lane markings. Alternatively a traffic circle (roundabout) or traffic control signals may be used.

On busy highways the safest answer is a grade-separated or multilevel, intersection which separates vehicles traveling in conflicting directions. But the construction of overpasses and underpasses makes this type of intersection very expensive, and its use is generally re-

The world's first iron bridge, built in Shropshire, England, in 1779.

stricted to freeways or points of particularly severe congestion. Cloverleaf and traffic circle intersections enable vehicles to travel from one route to the other. Conflict between cross traffic is eliminated, the only hazards being caused by vehicles entering and leaving the fast-moving traffic streams. This is minimized by the provision of acceleration and deceleration lanes (see TRAFFIC ENGINEERING).

Interstate Highway System

The world's most extensive national highway network. Started in the 1950s and completed in the mid-1970s, it consists of 41,000 mi. (66,000 km) of multi-lane divided highway linking 48 states and 90% of all cities with populations of over 50,000. The network cost about $50 billion and makes use of the latest design and engineering techniques. The sharpest curve is so gentle that the driver can see at least 400 yards (365 m) ahead, and the steepest gradient is only 1 in 20. Cloverleaf interchanges ensure safety and an uninterrupted flow of traffic.

Although comprising only a small fraction of the United States' total highway mileage, the Interstate Highway System is designed to take about 20% of the country's traffic.

Ion engine

A rocket engine that produces thrust by accelerating ions (atoms with their electrons removed) by means of an electro-static field. Both the United States and Russia are developing ion engines, and have successfully tested them in space. Mercury and cesium are generally used as propellants because they ionize readily. Ion engines would be of no use for powering launch vehicles, because they develop very low thrust, but they can produce pulses of thrust over periods of months or even years, and would thus be suitable for cruising in long-duration

space flights. In addition, by replacing chemical propellants for propulsion in space, they may allow takeoff weights to be reduced by 50%.

Iron Bridge

The world's first iron bridge, constructed across the River Severn at Ironbridge, Shropshire, England, in 1779. Built of cast iron by Abraham Darby III (grandson of the Abraham Darby who first smelted iron with coke 70 years earlier), it consists of a 100 ft. (30 m) semicircular arch.

Ironclad

Originally a wooden WARSHIP with iron plates covering (cladding) and protecting the hull. The idea first came from the French "floating batteries," ironclad barges carrying heavy guns, used in the Crimean War. This led to the first ironclad warship, the *Gloire* (launched in 1859), with $4\frac{3}{4}$-in. (11 cm) armor plating. The first battle between ironclads was the historic confrontation of the *Monitor* and *Merrimack* in the American Civil War.

J

Jet engine

A jet engine draws in air at the front, compresses it, and mixes it with fuel in the COMBUSTION CHAMBER. The resulting hot gases stream out of the jet nozzle, producing forward thrust by reaction in accordance with Newton's third law ("For every action there is an equal and opposite reaction"). While a propeller provides thrust by forcing a large volume of air back at a relatively slow speed, a jet engine ejects a comparatively small volume of gas at a very high speed. The greatest speed attained by a propeller-driven plane is about 550 mph (885 km/h), while the fastest jets reach well over 2,000 mph (3,218 km/h).

There are four basic elements in a jet engine: the compressor, which sucks air in at the front; the combustion chamber; the TURBINE, which is turned by the exhaust gases and drives the compressor (and, in the case of a TURBOPROP, the propeller); and the exhaust nozzle.

Compressors can be either centrifugal or axial. The centrifugal type distributes air to the combustion chambers from the perimeter of the impeler disk and can compress air to a ratio of about 5:1 in a single stage. In the more common axial

from a nozzle and this mixture is ignited. Exhaust gases pass backwards and drive turbines, the first (high-pressure) turbine powering the high-pressure compressor while the shaft from the second (low-pressure) turbine runs forward inside the high-pressure shaft to drive the low-pressure compressor.

Finally the exhaust passes out of the tail pipe, where an AFTERBURNER may be located. Power can also be boosted by 25% if water, or a water and alcohol mixture, is injected either into the compressor inlet or into the diffuser.

Reverse thrust is achieved by fitting clamshell vanes to the exhaust nozzle. These

The first two Heinkel jet engines had been unsuccessful because a small combustion chamber size had been dictated by the lack of ram effect at the air intake. The He 178's engine, the centrifugal S2, developed just under 1,000 lb. (454 kg) thrust and overcame this difficulty by spraying vaporized fuel into its 16 combustion chambers.

The Whittle-designed W.1 engine of 1,000 lb. (454 kg) thrust powered the Gloster E.28/39 research aircraft when it made Britain's first jet flight at Cranwell in May 1941, and in America the Bell P-59 Airacomet used two General Electric copies of the Whittle W.2B power

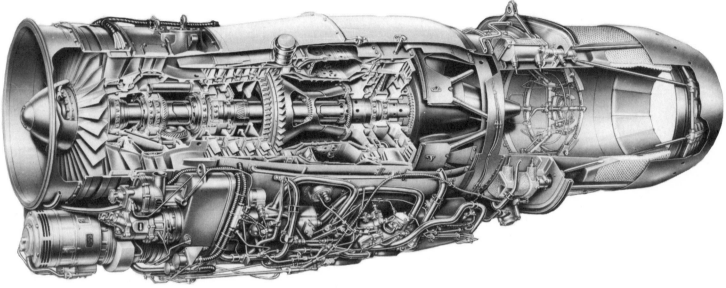

A cutaway view of a jet engine, the Rolls-Royce Turbomeca Adour turbofan. The rings of compressor blades can be seen at the left. With variable afterburning the 4,400 lb. (2,000 kg) thrust of this unit can be boosted by over 50%.

compressors the air passes along a series of perhaps nine rings of compressor blades that become progressively smaller and increase the degree of compression. A second spool, comprising another seven or so rings of blades, may be placed behind the first one to give the compression ratios of 25:1 or more.

The compressed air passes into the combustion chambers through a diffuser, which ensures that the air is at the optimum pressure and velocity for the best fuel combustion. Combustion chambers may be of the individual *can* type, the *annular* type (basically a single chamber that completely surrounds the engine), or the *cannular* (or turbo-annular) variant, which is a series of small flame tubes inside a common air casing that encircles the engine.

Jet engines usually have only two ignition sources, located in flame tubes on opposite sides of the power unit; at start-up the flame travels from these tubes to every other tube in turn via cross-ignition tube connections.

In the combustion chambers the compressed air mixes with fuel sprayed in

can be used to redirect the gas flow forwards, while swiveling nozzles are a feature of vertical takeoff and landing aircraft (see HARRIER; VTOL).

In bypass engines, some of the air from the first stage of an axial compressor is led down ducts that bypass the combustion chambers and discharge into the jet nozzle. This increases the mass of the air being accelerated out of the engine and hence increases the thrust. Turbofans have the first rows of the low-pressure compressor designed as fans to accelerate a cold air stream and thus provide a low-velocity jet efflux with accompanying high propulsive efficiency (in some engines this fan is at the rear and forms part of the turbine assembly).

History. Early development of the jet engine took place in Britain during the 1930s under the direction of Frank Whittle, who took out a patent on the principle in 1930. Parallel experimentation in Germany was initiated by Ernst Heinkel in 1936, and the world's first jet-propelled flight was made by the HEINKEL HE 178 in August 1939.

unit when it took to the air in October 1942.

During the latter stages of World War II the Germans developed the 1,980 lb. (898 kg) thrust Junkers Jumo 004 axial-type engine, which powered both the Messerschmitt 262 fighter and the Arado 234 bomber. British jet engine development tended initially to concentrate on centrifugals (Rolls-Royce Derwent and Nene) and the sale of 55 of these engines to the Soviet Union in 1948 had an influential effect on early Russian jet engine development. In America the 4,600 lb. (2,086 kg) thrust J-33 centrifugal that powered early military jets was followed by the axial J-47 developing 7,500 lb. (3,401 kg) thrust, and the axial has now virtually supplanted the centrifugal. Afterburning had been applied to the J-33 by 1952, and bypass engines were coming into service in 1959, with turbofans making their appearance by the early 1960s. Current research concentrates on increasing efficiency and power, and on reducing noise (by for example higher bypass ratios). (See also PULSE JET; RAMJET.)

Jet stream

A strong, narrow current of air flowing at speeds of from 70 to over 300 mph (110 to over 480 km/h), at altitudes of from 6 to 31 mi. (10 to 50 km). These currents are generated by energy released during the massive heat transfer occurring between cold air from the poles and warm air from the tropics. They flow eastward and are usually a few miles deep, up to about 100 mi. (160 km) wide, and well over 1,000 mi. (1,600 km) in length. The strongest jet streams occur over Japan.

Discovered by World War II pilots flying over Japan and the Mediterranean, they have become increasingly significant with the spread of high altitude air transportation. Planes heading into a jet stream require additional fuel, while the

The famous pioneer English aviator, Amy Johnson, the first woman to fly solo from England to Australia (1930).

Traditional Chinese junks. During the age of sail these were probably the most efficient sailing ships of all, despite their clumsy appearance.

turbulent airflow commonly found at the margins of a jet stream represents a considerable hazard.

John Bull

John Bull was a 10-ton locomotive built in England and delivered to the Camden & Amboy Railroad. On November 12, 1831, it hauled the first passengers to ride behind a steam locomotive on a regular railroad in New Jersey. *John Bull* was the first locomotive to run on any part of what later became the Pennsylvania Railroad.

Johnson, Amy (1903-1941)

Pioneer English aviator who in 1930 became the first woman to make a solo flight from England to Australia (in 19 days). In 1931 she flew to Tokyo and back. In 1932, with her husband J.A. Mollison, she set a record for the flight to the Cape (South Africa), and in 1936 she improved on this record. She flew air ferry services in World War II until her death in a crash in 1941.

Jumbo jet

The name given to the present generation of huge passenger jet airliners capable of holding 400 or more passengers, especially to the BOEING 747.

Jumbo rig

A multilevel platform used in rock tunneling for drilling a series of holes into the tunnel face simultaneously (see TUNNELING).

Jump jet

A term applied to jet planes that can take off and land vertically, such as the HARRIER (see VTOL).

Junk

Traditional Chinese seagoing sailing vessel, originating in ancient times but still in use today. With flat bottom, high stern, and from three to five masts carrying square sails (often made of matting and held flat by horizontal lengths of bamboo), junks are extremely strong, but slow.

Junkers J1

The first all-metal airplane, designed by Hugo Junkers (1859-1935), who became one of Germany's top airplane designers. First flown in 1915, the J1 was an experimental iron monoplane with cantilever wings of 42.5-ft. (13 m) span. Its overall length was 28 ft. (8.5 m); maximum loaded weight 2,380 lb. (1,080 kg); and maximum speed 106 mph (170 km/h).

K

Kaiser

American automobile introduced in 1946 by the Kaiser-Frazer Corporation. One of the first cars with "modern" styling, it set a trend followed by most other manufacturers for aerodynamically designed cars with similar lines at front and rear. During 1947-48 the Kaiser outsold all other independents, but although the company went on to introduce other inspired designs, it failed to hold its position and disappeared in 1955.

Kayak

A long, narrow, enclosed one-man CANOE used by Eskimos for hunting and fishing, and propelled with a double paddle. Consisting of a wooden framework covered with sealskin, it weighs only about 60 lb. (27 kg) and is self-righting. Modern sporting kayaks are usually made of glass reinforced plastic.

Keel

The structural "backbone" of a boat or ship's hull, running longitudinally along the center of the bottom. It may be made in a single piece, or in a large timber vessel, of several lengths fixed securely together. The keel is the central timber, on which the whole boat is built up. To it are attached stempost, sternpost, and ribs.

In early square-rigged sailing ships the keel's role was almost entirely structural, but in modern fore-and-aft rigged fast sailing craft the keel normally projects well below the hull to provide the vessel with a good "grip" in the water, that is, to prevent it from slipping sideways when under sail (see also CENTERBOARD).

Ketch

A two-masted fore-and-aft rigged sailing vessel, with gaff-rigged main and mizzen sails. Ketch-rigged trawlers and coastal freighters (often called billyboys) were common from the 18th century until the early years of the 20th century.

Kettering, Charles Franklin (1876-1958)

An American inventor, many of whose ideas contributed to the development of the automobile. He invented the electric starter, and improved ignition and lighting systems. In his position as research director for General Motors (from 1920 to 1947) he did important work on automobile paints, and on antiknock and leaded gasoline. Later, he improved the efficiency of the two-stroke diesel engine, and developed a high compression gasoline engine.

In the aerospace field he founded the Dayton-Wright Airplane Company in 1914, and developed a propeller-driven guided missile.

Kiel Canal

One of Europe's main waterways, cutting through the German province of Schleswig-Holstein to connect the North Sea with the Baltic. Some 60 mi. (96 km) long, it runs from Brunsbüttelkoog, near the mouth of the Elbe River, to Holtenau, near Kiel on the Baltic. The alternative route, before the canal was built, was around the Jutland peninsula, a distance of more than 300 mi. (480 km). The Kiel Canal was completed in 1895 and subsequently enlarged to a depth of 36 ft. (11 m) and width of 144 ft. (44 m). It is often called the North Sea-Baltic Canal, or, in German, the Nord-Ostsee Kanal.

Kite

The oldest form of aircraft known, a kite is basically a tethered glider. It obtains lift from air striking its under-surfaces, which are inclined at an angle to the wind. It is the true ancestor of the AIR PLANE; the WRIGHT BROTHERS pioneering *Glider No. 1* was first flown as a kite. Kites, capable of lifting men and thereby the first man-carrying aircraft, were known to the Chinese around 1000 B.C. Introduced to Europe in about the 13th century, they were employed by the British Royal Navy from 1806, being first used for dropping propaganda leaflets over the French coast in the Napoleonic Wars. The box kite of two square cells joined by booms, providing the basic configuration of some early biplanes, was introduced by the Australian, Lawrence Hargreaves, in 1893. Kites are now flown for amusement, and the word is also a slang term for an airplane.

A kite balloon is a balloon with large air lobes acting as stabilizers to keep it heading to wind and so prevent spinning. Kite balloons were used for observation purposes in World War I, and as "barrage" balloons in World War II.

Knocking

A metallic banging noise emanating from a gasoline engine using the wrong grade of fuel. It is caused by uneven burning of the fuel mixture in the cylinders, and is properly termed detonation (see GASOLINE).

Knot

The traditional measure of speed at sea and in the air, equaling a NAUTICAL MILE an hour. A nautical mile is 6,076.12 ft. (1,852 m), thus a speed of 20 knots is equivalent to approximately 23 mph (37 km/h) (see LOG).

Kon Tiki

The primitive balsa raft on which the Norwegian scientist Thor Heyerdahl and five other men crossed the Pacific in 1947, drifting with the wind and the ocean currents. The voyage lasted 101 days, from Peru on the western coast of South America to an island in the Tuamotu group east of Tahiti in the Pacific, a distance of 4,300 mi. (6,900 km). The raft was built of local balsa logs in Peru, and the journey was undertaken to discover whether the Polynesian islands could have been colonized from South America.

L

Lafayette

A celebrated early LOCOMOTIVE built in 1837 by William Norris of Philadelphia. It was a 4-2-0 machine with outside cylinders and a high, domed firebox. The wide-mouthed chimney was longer than the boiler. This very successful type of locomotive was particularly well-known for its grade-climbing abilities.

Laminar flow

Also called streamline flow or viscous flow, a kind of fluid flow in which the particles are in continuous, steady motion in a regular path. A state of laminar flow will exist in a fluid up to a certain velocity, after which the flow pattern becomes random and haphazard (turbulent). The point at which this occurs in a given fluid is defined by REYNOLD'S NUMBER. (See AERODYNAMICS; FLUID MECHANICS.)

Landing craft

Naval vessel for landing troops and equipment in seaborne assault operations. The conventional landing craft simply grounded on the beach, and troops and vehicles moved out over a large bow ramp. The more advanced LST (Landing Ship Tank) has a long, automatically extending ramp for landing troops and vehicles, while amphibians exit through stern gates. Modern assault landing craft also include the helicopter carrier, which lands its massive load (a Marine battalion complete with guns, vehicles, and equipment) by helicopter; and giant 40,000-ton vessels with a full-length flight deck for helicopters over a "dock well" where landing craft are carried.

Langley, Samuel Pierpont (1834-1906)

American scientist whose pioneer studies of AERODYNAMICS enabled him to build a number of successful model powered airplanes. Most famous was his 1896 steam (and later gasoline) engined tandem winged *Aerodrome*, which had a

The balsa raft Kon Tiki *which crossed the Pacific ocean in 1947, covering 4,300 mi. (6,900 km) in 101 days.*

span of 16 ft. (4.8 m) and made flights of up to 4,200 ft. (1,280 m), much farther than had previously been achieved. With government finance he built a full-scale manned version which was tested on October 7 and December 8, 1903 (the latter date being 9 days earlier than the WRIGHT BROTHERS' first success). Both attempts failed, partly because of a faulty launching catapult. In 1914 Glen CURTISS made some modification and flew Langley's *Aerodrome*.

Languedoc Canal

Also known as the Canal du Midi, this canal in southern France forms with the Garonne and Aude rivers a waterway connecting the Bay of Biscay on the Atlantic Ocean with the Mediterranean. Its construction, completed in 1692 after 26 years work, was a civil engineering milestone. The 150 mi. (240 km) long canal includes 106 locks, three large aqueducts, and a tunnel. The tunnel, near Béziers, was one of the first tunnels ever built by blasting with explosives (black powder).

LASH (lighter aboard ship)

See CANALS AND INLAND WATERWAYS; FREIGHTERS.

Lead-acid battery

The most widely used electric-storage BATTERY. It has lead plates immersed in a dilute solution of sulfuric acid, and is a secondary-cell type which can be recharged after it has run down.

Leaf spring

Spring consisting of overlapping steel strips, or leaves, of graduated length. They are clamped together at intervals,

The Soviet icebreaker Lenin. *Built in 1957, and the first nuclear powered surface ship, she can steam steadily through ice 8 ft. (2.4 m) thick.*

with the shorter leaves in the middle, curve upwards slightly, and are generally termed semi-elliptic. The rear suspension of most American cars and trucks incorporates leaf springs. They are attached to the vehicle body at the ends, and are clamped at the middle to the rear-axle assembly.

Le Mans

City in northwest France famous for its annual automobile race, the Le Mans 24-hour Grand Prix d'Endurance. The first race took place in 1923 on an 11.4-mi. (18.3 km) road course which was only

partly paved. Since then the circuit has been fully paved, straightened, widened, and reduced to a length of 8.4 mi. (13.5 km). The winner is the car that travels the greatest distance. In the traditional Le Mans start the drivers ran across the road to their cars when the starting flag was dropped. Today they sit securely harnessed in their vehicles, but do not start their engines until the signal is given.

Lenin

Soviet ICEBREAKER built in 1957, the world's first nuclear-powered surface ship. With a length of 440 ft. (134 m) and displacing 16,000 tons, the *Lenin* can maintain 2 knots when clearing a passage through ice 8ft (2.4 m) thick. Nuclear propulsion enables her to stay at sea almost indefinitely, of particular importance in an icebreaker, and she keeps shipping routes open for up to four months longer than was previously possible.

Lenoir, Jean Joseph Étienne (1822-1900)

French inventor of Belgian ancestry who made and marketed the first commercially successful INTERNAL COMBUSTION ENGINE in 1860. Essentially a converted double-acting steam engine, it had a two-stroke cycle, ran on coal gas, and was widely used for pumping and other work despite its very low efficiency.

In 1860 Lenoir fitted one of his gas engines to a road vehicle, and in 1862, having devised a carburetor, adapted the engine to run on liquid hydrocarbon fuel, thus making the world's first liquid-fueled internal combustion-engined automobile. Although it worked, it was not a great success, and Lenoir turned his attention to constructing the world's first motorboat (1864). Lenoir also devised an electric brake for trains.

Leonardo da Vinci (1452-1519)

Italian artist, sculptor, and scientist who proposed a host of ideas in the field of transportation (among others). Many brilliantly foreshadowed the future, but were of no immediate practical value as they were so far ahead of existing technology.

One of the great pioneers of aviation, Leonardo studied bird flight and aerodynamics, and his famous *Notebooks* include much on the principles of flight. He made a model helicopter powered by a clock spring, with a helical screw "rotor;" he sketched a bat-like flying machine and drew detailed plans for a wing-flapping mechanism with a system of cables and pulleys to enable the pilot to move wings and tail like a bird; and he suggested the

A modern U.S. Navy amphibious assault ship landing craft. The gantry crane at the bow supports a ramp for rapid offloading of tanks and other vehicles.

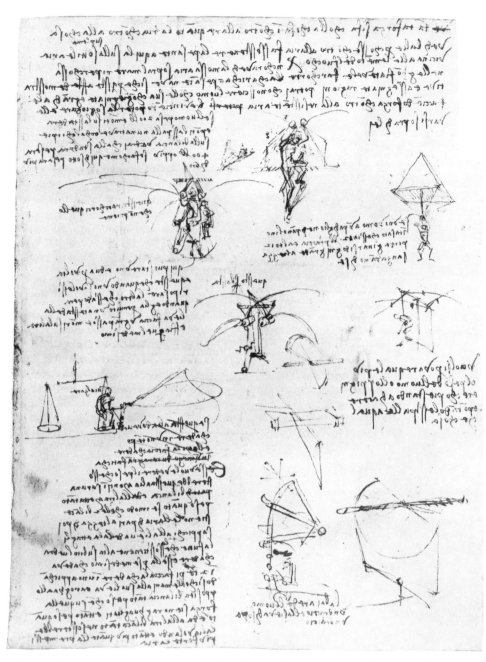

Sketches from Leonardo da Vinci's notebooks, showing his proposals for a helicopter with a screw-like "rotor," and for a parachute.

parachute (in the form of a cloth pyramid). Leonardo also made many studies for the construction of canals, and his *Notebooks* include designs for machinery for constructing the cuts and removing the material excavated. He invented the swinging (or mitre) lock gate, and built several locks thus equipped.

He sketched a diving apparatus in which the diver breathed through a tube leading to the surface (an idea which is in fact not practical at depths of more than a few inches). He also sketched designs for submarines, paddlewheels, bicycles, and driving chains; he worked out gear ratios and efficient shapes for gear wheels; he made an extensive study of friction, and suggested the use of roller bearings; and he proposed a traffic control system, with pedestrians and wheeled vehicles on different levels.

Lesseps, Ferdinand de (1805-1894)

French diplomat and engineer responsible for building the SUEZ CANAL. De Lesseps became interested in the possibility of a canal through the Isthmus of Suez while serving as a vice-consul in Alexandria. In 1849 he retired from the diplomatic service, and secured from the Egyptians a concession to cut the canal in 1854. His plans were modified by engineers, and work began in 1859. The canal was completed in 1869.

De Lesseps spent some years working on schemes for railroads, but in 1879 was persuaded to undertake the construction of a canal across the Isthmus of Panama. A private company, the French Panama Canal Company, was formed, and work began in 1880. De Lesseps planned a sea-level canal, but underestimated the difficulties of the task, and after 10 years the company was forced into liquidation. Financially ruined, he was tried for mismanaging the company's affairs and sentenced to five years' jail; the sentence was quashed on appeal.

Level crossing

Also known as a grade crossing, this is a place where railroad and highway cross each other on the same level. Most early crossings were unprotected, but as road traffic was slight, and as trains announced their approach with loud whistles or bells, accidents were rare. Similar unguarded crossings still exist in little-frequented areas such as farmland. In 1954 there were more than 250,000 grade crossings in the United States. Today the growth in speed and density of road and rail traffic has made unguarded crossings highly dangerous, and most are protected by automatic signals, flashing lights, or similar warning devices, or in some countries by automatic gates or half barriers. However, in spite of such precautions, disasters still occur, and the only safe answer is to take the highway over or under the tracks on a bridge or underpass. Unfortunately, the cost of such grade separation, especially in towns, is so high that it is normally only undertaken in the most urgent cases (except on new railroads, which are normally completely grade-separated).

Liberty ship

Type of merchant ship built in the United States as part of an emergency program during World War II. Also known as Ec-2 ships, they displaced 10,490 tons, were 441 ft. (134 m) long, and could cruise at 11 knots. They were simple, rugged vessels powered by reciprocating steam engines (some coal, some oil-fired). Prefabricated construction methods were used because speed was vital, and a record was set when one vessel was completed (from laying the keel to delivery) in only 14 days.

The initial scheme was for 200 ships, but after the attack on Pearl Harbor the program was expanded and altogether 2,610 Liberty ships were built.

Lifeboats

Small craft for sea rescue work. Those carried aboard large ships for the safety of passengers and crew are usually smaller and less complex than shore-based rescue craft, but they are normally equipped with emergency provisions,

A recent shore-based self-righting rescue lifeboat.

charts, water distillation plant, radio, and searchlights. They are powered by diesel engines, and are fireproof and almost unsinkable. Lifeboats on oil tankers are specially designed for safe launching in oil-covered waters.

Shore-based lifeboats, which may be moored in the water or kept on special slipways to permit rapid launching, are designed for safety and maneuverability in the roughest surf and seas. Built either of steel and aluminum, or with traditional double-hulled timber construction, they are very strong, and with reserve buoyancy can keep going even when partly damaged. Various self-righting devices are employed, one of the most common involving the transfer of water from one tank to another. Powerful twin diesel engines give speeds of about 15 knots. Special equipment carried includes radio, radar and echo sounding devices, and for the actual rescue work, line throwing apparatus, a BREECHES BUOY or similar rescue apparatus, and scrambling nets.

Lift

The upward thrust created by the movement of an AIRFOIL through air or water that raises an aircraft off the ground, and a HYDROPLANE craft out of the water. The principal function of an airplane's wings is to provide lift. This is achieved by accelerating the airflow around an airfoil of cambered section. As the leading edge of a moving wing separates the air, the flow has to speed up to pass around the curve of the CAMBER. This camber is normally greater on the upper surface than the lower, so the molecules of air have to travel much faster around the upper surface if they are to maintain their position relative to the molecules passing below the wing as the air leaves the wing's trailing edge.

It is a law of physics that increasing the speed of a flowing gas (or liquid) results in a pressure reduction (BERNOULLI'S PRINCIPLE). Hence accelerating the airflow around the cambered upper surface reduces the pressure above the wing, thus creating lift by "negative air pressure," or suction. Depending on the wing's ANGLE OF ATTACK this suction above the

wing may be supplemented by increased pressure from air striking the lower surface. During a landing approach the angle of attack is increased to augment lift. This is necessary to compensate for loss of suction lift caused by the lower airspeed. However, beyond an angle of attack of about 15 to 20 degrees the airflow over the top of the wing breaks down, causing STALLING.

Other devices depending on precisely the same principle include helicopter and autogiro rotors, hydrofoil foils, submarine hydroplanes, ship fin stabilizers, and sailboat sails (which work in a horizontal plane, thus producing forward movement). The principle is used in reverse to hold a racing automobile to the ground (see also AERODYNAMICS).

Light aircraft

The term "light aircraft" generally includes all planes with an overall weight of less than 6,000 lb. (2,722 kg). The earliest example of a machine designed for cheapness and simplicity of operation by a private pilot was perhaps the Demoiselle of 1909. With a bamboo and piano wire AIRFRAME covered by fabric, and a 30 hp engine, it could only carry pilots

Santos Dumont's Demoiselle, *one of the first light aircraft. Given a light enough pilot it was a successful plane.*

A typical modern low wing light aircraft, the Piper Cherokee. Although designed for personal use at relatively low speeds (up to around 150 mph, 241 km/h) such planes may be equipped with advanced navigational aids and an automatic pilot.

weighing less than about 120 lb. (54 kg). After World War I, huge military surplus stocks coming onto the market inhibited the light plane industry. In France the Farman David biplane, with a 50 hp Gnome engine, entered production with some success, to be followed by the Farman Sport of 1923. Under the stimulus of competitions, the German aircraft industry developed a number of interesting designs during the mid-twenties, including the first all-metal light plane to be series built, the Dornier Libelle flying boat. In 1925 the British de Havilland Moth, over 1,900 examples of which were subsequently constructed, made its appearance. Production of the two-seat Avro Avian of 1926 ran to about 740, and over a thousand Klemm Kl 25s were built in the late twenties.

Light racing planes were numerous in the early thirties, particularly in America, and the first of over 8,000 de Havilland Tiger Moth biplanes appeared in 1931, the year that saw the introduction of the highly successful 37 hp Taylor J-2 Cub and the Aeronca C-3 in America. Experiments in Europe with ultra-light aircraft such as the Flying Flea were largely a failure.

More powerful new versions of the ubiquitous Cub were marketed in America during the late thirties, and several outstanding light aircraft were developed during World War II, such as the Fiesler Storch in Germany, and the Taylorcraft Auster.

The Cessna 120/140 series appeared in 1948, and the later 150 became one of the most widely used two-seat light planes ever built, with over 15,000 coming off the production lines by the early seventies.

American aircraft now predominate in the light plane market, with the Cessnas (four-1 and six-seaters) and Pipers (Comanches, Cherokees, Super Cubs) being particularly successful, while over 10,000 Beechcraft Bonanzas have been built. The Pitts Special biplane has been an outstanding aerobatic aircraft.

In some planes (for example the French Rallye), a system of slats makes it almost impossible to spin, and difficult to stall. Because of the efficiency of propellers at low airspeeds, jets have not replaced air-cooled PISTON ENGINES in light aircraft.

Lighter

Flat-bottomed barge-like vessel used to carry cargo to and from ships in docks or open roadsteads. Some lighters are self-powered, others are "dumb" and must be towed. Special lighters in the form of floating containers are loaded complete with cargo on LASH (lighter aboard ship) ships (see CONTAINERIZATION; FREIGHTERS).

The Tongue *lightship stationed in the Thames Estuary, England. Many lightships have been replaced by large automatic navigational buoys, or by lighthouses.*

Lighthouses and lightships

A lighthouse is a structure, normally tower-shaped, carrying a powerful light to guide and warn shipping. A lightship is a permanently moored vessel serving a similar purpose.

Lighthouses may be built along the shore, or out at sea on rocks or sandbanks. The earliest were on the coast; the most famous, the Pharos of Alexandria, was one of the seven wonders of the ancient world. The first fully exposed structure was the famous EDDYSTONE LIGHTHOUSE (1699). The second Eddystone lighthouse pioneered interlocking block construction, but today most lighthouses are built of concrete or steel. On shore, or on solid rock foundations at sea, construction is fairly straightforward, although any offshore structure must be immensely strong to withstand the tremendous force of heavy seas.

Until recently it was impossible to build a lighthouse on sandbanks or other soft ground, and a lightship was used. The first lightships were converted merchant vessels, but modern ones are specially built and carry all normal lighthouse signaling equipment. However, where possible, their place is now taken by a large automatic navigational BUOY or by a lighthouse. Two types of construction are used. In one, a massive empty CAISSON is sunk into the seabed and filled with concrete, thus providing a solid foundation for the actual lighthouse. The other, often called a light tower, is similar to an offshore oil or gas drilling rig, with a large deck supported on steel piles which are driven 150 ft. (45 m) or more into the seabed.

A novel design pioneered in Sweden is the "float out" lighthouse. Built on shore and floated into position, its hollow concrete base is then filled with sand to provide weight and stability.

Until the late-18th century a blazing coal fire provided the brightest light. Then, in 1782, a Swiss scientist invented a smokeless oil lamp, which continued in use until the appearance of the much brighter incandescent oil lamp. Oil was eventually superseded by acetylene, which can be much more easily controlled. This has made possible the development of automatic unmanned lighthouses, and although electric light is the normal illuminant today, acetylene is still widely used. Electricity was first tried as early as 1858 but only came into general use in the 1920s. For most purposes conventional filament lamps of up to about three kilowatts are used, although when extra-powerful lights are needed arc lamps are fitted. Experiments are also being made with electronic flash tubes similar to those used in photography. Their extremely short flash is exceptionally bright and distinctive.

Various optical systems are employed in which lenses and mirrors concentrate the light into a compact beam, increasing its effective brightness and range enormously. The actual range depends on the light's power, its height, and of course on weather conditions. The 600,000-candle-power light of the world's tallest lighthouse a 348-ft. (105 m) tower near Yokohama, Japan, can be seen at a distance of 20 mi. (32 km).

The light is normally made to flash rhythmically, and a lighthouse has its own distinctive light signal by which it can be quickly recognized. Light signals are little use in dense fog, and lighthouses and lightships are normally provided with distinctive sound signals, and also transmit radio and radar beacons (the latter are known as racons).

Otto Lilienthal making a flight in his hang glider. He amassed much valuable information in over 2,000 successful flights before crashing to his death in 1896.

Lilienthal, Otto (1848-1896)

German pioneer aviator, known for his experiments with manned gliders. While still boys he and his brother Gustav (1849-1933) tried to make themselves gliding wings, and constructed models with flapping wings. After many years of experiments he made his first successful flight in a delicate batwing glider in 1891, over a distance of 100 ft. (30 m). He made more than 2,000 flights over a period of five years, covering distances of 650-980 ft. (200-300 m). On August 9, 1896, his glider went into a sudden dive and he broke his back. He died the next day. Lilienthal's book *The Flight of Birds as a Basis for the Art of Flying* (1889) is a basic work in aeronautics.

Limousine

A large, luxurious closed sedan, especially one driven by a chauffeur, who is often separated from the passengers by a glass partition. Very large, sometimes "stretched" sedans used to transport passengers to and from airports or stations are also called limousines. The word is derived from the French and means "hood," coming from the costume worn in a region in west-central France called Limousin. The name was first applied to an automobile with a closed passenger compartment and a hood or roof extending forward over the driver's seat.

Lindbergh, Charles Augustus (1902-1974)

American aviator who made the first solo crossing of the Atlantic Ocean. Lindbergh learned to fly at the age of 20, and toured the country barnstorming. He then attended army flying school and became an airmail pilot before deciding to try for the $25,000 prize offered for the first New York-Paris nonstop flight. He made his historic flight on May 20-21, 1927, in a single-engine Ryan monoplane, *Spirit of St. Louis*. To save weight for extra gasoline he flew without radio or fuel gauges. The flight covered a distance of 3,609 mi. (5,809 km), in 33½ hours.

With his wife, Anne Morrow Lindbergh, Lindbergh made many pioneering flights in the 1930s, and he was technical adviser to two airlines. After Pearl Harbor he flew 50 combat missions in the Pacific.

Linear induction motor

A form of electric motor which is likely to revolutionize high speed rail transportation. The field coils of this motor are laid out in a line instead of in the circular form used in ordinary electric motors. The effect is to produce a magnetic field which sweeps from one end of the motor to the other, whereas in a normal induction motor it sweeps around in a circle, carrying the rotor with it, thus producing rotary motion.

In a linear electric motor as applied to railroads, the field coils are mounted on the vehicle and the "rotor" takes the form of a steel or aluminum plate fixed in position along the whole length of the track.

Linear induction motor "locomotives" such as this experimental American version are likely to revolutionize high speed rail transportation, bringing speeds of 300 mph (480 km/h) or more.

There is no physical contact between the coils and the plate. When current is passed through the coils, the sweeping effect of the magnetic field tries to push the "rotor" under and away from the coils; but as the "rotor" is fixed, the coils, and the vehicle to which they are attached, move forward. Since the wheels only carry the load and do not have to transmit power, there is no wheelslip on starting. Braking is accomplished by reversing the field and is not dependent on friction between wheels and track.

In fact, trains using this motor are unlikely to run on wheels. The linear motor can provide propulsion and guidance for tracked "hovertrains" (see AIR-CUSHION VEHICLES), or for "mag-lev" trains in which the train is held off the track by magnetic levitation (i.e. by opposed magnetic forces). The Japanese have a working model of the latter idea, and expect to put a 300 mph (480 km/h) train in service in 1980. With no moving parts and no friction, there will be no wear and no noise except the rush of air.

Liner

An oceangoing ship that runs a scheduled service on a specified route (as distinct from a TRAMP). The passenger liner era began with the race between the paddle steamer *Sirius* and the *Great Western* in 1838 to be the first steamship across the Atlantic. Two years later Samuel Cunard of Britain founded the Cunard Line, and soon French, German, Italian, and American lines joined the competition to provide the largest, fastest, and most comfortable transatlantic "ferry" service.

Famous liners of the late-19th century include the *Scotia*, Cunard's last and most elegant paddle steamer, and the German *Kaiser Wilhelm der Grosse*. The early years of the 20th century saw the launching of such celebrated liners as the sister ships MAURETANIA and LUSITANIA (1906) and the ill-fated TITANIC (1912), while during the 1930s a new generation appeared setting new standards of design and comfort. Best known were the QUEEN ELIZABETH, the QUEEN MARY and the French *Normandie*, all of which carried some 2,000 passengers at average speeds of over 30 knots. The UNITED STATES, the world's fastest liner, was launched in 1952, and the longest, the FRANCE, appeared 10 years later.

In recent years all these giants have been forced out of business as more and more people travel by air. The passenger liners of today are smaller, and most have given up their "ferryboat" role to become floating hotels providing vacation cruises. (For cargo liners, see FREIGHTERS.)

Live axle

The conventional beam-type rear driving axle, used in most American autos and trucks, in which the axle is fixed rigidly to the wheels. It incorporates the right-angle drive, differential, half-shafts, and hub mountings in one unit. Independent suspension of the rear wheels is not possible with a live axle.

Liverpool & Manchester Railway

Opened in England on September 15, 1830, this was the first public railroad in the world to be worked entirely by steam locomotives. (The STOCKTON & DARLINGTON, opened on September 27, 1825, used steam for passengers on the opening day only.) It was also the first with proper stations, timetables, and a signaling system. Before opening, it was the scene of the Rainhill locomotive trials, won by the ROCKET which reached 24.1 mph (38.5 km/h) with a full load, ensuring that the new line would be worked by steam locomotives rather than cable haulage. The opening of the railroad by the Duke of Wellington is generally agreed to mark the beginning of the "Railroad Age." It also brought the first railroad accident when William HUSKISSON, a Member of Parliament, was run down by the *Rocket* and died the same day. The line, 30 mi. (48 km) long, included the Olive Mount cutting, 2 mi. (3.2 km) long and 100 ft. (30.5 m) deep at some points, and the crossing of a quagmire, known as Chat Moss, by using hurdles and heather to form a "floating road" for the track.

Lock

Locks, the simplest structures which can connect two bodies of navigable water at different levels, are widely used on canals, river navigations and at dock entrances. The idea is a very old one, but many changes have been made since the first (known) locks were built in China in 984 A.D. Most modern locks consist of an open rectangular concrete chamber with watertight steel gates at each end, inside which a vessel can be positioned while the water level rises or falls. When the water in the chamber reaches the correct level, the appropriate gate is opened and the vessel leaves.

The world's first railroad locomotive, Richard Trevithick's Penydarren of 1804. It hauled a 25 ton load at about 5 mph (8 km/h).

This, the pound or chamber lock, has superseded earlier types. It mostly has paired mitre gates at both ends, each rotating about its outer edge, meeting to form a V pointing upstream. Other types used are guillotine gates (rising vertically), flap gates (hinged about their lower edge) and sector gates (whose water-face is part of a cylindrical surface). In docks, a greater variety is used including traversing caissons (moved sideways on rails) and floating caissons (floated into place).

Locomotives

The first locomotive to haul a load on rails was built in 1804 by a Cornish engineer, Richard Trevithick, for the 9 mi. (14 km) Penydarren Iron Works plateway in Wales. The 5-ton locomotive had a single large cylinder mounted on top of the boiler and a very large flywheel to compensate for the absence of a second cylinder. It hauled a load of 25 tons at about 5 mph (8 km/h), but proved too heavy for the track and was abandoned. Trevithick built other locomotives and in 1808 he brought one to London and demonstrated it on a circular track. Called CATCH-ME-WHO-CAN, it hauled a single carriage at about 12 mph (19 km/h), and many people rode on this first mechanically-hauled passenger railroad. Trevithick, the true father of the steam locomotive, anticipated many features taken up and elaborated by other engineers, such as the return flue boiler and the use of exhaust steam to increase the draft in the chimney. Despite the evidence given by his locomotives that smooth wheels on smooth rails gave sufficient adhesion (grip) for normal haul-

age, many engineers continued to believe that a rack mechanism was necessary, or that trains would have to be cable-hauled by stationary engines. The first commercially successful locomotive built by John Blenkinsop in 1812, was in fact driven by a toothed wheel engaging a rack on the rail.

The development of the locomotive was carried on by William Hedley, and by George STEPHENSON, who produced the famous ROCKET. This defeated all comers at the Rainhill trials in 1829 and thus ensured that the LIVERPOOL & MANCHESTER RAILWAY would be worked entirely by steam when it opened in 1830, ushering in the true "Railroad Age." In the United States, the first steam locomotive was built by Colonel John Stevens, a distinguished pioneer of steam, canals, and railroads, and ran for a time on a circular track on his Hoboken estate. At about the same time the countries of Europe began to build steam locomotives and Marc Seguin in France invented the multitubular boiler, also invented, apparently independently, by George and Robert Stephenson and incorporated in the *Rocket*.

Development of the steam locomotive.

The *Rocket* owed its supremacy to the bringing together of all the essentials of the steam locomotive: two cylinders with their cranks at right angles so that one of them would always be in a position to produce power to start the locomotive; the blast pipe to take exhaust steam up the chimney and thus give a forced draft to the fire; the multitubular boiler which took the heat in small tubes through the

Steam locomotives were robust and long lived (this one was in service on the Boston and Maine Railroad from 1913 to 1954), but they were less efficient and required greater manpower than diesels.

boiler, giving a huge heating surface to produce steam quickly; and smooth wheels to run on smooth rails.

Later, in 1843, came the link motion, an invention of William Howe and Robert Stephenson. This made it possible to cut off the supply of steam to the cylinders at any point in the stroke, thus producing great economies. The effort of starting a train is much greater than that needed to keep it moving, so steam is supplied to the cylinders for most of their stroke on starting; but as speed increases steam may only be needed for about 15% of the stroke, the rest of the stroke being supplied with power by the expansion of the steam already in the cylinder. The other great advance, in the last years of the 19th century, was to pass the steam from the boiler through small tubes inside the boiler tubes on its way to the cylinder, heating it further and making it expand still more. This "superheating," as it was called, also produced great economies. In essence, although they increased in size and refinement, all steam locomotives since 1829 were improved versions of the *Rocket*. Apart from experiments with steam turbines, the prin-

ciples remained essentially the same. The *Rocket* had only one pair of driving wheels. Later and bigger locomotives have had first 4, then 6, and up to 10 or 12 wheels coupled together so that more of the locomotive's weight could be applied to increasing the driving wheels' adhesion.

The largest steam locomotives were all articulated: they had two engines (both receiving steam from the same boiler), and two sets of cylinders and driving wheels. The front set was mounted on a swiveling bogie to permit negotiation of sharp curves. Articulated types included the Mallet, one of which had three sets of driving wheels and a wheel code (see below) of 2-8-8-8-4, and the Beyer-Garrett in which the boiler was mounted between the engines rather than above them (giving a double wheel code such as 4-8-2 + 2-8-4). Mallets and Beyer-Garretts were particularly valuable on light track as the weight was spread on an unusually large number of wheels (see also BIG BOY).
But the steam locomotive was never a really efficient machine; only 7% or so of the fuel's thermal value could be used, and there was a constant search for

something better. Perhaps the ultimate was the *Jawn Henry* steam turbine-electric locomotive built for the Norfolk & Western Railroad in 1954. With tender, it weighed 591 tons, and had a maximum tractive effort (pulling power) of $87\frac{1}{2}$ tons.

Wheel codes. Steam locomotives are often described by type names, such as Pacific, Atlantic, or American. The names refer to the wheel arrangement. A locomotive with a leading 4-wheel bogie, 6 coupled driving wheels, and a trailing 2-wheel truck under the cab, is described as a 4-6-2. With no leading wheels, 6 driving wheels and a 2-wheel truck the wheel code is 0-6-2, and so on. Pacific is the name applied to all 4-6-2 locomotives; Atlantic to 4-4-2s; and American to 4-4-0s. This code is used in the United States, in Great Britain and most other parts of the world. In Continental Europe, however, the axles are counted, not the wheels, so a Pacific is 2-3-1.
Electric and diesel locomotives have different wheel code systems. Here the first and third figures represent the number of leading and trailing axles (as with steam locomotives in the European system), but the driving axles are shown by a letter. Where the driving wheels are coupled and all the driving axles are turned by a single motor, hydraulic unit, or the like, "A" represents one axle, "B" two, and so on. However, if each axle has an individual motor, and the wheels are not coupled, a small "o" is added: thus "Co" means three driving axles each with its own motor; while Co-Co (a common class of electric locomotive) has two 6-wheel bogies, all 6 axles being driven by separate motors.

Diesel locomotives. The first true diesel locomotive was built by Rudolf DIESEL in collaboration with a German engineering firm in 1912. The diesel engine, applied to a locomotive, is much more efficient than a steam engine, making use of up to about 25% of the thermal value of its fuel. It can run for much longer periods than a steam locomotive before returning to its depot for servicing. Also, with no head of steam to raise, it can be started at the touch of a button, and stopped when standing by.
Unlike a steam engine, a diesel develops power only when turning over at some speed, and must therefore be connected to the driving wheels by some form of transmission. In relatively low power units such as those in diesel railcars, this can be similar to that of an automobile, with a slipping clutch. But larger locomotives for heavy trains need greater efficiency (only possible with diesels

One of the streamlined Hudson type steam locomotives from the golden age of steam which hauled the famous Twentieth Century Limited train.

and the New York "El" (elevated railroad) was converted to electric traction in 1900. Electric locomotives pick up their power from a third rail, or from overhead wires, and simply convert electrical to mechanical energy. This frees the locomotive of all the heavy and bulky components used in steam and diesel locomotives (boiler, fuel, engines, and generators), allowing much more space for the efficient use of power. The power may be picked up from an extra rail on the track, in which case it is direct current (d.c.) at comparatively low voltage, or from an overhead wire. This can also be d.c. but modern practice is to put high alternating current (a.c.) voltages through overhead wires. In the locomotive it can be stepped down by a transformer to a suitable voltage for a.c. motors. The characteristics of d.c. motors are more suitable than a.c. motors for railroad purposes, so the power, after stepping down, is often converted on the locomotive to direct current for the motors.

Power to the electric motors cannot be controlled by a simple regulator or throttle, as in steam or diesel locomotives, but demands an elaborate system of transformer tappings, or electrical resistances which can be switched in or out of circuit as required. A new and

when running at a steady speed), and something more robust and flexible than a clutch. They usually have electric or hydraulic transmissions.

Electric transmissions are the most usual, except in some parts of Europe, and consist of an electric generator coupled to the diesel engine, with electric motors driving the wheels. This gives a very flexible drive. The wheels can be driven by one large motor (or one in each bogie), but it is more usual to have individual motors for each axle.

motives are usually fitted with controls which allow several units to be driven together by a single crew on the front locomotive, but individual locomotives can develop as much as 6,600 hp (compared to a maximum of about 500 hp with mechanical drive).

The first diesel-electric locomotive built in the United States was completed in 1923. The first diesel-electric shunter was placed in service in 1925, and the first diesel-electric hauled passenger train appeared in 1934 on the Burlington

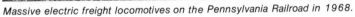

Massive electric freight locomotives on the Pennsylvania Railroad in 1968.

Typical modern electric locomotive of British Rail.

The diesel-hydraulic locomotive has some advantages in that the components of the drive system are lighter. The torque converter used is a reaction turbine. The engine drives an "impeller" which transmits its power, through the fluid in the converter, to a turbine wheel which drives the output shaft. There may be two or three torque converters for different locomotive speeds, or an automatic gearbox.

Diesel-electric or diesel-hydraulic locomotives

and the Union Pacific railroads. In Britain, the first main-line diesel-electric locomotive did not enter service until 1947, by which time diesel locomotives had established themselves firmly in many parts of the world.

Electric locomotives. Electric traction has a longer history than diesel power. The world's first main-line electrification was inaugurated in 1895 on a short stretch of the Baltimore & Ohio Railroad,

effective method of control uses thyristors, a method pioneered in Sweden. Many trains are not powered by locomotives, but by motive power installed along the length of the train. The most familiar are electric suburban trains with motors on nearly every car, but there are also high speed gas-turbine trains of this type, and diesel trains with engines in "power cars" at one or both ends. There are also other variations in use.

143

Electric traction gives better acceleration than other types, and is cleaner, quieter, and faster. The SPEED RECORD for a conventional train on conventional tracks has been held since 1955 by two French electric locomotives; and Japan's Hikari Express "bullet trains," which provide the world's fastest passenger services (averaging 112 mph, 180 km/h) are electric. However, an electric line, with its third rail or overhead cables, is very expensive to set up. Electric traction is therefore normally reserved for very busy routes which justify the initial expense. For high speed services on unelectrified routes, increasing use is being made of gas turbine locomotives, which are significantly faster than diesels.

Gas turbine locomotives. The world's first gas turbine locomotive was built in Sweden in 1934, and this form of motive power has been used for many years in the United States and the Soviet Union for freight train locomotives. In recent years gas turbine power has been developed for high speed passenger trains. Canada inaugurated a "Turbo Train" service between Toronto and Montreal in 1969, and France followed in 1970. One version of Britain's APT (ADVANCED PASSENGER TRAIN) is gas turbine powered; and several passenger train experiments have been made in the United States. France's new prototype TGV turbotrain has a design speed of 190 mph (306 km/h).

The future. Looking beyond the development of advanced electric and gas turbine locomotives, running on conventional tracks, with design speeds of up to about 200 mph (320 km/h), the high speed inter-city trains of the future are likely to be tracked AIR-CUSHION VEHICLES or trains held off special track by magnetic levitation, with propulsion by LINEAR INDUCTION MOTORS. Japanese National Railways are currently developing a "mag-lev" linear induction train with a design speed of over 300 mph (480 km/h), which is expected to enter service in 1980, and the United States and other countries have similar if less advanced projects.

Log

A device for measuring a ship's speed. It originally consisted of a log of wood attached to a line knotted at regular intervals. The log was dropped into the sea and the number of knots slipping through the crewman's fingers in a specific time was counted. The knots were so spaced that each one represented a speed of one nautical mile an hour (one KNOT). The modern log takes the form of a PITOT TUBE projecting through the hull into the water, which allows speed to be calculated from water pressure.

London Bridge

A bridge across the River Thames in southeast London, England, between Southwark Bridge and Tower Bridge. The present triple-arch, reinforced-concrete bridge was completed in 1971 after four years' work. It replaced a five-arch stone bridge designed by John Rennie, which itself replaced the famous Old London Bridge.

Rennie's bridge was completed in 1831 and widened in 1902. When the decision was taken in 1967 to replace it, it was offered for sale. Eventually McCulloch Oil Corporation in the United States bought it for nearly $2.5 million and proposed to make it the centerpiece of a new city they

The old London Bridge. Completed in 1209 and in continuous use for over 600 years, it was until the 1740s the only bridge across the Thames in London.

were building in Arizona (Lake Havasu City). They began shipping the bridge, or rather the stone facing of it, in 1968. It was reassembled stone by stone on a reinforced-concrete structure and opened in 1971.

Old London Bridge, subject of the traditional song "London Bridge is Falling Down," was constructed of stone between 1176 and 1209 and was in continuous use for more than 600 years. It was the only bridge crossing the Thames in London until the building of Westminster Bridge in the 1740s. Some 905 ft. (275 m) long, with 19 arches, it carried houses and shops, and was provided with a drawbridge for defense and to allow the passage of ships.

Longship

A double-ended vessel with sail and oars, the traditional ship of northern Europe and Scandinavia from ancient times until around 1200 when the stern rudder was introduced. The Vikings sailed to America in longships in the year 1000, and similar craft appear on the Bayeux Tapestry, which depicts the Norman conquest of England in 1066.

Loran

This very accurate LOng RAnge Aid to Navigation measures the different times taken by pulses from two separate (master and slave) transmitting stations to reach the receiver on a ship or aircraft. A video representation of the two pulses is superimposed by the operator and a digital readout gives the time separation (in microseconds) between them. Special charts are then used to establish the position. Master and slave stations are usually about 300 mi. (480 km) apart, operate at frequencies of 1,700 to 2,000 kilohertz, and have a useful range of some 700 mi. (1,126 km) by day (and double this distance at night).

Lubricant

A substance designed to reduce friction and wear between moving parts by interposing a barrier which prevents the surfaces from touching. However smooth surfaces may appear, on a microscopic scale they are quite rough. In fluid lubrication the surfaces are separated by a thick layer of lubricant. In boundary lubrication the layer is only a few molecules thick and there may be limited contact between the surfaces. This condition often occurs on starting and stopping of the moving parts. When speed increases, the lubricant layer tends to thicken and full fluid lubrication results.

The lubricant most widely used in gasoline and diesel engines, gearboxes, and other moving parts of vehicles is petroleum oil. Vegetable oils, such as castor oil, may be used for special purposes. Synthetic oils are widely used in aero engines as they are better able to withstand the severe operating conditions brought about by extreme temperature and pressure. Chemically these products are organic oxides, esters, silicones, and fluorocarbons.

One of the most important properties of a

An early American electric locomotive. Despite this and other early types, the United States still lags behind most advanced nations in railroad electrification.

With six coupled driving wheels, a two-wheeled swiveling truck at the front, and four trailing wheels under the cab, this Sharp and Fellows locomotive typifies the age of steam in America.

This Alweg monorail travels along a concrete beam on rubber-tired driving wheels. Although most often employed in the past for their tourist appeal (at Disneyland, for example) monorails are now being seriously considered for urban and inter-urban rapid transit systems.

Canadian Pacific's diesel hauled transcontinental express, the Canadian. The train takes just over 70 hours to travel the 2,881 mi. (4,636 km) between Montreal and Vancouver.

lubricating oil is viscosity, or "thickness." If an oil is too viscous, it will impede movement. If it is not viscous enough, the lubricating layer will be too thin to prevent contact between the surfaces, and wear will result. Viscosity decreases as temperature rises, a fact which creates problems in internal combustion engines, whose temperatures may vary from below zero on starting to a few hundred degrees. Engine oils are therefore formulated to have as consistent a viscosity as possible, so that they are neither too thick when cold nor too thin when hot. Such oils are termed multigrade. An oil's viscosity is described in terms of standard SAE (Society of Automotive Engineers) numbers. A typical multigrade oil has a rating of SAE 20W/50; this indicates that it has the viscosity of an SAE 20 oil at 0°F (-18°C) and of an SAE 50 oil at 210°F (99°C). Special EP (extreme pressure) lubricants are often used in auto gearboxes and rear axles to prevent siezing. They contain sulfur compounds which form a film on metal surfaces, thus preventing direct contact.

Engine oils have other functions apart from lubrication. They act as a coolant to carry away part of the engine heat, and as a seal to prevent gas escaping past the pistons. In addition they are usually slightly alkaline to absorb and neutralize acid combustion products, and they contain a detergent dispersant which helps to hold carbon and other residues in suspension and prevents them from being deposited in the engine.

Grease, a semi-solid product which consists of a liquid lubricant thickened with soap or other material, is another major lubricant. The soap may be the fatty acid salt of various metals, including calcium, barium, aluminum, lead, zinc, and lithium. Other thickening agents include finely divided clay, colloidal silica, and carbon black. Greases are preferred to oil for lubricating slow-moving machinery parts, for they have much higher shear resistance and can thus support heavier loads.

A third class of lubricant is the solid type. Graphite and molybdenum disulfide are examples. They provide lubrication by virtue of their molecular structure, which is laminar, or layered. They are able to resist high pressures and temperatures. Talc, soap, and wax also have some applications in the lubrication field.

Lubrication system

Every engine must have an efficient lubrication system to reduce friction between moving parts, carry away excess heat and prevent internal corrosion. In the gasoline engine lubrication system a reservoir of oil is carried in a sump at the bottom of the crankcase. Oil is drawn from the sump

and pumped via a filter through channels to the main bearings, from where it travels through passages to the crankshaft bearings and the rocker arms. The oil from the rocker box returns to the sump via the piston rod guides. Oil emerging from the crankshaft bearings is thrown onto the cylinder walls, providing lubrication for the pistons. The oil pump is usually of the gear type, forcing the oil along by rotating, meshed gears. Rotary pumps are also used and these propel the oil with a lobed rotor. To assist oil cooling, the surface of the sump is usually fluted, allowing better heat transfer. High-performance autos are often fitted with oil coolers which work on the same principle as the cooling system radiator.

Lunar orbital rendezvous

The technique which Apollo astronauts used to reach the Moon, land and return to Earth. The Apollo spacecraft consisted of three modules: command module (CM) for the crew, service module (SM), and lunar excursion module (LEM). On the launch pad the command and service modules (CSM) sat on top of the fragile LEM, which was inside a protective housing joined to the third stage of the Saturn V launching rocket. This configuration allowed the CM, with astronauts aboard, to separate from the rest in the event of an emergency. Once in orbit the CSM separated from the LEM housing, and the LEM was docked with the CM, the spacecraft now being powered by the SM's rocket motor. Once in lunar orbit two of the astronauts transferred to the LEM, separated from the CSM, and descended to the lunar surface. The CSM

with one astronaut aboard continued in orbit.

The LEM was made in two sections: for takeoff from the Moon the lower, descent stage was uncoupled and served as a launching pad for the upper, ascent stage. Takeoff was timed so that the ascent stage would rendezvous with the CSM in orbit, hence the term lunar orbital rendezvous. After rendezvous the crew of the LEM transferred to the CSM, and the LEM was discarded; the SM's engines then fired to take the spacecraft out of lunar orbit and into a transearth trajectory. Just before reentry into the atmosphere the SM was jettisoned, leaving only the CM to return to the Earth (see also SPACE FLIGHT).

Lunar roving vehicle

The correct name for the MOON BUGGY used by the American astronauts who explored the surface of the moon (see also LUNOKHOD).

Lunokhod

The Russian word for MOONWALKER, the name given to the first wheeled vehicle to travel over the moon's surface.

Lusitania

Famous British Cunard liner, sister ship of the MAURETANIA and launched in 1906, sunk without warning by a German submarine on May 7, 1915. She sank within 45 minutes, giving no time to load and launch the lifeboats, and 1,198 people drowned, including 124 Americans. This attack was an important factor in bringing about the entry of the United States into World War I.

The famous Cunard liner Lusitania *sinking after being torpedoed without warning in 1915. 1,198 people died in the disaster.*

M

Macadam

A form of road construction in which the foundation is shaped to the intended surface camber to facilitate drainage, the road base is formed of two layers of broken stone of about 3 in. (75 mm) diameter, and the surface is formed of a well-rolled layer of angular stone fragments up to 1 in. (25 mm) in size. Today a binder such as asphalt cement or hot tar is usually added to prevent the "tarmacadam" surface from breaking up. Macadam is named after the Scottish engineer James McAdam (1756-1836), who pioneered this method of construction, which was much simpler and cheaper, and almost as effective as that of his famous contemporary Thomas TELFORD.

Mach number

A measure of speed by comparison with the speed of sound, named after the Austrian physicist Ernst Mach (1838-1916). The speed at which sound waves travel varies according to the conditions (principally temperature) of the air through which they are passing. At sea level the speed of sound is approximately 760 mph (1,223 km/h), while at 37,000 ft. (11,277 m) it falls to about 660 mph (1,062 km/h). The pressure waves resulting from an aircraft's passage through the air also travel at the speed of sound, which is therefore a critical factor in high speed flight. The Mach number 1 has consequently been accorded to the speed of sound, whatever the altitude of the aircraft may be. Hence Mach 0.5 is half the speed of sound, and Mach 2.0 is twice the speed of sound.

Mackinac Bridge

Suspension bridge crossing the Mackinac Straits, between Lakes Michigan and Huron, and linking Mackinaw City with St. Ignace. Its total length is 19,205 ft. (5,854 m), with a main span of 3,800 ft. (1,158 m). It was opened in 1957 and ranks as the world's third-longest suspension bridge.

Magneto

An electric generator used for gasoline engine ignition when no battery is fitted, especially on piston aero engines, and on many motorcycles, boats, and early automobiles. A magneto converts mechanical energy, derived from cranking the engine, into electric current, and consists essentially of an armature rotating between the poles of a permanent magnet. The armature carries both primary and secondary COILS and a CONTACT BREAKER,

Vessels entering locks in Britain's Manchester Ship Canal which links the inland city of Manchester with the Irish Sea.

and the magneto is thus an independent and self-contained unit. Rotating the armature between the poles of the magnet generates an alternating current in the primary coil. When this current is momentarily interrupted by the contact breaker a high voltage current is induced in the secondary coil, and is transmitted by a DISTRIBUTOR rotor to the SPARK PLUGS. Multi-cylinder aero engines require magnetos capable of delivering 50,000 sparks per minute. Automatic timing devices to compensate for increasing engine speed are commonly used, and double contact breakers may be employed to provide a special additional advance for maximum cruising performance.

Mallard

One of the most famous of the streamlined "A4" Pacific steam locomotives built by Sir Nigel Gresley for the London & North Eastern Railway in Britain in the 1930s. In the course of brake trials in 1938, with a seven-car train, including a DYNAMOMETER car, *Mallard* covered 5 mi. (8 km) at an average of 120.4 mph (193 km/h), and reached an authenticated maximum of 126 mph (203 km/h), the world record for steam locomotives. *Mallard* is preserved in the Railway Museum at York.

Manchester Ship Canal

This connects the inland city of Manchester, England, with the Mersey River estuary, which leads to the Irish Sea. Opened in 1894, it is 36 mi. (58 km) long, from 28-30 ft. (8.5-9.1 m) deep, and varies in width from 90-180 ft. (27.4-55 m). With direct links to Britain's major rail and canal systems, it made possible the rapid development of Manchester and the surrounding industrial region.

Manhattan

150,000-ton American tanker, fitted out as an icebreaker to become the first commercial ship to navigate the NORTHWEST PASSAGE, plowing straight through the pack ice. The experimental voyage was undertaken in 1969 to explore the feasibility of shipping oil by sea from Alaska, and thus saving the expense of laying a pipeline. In the event, the *Manhattan* had on several occasions to be rescued from the ice.

Manifold

A branched pipe with one inlet and several outlets or vice versa. In a gasoline engine, for example, the inlet manifold takes the fuel mixture from the carburetor and distributes it to the cylinders. It also assists the vaporization process.

Engines with multiple carburetors have more than one inlet manifold, each of which may serve a single cylinder. The exhaust manifold carries the exhaust gases from the cylinders to the exhaust pipe. Various designs may be used: the longer the branches, the less is the back pressure on the engine. Usually the inlet manifold is positioned directly above the exhaust manifold, the heat from which helps vaporization of incoming mixture.

Man-powered flight
See PEDAL PLANE.

Maps
Maps are representations of the surface of the earth or a part of it on any plane surface, at a reduced scale. They fall into three broad categories: political, portraying political administrative divisions; topographical, portraying physical features of the earth's surface; and thematic. Thematic maps may be prepared on a topographic base map, or they may be compiled from statistics to show the characteristics of social and economic phenomena. Transport maps are thematic; they show the location, extent, and characteristics of road, rail, air, and sea communications. One of the main uses of transport maps is for navigation, but they are also important for regional planning and in the organization of transport systems.

The design of a map depends on its purpose. Thus a tourist road map has different requirements from one designed for the trucking industry. A large scale map such as a city plan portrays a small area in great detail, whereas a small scale map (for example, a route planning map of a continent) portrays a large area with corresponding loss of detail.

Projections. Problems arise in reproducing the features of the earth's spherical surface on the plane surface of a map, and the various projections used (these include zenithal, cylindrical, and conical types) each have particular advantages. The Mercator projection, a cylindrical type, is often employed in navigation and air route maps because a course between two given points can always be plotted on a straight line. A disadvantage is that areas in high latitudes are distorted; for example, the size of Greenland is much enlarged. The Lambet Conformal Conic projection is widely used in air navigation because it represents great circles as straight lines (see GREAT CIRCLE ROUTE). Other types include equal area projections, such as the Mollweide Projection, which are particularly useful for world distribution maps.

Methods of representation. Information may be represented in a variety of ways. Symbols, lines, or shading may be used, or the information may be written on the map. Linear symbols are particularly effective on transport maps for differentiating between the variety of road and rail types, and are easily amended to incorporate changes in road or rail classification. For the compilation of most transport maps the cartographer relies on statistical information. One widely used method of representing such information relating to the characteristics of transportation, such as frequency, capacity, density of traffic, and the like, is the *flowline* map.

Bar graphs are another type useful for comparative studies of transport over a given time (for example the volume of traffic using various ports over a given period), and provide valuable information for regional planning. *Choropleth* maps are used for representing information relating to transport networks, such as frequency of rail passenger services in a city. *Isopleth* maps are compiled to show the accessibility of a region by road and rail transport, and to analyze the historical development of transport networks. The rail networks of large cities are often represented in a diagrammatic form known as a *cartogram*.

Compilation. The statistics used in compiling maps are obtained from various sources and include the figures for transport and trade published regularly by international agencies, such as the United Nations, as well as by national agencies such as the Interstate Commerce Commission, which issues statistics on rail traffic in the United States. There is also a wealth of unpublished information; for example, records relating to the principal highways are maintained in nearly every state. Details recorded include width, surface type, condition, and gradient, as well as data on traffic flow, speed, and accident rates. The statistics for air and sea transport are generally available for most countries, whereas those for road and rail transport are very variable, making comparative studies between countries difficult. Some transport maps are based on topographic maps; these include some road and rail maps which show only the location and classification of the road and rail types. Little information is given regarding the types of traffic that can use them or the nature of the routes in terms of speed, facilities, or scenery. It is expected that future developments in cartography will allow the inclusion of this information on road maps.

Maps are updated by using information from new surveys such as those carried out by the General Drafting Company in the United States, by incorporating new statistical information, and by the use of aerial photographs.

History. The oldest known maps are Babylonian, and date from around 3800 B.C. Early maps were strictly practical; they showed routes, and delineated boundaries. The Greeks had a more abstract interest in cartography and produced highly speculative maps of the world. They also made quite detailed representations of the Mediterranean area. They had already assumed that the earth was a sphere, and their considerable cartographic skills culminated in the work of Ptolemy (90-168 A.D.), whose famous world map remained a standard reference source for some 1,400 years. It included a comprehensive system of geometrical coordinates, enabling any point to be described in terms of lines of latitude and longitude.

Ptolemy naturally omitted the American continent, and significantly underestimated the size of the earth. These faults were rectified by 16th century cartographers (including Mercator) who benefited from the discoveries of Columbus and others, and during the following centuries greater detail and accuracy became possible with further discoveries and improved methods of navigation. The International Geographical Congress of 1891 proposed the compilation of an International Map of the World (IMW), a project which has recently been revived. Today modern technology and the use of satellites in surveying and photography, has made it possible to produce accurate small scale maps of the world, although very large areas remain unmapped in any detail. In the early 1970s less than 20% of the world's land area was covered by maps with scales as large as 1:50,000 (about 1 in. to 1 mi.), while about 60% was covered by topographical maps with scales of around 1:250,000 (see also CHARTS).

Marcus, Siegfried (1831-1898)
One of the earliest automotive pioneers. Working in Vienna, Austria, he constructed his first automobile in 1864. A crude four-wheeler with a single-cylinder internal combustion engine, it had no clutch and the rear wheels had to be lifted off the ground when starting. Dissatisfied, Marcus turned to other inventions, and did not produce his second automobile until 1875. This made a successful 16-mi. (26 km) run, was capable of 4 mph (6.4 km/h), and in 1950 was overhauled and driven in Vienna. He built two more automobiles, but lost interest

when complaints about their noise forced the police to prohibit them from the streets.

Marie Celeste

American brig found abandoned in the Atlantic in 1872. The "ghost ship" was in good order, and the disappearance of the crew has never been explained. Her cargo was crude alcohol, from which vapor can cause a loud but harmless explosion. Possibly such an explosion occurred, and the crew abandoned ship, later to be overwhelmed by a storm.

Marine engines

See SHIPS.

Mass production

The basis of modern manufacturing practice, mass production involves making goods in large quantities at low unit cost. Essential features include the use of specialized precision machine tools to produce standardized, interchangeable parts, and the breakdown of the whole production process into a series of specialized tasks which can be carried out quickly by workers or machines performing simple and repetitive operations (see ASSEMBLY LINE). Production planners use analytical techniques including computer-generated specifications, to achieve optimum output, ensuring that each task is performed in the shortest possible time, and that all parts arrive at the right place at the right moment. They are also able to introduce a certain amount of flexibility so that, for example, in the auto industry they can offer a selection of models and colors without sacrificing the benefits of mass production.

American inventor Eli Whitney became one of the earliest pioneers of mass production when he used precision machines to make interchangeable parts for muskets in 1798. A little later Britain's Marc Isambard BRUNEL used mass production techniques to build pulley blocks for sailing ships. It was Henry FORD, using these ideas for the complex process of automobile manufacture, who has become associated with the techniques of modern mass production.

Master cylinder

A component in a hydraulic braking system (see BRAKING SYSTEMS; HYDRAULIC SYSTEMS).

Mauretania

One of the most famous of all the old Atlantic liners. Launched in the same year as her sister ship LUSITANIA, she was 766 ft. (233 m) long and displaced 31,938 tons. The two ships were the first turbine-engined liners, their four turbines developing 70,000 hp and giving a speed of 27 knots. Winner of the BLUE RIBAND in 1909, the *Mauretania* held it for over 20 years.

Mercedes-Benz

German automobile first produced in 1926 by the merging of companies started by Gottlieb DAIMLER and Carl BENZ. The name Mercedes was originally given to a new model built by Daimler in 1901. Designed as "the car of the day after tomorrow," it was so popular that the German Daimler company adopted Mercedes as the name for all subsequent automobiles. After the merger Daimler-Benz developed new models from the earlier Mercedes and Benz automobiles. One of the most successful was the supercharged 6.25-liter K model, at the time the world's fastest touring car. During the 1930s the company produced advanced sports and racing automobiles, several of which broke world speed records (which included, in 1938, a flying

kilometer at 268.9 mph, 432.8 km/h; this remains an all time record on a public highway). Today Mercedes-Benz holds its position as the leading German make of high-quality automobiles, which range from family sedans, many available with diesel engines, to luxury limousines and high-speed sports models.

Merchant marine

The merchant shipping fleet of a nation. The merchant fleets of the world include some 58,000 ships with a total gross registered tonnage of approximately 250,000,000. Before World War II the nations of Western Europe together with the United States and Japan between them owned 90% of the world's fleet, and until recently Britain retained her traditional position at the top of the league. However, the period since 1945 has seen the rapid rise of the Soviet Union's merchant marine, and of the FLAGS OF CONVENIENCE countries, notably Liberia and Panama. Registering under a foreign flag allows the shipowner to avoid the taxation and stringent rules and regulations of his own country. In 1967 Liberia took over Britain's leading position, and today over a fifth of the world's tonnage sails under flags of convenience.

The world's largest fleets are those of Liberia (44,444,000 gross tons), Japan (34,929,000), Great Britain (28,625,000), Norway (23,507,000), the Soviet Union (16,734,000), Greece (15,329,000), and the United States (15,024,000). Of the total over a third consists of tankers, and nearly a quarter of other bulk carriers. The United States fleet of some 3,300 ships has a slightly lower percentage of tankers, while the fleets of Panama and Liberia have around 60%.

Every nation regards its merchant marine as an important national asset, and one which can be called upon in time of war. Many protect their fleet's interests by, for example, charging higher port dues on foreign ships, or (as in the United States) by reserving all coastal trade and a large part of international government-financed cargo for vessels flying the national flag. The United States and Japan are unusual in giving direct subsidies to shipping operators, but many other countries provide assistance in the form of special loans or tax exemptions.

Regulations and administration. Many national and international organizations exist to ensure high standards of safety and to regulate training, conditions of service, and the like. At a national level, Chambers of Shipping organized by shipowners look after the interests of the industry, dealing with such matters as

Mass production methods being used in the production of automobile parts.

Tanks are the most heavily armed and armored military vehicles. The photograph shows a U.S. Army Sheridan type.

training and recruitment, safety, research, and various policy matters. Government agencies such as the United States Federal Maritime Commission draw up safety regulations and training requirements and ensure that they are followed. The U.S. Maritime Academy provides graduate courses for officers.

At an international level, the International Chamber of Shipping and the International Shipping Federation (both based in London) coordinate international research, provide expert technical advice, and generally promote the interests of merchant shipping; while the Inter-Governmental Maritime Consultative Organization and other United Nations agencies take up general aspects such as the development of trade, and oil pollution.

Another important aspect is the registry and classification of merchant shipping. To establish adequate standards of strength and safety, shipbuilding is usually supervised by surveyors working either on behalf of the government or of a classification society such as the American Bureau of Shipping in the United States. This Bureau works in cooperation with the world's largest and most influential classification society, Lloyds Register of Shipping (London). As a result of such surveys, and of subsequent regular inspections, Lloyds Register provides an up-to-date register of the

A U.S. Army M-113 armored personnel carrier demonstrates its ability to negotiate difficult terrain. Wheeled types are also used, often with "run flat" tires.

materials, construction, machinery, equipment, safe-loading capacity, and present condition of all merchant ships in the world of over 100 tons gross.

Yet despite the role of all these organizations, standards of training, maintenance, and ship operation are still very uneven. It is one thing to work out desirable rules and regulations, but quite another to enforce them internationally.

Mersey Tunnel

The longest road tunnel in Britain. It carries traffic under the Mersey River between Liverpool and Birkenhead. The tunnel is 2.13 mi. (3.4 km) long. With an internal diameter of 44 ft. (13.4 m), it has a four-lane roadway 36 ft. (11 m) wide

and carries almost 7,500,000 vehicles a year. The tunnel was begun in 1925 and opened in 1934.

One tube of a new Mersey road tunnel linking Liverpool and Wallesey was opened in 1971. A parallel tunnel is still under construction.

A rail tunnel under the Mersey was opened in 1886.

Metro

The word used to describe a subway in many European and South American countries, in Canada and the Soviet Union, and in some American cities (e.g., Washington, D.C.). The name came from London's Metropolitan Railway, opened on January 10, 1863, but has been replaced in London itself by "Underground" or "Tube" (although the original name is retained for that particular line in the subway network) (see SUBWAYS).

Military vehicles

The great majority of military vehicles, those used for supply and general transport, differ little from many in civil use. They include heavy trucks and jeep-type vehicles, often with additional gears and four-wheel drive so that they can operate on tough terrain, and often adapted so that they can run in water up to about 3 ft. (1 m) deep. Some are equipped with integral floating tanks for amphibious work (see AMPHIBIOUS VEHICLES) and are propelled in water either by their road wheels or by rear propellers.

The most widely used armored vehicles are personnel carriers such as the American M 113. Both wheeled and tracked types are used, the former often being fitted with special "run-flat" tires which reduce their vulnerability. For reconnaissance work small armored cars are employed, such as the American tracked M 114, while larger vehicles are used as command posts, ambulances and so on. The standard Soviet BRDM armored car has a machine gun turret or missile launcher, and specialist versions are equipped for repair work, or for chemical warfare decontamination. Bridging vehicles include traveling pontoon units, and amphibious tanks adapted to transport and launch floating bridge frames. Tanks, the most heavily armed and armored military vehicles, are invariably tracked and include fully amphibious types. Additional military "vehicles" include a variety of self-propelled guns and missile launchers, and AIR-CUSHION VEHICLES.

Miraflores Locks

Set of locks in the Panama Canal, lying 8 mi. (12.8 km) from its Pacific Ocean end and linking the ocean with man-made Mi-

A craftsman at work on a 1:100 scale model of a supertanker, with completed models of other freighters. They are built to order for museums and shipbuilding yards.

raflores Lake. The lake lies 54 ft. (16 m) above mean sea level. The locks are double-chambered, and passage normally takes about an hour.

Mobile home
See TRAILER.

Models
Miniature replicas have been a feature of human history since man first became capable of using tools and fashioning articles. Much important archaeological information has been culled from models found during excavations or in tombs, including evidence of the construction employed in early wheeled vehicles, indications of how the first sailing ships were rigged, and the nature of the harness used for hitching horses to chariots.

Experimental models. A great deal of technical experimental work can be carried out quickly and inexpensively using models. The design of ships' hulls has been facilitated by work with models made of balsa, laminated hardwood or a mixture of paraffin and beeswax. Special tanks are available in which artificial waves of different types can be propagated and simulated wind effects are produced. The model is towed through the water and electronic machines measure its behavior in calm conditions and its response to wind and waves (to what degree it will pitch and roll, etc.). Experiments to determine how effective the hull shape is under the influence of propulsive forces can also be undertaken. The first testing tank for evaluating hull design was built by the British admiralty 1870 for William Froude (1810-1879), who postulated that the total resistance of a hull consisted basically of two com-

ponent resistances: friction between the surface of the hull and the surrounding water, and residuary resistance (inclusing resistance due to wave generation, etc.). Froude's pioneer experiments with model ships established the validity of his concept.

Models of flying machines were assembled as a means of experiment from a very early date. As long ago as the early 14th century string-pull toy "helicopters" were in existence — models derived from the principle of a windmill's blades that were forerunners of the airscrew first used by Blanchard (on a balloon) in 1784. Model flying machines were subsequently build by Tito Livio Burattini in Poland and Robert Hooke in England during the 17th century. Later pioneers in the development of heavier-than-air craft who used models as research tools included Launoy and Bienvenu (who demonstrated a miniature helicopter in Paris during 1784), Sir George Cayley (1773-1857) and William Samuel Henson (1812-88) in England, John Stringfellow (1799-1883) — Henson's collaborator, and Alphonse Penaud (1850-80) who used twisted rubber to power his projects. Some of these models were quite large: Victor Tatin (1843-1913) built a monoplane in 1879 that spanned 6.2 ft. (2 m).

S.P. Langley (1834-1906) constructed 30 or 40 rubber-powered models in America during the late 19th century and also tried unsuccessfully to use steam engines before installing a small gas engine in a model that took to the air in 1903 — the first gasoline-powered aircraft to fly.

Aircraft models are extensively used for WIND TUNNEL experiments, and during design work on a new airplane scale models are constructed to help the project engineers evaluate progress. A

full-size mock-up is normally produced as a final preliminary before assembly of an actual flying prototype is commenced. Automobile manufacturers also make use of models, particularly in styling departments, where new body shapes are worked out three-dimensionally to determine their esthetic appeal to prospective purchasers and also to ensure that the design will be amenable to assembly line production methods.

Models as a hobby. Constructing models did not become a widespread leisure acitivity until the 20th century. Not until the 1900s were suitable tools and materials available for model making, together with new synthetic substances and techniques for casting metals at low temperature.

Today model making as a hobby is broadly divided into working models and static replicas. Powered model airplanes, boats and cars use diminutive internal combustion engines and are often radio-controlled or attached to control lines. Plastics technology has made available a wide range of beautifully detailed kits which can be assembled without too much difficulty and for the average constructor yield results that are far superior to anything which could be achieved with the old-type wooden kits. Specialists use commercial plastic kits as a basis for building elaborate replicas to very high standards of authenticity.

It takes a kit manufacturer over a year to prepare a new plastic kit. Detailed plans have to be obtained and drawings (larger than the proposed model) are made. The components into which the subject can best be broken down are decided upon, and a pattern is made up — sometimes carved in a fine-grained wood, or else worked in metal (e.g. brass). An epoxy-resin female mold is then produced and a pantograph die-sinker scales this down to the required size for the metal mold. Once the two halves of the mold are available, they are etched to provide the fine detail (rivets, panel lines, etc.). If moving parts are being incorporated, the task will take longer and involve greater complication.

Preservation. Modern technology is rapidly supplanting some old-established industrial processes and transportation concepts, and models are in many cases the best way of maintaining a record

of past engineering constructions when the originals cannot be preserved. The railroad steam locomotive is an example of this process. Many superb models of them have been made that demonstrate the details of their construction, and some of these "miniatures" are large enough to be fitted with working steam engines that enable them to pull cars carrying people.

Among the earliest formal ship models were the examples prepared by the French royal naval yards to depict every ship they built — a procedure ordered in 1679 by Jean Baptiste Colbert, Louis XIVs minister of marine, to establish a

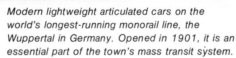

Modern lightweight articulated cars on the world's longest-running monorail line, the Wuppertal in Germany. Opened in 1901, it is an essential part of the town's mass transit system.

An experimental monorail in Japan. Like the German Wuppertal illustrated (above), the cars are suspended on cranked arms.

precise standard for future vessels. Partly because of the existence of these superb models, the French government established a maritime museum early in the 19th century in which many of then were exhibited.

In addition to ships, and trains, there are a great number of beautiful and marvellously accurate models of all forms of transport in museums and private collections throughout the world. Thanks to the compulsion for detail of generations of model makers, the development of transportation has been faithfully preserved in miniature.

Model T
The designation of the famous TIN LIZZIE, of which millions were produced between 1908 and 1927 by Henry Ford.

Monocoque construction
A method of construction in which the body skin or shell carries most of the structural load. "Monocoque" means "single shell" in French. Airplane fuselages are frequently of monocoque or semi-monocoque design, the latter signifying that they may have some supporting stiffeners and ribs. Many automobiles are of similar design, with the body shell acting as combined body and chassis. This is often termed UNITARY CONSTRUCTION.

Monoplane
An airplane with only a single pair of wings is known as a monoplane. Almost all modern aircraft are of this configuration; the wing loading is higher than that of a BIPLANE but drag is substantially reduced and performance is consequently much superior.

Monorail
A railroad with cars running on or suspended from a single rail. The theoretical advantages of such a system are that it minimizes friction, and occupies little space. An elevated monorail can be built on a row of single supports above the center of a highway without interfering with road traffic or taking up any useful space. The two main types in use today are the Alweg and Safege systems. On the former the cars run on rubber-tired wheels on top of the rail, which is a massive elevated concrete beam. They are guided and held upright by small horizontal wheels running in grooves along either side of the beam, and powered by electricity. Alweg monorails are in use on short routes in Japan and the United States.

In the French Safege system the cars are suspended from the rail, which is a box girder with a longitudinal slit in the lower surface to hold the car supports. The rubber-tired wheels run inside the girder on either side of the slit (so the system is technically not a monorail). Traction is again electric.

Monorails are most highly developed in Japan, where several are already in operation, and many more are planned for urban transit. Monorails of the future will probably be tracked AIR CUSHION VEHICLES (or be magnetically suspended), thus avoiding friction, and are likely to be propelled by silent LINEAR INDUCTION MOTORS.

Successful early monorails include the Lartigue system, which ran on A-shaped trestles that were easy to lay (or to move to a new site), and the German Wupper-tal line, which has been in operation since 1901. Here the cars are suspended on a cranked arm from a rail running for most of its length above a river.

Mont Blanc Tunnel

This runs under the Alps beneath Europe's highest peak, Mont Blanc. The longest road tunnel in the world, it has a total length of 7.2 mi. (11.6 km), and a diameter of about 30 ft. (9 m). There is one traffic lane in each direction, each being 12 ft. (3.7 m) wide. Work began in 1959, and the tunnel was opened on July 16, 1965. Construction cost was about $6,700,000. The tunnel provides a short-ened and year-round road link between France and Italy. It runs from Pèlerins, near Chamonix, France, to the village of Entrèves, Val d'Aosta, Italy.

Mont Cenis Tunnel

Railroad tunnel under the Alpine peak of Mont Cenis, also known as the Fréjus Tunnel 8.5 mi. (13.7 km) long, and about 4,000 ft. (1,220 m) above sea level, it runs between Modane, France, and Bar-donècchia, Italy. Work began in 1857, and the tunnel, the first through the Alps, was opened in 1871.

Montgolfier brothers

French inventors of the hot air balloon, and builders of the first man-carrying bal-loon. Joseph Michel (1740-1810) and Jac-ques Étienne (1745-99) were mill own-ers who conducted scientific experiments in their spare time. In 1782 they began ex-perimenting with paper bags filled with hot air, which they sent aloft. On June 5, 1783, they gave a public demonstration of a 30 ft. (9.15 m) diameter hot air balloon. Made of linen lined with paper, and infla-ted with hot air from a furnace, it reached a height of 6,000 ft. (1,830 m). On Septem-ber 19, 1783, at Versailles, the Montgol-fiers demonstrated a larger balloon which carried a sheep, a duck, and a rooster in a basket suspended underneath, the first living creatures to make a balloon ascent. The flight lasted about eight minutes. While Joseph worked (inconclusively) on the problems of control and propulsion, Étienne built a much larger balloon which carried its own fire and could therefore stay in the air for longer periods. It lifted the first human to leave the earth (the physicist de Rozier), on October 15, 1783, in a tethered flight, and achieved the first free flight on November 21 (see BALLOONS). Étienne never made an ascent, and Jo-seph made only one (which nearly ended in disaster), but the brothers were widely acclaimed and honored for their work, which paved the way for the development of hydrogen balloons.

The NASA moon buggy used by American astronauts for transportation on the moon. It had a top speed of 10 mph (16 km/h).

Moon buggy

Popular name for the Lunar Roving Veh-icle used for transportation on the moon by American astronauts from Apollo 15, 16 and 17. The buggy was a collapsible vehicle made from aluminum tube and wire. It was about 10 ft. (3 m) long, and its four wheels were driven by a battery-powered electric motor, giving it a top speed of 10 mph (16 km/h). The greatest distance travelled in an LRV was 22 mi. (35 km) by the Apollo 17 crew. Develop-ment of the buggy cost more than $13 mil-lion (see also LUNOKHOD).

Moonwalker

Lunokhod in Russian, the first wheeled vehicle to travel on the moon. Lunokhod 1 rolled out from the Russian lunar probe Luna 17 in 1970 and survived for a total of 322 earthdays. In all it traveled about 2 mi. (3 km). It had eight wheels driven by electric motor powered by batteries that were kept charged by solar cells in the vehicle's hinged "lid." It was guided re-motely by scientists on earth looking through its two television-camera "eyes."

Moped

A light motorcycle with pedals and a frame similar to that of a bicycle. The pe-dals are used for starting, for assisting initial acceleration, and for supplement-ing the engine on steep hills. Typically a moped has a 50-cc, two-stroke engine, fly-wheel generator, and three-speed gear-ing. Mopeds developed from convention-al bicycles to which small power units had been attached. Many modern mopeds however, are quite similar mechanically to motor scooters, except that they have a larger frame and larger wheels.

Moscow Canal

Waterway in the Soviet Union linking Moscow with the Volga River. Formerly called the Moscow-Volga Canal, it runs for 80 mi. (128 km) from the Moskva River to the Volga at Ivankovo, which lies at the eastern end of the Volga Reservoir. With 11 locks and 3 artificial lakes, one of which (the Khimki) forms Moscow's main port area, the canal has a minimum depth of 18 ft. (5.5 m). The locks are 950 ft. (290 m) long and 100 ft. (305 m) wide, so the canal can be navigated by shallow draft seagoing ships and provides an im-portant link between Moscow and the So-viet Union's western sea outlets.

Motion sickness

Sickness experienced by many people when traveling by sea, air, or in a road vehicle. The feeling is caused by unnatu-ral and irregular accelerations which may be the result of, for example, a ship pitching and rolling in waves, or an auto-mobile repeatedly speeding up and slow-ing down or traveling over an uneven surface. Many theories have been ad-vanced about the causes of motion sick-ness, and to explain why it affects some people but not others, but little is actu-ally understood about the subject. One undoubted factor is the functioning of the balance mechanism in the inner ear. This responds to changes in direction of movement and to gravity, and as well as enabling the brain to maintain the body's balance, it plays an important part in coordinating eye and body movements. Faced with the unnatural motion of a ship, automobile or aircraft, the balance mechanism fails to maintain a state of equilibrium, and it is generally assumed that this somehow causes not only the inability to keep one's balance but also all the other symptoms of motion sickness (drowsiness, sweating, salivation, and nausea).

Vision is a further contributing factor. The eye sees one frame of reference (the apparently stationary features of the inside of the vehicle) while the balance organs feel another (the actual motions of the vehicle). A driver or pilot rarely if ever experiences motion sickness. He is concentrating (which in itself helps to give immunity), and his eyes are fixed on the stationary world ahead.

Ingenious experiments have been tried to reduce the motions that cause travel sickness. In one, a ship was provided with a swinging public cabin which was supposed to remain steady when the vessel rolled. The idea was however bound to fail, for it took no account of pitching, yawing, heaving, and surging. Today ships are fitted with stabilizers, most aircraft fly above turbulent air, and improved suspension systems provide a smoother ride in road vehicles.

A motorboat constructed of plastics, and propeled by twin outboard motors. Turning the wheel turns the motors, thereby altering their angle of thrust.

Motorboat

Small craft powered by an internal combustion engine, or, rarely, an electric motor. Motorboats range in size from miniature one-man racing boats, through utility family or fishing craft of about 20 ft. (6 m) in length, to seagoing vessels over 100 ft. (30 m) long.

Smaller motorboats usually have gasoline engines similar to those used in automobiles or motorcycles, while larger craft often have diesel engines. There may be a gearbox providing a range of speeds and reverse, or the engine may run at a constant rate with changes in speed and direction of thrust being achieved by altering the pitch of the propeller blades.

The engine may be inboard (built in with propeller and shaft permanently installed), OUTBOARD (slotted over the stern and detachable), or inboardoutboard (with fixed inboard engine but movable shaft and propeller). With the two latter types, the boat is steered by turning the propeller to alter the angle of thrust, but an inboard engined boat is steered with a RUDDER.

There are two main hull types: displacement, and planing. A displacement motorboat sits in the water and travels through it, while a planing hull is designed to rise up at speed and to skim along the surface, thus reducing DRAG to a minimum and permitting much higher speeds in reasonably calm water. However in rough conditions the more seaworthy and stable displacement type can safely maintain a higher speed than a hydroplane (the name given to planing motorboats).

Motorcycle

Motorcycles range in size from lightweight machines with engines of around 100 cc to the largest which have engines as big as that of a small automobile and are capable of high speed and very rapid acceleration. Both two- and four-stroke engines are used. The former, running normally on a mixture of gasoline and oil, are cheaper, more economical and simpler to maintain, but require more frequent decarbonization and are prone to difficulties when starting. Four-stroke engines are most popular, espcially on large machines. They are smoother running and give greater power for a given capacity.

Although most motorcycles have single cylinder engines, twin cylinder versions are not unusual, and three or four cylinders are occasionally employed. One of the fastest racing machines ever built, a 748 cc Kawasaki which was capable of 185 mph (297 km/h), had three cylinders. Twin cylinders may be arranged vertically, in V formation, or horizontally opposed. The engine is almost invariably air-cooled, with the exhaust side at the front and the cylinder heads finned. Ignition is usually by coil, although on many small two strokes the spark is produced by a magneto. Transmission from engine to gearbox and from gearbox to rear wheel is most often by chain. The gearbox may have as many as six gears, with gear change being effected by a pedal. Another pedal controls the rear brake while handlebar controls govern clutch, throttle, and front wheel brake. The engine is normally started with a kick-starter mounted on the gearbox, but some machines are fitted with electric starters.

A typical medium-sized motorcycle suitable for general personal transportation, this 175 cc twin cylinder 4-stroke Honda CD 175 has a top speed of 77 mph (124 km/h) and a fuel consumption of 84 mpg.

However, many individuals, especially children and old people, still suffer from motion sickness. There are many ways of avoiding or at least of reducing its effects. These include lying flat on the deck of a ship, midway between bow and stern where motion is least pronounced; keeping the mind occupied, and the eyes shut. Alternatively one of the various drugs available may be taken.

Large high-speed craft such as naval patrol boats are often powered by gas turbine engines, and some can exceed 50 knots.

Propulsion is normally by screw propeller, although WATER JETS are useful in shallow or weed choked water and for towing water-skiers (to whom the propeller represents a considerable hazard). Speed record breakers are jet propelled.

Powerful motorcycles such as this 750 cc Triumph are capable of high speed and very rapid acceleration.

History. Various experimental steam powered motorcycles were constructed during the late 1860s and the 1870s, including one by L.D. Copeland of Philadelphia, but the first gasoline engined motorcycle was built by Gottlieb Daimler in Germany in 1885. A wooden-framed machine with a single cylinder four-stroke engine, its top speed was 12 mph (19 km/h). The first practical motorcycle in series production appeared in 1894. Built in Munich, Germany, by Hildebrand and Wolfmüller, it had a 760 cc water-cooled engine and, with a top speed of 24 mph (38 km/h) was faster than most automobiles of the time. Over 1,000 were produced before the firm went out of business in 1898.

Between 1897 and 1904 a number of interesting attempts were made to adapt pedal bicycles with the addition of a lightweight motor. These were the real forerunners of the automobile in Great Britain.

In the United States the first motorcycles in production were the Indian (1901) and the Harley-Davidson (1903). Popularity increased gradually over the years, and especially after 1910, by which time belt drive (smooth, quiet and simple, but inclined to slip in wet weather) had given way to chain drive, and machines with two or four cylinders were common, as was the motorcycle and sidecar combination. Extensive use of motorcycles during World War I increased their popularity, which continued until the beginning of the economic depression in 1929. Well known United States models of the 1920s included the 1,145 cc Henderson, the 1,229 cc Indian Ace, and various machines by Pierce (sister company of the famous automobile manufacturers Pierce-Arrow).

In general, improvements to motorcycles have paralleled those of the automobile. During the 1930s the side-valve engines were gradually replaced by overhead valve machines. More recent technical advances include torque converter transmission, air suspension, and shaft drive. The motorcycle's great attraction has always been in sport and enjoyment, rather than in the practical business of getting from place to place. This appeal is reinforced by the comparative simplicity of the machine and the accessibility of its parts, features which enable the enthusiast to do his own maintenance.

Motorcycle sports. These include drag racing (see AUTOMOBILE RACING), speedway races on short oval dirt tracks, and straightforward races on closed road circuits, with events for pure racing machines and for sports models. At the top of the scale come Class A Grand Prix machines complete with aerodynamic bodywork and supertuned engines, but there are also events for 50 cc motorcycles. Moto-cross, long popular in Europe, and introduced to the United States in 1970, takes place on rough terrain with the maximum of mud, hillocks and sharp turns. Other events include hill climbs, rallies and reliability trials, and speed trials. Since 1962 the world speed record on a motorcycle has stood at 224.57 mph (361.41 km/h), and was achieved by W. A. Johnson (United States) at Bonneville, Utah, on a 667 cc Triumph T. 120.

Motor ship

A ship powered by an INTERNAL COMBUSTION ENGINE (as distinct from a steam ship). The first oceangoing motor ship, *Selandia*, was launched in 1911, but it was not until the 1960s that the total tonnage of motor ships overtook that of steamers. Today, out of a world merchant fleet of some 58,000 ships, over 50,000 are diesel-powered. The cheaper and less complex steam turbine retains its importance only for very large vessels such as supertankers.

Internal combustion engines have several advantages over steam turbines: they have a higher thermal efficiency and are therefore more economical to run; requiring no boilers, they occupy less space; and they can be started at the touch of a button with no delay for building up steam.

Selandia's engines were four-stroke, but the majority of motor ships today have single-acting two-stroke engines fitted with turbochargers (SUPERCHARGERS driven by turbines powered by the exhaust gases) which increase power by nearly a third.

Mount Clare Station

This railroad station near Baltimore was opened on January 7, 1830, on land transferred to the Baltimore & Ohio Railroad by a farmer named Charles Carroll. A tablet on the building claims that it is the first passenger and freight station in America and the oldest in the world. When it was opened, horses were pulling trains between Baltimore and Ellicott Mills. There were, in fact, railroad stations operating in Britain and elsewhere before Mount Clare was built.

The Mount Washington Cog Railroad

This is the oldest mountain-climbing cog (or rack) railroad in the world. It was the idea of Sylvester Marsh of Chicago who built first a model, then the first section of track and a locomotive, at his own expense. Demonstrations in 1866 at Cold Spring Hill, at the foot of Mount Washington, raised interest and a company was formed to build the whole line, which was opened to the foot of Jacob's Ladder by 1868 and to the summit, at 6,293 ft. (1,918 m), in July 1869. It is $3\frac{1}{4}$ mi. (5.2 km) long and has an average gradient of

Two powered narrow boats lashed together, transporting coal along an English canal. These small barges carried about 25 tons of cargo.

A 19th century engraving of the Mount Washington Cog Railroad. The world's first mountain-climbing cog or rack railroad, it was completed in 1869.

25%. The original 8-ton locomotive, *Old Peppersass*, is still displayed at the foot of the incline.

Muffler

Also called a silencer, the muffler is the component in a vehicle's EXHAUST SYSTEM designed to slow down and silence the gases exhausted from the engine cylinders. The usual baffle type consists of a chamber containing baffle plates at right angles to the gas flow. The flow is slowed down as the gases weave between the plates, or through perforations in them. The main drawback of this type is that it sets up a certain amount of back pressure in the exhaust system which tends to reduce power output.

Sports and high-performance automobiles therefore often have a "straight-through" muffler, in which the gases pass through a central pipe which has perforated sides. Absorbent material such as fiberglass is packed round the pipe. The gases expand through the perforations and are thereby slowed down and silenced. A variation of this type contains hollow resonance chambers rather than absorbent packing.

N

Narrow boat

Name given to a type of small barge used on English canals. Carrying around 25 tons of cargo, and with a crew of two adults and a boy, they were specifically adapted to England's comparatively narrow canals, and to passage through the many miles of canal tunnels. With the arrival of the railroads their small capacity made them uneconomical for most cargoes, but in recent years narrow boats have achieved considerable popularity as pleasure craft for cruising holidays.

Narrow gauge

A railroad with a distance between the rails of less than the standard gauge of 4 ft. 8½ in. (1.435 m). Narrow gauge railroads have proved particularly successful in hilly country where they are able to make tighter curves than is possible with standard or broad gauges. Another significant advantage is cheapness, of track, bridges, tunnels, locomotives, and rolling stock. The principal drawback is the reduction of stability, and the consequent limitation in speed. One of the most popular narrow gauges is 3 ft. 6 in. (1.067 m), on which locomotives and rolling stock may be as large as much of that used on standard gauge lines. Metergauge (3 ft. 3⅜ in.) is popular in India, South America, parts of Africa, and parts of the Far East. A 3 ft. (0.91 m) gauge is used in parts of Central and South America and Mexico. The really narrow gauges (2 ft. 6 in., 0.76 m, and 2 ft., 0.61 m,) are found mainly in the hilly sections of the Indian subcontinent and South America. Many countries, however, have some narrow gauge railroads, which are not necessarily part of the main network; many serve local industries.

Nash

American automobile manufacturer. The company was founded in 1917 by a former president of GENERAL MOTORS, Charles W. Nash. It acquired the firms of Mitchell and Lafayette in 1924, successfully survived the Depression, and in 1954 was amalgamated with Hudson to form American Motors. The name Nash survived until 1957, as did the company's most famous automobile, the Rambler.

Natchez

Celebrated Mississippi sidewheel steamboat. In 1870 she took part in a famous race with her rival *Robert E. Lee*, from New Orleans up the river to St. Louis. Although the *Natchez* lost, she was considered to be the faster boat.

Nautical Almanac

An annual publication which first appeared in 1766, giving the distance of fixed stars from the moon at specific times for each day of the year, and other information about the positions of the sun, moon, planets, and stars. The main object was originally to provide navigators with a means of telling the time at sea to enable them to determine longitude. Finding longitude had earlier been a process of inspired guesswork, based on dead reckoning, and wild (and often dangerous) errors were common. The Nautical Almanac was some help, but the problem was finally solved only with the invention of the CHRONOMETER.

Today the Nautical Almanac includes a wider range of accurately computed information about the stars and planets, which is used in conjunction with SEXTANT and chronometer for finding longitude and latitude (see NAVIGATION).

Nautical mile

Measure of distance used at sea and in the air. In theory it equals one sixtieth of a degree (or one minute) of latitude, but since the earth is not a perfect sphere it varies slightly at different latitudes. The United States nautical mile of 6080.2 ft. was superseded in 1959 by the international nautical mile of 6076.12 ft. (1852 m). A KNOT is a speed of one nautical mile an hour.

Nautilus

United States submarine, the world's first nuclear-powered vessel, launched on January 21, 1954, and named after the earlier craft of Robert Fulton (see SUBMARINES) and of Jules Verne's science fiction classic. The *Nautilus* was the first submarine capable of operating deep under the surface for virtually unlimited spells of duty. With a length of 319 ft. (97 m) and displacing 3,180 tons, she exceeds 20 knots when submerged, can cruise for over 80,000 mi. (128,747 km) without refueling, and in 1958 became the first vessel to travel under the North Pole.

In addition to the nuclear reactor, which is fueled by enriched uranium 235 and used to drive a steam turbine, *Nautilus* is also equipped with a conventional diesel engine. She has six torpedo tubes at the bow, and can dive to a maximum of 750 ft. (230 m).

facilitated by the use of computers. Given a specified length, breadth, draft, and speed, together with details of the type and quantity of cargo or armaments to be carried, and the route, it is possible to produce many designs which will meet the requirements and comply with all the safety and other regulations. Using computers a series of designs can be prepared and assessed.

Unless the design is very close to that of an existing ship, it is usual to build a model and to test its stability, maneuverability, wave-making qualities, and so on in a test tank before drafting the final blueprints.

For an explanation of the basic elements underlying ship design (buoyancy, stability, and strength) see SHIPS.

Navigation

The science of finding the way at sea, in the air, or in space. Today, ships and aircraft carry complex instruments and electronic equipment to fix their position, to chart their course and even to operate the controls. Early seamen had no such aids. They relied on instinct and observation. They learned to see over the horizon by noticing reflections on cloud. They followed prevailing winds and currents, or migrating birds. And eventually they learned to estimate direction from the sun, and latitude (distance north or south) from the stars.

or west until he reached home. This is celestial navigation at its simplest, but it enabled the Polynesians to travel thousands of miles across the Pacific.

The Vikings used the Pole Star for the same purpose, to determine latitude. Because the position of the Pole Star is fixed in the sky, at any one place its altitude (height above the horizon) is constant. At the North Pole it is directly overhead, its altitude is 90°. On the Equator it is on the horizon, its altitude is 0°. Thus, in the Northern Hemisphere, the mariner had only to measure the altitude of the Pole Star to find latitude.

Later navigators used the midday altitude of the sun, and the altitudes of the planets (compared to their altitudes at the Equator as tabulated in almanacs) to find latitude.

At first altitude was measured in handbreadths, but various instruments were devised, including the ASTROLABE, the cross and back staffs, and finally the SEXTANT. Parallel improvements occurred in the preparation of detailed tabulated information in almanacs (see NAUTICAL ALMANAC), giving the positions of stars and planets throughout the year. In the mid-18th century the chronometer was invented, and at last accurate position fixing became a reality.

Shooting a fix. Selecting a star, or the sun, the navigator finds from the almanac

The world's first nuclear powered vessel, the U.S. submarine Nautilus, *seen here shortly after her launching in 1954.*

Naval architecture

The science of ship design. The naval architect is invariably asked to design a ship for a particular job, whether it be an aircraft carrier, an oil tanker or a coastal freighter. The specification may be very general (e.g. an oil tanker of a certain tonnage and a certain speed), or it may be very detailed, listing exactly what engines, machinery, handling gear, and so on are required.

Whenever possible an existing vessel of similar specifications is taken as a starting point, although the complex and lengthy procedure of designing a ship from scratch has in recent years been

Finding accurate longitude (distance east or west) only became possible after the invention of the CHRONOMETER in the mid-18th century. Until then, navigators had mostly to rely on dead reckoning, a process of estimating from speed, course, and time how far and in what direction the vessel had traveled since the last known position.

Celestial navigation. Knowing that a particular star passed directly over his island, the Polynesian mariner returning home from a long voyage sailed north or south until that star was overhead, and then followed the course of the star east

the point on the earth's surface at which it is, at that precise moment, directly overhead. This is called the substellar point. Using the sextant he now finds how many degrees from the zenith the star is at his position. This angle is the co-altitude. Each degree of co-altitude represents one degree of latitude, or 60 NAUTICAL MILES. If the co-altitude were, for example, 5°, the navigator would know he is somewhere on a circle with its center at the substellar point and a radius of 300 (5 x 60) nautical miles. The process is repeated with two further stars, and the point at which the three circles intersect is his position.

Sextant and almanac can of course be used to find latitude in the traditional way, and with the help of the chronometer, to find longitude. The ship's chronometer shows the time at the zero meridian of longitude (Greenwich, London). Taking a series of readings of the sun's altitude with the sextant the navigator finds local time, and hence how far ahead (east) of or behind (west) of Greenwich he is. Each hour of difference represents 15° of longitude. Aircraft are equipped with an ARTIFICIAL HORIZON instrument, since the actual horizon is often indistinct or invisible. However, although celestial navigation was used in the early days of flight, modern planes fly too fast for it to be of much value.

Electronic position fixing. Early electronic navigational aids made use of the RADIO DIRECTION FINDER. This enabled ships nearing land to fix their position by using directional aerials to find the bearings of two or more shore-based transmitters. No special equipment was needed on board, but the range was limited. The more advanced systems of today such as LORAN, DECCA NAVIGATOR, and Omega, rely on receivers that compare the times taken by signals from several associated but widely spaced transmitters to reach the craft. These hyperbolic systems are used by both ships and aircraft, and enable the navigator to fix position quickly and accurately in areas covered by the transmitters.

Satellite navigation and Doppler. Some craft are equipped to determine position with the help of navigational satellites. This normally involves use of the Doppler effect. When an aircraft flies past, for example, the pitch of its engine noise becomes higher as it approaches and then lower as it recedes. The aircraft's speed can be calculated by measuring the change in pitch, and its distance can be worked out from the abruptness with which the pitch drops. The navigation satellite transmits a steady frequency radio signal. Instruments on the craft measure the change in frequency due to the Doppler effect as the satellite passes by, and from this calculate the satellite's distance and (since the satellite's position is known) the ship's location.

Dead reckoning. Starting from a known position, the navigator can deduce his subsequent position if he knows for how long, at what speed and in what direction he has since been traveling. This is known as Dead (from "deduced") Reckoning. Speed was estimated with the help

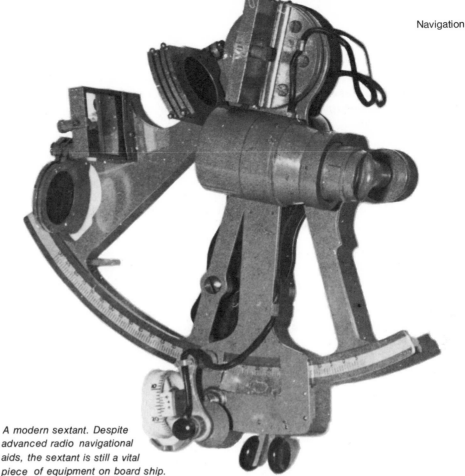

A modern sextant. Despite advanced radio navigational aids, the sextant is still a vital piece of equipment on board ship.

of a LOG, direction with a magnetic COMPASS, and elapsed time with a sand glass. The information was recorded on a traverse board. However, the log and compass were not particularly accurate, and neither took account of sideways drift due to wind or current. Estimating this was a question of inspired guesswork. Electronic position-fixing systems do not cover the world, and celestial navigation cannot be used when the sky is overcast, and so dead reckoning is still a vital aspect of navigation. Because ocean currents are comparatively slow and predictable, their influence can be taken into account with little difficulty, and on surface ships dead reckoning involves nothing more sophisticated than the log and the GYROCOMPASS. However, in advanced ships the two are often linked to a computer, an automatic pilot, and an automatic plotter which records progress on a chart. Accurate fixes are made at intervals by celestial or electronic means to correct the inevitable errors in the process.

Navigation under the sea. Nuclear submarines present a completely different navigational problem. They remain submerged for weeks on end, totally isolated from normal systems, and must rely entirely on dead reckoning. The log and gyrocompass method is far too inaccurate. Instead INERTIAL GUIDANCE systems are used, in which three gyroscopes set at right angles to each other in three planes provide a steady frame of refer-

ence. Very accurate ACCELEROMETERS sense the slightest deviation from this frame of reference, and on the basis of their measurements a computer plots distance and direction traveled. Inertial navigation, which was used by the NAUTILUS in her historic voyage under the North Pole in 1958, produces errors of less than a mile after a week's continuous cruising.

One other method of navigation available to nuclear submarines (and surface vessels) is to monitor carefully the contours of the sea bed, an increasingly practical proposition with the development of sophisticated ECHO SOUNDERS and detailed charts of the ocean floor.

Aerial dead reckoning. A similar inertial guidance system is sometimes used in aircraft, although the standard method of dead reckoning in the air involves the gyromagnetic compass (a magnetic compass isolated from changes of speed and direction by a gyroscope) and Doppler. The latter is used to determine speed of travel over the ground. A steady frequency radio signal is transmitted to the ground, and the reflected frequency measured to determine speed (the higher the reflected frequency the greater the speed). Signals at right angles show sideways drift.

At the opposite end of the speed scale, Doppler is also used when maneuvering giant ships. A tanker responds very slowly, and is so long that it is almost impossible to gauge its movements visually.

Doppler installations at bow and stern (or on shore aimed at bow and stern) show speed, and the relative movements of the two ends of the ship.

Planning the route. The navigator uses speed, time, and direction to deduce position, and to plot his future course. In civil aviation a detailed flight plan must be completed before takeoff. The plan shows intended speed and height, and the route, which is divided into sectors. The equally vital fuel flight plan shows the amount of fuel allowed for each sector (and the reserve). With high-speed flight and crowded air routes, accuracy is critical. Hence the importance of adhering to the estimated course and speed, and therefore of allowing in advance for wind conditions. At sea, similar precautions are not normally considered necessary except on unusually crowded sealanes. The rate of travel is much slower, and the length of the voyage is likely to be measured in days or weeks rather than hours. The strength of currents and tidal drifts cannot be predicted sufficiently far in advance, and in any case a ship may have to depart radically from its course to avoid bad weather.

Navigation lanes and radio beams. On long-distance flights dead reckoning and the electronic position-fixing systems already described are important. But in busy air corridors, and especially in the vicinity of airports, more specific navigational guidance is needed to ensure safety. This is provided by radio beacons transmitted from series of ground stations. Each airway and lane is clearly defined by these beacons, and a "fly left, fly right" indicator shows whether the plane is on course. The most widely used system is known as VOR (very-high-frequency omnidirectional range). With this system, signals radiate out in all directions, enabling the pilot to navigate along any of the infinite number of "spokes" towards or away from the beacon. In conjunction with DME (distance measuring equipment) VOR can also be used to fix position.

In addition, the air-traffic control service monitors all aircraft in its control zone, and all pilots must follow its instructions. (See also GROUND-CONTROLLED APPROACH; INSTRUMENT LANDING SYSTEM.)

Other related entries include BUOYS; LIGHTHOUSES AND LIGHTSHIPS; and RADAR (used for collision avoidance and for "seeing" the coastline at night and in bad weather).

New Orleans Bridge
Cantilever structure connecting the main part of New Orleans with Algiers, or New Orleans West, on the opposite bank of the Mississippi River. Known formally as the Greater New Orleans Bridge, the structure is 1,575 ft. (480 m) long, the third longest cantilever span in the world when it was opened in 1958.

New Tokaido Line
Providing the fastest railroad passenger service in the world, the New Tokaido Line is the first of Japan's new high-speed railroads. It was realized soon after World War II that the country's 3 ft. 6 in. (1.067 m) gauge network would soon become inadequate, and the standard GAUGE New Tokaido Line was built to link Tokyo and Osaka. Curves and grades permit high-speed operation throughout the line, there are no grade crossings, and a high degree of automation is used (including a system which stops the trains automatically in the event of an earthquake). Completely new electric "bullet" trains were designed, and when the line opened on October 1, 1964, 16-coach trains covered the 320 mi. (515 km) at an average speed of 103 mph (166 km/h), with a top

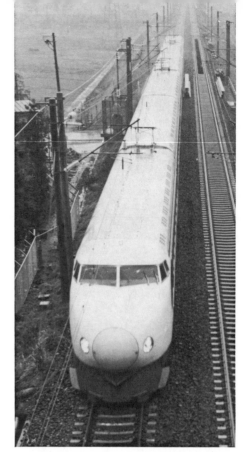

A "bullet train" on the world's fastest passenger train service, Japan's advanced New Tokaido Line. Top speed is around 160 mph (257 km/h).

speed of 130 mph (209 km/h). The line was extended to Okayama in 1972, top speed has now been raised to 159 mph (256 km/h), and a nationwide network of similar lines is planned (parts of which are already under construction).

New York State Barge Canal System
Waterway system linking Lakes Champlain, Erie, and Ontario with the Hudson River. It has a total length of 524 mi. (843 km), and consists of four canals — Cayuga and Seneca (92 mi., 148 km), Champlain (60 mi., 97 km), Erie (363 mi., 584 km), and Oswego (24 mi., 39 km). There is a total of 57 locks. The old ERIE CANAL, enlarged and in sections relocated, forms the main branch of the system, which was completed in its present form in 1918.

Noise control
Noise has become a serious problem in all modern modes of transportation. In the case of airplanes and roads through built-up areas, it is a more significant problem than pollution from engine exhaust. Medical opinion now universally acknowledges the deleterious effect of noise over 90 decibels (dB).

All road vehicles are required by law to have mufflers, but the degree of noise permitted varies with the vehicle. Large motorcycles, for example, can be restricted to a maximum of 85 dB and automobiles to around 88 dB, but heavy trucks will need to operate at a few more

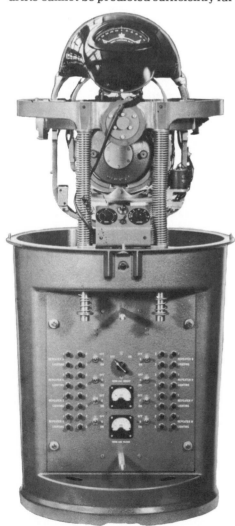

A gyrocompass. Unaffected by either deviation or variation, this instrument provides a more reliable guide to direction than the magnetic compass.

decibels. Screening is of some benefit in reducing overall traffic noise on comparatively narrow roads, a vertical wall being the most efficient, but on wide highways the value is limited.

Aircraft noise is a major problem, since most large civil airports are located near densely populated areas. Minimum Noise Routing (MNR) can be used to keep aircraft away from major conurbations, providing the procedure does not impose uneconomic penalties (fuel, time) on the operators. Silencers for jet engines are available, but fitting them to the older types of airliner involves withdrawing the aircraft from service, installation costs, and a weight penalty that reduces performance. Much of the objectionable noise created by turbofan-powered aircraft is caused by the fan itself, and the single-stage fans without inlet guides introduced in 1968 are less noisy than earlier two-stage systems.

ICAO recommendations for aircraft noise restriction do not apply to older airliners. For modern subsonic airliners, however, they propose a maximum noise level of 108 EPNdB (Effective Perceived Noise in decibels, a measure which takes into account the high-frequency emissions of jet engines to which the human ear is particularly sensitive).

For takeoff, readings are measured 21,000 ft. (6,500 m) from the start of the takeoff run and also at a point 2,100 ft. (650 m) to one side of the runway; during landing approaches the reading is taken 390 ft. (120 m) below the 3° descent path. American and British airport noise regulations are based on these recommended values. To reduce noise flight profiles may involve using less than maximum power, adopting a steep takeoff gradient so that a high takeoff thrust may be employed, or climbing out at a low air speed. But there is only limited scope for varying landing patterns. Movements of jet aircraft at night are restricted at many airports and prohibited at some. Servicing areas should be sound-proofed, with special mufflers for engine run-ups. This type of facility is also used on military airfields, but often the remoteness of such installations mitigates the noise problem.

A supersonic airliner presents even more serious problems, since at 60,000 ft. (18,300 m) it leaves a "boom path" 30 mi. (48 km) wide. The operation of these aircraft over land areas has met with considerable hostility.

Other sources of noise from transport media are hovercraft (mostly originating at the propellers) and speedboat engines, which are restricted by noise regulations framed by the Union of International Motor Boating.

North Sea Canal
A waterway running from the IJ River at Amsterdam, the Netherlands, to IJmuiden on the North Sea, the North Sea Canal is 18 mi. (29 km) long, around 700 ft. (210 m) in width and 40 ft. (14.9 m) deep. Built between 1865 and 1876, it has made Amsterdam one of the world's major seaports. There are large lock gates at IJmuiden whose principal task is to keep out the salt seawater. The salt that does enter is washed out again with fresh water from the IJsselmeer (Formerly part of the Zuider Zee).

Northwest Passage
The sea route through the Canadian Arctic Archipelago, linking the Atlantic and Pacific Oceans. The Northwest Passage is more than 3,500 mi. (5,600 km) long from the entrance to Davis Strait at the eastern end to Bering Strait at the western end. The tortuous channels through the Arctic Archipelago total about 900 mi. (1,450 km). Explorers began seeking a northwest route to the East as long ago as the end of the 15th century, but only

in 1903-06 did the Norwegian explorer Roald Amundsen become the first man to conquer the entire route by sea. U.S. and Canadian ice-breakers have forced passages many times since, but probably the most notable recent transit was that of the MANHATTAN.

Nuclear propulsion
Propulsion system in which an atomic reactor generating enormous heat through nuclear fission is used to drive a turbine. The reactor is normally of the thermal or pressurized-water type, in

which the fast neutrons emitted in fission are slowed down by a moderator to normal thermal speeds. The nuclear core is enclosed in a water-filled pressurized vessel.

The water in this primary circuit is heated to about 650°F and pumped to a heat exchanger. There water in the secondary circuit (which is isolated from the primary circuit and therefore uncontaminated) is heated to produce steam which drives a turbine. The turbine is normally coupled to the propeller shaft through reduction gears, as in conventional marine steam turbine engines, but occasionally turbo-electric drive is employed.

The fuel is Uranium 235, a heavily enriched form being used in order to save space. The nuclear reactor is controlled by control rods which absorb the neutrons emitted in fission. The deeper the rods are inserted into the reactor core the more neutrons they absorb, and the lower the amount of heat generated. The reactor is heavily shielded to eliminate radiation danger even in the event of a major fault.

The U.S. ship Savannah, the world's first cargo ship with nuclear propulsion. Although not an economic proposition at the time of Savannah's launching (1959), with increased oil prices nuclear propulsion is now being seriously considered for freighters.

Other types of nuclear reactors may be used in the future. One possibility is the pressurized gas reactor coupled directly to a gas turbine engine, in which no intermediate heat exchanger is needed. Fast reactors are generally smaller than thermal types, since they need no moderator, and when they reach a sufficiently high stage of development and safety they too may be used.

Nuclear propulsion has several great advantages, especially for submarines (see NAUTILUS, the world's first nuclear-powered craft). Because the reactor uses no

The U.S. Navy's Flip ship is used to measure the ocean's heat flow, take profiles of currents, and study heat transference from the surface to the ocean depths. The ship has been in operation since 1962.

oxygen and produces no fumes, a nuclear submarine never has to surface to "breathe" (see SUBMARINE). And, an advantage for all types of ships, a reactor generates an enormous amount of heat from a very small quantity of fuel. It can therefore be used to drive very powerful engines over virtually unlimited distances. A typical modern nuclear ship has a cruising range of some 400,000 mi. (640,000 km). The newest U.S. aircraft carriers are capable of cruising for 13 years without refueling. These factors are of the greatest importance to WARSHIPS, and to certain specialist vessels of which the ICEBREAKER is one example (see LENIN).

On the other hand, nuclear propulsion systems are very expensive. Several nuclear merchant ships have been built (including the SAVANNAH, the West German *Otto Hahn*, and the Japanese *Mutsu*), and although they are technically highly successful, economically they cannot justify themselves. However, nuclear propulsion plants are likely to become cheaper and smaller, and may in the future become standard in all large ships.

Nuclear-powered aircraft. A great deal of research was conducted in the United States in the 1950s on the possibility of nuclear-powered military aircraft, but it was eventually decided that the advantage (the ability to remain airborne for very long periods) did not justify the expense and the possible dangers (in the event, for example, of a crash). However, many experts foresee the arrival of the nuclear-powered military aircraft in the near future.

O

Oceanography

The study of all aspects of the oceans and seas. Physical oceanography is concerned with temperature, pressure, density, and salinity; with waves, tides, and currents both on and under the surface; and with the interaction between the sea and air.

The subject is important in climatology and weather forecasting; in understanding how waves are formed, how they interact, and in predicting wave-patterns and strength (for the benefit both of ships at sea, and of ship designers); and, of course, in exploiting the sea's natural resources.

Many different research and exploration vessels and underwater sampling equipment are employed. Surface vessels include the remarkable FLIP (floating instrument platform), which when "flipped" up into the working vertical position projects 300 ft. (90 m) under the surface for coustical research, and the *Glomar Challenger* which is specially designed to remain stable in heavy seas, and can maintain its position accurately for weeks at a time while drilling the ocean bed at depths of over 20,000 ft. (6,000 m). Fixed research platforms range from oil-rig-like structures "spudded" into the sea bed, and floating platforms anchored out at sea, to unmanned oceanographic buoys which can record and transmit up to 100 different measurements simultaneously over long periods of time. Underwater craft include submersibles (see SUBMARINES) and the so-called "undersea habitats," in which "oceanauts" can live and work for weeks on end. (See also ECHO SOUNDERS; HYDROGRAPHY; SONAR.)

Octane number

A measure of a gasoline fuel's resistance to KNOCKING in an internal combustion engine. The octane rating system was developed to standardize anti-knock ability, and is calculated by comparing a gasoline's knocking tendency with that of two standard test fuels (isooctane and heptane). The equivalent for diesel fuel is the CETANE NUMBER.

Odometer

A mileage recorder incorporated in a vehicle's SPEEDOMETER and driven through gearing from the speedometer shaft. Some speedometers incorporate two odometers, one showing the total mileage

the vehicle has traveled, the other, which can be reset, showing the trip mileage.

Ohain, Hans von

Pioneer German turbojet designer. While a student of applied physics and aerodynamics at Göttingen University in the 1930s, von Ohain obtained patents on a centrifugal turbojet design. He joined the Heinkel company and in 1937 demonstrated his first engine, which developed 550 lb. (250 kg) thrust.

A power unit scheduled for installation in a Heinkel airframe was tested in 1938 but proved unsatisfactory. In an attempt to hold down the diameter of the engine, the diameter of the compressor had been made too small and the combustion chambers were too cramped. However, a redesigned version, the He S-3b, was successfully used in the Heinkel 178 to power the world's first turbojet flight (August 27, 1939) (see JET ENGINE).

Oil

Substance used for lubrication or as a fuel. In the field of transportation most oils are derived from PETROLEUM which is knows as crude oil. The word derives from the Latin *oleum*, meaning olive oil. Petroleum means "rock oil," and is a mineral oil, as opposed to vegetable oils such as linseed oil, and animal oils such as whale oil.

Petroleum is distilled into a number of fractions most of which are called oils. The exception is the first fraction: light, low-boiling GASOLINE. Then in order of increasing boiling point come kerosene (paraffin oil) gas oil, diesel oil, and fuel oil, all of which are used as FUELS, followed by the thickest and highest boiling oils used for LUBRICATION. Most engines are lubricated by mineral oils, though some racing engines use castor oil, of vegetable origin. Aircraft engines, which are subject to particularly severe operating conditions, use synthetic oils for lubrication, including certain organic oxides, esters, silicones, and fluorocarbons.

Olds, Ransom Eli (1864-1950)

American automobile pioneer. Olds was trained in the steam-engine factory run by his father, Pliny F. Olds, at Lansing, Mich. There he began to build steam-powered carriages and in 1896 constructed his first gasoline-driven automobile. Three years later Olds and some colleagues founded the Olds Motor Works in Detroit, and began construction of the first Oldsmobile cars, including the famous 3-hp "curved dash" Olds that was probably the first volume-produced automobile. Its enormous success (5,000 were sold in 1904 alone) encouraged hundreds of other firms to set up in business. In 1904 Olds broke away from the Olds Motor Works and set up a rival firm, the Reo Motor Car Company, which he headed until 1936.

Orbital velocity

The speed necessary to sustain an object in orbit around a star or planet. The greater the gravitational force, the greater the speed necessary; orbital velocity therefore varies with altitude, and with the mass of the star or planet being orbited. At a height of 100 mi. (160 km), the orbital velocity of an earth satellite is about 17,500 mph (28,000 km/h), and the orbital period is just under 90 minutes. At greater altitudes the velocity decreases, and the period increases. At 22,300 mi. (35,900 km), the orbital velocity is about 6,900 mph (11,000 km/h) and the orbital period exactly 24 hrs. An orbit at this altitude is called a stationary orbit because the satellite rotates at the same rate as the earth does and therefore appears stationary in the sky. This kind of orbit is used for many communications satellites.

Orient Express

The legendary luxury train running between Western Europe and the Gateway to Asia which features in so many romantic spy stories of the era. The first train bearing this illustrious name left Paris bound for Vienna and Bucharest on June 5, 1883. Two years later the lines were linked up to allow this first international express to reach Constantinople. In its heyday, the train consisted of the resplendent blue coaches of the WAGON-LITS Company. It survived the breakup of great empires and two world wars, but its former glory is now very much overshadowed by the more recently inaugurated TRANS-EUROPE EXPRESSES.

Ornithopter

An aircraft designed to fly like a bird by flapping its wings. Although experiments continue to be made, human muscles alone are usually considered to be too weak to flap wings large enough to support a man's weight, and mechanical power has not so far been successfully applied to this problem (see PEDAL PLANE).

Otto cycle

An alternative name for the FOUR-STROKE CYCLE utilized in the gasoline and DIESEL ENGINE. It is named for Nicolaus August Otto (1832-91), the German engineer who built the first four-stroke engine in 1876. The idea was, however, worked out by the French engineer de Rochas and patented by him in 1862. Otto applied the four-stroke principle to a very successful stationary engine burning coal gas, and himself patented the idea, thereby preventing Carl BENZ and others from using the four-stroke engine until Otto's patent was revoked in 1886.

Outboard motor

Detachable internal combustion engine for small boats. It is clamped or bolted over the stern, or occasionally positioned in a well in the hull. Engine, drive shaft, and propeller are designed as a single unit for portability and simplicity of fitting. The outboard motor pivots on its mount so that the angle of thrust can be altered for steering. Apart from portability, the outboard motor has two other advantages. It eliminates the need for a propeller shaft passing through the boat's hull, and it can easily be raised for passage through shallow or weedy water.

Outrigger

On a rowboat, a bracket projecting from the side holding the oarlock or rowlock which carries the oar. It enables the rower to obtain more leverage. On a canoe,

an outrigger comprises struts extending out from one or both sides at the end of which is lashed a crosspiece that acts as a float. Used traditionally in the South Seas, Indonesia, and East Africa, it gives the craft more stability.

Overdrive

A unit fitted to a manual gearbox to give an extra, higher gear. Often overdrive works on both the third and the top gears of a four-speed gearbox. Its purpose is to reduce engine revolutions and thus save fuel when cruising. Cutting-in overdrive may reduce engine revs by about 500-700 rpm. The overdrive unit contains an EPI-CYCLIC-GEAR train similar to that in an automatic gearbox, and a cone clutch. When overdrive is disengaged, the whole epicyclic unit rotates, and the input and output shafts turn at the same speeds. When overdrive is selected, the cone clutch locks the sun wheel to the unit housing, causing the annulus, which is attached to the output shaft, to be driven around at a higher speed than the input shaft.

Overhead cam (OHC)

See CAMSHAFT.

Overhead Valve (OHV)

See VALVE GEAR.

Oversteer

A condition in which a driver has to turn the steering wheel of his vehicle less sharply than he would expect when cornering. It is caused by differences between the slip angles of the front and rear TIRES. The slip angle is a measure of the extent to which a tire diverges from its correct position under cornering stresses. Oversteer occurs when the slip angle of the rear tires exceeds that of the front tires. Contrast UNDERSTEER.

Outriggers are used to provide stability on narrow-hulled canoes and on some shallow-draft tall-masted racing sailboats.

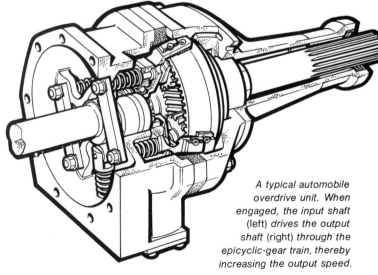

A typical automobile overdrive unit. When engaged, the input shaft (left) drives the output shaft (right) through the epicyclic-gear train, thereby increasing the output speed.

P

Pacific class locomotives

With a leading four-wheel truck, six coupled driving wheels and a two-wheel trailing truck, Pacific class steam locomotives were among the best ever designed for high-speed passenger work. They hauled many of the most famous steam "flyers," and include the streamlined British *Mallard*, which holds the world speed record for steam locomotives (126 mph, 203 km/h). A Pacific locomotive, with streamlining designed by Raymond Loewy, was used on the Pennsylvania Railroad in 1936. Pacifics were also used on the New York Central, but for heavy American trains larger fireboxes proved necessary, leading to the use of a four-wheel trailing truck.

Pacific Great Eastern Railway

Now the British Columbia Railway, it has nearly 900 mi. (1440 km) of track stretching northward from North Vancouver to Prince George, Dawson Creek, and Fort Nelson, with a long branch under construction from just north of Prince George to the northwest. There are 100 diesel locomotives and over 5,000 freight cars. Passenger services are maintained by diesel railcars but there are also 14 passenger cars for use in locomotive-hauled trains.

Packet

Name given to a vessel carrying passengers and mail on a regular service between two ports. The earliest transatlantic steamers, for example, were known as Atlantic packets.

Paddle steamer

A steam ship propelled by paddles rather than screw propellers. All the well-known early steamships had paddle wheels, either at the stern (sternwheelers) or at each side (sidewheelers). But by the 1840s it had become clear that for oceangoing vessels and warships the paddle had considerable disadvantages. It was vulnerable to enemy action and to heavy waves; and when the ship rolled one paddle spun helplessly in the air while the other was too deeply submerged. However, on calm inland waters the paddle wheel's efficiency equals that of the propeller, and paddle steamers remained popular for river transport throughout the 19th century. Today most paddle steamers are pleasure boats.

Panama Canal

Artificial waterway linking the Atlantic and Pacific oceans through the Isthmus of Panama. Opened in 1914, it shortened the sea voyage between the United States east and west coasts by up to 9,000 mi. (14,000 km), from Britain and Europe to the west coast by a similar figure, and from Europe to Australia by 2,000 miles (3,200 km).

Annual traffic has risen from around 1,700 ships carrying 6 million tons of cargo in the early years, to over 15,500 ships and 132 million tons in 1970. Although only about 11% of ships using the canal fly the United States flag, approximately 70% are engaged in trade to or from the United States, and the canal is thus vital to the national economy (and to defense).

The original proposal by de Lesseps, the builder of the SUEZ CANAL, was for a sea level canal, but his scheme failed. The United States then gained control of the Canal Zone (for which it makes an annual payment), and began construction in 1904. The canal has short sea level

A ship approaching locks at the southern end of the Galliard Cut in the Panama Canal. The signals at the right indicate when the Cut is clear, as ships are not normally permitted to pass there.

sections at either end, but the majority of its 50 mi. (80 km) length is elevated. Three locks at each end raise ships 85 ft. (26 m), the raised section comprising Gatun Lake and Gaillard Cut. Each lock is paired to allow two-way traffic, each lock chamber being 1,000 ft. (300 m) long, 110 ft. (32 m) wide, and 41 ft. (12 m) deep. Large vessels are towed through the locks by "mules," electric locomotives running alongside.

The actual time taken for a ship to pass through the canal is about eight hours, although the overall passage including waiting, taking on a pilot, etc., is nearly twice as long.

The canal is crossed at the Thatcher Ferry Bridge by the PAN-AMERICAN HIGHWAY, while a railroad and highway cross the Isthmus close to the canal.

In its present form the Panama canal can accommodate all but the largest ships. Discussions have been taking place for some years on the possibility of widening

At sea paddle wheels are inefficient and vulnerable, but on riverboats like these early Mississippi paddle steamers they are as effective as propellers and can operate in shallow waters.

and deepening the existing canal and locks to permit passage of more and larger ships (e.g. supertankers, and aircraft carriers), or of replacing it with another canal.

Pan-American Highway
Road system, planned to be 15,700 mi. (25,300 km) long, linking the major cities of North, Central, and South America Planning of the system began at an International American Conference in 1923. Part of the highway system has been specially built, but most of it consists of designated highways in the individual countries. The system begins at the U.S.-Mexico border, with four routes running south to Mexico City, and then through the nations of Central America to Chepo, Panama. At that point 500 mi. (800 km) of thick jungle, the Darien Gap, interrupts the highway. A route through the difficult terrain was surveyed in the early 1970s. In South America the highway runs down the western coast from Colombia to Puerto Montt in Chile, with branches leading eastward.

Pan American World Airways
One of the largest and oldest established airlines, Pan American operated flying boats between Key West and Havana in 1927. By the early 1930s the Pan American system had spread across the Caribbean to South America, and Pan Am flying boats pioneered Pacific routes to Manila and Auckland. In 1939 Pan American flying boats helped to inaugurate North Atlantic air services.
Pan American's four-engined aircraft have been known as clippers since the launching of the S-40 American Clipper flying boat in 1931. By the mid-1970s the jet clipper fleet comprised 130 aircraft which in 1974 carried 9.6 million passengers.

Panhard-Levassor
Leading French automobile manufacturer founded in 1889. The firm began by building "horseless carriages" typical of the time. Then in 1891 they evolved an entirely new type of vehicle which set the pattern for the future. With the engine at the front under a hood (instead of at the middle or rear), a gearbox (instead of belts and pulleys), a foot-controlled friction clutch and rear wheel drive, it has been called the first true automobile. Until the appearance of the Mercedes in 1901 (see MERCEDES-BENZ) Panhard led the automobile world in competition and design. Thereafter it retained an important if conservative position, developing quieter and more luxurious automobiles, and specialist racers. After World War II the

firm turned to the utility automobile field with their successful Dyna range, which included some high-performance models. In 1965 Panhard was acquired by CITROËN, and in 1967 the name disappeared.

Pantograph
An apparatus mounted on top of an electric locomotive or streetcar to collect current from an overhead wire. There are various types, but generally the arms supporting the actual contact strip are hinged and provided with springs to allow the equipment to respond to varying heights of the overhead wire. The actual contact strip is often wide and the overhead wire is staggered so that wear on the strip is equalized as much as possible. Pantographs can be lowered away from the wire when not in use.

Parachute
A parachute is an umbrella-like device used to slow down a body falling, or traveling horizontally at high speed, through the air. It consists of a canopy to which rigging lines and a harness are attached. A number of panels (gores) are sewn together to form the canopy, the traditional silk having now been largely replaced by synthetic fabrics.
Parachutes may be used for saving life in emergencies; for paratroop operations, when large canopies with a slow rate of descent ensure the safe landing of a heavily-laden soldier; for supply dropping; for spacecraft recovery (for which clusters of parachutes are often deployed); for braking high-speed aircraft after touchdown; and for sport, in which case the canopy has one or more openings to facilitate guidance during descent. Flat parachutes open quickly and are very reliable; they have a central vent and the rigging lines pass completely over the canopy, which will lie flat when spread out on the ground. Shaped parachutes, which are sometimes almost hemispherical, cannot be laid out flat. The deployment of parachutes may be carried out by an auxiliary parachute, by a pilot parachute and sock, or by a ripcord (which may be operated manually, by an automatic timing device, or by a static line attached to the aircraft). Ejection seat parachutes are positively opened by drogue and designed to withstand the high speed ejection.
Leonardo da Vinci drew sketches of a parachute device, but the first successful demonstration was not made until 1783 when the Frenchman Louis-Sébastien Lenormand jumped from a tower. The first successful descent from an airplane was made by U.S. Army Captain Albert Berry in 1912.

Parachutes provide an effective form of aerodynamic braking in a variety of applications. They are seen here providing a soft splashdown for a returning Apollo spacecraft.

Parsons, Sir Charles Algernon (1854-1931),
British engineer who invented the multi-stage STEAM TURBINE engine in 1884. The "Parsons turbine," as it was called, was first used for generating electricity in power stations. After the success of his turbine-propelled vessel TURBINIA (the world's first) in 1897 it revolutionized marine propulsion.
Parsons also invented a mechanical reduction gear to allow his marine turbines to turn at the high speed necessary for their efficiency while rotating the propeller at the much lower speed necessary for hydrodynamic efficiency (see CAVITATION). Parsons also invented antiskid chains for automobile wheels.

Pavement
The pavement is the surface of a road or similar area, and is laid on a prepared base course. The commonest type is the flexible pavement, which is composed of asphalt and called black-top paving. In paving operations a truck tips hot asphalt ahead of a spreader which spreads the mixture evenly to the desired thickness. Then it is rolled. Usually the pavement is built up in several passes. Rigid pavements are constructed of concrete and are laid by "slip-form" paving machines which lay, compact, and form the edges of the concrete in a single operation. A reinforcing steel mesh is placed on the first layer and overlaid by the top layer, which is brushed to give a nonskid surface. (See also HIGHWAYS.)

Pedal plane

A pedal plane provides the most practical means so far devised of achieving man-powered flight. The source of power is a pedal-driven propeller.

A man pedaling can generate about 2 hp for a brief period (sufficient for takeoff), and can then maintain about 0.5 hp. Weight and DRAG are the principal problems, but to minimize induced drag and at the same time cruise at very high LIFT coefficients it is necessary to have an exceptionally low wing loading. This has led to wings of up to 82 ft. (25 m) span with a 15:1 aspect (length to width) ratio, resulting in a weight and drag penalty.

Lightweight wood is generally favored for wing structure, possibly with a light fabric covering supported by foam plastic or impregnated paper honeycomb. To keep propeller turbulence away from the wings a pusher layout is desirable, the airscrew itself requiring a diameter of 6-9 ft. (1.8-2.7 m) for maximum efficiency. A twin-boom layout, a tail-less configuration or a canard could be employed, or the propeller could be located above or below a normal fuselage.

Chain or belt drive is the usual choice for power transmission, but frictional and other losses must be reduced to an absolute minimum. For takeoff it is necessary to drive the undercarriage as well as the propeller. The torque transmitted to the propeller is inevitably erratic, due to the limitations of the human machine. There is some evidence that the use of two men would be mechanically advantageous, despite the additional weight. Success in this field has been limited, although a number of pedal planes have been constructed. Two British designs with wing spans of about 82 ft. (25 m) were flown in the 1960s. Both took off under their own power, and one of them was airborne for over half a mile. The gross weights of these two aircraft (including pilot) were 249.7 lb (113.5 kg) and 267.5 lb (121.6 kg). On June 29, 1972, RAF Flight Lieutenant John Potter covered the greatest distance so far attained (1,355 yd., 1.23 km) in the 80 ft. (24.3 m) span *Jupiter*. A large cash prize still awaits the first pedal plane to achieve a controlled figure-of-eight maneuver without losing height.

Penn Central Railroad

The largest railroad in the United States, formed out of the former Pennsylvania, New York Central and New Haven Railroads. The system covers the major population centers of Boston, New York, Philadelphia, Pittsburg, Detroit and Chicago. Its 20,000 mi. (32,000 km) of track extend over 16 states and two provinces of Canada and carry nearly 3,000 trains daily. The Penn Central has always been one of the more progressive railroads in the United States, with the greatest length of electrified track and a large number of cars designed for "Trail Van" container services (it is a major carrier of the U.S. mail in exclusive container trains).

Performance

In the transportation field, criteria of performance are usually measurements of the movement of goods or people from place to place.

The most basic of these factors is distance traveled compared with time taken, expressed in miles or kilometers per hour in most cases, although very high speeds such as those associated with space flight may be expressed in feet per second. However, although a small fast vehicle with a maximum capacity of one ton may be able to carry this quantity of goods to its destination in a very short time, it would have to make ten separate trips to carry ten tons. A larger, slower vehicle with a ten-ton capacity would in fact be more efficient. To compare this kind of performance the ton-mile (or tonne-kilometer) is used, one ton-mile corresponding to the amount of work required to carry one ton a distance of one mile. Airlines assess their operating efficiency in terms of passenger-miles, which provide a means of relating the distance flown to the load carried.

Air freight cannot easily be evaluated purely on the basis of weight, since many articles are sent by air because of their high value but relatively small size. Instead, the revenue ton-mile (or revenue tonne-km) is used, since this reflects the value of the consignment.

Periscope

An optical instrument which enables an observer to see over or around an obstacle without himself being seen. It consists basically of a tube with a prism at each end. Light striking the top prism is reflected through 90° to pass down the tube where it strikes the lower prism. There it is again reflected through 90° to the eyepiece. In advanced models, lenses between the prisms enlarge the image and extend the field of view.

A periscope was first fitted to a submarine in 1854. In its modern form the submarine periscope extends to a length of about 40 ft. (12 m), has special filters for different light conditions, and is adapted for viewing the sky as well as the surface. It can be used for celestial navigation, and for photography.

Periscopes were widely used by soldiers in World War I to view the action from the relative safety of a trench. They were later fitted to tanks and other armored vehicles, and for rear vision, to automobiles towing trailers.

Personal rapid transit (PRT)

The collective name given to a variety of novel modes of passenger transport which consist essentially of relatively low capacity vehicles operating under full automatic control on exclusive guideways and designed to transport family-sized groups of passengers. The ultimate in such a concept would involve a comprehensive network of guideways throughout a city on which two- or four-seater vehicles await the arrival of passengers at frequently spaced stations. On arrival at his nearest station, the passenger would obtain a ticket for his desired destination from a machine. He would then occupy the first available vehicle and use the ticket as a means of passing instruc-

The pilot of a successful British pedal plane demonstrates the mechanism. During an actual flight he is enclosed in a canopy.

An experimental computer-controlled personal rapid transit system in Germany. The cab travels on top of the elevated rail in one direction, and is suspended beneath it in the other. The passenger feeds the data system with the desired destination; the computer determines the best route and sends the cab on its way.

tions to the car as to his destination. The car would then be automatically routed to the indicated destination via the quickest available route, bypassing all other stations and any potentially congested sections of the network. When not in use, the vehicles are automatically redistributed around the system in anticipation of expected demands.

Many such systems have been devised and patented and a number have been fully demonstrated. Rudimentary versions of them, consisting of automatically operated carriages on concrete guideways capable of shuttling fifty to a hundred people at a time between airport terminals may be seen at such airports as Houston, Dallas/Fort Worth and Seattle-Tacoma. The U.S. Department of Transportation has funded a much larger scale demonstration on the campus of West Virginia University at Morganstown. Here, eight-seater cars were operated on 2¼ miles of largely elevated guideway linking the campus with the downtown area. During the hours of peak demand they were operated on a fixed schedule, but outside these periods they were demand activated.

Though technically a success, the experiment failed economically and revealed certain problems which have yet to be overcome — fears of the automation, for example, and vandalism. It is also apparent that such systems are unlikely to have an application except for passenger movement in concentrated areas of activity such as airports and the hearts of the larger central business districts.

The Ford Motor Company's research into PRT has led to a recently demonstrated system called ACT — Activity Center Transportation. The Ford ACT consists of 12 seat, 12 standee vehicles running on rubber tires within a channeled guideway. As with all such developments, the key element is the computerized control system. This has to route the vehicles through the network, maintain safe headways, and control switching operations and the smooth merging and spacing of vehicles at junctions. In the ACT vehicle, wayside units under central control relay instructions for speed, lane switching, station stops, etc., to onboard controllers. Another patented system, the Bendix "Dashaveyor" has larger vehicles, with a rush hour capacity of 40 or more passengers, which can be operated singly or in pairs. A full scale installation is proposed for the Metropolitan Toronto Zoo. In Britain, the Hawker Siddeley Company and the GEC, in conjunction with the Government Transport and Road Research Laboratory, have been researching into possible applications for similar PRT systems. One would involve small vehicles and is called "cabtrack." This would be entirely demand activated and provide non-stop point-to-point routing of small automated cabs.

The other more immediately practical system is the "Minitram." This is an intermediate capacity system capable of carrying up to 20,000 passengers per hour each way in driverless train sets running on lightweight guideways. These guideways can be readily grafted into existing built-up areas because of the relatively tight curves and steep gradients that can be negotiated by the vehicles. The principal difference between the two systems is that the Hawker Siddeley vehicles incorporate pneumatic tires on concrete tracks, whereas the GEC vehicles have more conventional steel wheels on steel rails. The latter give more economical running, but the track alignment is less flexible. Research and development by the two companies has now reached the stage where a full-scale demonstration project within a city center is needed to finally prove the viability of the concept. German and Japanese firms are also very active in this field. Krauss-Maffei of Munich, for example, are developing a guideway system where vehicle support, guidance, and propulsion are all by electromagnetic means — propulsion by LINEAR INDUCTION MOTORS and support and guidance by electromagnetic levitation. In principle, any of these PRT systems could provide a very attractive and far less damaging alternative to the use of the auto in downtown areas, but with questions still remaining as to their economic viability and social acceptability, it may be some time before they come into universal use.

Petrol
The English term for GASOLINE.

Petrol engine
See GASOLINE ENGINE.

Petroleum
Crude oil, the world's most important source of energy, and a rapidly dwindling one. At the present annual rate of consumption, some 60 million barrels a day, the known reserves of petroleum will hardly take us into the next century. Dramatic increases in petroleum prices in recent years by OPEC (the oil-producing and exporting countries) have helped to limit consumption a little but not much. The United States is one of the world's biggest petroleum producers,

The drill pipe of a petroleum drilling rig is withdrawn for examination and possible renewal. Once the drill has reached a considerable depth this is a lengthy process, as the entire drill pipe must be raised and stacked.

with an output of more than 11 million barrels a day. But it is by far the world's biggest consumer, requiring it to import large quantities from other countries, notably Venezuela. In fact it consumes more than a fourth of all the oil produced in the world.

The oil industry was born in 1859, when E.L. Drake began drilling near Titusville, west Pennsylvania, in the Appalachians. Most petroleum production in the United States today is concentrated in Louisiana, Texas, and Oklahoma, major amounts also being produced in Kansas, Arkansas and southern California. Soon to be tapped is the Northern Slope of Alaska, from which oil will flow via the 798-mi. (1,285 km) TRANS ALASKA PIPELINE. Other major oil-producing regions in the Americas are Alberta in Canada, the Tampico fields on the Gulf coast of Mexico, and Lake Maracaibo in Venezuela.

The world's main oil-producing region, however, is the Middle East, with Saudi Arabia, Kuwait, Iran, and Iraq being the leading countries. This region also has more than 60% of the world's oil reserves, compared with the United States' 10%. Libya, in north Africa, is also a major oil producer. So is the Soviet Union, which has about 10% of world total. China, which probably has even more, has just begun extensive exploration and production. Large quantities are also being found off the coast of Africa. Until recently Western Europe had no major oil fields, but oil in vast quantities has now been discovered under the North Sea, and has begun flowing. Britain, for example, expects to be self-sufficient in oil by 1980.

Nature and origins. The word "petroleum" is derived from the Latin *petra* and *oleum* ("rock oil"). Petroleum comes from the ground as a thick greenish-brown or black liquid. It is a complex substance made up of a mixture of organic compounds called HYDROCARBONS, compounds of hydrogen and carbon only. As such it would have limited use, but it can be separated into fractions with different boiling points. By fractionally distilling crude oil we get in order of increasing boiling point the major fractions gasoline, kerosene, gas oils, diesel oils, and residual fuel oils, all of which are important fuels, together with lubricating oils, greases, wax, and bitumen.

Petroleum is thought to be the remains of organisms that lived in the warm seas that covered our planet hundreds of millions of years ago. These organisms were probably simple, single-celled plants and animals. As they died their bodies accumulated on the seabed and became

A typical offshore oilrig in the North Sea. An increasing proportion of the world's petroleum is being obtained from under the sea, the high value of the product justifying the enormous expense involved in such operations.

covered with silt and clay. In time, measured in millions of years, the organic remains changed into oil, under the influence of agencies such as heat, pressure, and possibly anaerobic bacteria. Gradually the droplets of oil migrated, under various influences, from the muds and clays in which they formed into porous rocks such as limestone and sandstone. The oil migrated up through the rock strata until it reached impervious strata, where it became trapped and accumulated as a reservoir or pool. The oil is trapped in locations such as rock folds, where faulting has caused an impervious rock stratum to interrupt the porous stratum, or where salt domes have penetrated the strata. The oil-forming process invariably resulted in the production of natural gas as well, and this is always present in certain quantities where oil deposits are exploited.

Prospecting and drilling. In the early days of the petroleum industry, oil prospecting consisted merely of looking for tell-tale seepage of oil through the ground. But few deposits lie close to the

surface, and it soon became necessary to adopt a more scientific approach. Today prospecting is a highly complex affair aimed at finding the kind of sedimentary rock strata where oil may be expected to accumulate. It involves detailed surface and aerial mapping and geological testing of the surface rocks, aerial gravity surveys, and seismic exploration. In the latter, explosive charges are set off in the ground, and shock waves reflected by rock strata are analyzed.

The main method used for reaching the oil is rotary drilling from a drilling rig, which is easily recognized by its tall derrick. The process consists of boring into the ground with a bit on the end of a long drill pipe. Various bits may be used, depending on the type of strata being penetrated. The drill pipe is made up of 30-40 ft. (10-12 m) sections of pipe screwed together, the one attached to the bit being the collar, and the top one the kelly. The kelly, a tube of square or octagonal cross-section is gripped and rotated by a turntable. A fine drilling mud is pumped down the drill pipe and through the bit, and up through the bored hole. The circulating mud provides lubrication for the bit and flushes out the rock cuttings. It also provides a hydrostatic seal against oil blowouts.

New sections of pipe are added as necessary, but when the drill bit wears out the whole drill pipe, which may be thousands of feet long, has to be withdrawn. When an oil-producing zone is reached, the borehole is lined with a casing and capped with a network of valves called a Christmas tree, which controls the oil flow from the well.

For exploration offshore, drilling is a more difficult process. In shallow water it may be done from mobile drilling platforms that rest on the seabed, such as the jack-up (self-elevating) type, which is floated into position, and then elevated as its legs are extended to the seabed. Often floating, semi-submersible platforms are used instead. The drilling platform rests on massive floating legs ballasted with water so that they sink to a depth of 100 ft. (30 m) or so. These platforms and the production platforms that succeed them, are complex structures costing tens of millions of dollars and may be manned by as many as 75 men. Oil from a producing well, may be piped directly to refineries for REFINING via PIPELINES or to storage tanks at seaports, from where it is transported by TANKER.

Until the mid-19th century petroleum was used primarily as an illuminant and, in the form of bitumen, for waterproofing ships and building roads. With industrial growth and the invention of the gasoline engine, it became essential for lubrication and as a fuel.

Today virtually all forms of transportation are fueled by various fractions of petroleum, the only significant exceptions being those using nuclear or rocket propulsion, and electric traction. As much electricity is generated by oil-fired steam turbines, many electric vehicles depend on petroleum as well. Current research to find alternative fuels for use in transportation has been accelerated as much

Auguste Piccard (center) beside one of his pressurized spherical gondolas which during the early 1930s were carried by balloon to altitudes of over 50,000 ft. (15,240 m).

by problems as by long-term shortages in oil supply (see ELECTRIC CAR and STIRLING ENGINE).

Photogrammetry

The art of SURVEYING or measuring by taking photographs, particularly aerial photographs.

Photon engine

A kind of rocket motor that has been proposed for propelling spacecraft in the distant future. The idea behind it is to convert energy into light and to use the light for propulsion. The photons in the light, traveling at the speed of light, would theoretically develop thrust in the same way as the molecules of an exhaust gas.

Piccard, Auguste (1884-1962)

Swiss physicist, member of a family of explorers and scientists. Piccard designed a pressurized gondola for a balloon, and with it made a world-record ascent of 51,775 ft. (15,781 m) in 1931, accompanied by Paul Kipfer. The following year he set a new record with an ascent of 53,153 ft. (16,201 m), his companion being Max Cosyns. Later, Piccard designed a revolutionary diving vessel, the BATHYSCAPH, and in 1953 he descended to 10,300 ft. (3,140 m) in the waters of the Pacific Ocean. In another bathyscaph, Piccard's son Jacques descended 35,800 ft. (10,912 m) in 1960.

Pick-up

A utility vehicle with an enclosed compartment and an open rear section, with low sides and an opening tailgate. Some are based on light trucks, while others are modified sedans or station wagons, with sedan-type lines and a comfortable driver's compartment.

Piggy-back transport

A term applied to the practice of transporting truck-trailers on railroad flat cars (see RAILROAD).

Pilot

An experienced seaman with detailed knowledge of local waters and conditions, whose job it is to navigate ships entering or leaving port. The ship's captain navigates his vessel on the open seas, and when entering a port for which he has a pilotage certificate, provided that his ship is a freighter. But elsewhere (and in the case of passenger ships, everywhere) he must take on a pilot to conduct his ship along the final stretch. Pilotage is also compulsory through certain roadsteads, rivers, and channels — wherever, in fact, detailed knowledge and experience of local problems and conditions are essential to safety. The pilot receives a fee, paid by the shipowner, based on the tonnage and draft of the vessel.

The word pilot is also of course used for the person in control of an aircraft.

Pinking

A metallic knocking noise heard sometimes in an internal combustion engine when the driver accelerates. It is properly called detonation (see GASOLINE).

The Middle East is one of the world's main sources of petroleum. The photograph shows oil tankers loading at the automatic crude oil jetty on Kharg Island in the Persian Gulf.

Pipelines

Pipelines are systems of pipes used to transport petroleum products, natural gas, and some other substances over long distances. The most extensive petroleum and gas carrying networks are in North America. The United States alone has about 200,000 mi. (320,000 km) of major pipelines. The world's longest pipeline is the TransCanada, which carries natural gas for nearly 4,500 mi. (7,200 km). It will be surpassed shortly by a Russian line that will extend 5,600 mi. (9,000 km) from Siberia to Leningrad. The 1,775 mi. (2,860 km) Interprovincial pipeline from Edmonton, Alberta, to Buffalo, New York, is the world's longest oil line. The United States has several pipelines exceeding 1,000 mi. (1,600 km), including those used to transport petroleum from the oil fields of Texas and Louisiana to the Midwest and to the Eastern states. One of the most famous systems is the Little and Big Inch oil line from Texas to Pennsylvania. Typical flow through these lines is about 400,000 barrels (about 1,700,000 U.S. gallons) a day.

Russia has extensive systems to transport petroleum and natural gas from its remote northern fields to centers throughout the country and to other countries of the Soviet bloc, while in the Middle East pipelines carry oil from the desert to the Persian Gulf and the Mediterranean. Much North Sea gas and oil is transported to coastal terminals by pipeline. Many existing pipelines have a relatively small bore. The so-called Big Inch was one of the first large-bore lines, with a diameter of 24 in. (61 cm), while the Super Inch carrying gas to San Francisco is 36 in. (91 cm). Parts of the TransCanada pipeline are 42 in. (107 cm), and 48-in. (122-cm) pipelines are being built.

Pipeline operation. A pipeline system is very much like a railroad network. Branch or gathering lines lead from the oil-well heads and converge on a central point where they join the trunk line. This may take the oil to the refinery, or to a port for transportation by tanker. The refined products may also be sent to consumers by pipeline.

Pumps are located at intervals of up to about 150 mi. (250 km) along the pipeline to keep the liquid or gas flowing, and in a cold climate the line may need heating if the liquid is of high viscosity. Batches, or slugs, of different liquids, such as different grades of petroleum, can be transported along the same pipeline. Some mixing naturally occurs at the interfaces, but not to any important degree. Since the operating engineers know the rate of flow of the fluid through the pipeline, they can calculate when a particular slug

A section of 48 in (122 cm) pipeline set out prior to burial, in Alaska.

is due or finished. Sometimes a radio-isotope is injected at the head of a slug, and the engineers detect its arrival with a Geiger counter.

Design and construction. Despite the very high capital outlay involved, a pipeline generally provides the cheapest means of transporting oil long distances overland. Operating costs are relatively low, and the greater the pipe diameter, the lower the cost per unit transported. In addition, if the pipeline is buried no land is wasted, and there is minimal despoliation of the environment. In the case of offshore oil, it is usually cheaper to carry the oil from production rig to shore by tanker. However, bad weather can delay tankers, and the very high initial cost of laying a submarine pipeline may be justified by the reliability achieved. The many factors influencing pipeline design include the desired capacity, the pressures to be encountered, the choice of routes to be taken, the materials for construction and methods of manufacture, whether the pipe will be underground, whether it will need heating, whether there will be objections on envi-

ronmental grounds, and so on. To estimate the pumping requirements for the desired flow, the designers work out the pressure losses that will occur in the pipe. These depend on the velocity and viscosity of the fluid, the length and diameter of the pipe, and friction between fluid and pipe. In addition to the pipe losses, those due to gradients and changes in direction along the route must be calculated (see FLUID MECHANICS). When all these pressure losses have been allowed for, suitable pumping machinery can be designed. The exact location of the pumps depends on the terrain; they must be closer together in mountainous districts, where larger pressure heads need to be overcome, than on flat land. Valves are required at intervals along the main and branch lines to direct and regulate the flow: those on 48-in. (122 cm) pipes are nearly 30 ft. (9 m) high overall and weigh up to 30 tons.

Pipelines for transporting petroleum and gas are invariably made of steel and are usually of seamless construction. Before the pipe is laid it is given a protective coating of bituminous paint or waterproof tape which helps to prevent chemi-

Sections of 48 in (122 cm) pipeline being double jointed to ensure a perfect seal. Each joint is tested, and after laying the pipeline is again rigorously checked for leaks.

into the pipe under pressure. With large-bore pipes, the considerable amount of water necessary is not always available and crude oil may have to be used (with the risk of large-scale spillage if the pipe breaks). If the hydraulic tests are satisfactory, the pipeline is lowered into the trench by side-hoist crawler tractors, the soil is replaced and rolled firm, and any disturbances to the environment are remedied.

Among the main problems of the pipelaying operation are the organization of the labor force and the maintenance of a steady supply of materials so that the operation proceeds smoothly. These problems become acute in remote regions, where road or rail communications may have to be built before work can begin, as was the case with the TRANS ALASKA PIPELINE SYSTEM.

Freight pipelines. Solids as well as liquids may be transported by pipeline, though at present this is only done on a modest scale. The usual method is to transport solids in the form of a slurry mixed with a fluid (usually water). The largest slurry pipeline in the United States is a 250-mi. (400 km) line of 18-in. (46 cm) diameter, which transports coal at the rate of 600 tons per hour. The operating costs of such a system can be more than 60% cheaper than rail transportation, and over 80% cheaper than by truck. Where the solids being handled must be dry, the cost increases because of the extra plant necessary for processing.

Experiments are now well advanced in the United States and in many other countries on the capsule pipeline. A great deal of the freight carried by road and rail is comparatively small, and could be more economically carried within capsules traveling along pipelines. It has been estimated that a single 8-in. (20 cm) diameter pipeline has a potential carrying capacity greater than a railroad carrying 20 trains a day. Several capsule pipelines are already in commercial operation. One in Hamburg, Germany, has been carrying letters between post offices at a rate of up to one million a day since 1967.

The capsule pipeline is by no means new. Small-scale versions have been used in department stores for years to carry cash between departments. Like these cash-delivery systems, the larger capsule pipelines in operation work by air pressure. The capsules fit snugly into the pipes and have wheels around their circumference to reduce friction with the pipe walls. Jet pumps are installed at intervals along the pipeline to keep the air flow at the required level.

cal salts in the soil reaching the steel and causing CORROSION. Alternatively, CATHODIC PROTECTION may be used, in which the steel is made the cathode in an electrolytic circuit and therefore does not corrode.

Pipelaying is a highly mechanized operation. Once the ground has been cleared and the trench dug, pipes are laid beside the trench and are then welded together. Crawler tractors with side hoists lift the pipeline, and machines move along cleaning and coating it with paint or tape. The joints are hydraulically tested for leaks as work proceeds. Where possible, this is done with water, which is pumped

Special tractors are used for stacking double jointed lengths of pipe, and for lowering them into position during the actual laying operation.

Piston

A disk or short cylinder that fits snugly inside a larger cylinder and is moved back and forth within it by the pressure of a fluid, either a gas or a liquid. Pistons are employed for a variety of purposes in a variety of machines. Their best-known use is in reciprocating steam, gasoline, and diesel engines, in which the piston is moved by an expanding fluid (steam or hot combustion gases). The movement is transmitted via a CONNECTING ROD to a CRANKSHAFT to convert it into rotary motion. To make the piston gas tight in its cylinder, a number of piston rings are fitted in grooves around it. The crown of the piston in a gasoline engine is usually flat, but some designs have a hollow crown, which forms the combustion chamber. Many diesel engine pistons also have a hollow crown. The crown of a two-stroke engine piston has a curved projection on it to assist expulsion of the exhaust gases.

Piston engine

Reciprocating engines, developed from auto engines in the early days of powered flight, are today used almost exclusively in LIGHT AIRCRAFT. There are two basic types: RADIAL ENGINES, which are air-cooled and have the cylinders arranged radially around a central crankcase; and in-line engines with the cylinders often in V formation. Larger in-line power units are normally liquid-cooled, using ethylene glycol. Lubrication is customarily on the dry sump principle to ensure an adequate oil supply in any flight altitude. Sleeve valve engines are smooth in operation and retain positive timing at high revolutions. In very powerful engines the heat to which exhaust valves are subjected is a limiting factor, but sleeve valves can be used in units developing over 3,000 hp.

SUPERCHARGERS are fitted to boost the power output for takeoff and at high altitude. They are usually either of the centrifugal type (one- or two-stage, one- or two-speed), or are exhaust driven (turbo-superchargers).

Aero-engine CARBURETORS may be required to handle 200 gal. (909 l) of fuel an hour and must be capable of functioning during aerobatics. Fuel injection into the supercharger is frequently used to ensure engine operation during negative-G maneuvers. (See also RECIPROCATING ENGINE.)

Pitot tube

A device for measuring the flow velocity of air or water, the pitot tube is named after its inventor Henri Pitot (1695-1771). One of its many applications is speed in air indicators (see AIRCRAFT INSTRUMENTS), in which the pitot tube (or pressure head) projects forward into the air. As the aircraft flies forward, air is forced into the pitot tube and passes into a capsule within the air speed indicator which then expands and moves a needle around the dial.

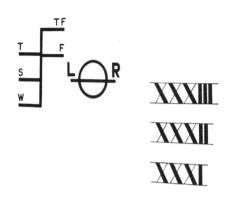

The circular Plimsoll Line, with the more detailed load lines for various sea conditions to the left. The Roman numerals are draft marks from which the vessel's total displacement can be calculated.

Plimsoll Line

Popular name for the load lines painted on the hull of every large merchant ship to show how deep in the water the ship may be loaded. Strictly speaking, the Plimsoll Line is the circular mark, and the line through its center shows the maximum depth of loading permitted in summer in salt water. Through the influence of the shipping reformer Samuel Plimsoll, the mark became compulsory in 1876 on all cargo ships using British ports, and it was soon adopted internationally.

Other marks indicate safe loading depths for W (winter), WNA (winter North Atlantic), TF (tropical fresh water), and so on. They are based on the fact that ships are more buoyant in salt water than in fresh, and can safely be loaded more deeply in calm than in heavy seas.

Pneumatic tube trains

A transportation system envisaging the use of cylindrical, pressure-tight trains traveling on wheels or roller bearings through underground steel tubes; acceleration and deceleration being applied by air pressure assisted by gravity. Stations spaced at intervals of a $\frac{1}{4}$ mi. (.4 km) to 10 mi. (16 km) apart would be some 50-100 ft. (15-30 m) underground with the connecting tunnels built on a sag profile between them. After passengers have boarded the train at normal atmospheric pressure, the tube in front is evacuated to approximately one-fortieth of an atmosphere. This provides the initial impetus for the train which is speed down the sloping tunnel by the force of gravity. The pressures fore and aft are so adjusted that the train has sufficient momentum to carry it on and up once more to the next station. Normal atmospheric pressures are maintained in the stations themselves by means of valves. Unprecedented reliability, safety and economy are claimed for such a system together with high journey speeds and complete avoidance of environmental nuisance.

Polar route

A GREAT CIRCLE ROUTE over (or under) the Arctic which shortens flights (or sea passages by submarine) between the eastern and western hemispheres. The Polar air route was pioneered by Scandinavian Airlines System in 1954, the undersea route by the U.S. submarine NAUTILUS in 1958.

Pollution

Contaminating or damaging the environment. In the field of transportation several sources of pollution exist. Potentially the most damaging perhaps is the pollution of the air by exhaust emissions from engines in general and the gasoline engine in particular. The gasoline engine gives rise to a number of polluting emissions, among them carbon monoxide, unburned hydrocarbons, nitrogen oxides, and lead. In a standard engine the amount of pollutants emitted per vehicle-mile are about 1.6 oz. (45 g) of carbon monoxide, 0.175 oz. (5 g) of hydrocarbons and 0.21 oz. (6 g) of nitrogen oxides. Carbon monoxide, formed by the incomplete combustion of gasoline, is the most deadly because if breathed even in small quantities it will kill. It combines with the hemoglobin of the blood, preventing it from carrying oxygen to the body cells. Even minute amounts will slow down a person's reactions. Unburned hydrocarbons, though not poisonous in themselves, are a major pollutant because they combine with nitrogen oxides in the presence of ultraviolet rays in sunlight to form what are called photochemical oxidants. These substances form with liquid and solid particles the suffocating smoky fog we call smog. Smogs are particularly prevalent in geographical regions where a phenomenon called temperature inversion takes place, which effectively traps the polluted air. The most notable example is the Los Angeles basin.

Volatile lead compounds are produced in the engine exhaust from the breakdown of lead tetraethyl, a gasoline additive that raises the octane rating and promotes smooth burning of fuel mixture in the cylinders. Lead is a hazard because it accumulates in the body.

A pollution test. While the stationary car is driven on a dynamometer, special equipment measures and compares the level and composition of exhaust emissions.

A variety of EMISSION-CONTROL SYSTEMS have been developed to reduce the emission of carbon monoxide, hydrocarbons, and nitrogen oxides. They include crankcase breathers, catalytic and thermal converters, and manifold reactors. Engines have been modified to permit more efficient combustion. In principle the catalytic converter is one of the most effective of the anti-pollution devices, but in its present state of development it is unreliable and unsuited for use with leaded fuel, for lead inhibits the catalytic action. The unreliability of the converter was the major reason why American auto manufacturers were unable to meet the standards laid down in 1970 for the emission requirements of 1976 vehicles, which required an emission-level reduction of up to 90%. Apart from the extra cost of anti-pollution devices, they have the disadvantage that they cut gasoline mileage by between 15 and 30%.

The jet plane also contributes its share of exhaust-fume pollution, and it has been suggested that high-flying supersonic planes may even significantly disturb the earth's protecting ozone layer. But the main concern with planes is noise. The noise of a jet taking off 2,000 ft. (600 m) away is louder than someone shouting in your ear 6 in. (15 cm) away. Persistent noise of this kind can give rise to irritation, hypertension, and even heart attacks. Traffic and subway noise can be almost as bad. On the decibel-rating scale the jet takeoff would rate about 105; a train coming into a subway station about 95, and a heavy truck at 50 ft. (15 m) about 90.

Several means are available for reducing the noise pollution of jets, including using different takeoff and landing techniques, improving engine silencing, and so on. But one thing that cannot be silenced is the SONIC BANG made by a plane when it goes through the "sound barrier." This can affect a region up to 50 mi. (80 km) on either side of the flight path. The problem will become acute when supersonic planes begin commercial flying on a large scale, though much of their supersonic flight time will be spent over the sea. Pollution of the seas is another serious problem, brought about primarily by oil. Crude oil is carried in tankers from oil-producing regions often thousands of miles to the refineries. The latest supertankers have a carrying capacity of hundreds of thousands of tons. If these or indeed any tankers are involved in collisions, colossal spillage can and does occur, harming wildlife and caking the beaches. Spraying with detergents helps to disperse the oil but itself does environmental harm. As well as accidental discharge, oil is often deliberately discharged when tank cleaning is in progress. This is generally punishable by law, but is almost impossible to detect when it is done on the high seas.

Pontchartrain Causeways

Twin-bridge system linking New Orleans with Mandeville, La., on the opposite side of Lake Pontchartrain, considered the world's longest bridge. The two causeways are 23.87 mi. (38.42 km) long, and each carries two lanes of traffic, supported on a long series of piers and cantilevers. The first was completed in 1956, the second in 1969.

The results of oil pollution at sea. A helicopter drops a drum of detergent in cleaning-up operations.

A modern pontoon bridge being set up across the River Main in Germany. The next section can be seen being brought into position.

Pontoon bridge

Pontoon bridges rest on securely anchored floating pontoons instead of on piers, and are most often used as a temporary expedient, expecially for military purposes. Permanent floating bridges are expensive to maintain, and they obstruct navigation. The world's longest pontoon bridges cross Lake Washington (6,560 ft., 2,000 m, span) and the Hood Canal (7,131 ft., 2,180 m, span) near Seattle, and are concrete structures with central opening sections to allow shipping to pass.

Pony Express

Famous though short-lived mail service operated between St. Joseph, Mo., and Sacramento, Cal. It was opened on April 3, 1860, to carry mail over the 1,840 mi. (2,960 km) route in 10 days, as compared to the 22 days taken by the Overland Mail stagecoaches.

About 160 relay stations an average of 11 mi. (18 km) apart were located along the route, with "home stations" every 75 mi. (120 km). Skilled riders rode from one home station to the next, changing horses at the intervening relay stations. The average change time was two minutes. The fee for each letter was $5 (later reduced to $1). Despite attacks by Indians, the mail was lost only once. The Pony Express service ended on October 24, 1861, when the transcontinental telegraph was opened.

The pony express carried mail on the 1,800 mi. (2,897 km) route between St. Joseph, Missouri, and Sacramento, California.

Ports and harbors

A port is generally a city where sea and land transportation systems meet, while a harbor is a protected area of water where ships can anchor in safety. The working areas of ports and harbors where ships actually load and unload are known as DOCKS.

Virtually all large ports are within a harbor or on a river or sheltered estuary, but many small ports, especially in underdeveloped countries, are open to the sea. In this case ships normally anchor in the roadstead and load and discharge their cargo using LIGHTERS, a procedure which doubles the amount of handling involved. Small, unprotected ports like this are adequate where the volume of trade is low and where weather conditions are generally calm. But as trade increases there comes a point at which the expense of building an artificial harbor, or of moving the port to a sheltered position, is justified.

Giant tankers with drafts of up to 90 ft. (27 m) or more cannot berth at any conventional port, and special offshore ports must be built. There have been plans for several of these in the Gulf of Mexico and off the Atlantic coast.

Artificial harbors. Such harbors are formed by the construction of massive BREAKWATERS to create a sheltered basin. It may also be necessary to dredge the basin and approach channels to provide sufficient depth for large ships. Wherever possible, artificial harbors are sited where the natural coastline affords some protection, as for example in a shallow bay, or in the lee of a headland. Many of the harbors on the Great Lakes are of this kind, including Chicago, Cleveland, and Milwaukee, as is that at Long Beach, California. But it is sometimes necessary, for strategic or commercial reasons, to build a harbor on an unsheltered stretch of coast, as for example at Dover in southeast England, where the breakwater is over 2 mi. (3.2 km) long.

Natural harbors. These take advantage of natural features, and their very existence accounts for the foundation and success of many of the world's great cities. New York, for example, is the largest port in the world, with 75.5 mi. (121.5 km) of waterfront and covering over 92 sq. mi. (238 km²). The bay of Rio de Janeiro, protected on either side by headlands, provides a large natural harbor 15 mi. (24 km) long. Other bay harbors include those at San Francisco, and at Sydney (Australia).

River and estuary ports. Many important ports lie some miles inland at the head of river estuaries, as, for example, London.

Part of the artificial harbor at Dover, England's busy Channel port. The well known steep chalk cliffs and strong currents would otherwise provide poor facilities for oceangoing vessels.

Where tidal variation is considerable, the working areas of the port are separated from the river by locks. But where the rise and fall of the tide is slight, berthing facilities may take the form of simple shoreline WHARFS and QUAYS. The port of Rotterdam in the Netherlands began in this way, but as traffic increased it was extended downstream, large artificial basins were constructed to provide more berths, and in recent years it has been further enlarged with a new artificial harbor built in the sea at the mouths of the Rhine and Meuse rivers. Now known as Rotterdam-Europoort, it has become the world's busiest port in the tonnage of cargo handled. It is a free port; that is, no customs duty is payable on goods transported to and from the port. Hence a wide range of processing industries has been developed in the port, with raw materials brought in, processed, and shipped out duty-free.

Inland ports. Road and rail facilities are as important to a port as the facilities provided for shipping, but moving goods by water is normally considerably cheaper than moving them by land and so a port is always situated as close as possible to the industrial or commercial hinterland that it serves; many are well inland. Houston, Texas, linked to the Gulf of Mexico by the Houston Ship Channel, is 52 mi. (84 km) from the sea, while Albany is 150 mi. (241 km) up the artificially deepened Hudson River.

Ports not only serve existing industry and commerce, but also encourage their development. Rapid industrial expansion has occurred in the Great Lakes area since the opening of the SAINT LAWRENCE SEAWAY turned cities such as Chicago and Duluth into important seaports, despite their distance (2,000 mi.; 3,200 km) from the ocean.

As trade increases and ships become larger and more specialized, ports and harbors require deeper channels, more and longer berths, more specialized handling gear, and sophisticated traffic control systems. Harbor RADAR is widely used to monitor and control all shipping movements.

Power
The rate of doing work. The power output of many engines is expressed in terms of HORSEPOWER, originally the rate at which an average horse could work. British engineer James WATT defined horsepower as a rate of working of 33,000 foot-pounds per minute. In electrical terms power is defined in terms of watts, 1 watt being equivalent to a rate of working of 10^7 ergs or 1 joule per second; 746 watts are equivalent to one horsepower.

The power of a jet or rocket engine is invariably expressed in terms of pounds thrust (see JET ENGINE).

Prandtl number
A number of importance in AERODYNAMICS and FLUID MECHANICS generally, named after German mathematician Ludwig Prandtl (1875-1953). It is a function of viscosity, specific heat at constant pressure and thermal conductivity. Prandtl was the person who first introduced the theory of the boundary layer, the thin fluid layer attached to a body moving in a fluid (see BOUNDARY LAYER).

Preselector gearbox
A gearbox fitted to some early automobiles in which a gear was selected first but changed only when a pedal was depressed. It was a precursor of the EPICYCLIC-GEAR automatic gearbox and like it was linked to the engine by a fluid coupling. After a gear had been selected, depression of a pedal actuated the brake bands of the epicyclic-gear train, enabling the appropriate gear change to take place. (See also AUTOMATIC TRANSMISSION.)

Pressurization
At high altitudes aircraft and spacecraft cabins must be pressurized to protect crew and passengers from the dangerous effects of low pressure and the oxygen deficiency that accompanies it. In addition pressurization is important during descent to prevent pressure inequalities causing discomfort or damage in ears, sinuses and intestines. Without pressurization, oxygen starvation causes loss of efficiency at altitudes above 10,000 ft. (3,048 m), while at 20,000 ft. (6,096 m) unconsciousness may occur within a few minutes (see AVIATION MEDICINE). Airliner cabins are usually pressurized to the equivalent of an altitude of about 5,000 ft. (1,524 m), air being continuously pumped in and leaked out to maintain its freshness. The pressurized air may be obtained either from a mechanically-driven blower (the normal system in piston engined planes), or from the compressor system of one or more of the jet engines. Since engines may only be idling under certain conditions (during descent, for example), the air supply from the compressor may be inadequate. The engine from which the cabin air is drawn may therefore have to be speeded up, or facilities may be provided to draw air from three or four engines. Before being fed to the cabin the air must be cooled by expanding it through a turbine and passing it into a heat exchanger.

Pressurization is also used to prevent water entering manned undersea chambers that are open to the water, such as CAISSONS, DIVING BELLS and undersea habitats, and (for the same reason) in tunneling shields (see TUNNELS). When the depth, and therefore the pressure, is very great, special precautions are needed to avoid oxygen poisoning, as at high pressures the body absorbs excessive amounts of gas (see DIVING).

Proa

Sometimes called a flying proa, this is a specialized sailboat whose crew sit on an outrigger "car" which projects from the main hull and is fitted with a planing shoe. In 1975 the 55-ft. (17 m) long British flying proa *Crossbow* became the first sailboat to exceed 30 knots (about 35 mph; 56 km/h).

Propellant

A substance burned in a rocket motor to provide the stream of hot gases that produces THRUST. It comprises a FUEL and oxidizer (a substance that provides oxygen for combustion). The propellants may be liquid or solid. Liquid propellants in general are more powerful than solid propellants and can more readily be controlled (see ROCKETS).

One of the most common liquid fuels is kerosene, which is usually combined with liquid oxygen as the oxidizer. Liquid hydrogen is another widely used fuel. Like liquid oxygen (-361°F, -183°C) it is very cold (−487°F, −253°C) and is termed a cryogenic propellant. Alcohol and hydrazine are also used as fuels. Nitrogen tetroxide is another oxidizer. Hydrazine and nitrogen tetroxide are *hypergolic* fuels used in combination which ignite spontaneously when they are mixed.

One traditional solid propellant used in firework rockets is gunpowder, a mixture of charcoal and sulfur with potassium chlorate as the oxidizer. Modern solid propellants are made up of an oxidizer bonded with a synthetic rubber.

Propeller

A screw-like device which develops thrust when it rotates, used to propel most ships and many airplanes, and to lift helicopters. The airplane propeller, or airscrew, obtains thrust from a large mass of air moving at low velocity, whereas with a JET ENGINE thrust is obtained from a small mass of gas moving at high velocity. At moderate speeds, up to about 500 mph (800 km/h), propellers provide more economical propulsion than jets, and many transport planes are fitted with them. Most are TURBOPROP craft, with their propellers turned by GAS TURBINES. Many propeller-driven, low-speed light airplanes have gasoline-burning PISTON ENGINES.

A typical airscrew has two or more blades, often three or four, radiating from a central hub. They are sited so as to form part of a spiral surface, like segments of a screw thread. They are twisted along their length and strike the air at a certain angle of attack. They have an AIRFOIL cross-section, being rounded at their leading edge and sharp at their trailing edge (see AERODYNAMICS). When

A Kort nozzle marine propeller unit. Enclosing the screws in nozzles increases thrust by up to 25%.

they rotate they develop thrust in much the same way as an airplane wing develops lift, creating reduced pressure in front and increased pressure behind. The angle at which the blades are set on the hub, called the pitch, determines how far the propeller screws itself through the air on each rotation. A low-pitch setting makes best use of engine power at low speeds (during takeoff, for example), while a high or coarse-pitch setting is suitable for high speeds. A fixed-pitch, or constant-pitch propeller is most efficient only at one air speed. Therefore modern airplanes and other airscrew propelled craft (e.g. AIR-CUSHION VEHICLES) have variable-pitch propellers; their adjustment may be manual, but it is often automatic. The pitch can also be reversed, and this provides a means of braking on landing.

Marine propellers. Usually manufactured from manganese bronze, a marine propeller operates on the same principle as an airscrew, but usually has very much broader blades. Some are really massive; those of the supertankers GLOBTIK TOKYO and GLOBTIK LONDON, for example are more than 30 ft. (9 m) across and weight 58 tons. As with the airscrew a fixed-pitch marine propeller gives optimum performance at one speed only. At other speeds more slip will occur between the propeller and the water, thus reducing efficiency. Variable-pitch propellers are therefore also used.

As the speed of a propeller increases there is a greater tendency for CAVITATION to occur. This is a phenomenon in which bubbles form in the wake of a spinning blade, causing reduced thrust

This massive Soviet snow-clearer does the work of 20 conventional bulldozers. It can deal with large drifts, moving some 1,200 tons an hour. (See Public Service Vehicles).

and erosion. Special super-cavitating propellers have been designed for high-speed craft to minimize this effect.

Two special marine propellers are the Kort nozzle unit, in which the screw is shrouded in an open-ended cylinder, thereby increasing thrust by up to 25%, and the cycloidal propeller. This is similar to a small feathering paddle wheel, but it is mounted underwater on a vertical instead of a horizontal axis. By altering the relative angle of the blades the direction of thrust can be altered, and no rudder is needed. Cycloidal propellers are especially valuable for shallow water operation. In conjunction with pivoting vanes to alter the direction of thrust the

Modern fire engines at work. Rapidly extending ladders and high-capacity high-pressure hoses are essential features.

Kort nozzle unit gives better maneuverability than a conventional propeller and rudder combination, and is widely used on tugs, fishing and research vessels.

Propeller shaft
See DRIVE SHAFT.

Public service vehicles
Road vehicles designed for transporting passengers in large numbers, usually on scheduled routes, and a multiplicity of specially built vehicles to provide municipal services. (See BUS; STREETCAR; TROLLEYBUS.)

Pullman Cars
These were the brainchild of George M. Pullman (1831-97), a Chicago contractor who in 1859 converted two existing passenger cars of the Chicago & Alton Railroad to SLEEPING CARS. This successful experiment led him to build the first specially built Pullman sleeping car in 1864. It went into service in 1865 and was named *Pioneer*. His cars were in great demand, especially after he had introduced, in 1867, covered vestibules which provided a safe, weatherproof connection between cars, giving passengers the freedom of the whole length of the train. He also introduced sleeping cars complete with kitchens and tables, in 1867 and restaurant cars in 1868. The name "Pullman" came to be synonymous with luxury and trains with Pullman cars charged higher fares. Many modern luxury trains in all parts of the world owe much to Pullman's ideas.

Pulse jet
In a pulse jet engine there are no rotating parts. Air is sucked into the COMBUSTION CHAMBER through a number of valves which are spring-loaded in the open position. Fuel injected into the combustion chamber is ignited and the resulting expansion of gases forces the air-intake valves shut, allowing the exhaust only one means of exit (backwards down the jet pipe), thus creating forward thrust. When the combustion chamber is emptied, the spring-loaded intake valves reopen and the cycle begins again.

This type of jet engine found limited application for driving the rotors of helicopters with an engine attached to the tip of each blade. By careful design of the air intake duct it is possible to control the changing pressures of the resonating cycle without using valves, but pulse jets have not been widely used because of their high fuel consumption, vibration, and inferior performance compared with a conventional JET ENGINE.

Q

QE 2
British passenger ship launched in 1967, well after the end of the great LINER era, and the only giant passenger vessel still in service. Her success is due to several factors. First, she is a luxurious floating hotel, providing vacation cruises as well as a transatlantic "ferry" service. Second, with a lightweight aluminum superstructure her draft is only 32.5 ft. (9.8 m), and she can therefore berth at a wide range of ports (unlike her predecessors). Third, she is the world's most efficient merchant ship (she consumes half as much fuel as the first QUEEN ELIZABETH) and is therefore economic to run. With a length of 963 ft. (293.5 m), a gross tonnage of 65,863, and a cruising speed of 28.5 knots, the *QE 2* carries 2,025 passengers and a crew of 906.

Quay
An artificial landing place where ships tie up for loading and discharge. Quays may lie along the edge of the shore, or they may project into the water to provide berthing facilities on both sides.

The world's only remaining large passenger liner in service, Cunard's 963 ft. (293.5 m) long QE 2. She carries over 2,000 passengers at a cruising speed of 28.5 knots.

One of the most famous ships of the liner era Cunard's Queen Mary. *Launched in 1934, she is seen here on her last voyage to her present mooring at Long Beach, California.*

Quebec Bridge

A CANTILEVER BRIDGE across the St. Lawrence River, in Quebec, Canada, with the world's greatest cantilever span (1,800 ft., 549 m). Completed in 1917, it is of double-trussed design (compared with the triple-trussed cantilever FORTH RAIL BRIDGE) and has an overall length of 3,239 ft. (987 m) with railroad tracks and two automobile lanes.

Queen Elizabeth

British passenger LINER designed to join her sister ship QUEEN MARY on the weekly Southampton - New York service. Slightly larger than *Queen Mary*, with a length of 1,031 ft. (312 m) and a gross tonnage of 83,673, she was launched in 1938. Both Queens spent the war as troopships, carrying between them over a million and a half passengers on war service. The *Queen Elizabeth* did not sail on the commercial transatlantic run until 1946. She was withdrawn from service soon after *Queen Mary* (both ships were running at a loss), and was destroyed by fire in Hong Kong in 1972.

Queen Mary

Famous British transatlantic passenger LINER launched in 1934, and one of the first merchant ships to be fitted with stabilizers. Carrying 2,139 passengers and a crew of 1,101, she was 1,020 ft. (309 m) long, with a gross tonnage of 81,237. In 1938 she took the BLUE RIBAND from the French liner *Normandie*, with an average speed of 31.69 knots, and held it for 14 years. In 1967 she was withdrawn from service, and today she is permanently moored at Long Beach, California, ending her days as a museum and conference center.

R

R 34

British rigid AIRSHIP. Its design was based on that of a German zeppelin which came down in England during World War I, in 1916. In July 1919 the *R 34* became the first aircraft of any type to make a round-trip crossing of the Atlantic, from Scotland to America and back to England.

R 101

Large rigid British AIRSHIP intended (with the *R 100*) to initiate a network of air routes throughout the British Empire. It made its first flight in 1929. On October 4, 1930, en route from Britain to Egypt and India, it crashed near Beauvais in northern France and was destroyed by fire, thus ending the airship experiment in Britain.

Rack and pinion

A common type of steering arrangement in which a pinion at the end of the steering column turns, and moves a toothed rack beneath it from side to side (see STEERING SYSTEM).

Rack railroad

On a rack railroad traction is by a rack-and-pinion mechanism and there is no drive to the wheels. The train's engine turns a toothed wheel (the pinion) which engages in the teeth of a rack rail. Several early LOCOMOTIVES used this system, as it was thought that smooth wheels on smooth rails would provide insufficient grip or adhesion. This belief was soon disproved, but the idea is used on steep mountain railroads where normal adhesion is inadequate.

Several systems are employed, including the Riggenbach, which locks the pinion to the track to prevent derailment; the Abt, which has two racks side-by-side with the teeth staggered, to ensure continuous engagement of the pinion; and the Lochner, which uses two racks, one on either side of a single bar, and two horizontal pinions, thereby ensuring a positive grip and guiding the cars (whose wheels are unflanged and can therefore follow very sharp curves easily). The Lochner system was designed specifically for the world's steepest rack railroad, which climbs Mount Pilatus in Switzerland and has a maximum gradient of 1:2. In a few places a rack system is used to supplement normal traction on severe grades. (See also MOUNT WASHINGTON COG RAILROAD.)

Radar

Without radar for AIR TRAFFIC CONTROL and for NAVIGATION and guidance on water, modern transportation systems would be limited in scope, slower, less safe and less efficient. Although the term radar (RAdio Direction And Range) was coined in America, the technique was being developed simultaneously in Britain and Germany as well. Conventional radio direction finding used before radar, required the operation of at least two intersecting beams if range as well as direction was to be obtained. With radar, the direction and range not only of physical features on land and ships at sea but also of aircraft can be detected by a

Railroad history on display. On the right is a classic American-type
steam locomotive of the 19th century; on the left, a locomotive from the
end of the steam era; and in the center a powerful modern diesel-
electric freight locomotive.

Early steamboats, 1817. Even small coastal or inland craft such as
these still carried sails, which remained a feature of oceangoing
steamships throughout most of the 19th century.

The radar screen of a ship in the Thames in the Pool of London, England. The image of Tower Bridge can be seen in the straight-ahead position.

single transmitter/receiver. Furthermore, radar operates without the knowledge or cooperation of the target, whereas ordinary radio direction finding requires the target to transmit for a fix.

Principles. Radar employs very short-wave radio transmissions, which are reflected back from the target, the time taken for this double journey being registered on receiving equipment that incorporates a cathode ray tube. The receiver is calibrated to indicate how far away the target is, depending on how long the radar echo takes to return to its source.

The display screen of a radar unit makes use of the electrons discharged from the cathode of a cathode ray tube. These negatively-charged electrons are emitted from a similarly negatively-charged metal cylinder (a grid) with a small aperture at its outer end. They then pass through a series of anodes, which because of their positive charge attract the electrons and form them into a stream (or ray). The end of the cathode ray tube is coated with a material that glows (fluoresces) when the electron stream strikes it to give a bright spot, which can be dimmed or brightened as required by adjusting the negative charge on the grid to increase or suppress the flow of electrons. Focusing is effected by a control on one of the anodes.

Before finally reaching the screen, however, the ray passes between two pairs of charged plates (vertical X-plates, horizontal Y-plates). The negatively-charged electron stream can then be deflected by imparting positive (attracting) or negative (repelling) charges to the plates. Changing the electrical potential of the plates in this way enables the ray to be oscillated across the fluorescent screen 100 times or more a second. It is this rapidly oscillating ray that enables radar sets to compute ranges to an accuracy

of a few yards over many miles, using radio waves that take only 10.7 microseconds to echo off a target a mile away, or 214 microseconds to return from one 20 miles distant.

By balancing the negative and positive potentials of the X- and Y-plates, the electron beam can be made to originate from one side of the fluorescent screen and travel across it.

When a pulse is directed at a target by a radar transmitter, a corresponding locking pulse is sent to the receiver and starts the cathode ray spot moving across the fluorescent screen from the left hand side by increasing the positive potential of the right hand X-plate. The returning echo is amplified and fed to the receiver where it causes a momentary increase in the negative potential of the bottom Y-plate. Although the indicating spot is moving back and forth across the screen in a millisecond or less, to the human eye it looks like a bright line with a permanent blip in it. An operator manipulates a control to keep the front edge of this blip aligned with a vertical hairline on his cathode ray tube and so automatically registers the range on an adjacent scale that is correlated with the characteristics of his radar set.

Direction and bearing. The aerials used for radar direction finding are separated by a short horizontal distance so that a differential signal originating from each will disappear or cancel out when they are aligned with the target's bearing (a special switch enables the size of the blip

Large dish-type radar antennae in an air traffic control system.

Radar scanners on the mast of a naval frigate. The scanners rotate to provide continuous images on the screen of objects in the ship's vicinity in all directions.

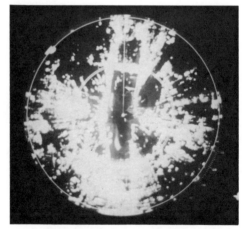

A radar "photoplot" screen on a modern ship. The latest systems plot the course of the ship in relation to other ships in the vicinity, and display a warning and suggested course-alteration if there is any danger of a collision.

on the cathode ray tube to indicate whether the target is ahead of or behind the receiver).

On the cathode ray tube that indicates bearings, the vertical trace employed is interrupted by two colored blips — a green one and an orange one. The green blip is caused by the range signal plus any signal received from the bearing aerials; the orange blip represents the range signal minus any signal from the bearing aerials. When the bearing aerials are correctly aligned, they generate no signal, so the green and orange blips are the same size (they both represent only the range signal), but if any bearing signal is coming in, the two colored blips will be of different size and the operator must use his controls to equalize them by altering the orientation of his aerials. Angle of sight is similarly recorded on another cathode ray tube, using an upper elevation aerial and a lower elevation aerial. Rotating aerials at the base of parabolic metal reflectors can be made to switch in and out either above and below

or to either side of a target, thus projecting two blips onto a cathode ray tube which have to be kept the same size. If one grows larger than the other, it means the target has moved directly into the path of the aerial instead of being bracketed by it and a correction must be made. For the location of aircraft, special instruments convert slant range (line-of-sight range) into ground range and height.

Navigational radar. In navigational radar, the Plan Position Indicator (PPI) display is used. This comprises a scanner (aerial) electrically coupled to coils around the neck of a cathode ray tube

which deflect the electron beam in the same way that the X- and Y- plates do. The center of the screen represents the position of the ship or aircraft, and as the scanner rotates so the beam oscillates backwards and forwards to the margin of the screen in concert with the direction in which the scanner is pointing. The light spot is located at the center of the screen when a pulse is transmitted, the current through the coil windings being zero, but as the current builds up it moves out at a constant speed in a direction perpendicular to the axis of the coils. The bias voltage between the grid and the cathode suppress the electron beam until an echo is received. When this echo arrives at the receiver, the grid bias is changed to allow the electron beam to become visible. The image of the echo appears on the screen, which because of its fluorescence retains a fading afterglow until the next sweep of the scanner re-activates the reflection.

Ship-borne navigational radar must not be mounted too high on the vessel, or it will be unable to detect marker buoys. If two scanners are used (one for transmitting, the other for receiving), there is no need for a transmit/receive switch and minimum ranges of only 20 yards are possible.

Nautical PPI sets have a video gain control (which must be used with care, for at its maximum setting there will be considerable "grass" interference), a suppressor control to restrict the small specks and spots caused by echoes from the waves of the sea, a range switch (maximum range for ship-borne radar is about 30 miles, for radar transmissions travel almost rectilinearly and do not follow the curvature of the earth), and an FTC (fast-time-constant) switch to sharpen the contrast between the required echo and one caused by the presence of snow or heavy rain.

Atmospheric effects. The effect of the atmosphere on radar waves is small, although there is a tendency for them to be defracted slightly downwards under normal meteorological conditions. A steep temperature gradient in the atmosphere or a vertical increase in relative humidity can lead to sub-refraction and shorten the range, while conditions in which air from a warm land mass moves out over the sea may result in super-refraction and increased range. Cumulo-nimbus and cumulus clouds contain heavy concentrations of rain drops, hail and snowflakes, which will return an echo. Aircraft radar is used to detect these bad-weather clouds so that the pilot can avoid them.

New uses. While the military uses of radar have been constantly extended, its application to civil transport at sea and in the air has greatly increased the safety of ships and aircraft.

As the density of air traffic increased, secondary surveillance radar (SSR) was developed for airport controllers. This system is a communication channel which receives coded emissions from a transponder in an aircraft. The identity of the airplane can thus be established as well as its range, azimuth, and height. Additional information from the aircraft can also be transmitted and thrown onto the radar screen, special positions on the display being available for encoded notification of in-flight emergencies (including hi-jacking) or communications failure.

Radial engine
Gasoline-powered aero-engines in which the cylinders are arranged in circular fashion around the crankcase are known as radial engines. Up to nine cylinders can be incorporated in a single circular row, one of the connecting rods being a strongly constructed master rod that receives the thrust delivered from the other connecting rods. A two-throw crank can enable two rows of cylinders to be employed.

Air cooling is used for radial engines, which are capable of producing very high power outputs, especially if sleeve valves are employed, since these have a higher maximum operating temperature than comparable poppet-type exhaust valves.

The principal disadvantage of radial engines is their frontal area which imposes a severe drag penalty compared with a liquid-cooled in-line power unit.

Radiator
Part of the COOLING SYSTEM of an engine in which cooling of the hot circulating fluid takes place. It is really a misnomer because cooling takes place by conduction rather than by radiation. Hot water from the engine passes into the header tank of the radiator and flows downward through narrow tubes in the radiator core to the bottom tank. From there it is pumped back through the engine. The core tubes are fitted with fins to offer as big a surface as possible for cooling by the air that is drawn through the radiator by a fan.

Water is added to the radiator through a filler cap, which incorporates a spring-loaded valve. This allows the pressure in the header tank to rise above atmospheric, thereby raising the boiling point of the water. If the pressure rises too high, however, the valve opens and steam escapes through an overflow. Many modern engines have a sealed radiator, which

has an expansion tank to take the overflow. Water flows into and out of the tank as the temperature of the water in the radiator rises and falls.

Radio direction finder
A device used to determine the bearing of a radio signal. It consists of a conventional radio receiver with a directional antenna, usually in the form of a loop which can be rotated about its vertical axis. By turning the antenna to find the points of strongest and weakest reception, the direction of the transmitter can be found.

The radio direction finder is used in NAVIGATION, either as a compass, using just one bearing, or as a means of fixing position, especially in poor visibility near land. In this case bearings are taken on two transmitters. The system has the advantage of simplicity since no special equipment is needed on board, but its range is limited. The radio direction finder can also be used from a shore station to take bearings on ships or aircraft — thus the importance of maintaining "radio silence" in military operations.

Raft
One of the earlier types of watercraft, made by tying logs, planks, or reeds together into a floating platform. The voyage of the KON TIKI demonstrated their oceangoing potential, but rafts have most often been used on inland or coastal waters. Examples include the Brazilian balsa *jangada*, and the Peruvian *caballito*, which is made by lashing conical bundles of reeds together. Both are still used today.

A boat relies on its watertight shell to keep it afloat, and may be built of materials that are heavier than water, but a raft depends entirely on the buoyancy of the materials. In certain conditions this can be a great advantage. The Taiwan raft, built of long curved bamboo poles, is designed to ride safely in heavy surf which would quickly swamp a normal boat.

Railcar
Railcars are self-propelled passenger cars used on light traffic railroad routes. They are usually lightweight direct drive diesel-powered vehicles, but electric railcars are sometimes used for offpeak or special services. Railcars may be single vehicles, or may comprise two- or three-car sets which for peak services can be coupled into four- or six-car trains driven from the cab of the front set.

A "Vert-A-Pac" freight car in which 30 automobiles are carried nose down and are fully enclosed for protection.

Railroad
A guideway of two parallel steel rails along which locomotives and cars travel on flanged wheels. The two basic features that make railroads the most efficient mode of land transportation for large and heavy loads are that the flanged wheels follow the rails automatically, and that there is very little friction between steel wheels and steel rails. A train can run on a narrower road than a steerable road vehicle, and because of the low rolling friction a locomotive can haul about 10 times as heavy a load as a truck of the same power; savings in fuel and manpower are of the same order. The lack of friction has one disadvantage; with conventional wheels and track a train cannot climb a steep grade, so

A modern long distance diesel electric hauled passenger train, The Empire Builder. *With every luxury, including in this case "penthouse-high" seats in special observation cars, such trains are attracting passengers back to America's railroads.*

railroads are always made as level (and as straight) as possible. For this reason BRIDGES and TUNNELS are far more important to railroads than they are to highways. Where a severe grade must be surmounted, the track is laid out in large loops or spirals, as for example in the St. Gotthard line which crosses the Swiss Alps with the aid of three spiral tunnels. In extreme conditions, notably in the Peruvian Andes mountains, a zigzag track is built, on which trains travel forwards up one stretch and backwards up the next. The steepest grade on any normal railroad today is 1 in 11, although RACK RAILROADS climb grades of up to 1 in 2.

The track. The distance between the rails is normally 4 ft. 8½ in. (1.435 m), known as standard gauge, although broad and narrow gauge tracks are used in various parts of the world (see GAUGE). The more common alternatives include meter (3.28 ft.) gauge, in Brazil, East Africa, etc.; 3 ft. 6 in. (1.07 m) gauge, in much of Japan, Australasia, and central and southern Africa; and 5 ft. (1.52 m) gauge, in Spain, and parts of India and South America.
Railroad track has remained unchanged in principle for well over a century, but materials and methods have improved. The basic idea of a well-drained bed with fairly deep foundations to spread the load evenly over the subsoil is still fol-

lowed. The foundation of broken stone supports the crossties, which have smaller stones (ballast) placed between them. Timber crossties are still widely used, although reinforced concrete types are increasingly common. The steel rails, nearly always flat-bottomed, rest on resilient pads of rubber or plastic; these in turn rest on metal plates which distribute the load on the crossties. Spikes or clips attach rails to ties.
The rails, which can weigh 130 to 150 lb. a yard (about 60 to 70 kg a meter), are usually welded together end-to-end in lengths of a mile or more to cut down wear on rails and cars at joints, and to give a smoother and quieter ride. The spacing of ties depends on the traffic to be carried and the practice of the country concerned. The United States is probably the most liberal in its use of ties, with up to 3,500 per mile (2,175 per km) on some sections of track.
As trains must slow down drastically to take sharp curves, the tendency today is to build new tracks with very large radius curves (and with superelevation of the outer rail) to permit high-speed operation.

Motive power. During the first 100 years of the railroads steam traction was almost universal, and it is still used in many parts of the world. But in modern networks such as those of the United States, western Europe, and Japan, steam

has been replaced by diesel, electric, and gas turbine power. Electric traction is generally considered the most efficient and economical system, given cheap electricity, and sufficient traffic to justify the very high initial expense. On short distance suburban networks the electric current is normally carried on a third rail in the form of a relatively low voltage direct current (600 to 3,000 volts). However on long routes the expense of the frequent substations necessary becomes prohibitive, and a high voltage (25,000 to 50,000 volts) alternating current supply carried on overhead cables is usual.
Extensive electrification has been carried out in most west European countries, in Japan, and in the Soviet Union, but in the United States the vast majority of trains are still diesel hauled. The diesel has the great advantage of independence, and of an efficiency roughly four times that of steam, but it lacks the power and speed of the electric, and is costly and complex. Modern railroad systems normally reserve electrification for busy short and medium distance intercity routes, employ gas turbine powered "turbotrains" for high-speed passenger trains on unelectrified lines, and use diesels for the rest.
In the United States the long dominant position of the diesel is now being challenged by increasing electrification, and increasing use of turbotrains. The high

price of oil is one factor. Another is the federal government's effort (and financial assistance) to rescue the railroads from their near-extinction of a few years ago. The Black Mesa and Lake Powell Railroad in Arizona, an 81 mi. (130 km) line linking a coal mine and a power station, was opened in 1973 with automatic operation, and a 50,000 volt 60 hertz system which was expected to become the national standard. (See also LOCOMOTIVES, and LINEAR INDUCTION MOTOR.)

Passenger transportation. Fifty years ago about 75% of passenger transportation was by rail. In the early 1970s the figure for intercity travel in the United States was 1%. However rail transportation continues to play an important role in suburban commuter traffic (see BAY AREA RAPID TRANSIT, and SUBWAYS), and is showing signs of a limited revival on intercity routes following the introduction of high-speed services by AMTRAK (National Railroad Passenger Corporation). These include the electric Metroliners running between New York City and

speed, and are generally cheaper, more comfortable, and more convenient.

Freight transportation. The railroads have suffered increasingly from competition from trucks (see TRUCKING), which can provide a more flexible service, and from PIPELINES, which are the cheapest mode of transportation for bulk liquids. However, with the rise in overall production, the railroads have continued since the earliest years to carry ever larger volumes of freight. Today trains carry some 40% of the overall volume of freight transported in the United States. Traditional railroad freight systems involve the assembly of loaded cars from various sources and for various destinations in a CLASSIFICATION YARD. There electronic scanning devices and a centralized computer control system organize the cars into sidings by destination, and only when enough cars for a given destination have been assembled will they be dispatched. Today this time-consuming procedure is avoided whenever possible. General merchandise is increasingly pre-packed in containers

modity in specialized cars on a predetermined route have cut costs and attracted business to the railroads. Freight carried in this way includes coal, grain, chemicals, ores, automobiles, and (on routes which do not justify a pipeline) petroleum. Recent developments include three-deck fully enclosed cars holding up to 18 new automobiles (for example the RailPac, and the articulated Autoguard), and 40-car "tank trains." These carry 1,000,000 gallons of petroleum, and are interconnected so that loading and discharge (at the rate of 3,000 gallons a minute) is from a single point.

Signaling and automation. Trains following each other along a track must be regulated to avoid collision. In the traditional and widespread block system the line is divided into lengths (blocks) with an automatic switch on the track at the start of each block. As a train enters one block it automatically puts the signal to danger, thereby preventing another train entering the block. The signal clears when the block is empty. Where there is relatively little traffic, train control may simply involve adhering to a timetable; in the event of a delay the driver can communicate by microwave radio with the traffic control officer, who can delay or reroute other trains as necessary. On busy lines all switches and signals are often remotely controlled from a central traffic control office, where an electronic display panel shows the track layout, the position of all trains, and the state of all switches and signals. With the addition of computer control fully automatic operation is possible, and can be extended to provide automatic control of train speed. A number of lines, including Japan's New Tokaido Line and San Francisco's Bay Area Rapid Transit system, are already on fully automatic control, and with the increase of high-speed high-frequency services the system is likely to become widespread. (See AUTOMATIC TRAIN CONTROL; AUTOMATIC WARNING SYSTEM; SIGNALING IN TRANSPORT.)

The world's largest networks. The United States, with a route length of 208,035 mi. (334,800 km), has the largest railroad system in the world, followed by the Soviet Union (159,754 mi., 257,100 km), Canada (44,179 mi., 71,100 km), India (37,282 mi., 60,000 km), and Australia (25,041 mi., 40,300 km). In passenger transport Japan's network of 17,336 mi. (27,900 km) is by far the busiest, with an annual passenger mileage over 20 times that of the United States. In terms of freight transportation the Soviet Union's network is the busiest, followed by that of the United States.

Each of these typical bulk freight cars carries 100 tons of cement and is pneumatically discharged. Specialized cars and handling systems save time and therefore money.

Washington D.C., and a number of new turbotrain services. In Japan, Europe, and Britain, fast intercity services are far more highly developed, notable examples being Japan's NEW TOKAIDO LINE, Britain's "Inter City" services, and Europe's TEE (Trans-Europ Express) trains. For journeys of up to about 300 mi. (482 km) railroads can compete successfully with air travel in overall arrival

(see CONTAINERIZATION) which are taken by truck to specialized container terminals where they are loaded onto trains running fast shuttle services which avoid classification yards and intermediate terminals. Alternatively complete truck trailers are loaded onto flat cars in the so-called "piggyback" system (also known as TOFC: trailer on flat car). Similar "unit trains" carrying a single com-

Railroad history

The history of railroads begins in the mines of Europe, where in the 16th century flanged-wheel cars running on wooden rails were being used for coal transport from the mine face to stacking grounds on the surface. By the 17th century these primitive railroads had been extended in Britain and parts of Europe so that larger carts, drawn by horses instead of being pushed by men and women, could carry the coal down to river banks for transport by ship or barge. In 1776 the wooden rails were covered by angled iron plates to reduce wear, the angle edge keeping the wheels to the track. Cast iron rails came in 1789, the invention of William Jessop, an Englishman, and then followed wrought iron and eventually the steel rails of today. From Jessop's time on plain rails and flanged wheels were used.

The first public railroad to be sanctioned by Parliament in Britain was the Surrey Iron Railway, opened in 1803, and others followed. In 1825, the STOCKTON AND DARLINGTON RAILWAY became the world's first public railroad to use steam locomotives (for freight only, after the first day), and in 1830 the LIVERPOOL AND MANCHESTER was opened. With all its trains hauled by LOCOMOTIVES, and with timetables, a signaling system, and proper stations, the Liverpool and Manchester ushered in the "Railroad Age."

The Best Friend of Charleston (1830), the first successful American built steam locomotive, hauled trains on the South Carolina Railroad, America's first all-steam public railroad.

Pioneers in the United States. A short wooden-railed line was opened in 1795 on the slopes of Beacon Hill, Boston, to carry materials used in the building of the State House, and other short lines followed, all of wood and all using horses or mules to pull the cars. A notable gravity railroad was built in 1829 by the Delaware & Hudson Canal Company to connect its mines in the Honesdale, Penn., area with the company's canal running towards New York. Gravity railroads used the natural slope of the ground to take the loaded cars down to the river, and animals to haul the empty cars back. In 1825, Colonel John STEVENS built and demonstrated a small steam locomotive which ran on a circular track on his private estate. This was 21 years after TREVITHICK's 1804 triumph in Britain with a steam locomotive which hauled a 25-ton load along a 9-mi. (14.5 km) Welsh plateway, but still four years ahead of the first French locomotive, built by Marc Seguin. In 1829 the imported British locomotive STOURBRIDGE LION proved too heavy for the wooden rails. Later the same year Tom Thumb, a light locomotive built by Peter Cooper of New York, was tried out on the newly-opened railroad at Baltimore and became the first American built locomotive to run on a public railroad.

The BALTIMORE & OHIO, opened for regular traffic on May 24, 1830, was the first public railroad to carry passengers and freight in the United States, closely followed by the South Carolina in December 1830, which was the first to be operated by steam power. This year of 1830 marked the real beginning of railroad development in America, and five years later there were 1,000 mi. (1.600 km) of track. New York could be reached from Washington by rail in 1838. By 1850, the year Congress passed the first act granting land to railroads, there were 9,000 mi. (14,484 km) of route in operation.

A classic American steam locomotive on the Northern Pacific Railroad at the turn of the century, with high roofed passenger cars typical of the period.

Such land grants, which continued for over 20 years, encouraged the building of railroads in virgin territory.

Population swiftly followed the rails, and the country was opened up by the railroads. The culmination came on May 10, 1869, when the East and West Coasts were linked by the meeting of the UNION PACIFIC and CENTRAL PACIFIC at Promontory, Utah. By 1860, just before the Civil War, there were already 30,000 mi. (48,280 km) of railroad in the United States. Between 1880 and 1890 the network expanded enormously; 70,300 mi. (113,136 km) were added in these 10 years. The peak was reached in 1916, when there were 254,000 mi. (408,773 km) of railroad. In 1975, despite the growth of highway traffic, there were still 241,400 mi. (388,495 km) of railroad in existence.

Mileage does not tell the whole story. Most of the early lines had only single tracks and ran very few trains, but over the years routes have been doubled, trebled and quadrupled to meet the demand for rail transport. The many separate railroads of the early years have gradually been welded together to form fewer and larger companies, so that through journeys in a single train are possible, eliminating the need to change trains every few hundred miles.

Depots, yards, rolling stock, and locomotives have all grown over the years, and a modern diesel or electric locomotive has a power output undreamt of in the pioneer days. All the very early railroads were hauled by men or animals, with occasional experiments in sail power, but after the 1830s steam locomotives were to reign supreme for over a century. They grew from Stephenson's tiny ROCKET to 600 ton monsters like the Union Pacific's BIG BOY class, developing over 6,000 hp.

Electric and diesel. Electricity was used by Werner von Siemens to draw a small exhibition train in Berlin in 1879, and it was soon realized that here was a clean, efficient, new way to power trains. London's first subway line, opened in 1863, was steam-hauled, but trains on the first full-scale deep "Tube" subway in London, the City & South London, opened in 1890, were hauled by electric locomotives. Since then, most important European railroad routes have been electrified, and almost without exception subways everywhere use electric traction. An important step came when Frank J. Sprague, in the United States, perfected the multiple-unit system which allows electric motors to be installed in the cars of a train, all being simultaneously controlled by the driver in the front cab.

This eliminates the use of locomotives and "running-round" at terminals. Multiple-unit trains are normally used for suburban or medium-distance services, locomotives having some advantages for long journeys.

Electrification, except for SUBWAY and rapid transit lines, has made little progress in America — Penn Central is the only system with substantial electrified mileage. This is undoubtedly due to the availability of domestic oil supplies which has favored diesel locomotives, enormous numbers of which are in use in the United States, where they first came into service in 1925. In the rest of the world as well, diesels have supplanted steam. They require far less maintenance, smaller crews, and they give some of the advantages of electrification without the need to install costly substations, overhead wiring or third rails (see LOCOMOTIVES).

A typical modern European electric passenger train.

Passenger and freight cars. The passenger cars of early railroads, either open and four-wheeled with wooden seats, or closed and resembling two or three stagecoach bodies put together and mounted on a single railroad car frame, have improved beyond recognition. Sleeping cars of a sort were first seen in the United States in 1837 and George M. PULLMAN's luxurious custom-built cars began appearing in 1865. Dining cars came in 1863, on the Philadelphia, Wilmington & Baltimore Railroad, and the first real Pullman diner ran in 1868. Air conditioning was introduced in the late 1920s.

Small, all-purpose, freight cars have given way to specialized equipment, often of giant size, designed to carry particular loads and fitted with apparatus to speed

loading and unloading: for example, hopper cars for minerals and coal with special doors for bottom discharge; cars for oil products and chemicals with special outlets for pumping purposes; and cars for cement and powdered products fitted for compressed-air loading and discharge.

Recent Developments. These include the increasing use of gas turbine power for high-speed passenger trains on unelectrified lines; experiments with tracked AIR-CUSHION VEHICLES and the LINEAR INDUCTION MOTOR; and increasing use of automation in freight yards, and for control and safety on high-speed surface and subway routes. But despite technical progress, railroads are very expensive to run and maintain. Few are able to operate at a profit under present conditions and most are state subsidized. In the United States the government sponsored AMTRAK (National Railroad Passenger Corporation) had to be founded in 1970 to rescue the railroads, which seemed (especially in the passenger field) to be in danger of extinction. Nevertheless, when the real cost, both in money and environmental damage, of alternate means of transportation is calculated, the railroad emerges with a reasonably bright future.

Rails

The first railroad consisted of wooden baulks on which the wheels of horse-drawn carts could run, the driver being responsible for keeping the cart on the track. As the wood wore quickly, cast iron plates were later nailed over the baulks, and in Sheffield, England, the plates had flanges to keep the wheels on the track. In 1789, William Jessop designed and laid cast iron rails on cross-ties; each rail was about 3 ft. (1 m) long, was fitted into the end of the next, and required flanged wheels. Jessop's rails were the ancestors of modern types. Wrought iron rails followed, but the great advance came in 1857 when the first steel rails were laid on the Midland Railway in England. They lasted 16 years in a location where iron rails had to be replaced every three months. Early "bullhead" rails had to be fastened into special "chairs" by wood blocks or steel spring components known as "keys." Today most railroads use "flat-bottom" track which is fastened to cross ties by spikes or clips. To avoid wear and jarring at joints, rails are usually welded in the factory to lengths of 600 ft. (180 m) or more and then welded when laid to much longer lengths. They are anchored firmly to prevent undue expansion or contraction on hot or cold days.

Rally

Competitive automobile event, often over long distances, held on public roads. The roads are not closed to other vehicles, and contestants must comply with normal traffic regulations. A rally is therefore not in a strict sense a race, although the course may include a number of off-the-road stretches where high speed is tested.

The primary object in a rally is to maintain specified average speeds over each leg of the route, and to show driving skill, particularly on special stretches of difficult terrain. All vehicles are inspected to ensure that they comply with stringent local or international regulations.

Europe has always been the main home of rallying, with countless local events as well as international ones, of which the most famous is the annual Monte Carlo Rally. However, the sport has spread around the world, with annual events such as the East African Safari Rally, and such occasional world events as the London to Sydney (Australia) Rally in 1969, and the World Cup Rally from London to Mexico City in 1970.

Ramjet

The ramjet is the simplest form of the jet engine. It has no moving parts. The motion of the aircraft itself "rams" highly compressed air into the engine. Air enters the engine through an intake incorporating single- or double-cone center bodies designed to decelerate the flow into a combustion chamber, where fuel is injected to provide an inflammable mixture. Ignition may be achieved initially by means of a pyrotechnic flare, and it is then stabilized by a baffled section at the after end of the combustion chamber. Forward thrust is generated as exhaust gases pass backwards down the nozzle.

To start a ramjet, forward motion must be imparted to it so that air enters the intake. This has largely limited its application to missiles, and ramjet engines have therefore been designed only for short periods of operation during which they run at full power.

Ram wing

A ram wing develops lift by the conventional aerodynamic method (see LIFT), and in addition makes use of "ground effect" like an AIR-CUSHION VEHICLE. Flying close to the sea the "wing-in-ground-effect" (WIG) machine may provide a valuable new type of aircraft for transporting heavier loads than can be carried by conventional airplanes at higher speeds than are possible on a normal air-cushion vehicle.

A prototype Soviet WIG craft with a design speed of 300 knots and a weight of 500 tons, making it the world's heaviest aircraft, has already been flight-tested over the Caspian Sea. Thrust from its eight turbojets, which are mounted on stub wings near the nose, is deflected downwards to create a lifting air-bubble under the main wings. Once airborne, the thrust is directed over the main wing to give additional aerodynamic lift.

In the United States several WIG machines proposals have been suggested, including one with a reversed delta wing designed by Alexander M. Lippisch, originator of the DELTA WING and designer of the Me-163 World War II rocket fighter plane.

Reciprocating engine

Engine in which pistons are driven back and forth in cylinders. In most instances the reciprocating motion has to be converted into more useful rotary motion which can turn the driving wheels of a vehicle or a ship's propeller. This is accomplished by means of a connecting rod and crankshaft. Contrast ROTARY ENGINES and TURBINES.

In the early days of automobiles the British Red flag law required a man carrying a red flag to walk in front of a motor vehicle.

Red flag law

Popular name for the Locomotives on Highways Act passed by the British government in 1865 restricting the speed of powered road vehicles to 2 mph (3.2 km/h) in towns and 4 mph (6.4 km/h) on other public roads and highways. In addition until 1878 a man was required to walk in front of the vehicle carrying a red flag, to warn other road users of their imminent "danger."

The law was the culmination of a series of private and parliamentary actions designed to force steam coach operators out of business. It also effectively restricted early automobile activity. The law was finally repealed in 1896.

Refining

PETROLEUM refining is a process of manufacturing useful products, such as gasoline, from crude oil, which is a complex mixture of hydrocarbons. The first stage in the refining process is straight distillation, or fractionation, in which the oil is vaporized by circulating it through a heated furnace. The vapor is fed to a bubble-tray fractionating column, which has numerous levels maintained at different temperatures (low at the top and high at the bottom). The hydrocarbon constituents separate out at the different levels according to their volatility, and include in decreasing order of volatility gasoline, kerosene, diesel and other fuel oils, and lubricating oils.

Gasoline is the most valuable fraction, and subsequent refinery processes seek to increase gasoline yield and quality (OCTANE NUMBER) by such processes as cranking, reforming, hydroforming, polymerization, alkylation, and isomerization. CRACKING is a process in which heavier oil fractions are broken down (or "cracked") into lighter ones by the application of heat and by catalytic action. Hydro-

forming is a reforming process carried out in the presence of hydrogen. With these processes gasoline can be produced from less valuable heavy fuel oils. Whereas cracking involves the breakdown of large molecules into smaller ones, polymerization involves the buildup of large molecules from smaller ones. Low-molecular weight gaseous hydrocarbons such as olefins are produced during cracking operations. They may be used as a cheap fuel in the refinery, or they can be polymerized: their molecules can be made to combine with each other, under heat and pressure in the presence of sulfuric acid, to form high-octane gasoline. Alkylation involves the combination of saturated hydrocarbons such as isobutane with unsaturated hydrocarbons to give larger molecules of higher octane rating, such as isooctane. Isomerization is a catalytic process for converting normal butane into the more valuable isobutane used in alkylation.

In addition to hydrocarbons, petroleum contains various harmful substances, the most important of which are sulfur compounds which in fuels can cause engine inefficiency and corrosion, and polluting and foul-smelling exhaust gases. In refining, various processes are used to remove these substances, including sulfuric acid, clay, and hydrogen treatments, and the use of molecular sieves.

Renault

Leading French automobile company founded in 1898. In its early years the firm (the first to use a drive shaft instead of chain-drive) was best known for its quality limousines, its taxicabs (which dominated the streets of Paris), and its racing successes. But by 1914 Renault was producing one fifth of all private automobiles in France.

During and after World War I, Renault built aircraft engines and tanks. Between the wars production included several large family models. In 1944 the company was nationalized.

The notable rear-engined Dauphine appeared in 1956 and became the first French car to reach sales of two million. It was followed in 1962 by the front-wheel drive "4," which still retains its position as one of Europe's leading economy cars.

Today, Renault, with a comprehensive range of front-wheel drive automobiles, is a leading worldwide concern with factories or assembly plants in 27 countries (including several in Eastern Europe). Other Renault products include tractors and machine tools.

Rev counter

The colloquial term for a revolution counter, or TACHOMETER, which measures the rate of rotation of an engine.

Reynolds number

A non-dimensional number named after British physicist Osborne Reynolds (1842-1912) of great importance in AERODYNAMICS and FLUID MECHANICS generally, which provides a criterion by which the behavior of a fluid can be predicted. It is a function of the velocity of flow, the diameter of pipe, and the density and viscosity of fluid.

In general, if the Reynolds number in a fluid is less than about 2,000, then flow of that fluid will be smooth and streamline, or laminar (see LAMINAR FLOW). At Reynolds numbers greater than 2,000 the

Early rickshas were drawn by a man on foot, but more modern types such as the Indian one shown are pedaled.

fluid tends to become haphazard or turbulent (see TURBULENT FLOW).

Rhine-Main-Danube Waterway

An ambitious international waterway planned for completion by the 1980s, the Rhine-Main-Danube Waterway will allow vessels to travel between the North Sea and the Black Sea. The route incorporates the rivers Rhine and Main, and artificial canals and canalized rivers which link Bamberg (on the Main) with the Danube near Kelheim. Sections of the Danube have been improved and deepened to assist navigation. The notorious Iron Gate rapids at Djerdap on the Yugoslav-Romanian border have been tamed by damming. The dams form part of hydroelectric power schemes.

Ricksha

Two-wheeled passenger cart formerly used as a form of taxi in China and Japan, also called a jinricksha. It was invented in the 1880s. The ricksha was pulled by a man running along between the shafts, holding one in each hand. Rickshas have now been replaced by *pedicabs*, tricycles designed to carry a passenger.

Riverboat

Shallow draft boat for use on rivers. In the early days all riverboats were propelled by paddles, which have a shallow draft and, when placed at either side, permit good maneuverability (an important feature for riverboats). Today the same advantages are achieved with bow thrusters (see SHIPS) and vertical axis Voith-Schneider propellers (see PROPELLERS). The majority of modern riverboats are pleasure craft, or ferries, cargo normally being carried in BARGES.

Rocket

The *Rocket* was a famous pioneer steam LOCOMOTIVE built by George and Robert STEPHENSON to enter the Rainhill trials, which were held in October 1829 to determine the type of power to be used on the new LIVERPOOL AND MANCHESTER RAILWAY. The locomotives had to haul three times their own weight, and to cover the $1\frac{1}{2}$ mi. (2.4 km) course 10 times each way, after which fuel and water could be taken on and another 10 round trips made at an average of not less than 10 mph (16 km/h). The *Rocket* was the only locomotive to fulfill all requirements, maintaining an average of 13.8 mph (22.2 km/h) and a maximum of 24 mph (38.6 km/h) with full load, as well as reaching 29 mph (46.7 km/h) running light.

The *Rocket* was the first locomotive to combine most of the developments made up to that time, including the multiple fire-tube boiler. It was faster, lighter, more powerful and more reliable than its predecessors, and it established a pattern for steam traction. However, its greatest achievement was to ensure that all trains on the Manchester and Liverpool Railway would be worked by steam. This was the first all-steam public railroad, and its opening in 1830 is generally regarded as the start of the "Railroad Age."

A Mississippi riverboat, the all steel Admiral. *Based at St Louis, the* Admiral *carries 4,000 passengers and is the world's largest riverboat.*

Rocket

A device used for propulsion which works on the reaction principle, forward propulsion deriving from reaction to a jet of gases streaming backwards out of a nozzle. It differs from the JET ENGINE, which also works by reaction, in that it carries an oxygen supply to burn its fuel, whereas the jet engine obtains its oxygen from the air it takes in from the atmosphere. Being thus self-contained, the rocket can function in airless space. In fact it works better there than in the atmosphere, which tends to spoil the jet action. Not only is the rocket the only engine capable of working in space, it is the only engine able to develop enough power to launch a body into space. To achieve orbit at an altitude of 100 mi. (160 km) a satellite must be boosted to a speed of about 17,500 mph (28,000 km/h). To achieve such speeds for reasonable weights takeoff thrusts of millions of pounds are required; the powerful *Saturn V* moon rocket, for example, developed no less than $7\frac{1}{2}$ million lb. ($3\frac{1}{2}$ million kg) thrust at takeoff.

Apart from space launchings the biggest use of rockets is in missiles, which vary in size from small ones fired in salvoes from ground-attacking aircraft to intercontinental ballistic missiles (ICBMs)

Thrusters of the powerful Soviet A-2 Vostok rocket are seen here as it is carried out on its special flatcar to launch the Soyuz 18 spacecraft (May 1975). 125 ft. (38 m) long, with a first-stage thrust of 1,124,350 lb. (510,000 kg), it also has a top stage producing 270,000 lb. (122,000 kg) of thrust. The four outer engines fall away while the center continues burning.

with multiple nuclear warheads capable of destroying targets several thousands of miles away. They have a pre-programmed INERTIAL GUIDANCE system to help guide them to their target. Military aircraft and ships are equipped with a variety of missiles that may be guided in one of several ways: visually, by means of radar, by signals through a wire, by infrared homing devices, by television eyes, and so on. Rockets are also used to send instruments into or sound the upper atmosphere to obtain meteorological and other scientific data.

Rockets have also been used to propel airplanes, one of the earliest being a Messerschmitt 163 interceptor in World War II. In 1947 the rocket-powered Bell X-1 became the first aircraft to exceed Mach 1 (the speed of sound). The current fixed-wing air-speed record is held by the rocket-powered North American Aviation X-15A-2, which achieved a speed of Mach 6.7 (4,534 mph, 7,297 km/h) in 1967 (see X-1 and X-15). Rockets are not used as a primary means of propulsion in modern production aircraft, but rather as boosters for use to assist takeoff or in combat to achieve a rapid rate of climb.

History. The rocket is believed to be an invention of the Chinese, and the first report of its use, in warfare, dates from 1232. Over the centuries it was used from time to time in European warfare, but by the 1800s rocket missiles had been developed, notably in Britain by William Congreve and his son, into quite an ef-

fective weapon. By the turn of the century a few visionaries were beginning to suggest the use of rockets for space travel and one, Konstantin TSIOLKOVSKI, foresaw that this could be achieved only with liquid-propellants and a step rocket. Hitherto rockets had been propelled by gunpowder, a solid propellant. However, it was not until 1926 that the first successful liquid-propellant rocket was fired, by Robert Hutchings GODDARD in the United States. He used gasoline and liquid oxygen as propellants. In the 1930s German scientists were actively engaged in rocket development and in 1942, at Peenemünde on the Baltic, made the first successful firing of the 47-ft. (14 m) V-2 ballistic rocket, subsequently used to bombard London. Its propellants were alcohol and liquid oxygen. The V-2 was the direct ancestor of virtually all liquid-propellant rockets produced since. A team of German rocket scientists, headed by Wernher von Braun, continued their research and development of the V-2 in the United States, while another group went to Russia. Russia launched the first space rocket in 1957, two months before the United States launched their first (see SPACE FLIGHT).

Rocket Motors. Rocket motors are classed by the type of propellants (solid or liquid) they use. Solid-propellant motors are the simplest in construction and operation. The motor consists simply of a casing filled with propellant, narrowing to a throat and then expanding into a nozzle at the rear. The casing itself forms the

Atlas-Centaur rocket used to launch the Intelsat communications satellites. The 117 ft. (35.7 m) rocket combined the Centaur with 30,000 lb. of thrust (13,600 kg.) with the three-engined Atlas, whose two outer engines each developed 185,000 lb. of thrust (84,000 kg) before falling away after 2.5 minutes. The third engine sustained the flight with 60,000 lb. of thrust (27,300 kg).

combustion chamber. The charge of propellant, called the grain, is not usually packed solid in the casing but has a hole down its center. Burning of the propellants takes place not just at one end but radially from the center outwards. The rate of burning depends on the actual cross-section of the grain. Modern propellants usually consist of an oxidizer dispersed in a synthetic-rubber fuel (see PROPELLANT).

The liquid-propellant rocket motor is considerably more complex and consists of storage tanks for the propellants, thrust or combusion chamber, igniter, turbopumps, gas generator, and associated valves and control devices. The storage tanks occupy the greater part of the volume of space rockets, for vast quantities of propellants need to be burned to give the required thrust. Up to 3 tons of propellants per second are burned in some rockets. In most rockets bipropellants are used, that is, fuel and oxidizer are separate; liquid hydrogen or kerosene as fuel and liquid oxygen as oxidizer is a typical combination. In some rockets, however, monopropellants are used, including high-strength hydrogen peroxide and hydrazine. These are decomposed into a propelling gas by reaction with a catalyst.

A measure of the effectiveness of a propellant is given by specific impulse, which is the thrust per pound per second. It is given in units of seconds, and increases with increase in combustion-chamber temperature and pressure. Propellants producing low molecular exhaust gases have the highest specific impulse.

Two main methods are used to get the propellants into the combustion chamber. The simplest way often used in small rockets, is to use a pressurized inert gas such as helium or nitrogen. In large rockets a turbopump is used, however, which consists of a turbine that drives centrifugal impellers in the propellant-supply lines. The turbine is spun by gas produced in the gas generator, sometimes from the decomposition of hydrogen peroxide and sometimes from the reaction of the main propellants.

The propellants enter the combustion chamber through one or more injectors with many orifices and mix thoroughly in a fine spray. When the rocket is first started up, the propellants must with certain exceptions be ignited. Thereafter they will burn continuously, being set alight by the heat and already burning fuel as they enter the combustion chamber. Hypergolic propellants such as dimethyl hydrazine and fuming nitric acid are an exception in that they ignite spontaneously when they mix. In fact they are sometimes used as a source of ignition

for other propellant combinations. Other rockets utilize electrical high-energy (high-current) or pyrotechnic ignition.

Cooling. The burning propellants create a temperature often exceeding 3,000°C, and the combustion chamber must therefore be suitably designed to withstand this. One common way of doing this is by regenerative cooling. The walls of the chamber and nozzle are constructed with a double skin, and cold fuel from the storage tank is circulated through them before it enters the injector. This has a dual purpose of preheating the fuel as well as cooling the chamber walls. By regenerative cooling the temperature of the walls can be kept down to about 600°C and conventional high-temperature alloys can be used for construction. The five RP1 and six J2 engines of the *Saturn V* rocket, made by Rocketdyne, were all

Saturn V heads for the moon with Apollo 16. This immensely powerful rocket is 363 ft. (111 m) high overall with a first-stage thrust of 7,600,000 lb. (3,450,000 kg) produced by five engines. Second-stage thrust, also produced by five engines, is up to 1,160,000 lb (526,000 kg). One engine top stage develops up to 230,000 lb. (104,000 kg). Total lift-off weight is 2,850 tons.

regeneratively cooled. Their combustion chambers and nozzles were made of high-strength stainless-steel tubes stacked on top of one another, contoured and brazed.

The Rocketdyne RS18 engines used for the Apollo lunar landing module used a combination of ablative and film cooling. In ablative cooling the inner walls of the chamber and nozzle are coated with a material similar to that used for a re-entry vehicle's heat shield: cooling is

achieved by the coating melting and then boiling. In film cooling one of the propellants enters the combustion chamber through orifices in the walls which are lined with a refractory ceramic material such as zirconium oxide.

Control and stability. The combustion chamber in most rockets is mounted on gimbals so that it can be moved several degrees about two axes at right angles. This is often done by means of rams actuated by pressure from the gas generator. The purpose of gimbaling the chamber is to provide flight trajectory control by directing the rocket exhaust jets in different directions. Control may also be effected by deflecting the jet stream by means of vanes or by jets of high-pressure gas. Various methods are used for stabilizing rocket flight. Simple rockets traveling through the air have tail fins, which act in the same way as in the flight of a dart. Others are spin-stabilized, the rocket being fitted with a series of nozzles so that the exhausting jets impart a spin to the body. Stabilization is also often aided by means of gas jets around the outside of the rocket casing.

Types of motor. Liquid-propellant rockets are very much more powerful than solid-propellant types and have greater flexibility of operation. They can be shut off and re-started by opening and closing appropriate valves. Solid-propellant rockets lack this re-start capability, though hybrid motors, containing solid and liquid propellants, do have it. Solid-propellant rockets have the advantage that they are simple and can be stored, ready for use, for long periods. This is naturally a great advantage for military missiles. Most liquid-propellant rockets require filling with propellants just before takeoff. Handling liquid rocket fuels is also more difficult, and can be dangerous, for they may be toxic, highly flammable, corrosive, or cryogenic (at very low temperature, e.g. liquid oxygen, −183°C).

Other types of rocket motor are under active development including the nuclear rocket and ion rocket (see ION ENGINE). In the nuclear rocket, propulsion is provided by a stream of hydrogen gas accelerated to high speed by heating in a nuclear reactor. One designed in the United States by Aerojet, called NERVA (nuclear engine for rocket vehicle application), has already been successfully fired. (See also PHOTON ENGINE.)

Actual rocket launch vehicles are made up of two or more rocket stages on top of one another, this being the principle of the STEP ROCKET. This permits a higher overall power-to-weight ratio than is possible with a single rocket.

Rockoon

A contraction of *rocket* and *balloon*, it is a ROCKET that is lifted to high altitude by BALLOON before it is fired. In this way the effects of atmospheric DRAG are minimized.

Roebling

Family of American civil engineers, pioneers of the modern suspension bridge.

John Augustus Roebling (1806-1869) was born at Mühlhausen, Prussia, and came to America in 1831. He set up the first American wire rope factory and applied his talents to the design of suspension bridges. He constructed several suspended aqueducts, and built suspension bridges at Pittsburgh, Niagara Falls, and Cincinnati. They were longer and stronger than any suspension bridges that had gone before, a feat made possible by Roebling's pioneering use of steel wire-cable. In 1869 he began work on New York's BROOKLYN BRIDGE across the East River, but died as a result of an accident while surveying the site.

Washington Augustus Roebling (1837-1926), son of John Augustus, succeeded his father as chief engineer of the Brooklyn Bridge, which he completed in 1883. During the work he contracted caisson disease, which left him a permanent invalid, and he supervised construction of the bridge from his sickbed.

Rolling stock

Rolling stock is the collective name for all the running equipment of a railroad company: that is, locomotives, freight cars, and passenger cars. The term is also applied to the trucks, trailers, and so on, of a trucking company.

Rolls-Royce

Important British manufacturer best known for its aircraft engines and quality automobiles, but which also produces marine and rocket engines, industrial gas turbines, railroad and nuclear propulsion equipment.

The company was founded in 1906 by Henry Royce, an outstanding engineer and designer, and C.S. Rolls, a pioneer motorist and aviator. The success of the firm's first automobile, the celebrated Silver Ghost, and of later models up to the present day, has been based on advanced design, painstaking care and superb engineering. The Silver Ghost set new standards of quality, reliability, and performance, and the Rolls-Royce continues to maintain its reputation as "the best car in the world."

Aircraft-engine production began during World War I with the Falcon, which powered the famous Bristol F.2B fighter. In World War II the Merlin, a landmark in quality and reliability, powered more allied aircraft than any other engine, including the Spitfire, Hurricane, Mosquito, Mustang, and Lancaster. After the war the company became a world leader in jet propulsion. Today the Rolls-Royce RB 211 turbofan is fitted to the Lockheed Tristar airbus; the unique vectored-thrust Pegasus powers the VTOL Harrier; and the Conway powers the VC 10 airliner. Other Rolls-Royce engines include the Tyne and Dart propjets, and the Olympus, used in the supersonic airliner CONCORDE.

Roman roads

By the peak of the Roman Empire the network of Roman roads extended to all parts of the empire, included 29 military highways radiating from Rome itself, and covered a total of nearly 53,000 mi. (85,295 km). The roads were built as straight as possible, even if this involved crossing mountains, marshes, or other natural obstacles, and they were constructed to last, with deep, solid foundations. A typical Roman road was about 21 ft. (6.4 m) wide, although some major highways were over 80 ft. (24 m) wide including the grass shoulders provided for horsemen. The ground was excavated to firm subsoil, on which a bed of well-rammed sand was made. There followed a layer of large stones or rubble, sometimes set in mortar, and two layers of concrete known as the *rudus* and the *nucleus*. The top surface (the *summa crusta*) consisted of fitted polygonal flagstones. The complete pavement was from 3 to 6 ft. (1 to 1.8 m) thick.

A classic Rolls-Royce automobile, a symbol of luxury and quality since the firm's foundation in 1906.

Although severely fractured by a heavy metal object, this laminated glass windshield has remained in place, has stopped the object's flight, and retains a reasonably clear view ahead for the driver, making it in all respects superior to simple toughened glass.

Rotary engine

Steam and gas turbine engines produce rotary power directly, but the term rotary engine is normally reserved for internal combustion engines in which reciprocating pistons are replaced by a rotor which turns the drive shaft. There is thus no need for CONNECTING RODS or CRANKSHAFT, and rotary engines turn more smoothly than reciprocating types, are smaller, simpler, and have very few moving parts.

The most highly developed rotary engine is the WANKEL ENGINE, which has a triangular lobed rotor turning eccentrically in a broad figure-of-eight chamber. The rotor's three apexes are in continuous contact with the casing, thus forming three rotating combustion chambers. The engine works on the FOUR-STROKE CYCLE, each stage in the cycle taking place in a different section of the casing. Three power "strokes" take place for each revolution of the rotor, compared to the one power stroke for every four strokes of a piston. The main drawbacks of the Wankel are high fuel consumption, and the difficulty of making an efficient seal between rotor apexes and casing.

Another interesting rotary design is the British Tri-Dyne engine, which has three interacting rotors: a large power rotor, a small combustion rotor, and a barrier valve. The power rotor turns in the opposite direction from the others. It has three lobes, and the smaller rotors have three curved cavities which match the lobes. The relative rotation of the combustion and power rotors provide induction, compression and exhaust stages in a four-stroke cycle. The cavities of the combustion rotor form successive combustion chambers as it rotates. Although more complex than the Wankel, the Tri-Dyne has the advantage of avoiding the rotor-to-casing seal problem.

Rotor arm

The rotor arm is a component fitted to the top end of the DISTRIBUTOR shaft. It carries a brass contact plate which is in permanent contact with a spring-loaded brush connecting with the high-voltage lead from the COIL. As the rotor arm turns, the tip of the contact passes close to SPARK-PLUG lead contacts set in the distributor head. The rotor arm thus leads the high voltage current from the coil to each spark plug in turn.

Rotor ship

The rotors of a rotor ship were huge funnel-like metal towers some 50 ft. (15 m) tall and 12 ft. (3.6 m) in diameter, which were revolved at about 100 rpm by a small engine. A wind meeting the spinning rotors was deflected and rarified on one side, thereby causing suction ahead of the rotors and high pressure behind them, the two forces combining to move the ship forwards. Invented by the German engineer Anton Flettner in the 1920s, the idea worked, but it was not practical as it depended on the presence of a good wind.

Roundabout

See TRAFFIC CIRCLE.

Rowboat

Small boat built to be propelled by oars (see BOATS).

Rudder

Flat hinged control surface at the stern of a ship or aircraft, used for steering. When the rudder is turned to the left, the stream of air or water meeting it pushes the stern of the craft to the right, thus causing a left turn. The rudder is very small in relation to the craft, and much of its effect depends on speed; once a turn has been initiated by the rudder, momentum and aerodynamic or hydrodynamic forces will continue it. On a large ship moving at slow speed the rudder has little effect, and is often supplemented by "bow thrusters" (see SHIPS). To make a smooth banked turn in an aircraft, rudder and AILERONS must both be used.

Runways

See AIRPORTS.

S

Safege system

The Safege system is a French MONORAIL design in which the car is suspended from a four-wheel electric powered truck which runs inside an overhead box girder. The car supports pass through a slot in the underside of the girder. The rubber-tired wheels run on each side of the slot, and horizontal wheel bearings on the sides of the girder steer the trucks. Speeds of over 60 mph (96 km/h) were achieved on the trial track in France, and several Safege monorails are now in operation on short routes in Japan.

Safety glass

Used for automobile and airplane WINDSHIELDS safety glass is strong and does not shatter into sharp splinters when it breaks. Both toughened plate glass and laminated glass are used. Laminated glass consists of a glass-and-vinyl sandwich, a thin vinyl sheet being bonded between two sheets of glass under heat and pressure; the thicker and the greater the number of layers, the stronger the result. If it does break, the splinters remain attached to the vinyl.

Toughened plate glass is made by rapidly chilling the sides of a hot glass sheet with cold air. This greatly strengthens the glass and makes it resistant to fairly heavy impacts. When toughened glass does shatter, it disintegrates into thousands of small rounded pieces which cannot cause bad cuts.

Laminated glass is both stronger and more flexible than ordinary toughened glass and is compulsory for American auto windshields. Airplane windshields, which have to be capable of withstanding, for example, the high-speed impact of birds, are made of a combination of several layers of toughened and laminated glass up to several inches thick.

An oceangoing sailboat with typical Marconi (Bermuda) mainsail and large Genoa jib.

Sailboat

Sailing yacht or dinghy used for pleasure and sport. Some sailboats, such as the scow, are designed for specific conditions, or even for a particular race. In the famous Bermuda Race, for example, the winds normally blow at right angles to the course, and the rigging, hull, and ballasting may be adapted for precisely those conditions. But most sailboats are designed for sport and racing in a wide variety of places. They range from small beginner craft like the 8-ft. (2.5 m) Optimist pram, through high-performance Olympic racers to 35-60-ft. (10.6-18.3 m) oceangoing sailboats which, as Sir Francis Chichester and others have shown, can be sailed singlehanded round the world, or (more normally) raced by larger crews in events such as the Admiral's Cup and the Bermuda Race. Two of the most popular small sailboats of today are the Star, a 22 ft. 8½ in. (7 m) KEEL boat; and, with over 15,000 examples around the world, the Snipe, a 15 ft. 6 in. (4.7 m) daggerboard sloop (a daggerboard is a type of CENTERBOARD).

Rig design. Most small sailboats have a mainsail and jib, to which a spinnaker may be added when sailing with the wind. Larger craft often have two-masted yawl or KETCH rigs. Many experts believe that a single-sail rig is the most efficient, except in very light wind conditions, and this arrangement is becoming more popular.

By far the most common type of mainsail is the triangular Marconi (or Bermudan) sail, and it is often accompanied by a Genoa (or masthead) jib which may overlap the mainsail by up to two thirds the length of the boom. This gives much more power than the conventional shorter and non-overlapping jib. Sails are commonly of artificial fiber with a highly polished surface.

With mainsail held tightly to the mast in a "sail track," rather than by hoops, and with a streamlined and in some cases rotating lightweight mast (normally hollow, and often of extruded aluminum), which acts with the mainsail as part of an overall airfoil shape, the modern aerodynamically efficient rig gives greatly increased power from smaller sail areas. And with less sail area, and shorter mast, less ballast is needed to keep the boat stable, permitting still greater speeds.

Multihulled boats and scows. A conventional sailboat is, with its mast and sails, very tall in relation to its beam, and for stability the hull must be counterbalanced with heavy ballast. Thus the sails have to move a great deal of dead weight. Multihulled boats have a very broad effective overall beam. They are therefore very stable and can carry more sail than a normal boat, need no ballast, and are very light. Their only problem is that if (as does happen occasionally) they capsize, they do not, unlike a properly designed and ballasted single-hulled boat, right themselves automatically (see CATAMARAN).

To a certain extent the scow makes use of the same principle, but its two hulls are connected by a flat bottom. The scow, strictly a racing sailboat for use only on well-sheltered waters, has an unusually broad beam, and a draft of only a few inches. Its shape has been described as an "elongated saucer." With two centerboards (called bilge- or lee-boards) and two rudders, it is designed to sail heeled over at an angle of about 20°. In this position the bilgeboard and rudder on one side (equivalent to one hull of a multihulled boat) are vertical in the water, while the other set is more or less in the air. Scows are very light, and like multihulled craft they skim (plane) along the surface at high speeds. They are especially popular in and around Wisconsin.

Materials. Since the early 1960s sailboats have increasingly been built of man-made materials, and particularly of fiberglass. This cuts the cost by nearly half as compared to traditional timber construction, is impervious and rotproof, and is significantly lighter and therefore faster. Both steel and aluminum are also used, as is ferrocement. However some designers have recently been returning to wood, and have achieved still greater strength and lightness (compared even to plastic) by using timber saturated in epoxy resins.

Iceboats. Many of the recent advances in sailboat design were pioneered in iceboats. Instead of allowing the wind simply to push them along (in which case it is impossible to exceed the wind speed), iceboats sail across the wind, to make use of both the actual wind and of that caused by their own motion. In this way they can travel up to five times as fast as the actual wind. Speeds of 140 mph

Large sailboats racing. The billowing spinnakers, held out by a boom on the opposite side from the mainsail, increase speed in a following wind.

(225 km/h) have been recorded, making iceboats the fastest means of non-mechanical transportation.

Today they are used only for sport, but in the Netherlands during the 18th and 19th centuries merchant seamen fitted skate-like runners to their flat-bottomed canal sailboats so that they could continue trading during the icebound winter months.

Sailing ships

For some 3,500 years sailing ships were the merchantmen of the world, but the period of sail-powered warships lasted only some 300 years (roughly from 1550 to 1850). A warship must above all be fast and maneuverable, and in these respects sailing ships lagged behind rowed vessels until the 16th century. For merchantmen, on the other hand, carrying capacity is all-important, and although sails produced less speed, and had often to follow indirect routes to catch the wind, they took up no cargo room. Sailing merchantmen continued in service long after the advent of steam. They

English and Spanish galleons of the 16th century. The basic design of large sailing ships altered little until the early 19th century.

needed no coaling stations, and with a supply of live chickens and pigs on board they could stay at sea for months on end on voyages of 10,000 mi. or more. Where speed was unimportant and cheapness

vital, as for example in the South American nitrates and guano trade, large windjammers continued to earn a living well into the 1930s.

Early history. The oldest extant illustrations of sailing ships are from Egypt, and date from about 4000 B.C. The craft had a square sail set on a bipod mast near the bow, a satisfactory arrangement for sailing with a following wind. Altering course would however have been difficult, since the forward position of the sail would always pull the bow into the wind.

By about 1500 B.C. Egyptian ships had a single central mast, in which position there would be no tendency to turn the bow. In addition there was a system of braces and sheets with which the sail could be held at an angle to the wind, and of brails for reducing sail area. Very few further improvements could be made to the square sail rig, and these ancient Egyptian ships could sail with the wind blowing from the side.

The main weakness of the Egyptian ships was in the construction of the hull, which had no frame and was made up of brick-like blocks of wood pegged together. However the Phoenicians and Greeks developed strong framed and planked Carvel-built hulls, and by the time of the Romans the sailing ship had reached a new level in size, seaworthiness and maneuverability (see CARVEL CONSTRUCTION). Roman grain ships of the 2nd century measured about 180 ft. (55 m) in length. The single mast carried one or two triangular topsails above the mainsail, while at the bow a sharply angled spar foreshadowed the later bowsprit, and carried a small

The Chinese junk is one of the most aerodynamically efficient of all traditional sailing ships, and yet its simple rig was never adopted in the west.

square sail known as the artemon. This added a little power, but its primary purpose was to steady the ship and make it easier to steer.

Development of the fore-and-aft rig.
This enables a ship to sail faster and much closer to the wind than is possible with square sails. There is evidence that in classical times some large vessels had fore-and-aft artemon sails, but more important was the lateen type of mainsail. Roughly right triangular in shape, with its long leading edge attached to a thin spar, the lateen sail may have been of Arab origin (see DHOW). The rig became popular in the Mediterranean around the 9th and 10th centuries, generally on small coastal vessels for which maneuverability and the ability to sail to windward were vital.

In the Far East the JUNK had advanced rectangular fore-and-aft lug sails. These were easy to handle, and made the vessel one of the most aerodynamically efficient sailing ships of all. Yet the rig was never adopted in the West, where the square sail retained its dominance throughout the sailing-ship era. Had the clippers of the 19th century and their successors been rigged like junks, they might have been even faster, and they would undoubtedly have required much smaller crews. The junk was also notable for its stern rudder. The lateral rudder or steering oar was not supplanted in northern Europe until around 1200, and survived in the Mediterranean until the 14th century.

From longship to carrack. The craft in which the Vikings sailed to America almost 1,000 years ago, and in which the Normans invaded England in 1066, were sturdy double-ended LONGSHIPS of CLINKER CONSTRUCTION, equipped with a single square sail, and oars. The Vikings developed a method of holding the square sail's leading edge taut when sailing to windward (using bowlines), the first significant improvement to the square rig as evolved by the ancient Egyptians.

In northern Europe fighting "castles" at bow and stern turned the longship into the vessel used by the Crusaders, and for trading the cog was developed. In the Mediterranean and Portugal the principal sailing ships of medieval times were the carrack and the caravel. The latter had two or three masts, with either lateen or square sails, or both. In its lateen-rigged form it was the vessel used by the Portuguese to open the trade routes round Africa to India.

On Columbus' famous voyage of discovery in 1492 one of his ships the *Niña*, was a lateen-rigged caravel (she was refitted en route with square sails to take better advantage of the following winds), while his flagship *Santa Maria* was a carrack. Deeper and broader than the caravel, the carrack had high overhanging castles at bow and stern, from two to four masts, and a bowsprit carrying an additional square sail. By the end of the 15th century the three-master was common, usually (as on *Santa Maria*) with square sails on fore and main masts, and lateen on the after mast (or masts).

The golden age. The 16th century saw the growth in size of the carrack, and the development from it of the slimmer but more lofty GALLEON. During the following two centuries ships grew longer and the number of sails was extended until by the 1820s square sails stood six high on each mast, with a collection of fore-and-aft sails at bow and stern (see FULL-RIGGED SHIP). Yet despite the massive increase in sail area top speeds did not exceed 10 knots. The fault lay not in the rig, but in the heavy round-bowed hulls. The lighter and more streamlined CLIPPERS of the 19th century regularly topped 20 knots.

Two barks (center and right) *and a full-rigged ship taking part in a recent "tall ships" race. Vessels like these continued in service as freighters well into the present century.*

The Clippers sacrificed everything for speed, and when competition from steam rendered their particular virtues obsolete, a new generation of sailing ships appeared, with fuller hulls (later of iron and then steel) and simplified rigs to reduce crew-size. These included huge square-rigged windjammers, and fore-and-aft rigged SCHOONERS. (See also BARK AND BARKENTINE; BRIG AND BRIGANTINE; CUTTER; FRIGATE; KETCH; SHIP O' THE LINE; SHIPS; SLOOP.)

This photograph emphasizes the streamlined lines and great wingspan of modern sailplanes.

Sailplane

Sailplanes, or gliders, are unpowered heavier-than-air planes. They are usually towed up into the air by a small powered airplane and released at an altitude of 2,000 to 3,000 ft. (610 to 915 m), but can also be launched like a kite by an automobile or a winch; more primitive methods include pushing or catapulting the glider off a hilltop, while modern powered sailplanes or "motor gliders" have an auxiliary engine for takeoff and for emergency use in the air. Once aloft, sailplanes can simply glide back to earth, or they can make use of rising currents of air for soaring, and by spiralling up such upcurrents or "thermals" they may ascend to heights of over 10,000 ft. (3,050 m) and remain airborne for many hours. Modern sailplanes have made flights of over 900 mi. (1,448 km), climbed to over 40,000 ft. (12,192 m), and reached speeds of 145 mph (233 km/h). Although flown mainly for sport, sailplanes have been employed as troop carriers, and are used in meteorological and aeronautical research.

Any plane can glide, but a normal powered craft will descend rapidly as it is relatively heavy and its wings are designed to provide high LIFT only at fairly high airspeeds. A sailplane designer seeks to achieve maximum lift with minimum weight and DRAG. Long, narrow wings are used, sometimes with an aspect (length to width) ratio as high as 20:1 to produce the greatest efficiency with minimum induced drag, and any taper is usually straight rather than curved to simplify construction. For maximum performance the wing's AIRFOIL shape is a thin laminar flow cross-section (see AERODYNAMICS; WING), and as such is very sensitive to any surface irregularities; even dust and raindrops need to be removed before flight. Construction materials include plywood, aluminum, fiberglass, and fabric, for minimum weight. With high aerodynamic efficiency and low weight, a sailplane descends at a

very shallow angle, and performance is a measure of this angle expressed as the ratio between distance traveled horizontally and loss of altitude. Thus a medium performance sailplane with a glide ratio of 25:1 sinks 1 ft. (0.3 m) for every 25 ft. (7.5 m) of forward travel, and has a "sink speed" of 2½ ft. (0.8 m) per second. The glide ratio on a high-performance sailplane may exceed 40:1

Controls and instruments. Cockpit controls comprise a column for the elevator and ailerons, pedals for the rudder, and a hand operated spoiler lever. This raises hinged wing panels to reduce lift (see AIR BRAKES) and is mainly used to increase diving angle during a landing approach. It is also sometimes needed to reduce excessive speed in a dive, or to control excessive lift in a particularly strong upcurrent.

Long, narrow ailerons are usual, while elevators may be attached to a fixed tailplane in the normal way or an "all flying" tail may be used. Some sailplanes have V or T shaped tails (the latter design increases the effect of the fin), but a conventional inverted T is usual.

The instruments include ALTIMETER, airspeed indicator, COMPASS, turn-and-slip indicator, ARTIFICIAL HORIZON (see also AIRCRAFT INSTRUMENTS), and a variometer which responds to changes in pressure and indicates rate of climb or sink. In addition sailplanes designed for AEROBATICS may have an ACCELEROMETER as a precaution against excessive acceleration (which can damage the structure), while those designed for long distance and high altitude flights normally carry a two-way radio and oxygen.

History. Gliders were the earliest successful man-carrying heavier-than-air flying machines. The first to fly (1853) was built by Sir George CAYLEY, and this was followed during the 1890s by the hang gliders of Otto LILIENTHAL (Germany), Percy Pilcher (Britain), and Octave

CHANUTE (United States). Their experience and successes encouraged and assisted the work of the WRIGHT BROTHERS, and in recent years has led to the popular sport of hang gliding.

Hang gliders are controlled by body movements, and the early types were not designed for soaring. The first soaring flight was achieved in a Weiss glider in England (1909), but most pioneering work in sailplane design and the use of air currents took place in Germany in the 1920s and 1930s, during which period the variometer was evolved, sailplanes were equipped with instruments for cloud flying, and more robust construction enabled the craft to withstand turbulence. After World War II synthetic waterproof adhesives became available, together with the results of wartime research on airfoils, and during the 1950s low-drag wing designs developed by NACA came into use, as did fiberglass construction. A further reduction in drag was achieved in 1960 by adopting a reclining position for the pilot, and this was followed by the development of metal construction, retractable undercarriages, and various other refinements.

Saimaa Canal

An important waterway linking Lake Saimaa, Finland's largest lake, with the Gulf of Finland. The Saimaa Canal is 36 mi. (58 km) long, and was completed in 1856. The lake is almost 250 ft. (76 m) above sea level, and the canal was originally built with 28 locks. These were replaced by eight large locks during modernization in the 1960s.

Saint Gotthard Tunnel

Swiss railroad tunnel under the Alps, below the St. Gotthard Pass. It runs for 9.3 mi. (15 km) from Göschenen to Airolo, rising to 3,786 ft. (1,154 m) with the help of a spiral layout. It was completed in 1882 as the final link in the route between Lucerne, Switzerland, and Milan, Italy.

Saint Lawrence Seaway

One of the greatest engineering feats of modern times, the seaway enables ocean-going ships to sail to the Great Lakes, and has brought industrial expansion to the densely populated hinterland of North America. Strictly speaking the seaway is the 182 mi. (291 km) stretch between Montreal and Lake Ontario, and the main part of the operation was to make this section navigable; but the name St. Lawrence Seaway is generally applied to the entire system from the sea to the head of the Great Lakes 602 ft. (273 m) above sea level, comprising a total of 9,500 mi. (15,300 km) of navigable waterways with an overall length of 2,342 mi. (3,769 km).

The entire project, which was jointly financed by Canada and the United States, involved the construction of larger and deeper locks and canals between Montreal and Lake Ontario, the clearing of shoals from the Thousand Islands section, the deepening of the Welland Canal, the construction of two canals and five locks around the Soulanges and Lachine Rapids, the deepening of channels between the lakes and of several harbors, and the construction of a series of dams for hydroelectricity generation.

It has been estimated that in the first ten years the seaway saved about $500 million in transportation costs (roughly $1 for every ton transported). The main cargoes are iron ore traveling from Quebec and Labrador to United States steel mills, grain from the interior for

A massive floating salvage crane preparing to lift a sunken ship off a sandbank.

export across the world, and coal. Bulk cargoes account for more than 80% of traffic, although general cargo ships from over 30 countries use the seaway, which is also a major route for exports such as automobiles, meat, and steel products from the Great Lakes cities.

With a minimum depth of 27 ft. (8 m), and with locks able to take ships up to 730 ft. (221 m) long and 75.5 ft. (23 m) wide, the seaway when opened could take the majority of freighters. However by today's standards vessels able to navigate the seaway are comparatively small (with a capacity of about 27,000 tons).

Various schemes are now underway to keep the Great Lakes open around the year, including the use of icebreakers.

Saloon

See SEDAN.

Salvage

The rescue of a ship in peril at sea, and the process of raising ships, or their cargoes, or other objects from the seabed. Despite all modern navigational aids and safety precautions, accidents at sea are still common. In an average month some 15 vessels sink, and around 500 suffer serious damage.

If a ship is in trouble, but in no immediate danger of sinking, special ocean-going salvage tugs are sent to the scene. They carry divers, underwater cutting and welding equipment, powerful fire-fighting pumps, winches, towing apparatus, etc. They patch the ship up when necessary and tow it back to port. If the ship is aground, or stranded on rocks, the salvage tugs usually attempt to tow it clear. If one end is hopelessly stuck or damaged, the salvors may literally cut the vessel in half, and tow the salvageable part to a shipyard where a new end can be built on.

Various methods are used to raise a sunken ship, but first the site, and the vessel, will be examined by divers, or from a submersible. Sometimes it is possible to seal all openings in the hull and pump it full of compressed air, thus refloating it. Where tidal rise and fall is adequate, cables can be passed under the ship and attached, at low tide, to lifting pontoons. As the tide rises, the sunken ship rises clear of the bottom, and the pontoons are towed to shallower water where the process is repeated. Alternatively, the pontoons

Push-button control of locks speeds the passage of ships through the St. Lawrence Seaway, which enables oceangoing vessels to reach Great Lakes ports such as Duluth and Chicago.

may be filled with water and sunk, one on each side of the vessel. Cables passed under the ship are attached to the pontoons, and as the water is pumped out of the pontoons they refloat, bringing the wreck with them.

If the ship is very deeply submerged, or very badly damaged, operations may be limited to the salvage of valuable cargo by divers.

Sampan

Name given by people of the western world to small boats of Far Eastern waters. Many are propelled by a single oar at the stern, but larger sampans have sails (on one or two masts) or an engine.

San Francisco-Oakland Bay Bridge

One of the world's great bridges, linking San Francisco with Oakland across San Francisco Bay. Completed in 1936 it is a total of 8.25 mi. (13.2 km) long, consisting of 10 twin-decked suspension and cantilever spans, plus a tunnel through Yerba Buena Island. Between San Francisco and Yerba Buena Island are two end-to-end suspended spans 2,310 ft. (704 m) long. The central anchorage between the spans was driven 265 ft. (80 m) down to bedrock.

Santos-Dumont, Alberto (1873-1932)

Brazilian-born aviation pioneer who lived most of his life in France. He built in all some 16 small, nonrigid AIRSHIPS, winning a prize in 1901 for a return flight from Saint-Cloud to the Eiffel Tower. He turned his interests to airplanes after the Wright Brothers' pioneer flights in 1903, and on November 12, 1906, made what is generally considered the first powered flight in Europe. Two years later he pioneered the world's first light monoplane, the Demoiselle.

Sault Ste Marie Canals

This is an alternative name for the SOO CANALS between Lake Huron and Lake Superior.

Savannah

The name of two famous United States ships. The earlier, a three-masted full-rigged ship, became in 1819 the first vessel with a steam engine to cross the Atlantic. However, the engine was no more than a 90-hp auxiliary, and it was used for only 85 hours during the 27-day crossing. In the following year it was removed. The first ship to cross the Atlantic under sustained steam power, in 1838, was the Sirius.

The second Savannah, launched in 1959, was the world's first nuclear-powered cargo ship. Built as an experiment to demonstrate the value of nuclear power for merchant shipping, she was 595.5 ft. (181.5 m) long, carried 9,400 tons of cargo and 60 passengers, cruised at 21 knots, and could stay at sea for 300,000 mi. (480,000 km).

The Savannah, like the West German and Japanese nuclear merchantmen that followed, was a technical success but operated at a loss and was retired.

Schlieren photography

Schlieren photography is a system of spark photography used in WIND TUNNELS to photograph shock waves set up by models of aircraft that are under test. It involves recording the deflection of a beam of light as it passes through areas of changing density or pressure. The principle was first studied by Jean Foucault (1819-68).

Schooner

Fore-and-aft rigged sailing ship with two or more masts. The topsail schooner carries a square topsail on the mainmast in addition to the usual gaff mainsail. Fast and maneuverable, and (compared to the full-rigged ship) easy to handle, the schooner was first used by the Dutch in the 17th century. It was developed in the famous late-18th-century Baltimore clippers (strictly "clipper schooners;" their rig bears no resemblance to that of the true CLIPPERS).

Schwarz, David (1845-1897)

Hungarian-born dirigible pioneer. Although engaged in the lumber business and not an engineer, he designed an advanced airship with a conical aluminum nose and a sheet alloy nacelle. He died in Vienna after suffering a stroke, but his wife arranged for construction of his project to be completed. It crashed after taking off from Templehof on November 3, 1897, piloted by Jaegels Platz.

Invented in the Netherlands in the late 17th century, the schooner was the first fast and maneuverable sailing ship of the western world. The photograph shows a modern three-master.

An assortment of sampans in Singapore harbor. The term covers a wide variety of boats.

Scooter, motor

Type of motorcycle which appeared briefly after World War I (and in one version was literally a scooter, with no seat), and was developed in the years following World War II in Italy by such famous firms as Vespa and Lambretta. Designed for comfort, and ease of driving, rather than for speed and sport, the motor scooter has a hand operated gear change and a small enclosed engine normally in the 90 to 150 cc range giving top speeds of around 50 mph (80 km/h).

The rider sits inside the frame protected from the weather by a combined foot-board and front apron, and often a wind-shield. The small-diameter broad-tired wheels produce a low center of gravity and a smooth ride. They are easily removed since they are bolted on like automobile wheels.

The scooter reached a peak of popularity in the 1950s, but numbers declined as greater affluence enabled more people to buy small automobiles.

Screw propeller

A screw propeller is the most common means of propulsion on boats and ships.

Seaplane

Seaplanes are airplanes designed to land on and take off from water. A "float sea-plane" is essentially a normal plane with its landing wheels replaced by floats, while a FLYING BOAT has a boat-like hull. Seaplanes normally have two large floats, although some have a single float on the fuselage and small stabilizers on the wings. Needing neither expensive runway nor complex UNDERCARRIAGE gear, seaplanes are useful in remote or under-developed areas with extensive lakes or rivers, but the unretractable floats create considerable aerodynamic DRAG.

Sea routes

Trading routes followed by merchant shipping. In the earliest days ships simply kept the coastline in sight. Later, as sea-men learned to find their way across the oceans (see NAVIGATION), trading routes were developed around the world, although it was not until the mid-19th century that the routes were systematically studied and listed, notably in the pioneer-ing Pilot Charts of Lieutenant Matthew Fontaine Maury of the U.S. Navy. Throughout the era of sail, the routes and the timing of voyages depended very much on the prevailing winds. The patterns of these winds were charted during the great voyages of discovery of the 15th and 16th centuries and since the square-rigged ships sailed best with a following wind, the captains chose their routes accordingly. Even the Chinese with their

Widely used in Europe during the 17th and 18th centuries, and also popular in New York City and Philadelphia, sedan chairs occupied much less road space than horsedrawn coaches and thus helped to reduce traffic congestion. The two engravings show models of the 16th and 18th centuries.

fore-and-aft rigged junks timed their voy-ages to run before the monsoons. However, with the appearance of the steamship in the 19th century, winds and currents became of much less signifi-cance, and shipping began and has con-tinued to follow GREAT CIRCLE ROUTES. Re-presenting the shortest possible distance between two places, these are adhered to except when avoiding ice, bad weather, or — of course — land. A network of major routes soon developed, and has al-tered little in the last 100 years, although many new routes have been added by the oil tanker trade. These include several radiating from the Persian Gulf and the Middle East (to Europe, Japan, and North America), and from the Caribbean (to North Africa and Europe).

On particularly busy sea routes such as the North Atlantic crossing, clearly de-fined lanes have been internationally ad-opted, with separation of east- and west-bound shipping; while where the lanes themselves are crowded and crossed by other routes (as for example in the Straits of Dover between England and France), marking buoys and a traffic control sys-tem are employed.

The busiest sea routes of today are those across the North Atlantic and Indian oceans and down the east coast of South America. A high proportion of them come to a focus at the PANAMA and SUEZ CANALS, both of which shorten many voyages dramatically.

Seat belt

A seat belt is a passenger safety harness worn by passengers in aircraft, and fit-ted to the front and sometimes to the rear seats of automobiles, to prevent the wearer from being catapulted forward by intertia during an impact.

Statistics show that the risk of serious injury in an automobile is at least halved if a seat belt is worn. In many countries new automobiles must be fitted with seat belts by law, although the drivers are not compelled to wear them. However, many cars are now being fitted with devices that require the seat belts to be engaged before the engine ignition will function. The commonest type of seat belt has a lap and diagonal shoulder restraint. The fixed type has three anchorages to the car chas-sis or strong body members, (two on the floor and one higher up for the diagonal shoulder strap). The straps are fastened by a quick-release mechanism. Once fast-ened, the fixed type does not permit the wearer to move forward more than a frac-tion. The inertia-reel type allows much greater freedom in normal circumstances, only locking in the event of a sudden move-ment. The pendulum type has the same advantage. When the vehicle is traveling at a steady speed, the pendulum stays in a neutral position, and the wearer of the belt can move freely. But any sudden change in speed or direction deflects the pendulum and thus locks the seat belt in position.

Sedan

An enclosed automobile with seating for four or more people, and with either two or four doors. The first automobiles were all open, having at most a folding top for weather protection, and for many years the CONVERTIBLE was more popular than the sedan.

Sedan chair

A cabin carried on two poles by two men, containing one passenger. It was used in Europe from the 17th to the early 19th centuries. Some chairs plied for hire; others were privately owned. The passenger entered through a door at the front; the roof also opened. The less common *sedan-cart*, or *roulette*, was mounted on wheels and drawn by one man.

Seikan Tunnel

Due for completion in 1979, the Seikan underwater tunnel will provide a link between the Japanese islands of Honshu and Hokkaido. It will be the world's longest railroad tunnel, running 33.6 mi. (54 km) under the Tsugaru Strait, at a depth of 460 ft. (140 m) below the seabed and will link Tappi Saki, in Honshu, and Fukushima in Hokkaido. The underwater section, bored through solid rock, is 14.5 mi. (23.3 km) long, making it the longest underwater tunnel in the world. The tunnel will be equipped with twin rail tracks capable of taking high-speed "bullet trains" similar to those on the NEW TOKAIDO LINE. These will take 8 minutes to travel between the islands, compared to the 4½ hours taken by the present ferries.

Selfridge, Thomas Etholen (died 1908)

The first person to be killed in an airplane crash. Selfridge, a lieutenant in the U.S. Army Signal Corps, was a passenger with Orville Wright near Washington, D.C., when a propeller blade broke, severing a control wire, and causing the plane to crash on September 17, 1908.

Servo-assistance

Servo-assistance involves the use of a device to magnify a feeble effort applied to operate a mechanism. Its commonest application is in automobile and truck braking systems, especially those using DISK BRAKES, which require greater effort than DRUM BRAKES. A servo-brake (power brake) unit may operate from the vacuum in the engine inlet manifold or from a separate vacuum pump. In a simple engine-vacuum unit the vacuum is normally connected to each side of a large booster piston. Atmospheric air can be admitted by a diaphragm-operated air valve to one side of the booster piston, causing it to move and apply increased pressure to the hydraulic braking system. The air valve is forced open by fluid entering the unit from the brake master cylinder when the driver depresses the brake pedal.

The servo-unit is not an "all-on" or "all-off" system. The air valve closes when the desired braking effect is achieved. The degree of servo-assistance is proportional to the pressure applied to the brake pedal. When the brake pedal is released, the air valve closes and engine vacuum is reconnected to the "atmospheric" side of the booster piston, which is returned by spring to its original position. This releases the pressure of the hydraulic fluid in the braking system and releases the brakes.

Servomechanism

Automatic control system in which feedback of information is used to correct error. Sensing elements continuously or intermittently monitor actual performance of a task, and feed that information to a controller, which compares the actual performance with the desired performance. If there is any error, the controller acts via a servomotor to correct it. The AUTOMATIC PILOT is an example of servomechanism. The controls are set to give a certain course, altitude and speed. Any differences are automatically signaled to servomotors which correct rudder, elevators or throttle as necessary.

In such a system provision is made to amplify the signals so that they are strong enough to activate the motor. This gives rise to the term SERVO-ASSISTANCE, meaning the use of a device to amplify a low effort, as in servo-assisted (power) braking.

Severn Bridge

A SUSPENSION BRIDGE across the River Severn estuary in southwest England. Completed in 1966, this 3,250 ft. (990 m) span bridge is of extremely economical design. The bridge deck is made up of hollow torsion box sections streamlined aerodynamically. The suspension towers, 395 ft. (120 m) high, weigh a mere 4½ million lb. (2 million kg) compared with the 60 million lb. (27 million kg) towers of the VERRAZANO-NARROWS BRIDGE.

Sextant

Optical precision instrument used in NAVIGATION at sea for measuring the angle above the horizon (the altitude) of stars and planets. In conjunction with an accurate CHRONOMETER and a NAUTICAL ALMANAC, the sextant is used to determine latitude and longitude, and thus to "fix" the ship's position.

The word sextant means "one sixth of a circle," and the instrument consists of a fixed arc of a circle and a moving index arm, a telescopic eyepiece, and a system of mirrors. The navigator sights the horizon through the eyepiece and moves the index arm (which rotates a mirror) until the image of the sun or other celestial body (reflected in the mirror) appears to sit on the horizon. The position of the index arm on the calibrated fixed arc shows the sun's angle above the horizon. The advantages of the sextant over earlier aids for measuring altitude (such as the ASTROLABE) are its accuracy and the fact that movements of the ship do not affect the reading.

Shenandoah

The first rigid AIRSHIP to be filled with nonflammable helium instead of the customary and often disastrous hydrogen. Some 680 ft. (207 m) long, she was commissioned by the U.S. Navy in 1923, and took part in naval exercises for two years until she broke up in the air during a storm. Fourteen people died, but 27 rode safely to the ground on broken-off sections of the airship.

Ship o' the Line

Large warship in the days of sail which entered battle "in line." They included so-called first-, second-, and third-rate ships. The technique of deploying men of war in a long line was developed in the late 1600s.

The U.S. Navy airship Shenandoah. *Commissioned in 1923, it was the first to be filled with helium instead of the then usual and highly dangerous hydrogen.*

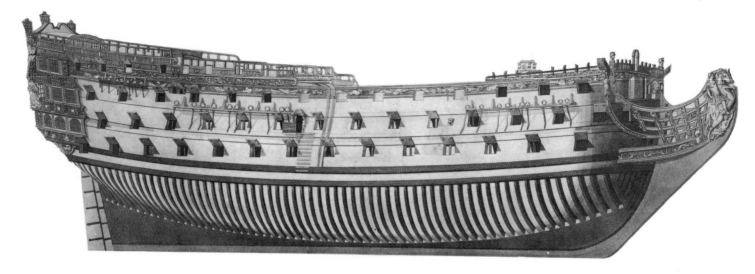

A contemporary etching of The Royal George, *showing the construction of a late 18th Century British warship.*

Ships

The first vessels which could reasonably be called ships rather than BOATS were probably those built in Egypt about 1500 B.C. Fitted with a single square sail and with oars to overcome the limitations of rig and weather, they voyaged down the Red Sea and some distance along Africa's eastern coast. The hulls of these early vessels were constructed of brick-like blocks of wood which were simply pegged together. Although the timbers were very thick, the hull had little strength because it lacked a structural frame. It was in fact held in shape by thick ropes. These were passed lengthwise round the hull, and crosswise at each end, to stop the hull collapsing outwards. An additional rope was fixed at bow and stern and stretched tightly over forked supports on deck. Known as the truss, it helped to prevent the ship from bending in the middle when riding over a wave.

This curious method of construction was dictated by the available materials (acacia trees). Even earlier the Minoan Civilization of Crete had already evolved the system which was to make possible the building of larger, faster, and more seaworthy ships — the framed and planked hull. The basic method of ship construction until the 19th century, it used a strong skeleton built up on the main structural timber, the keel. To this were attached stem and stern posts and ribs, and the whole covered with longitudinal planks which may overlap (CLINKER CONSTRUCTION) or meet edge to edge (CARVEL CONSTRUCTION). Heavy timbers fixed wise along the sides were added by the Minoans to help the hull survive its normal naval role of a battering ram. These "longitudinals" (or whales) were retained on merchant ships for added longitudinal strength.

Round ships and long ships. The Phoenicians, the merchantmen of the ancient Mediterranean, are reputed to have sailed around Africa in about 600 B.C. and they undoubtedly made regular voyages to Spain and Britain. They developed two distinct types of ship: the long ship or war GALLEY, sleek, fast, and propelled by oarsmen with an auxiliary sail; and the tubby trading round ship, slow but capacious, powered by sail with auxiliary oars. Their warships were later developed into the 150 ft (45 m) long BIREMES and quinquiremes of ancient Greece, while their round ships reached maturity in the sturdy grain ships of ancient Rome. With a length-to-beam ratio of about 3:1 compared to the galley's 8:1, they could carry some 300 passengers and 250 tons of cargo. Over the following centuries the bireme developed into the huge galleys and galleases of the last great sea fight between rowed ships, the Battle of Lepanto in 1571 (see WARSHIPS), and from the round grain ship evolved the fore-and-aft rigged CARAVEL (see SAILING SHIPS).

The East and the North. Meanwhile very different types of ships had been developed in China, and in northern Europe. The Chinese progressed from the dugout canoe to a square raft made by joining two dugouts with planking, and thence by building up wall-like sides on the raft, to the junk. With the addition of a wedge-shaped bow, internal walls (bulkheads) to subdivide and strengthen the hull, a high stern, very efficient fore-and-aft sails, and a revolutionary stern rudder, the junk became the world's largest, strongest, and most efficient ship, and held that position throughout the 15th to 18th centuries.

In the north, the Vikings produced their famous LONGSHIPS in which they sailed to America. Considerably broader than the Mediterranean galley, with high pointed bow and stern and the stronger if less streamlined Clinker construction, they were well adapted to the rough northern seas. The longships were among the earliest vessels to have concave hull lines at bow and stern, a design that improves stability, speed and resistance to sideways drift, but reduces carrying capacity. With fighting platforms ("castles") at bow and stern, and with, for the first time in western waters, the more efficient stern rudder replacing the steering oar, the longship evolved into the larger craft of the Crusader armies, and into the broader and deeper hulled trading cog.

Golden age of sail. Probably in the 13th century the northern square-rigged cog sailed to the Mediterranean and met the southern fore-and-aft rigged caravel. During the next 100 years the two designs were merged in the carrack, the direct ancestor of the GALLEON, the SHIP O' THE LINE and the EAST INDIAMAN (see also FULL-RIGGED SHIP). No significant advances occurred except in detail until the appearance of the SCHOONER, and the CLIPPER, whose underwater hull shape remains today a common design for fast ships. With concave V-section at the bow (to cut through the water) gradually broadening to a U amidships (for maximum capacity), and narrowing again at the stern (for minimum drag), it is a much enlarged and more streamlined descendant of the Viking longship.

Steamships. The first steamboat to succeed in moving against the current was the French *Pyroscaphe* of 1783, and during the following years several other pioneers constructed working if impractical steam powered craft. In 1801 William Symington devised an efficient way to convert the reciprocating steam engine's up-and-down motion into a rotary one on his CHARLOTTE DUNDAS. And with the commercial successes of Robert Fulton's CLERMONT (1807) in America and of Henry Bell's *Comet* in Britain, the steam era had begun. However, more than 50 years would pass before ship designers and seamen trusted the new invention sufficiently to abandon sail altogether. The *Sirius*, the first ship to cross the Atlantic under sustained steam power (1838), could set a large area of sail, and still in the 1890s many steamers carried auxiliary sails.

The first steamships were all wooden (although many had copper-clad bottoms), and were propelled by paddles, until the appearance in 1843 of Brunel's GREAT BRITAIN. The "forefather of all modern ships," she was the first all metal ocean-going ship, and the first large vessel with screw propulsion.

Riveted steel plates replaced iron in the late-19th century (and have since been superseded by welded hulls); the turbine ousted the reciprocating steam engine early in the present century, and was soon followed by the marine diesel engine; and ships have become ever larger, faster, more efficient and more specialized (See BULK CARRIERS; FREIGHTERS; LINERS; SUBMARINES; TANKERS; WARSHIPS, etc.)

Stability and strength. Apart from the primary requirement of BUOYANCY, a ship must be able to pitch and roll in the waves without capsizing. That is, it must be stable. A vessel's center of gravity remains (with a given cargo) always at the same point. But when the vessel heels to one side its center of buoyancy (the center of gravity of the part underwater) moves out towards that side. A ship must be designed so that when it heels the upward force of buoyancy and the downward force of gravity combine to right it. If the center of gravity is too high, the forces will combine to turn the ship over. As a ship rides across the crest of a wave, bow and stern tend to droop. When bow and stern are on separate crests, the middle tends to sag. A ship may pitch up over one wave and slam down into the next. STABILIZERS are normally fitted to control roll, but pitching, heaving, and yawing cannot be damped out, and the most the ship designer can do is to test models in wave tanks to check their performance in heavy seas.

A Spanish carrack of the 15th century. The predecessor of the galleon, the carrack combined features of the caravelle and the cog.

A Roman grain ship of the second century. Steering by a stern rudder did not appear in the west until a thousand years later.

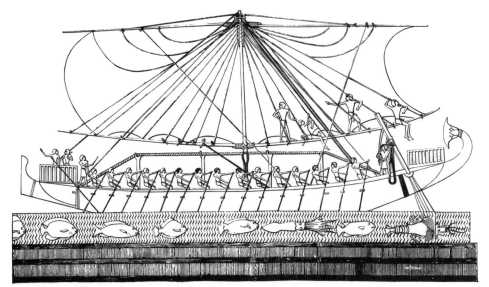

An Egyptian ship of around 1500 BC. Binding ropes can be seen at bow and stern, as can the longitudinal truss which helped prevent the vessel bending in the middle.

The hull is essentially a very large and complex steel girder, specially reinforced to withstand the enormous stresses imposed on it by heavy seas. The interior of the hull is subdivided by bulkheads into a number of watertight compartments to make the ship reasonably unsinkable in the event of being holed. The degree of subdivision for different types and sizes of ships, and especially (since the sinking of the TITANIC) for passenger ships, is specified in maritime safety regulations, as indeed are most aspects of ship design and construction.

The exterior lines of the hull are designed (and tested in wave tanks) for minimum drag and wave-making, for maximum performance in rough seas, and for maneuverability. Raised decks may be built on the main structure of the ship, in which case they are part of the superstructure. Alternatively they may be constructed as part of the hull, and

New ship designs are tested in wave tanks to check their performance, and their behavior in a wide variety of wave sizes and patterns.

several engines to be coupled to the same propeller, thus simplifying engine repairs at sea, and saving time when maneuvering: the propeller can be quickly changed from a forward running to a reversed engine.

The paddle wheel is only used on calm water excursion steamers (see PADDLE STEAMER). Occasional experiments have been made with water-jet and airscrew propulsion, especially for use in shallow water. One of the most successful modern inventions in ship propulsion is the Kort Nozzle unit, in which the propeller is encircled by a short open-ended cylinder. The system increases the propeller's effectiveness by about 25%.

Modern trends and ideas. Welded steel is the normal material for ship construction, although aluminum alloys are now often used for superstructures, and for the hulls of high-speed ships. An interesting modern invention is the ram or bulbous bow. This takes the form of a bulb-shaped extension at the bow under the waterline to reduce drag.

Experiments have recently been made with fully automated remote-controlled ships, and on all large vessels automation, remote control, and complex monitoring equipment are employed to increase efficiency and safety and to cut running costs by reducing the size of the crew. Once at sea an automatic pilot holds the vessel on course. Automatic monitoring systems measure the performance of the engines, the temperature in the holds, and many other aspects of "ship condition," all of which are displayed on consoles in a central control room.

Increasing use is made of computers in ship design and construction, while in ship operation computers are important aids in data logging, alarm scanning, machinery control, weather routing, prediction of fuel consumption, and similar functions.

are called islands. Thus the so-called "three island" ship has raised decks at bow, stern, and amidships (forecastle, poop, and bridge). Many ships have only one or two islands, while the flush-decked ship has none.

Maneuverability. A large ship is one of the least maneuverable of all forms of transportation, with an enormous turning circle and stopping distance. Slowing is achieved by reversing (or altering the pitch of) the propellers, while steering relies on the RUDDER. A ship designed for maximum maneuverability is unlikely to be easy to hold on a steady course, and design is normally a compromise between the two virtues. To improve maneuverability at slow speeds, when the rudder has little effect, many large ships are fitted with a bowthruster. This employs a variable pitch propeller to thrust water out through a transverse tunnel in the bow, thus swinging the bow. On some smaller ships, especially fishing vessels and tugs,

the propeller is fitted in a vaned cylinder. Altering the angle of the vanes alters the direction of thrust, giving much better steering control than with a rudder.

Marine engines and propulsion. The vast majority of ships today are powered by DIESEL ENGINES and propelled by screw PROPELLERS, although less complex and costly STEAM TURBINES are still normally fitted to very large ships. Many warships are powered by GAS TURBINES, which occupy much less space than other systems, or have NUCLEAR PROPULSION, which gives virtually unlimited range. Occasionally diesel- or turbine-electric systems are used, as are combined diesel and gas turbine, or steam and gas turbine.

Whatever type of engine is used, it is normally coupled to the propeller through reduction gears. This allows the engine to run at an efficient high speed and the propeller to turn at its most effective speed of around 100 rpm. It also enables

Shipworm
The name of a group of marine bivalve borers which attack wood. Also called teredos, they are found in most seas and do considerable damage to wooden hulls, piles, and wharves. The commonest shipworm is *Teredos navalis*. During the 18th century the hulls of many wooden ships were clad with copper to prevent teredo attack and bottom fouling by barnacles.

Shipwreck
Despite modern navigational equipment and safety regulations, shipwrecks are still far from uncommon. An average of about 15 ships sink each

H.M.S. Shannon, *showing the transitional period between sail and steam in the 19th Century.*

month, and between 1963 and 1973, 64 vessels simply disappeared. Most were presumably overwhelmed in heavy seas so suddenly that there was no time to radio for help. A new Global Rescue Alerting Network (GRAN) is under development, employing satellites and an onboard device which automatically transmits an identification signal in the event of a disaster. Already the United States Automatic Merchant Vessel Reporting (AMVER) system keeps track of vessels with the help of computers.

Apart from heavy seas, the most common causes of total shipwrecks are fires and explosions on board, and grounding in fog, while the usual causes of "partial losses" (in which the vessel is not a complete wreck) are machinery damage and collisions.

Shock absorber

Part of a vehicle's SUSPENSION SYSTEM, designed to reduce or damp down the oscillations of the springs. A typical telescopic hydraulic shock absorber contains a piston moving up and down in a cylinder containing oil. The piston is attached to the upper part of the vehicle body, the cylinder to the wheel-carrying axle. When the wheel hits a bump, the cylinder moves upward, and the piston moves slowly down as oil is forced through a valve in it. When the wheel regains its former position, another valve in the piston opens allowing oil to flow back again relatively slowly. The resistance of the oil to flowing through the narrow valves in the pistons effectively eliminates much of the resonance in the springs.

Shockwave

See SUPERSONIC FLIGHT.

Signaling in transport

Signals are necessary in transport to control the movements of vehicles. In most instances the signal is directed at the person in charge of the vehicle, who is relied upon to take appropriate action; in the case of rapid mass transportation devices may be employed to enforce the message automatically.

Railroads. When the first railroad opened in 1825 it was single track and if two trains met the one that was nearest

a passing place had to back into it to permit the other to pass. The first double track railroad in Britain was between Manchester and Liverpool and a private police force patrolled each station to note when trains passed and to prevent others from proceeding until a certain time had elapsed. They used colored flags at first, but their task was made simpler by the use of trackside signals consisting of bars or disks controlled from a nearby position. With all levers controlling signals and points located at one place, the next step was to provide interlocking to prevent signals from being cleared unless the points were correctly set and no conflicting signals were cleared. These early time interval systems made no allowance for a train breaking down between stations. With the invention of the telegraph in 1840 a message could be sent between stations to say when a train had cleared the section and only then could trains be authorized to enter. With this development the railroads were safe even at high speeds, but there was always the possibility of men operating the equipment incorrectly or of engineers misreading the signals. Developments since that date have mainly consisted of checks or interlocks to avoid the results of human error. In many cases a loophole in the safety system has only become evident as a result of an accident. Further developments in signaling have permitted a more intensive service, still with perfect safety. But the operation of mechanical signals and points needs considerable effort and several men are required at a large installation. The application of electrical and electronic devices has considerably eased the signal-

The oil tanker Texaco Caribbean, *which sank in 1971 after colliding with a freighter. Despite all precautions and electronic aids, shipwrecks are still far from uncommon.*

On busy lines the traditional signalling system is usually replaced by colored light signals operated from a centralized traffic control center.

based on time, allowing one stream of traffic for a fixed time and then the other. This time will be arranged to be greater for the route likely to carry the most traffic. In a large city the traffic flows may change for different peak hours and the timing of certain phases may be altered for different times of the day.

To achieve more satisfactory control a device is required to detect the presence of vehicles. This may take the form of pressure pads in the road, or more recently, buried coils which detect the metallic mass of the vehicle. Thus a signal may be held at green if other vehicles are approaching. Alternatively, the major route may be kept at "clear" until a car is detected on the side road. Detectors can also sense a line of traffic and the cycle may be altered to clear it.

On roads with several successive sets of traffic lights, each set is linked to permit a group of cars to travel the section without meeting a set of red lights. This is possible by calculation of timings for the lights, taking account of the movements in both directions.

The control of traffic lights lends itself to a computer application. In city areas the computer can monitor street equipment to ensure its correct functioning, it may select a plan to optimize the cycle time at each intersection and it can send instructions to the street equipment to achieve this.

Latest developments provide facilities for clearing routes for fire engines or other high-priority vehicles. An infrared source on the vehicle giving a coded output is detected by roadside equipment which clears the route for it.

These automatic techniques have been applied successfully to signaling for land transport; for signaling to airplanes and ships see AIR TRAFFIC CONTROL; AVIONICS; COMMUNICATIONS IN TRANSPORT; NAVIGATION.

Signs, highway

The purpose of highway signs is (1) to advise drivers of their whereabouts, guide them to their destination, indicate highway facilities and guide them into lanes; (2) to warn drivers of actual or potential hazards; and (3) to announce mandatory or prohibitory regulations governing speed, direction of travel, and limitations on highway use.

Signs must be simple so that the information they convey can be readily assimilated by a driver, and they must also be easy to pick out despite the presence of other vehicles, trees, bushes and hedges, street furniture and shop awnings, or sunlight, or any curvature of the road. Some form of illumination for signs is

man's task and permitted control of large areas from one point.

On modern installations mechanical signals have been replaced by color light types operated by relay circuits. The relay is a device energized by an electric current and capable of switching several circuits. Relays are used to indicate switch positions and the location of trains, which in conjunction with contacts made by the signalman energize a final relay to give the signal a clear indication. Thus the electric circuitry supplements or in some cases also replaces the mechanical interlocking of early systems. One fundamental requirement of any piece of signaling equipment is that it will "fail safe," that is, if anything goes wrong with the device it must automatically give a "danger" signal.

To enforce the signals given to an engineman several types of Automatic Train Control (ATC) have been applied. In 1907

the Great Western Railway of Britain started using a system that sounds an alarm in the cab when a caution signal is approached. If the alarm is not acknowledged then the brakes are applied. On some systems an arm beside all stop signals is raised when that signal is at danger, if a train attempts to pass the signal the arm will strike a second arm on the train and apply the emergency brake. On the newer lines this is taken a stage further with coded information passed to the train from the running track to permit it to run automatically.

Highways. On the road fixed signs give information to the driver about hazards ahead or directions to destinations. Apart from the electronically controlled lane signs on highways, it is at intersections that instructions are given to stop or proceed in the familiar form of traffic lights. The cycle may simply be necessary at night, and this must be distinct from any competing lighting in urban areas. Floodlights may be employed, or (in rural districts) a reflective surface.

Conspicuous shapes are used, enhanced by color: triangles, hexagons and circles usually indicate mandatory or warning signs; the rectangular format is normally reserved for direction signs. Capital letters seem to have greater emphasis for STOP or GIVE WAY signs, but small ("lower case") letters are probably better for direction signs. The highway surface itself is used to point out parking prohibitions, lanes, passing restrictions, and the need to slow down or stop. Where possible, highway signs are now being internationally standardized, and most use symbols instead of wording.

Signs on a multilane highway give clear indications of a wide variety of routes.

Sikorsky, Igor (1889-1972)

Russian-born aircraft designer. Sikorsky constructed two unsuccessful HELICOPTERS in 1909-10, before turning his attention to a series of single-engined AIRPLANES. Then, with financial assistance from the Russian Baltic Company he built the first successful four-engined plane, *Le Grand* (1913), and its development, the Ilia Mourometz series, which equipped a Russian squadron during World War I. After the Russian Revolution, Sikorsky worked in Paris and then, in 1919, moved to the United States, where he established the Sikorsky Aero-Engineering Corporation in 1923 and soon turned his attention to FLYING BOATS. His company rented part of a factory on Long Island in 1927 and eventually moved to Bridgeport, Conn., in 1929. His S.38 twin-engined amphibian of 1928 was used by the U.S. Army and Navy and also by Pan American Airways. The S-40 was a four-engined flying boat supplied to Pan American, which christened the aircraft

the "American Clipper" (Pan Am's large airliners were all subsequently known as clippers). The S-42 flying boat of 1934 was designed for trans-ocean travel and in Pan American service pioneered the Pacific air routes and participated in the first commercial North Atlantic services. Igor Sikorsky renewed his interest in helicopters during the late 1930s, producing several pioneering models including the VS-300 of 1939, and the R-4 (1944), the first helicopter to be extensively used by the armed forces. Subsequently the company produced the successful S-51, S-55, and S-58 designs.

Simplon Tunnels

Longest railroad tunnels under the Alps, running from Brig, in Switzerland, to Iselle, in Italy. Work on the first began in 1898 and was completed in 1906. The tunnel is 12 mi. 537 yd. (19.36 km) long. The second tunnel was begun in 1918 and completed in 1922. It is 22 yd. (20 m) longer than the first tunnel, and ranks as the world's longest rail tunnel.

Simulator

To reduce the heavy costs in flying aircraft for training, as well as to prepare pilots for actual flight, ground rigs are used to simulate the experience of flying. Simulators date back to World War I, when they were used for aerial gunnery training. In World War II, flying training often included periods in Link ground trainers. In these the pilot could experience changes of attitude as he manipulated controls and a course plot was traced on an instructor's desk.

Modern flight simulators may have a complete flight deck made from the nose section of an actual aircraft for the trainee, while instructors have a separate console with duplicated controls. The

whole may need a hangar-sized building. The pilot under training can experience, through multi-axis motion systems, movement from slight bumping through taxiing over "cats-eyes" on the runway, to aerobatics. Closed-circuit color television, scaled moving terrain complete with airfield lighting systems, windshield view giving apparent changes in weather conditions and appropriate associated noises — all these are designed to add realism. The instructors can induce situations and monitor pilot reactions, aided by computers monitoring instrument settings. A record is made on sound and video tape so that a "flight," or parts of it, can be analyzed and discussed at the de-briefing stage. When a pilot is fully conversant by simulator rating, he proceeds to actual flying.

Ski lift

Device for carrying or towing skiers up snow slopes at ski resorts. In the towing type the skier stands on his skis, in well-defined tracks, and either fastens a rope around his middle or sits on a metal support. The support may be a T-shaped bar held between the legs, or a larger T-bar with one skier on each arm. The rope or rod is then clipped to an endless rope which moves up the ski slope, and the skier is towed uphill. Chair lifts work on a similar principle, but actually lift the skier clear of the ground. On some high ski slopes cable-cars, known as téléferiques, are used. Ski lifts were developed in the 1920s and 1930s.

Sled

Vehicle using runners instead of wheels, also called a sledge or sleigh. The sled was one of the earliest vehicles known, and probably developed from the *travois*. Used by the American Indians, and still in use by primitive peoples in some underdeveloped countries, the travois consists of two poles with a net or crosspiece lashed between them. A harness enables the poles to be pulled by an animal such as a dog or a horse. The ends of the poles drag on the ground. Loads are slung between the poles.

A modern sled has two parallel runners extending the length of the vehicle, and turned up in a curve at the front so that they will glide more easily over the ground. The runners are generally faced with strips of iron or steel so that wear is minimized. Sleds can be used on ordinary ground, but today they are almost exclusively employed for traveling over snow and ice, and in the Arctic and Antarctic they were once the only practical means of transportation.

Motive power. This may be provided by horses, reindeer, or teams of dogs. The dogs mainly used are the Husky, which originated in Greenland, and the Alaskan Malamute. Husky-German Shepherd and Husky-Collie crosses are used for sled-racing in parts of Canada. There are a number of ways of hitching a dog-team to a sled: in one, a single trace runs between the lead dog and the sled, and the rest of the dogs are hitched to the trace on either side; in the second, the dogs run

are used exclusively for downhill races. A toboggan is a runnerless sled, made of wood or metal, with the front curved up like an ordinary sled. The original toboggans were used for transportation by American Indians, but today toboggans are used almost soley for sport. A luge toboggan has runners, and is a lightweight kind of sled also used for sport. It carries only one person.

A 19th century sloop with mainsail, jib, and one topsail.

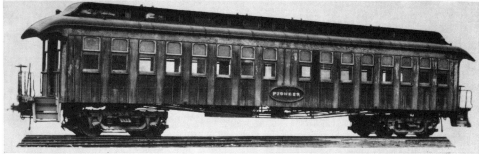

The upper photograph shows George Pullman's first sleeping car, remodeled from a day car, while the lower one shows his first purpose-built sleeping car, the Pioneer of 1864.

in line between two parallel traces; in the third, favored in eastern Greenland, the dogs are fan-hitched, each being connected to the sled with its own trace. Sometimes human power is used to pull a sled, and in favorable conditions sails have been used, notably by the Norwegian explorer Fridtjof Nansen when he made the first crossing of Greenland in 1888.

Kinds of sleds. Sleds vary from place to place, and also according to the use to which they are put. The troika is a Russian sleigh, light in construction, which is pulled by three horses. Troikas were used in many Soviet cities as well as in the country during the winter months. The Nome sledge, named for Cape Nome, Alaska, is an Alaskan type of sled; it is long and narrow, and very strong. The Nansen sled, named for Fridtjof Nansen, is wider than the Nome sledge, and is the kind favored by polar explorers.

The bobsled is a steerable sled with four runners, mounted in pairs. The front runners are attached to an axle, and can be turned either by ropes or by a steering wheel linked to them by steel cables. A brake shaped like a farm harrow is mounted between the rear runners. Bobsleds carry either two or four men, and

Sleeping car

Railroad car designed for overnight passenger travel. The first ran between Harrisburg and Chambersburg on the Cumberland Valley Railroad (later part of the Pennsylvania Railroad) in 1837 and was invented by that railroad's manager, Philip Berlin. Other early makeshift sleeping cars came into service elsewhere but a major advance came in 1856 when the Illinois Central brought its six "Gothic" stateroom cars, each nearly 50 ft. by 10 ft. (15 m by 3 m), into operation. The next improvement came in 1864, when George M. Pullman, after building some experimental cars by converting ordinary passenger coaches, built his first Pullman sleeping car. It had upper berths that folded down from the roof, and lower berths formed out of day seats. Sleeping cars of Pullman design spread rapidly to most parts of the world. A typical modern sleeping car has six double and 12 single bedrooms. The "slumbercoach," with 40 beds in smaller rooms, has also been devised to provide cheaper accommodation.

Slipstream

The airflow generated by an aircraft's power unit(s) is known as a slipstream. In jets, the hot exhaust gases are necessarily discharged clear of the airframe

and aerodynamic effects are nil. Propellers, however, project air backwards, and in single-engined aircraft a rotating column of fast-moving air is pushed back down the fuselage. This slipstream is more pronounced on one side than the other (due to the direction of the propeller's rotation) and causes yaw, particularly when the throttle is opened.

Sloop

A single-masted fore-and-aft rigged sailing vessel with mainsail and jib, and sometimes carrying one or more topsails. Originally the sloop was a small three-masted full-rigged warship with about 20 guns, one class smaller than the CORVETTE. Today the sloop is virtually indistinguishable from the CUTTER.

Snowmobile

Small motorized vehicle for transport on snow, with one or two skis at the front, and propulsion by tracks at the rear. Snowmobiles are popular for recreation, racing machines reaching over 100 mph (160 km/h), and are also used in rescue, police, and maintenance work. Snowmobiles are used for herding reindeer and for general purposes in the far north, where they have largely superseded the dog-drawn sled.

Soil mechanics

Soil mechanics is the study of the composition and properties of soils, important in the building of roads. Soil mechanics is to a large extent an empirical science. It is particularly concerned with the bearing strength of soils, which is affected by particle size, the presence of air and water and the percentage of organic matter. In general a good base for road construction is provided by soil consisting of particles of different sizes in even proportions. This is a well-graded soil which can be consolidated or compacted into a good load-bearing surface. Poorly graded soils on the other hand have uneven distribution of particle sizes, cannot readily be compacted, and remain weak. Where this kind of soil is encountered, it must be stabilized with additional soil, cement, lime or bitumen.

Solar cell

Solar cells convert the energy of sunlight into electricity, and are widely used to supply power on satellites and deep-space probes. They have also been used experimentally to power automobiles. The electricity generated may be stored in conventional storage batteries. The most common type consists of a wafer-thin sheet of silicon. When photons (particles of light energy) fall on it they release electrons, and thus produce an electric current. Thousands of such cells are needed to generate an appreciable voltage. The solar arrays in the Skylab space station comprised 238,000 cells and were capable of generating some 16,000 watts.

At this time solar cells are neither powerful nor cheap enough for general use, but research at establishments such as the Delaware Institute of Energy Conversion suggests that future types may be able to generate electricity at a competitive price.

Solenoid

A solenoid is a coil of wire which acts as a magnet when a direct current is passed through it. It forms the heart of relay devices in which a small current in one circuit triggers a large current in another circuit. The most familiar use of a solenoid is to close the STARTER-MOTOR circuit in an automobile engine. Turning the ignition switch allows current to flow in the solenoid, which thus becomes a magnet and attracts a soft iron plunger which completes the circuit between starter motor and battery. This arrangement isolates the ignition switch from the very heavy current used by the starter motor.

Soo Canals

Artificial waterways providing a navigable link between Lakes Huron and Superior, also known as the Sault Sainte Marie Canals. The two parallel canals bypass the rapids of the St. Marys River, the natural link between the lakes, which forms the Michigan-Ontario boundary and has a 19 ft. (5.8 m) drop over a short distance. The American Canal is 1.6 mi.

(2.6 km) long. It consists of two channels, each with two locks. The American North Canal is 280 ft. (85 m) wide and 23 ft. (7 m) deep; the South Canal is 304 ft. (93 m) wide and 23.5 ft. (7 m) deep. The canals were built between 1881 and 1919. The Canadian Canal is 1.3 mi. (2 km) long, 150 ft. (46 m) wide and 25 ft. (8 m) deep, has one lock, and was completed in 1895.

The array of solar cells projecting from this space probe generate electricity from the sun to power the craft's electrical systems.

Sonar

A method of detecting the presence and distance of underwater objects by ultrasonic echoes. The term is a contraction of the name Sound Navigation and Ranging. Developed during the two world wars for submarine detection, sonar is similar in principle to RADAR but employs sound instead of radio waves. In its earliest form it was used simply to detect depth (see ECHO SOUNDER), but modern side-scanning sonar systems can, for example, produce "pictures" of the seabed almost as graphic as photographs of land features taken from the air.

The sonar transducer, normally carried in a towed "fish" to minimize interference from ship-generated noise, radiates ultrasonic beams to both sides, at right angles to the ship's course, and thus scans two broad strips of seabed at once. The actual beam is very narrow, and it scans rapidly back and forth to give a detailed picture that may be displayed on a screen, or be automatically recorded on a paper strip.

The higher the frequency of the sound the greater the detail, but the lower the range. The greatest ranges so far achieved are in the region of 6 mi. (10 km).

Sonar is invaluable in mapping the seabed, and in surveying the site or route of proposed underwater projects (harbor works, pipelines, etc.). Many fishing vessels are now equipped with horizontal-scanning sonar for locating shoals of fish (at distances of up to about 1,100 yd., or 1 km), and with conventional sonar for determining the exact depth of nets. An interesting experimental possibility for a sonar-type device is as a guide for blind people.

Military applications include sonar-guided homing torpedoes, mine detection, and submarine hunting. Extra high-powered systems are used, with special equipment to overcome sonar's main limitation, interference from background noise (from water movement, from fish, and from other ships). Sonar can also be used simply as a listening device, to detect other vessels' presence by their noise.

Sonic bang
See SUPERSONIC FLIGHT.

Sound barrier
See SUPERSONIC FLIGHT.

Southern Pacific Railroad

Now part of the Southern Pacific Transportation Company, the Southern Pacific Railroad operates some 13,700 mi. (22,048 km) of railroad extending from California to ports on the Gulf of Mexico, with several branches. It has over 2,300 diesel locomotives and 90,000 freight cars.

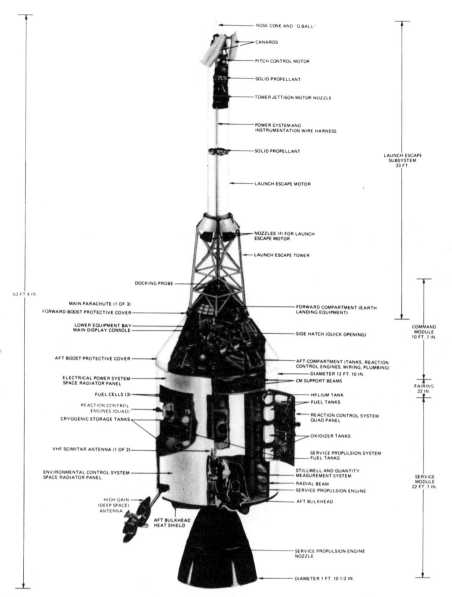

NOSE CONE AND "Q BALL"

CANARDS

PITCH CONTROL MOTOR

SOLID PROPELLANT

TOWER JETTISON MOTOR NOZZLE

POWER SYSTEM AND INSTRUMENTATION WIRE HARNESS

SOLID PROPELLANT

LAUNCH ESCAPE MOTOR

LAUNCH ESCAPE SUBSYSTEM 33 FT.

NOZZLES (4) FOR LAUNCH ESCAPE MOTOR

LAUNCH ESCAPE TOWER

DOCKING PROBE

63 FT 4 IN

MAIN PARACHUTE (1 OF 3)

FORWARD BOOST PROTECTIVE COVER

LOWER EQUIPMENT BAY MAIN DISPLAY CONSOLE

AFT BOOST PROTECTIVE COVER

ELECTRICAL POWER SYSTEM SPACE RADIATOR PANEL

FUEL CELLS (3)

REACTION CONTROL ENGINES (QUAD)

CRYOGENIC STORAGE TANKS

VHF SCIMITAR ANTENNA (1 OF 2)

ENVIRONMENTAL CONTROL SYSTEM SPACE RADIATOR PANEL

HIGH GAIN (DEEP SPACE) ANTENNA

AFT BULKHEAD HEAT SHIELD

FORWARD COMPARTMENT (EARTH LANDING EQUIPMENT)

SIDE HATCH (QUICK OPENING)

COMMAND MODULE 10 FT. 7 IN.

AFT COMPARTMENT (TANKS, REACTION CONTROL ENGINES, WIRING, PLUMBING)

DIAMETER 12 FT. 10 IN.

CM SUPPORT BEAMS

FAIRING 22 IN.

HELIUM TANK

FUEL TANKS

REACTION CONTROL SYSTEM QUAD PANEL

OXIDIZER TANKS

SERVICE PROPULSION SYSTEM FUEL TANKS

STILLWELL AND QUANTITY MEASUREMENT SYSTEM

RADIAL BEAM

SERVICE PROPULSION ENGINE

AFT BULKHEAD

SERVICE MODULE 22 FT. 7 IN.

SERVICE PROPULSION ENGINE NOZZLE

DIAMETER 7 FT. 10 1/2 IN.

Apollo spacecraft command and service modules with the launch escape system still attached.

Space flight

In 1865 French novelist Jules Verne published *From the Earth to the Moon* and launched a new genre in literature, science fiction. In it he propelled his heroes to the Moon by an enormous cannon at a speed of 7 miles (11 km) a second, from a launching point located in southern Florida. Just over a century later, in July 1969, a Saturn V rocket was launched from nearly the same spot thrusting *Apollo 11* astronauts to nearly 7 mi. (11 km) a second on their way to the Moon.

The Saturn V was the most powerful rocket ever constructed, the brainchild of Wernher von Braun, who directed the team in Germany which carried out the most important pioneering research on rocketry in the late 1930s (see ROCKET).

The Apollo mission, the first of six, was the culmination of 12 years of space flight, which began with the launching of the Russian satellites *Sputnik 1* (October 4) and *2* (November 3) in 1957. *Sputnik 2*,

weighing more than half a ton, carried the first space traveler, a dog called Laika. The United States launched its first satellite, *Explorer 1*, in the following January. *Explorer 1* was puny compared with the *Sputniks*, weighing a mere 23 lb. (10 kg), but it had highly sophisticated instrumentation and made the first major discovery of space travel, namely the Van Allen radiation belts. Three years later (on April 7, 1961) cosmonaut Yuri Gagarin in *Vostok 1* pioneered the next phase of space exploration by becoming the first man to orbit the earth. John H. Glenn in *Friendship 7* became the first American in orbit a few months later (February 20, 1962).

Since then many astronauts and cosmonauts have journeyed in space and 12 Americans have explored the moon on foot. Hundreds of satellites have been launched around the earth; they have helped global communications and weather forecasting and greatly extended scientific understanding of our planet and of the universe as a whole. In

addition, deep-space probes have been sent to the moon and other planets. Some are now on their way into interstellar space.

Earth satellites. Basic satellite theory is naturally connected with gravity, and Isaac Newton, who first advanced the law of gravity, was familiar with the theory. The reason why a satellite (or indeed the Moon) does not fall from the sky is because of its speed. Imagine that a body is launched parallel with the Earth from a high tower. At low speeds, it will arc downwards as gravity attracts it. But the faster it travels initially, the farther it will go before succumbing to Earth's gravity. At a certain very high speed it will curve downwards at the same rate as the Earth itself is curving. In other words it will remain the same distance above the ground, in orbit. The speed at which this happens depends on altitude, and is known as the orbital velocity. About 100 mi. (160 km) up, the orbital velocity is about 17,500 mph (28,000 km/h), and the period (the time it takes for the satellite to make one circuit of the Earth) is about 90 minutes. At 22,300 mi. up (35,900 km) the orbital velocity is only 6,900 mph (11,100 km/h) and the period is 24 hours.

In practice an altitude of 100 mi. (160 km) is rather too low for a satellite, for there is still sufficient air present to cause noticeable drag which will quite quickly slow the satellite down and cause it to succumb to gravity. If that happens, air friction in the thicker part of the atmosphere will burn it up like a shooting star, or meteor.

The 22,300-mi. orbit is interesting because its 24-hour period exactly matches that of the Earth. So a satellite launched in the direction of the Earth's rotation and positioned over the equator will appear from Earth to remain stationary in the sky. This so-called geostationary or synchronous orbit is often exploited in practice (see below).

Satellite orbits are elliptical in shape rather than circular, though most deviate only slightly from circular. The point in the orbit where the satellite comes closest to Earth (which is located at one focus of the ellipse) is called the perigee, and the farthest point the apogee.

Among the most important satellites are the communications satellites, which relay radio-telephone, telex, and television signals between ground stations. The present generation of Intelsat IV satellites are placed in geostationary orbits so that ground stations can "lock" their antennae permanently in position for transmitting and receiving. Intelsat IV satellites, which are some 17 ft. (5 m) high and 8 ft. (2.5 m) in diameter, are located above the Atlantic, Pacific and Indian oceans. Together they can provide almost complete global communication coverage. They are able to handle more than 7,000 voice channels simultaneously or 12 or more television programs. This capacity is only about half that of the next generation of satellites currently entering service, the Intelsat IVAs. Weather satellites also have proved invaluable, enabling meteorologists to

a body must have to escape from Earth's gravity: 25,000 mph, 40,000 km/h). As the spacecraft travels on its 240,000-mi. (385,000 km) journey, it is first slowed down by Earth's gravity and then accelerates as it reaches the vicinity of the Moon. By suitably adjusting its speed by retrorocket fire, the spacecraft can enter lunar orbit. By retro-firing again, it can descend from lunar orbit onto the surface, retro-firing all the time to slow it down for a soft landing. It cannot be

moving relative to every other body, the timing and the speed of launching of a probe are critical. Favorable launch windows occur periodically for each planet, when a probe can reach it with the minimum of trouble. A favorable launch window for Mars, for example, occurs about every two years.

All planets out to Jupiter have now been scanned by space probes, which have sent back television pictures from a few hundred to a few thousand miles out. *Mariner 10* (1974/5) showed Mercury to have a heavily cratered surface much like the Moon's, but failed to show any detail of Venus' cloud-obscured disk. Several Mariner probes have photographed Mars, showing a crater-strewn surface eroded by wind-driven sand. Most information came from the *Mariner 9*, which entered Martian orbit. Manned flights to Mars have been suggested but are not quite practical with existing technology. Even assuming great improvements in propulsion systems, such as nuclear rockets, the round trip would take nearly two years. Jupiter was scanned in two successive years (1973 and 1974) by *Pioneers 10* and *11*, which reached the planet after journeys of some 620 million mi. (1,000 million km). *Pioneer 10* is now on its way out of the solar system; *Pioneer 11* is heading for a rendezvous with Saturn in 1979.

Communications with a satellite do not pose any great problems, for the distances involved are not great. With deep-space probes on the other hand, the communications links are very tenuous. Deep-space tracking stations use huge (210-ft., 64 m) directional antennae to transmit signals to and receive them from probes. They need to be incredibly sensitive. The signals received from *Pioneer 10* near Jupiter had a power of only some 10^{-17} watt, and *Pioneer 10* was then so far away that the signals, although traveling at the speed of light (186,000 mi./sec, 300,000 km/sec), took three-quarters of an hour to arrive. Whereas practically all satellites and near-space probes are powered by solar cells, distant-space probes like *Pioneer 10* require radio-isotope thermoelectric generators (RTGs). Sunlight at such distances is not strong enough to power solar cells.

American astronauts leave their spacecraft at the end of a space flight. Final descent is slowed by parachutes. In the future many manned missions will takeoff and land in a reusable space shuttle.

keep a close eye on cloud cover and the general weather situation over the whole globe. Constantly circling low-level (ca. 600 mi., 960 km) satellites like the Nimbus series are being superseded by geostationary ones like SMS (synchronous meteorological satellite) and GOES (geosynchronous operational environmental satellite). The latter, for example, provides day and night pictures of nearly one-fourth of the Earth's surface, in visible and infrared light respectively. Similar to Nimbus in design is the Landsat Earth Resources Technology Satellite (ERTS) series designed to increase knowledge of Earth's resources and to collect environmental data from remote sensing platforms.

Reaching the Moon and planets. To propel a spacecraft to the Moon, it must be boosted from Earth orbit to a speed close to the Earth's escape velocity (the speed

slowed down aerodynamically of course because there is no air. (For the Apollo lunar landing techniques, see LUNAR ORBITAL RENDEZVOUS.)

To reach the planets a spacecraft must be boosted from orbit with a speed in excess of the escape velocity. To reach the inner planets Venus and Mercury a spacecraft must be launched against the directon the Earth is moving in its orbit. Then after escape it will end up traveling more slowly around the Sun than the Earth, and the Sun's gravity will cause it to move inward, toward the orbit of the inner planets.

To reach the outer planets (Mars, Jupiter, Saturn, and so on), a spacecraft is launched in the direction the Earth is traveling in its orbit so that after escape the spacecraft will be traveling faster than the Earth, and will therefore move out toward the orbiting outer planets. Because every body in the solar system is

Manned spacecraft
Manned spacecraft naturally have to be much bigger than ordinary satellites and probes to give the astronauts living space, to accommodate their life-support systems, and to provide the facility to get them back to Earth. The two major spacecraft designs have been the American Apollo and the Russian Soyuz. They are made up of a number of modules which

Spectacular spinnakers (foresails used to increase speed in a following wind) dominate this ▷
sailboat scene. The small craft in the foreground is rigged with a conventional Marconi mainsail
and a jib.

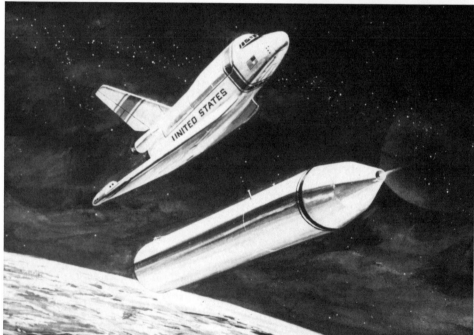

The upper illustration shows the space shuttle's solid rocket boosters falling away from the manned orbiter at an altitude of about 27 mi. (43 km) for recovery and reuse. In the lower illustration the empty propellant tank is jettisoned.

ide and odors, and controls humidity and temperature. For EVA (extra-vehicular acitivity) the astronauts don multi-layer spacesuits which may connect with the spacecraft's life-support system or with a portable system. The life-support systems are also concerned with such things as health and hygiene, waste disposal, sleeping facilities and the like.

These systems become more complicated during long-term missions such as Skylab, when three teams of astronauts visited an orbiting space station in 1973 and 1974 for periods of 28, 59 and 84 days respectively. The Skylab cluster was built around the second stage of a redundant Saturn rocket. It was fully equipped before launching and was the biggest piece of hardware ever manned in space, measuring in all 120 ft. (36 m) long and weighing nearly 200,000 lb. (91,000 kg). The experience obtained with Skylab proved conclusively that man is able to adapt to the unique weightless conditions of space with no permanent ill-effects (see AVIATION MEDICINE). (See also SPACE SHUTTLE.)

Space shuttle

A re-usable space launching vehicle being developed for use by NASA from 1980 on. Its use will permit great reductions in the cost of space launchings. At present the huge launch vehicle required to place a modest-sized satellite into orbit is wasted, since no part of it is recovered. With the shuttle, most of the hardware will be recovered and re-used. The space-shuttle program dates from design studies initiated by NASA early in 1970. Static testing of the main engines began in 1975, test flights in the atmosphere are scheduled for 1977, and orbital flights for 1979.

The shuttle consists of three main elements: a delta-winged orbiter, a large expendable propellant tank, and twin solid-propellant rocket boosters. On the launch pad the orbiter is mounted vertically on the expendable propellant tank, on each side of which are the solid boosters. The expendable tank stands about 184 ft. (56 m) tall, and is some 27 ft. (8 m) across. The orbiter itself is about 122 ft. (37 m) long and has a wingspan of 78 ft. (24 m).

At launch the twin solid boosters and the orbiter's three main engines fire simultaneously, producing a total thrust of more than 6,000,000 lb. (2,720,000 kg). The main engines will burn liquid hydrogen and liquid oxygen propellants. At an altitude of about 25 mi. (40 km) the solid boosters will be detached and parachuted back to Earth to be recovered and re-used. The orbiter continues feeding on propellants from the tank until just be-

each have different functions. In Apollo there were two main modules, the command (descent) module housing the crew, and a larger service (instrument) module, housing, for example, rocket motors, propellant tanks and fuel cells (for electricity and drinking water). The Soyuz craft is made up of an instrument module, and an orbital module.

Only the descent module returns to Earth. After retro-fire from the instrument module, the descent module separates and plunges Earthwards, re-entering the atmosphere. It is protected from the searing heat developed during aerodynamic braking in the atmosphere by the ablative

coating of a heat shield, which dissipates heat by melting and boiling. Lower down in the atmosphere parachutes open to slow it down further. Apollo astronauts always touched down at sea, but Russian practice is to touch down on land, using retro-rockets to achieve a soft, low-speed landing.

The vital life-support system of a manned spacecraft provides the astronauts with food, drink, and an environment in which they can live. It supplies oxygen or air under pressure, though not necessarily atmospheric pressure (Apollo's atmosphere was oxygen at 5 lb./sq. in.). It also has facilities for removing carbon diox-

A "tall ship" race. Vessels such as these carried cargos across the oceans well into the 20th century, and their reintroduction is under consideration (with simpler fore-and-aft schooner rig). In the distance, appearing under the full-rigged ship's bowsprit, is a bark.

An essential feature of ports and harbors, tugs like these are used to maneuver large vessels to their berths.

fore reaching orbit. Then the pilot switches to its internal propellant tanks, jettisons the external tank, and enters the required orbit. When its mission is over, the pilot fires the engines to provide retrobraking, and the orbiter descends from orbit, being braked aerodynamically as it re-enters the atmosphere. Because it has wings, it can be maneuvred in the air onto a suitable glide path and land on a runway like a conventional airplane. On return to earth the shuttle is refurbished as necessary and prepared for its next mission. One interesting feature of the orbiter design is the use of replaceable external insulation. Areas subject to high temperature (1,500°C+) on re-entry are insulated with silicon-carbide coated graphite or tiles of felted silica fibers. It is anticipated that an orbiter should be able to make at least 100 missions without a major overhaul.

The orbiter, which is designed for operation in a "shirt-sleeve" environment, normally carries a crew of three, but has the facility to accommodate four payload specialists who will not need detailed astronaut training.

Access to the payload bay, which measures some 60 ft. (18 m) long and 15 ft. (4.5 m) in diameter, is through an air lock. The maximum payload capacity for the orbiter will be about 65,000 lb. (30,000 kg) in a 170-mi. (280 km) high orbit. It is able to launch and retrieve smaller payloads up to 500 mi. (800 km) high. To reach satellites in higher orbits it may employ the services of a so-called space tug.

A typical use for the shuttle would be the placement in orbit of satellites. It will also be used to retrieve, repair, or revitalize satellites: many communications satellites, for example, have to be abandoned not because their electronics are faulty but because they have run out of maneuvering fuel to keep them in the required altitude and location.

Spark ignition

Spark ignition provides the means by which the fuel mixture in a gasoline engine is burned. The spark is provided by applying a very high voltage current to a spark plug so that the electricity jumps between the plug electrodes (see IGNITION SYSTEM).

Spark plug

The spark plug is a device that screws into the cylinder head of a gasoline engine, and has two electrodes across which a spark is made to discharge to ignite the fuel (see IGNITION SYSTEM). It consists essentially of two electrodes separated by a ceramic insulator. One electrode is grounded via the cylinder head; the other passes up through the plug body and is connected by a high tension lead to the DISTRIBUTOR. The correct gap between the electrodes is specified for every engine, and varies from 20 to 40 thousandths of an inch (0.508 to 1.016 mm). If the gap is too small the spark will not be strong enough, while if too large the current may be unable to discharge and the engine will misfire. Some plugs are intended to run hotter than others (the shape of the ceramic insulator affects the operating temperature). An excessively hot plug causes detonation and pre-ignition, while one which is too cool will carbonize rapidly.

Speed of sound

See SUPERSONIC FLIGHT.

Speedometer

A speedometer is a device that registers the speed of a vehicle by means of a needle moving over a circular scale or of a band moving along a horizontal scale. It is driven by a flexible cable which is usually turned by the gearbox output shaft. At the end of the cable is a permanent magnet located inside a drum. When the magnet rotates, the drum tends to turn with it, motion being partly resisted by a spiral spring. The faster the cable rotates, the further the drum turns, this being a measure of the vehicle's speed. The speedometer pointer is attached to the drum. In the band-type speedometer the drum is more elongated, and has a spiral line marked on it in such a way that the line moves back and forth over the horizontal scale as the drum turns.

The world's fastest conventional locomotive, this French CC-7107 electric unit hauled a three-car train at 205.6 mph (330.8 km/h) in 1955.

Speed records

A selection of progressive records is given for each mode of transport. Where no nationality is given, the vehicle is American. Starred entries are absolute speed record holders.

Railroad		mph	km/h
1829	Rocket (UK)	29.1	46.8
1839	Lucifer (UK)	56.75	91.3*
1890	Crampton (France)	89.48	144*
1893	Empire State Express	102.8	165.4*
1899	Burlington Route	130	209*
1903	Siemens and Halske (electric, Germany)	130.61	210.19*
1931	Kruckenberg (propeller-driven, Germany)	143	230.1
1953	SNCF No 7121 (electric, France)	150.9	242.9
1955	SNCF Nos 7109 and 9004 (electric, France)	205.6	330.9
1967	Aérotrain (tracked air-cushion, France)	233	375

A rocket-powered sled running on a test track reached 632 mph (1,017 km/h) in 1954 with a man on board, and more recently a similar but unmanned sled reached 3,090 mph (4,973 km/h).

Automobile		mph	km/h
1898	Jeantaud (electric, France)	39.24	63.17
1899	La Jamais Contente (electric, France)	65.79	105.92
1902	Serpollet (steam, France)	75.06	120.84
1904	Ford 999	91.37	147.10
1905	Napier (UK)	109.65	176.53
1914	Blitzen Benz (Germany)	124.10	199.72
1922	Sunbeam (UK)	133.75	226.50
1925	Sunbeam-Bluebird (UK)	150.76	242.63
1927	Sunbeam (UK)	203.79	327.97
1932	Napier-Campbell Bluebird (UK)	253.97	408.73
1935	Campbell-Special (UK)	301.12	484.62
1938	Railton (UK)	350.20	563.59
1947	Railton Mobile Special (UK)	394.19	634.40
1964	Proteus-Bluebird (UK)	403.01	648.58
	Spirit of America (jet)	526.28	846.97
1965	Green Monster (jet)	576.55	927.87
	Spirit of America-Sonic I (jet)	600.60	966.57
1970	The Blue Flame	622.40	1,001.67
	(rocket; during the run it briefly touched	650	1,046.50

The fastest speed ever reached by a diesel is 210 mph (337 km/h) in 1971, by the Corsair streamliner. The fastest by a motorcycle is 224.57 mph (361.41 km/h) in 1962, on a Triumph T-120. The greatest distance covered by a cyclist in a one-hour track race is 30 mi. 1,232 yd. (4,941 m), by the Belgian E. Merckx in 1972.

Boats			
1939	Bluebird (UK)	141.74	228.06
1950	Slo-Mo-Shun IV	160.32	257.96
1952	Slo-Mo-Shun IV	178.49	287.202
1955	Bluebird (UK)	202.32	325.53
1964	Bluebird (UK)	276.33	444.71
1967	Hustler	285.21	458.901

In 1967 Donald Malcolm Campbell was killed when Bluebird broke up at a speed of 328 mph (527.8 km/h).
The fastest inboard motor propeller craft is Mr. Ed I, which in 1971 reached 202.42 mph (325.76 km/h). The fastest with outboard motor is a Jones/Mercury which in 1960 reached 115.54 mph (185.94 km/h).

Aircraft			
Piston-engined			
1909	Wright Biplane	34.04	54.77
1910	Blériot Monoplane (France)	68.20	109.73
1913	Deperdussin Monoplane (France)	126.67	203.81
1922	Curtiss R-6	243.94	392.64*
1928	Macchi M-52 bis (Italy)	318.64	512.69*
1931	Supermarine S6B (UK)	407.02	654.90*
1939	Messerschmitt 209 V-1 (Germany)	469.22	754.97*
Jet-engined			
1946	Gloster Meteor F4 (UK)	615.78	990.79
1953	North American Sabre F-86D	715.75	1,151.64
1955	North American Super Sabre F-100C	822.27	1,323.03
1956	Fairey Delta 2 (UK)	1,132.01	1,821.39
1958	Lockheed Starfighter F 104A	1,404.09	2,259.18
1961	McDonnell Phantom 2, F4H-1F	1,606.51	2,585.43
1965	Lockheed YF-12A (a variant of this, the Lockheed SR-71, is currently the world's fastest jet, with a speed of around 2,200 mph, 3,540 km/h).	2,070.10	3,331.51
Rocket-powered			
1941	Messerschmitt 163V-1 (Germany)	623.85	1,004*
1947	Bell X-1	670	1,078*
1953	Douglas Skyrocket D-558-II	1,328	2,137.2*
1956	Bell X-2	2,094	3,369.9*
1960	North American X-15	2,196	3,543.1*
1967	North American X-15A-2	4,534	7,297

Space			
1961	Vostok 1 (USSR) earth orbit	17,560	28,260*
1966	Gemini XI earth orbit	17,943	28,876*
1968	Apollo VIII trans-lunar injection	24,226	38,988*
1969	Apollo X reentry	24,791	39,897*

Spirit of Saint Louis
Famous aircraft in which Charles LIND-BERGH made the first solo nonstop flight across the Atlantic, from New York to Paris in 1927. The plane was a modified Ryan Brougham single-engine high-wing monoplane with a Wright Whirl-wind radial engine and a top speed of some 120 mph (192 km/h). Its wingspan was 46 ft. (14 m), length 27 ft. 8 ins (8.4 m), and range 4,100 mi. (6,700 km). Most of the normal passenger space (the plane was a five-seater) was taken up by extra fuel tanks.

Sports car
A type of automobile designed for touring and sport, with (usually) only two doors and two seats. "Sporting" features such as rapid acceleration and good maneuverability are emphasized, rather than utility and comfort. Sports cars are normally convertible, and low on the ground. They are not necessarily faster or more powerful than larger sedans, but are often more highly tuned.

S.P.X.
Stepped piston crossover engine, whose British inventors claim it will revolutionize the design of both motorcycle and auto engines. The S.P.X. engine combines the simplicity of the TWO-STROKE CYCLE with the full flow pressure-lubricated crankshaft and connecting rods of the FOUR-STROKE CYCLE, thus eliminating the more expensive components of the four-stroke type — the valves, valve gear and camshaft. This is achieved by the ingenious use of a number of crossover ports between two cylinders mounted side by side which enable the pair to work in unison. Engines made up of any number of pairs can be built to power anything from a motorcycle to a marine engine. Production costs are estimated to be substantially lower than for conventional two-stroke engines, with satisfactory fuel economy, noise and emissions control.

In its final form, the S.P.X. will incorporate the STRATIFIED CHARGE principle, giving greater economy and purer emissions without any significant loss in performance.

SR-N4
Giant British amphibious AIR-CUSHION VEHICLE in service as an automobile and passenger ferry between England and the continent of Europe. Each of the SR-N4's four gas turbine engines powers a lifting fan and an airscrew. Speed is controlled by varying the pitch of the propellers, while direction of thrust is altered by turning the pylons on which they are mounted. Additional turning effect at speed is provided by twin rudder fins.

Spirit of St. Louis, *the Ryan monoplane in which Charles Lindbergh made his historic nonstop crossing of the Atlantic in 1927.*

Stabilizers

Devices to improve stability on aircraft and ships. On aircraft the design of the wing is usually inherently unstable and tends to push the front of the plane down. To counter this effect stabilizing fins are normally provided on the tail. These are in fact the main horizontal surfaces of the tail, and they provide negative lift, thus holding the tail down. They are fitted with ELEVATORS for pitch control. Experiments have also been made with stabilizing fins at the front of the plane, to hold the nose up.

The SR-N4 is 130 ft. 2in. (39.7 m) long and 76 ft. 10 in. (23.4 m) wide. It carries 34 automobiles and 174 passengers at up to 77 knots, making it much the fastest sizeable sea-going craft in existence. First introduced on the cross channel run in 1968 with fares midway between those for ship and plane, the SR-N4 was an immediate success, despite criticisms about its noise and vibration. The crossing time for the journey of some 25 miles (40 km) was about 30 minutes, which was not significantly longer than the air journey. In the succeeding years the price-differential with ships has disappeared, car/passenger air services have virtually ceased, and the SR-N4 continues to win traffic from the shipping companies.

SST

An SST (supersonic transport) is an airliner designed to fly at supersonic speeds. (See CONCORDE, TU-144, SUPERSONIC FLIGHT.)

A Lockheed SR-71, the world's fastest jet airplane in service. Made of titanium to withstand the great heat, it has a top speed of around 2,200 mph (3,540 km/h), and can reach an altitude of some 100,000 ft. (30,480 m).

By far the fastest sizeable seagoing craft in existence, the SR-N4 air-cushion vehicle carries 34 automobiles and 174 passengers at up to 77 knots.

On ships, stabilizers are fitted to counter roll. The simplest consist of longitudinal fins called bilge keels along either side of the hull. The most effective type, however, is the fin stabilizer which virtually eliminates roll. It consists of an adjustable fin at either side, linked to gyroscopes that detect the angle, speed and acceleration of roll. The gyroscopes adjust both fins to damp out the roll. A cheaper and rather less effective type often fitted to freighters is the flume stabilizer. In this two water tanks, one at either side of the ship, are connected by a pipe. When the ship starts a roll to one

Averaging up to 10 mph (16 km/h), stage coaches were the main means of long distance public passenger transportation from the late 17th century until they were superseded by the railroads in the 1840s. The illustration shows an American stagecoach of 1795.

side, the water is in the opposite tank, where it damps the roll. By the time the vessel starts a roll in the other direction, the water has crossed to the other side, and thus damps the new roll.

Fixed fin stabilizers have been tried at the bow to counter pitching, but they are not very successful.

Stacking

The almost simultaneous arrival of a large number of airliners at the same destination makes it necessary to evolve an orderly system of holding aircraft while they await their turn to land. Airliners are "stacked" at varying altitudes over a location some distance from the airport. As the lowermost machine is given permission to land, those above it each move to a lower level, while new arrivals join the top of the stack.

Stagecoach

Large, horse-drawn carriage conveying passengers over relatively long distances on a regular route. Introduced in England in 1640, and in North America during the 1750s, they were the first, and for a long time the only, major mode of long-distance public transportation. They took their name from the *stages* or stopping places along the route. These stages were up to 20 mi. (32 km) apart, and they formed the beginnings of countless new settlements. Four or six horses drew each coach, and the teams were changed at each stage. Journeys along the poor roads of the 18th and early 19th centuries often averaged no more than 4 mph (6 km/h), but as roads improved so

did speeds, and some main coach lines in Europe averaged 10 mph (16 km/h). The earliest stagecoaches carried up to eight passengers inside, and several outside on the roof. A large basket slung on the back of the coach could provide accommodation for a few more travelers. Stagecoaches run by such companies as Wells Fargo and Overland Mail played an important role in the opening of the West, but they eventually went out of service with the coming of the railroads.

Stalling (air)

So long as the airflow over a wing's airfoil is maintained, LIFT will be developed. If speed is reduced, lift can be increased by adopting a greater angle of attack (see WING): this augments both the pressure below the wing and also the backward downwash of air.

Once the angle of attack exceeds 15-20° (depending on the aircraft type), the drag becomes too great for forward speed to be maintained. TURBULENCE spills over the trailing edge and around the wing tips as air moves from the high pressure region below the wing to the low pressure area above it, and the airflow breaks down. The wing can no longer generate lift and becomes stalled.

If one wing drops when an aircraft stalls, a spin may develop unless corrective action is quickly taken. Shock stalls occur at sonic speeds and are due to a breakdown of the airflow as a result of shockwave formation.

Stalling (auto)

Internal combustion engines only develop power when turning over at fairly high speeds. Below a certain rate there is insufficient power to turn even the crankshaft and flywheel, and the engine stops. This is stalling. At higher speeds more power is developed, but it is still possible to impose too great a load for the available power, for example by climbing a hill in too high a gear, and thus to stall.

Stanley Steamer

The most famous American STEAM CAR, in production from 1897 until 1927. The

A "Gentleman's Speedy Roadster" Stanley Steamer of 1910. During the first decade of the 20th century steam cars enjoyed great popularity and were in many respects superior to gasoline automobiles.

first model proved an immediate success, and Stanley Steamers continued to be popular until about 1914, by which time electric self-starters had given the gasoline engine a distinct advantage. In 1906 and 1907 two Stanley Steamers, the *Beetle* and *Wogglebug*, achieved land speed records of 127.56 mph (204 km/h) and 150 mph (240 km/h).

Starter motor

A starter motor is an electric motor used to turn over an engine before it fires and is able to run under its own power. Before a gasoline engine, for example, can fire it must be rotated at a speed of at least 50 rpm, which requires considerable power. The starter motor is of simple, strong construction and consumes a very high current of about 300 amps. After a SOLENOID has activated the starter-motor circuit, the starter-motor shaft spins a toothed pinion into mesh with a toothed ring around the edge of the engine flywheel. Shaft, pinion and starter ring then rotate together until the engine fires. At this point the pinion is flung out of mesh with the starter ring. This type of arrangement is called a Bendix drive.

Station wagon

A type of automobile in which the main compartment is extended to the rear of the vehicle to provide more space, either for additional passengers or, with the seats folded flat, for luggage. A tailgate is fitted to give access through the back. The earliest station wagons were almost indistinguishable from open trucks, but by the 1930s most models had closed and often wood-paneled bodies.

Steamboat

Although strictly speaking any small vessel with steam propulsion is a steamboat, the expression is normally reserved for the river paddle steamers of the 19th century, and particularly for the legendary craft of the Mississippi and its tributaries. The most famous of all, the NATCHEZ and *Robert E. Lee*, were sidewheelers, but most later steamboats were less glamorous but more economical stern-wheelers.

Steam car

Over 20 years before the appearance of the first practical gasoline automobiles steam cars were in small-scale production. They were, however, essentially scaled-down railroad locomotives. They had large boilers, took 30 minutes or more to build up a head of steam, and required a chauffeur to stoke the fire. Then in 1888 Léon Serpollet of France perfected his multi-tube flash boiler, in which water is pumped into red-hot

coiled tubes and converted instantly into steam. When eight years later he replaced coke fuel with kerosene, his steam cars were in many ways superior to gasoline automobiles. The flash boiler eliminated the need for a large boiler and a potentially dangerous head of steam. The steam car was now no larger than a gasoline model; starting was almost as quick and much less strenuous; the engine was quieter and simpler to operate, and because steam engines need neither clutch nor gears the car was simple to drive. It was also very fast. In 1907 the STANLEY STEAMER *Wogglebug* attained 150 mph (240 km/h), a speed

that was not exceeded by a gasoline automobile until 1920.

Famous steam cars such as the Stanley and the White rivalled gasoline automobiles until the appearance of the electric self-starter in 1912, and their popularity continued to a lesser extent into the 1920s, when the most advanced model, the Doble, had electric ignition and took just over one minute to warm up.

The main disadvantages of steam cars are their complexity, and the nature of water which freezes easily and must be heated to a high temperature to generate steam. But they have many advantages as already mentioned, and they produce less pollution than gasoline automobiles. Several manufacturers are experimenting with them at present. One possibility under test in Japan is the replacement of water by special liquids which boil and freeze at much lower temperatures than water.

Steam engines

The essential principle of steam engines is the use of the pressure of expanding steam to push a piston in a cylinder, or to spin the vanes of a turbine. The greater the heat and pressure of the steam, the greater the engine's efficiency. Superheating involves passing steam from the boiler through tubes which are exposed to hot gases from the boiler furnace, thereby raising its temperature. Compounding involves allowing the steam to expand in stages; thus in a double expansion reciprocating engine the steam is partly expanded in a small high-pressure cylinder, and is then led to a larger

Henry Bell's Comet *of 1812, Britain's first commercially successful steamboat.*

low-pressure cylinder to provide additional power; while in a turbine each stage of expansion takes place at one row of blading, a hundred or more stages being possible to deal with steam pressures as great as 100 atmospheres. After use the steam may simply be exhausted to the atmosphere, which causes some back pressure and wastes water, or it may pass into a condenser where it is cooled and condenses to water virtually instantaneously.

In 1690 Denis Papin made a small demonstration model of a piston-and-cylinder arrangement, but Thomas Newcomen made the first practical industrial engine, in 1712. Strictly speaking this was an atmospheric engine, that is, steam was only used to produce a vacuum, thus enabling atmospheric pressure to move the piston. Various attempts were made to power boats with atmospheric engines, but their great bulk and low efficiency made them unsuitable. In 1769

James WATT began a process of improvement and adaptation. His great contribution was his invention of a separate condenser to cool the steam, but he also invented the double-acting engine, in which the piston both pushed and pulled, and the GOVERNOR. Watt's engines were relatively small and efficient enough to power the earliest successful steamboats (see CHARLOTTE DUNDAS; CLERMONT).

In 1800 Watt was still using steam at low pressure. Richard TREVITHICK then made a vital advance when he pioneered the use of "strong steam" at four or five times atmospheric pressure. His engines were much smaller, lighter and more efficient than Watt's, and with them he constructed the world's first steam locomotives and the first practical powered road vehicles. Most locomotives and steam coach designs were directly descended from Trevithick's engines, and like them dispensed with the condenser, although factory and marine engines continued to have condensers. Higher pressures, superheating, and compounding were developed to improve output, and the triple expansion engine became the commonest marine engine for three quarters of a century. The modern steam engine, however, is the compound turbine invented by Sir Charles PARSONS in 1883. It was adopted for electricity generation and for powering large ships, and has continued for both these purposes since the first decade of the 20th century. (See also STEAM CAR; STEAM TURBINE.)

Steam turbine

A type of steam engine similar in principle to the water wheel, in which steam issues at high pressure from fine nozzles onto vaned blades fixed to a shaft or rotor. The pressure of steam on the blades spins the shaft, which is then used to drive wheels, or a propeller, or an electric generator. The steam is provided by a boiler which may be heated by a furnace, or by a nuclear reactor. Although it was used in some railroad locomotives, the steam turbine's primary application in transportation has been in ship propulsion. All early steamships were powered by reciprocating steam engines. These proved very reliable, but they took up a great deal of space and were incapable of producing high speeds. A turbine generates much greater power in less space, it is more efficient and therefore more economical to run, it is lighter, and as all moving parts rotate it is smoother and mechanically much simpler.

As early as 1802 the American John Stevens built an experimental steam turbine powered boat. In the 1830s William Avery manufactured primitive turbines

A rack-and-pinion type steering system.

to power sawmills, and one of them was tried out on a railroad locomotive. But the first successful application was by the Englishman Charles Parsons in his TURBINIA. This small vessel, built in 1897 to demonstrate the turbine's potential to the British Admiralty, startled spectators by racing through the British fleet during a naval review at the then remarkable speed of 34.5 knots.

After this the turbine was soon adopted for large and high-performance ships. Today it has been generally supplanted by the diesel engine except in very large vessels, and in nuclear powered ships. Towards the end of the steam era, some steam turbine locomotives were built, but they were rendered obsolete by diesel and electric traction before any true evaluation had been reached.

Steerage

Term once used to describe that part of a passenger ship allotted to people traveling at the cheapest rate. Steerage passengers had few comforts, and were usually in the lowest part of a vessel. The term came into use early in the 19th century; earlier it described the second cabin of a ship, and originally was the place from which the ship was steered.

Steering system

In a typical steering system movement of the steering wheel turns a shaft in the steering column. This movement is translated by the steering gear into a side-to-side motion which is transmitted to the front wheels through suitable linkages. The steering geometry must take account

of the fact that when cornering the inner wheel follows a smaller circle than the outer one (see ACKERMAN STEERING). The steering gear may consist of a steering box in which a worm-and-nut or cam-and-peg mechanism swivels the wheels through drop arms and TRACK RODS, or it may be a simple rack-and-pinion. In this case a pinion turned by the steering shaft moves a toothed rack from side to side. This motion is transmitted to the wheels by short track rods with ball joints at each end to permit independent up-and-down movement when the vehicle travels over uneven ground. The steering shaft contains UNIVERSAL JOINTS for flexibility, and in most modern vehicles is designed to collapse on impact, thereby protecting the driver from severe chest injuries.

The steering ratio is a measure of the amount of steering-wheel turn needed to turn the front wheels one degree, and depends on the reduction afforded by the steering gear. The higher the ratio, the more the steering wheel must be turned for a given effect, and the lower the driver effort required. On the other hand, a high ratio makes rapid maneuvers difficult. A heavy automobile may have a steering ratio of about 25:1, requiring four to five turns of the wheel to achieve full lock. Many vehicles have hydraulic power-assisted steering (see HYDRAULIC SYSTEMS).

The positioning of the front wheels relative to the vehicle and the ground critically affects steering performance (see CAMBER; CASTOR ANGLE; TOE-IN, TOE-OUT).

Stephenson, George and Robert (1781-1848; 1803-1859)

George Stephenson, one of the great pioneers of locomotive building, was born in northeast England and became an assistant fireman at a coal mine at the age of 14. His skill as a mechanic brought him an appointment as an enginewright in 1812 at Killingworth Colliery. He became a friend of John Steele, who had worked with Richard TREVITHICK and had built a steam locomotive on Trevithick's principles. This was too heavy for the track and was converted to a stationary engine, but Stephenson studied it and Steele taught him all he

structing the LIVERPOOL & MANCHESTER RAILWAY, and the Stephensons' locomotive ROCKET was the winner of the trials held at Rainhill in 1829 to decide the form of motive power for the new line. George Stephenson's reputation was now made and the rest of his life was spent as an adviser and a designer of railroads. Robert specialized in locomotives and traveled for a time in America. He was also a civil engineer of great note and was responsible for building, among others, the 112-mi. (180 km) London & Birmingham Railway. He was regarded as one of the finest railroad engineers of his time.

A painting of the Stephenson family, including the famous railroad pioneers George and Robert, with an early colliery railroad scene in the background.

had learned from Trevithick. He also studied other early locomotives and in 1813 he was allowed to build a locomotive for Killingworth. A second locomotive followed in 1815. The elder Stephenson surveyed and built the 8-mi. (13 km) Hetton Colliery Railway, opened in 1822, and was appointed engineer-in-chief of the STOCKTON AND DARLINGTON RAILWAY in 1823. His son Robert helped with this work, and the $25\frac{1}{2}$-mi. (41 km) line opened in 1825, with a Stephenson engine, *Locomotion*, hauling the first train. (Horses were used for passenger traffic after the first day.) He was later appointed engineer in charge of con-

Step rocket

A combination of ROCKETS, one mounted on top of the other, used as a launching vehicle. Such a combination is necessary for space launchings, for example, because no single rocket can achieve a sufficiently high power-to-weight ratio to boost a payload to such a speed (at least 17,500 mph, 28,000 km/h) that it goes into orbit. Konstantin TSIOLKOVSKY advanced the step-rocket principle in the early 1900s. He suggested the use of parallel staging — with the rockets being placed side by side.

The end-to-end method now utilized is called tandem staging. The first stage of a

step rocket is the most powerful, lifting the biggest load through the densest part of the atmosphere and overcoming the greatest gravitational pull. It separates from the rest of the rocket when its propellants are exhausted. Then the second stage fires and thrusts the very much lighter rocket on its way. When in turn its propellants are exhausted, it separates and the third stage, if there is one, fires. In some rockets the first stage takes the form of solid-propellant boosters wrapped around the main body of the rocket (as in Titan III). This is in effect a mixture of parallel and tandem staging.

Stevens, John (1749-1838)

American lawyer and inventor, a notable pioneer of steamboats and locomotives. In 1802 he built a small boat with a steam turbine engine and screw propulsion. Both features were decades ahead of their time but sadly impractical as commercial ventures with the technology of the day. Two years later he constructed an improved twin-screw boat with a reciprocating high-pressure steam engine. Both craft attained speeds of 4 mph (6.4 km/h). In 1808 his 101-ft. (30.8 m) paddle steamer *Phoenix* became the world's first seagoing steamship by steaming from New York Harbor to Philadelphia, where it ran a regular service on the Delaware River to Trenton.

In 1812 Stevens wrote a pamphlet on the "Superior Advantages of Rail-ways and Steam-carriages over Canal Navigation," and in 1815 he obtained from New Jersey the first railroad charter issued in the United States (for a line from Trenton to New Brunswick). In 1825 he built the first American steam locomotive, and displayed it on a circular track on his estate at Hoboken, N.J. The small four-wheeled locomotive was driven by a pinion which engaged a rack rail laid between the running rails.

Stilwell Road

Wartime highway linking India with the BURMA ROAD during World War II. It ran for 478 mi. (769 km) from Ledo, in Assam, and was known as the Ledo Road until Chinese leader Chiang Kai-shek renamed it for General Joseph W. Stilwell, U.S. commander-in-chief in the China-Burma-India theater of war. Stilwell began construction of the road in 1942 to form a land supply route to China after the Japanese had seized a section of the Burma Road. At first the road terminated at Mogaung, Burma, but in 1944 a linking section to the Burma Road at Mu-se was begun. The road was completed in January 1945, and although abandoned by the United States 11 months later after the end of the war, it is still used by traffic.

The British-built locomotive Stourbridge Lion *introduced practical steam railroad traction to the United States in 1829.*

Stirling engine

An external combustion engine working on a principle patented in 1816 by a Scottish minister, the Rev. Robert Stirling (1790-1878). It is often called a hot-air or hot-gas engine as it involves cyclic heating, expansion, and cooling of air or another gas in a sealed system. A number of Stirling engines were manufactured but never achieved any great success. The idea has been revived in recent times, for these engines can use virtually any fuel efficiently and cause relatively little pollution. The Dutch company Philips has been prominent in Stirling-engine research, and has joined forces with Ford to develop a V-4 engine for the Pinto model.

In a typical Stirling-cycle engine a burner burns fuel continuously, heating gas compressed by a piston in a cylinder. The gas expands, pushing the piston down the cylinder. Gas behind the other side of the piston is forced out through a regenerator-cooler into an adjacent cylinder, where heat is again applied and the process is regenerated. A number of linked cylinders may be employed. The back-and-forth motion of the pistons may be converted to rotary motion by conventional means, via connecting rod and crankshaft, or it may be done more directly by means of a swashplate, which is a flat disk set at an angle on the drive shaft.

Stockton and Darlington Railway

The world's first public railroad using steam locomotives, the Stockton and Darlington Railway opened on September 27, 1825. After the first day steam was only used for freight haulage; passengers traveled in horse-drawn cars. The 25½-mi. (41 km) line was a notable feat for its time and was built by George STEPHENSON. Its main purpose was, as with so many early railroads, to carry coal from the mines to a navigable waterway. Stephenson not only checked and improved the original survey, but was responsible for the roadbed and route and all the civil engineering work. He also built the line's first locomotive, *Locomotion,* which hauled 90 tons and hundreds of passengers at 15 mph (24 km/h) on the opening day.

This railroad laid the foundation of George Stephenson's career, and helped to convince people that the steam locomotive was a practical form of motive power.

STOL

There are various means of obtaining STOL (Short Take-Off and Landing) performance.

In multi-engined airplanes, the power units may be mounted so that their thrust is directed backwards through high-lift FLAPS. This artificially speeds up the airflow and augments the lift.

Another method of increasing lift is to bleed compressed air from the engine(s) and expel it from slits located along the leading edges of the wings and tail. The injection into the BOUNDARY LAYER of this extra air represents a source of additional energy and inhibits the tendency of the airflow to breakdown in TURBULENCE as the speed drops. Compressed air bled from the engine compressor can also be liberated from slots located immediately in front of the flaps and ailerons. Vortex generators are small vanes 2-3 in. (5-7.5 cm) high located on the wing surface at an angle to the local airflow. As the stall is approached they create vortices which introduce energy from the smooth-flowing outside airstream into the sluggish boundary layer and delay the onset of turbulence.

Stourbridge Lion

The first locomotive to run on a standard railroad in the United States. A trial trip on wooden rails at Honesdale, Pennsylvania, on August 8, 1829, showed that the British-built, 6-ton locomotive was too heavy for the track, and it was converted for use as a stationary engine.

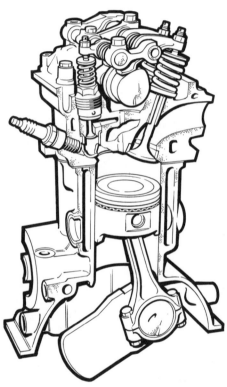

A stratified charge engine of the pre-combustion chamber type. By burning fuel more completely than the conventional gasoline engine, the stratified charge engine improves economy and reduces pollutant exhaust emissions.

Stratified-charge engine

The stratified-charge engine is a modified gasoline engine designed to reduce noxious exhaust emissions. The modification allows the engine to run on a much leaner mixture than usual, and results in more complete combustion. A layer of lean fuel-air mixture is coaxed into burning by the ignition of an adjacent fuel-rich layer. The rich mixture is fed to and ignited in a small combustion chamber located above the main one. An extra inlet valve is required for this, together with an extra carburetor. In an alternative and simpler layout there is no carburetor. A fuel injector injects fuel between spark plug and inlet valve (which admits only air). The mixture reaching the plug initially is rich and therefore ignites easily, and combustion spreads smoothly to the leaner mixture swirling in the combustion chamber. Honda of Japan was one of the first to demonstrate a successful stratified-charge engine.

Stratocruiser

Large, long-range airliner built by Boeing between 1947 and 1950. With four piston engines, a two-deck pressurized fuselage, and a cruising speed of some 340 mph (547 km/h), it carried up to 112 passengers. The Stratocruiser was one of the most comfortable and popular airliners of the pre-jet age.

Streamlining

The process of shaping an object so that it slips through the air (or water) with a minimum of DRAG. Water has about 800 times the frictional resistance of air, so streamlining is important to all water craft. On land, every cyclist and skier appreciates the effect of leaning forward, thus presenting the smallest possible surface to the air, and at high speeds streamling makes a dramatic difference. A well designed airplane wing traveling at 210 mph (336 km/h) has less drag than a one-inch (2.5 cm) diameter rod moving at the same speed: hence the relative inefficiency of early airplanes, which were a mass of struts.

This prototype automobile makes full use of streamlining to reduce drag to a minimum, thereby lowering fuel consumption and increasing speed potential.

With the notable exception of racing cars and of such bold experiments as the Chrysler Airflow of 1934, automobile designers have paid little attention to the subject. However, with increased oil costs streamlined automobiles have taken on a new significance as they use noticeably less fuel.

Several locomotives of the 1930s were given streamlined shapes. Today, as train speeds are raised to 150 mph (240 km/h) or more, all locomotives are designed on aerodynamic principles, and tested in wind tunnels.

Streetcar

Passenger carrying vehicle for urban and interurban transit running on rails laid in or beside the street. The main advantage of the system is that less power is re-quired to move a vehicle running on metal wheels and tracks than for a conventional road vehicle. In the early days an added attraction was that it was easier and cheaper to lay rails than to provide a good pavement. The principal drawback of streetcars is their inflexibility: they must follow the tracks, and changing the route involves major expense. However, with the existing problem of pollution from internal combustion-engined vehicles, it is possible that pollution free electric streetcars may be revived.

The first streetcars were introduced in New York in 1832. They were horse-drawn, and became an immediate success as they provided a much smoother ride than buses running on the rough-surfaced streets. The New York and Harlem Railway ran the first steam streetcars in 1837, while the first electric streetcars appeared in Germany in 1881. Power was transmitted along the rails, but less dangerous methods were quickly devised, usually with overhead cables linked to the streetcar by a trolley pole or similar mechanism.

Between about 1890 and 1920 electric tramways spread rapidly in the United States, Europe and elsewhere, providing urban and high-speed interurban transportation. Double deckers were normal in Britain, but most other countries preferred single deckers, often in two car units. Tramway mileage reached a peak in the United States in 1926, but by then competition from buses and automobiles was considerable, and by the end of the 1930s streetcars had virtually disappeared. In many Continental countries and in a few other places streetcars still play an important role in urban, and to a lesser extent interurban, mass transit.

This old-fashioned streetcar, seen here being turned at the end of the line, remains as a tourist attraction in San Francisco. Unlike most streetcars, which have electric traction, this one is cable hauled.

Streets

See HIGHWAYS.

A typical conventional submarine of World War II, with diesel engines for use on the surface and electric motors for submerged cruising.

Submarines

A submarine is essentially a double-hulled vessel whose buoyancy can be varied by altering the proportions of air and water in ballast tanks between the hulls. The hull is specially strengthened to withstand the great pressures deep under the surface.

The submarine's "flight path" through the water is controlled by small adjustable fins called hydroplanes, which can be angled to make the craft dive or ascend, and by a rudder. The basic control resembles an airplane's control column. The helmsman, or pilot, cannot however see where he is going and relies on instruments showing course, speed, and depth. To submerge, the ballast tanks are first flooded to provide a state of neutral buoyancy, and the submarine is then driven down using propeller and hydroplanes. To surface the craft is put into an upward angle, and at the same time water is pumped from the ballast tanks. While submerged, the submarine is kept in a state of neutral buoyancy according to depth and load. The balance is achieved by using compressed air to adjust the amount of water in trim tanks.

Early submarines had a watertight conning tower rising from the hull roughly amidships. This was the place from which the vessel was commanded when in action. In modern submarines this tower is a streamlined sail structure designed to flood when the vessel submerges. In both cases the tower contains the retractable PERISCOPE, and radio and radar antennae, as well as breathing tubes called snorkels (which were developed during World War II in Germany).

When fully submerged the submarine is almost completely cut off from the rest of the world. It can receive only special low-frequency radio transmissions, and it cannot transmit them. Nor can it make use of normal celestial or radio NAVIGATION systems, and relies instead on sensitive gyroscopes and accelerometers which detect and measure changes in position (see INERTIAL GUIDANCE). And it is cut off from normal air supplies. It does however have a very efficient "underwater eye" in the form of SONAR.

To transmit radio messages, to check position by conventional navigation methods, to view the surface and the sky, to use its radar, and to breathe (to take in fresh air and get rid of stale air and fumes), the submarine must ascend to periscope depth. Fresh air is all-important, and until the advent of NUCLEAR PROPULSION oxygen-supply problems severely limited the submarine's potential. Conventional oil-burning engines use up oxygen and produce noxious fumes, and thus cannot be run when fully submerged. In the past, submarines therefore needed two sets of machinery: diesel engines for cruising and battery charging on the surface or at snorkel depth, and electric motors for underwater propulsion. This restricted underwater cruising to a maximum of four days at slow speeds, or at most an hour or two at high speeds, after which the batteries had to be recharged. All early submarines were thus strictly speaking submersibles, capable only of short spells of duty under water.

With the advent of nuclear propulsion the problem disappeared. A nuclear reactor, like an electric motor, uses no oxygen and produces no fumes. In addition it requires minute quantities of fuel, and has a range of some 400,000 mi. (640,000 km) on one fueling. With equipment on board to produce oxygen and fresh water from the sea, the nuclear submarine can remain submerged for virtually unlimited periods. The first nuclear submarine, the U.S.S. NAUTILUS, was launched in 1954, and in 1958 became the first vessel to travel under the North Pole. In 1960 the U.S.S. *Triton* circumnavigated the globe underwater, covering 36,014 mi. (57,967 km) in 77 days at speeds of up to 30 knots.

Hull design. Early submarines were basically surface vessels adapted for underwater use. They had similar lines to those of a surface ship, complete with a superstructure to provide a main deck when the craft was cruising on the surface. The hull was thus not designed for maximum underwater efficiency, and its superstructure added considerably to the craft's drag. Nuclear submarines are designed solely for underwater operation, and a new hull shape has accordingly been evolved. First tested on an experimental vessel, the *Albacore*, and in 1959 adopted on the Skipjack class, the new streamlined design has a rounded bow and a tapering teardrop-shaped hull with no protruberances except the "sail" tower and the control surfaces. Officers on the *Albacore* coined the word "hydrobatics" to describe the submarine's airplane-like maneuverability, and the nuclear-powered Skipjack vessels are the world's fastest submarines, with a top speed of about 45 knots when submerged.

Research and rescue submersibles. With one exception (the *NR-1*, see below) all nuclear submarines are naval craft, equipped with torpedoes and a variety of missiles including ICBMs. They have become one of the key factors in modern warfare. Almost all early submarines were also warships, but in recent years a large number of small electric-powered submersibles have been developed for deep-water salvage, research, and rescue operations. Most are equipped with a variety of mechanical grabs remotely controlled from inside the craft, and with powerful lights, and photographic and television apparatus. One, the U.S. Navy's Deep Submersible Rescue Vessel (DSRV), is designed specifically to rescue crews of conventional submarines stranded on the seabed. It locks onto one of the damaged craft's escape hatches and can rescue 24 men at a time, operating at depths of at least 3,500 ft. (1,100 m). Later versions can dive still deeper, and should help to prevent such disasters as the loss of 129 lives that occurred when the U.S.S. *Thresher* sank off New England in 1963 in over 8,000 ft. (2,400 m) of water. Nuclear submarines can dive to depths of around 1,200 ft. (366 m), with the exception of the US Navy's *NR-1* Deep Submergence Search Vehicle (DSSV). Information about this remarkable seven-man craft is classified, but it can dive to at least 20,000 ft. (6,096 m). Previously the 73-ton *Aluminaut* had the greatest diving ability, being designed to operate at depths of up to 15,000 ft. (4,572 m). Its aluminum hull is only one-third the weight of a steel hull of the same size and strength. *Aluminaut* played an important part in the recovery of an unexploded nuclear bomb from the seabed off the coast of Spain at Palomares.

Smaller submersibles include the *Beaver*, which can carry five men to a depth of 2,000 ft. (600 m), and the 8-ton *Deep Diver*. This is designed to transport divers to and from the seabed, and to stand by in case of emergencies.

Submarine freighters. During World War II the Japanese built a number of very large I-400 class submarines for use as underwater aircraft carriers. Just over 400 ft. (122 m) long, they displaced 5,700

freighter. The Japanese I-400s were in fact employed in this role carrying supplies to islands in the Pacific.

Four or five hundred feet below the surface there are neither storms nor waves, and at such depths streamlined submarines can cruise faster and with less effort than surface ships. Moreover they can follow shorter routes by traveling under the polar ice cap, with dramatic savings in time and expense. For example,

comes less costly, the submarine bulk freighter will almost certainly be a commercial proposition, at least on certain routes.

Early submarines. A primitive rowed submarine was built in England in the 1620s, and was followed by many ingenious experiments, but the first submarine actually used in combat was David BUSHNELL'S *Turtle* of 1776. Shaped like an upended

The U.S. Navy Holland, *the first practical submarine. Electric motors gave it a submerged speed of two knots.*

With the arrival of nuclear propulsion in 1954 the true submarine, able to operate for indefinite periods underwater, was born. The photograph shows a modern naval nuclear submarine.

tons, and contained a hangar 102 ft. (31 m) long with a diameter of 12 ft. (3.7). The Soviet navy's Y class nuclear missile submarines have a submerged displacement of 9,000 tons and are 426.5 ft. (130 m) long. These two types represent the largest conventional and nuclear submarines yet built, and point to the possibility of the submarine

the surface voyage from Europe to Japan through the Suez or Panama Canals is roughly twice the length of the direct route under the arctic ice and through the Bering Strait. Submarines are well suited for carrying bulk cargoes such as oil, ore, and grain, which could be loaded and discharged through small openings in the hull. When nuclear propulsion be-

turtle, constructed of wood, and carrying one man, it had two hand-cranked screws for propulsion, a rudder, and a valve and hand pump arrangement for controlling buoyancy. Although an attempt to fix a mine on a British warship during the Revolution failed, the *Turtle* was the first effective submarine.

In 1801 Robert FULTON, better known for his steamboat CLERMONT, built the first *Nautilus*. With a propulsion by sail on the surface and by a hand-cranked screw when submerged, his invention had a limited success but failed to arouse any interest. The *Hunley*, the first submarine to actually sink an enemy ship (the Union warship *Housatonic*, in 1864) was basically a modified iron boiler, propelled by eight men cranking a screw. Unfortunately the submarine was also destroyed in the explosion.

The first practical submarines were the American *Holland* of 1897 and the French *Narval* of 1899, both of which had conventional engines for surface use and electric motors for submerged propulsion. The *Holland*, 53 ft. 3 in. (16 m) long and with a crew of nine, was adopted by the United States, British and Japanese navies. With the *Narval*, it was the direct ancestor of the larger and more efficient submarines of the two world wars.

One of the highly ornate stations on the Metro network of Moscow, Soviet Union. The stations were all designed by leading architects.

Subway

Subways are rapid transit urban railroads serving the busiest parts of a city and geared to handle intensive peak-hour passenger traffic. Although the term implies underground construction, the majority of subways are only partly underground, rising to the surface, or onto elevated structures, in suburban areas. Traction is invariably electric. The current is generally supplied by a third rail, usually outside the running rails and, especially in newer systems, carefully shielded as far as possible to protect staff walking alongside the track. A few subways use an overhead system, and London has a fourth rail between the running rails for the return half of the circuit. Power is usually direct current at 600 to 1,500 volts. Most systems use conventional flanged steel wheels on steel tracks, but Montreal and Mexico City have followed the example set by the Paris MÉTRO in 1956, and use rubber-tired wheels. These run on concrete beams, and have small horizontal rubber guide-wheels running on trackside guidebars. Normal track and rails are provided in case of punctures, and for use at switches. Although rubber tires provide a quieter and smoother ride, the complicated tracks necessary are expensive, and the system is unlikely to become widespread. It was considered and rejected by the planners of San Francisco's BAY AREA RAPID TRANSIT (BART) subway, and is being phased out in Paris.

History. The world's first subway was London's 3¾ mi. (6 km) Metropolitan Line linking the mainline station at Paddington with the City. Opened on January 10, 1863, it was constructed by the still common cut-and-cover method, and carried some 9,500,000 passengers in the first year despite the sulfurous fumes produced by the steam locomotives used. The first electric subway was also in London, and was opened on December 18, 1890. This, the City and South London Railway, was a "deep tube" line bored with a tunneling shield deep in the London clay.

Other cities soon followed London's example. In 1896 Glasgow, Scotland, opened its first subway, which was cable-hauled until its electrification nearly 40 years later. The United States' first underground subway was inaugurated in Boston in 1898, although Charles T. Harvey had built an experimental section in New York City's Greenwich Street in 1867, and New York's "subway in the sky" (the El) began services in the same year, using cable drive. The El transferred to steam traction in 1871, was later electrified, and widely extended, and has since been removed for esthetic reasons and because of the noise and traffic congestion it caused.

In 1897 the South Side Elevated Railroad in Chicago became America's first subway with the now standard multiple-

The subways of Tokyo, Japan, are so busy at peak hours that special oshiya ("pushing boys") are employed to push passengers into the already crowded trains.

A station on the Paris, France, Métro subway system. Television screens are installed to enable the driver to see at a glance when all passengers are clear of the doors.

unit system, in which every car has traction motors and controls. This allows a train to be controlled from any car; it avoids the wasteful use of a powerful locomotive to pull a short train outside the rush-hours; and at the end of the line the train can simply reverse direction. Almost half of the world's largest cities now have subway systems; another 20 have systems under construction; and at least 70 more have plans for them. This is because such railroads have so far proved the only practical way to move dense commuter traffic into and out of city centers. A single subway line can carry some 20,000 to 40,000 passengers an hour, far more than a multi-lane highway. However, a dense network of lines and stations is essential if a subway is to meet a city's mass transit needs, and average costs of subway construction exceed $50,000,000 per mile ($31,250,000 per km). Many cities are accordingly considering the possible alternative of

been extended and modernized, and are being increasingly automated.

With trains running at 1½ to 2 minute intervals at peak hour, efficient signaling and control is of vital importance. The block system (see RAILROAD) is normally used, and is often supplemented by an automatic warning system which either triggers an alarm in the cab or automatically applies the brakes should the driver ignore a "stop" signal (see SIGNALING IN TRANSPORT). Operation of all switches and signals is invariably from a central traffic control office, where the track layout is shown on a display panel, together with the position of all trains and the state of all switches and signals. On the London Underground automatic "program machines" contain the day's timetable in the form of a punched code, and set signals and switches in the correct sequence throughout the day. The machines can be set to route trains according to their description on a "first-

"read" the ticket at both ends of the journey and can decide whether it is correct (in value, date, etc.).

With stations often under ½ mi. (0.8 km) apart, and station stops of 25-30 seconds or longer, the most advanced automation and the fastest possible acceleration and braking cannot produce average journey speeds of much over 20-25 mph (32-40 km/h). However, even this is much faster than traffic on the congested streets overhead.

Suez Canal

An important ship canal linking the Mediterranean and Red seas, the 101 mi. (162.5 km) Suez Canal crosses the Isthmus of Suez from Port Said in the north to the port of Suez in the south. Constructed in the years 1859 to 1869 by a joint French and Turkish company, with the French engineer Ferdinand de LESSEPS in charge, the canal shortened the sea route between western Europe and India by about 6,000 mi. (9,600 km), and that between New York and India or Saudi Arabia by 3,600 mi. (5,794 km).

The canal was routed to take advantage of three lakes and has eight major bends which slow passage time, but there are no locks as it is at sealevel throughout. The lakes (Menzala, Timseh, and the Bitter Lakes) account for about one fifth of the total length. At the time of its closure after the June 1967 Arab-Israeli war the canal could accommodate ships with a maximum draft of 38 ft. (11.6 m) and a maximum length, determined by the sharpness of the bends, of 900 ft. (274 m). It had a minimum width of 179 ft. (55 m); its banks were reinforced where necessary to prevent erosion; and it was used by over 20,000 ships annually, averaging 56 a day, and representing some 15% of the world's sea traffic. Passing places were provided at regular intervals, but as these required one vessel to move out of the main waterway and stop, a convoy system was adopted. Two convoys traversed the canal in each direction daily, passing at two bypasses where the canal divides into two channels. The average actual transit time was 15 hours.

Salvage craft at work clearing the Suez Canal in 1974. The canal, which shortens the sea route between Europe and the east by some 6,000 mi (9,600 km), was closed in 1967 after the Arab-Israeli war of that year, and was reopened in 1975.

restricting automobiles in urban centers, and of providing special bus lanes. One bus lane into New York City proved able to transport 25,000 passengers an hour.

Modern networks. The world's most extensive subway system is London's "Underground" or "Tube." With 252 mi. (405 km) of track, and 279 stations, it carries some 650 million passengers a year. New York City's network is slightly shorter (231 mi., 372 km), but has more closely spaced stations (462 in all) and carries over 2 billion passengers annually, making it the world's busiest. With growing congestion on the surface leading to greater demands on subways, old-established networks such as those of London, New York, and Paris, have

come first-served" basis, and give warning to the central control officer of trains that are late or out of turn. On the most advanced lines, such as London's new Victoria Line and San Francisco's BART network, all operations including the driving of the trains are automatic. On the Victoria Line automatic driving is controlled by signals initiated by the train ahead and by program machines. On BART it is controlled by a central computer which works on information fed back to it automatically from all parts of the system. In both cases an attendant travels in the front of the train and can take over in an emergency.

Automatic ticket machines which can give change are becoming more common, as are automated turnstiles which can

In 1975 the canal reopened to full traffic, but the nature of that traffic had changed. In 1967 over 70% of the tonnage transported was oil. In the years of closure supertankers had been developed, and used the Cape route around South Africa. The canal in its present form cannot take tankers of over 50,000 tons deadweight, and is not an economic proposition for tankers of less than about 100,000 tons deadweight, so the future is uncertain. However, there are plans to deepen the canal to accept ships with a draft of 46 ft. (14 m) in the near future (and with a draft of 70 ft., 21 m, by 1982), and to straighten out the bends as necessary.

Originally in the hands of the Suez Canal Company, which was owned by a number of French shareholders and the khedive of Egypt, the canal came under British control in 1875 when the British government bought the majority holding. An international convention of 1888 declared the canal an international waterway, open to ships of all nations, but during the two world wars the British effectively prevented their enemies from using it. Since 1956, when the Egyptian government nationalized it, the canal has been controlled by Egypt.

Supercharger

Also called blower, a supercharger is an air pump or compressor fitted to some internal combustion engines to increase the amount of air taken into the cylinder during each intake stroke. This, with the passed through a heat exchanger, or intercooler, before it enters the engine cylinders.

Supermarine S6B

Famous British single-seater racing seaplane, from which the Spitfire fighter plane of World War II was developed. In 1931 the S6B was the winner of the Schneider Cup with a speed of 340.8 mph (545.3 km/h), and became the first airplane to exceed 400 mph when it set a new air speed record of 415.2 mph (668.2 km/h).

Supersonic flight

Sound is transmitted in waves, which travel at varying speeds according to the temperature and density of the medium through which they pass. In warm air at sealevel the speed of sound is about 1,100 ft. (335 m) per sec. (760 mph or 1,216 km/h), while at a height of about 37,000 ft. (11,000 m) its velocity is only 660 mph (1,056 km/h).

The world's first supersonic passenger transport, the Soviet Tu-144. The thin swept delta wing is designed for maximum control and efficiency when passing through the "sound barrier" and in supersonic flight.

addition of more fuel, boosts power output by up to 100%. Superchargers are used on most large diesel engines; on airplanes piston engines, enabling them to maintain power at high altitudes where the external pressure is low; and on many racing automobiles.

The most common form of blower is the centrifugal type, which is driven by a turbine from the engine exhaust, and is known as a turbocharger. The turbine in larger installations is of the axial-flow type, while smaller units have radial-flow turbines. The air compressed by the blower becomes hot, and is usually

At subsonic speeds, pressure waves preceding the aircraft cause the air ahead of it to begin moving out of the way before the plane actually arrives, so that the air is not subject to any compression. When the speed of sound is reached, the aircraft is traveling as fast as the pressure waves preceding it, and the air does not therefore begin to move aside ahead of the machine. As the wings meet this wall of air a shock wave (representing an increase in pressure due to compression of the air) is generated from the point on the upper surface at which the airflow is accelerated over the airfoil's curvature

to reach the speed of sound. Behind this shock wave there is an increase in air pressure and density, accompanied by a fall in the speed of the airflow, resulting in TURBULENCE, loss of LIFT and increased drag (shock stall). It is the rapid rise in drag caused by the airflow striking the shock wave that initially made supersonic flight difficult to achieve and maintain — the so-called "sound barrier." When a shock stall occurs and the airflow breaks down in turbulence behind the shock wave, the pilot experiences similar sensations to those associated with a normal stall: buffeting, shaking, change of trim, and loss of control. Instead of becoming sloppy, however, the controls may be too stiff to move, except with the aid of the trimmer. But while an ordinary stall occurs at a high angle of attack, a shock stall occurs when diving or in level flight, and the aircraft's nose must somehow be pulled up to overcome it.

Two basic solutions to the problem have been evolved: sweepback and laminar-flow airfoils. If a wing is swept back, the speed of the airflow across the chord is less (relative to the speed of the aircraft) than it would be over a straight wing because a proportion of the airflow's speed becomes directed along the wing instead of across it. As a result, the chord-wise airflow has a lower MACH NUMBER than would be the case with a straight wing at the same air speed, and the formation of sonic shock waves is deferred.

Sweepback also has the effect of making the chord effectively longer if it is measured parallel to the fuselage (in the direction of airflow); hence the wing section is proportionately thinner and produces less drag.

A straight wing begins to incur a sharp rise in drag at Mach 0.85, and the maximum drag is experienced at Mach 1.1. The higher the Mach number, the greater must be the sweepback if compressibility effects are to be delayed. A sweep of 45° will delay the onset of maximum drag until Mach 1.4, but 70° is necessary to achieve a further delay to Mach 1.5, and at Mach 1.7 the drag of a swept wing will be comparable to that of a straight wing (the drag coefficient of which begins to fall once the speed of sound has been exceeded). Straight wings are consequently often used on missiles and have also appeared on a number of high-speed aircraft (for example the F-104). A laminar-flow airfoil has an approximately equal convexity (often angular) both above and below, with a sharp leading edge. Sonic shock waves form above and below it as the speed of sound is approached, and just beyond Mach 1 this shock wave becomes established at the trailing edge, while a second shock wave begins to form slightly ahead of the leading edge.

Once above Mach 1, the second shock wave gradually moves back until it touches the leading edge, and the angles at which both shock waves leave the wing become progressively more acute. Beyond the speed of sound, the shock wave pattern stabilizes and flight becomes smoother. (Another device to facilitate the attainment of supersonic flight is AREA RULE.)

As shock waves from an airplane traveling faster than sound reach an observer on the ground, they give rise to sonic booms or bangs. Although the strength of these shock waves is attenuated by distance, the sudden increase in pressure (compressibility) which they represent is capable of doing considerable damage. The magnitude of sonic bangs will be greater if a large, heavy aircraft is involved, and the faster it flies, the more severe will be the shock waves generated.

Compressibility first became a problem during World War II, when fighters such as the P-38 and P-47 began to approach the speed of sound in power dives. The first man credited with reaching Mach 1 was Major Charles Yeager of the U.S. Air Force, who attained Mach 1.45 at 60,000 ft. (18,000 m) in 1947, flying the rocket-propelled Bell X-1 research plane. In 1949 the Douglas Skyrocket became the first supersonic jet-powered aircraft when Gene May flew it to Mach 1.03 at 26,000 ft. (7,900 m).

Supertanker

Also known as a VLCC (very large crude carrier), the name supertanker has been given to the generation of very large oil TANKERS such as GLOBTIK TOKYO.

Surrey

The Surrey was a light four-wheeled carriage originating in Surrey, England. It usually had two seats and a flat fringed canopy on top (see CARRIAGES).

The unusual "canard" layout of this Swedish Saab Viggen fighter is designed to combine efficient supersonic flight (the plane's top speed is 1,320 mph, (2,125 km/h) with STOL (short takeoff and landing) qualities.

Suspension bridge

A suspension bridge consists of a lightweight deck supported entirely by the steel rods on which it hangs. These rods, or suspenders, hang from massive steel cables which loop from shore to shore from the tops of high towers, and are anchored in the bedrock beyond the towers. The weight of a suspension

bridge therefore thrusts straight down through the towers and pulls inward on the anchoring cables. The weight of the supporting rods and cables is very much less than that of an arch or girder; this low dead weight, combined with the fact that the deck is supported throughout its length, makes the suspension bridge the only possibility for spans of over about 2,500 ft. (762 m). The nearest rival in this respect is a recent adaptation of the suspension idea, the cable-stayed bridge (see BRIDGES). At present the world's longest-span bridge is the VERRAZANO-NARROWS suspension bridge (4,260 ft., 1,298 m), but this will soon be exceeded by the 4,625 ft. (1,410 m) HUMBER BRIDGE in northeast England, due to be completed in 1978. The supporting cables of a suspension bridge are made up of thousands of strands of pencil-slim, cold-drawn, high-tensile steel, and are usually laid by means of a moving carriage using a method of "cable-spinning" devised by John ROEBLING for the BROOKLYN BRIDGE in the 1860s. After spinning, the cables are compacted by hydraulic machine and clamped in place with wire. An alternative method is to construct the cable of fewer but much thicker twisted wire ropes 2-3 in. (5-7 cm) in diameter. The twin suspension towers may be built of welded steel or reinforced concrete, and for long-span bridges they must be very high. Those of the Verrazano-Narrows bridge are 680 ft. (207 m) tall.

Extensive WIND-TUNNEL testing is done before a design is finalized. The Humber bridge, for example, is designed to withstand winds gusting up to 150 mph (240 km) at tower-top level (533 ft., 163 m).

Suspension system

A suspension system insulates a vehicle and its occupants from the effects of an uneven road surface, and is as important to road holding and safety as it is to com-

The cable anchorages nearing completion on the Staten Island end of the Verrazano-Narrows suspension bridge. Each strand of each cable is anchored at one end, taken across the towers (allowing for the catenary curve) and anchored at the other end. (See the article on this bridge for a photograph of the complete structure).

The layout of a hydropneumatic suspension system, providing independent and self-leveling suspension on all four wheels. The enlarged detail shows one of the hydraulic cylinders.

fort. The two major components are springs and SHOCK ABSORBER. When a vehicle hits a bump, the spring is compressed, storing energy which it releases when it expands. This cushions the impact, but at the same time it tends to make the vehicle bounce — a reaction prevented by the shock absorber. The TORSION BAR is another device used to absorb energy, and it is also used as an anti-roll device.

Both coil and LEAF SPRINGS are used in suspension systems and in some suspensions springing is provided by the compression of gas in a sealed chamber. Rubber is also often used. The most common type of shock absorber is the oil-filled telescopic type, but oil-filled rocking-lever types are sometimes used.

Practically all modern vehicles have independent front-wheel suspension. One of the commonest systems incorporates double wishbones, so called because of their shape. The wishbones are hinged at their wide end to the body or subframe of the vehicle and connect at their narrow end to swivel joints or a king-pin on which the wheel can swivel. A coil spring with a telescopic shock absorber inside is located between the upper and lower wishbones. Another front-suspension system is the simpler MacPherson strut, which consists of a hollow strut containing a shock absorber. The upper part of the strut is connected via a coil spring to a flexible mounting on the vehicle's body. The lower end of the strut connects with a triangular link hinged to the body or engine subframe.

Most vehicles have rigid-axle rear-suspension units incorporating leaf springs and telescopic shock absorbers. The leaf springs are located under each side of the body and attached to it at front and rear. In the middle they are clamped to the rear axle. Shock absorbers are located between the clamping points and the vehicle body. This arrangement is known as Hotchkiss drive. Several independent rear-suspension units are in use. Some use double wishbones or MacPherson struts. Some use trailing arms with coil springs and shock absorbers, the arms pivoting at right angles to the body. Others use semi-trailing arms which pivot obliquely to the body. The common feature of most independent rear-suspension units is the use of UNIVERSAL JOINTS at each end of the half-shafts, permitting relative movement between differential, half-shafts, and wheels.

Several interesting linked suspension systems have been devised in which front and rear units are connected. British Leyland's HYDROLASTIC SUSPENSION is an example. On their smaller automobiles Citroën use a mechanically linked suspension system incorporating a coil spring. On their larger models they use a HYDROPNEUMATIC SUSPENSION incorporating fluid and compressed gas.

Swing bridge

A swing bridge usually pivots like a turntable on a central pier, thus allowing river traffic to pass on either side of the pier. Its disadvantage is that it provides narrow channels for navigation. Some swing bridges, including the world's longest (the al Firdan Bridge over the Suez Canal in Egypt, with a span of 552 ft., 168 m) have two separate arms which pivot on piers at either end. Both types disrupt river traffic more than BASCULE or VERTICAL LIFT BRIDGES.

Swing-wing design

In an attempt to combine the low-speed virtues of straight wings with the high-speed advantages of swept wings, variable-geometry airplanes have been designed with "swing-wings" — wings that can be rotated to a straight position for landing and taking off, or swept back for maximum speed, with an intermediate cruising configuration.

Although the mechanical complexity of swing-wings results in a greater structural weight, the fact that drag is less and that maximum aerodynamic efficiency can be obtained at any given speed enables a lighter, less powerful engine to be used. A swing-wing aircraft will also use less fuel than a comparable fixed-wing machine because of its enhanced aerodynamic efficiency, and so any ad-

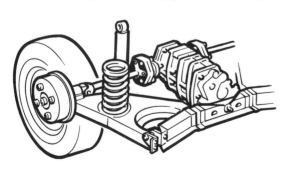

Semi-trailing independent rear wheel suspension used on a number of European cars.

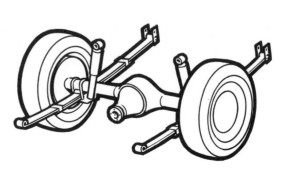

The conventional leaf spring and shock absorber suspension system used on the rear wheels of most automobiles.

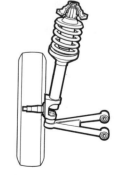

A typical independent front wheel suspension system, with single wishbone (pivoting on the chassis) and shock absorber.

ditional structural weight may be offset by reducing the fuel capacity.

The first swing-wing aircraft to enter military service was the General Dynamics F-111 tactical strike fighter, which was in production from 1965 until 1973. A strategic bomber variant of the F-111, the FB-111A, was also built in small numbers; the 76 machines constructed were allocated to two two-squadron bomber wings and a training unit. Maximum speed of the F-111 is Mach 2.5.

Variable-geometry wings have also been incorporated in the Grumman F-14 Tomcat two-seat fighter, designed for U.S. Navy use when the F-111 failed to meet naval requirements. Maximum speed is again in excess of Mach 2.

In Europe, the Panavia consortium has designed the MRCA (Multi-Role Combat Aircraft), designed to operate in strike, close support, air superiority, reconnaissance, and maritime roles. The use of swing-wing design is intended to provide a range of performance compatible with these varied service requirements.

The Soviet air force began receiving the swing-wing MiG-23 interceptor fighter in 1971; the design made its first public

The Sydney Harbour Bridge, New South Wales, Australia, is the strongest and one of the longest steel arch bridges in the world.

Variable geometry wings were first used on the F111 fighter shown in the photograph. After considerable initial problems the idea is now widely used, combining as it does the advantages of swept wings for supersonic flight and straight wings for low speeds.

appearance in 1967. Several squadrons of this Mach 2+ airplane were believed to be in service by 1973, and a swing-wing strategic bomber ("Backfire") joined the Soviet air force in 1974.

Switching

Diverting a railroad car or a complete train from one track to another. Indiv-idual cars for the same destination or route can thus be made up into a single train. This task is usually performed at low speeds by small powerful locomotives known as "switchers." The actual diversion is performed by moving specially shaped sections of track designed to form a continuous path for the wheels in either of two positions.

Sydney Harbour Bridge

The world's most massive steel-arch bridge, and one of the longest, the Sydney Harbour Bridge in New South Wales, Australia, has a span of 1,650 ft. (503 m) and accommodates two railroad tracks, eight traffic lanes, a cycleway, and a footway in its 160 ft. (48 m) width. Opened in 1932, it was built without the aid of temporary falsework by a cantilever method. Each half of the arch was built outward from its support, being restrained by temporary steel anchorages. The girders forming the arch were lifted in place by creeper cranes, which traveled along the top of the arch as it progressed.

Synchromesh

Synchromesh is a mechanism is a GEARBOX that synchronizes the speed of two gearwheels before they are allowed to mesh. This ensures a smooth gear change and avoids the grinding of gears common on early "crash" gearboxes. Cadillac and La Salle introduced the synchromesh gearbox in 1928.

In a gearbox a gear is selected when a sliding collar splined to a shaft is meshed with a gearwheel by means of side teeth called dogs. Synchronization between the two is achieved by means of conical surfaces on the outside of the gear and the inside of the collar. The two cones come together before the dogs meet and become synchronized, so that the dogs can slide smoothly into mesh.

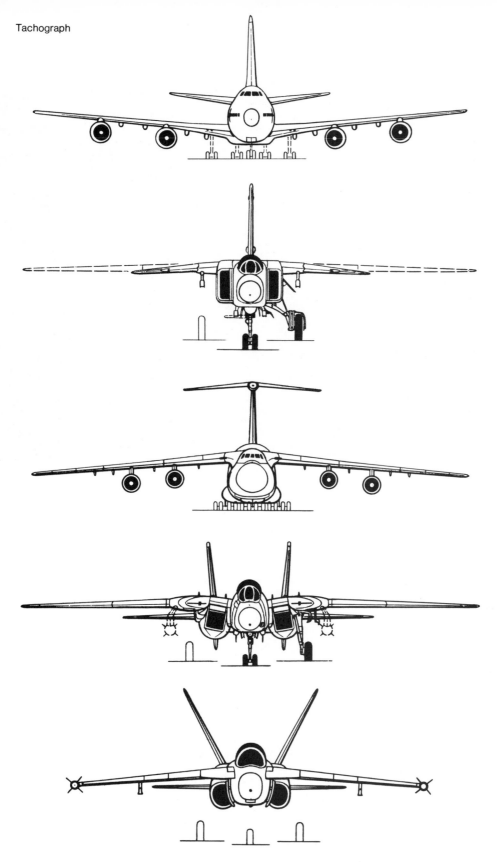

trically from the engine crankshaft, and is graduated in units of 100 rpm. On mechanical tachometers centrifugal force is used to compress or stretch a spring, which drives the instrument's pointer, while electrical types are simple electric generators.

Tacoma Narrows Bridge

The original Tacoma Narrows suspension bridge crossing the Narrows of Puget Sound achieved fame when it collapsed in a gale in 1940, after only four months' use. The bridge had a span of 2,800 ft. (853 m) and was unusually narrow (39 ft., 12 m) and flexible; instead of the usual deep trusses the deck was stiffened only by shallow plate girders. In a 42 mph (68 km/h) gale the deck began to oscillate in a wave motion up to 30 ft. (9 m) high and also swayed laterally. Within a few hours the bridge collapsed. Fortunately, a film was taken of the whole episode, providing a unique record of the effects of wind load on a full-scale suspension bridge. Since then every large bridge design has been tested aerodynamically, and there have been no similar disasters since. The new bridge completed across the Narrows in 1950 is significantly wider and more rigid, and incorporates longitudinal slots in the deck to minimize the formation of dangerous eddies in a strong wind.

Tail

To endow an airplane with directional stability it is equipped with a stabilizer (incorporating the ELEVATORS) and a fin (with the RUDDER). Together these constitute the tailplane. Without it, a con-

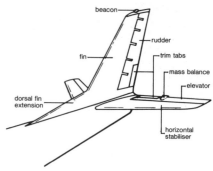

The labeled diagram (right) shows the names of the parts of an airplane's tail, while those above show the wide variety of tail configurations employed. They are, from top to bottom, Boeing 747, Mikoyan Flogger, Lockheed Galaxy, Grumman Tomcat, and Northrop 600.

T

Tachograph

A device for measuring and recording both time and distance traveled, the tachograph became a compulsory device on all new trucks in European Economic Community countries in January 1976.

Its purpose is to prevent truck drivers from driving for dangerously long periods, and to detect offenders.

Tachometer

Also called a "rev counter," a tachometer is an instrument that registers engine speed in revolutions per minute (rpm). It is driven mechanically or elec-

ventional (non-delta-wing) aircraft would tend to somersault either forwards or backwards. If the tail drops during level flight, however, the tailplane acquires a greater angle of attack (see WING) and its lift is therefore increased, raising the tail to the normal position. Should the nose fall, the tail plane acquires a negative angle of attack, its lift decreases and

This photograph of the bows gives some idea of the size of modern tankers, and of the problems of maneuvering them.

VLCCs (very large crude carriers) which are the largest mobile objects ever made by man. The largest of all at the time of writing was GLOBTIK TOKYO (483,644 tons deadweight). Much bigger tankers have been planned, but with the present drop in petroleum demand (over 35,000,000 tons of tankers are laid up) *Globtik Tokyo* may remain a record size for some time. These huge ships are built on the principle that the bigger the ship the more economic it is to operate. Most have a single propeller and a single boiler, and may therefore be rendered helpless by a comparatively minor mechanical fault. At the best of times, giant ships are difficult to maneuver, accidents have been far from uncommon, and an increasing number of people consider that VLCCs represent a major and unwarranted environmental hazard.

Tappets
Tappets form part of the valve-operating mechanism in an engine (see VALVE GEAR).

Taps
Abbreviation for TRANS ALASKAN PIPELINE SCHEME, a project begun in 1975 to transport oil from northern Alaska to a southern ice-free port.

Tay Bridge
Like the TACOMA NARROWS BRIDGE, the Tay Bridge in Scotland became famous as a result of a spectacular and tragic failure, which occurred on a stormy December night in 1879. The center part of the 2-mi. (3 km) bridge consisted of thirteen wrought-iron trusses supported by cast-iron columns on brick-and-concrete piers. For more than 18 months the bridge carried trains across the Firth of Tay without incident. Then on that night in December a complete train disappeared while crossing the bridge, with no survivors. All thirteen main spans came down, probably when a freak gust of wind hit the train broadside and imposed lateral stresses on the bridge structure that it could not withstand, partly because of its design and partly because of poor workmanship in construction.

Teleferique
An aerial ropeway carrying a CABLE CAR.

Telford, Thomas (1757-1834)
Scottish civil engineer famous as a pioneer road and bridge builder. In 1793 he was placed in charge of the Ellesmere Canal, for which he built two notable aqueducts over the Dee and Cairoig valleys in Wales. Then, in 1803, he was given the task of developing the Scottish Highlands, and constructed over 900 mi. (1,450 km) of roads, numerous bridges,

the tail drops to level the airplane again. The elevator controls diving and climbing maneuvers, and overrides the stabilizing effect of the tailplane.

Stability in the yawing plane is provided by the fin, with its hinged rudder giving directional control. Both the elevators and the rudder may be provided with trim tabs, usually controlled from the cockpit, which enable the flight attitude to be maintained.

"Tail first" aircraft (canards) have stabilizers located at the nose, with the wings moved to a position well aft. If the wings are substantially swept back, the wing tips themselves are far enough back to stabilize the aircraft and the machine may not need a tailplane.

Talgo
The Talgo is an advanced Spanish railroad train, its name deriving from "Train Articulé Léger Goicoechea et Oriel." Talgo is a lightweight train capable of maintaining relatively high speed on curves and over indifferent track, while giving comfort and safety to the passenger. Each car is short, has only two wheels, and is carried on a triangular frame with the apex of the triangle borne on the center of the single axle of the car in front. Each car is thus led around curves by the one immediately ahead, and as there is only one axle per car the wheels maintain a proper angle to the rails. There is no binding tendency as there is with cars with rigid wheelbases or even with pivoting wheel assemblies. The short cars are connected to allow passenger movement and have sheathing between them to give a "continuous" appearance. Hauled by diesel locomotives, Talgo trains have proved particularly successful in Spain, but experiments elsewhere, including the United States, have been inconclusive. (See also ADVANCED PASSENGER TRAIN (APT.)

Tankers
Ships designed to carry liquid cargo in bulk. Most tankers transport crude oil, but there are specialized vessels to carry wine, asphalt, liquefied natural gas, and molasses. For ease and speed the liquid is pumped into the holds or to the shore through pipes, and the process is automatically controlled by computer to maintain the ship's stability.

Virtually all tankers have their engines and other machinery at the stern, and most have the bridge and accommodation over the engines, so that the working areas of the ship are away from the cargo. In addition, the cargo space is isolated from the stern and from the bow (which often contains storage holds and ballast tanks) by pairs of watertight bulkheads.

Tankers vary in size from coastal craft of about 2,000 tons deadweight, to giant and the CALEDONIAN CANAL, as well as improving several harbors, including those at Aberdeen and Dundee.

Other notable achievements include famous suspension bridges over the Menai Strait and the River Conway in Wales, widespread canal work (including the construction of Sweden's Göta Canal), the building of London's St. Katherine's Dock, and the reconstruction of the London to Holyhead, Wales, road: The specification he adopted for the construction and alignment of this, his most famous achievement, were of such quality that much of his road has been incorporated in the present highway.

The Conway Suspension Bridge, Wales, one of many bridges built by the famous Scottish civil engineer Thomas Telford.

Temperature gauge

A temperature gauge is used to measure the temperature of, for example, the cooling water in a gasoline engine. The sensor placed in the water jacket is a thermosistor: a resistor whose resistance varies with temperature. As temperature changes, so does the current passing through the circuit incorporating the thermosistor and the temperature gauge. The gauge incorporates a bimetallic strip which is heated by this current. The strip, which consists of two metals of unequal coefficient of expansion, bends more or less according to the strength of the current, and moves the gauge pointer.

Tender

A car coupled to a railroad steam locomotive to carry supplies of water and fuel. When these are carried on the locomotive itself, it is known as a tank locomotive. An average tender of the last years of steam held about 25,000 gallons of water and 28 tons of coal.

A small rowboat towed behind (or carried aboard) a yacht is also called a tender.

Test pilot

Testing aircraft calls for the most skilled of pilots. The work falls into two categories: testing the prototypes and production testing before acceptance by the customer. Aircraft are not only tested to ensure that they are safe and that all systems function satisfactorily, but also to see that they meet the design specifications which an airline or military service has set. All aircraft must also meet stringent operation regulations made, in the case of the United States, by the Federal Aviation Administration. In military or airline service, new types of aircraft may pass through the hands of test pilots who will control the writing of operating manuals and help set any operating restrictions. After each major overhaul an aircraft will be test flown, but for such flights an ordinary pilot may aspire to the title of test pilot.

Test track

Track designed for testing supersonic aircraft, missile, and spacecraft equipment. On one, the Supersonic Naval Ordnance Research Track (SNORT) at China Lake, speeds of 3,090 mph (4,974 km/h) have been achieved. The track is very similar to normal railroad track, but is more precisely engineered, since for such high speeds it must be perfectly straight and smooth.

The equipment to be tested runs on a sled fitted with sliding metal shoes. Guide brackets on either side of each shoe keep the sled securely on the rails. The sled is rocket powered, and is decelerated at the end of each test run by water; the last stretch of the track is flooded for the purpose.

Such test tracks allow new materials and designs to be tested in safety before they leave the ground.

Thermostat

A thermostat is a device for maintaining a constant temperature. In a road vehicle's COOLING SYSTEM a thermostat is fitted to control the circulation of the coolant. It remains closed until the engine has reached its working temperature, thus preventing water from circulating from the engine into the radiator, and enabling the engine to warm up more quickly. One common type incorporates a concertina-like bellows containing a volatile liquid. When the water is cold the pressure inside the bellows is low, keeping the bellows compressed and a valve attached to it closed. When the water warms up, the pressure inside the bellows increases, the bellows expand, and the valve opens, allowing water through to the radiator. In another type the valve is opened by the expansion of a wax element when the normal operating temperature is reached.

Throttle

A throttle is a valve which regulates the flow of steam or fuel in an engine to control speed. In a gasoline engine it is in the CARBURETOR, and is usually a butterfly valve whose position is regulated by that of the accelerator pedal.

Thrust

Force generated by a jet or rocket engine, or by a propeller driven from a piston engine or turboprop, corresponding to mass multiplied by velocity.

A jet develops thrust by displacing a relatively small mass of air at high velocity; a propeller displaces a large mass of air at a low velocity.

Thrust bearing

A thrust bearing is one designed to resist end thrust. It may incorporate balls, rollers, needles or tapered rollers (see BEARINGS).

Timing

Timing in a gasoline engine refers to the timing of the spark in the IGNITION SYSTEM, and of the opening and closing of the inlet and exhaust valves (see VALVE GEAR), so that the various events occur at exactly the right moments in the FOUR STROKE CYCLE. Ignition timing is regulated by rotating the DISTRIBUTOR on its shaft so that the cams on the shaft open the contact breaker points (thereby causing a spark at the spark plug) at the correct moment in each cylinder: in most engines this is a little before the piston is at TOP DEAD CENTER. Fine adjustment is achieved by turning a screw on the VACUUM ADVANCE mechanism.

Valve timing depends on the correct adjustment of the timing chain or gears through which the crankshaft turns the camshaft (which operates the valves). Normally the valves are timed to open fractionally before the piston is at dead center, and to close fractionally after the dead center position at the other end of the stroke. This allows for the time taken for the valves to move, and permits the gases to start or stop flowing gradually.

Tin Lizzie

The Model T Ford, probably the most famous automobile of all time, and after the Volkswagen "Beetle" the best selling automobile in the history of the industry. A total of 15,007,033 were made between 1908 and 1927. Most early automobiles were expensive, unreliable, and suitable only for use on paved roads. Henry Ford decided to design and produce in quantity "a car for the great multitude," sturdy enough to go anywhere, cheap, easy to drive, and with a nationwide network of garages to supply spares and servicing. He dropped all other models and announced the Model T for 1909 at $850.

With a 2.9-liter, four-cylinder engine, a top speed of about 45 mph (72 km/h), pedal-controlled transmission, and a wide variety of body styles (and, until 1914, colors, after which it could be in any color so long as it was black), the Model T put America on wheels. Demand was so strong that Ford was led to introduce the mass-production techniques that revolutionized American industry, and the price of the Model T dropped year by year, reaching $260 in 1925.

Tire

The first powered road vehicles had wooden wheels with metal tires, but by the start of the automobile era solid rubber tires were usual, and in 1895 Edouard Michelin introduced the pneumatic tire to driving. The idea was first patented by the Scotsman Robert W. Thomson in 1845, and was reinvented by John DUNLOP who made the first pneumatic bicycle tires in 1888. Pneumatic tires not only provide a smoother ride but also have better adhesion and thus permit greater speed and safety. Until 1948 all tires had a separate inner tube, but in that year Goodrich introduced the tubeless tire, which has an inner lining of soft rubber. When it is punctured, the lining acts as a seal and the tire tends to deflate slowly; with a tubed tire deflation is more likely to be sudden, and therefore dangerous. The tubeless tire can be temporarily repaired with a rubber plug.

In the 1970s manufacturers began to offer "run flat" tires such as the Dunlop Denovo, which virtually eliminate danger after a blowout, can be run flat for 100 mi. (160 km) at up to 50 mph (80 km/h), and make the provision of a spare wheel

The Model T Ford, known as Tin Lizzie. The automobile in the photograph dates from 1927, the last year of production, by which time the Model T had become a functional small car.

unnecessary. Practically all tires are made of synthetic rubber blended to combine strength and flexibility, and to give resistance to gasoline and oil. Styrene-butadiene and polybutadiene rubbers are the most widely used synthetics.

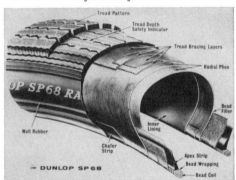

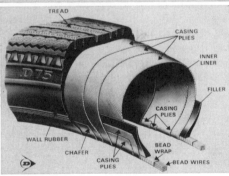

The two illustrations show the construction of a belted radial ply tire (above) and of the conventional bias ply type (below).

The tread pattern varies widely. While a fairly smooth tire is suitable for road-holding under dry conditions, on wet surfaces it will AQUAPLANE even at low speeds, owing to the build-up of a wedge of water beneath it. The tread is designed so as to channel water away from the contact zone, pushing or "pumping" it to the sides and rear. Winter tires have a deep, coarse tread and grooved shoulders to assist grip on a slippery surface, and some are fitted with steel studs.

There are three main types of tire construction. On the oldest, the bias-ply or cross-ply, the casing is made up of several layers, or plies, or corded fabric (usually rayon or nylon) with their cords lying diagonally to the center-line of the tire. Adjacent plies are laid with their cords in different directions. In belted bias-ply tires fiberglass belts encircle the tire between the tread and the plies, giving improved strength and directional stability and longer life.

The third type, the radial-ply tire, is also made up of overlapping plies, but the cords of the plies are at right angles to the center-line of the tire, and the belts are usually made of steel wire. The walls of the radial tire are more flexible than those of the bias-ply type, giving better adhesion on cornering. They also have less rolling resistance and a much longer life (25-30,000 mi., 40-48,000 km, compared with less than 20,000 mi., 32,000 km, for bias-ply tires). But at low speeds steering is somewhat harder and the ride less comfortable than with bias-ply tires.

Titanic

British liner announced as the largest, safest, and most luxurious passenger ship ever built, and claimed to be unsinkable. The *Titanic* struck an iceberg during her maiden voyage across the North Atlantic in 1912 and sank. There were 1,513 deaths.

Some 882 ft. (279 m) long, and carrying 2,206 passengers and a crew of 885, the *Titanic*'s hull was divided into 16 compartments and had a double bottom. There were too few lifeboats and there had been no lifeboat drill. After the disaster a new safety code was drawn up regulating such points as these and specifying adequate subdivision of the hull. The International Ice Patrol was also established.

Toboggan

A toboggan is a long, narrow SLED without runners, made from thin boards, and often curved at the front.

Toe-in, toe-out

Toe-in and toe-out are terms used to describe the slightly out of parallel alignment of a road vehicle's front wheels. This is necessary to counteract their natural tendency to deviate from the parallel caused by the steering system. Most rear-wheel driven autos have toe-in; the front wheels are set to point inward slightly. Many front-wheel drive autos have toe-out. The maximum amount of toe-in or toe-out required is about 3/16 in. (0.5 cm).

Toll road

See HIGHWAYS.

Tonnage

The tonnage of a ship may be a measure of the weight of the ship and everything on board (DISPLACEMENT tonnage); or of the weight of cargo, fuel, etc. that the ship can carry (DEADWEIGHT TONNAGE); or of the interior volume of the ship in units of 100 cubic feet (gross tonnage). Net registered tonnage, on which port and harbor dues are paid, is a measure of the volume of the actual cargo-carrying areas. Warships are normally measured in displacement tons, bulk ships in deadweight tons, and general cargo and passenger ships in gross or net registered tons.

Top dead center

The position of the piston at the top of its stroke in a cylinder is called top dead center. Ignition of the fuel mixture in a gasoline engine is timed to occur a fraction before top dead center (BTDC) (see TIMING).

Torque converter

A torque converter is a type of fluid coupling used, for example, in AUTOMATIC TRANSMISSION systems in automobiles and some diesel locomotives and railcars. It converts the torque of the engine into the higher torque required at low road (or rail) speeds, and is similar to the FLUID FLYWHEEL. It has a vaned impeller driven by the engine, and a vaned turbine connecting with the gearbox input shaft. The two face each other inside an oil-filled casing, with between them a vaned reaction wheel, or reactor. At low speeds the reactor is locked to the gearbox housing and cannot turn. It deflects the oil in such a way that the turbine receives extra thrust. As speed increases the reactor is allowed to freewheel, and it eventually spins at the same rate as the

Steam powered traction engines like this were used for heavy road haulage well into the present century.

turbine, thus causing no increase in torque.

Torque tube

A tube surrounding the PROPELLER SHAFT, bolted to the rear axle of a vehicle. It absorbs the torque reaction to the twisting force of the shaft.

Torrey Canyon

Notorious oil tanker sailing under the Liberian FLAG OF CONVENIENCE which ran aground off southwest England in 1967 in clear weather. The ship was broken up by the waves, and the oil polluted a long stretch of coastline. The captain had had no leave for over a year, and was physically unfit.

Torsion bar

A torsion bar is a steel bar often incorporated in a vehicle's SUSPENSION SYSTEM to resist twisting forces. It has one end fixed, while the other can be twisted by a lever. In the suspension system one end is fixed to the body, while the other is subject to leverage when the body rolls or pitches. The natural tendency of the bar to resist twisting reduces rolling.

Tower Bridge

Built between 1886 and 1894, Tower Bridge is a double-leaf simple BASCULE BRIDGE spanning the River Thames near the Tower of London in England. The bascule span provides an opening of 250 ft. (75 m) and the two side spans are each 270 ft. (82 m) long. The bridge carries a roadway 49 ft. (15 m) wide. A

footbridge, no longer in public use, runs between the central towers, 140 ft. (42 m) above the high-water level. Today the bridge is rarely opened, and there are plans to relieve it of road traffic by constructing a tunnel under the river.

Track circuit

The track circuit is the basis of most modern railroad signaling, and was first used in the 1870s. The track is divided into sections electrically insulated from those on either side, and in each section the two rails are also isolated electrically from each other. A low voltage is passed along one rail of a section, and across, at the end, via an electromagnet to the other rail and so back to the source. While the current flows, the magnet holds an armature; but when a train enters a section it short-circuits the current, and the magnet releases the armature. This can be used to indicate to a signal tower that a train is in the section, or to change signals automatically (see SIGNALING IN TRANSPORTATION).

Track-laying vehicle

A track-laying vehicle has caterpillar or CRAWLER TRACKS, such as a bulldozer and tank.

Track rod

A track rod is a bar or system of linkages that connects the front wheels of a vehicle so that they both turn when the steering wheel is turned (see STEERING SYSTEM).

Traction engine

Predecessor of the internal-combustion engined TRACTOR and truck, a steam-powered vehicle for hauling heavy loads on or off the road. From the 1830s wide use was made of stationary and portable steam engines for threshing and other farm duties. They were moved from place to place by horses. Then, in 1841, an English firm fitted a portable steam engine and belt-drive to a cart, leaving the horse to do the steering, and in 1849 the first true traction engine appeared. Complete with steering mechanism and a tender, it resembled a railroad locomotive.

America's first traction engines were built in the early 1860s to haul supplies in the West, and during the following 30 years traction engines were widely used for road haulage, for plowing and other farm work, in the logging industry (where giant three-wheelers pulled loads weighing 30 tons), and by traveling fairs.

Traction motor

A traction motor is an electric motor used to drive the wheels of a railroad locomotive or car, or of any other vehicle. The essential components are the stator, a casting which carries magnetic poles and windings (field coils) to produce the necessary magnetic field. These are arranged to leave space in the center for a rotor (or armature) which carries a number of coils, insulated from each other. The third main component is a commutator. When current is applied, a magnetic field is created by the field coils. The armature coils also carry current and the effect is that one by one each armature coil is given a twisting motion which causes the armature to revolve. The commutator is a device that supplies current to the right armature coil at the proper time and in the proper direction to continue the rotating motion. This rotation produces the power needed to drive the train. There are various types of traction motor, but basically all depend on the same principle. Locomotives may have up to six traction motors, each driving a separate axle, or can have one or two large motors, each driving a number of axles. The separate motors are more usual (see LOCOMOTIVE).

Tractor

A tractor is a powerful vehicle designed for relatively low-speed traction, generally off the road. (The term "tractor" also refers to the power unit used to haul trailers in trailer-trucks; for this, see TRUCKING.) Tractors have a wide range of uses in farming, construction work, road building, heavy industry, and materials handling. Fitted with suitable accessories they can become bulldozers, loaders, and excavators. They developed from the steam TRACTION ENGINES used from the late 1800s until the 1940s. By the turn of the 20th century gasoline-engine tractors were being produced in the United States, notably by Hart and Parr of Iowa, and by 1920 they were well established. Today, gasoline and diesel engines are the most common form of motive power; but engines burning kerosene and liquefied petroleum gas (LPG) are also used.

For general farm duty wheeled tractors are preferred, usually with large driving wheels on a wide axle at the rear and small steered wheels on a short axle at the front. On particularly sticky or light soil CRAWLER TRACKS may be used. These spread the tractor's weight over a larger area and provide better adhesion. Crawler-tracked vehicles in effect move along endless steel tracks which circle around wheels front and rear, being driven by those at the rear. Steering is effected by braking either of the driving wheels. For work on very uneven ground the front ends of the tracks are mounted so that they can rise and fall independently. For special duties on waterlogged or other unusually difficult terrain wheeled tractors with four-wheel drive are most successful.

One of the tractor's most important features is its power takeoff (PTO). With a pulley and belt drive fitted, this is used to power stationary machinery; with a

A view of London's Tower Bridge with the bascules raised to allow a Norwegian full-rigged training ship through.

A typical wheeled farm tractor. These versatile machines can haul heavy loads, and by means of a power takeoff can be used to power a variety of implements.

A massive 70 ton 524 hp crawler tractor (crawler tracks enable it to operate in conditions that would immobilize a conventional wheeled type) towers over a tiny lawn and grass tractor weighing just 745 lb (338 kg).

flexible shaft, it can drive implements mounted on or pulled by the tractor. The power takeoff is normally independent of the main transmission and can thus drive machinery at a constant rate regardless of the tractor's speed. Sometimes a hydraulic power takeoff system is fitted, and most tractors have a hydraulic ram mechanism. This may be used to raise and lower implements, or the tractor may carry hydraulic arms with a bucket attachment in front and a long-arm trenching device at the rear.

Trade winds

Steady and consistent winds that blow from subtropical belts of high pressure towards the equatorial belt of low pressure. With speeds of around 12 mph (19 km/h), they blow from the northeast in the Northern Hemisphere, and from the southeast in the Southern Hemisphere. At certain times reversed trade winds appear, notably in the Indian Ocean during summer when they form the southwest monsoon.

Columbus noted the existence of the trade winds during his first Atlantic crossing in 1492, and throughout the sailing era seamen followed the trades whenever possible. It was for example normal when crossing the Indian Ocean to sail west with the southeasterly trade wind, and east with the southwest monsoon.

Each belt is about 1,400 mi. (2,240 km) wide, stretching from roughly 5° to 25° latitude.

Traffic circle

A one-way circular system of traffic at an intersection, designed to promote a safe and continuous flow of traffic without the use of traffic lights. Normally a vehicle entering a traffic circle must give way to those already on it, but some circles are marked to give one route precedence.

Traffic control

The primary function of traffic control is to regulate the flow of conflicting traffic streams.

Traffic signals. The operation of electric traffic signals may be either by the passage of traffic over pneumatically-activated detectors aligned across the roadway (vehicle activation) or by a pre-set timing sequence (fixed-time).

Vehicle activation as a means of rationalizing traffic flow is finding increasing favor. There is a minimum running period that enables vehicles halted between the detector and the stop line to move off. The continual passage of a line of vehicles will prolong the green period, but there is a pre-set maximum to ensure that one stream does not secure a monopoly of the intersection.

To clear the traffic turning off across the oncoming stream, there may be a longer green for that lane than for through traffic, or alternatively the oncoming vehicles may be held for a late release after the red period.

Pushbutton-operated light signals for pedestrians may be provided if normal light sequences at busy junctions give walkers insufficient time to cross. Alternatively, a special phase for pedestrians may be incorporated in the timing sequence.

Control of traffic during rush-hour commuting is made more effective if all the signals in a given area can be coordinated. In some systems a master controller supervises the local controllers installed at each signal-governed intersection. This master controller determines a common operating cycle and overrides the local vehicle-activated control at certain points in the sequence to give a longer green time if conditions demand it.

United States cities employ a large number of fixed-time light systems, most of which are designed to give priority to traffic on arterial or radial routes. The fixed-time lights of a given area can, however, be wired or radio-linked to a central control. If it is determined by observation that certain traffic conditions occur at a given time each week, a light sequence to meet this situation can be devised and fed into the area at that particular time every week (predetermined fixed-time system). A further elaboration of this concept is to build up a "library" of predetermined signal settings designed to meet different situations. Transmissions from traffic sensors recording the flow of vehicles can then be used to automatically select an appropriate program for the situation as it develops.

The use of digital computers to govern traffic light signals was pioneered in Toronto in 1959. Loop detectors (usually

Increasing use is made of helicopters for surveying highway traffic conditions and informing ground patrols of potential or actual trouble spots.

located at mid-block) were connected by telephone lines to a central control and transmitted ten tones ranging between 350 and 2,600 cycles per second.

Other systems. To make the optimum use of multi-lane highways during rush hours, a system of changing the numbers of incoming and outgoing lanes can be used. This is called "tidal flow." The simplest system uses signs to indicate times and directions, but a police car is usually needed to clear a lane before it can be reversed. Movable barriers have also been employed, some of them electrically powered, but these are costly to provide and maintain.

Traffic control on arterial routes, particularly through cities, can be effected by remote control of diversion signs and speed limits. Closed-circuit television is

an important aid, together with sensors built into the road surface which either detect vehicles that remain stationary for more than, say, 10 seconds (thus indicating a hold-up), or else warn of a reduction in the rate at which vehicles are passing. Transmissions from this type of sensor can be routed to a central control where lights on a diagram will be illuminated and an audible warning tone will sound. (See also COMMUNICATION IN TRANSPORTATION.)

Traffic engineering

Traffic engineering takes into consideration the existing travel patterns of people living or working in a given area, together with the available transportation facilities, and the use to which the land in the area is dedicated (i.e. residential, industrial). It then seeks to find ways of speeding up the traffic flow, shortening

journey times, and reducing congestion both by recommending more efficient ways of using existing roads and by suggesting improvements to the road system.

The first step is usually a survey to determine the current traffic circulation, the area's annual rate of traffic growth, what additional traffic will be generated by any proposed new plan, and how much development is likely to be attracted to the area (since this will in itself increase the traffic volume). Individual travel patterns are assessed by questionnaire.

All this information can be reduced to coded data for processing and charts can be drawn up showing lines of varying thickness according to usage.

Among the criteria considered in assessing the viability of a proposed new plan

are the cost of the vehicles using the system (capital cost and depreciation), and the costs of road maintenance and traffic control personnel (police etc.). An evaluation must be made of money saved by reducing the number of accidents and the amount of time an individual spends sitting unproductively in traffic jams, against which must be set any social costs — for instance loss of amenity or property value if a new one-way system is partly routed through a residential neighborhood. Indirect costs are assessed for the effect a road improvement scheme might have on people's shopping habits or on decisions by industrial concerns about the siting of new factories. Relatively simple traffic measures may have quite startling effects. Erecting stop signs to bring traffic joining major roads to a halt before turning out of side roads may reduce accidents by 80% per million vehicle miles, at the expense of slowing down the traffic flow to a greater extent than a traffic light would. Staggering crossroads can produce an 85% reduction in accidents, while improvements in bridges or culverts and modifying the alignment of bends can bring something on the order of a 70% reduction.

More extensive alterations to roads may involve increasing lane widths, providing acceleration lanes, or easing gradients and curves.

Traffic characteristics are measured in terms of flow (vehicles per hour), concentration (vehicles per mile), speed, and journey time. A necessary evil in any system are intersections, which inevitably cause delays as competing traffic flows meet and merge; the only palliative is to ensure that, if possible, the capacity of intersections is in excess of requirements.

When traffic is heavy it is essential to maintain the flow, speed and concentration of vehicles. If a holdup does occur, any further traffic should be prevented from entering the area, since even a slight disturbance in the flow will cause rapid congestion buildup.

One-way streets reduce the points of conflict between traffic streams at intersections and have increased average speeds in London from 8-10 mph to 16-20 mph. The increased road width reduces the obstruction caused by parked vehicles, and other advantages are lower accident rates (especially to pedestrians) and a low initial cost that enables a one-way system to pay for itself in a few months. Disadvantages are increased vehicle mileage, possible loss of amenity in residential streets, and access problems for purely local traffic.

Prohibiting turns across oncoming traffic increases flow by 10-20%. Tidal flow involves allocation of extra traffic lanes to busier routes, with a concomitant reduction of the lanes available in the less congested direction. There must, however, be at least two low-flow lanes to allow for vehicles stopping. Flow reversal can be effected even on wide highways to accommodate morning and evening commuter traffic. With the use of computers, electronic monitoring devices, and television surveillance, traffic engineering is gradually becoming a less empirical science. It remains true that the problems of dealing with urban congestion are far too complex to be solved by engineers alone.

Trail bike

A motorcycle intended for use off the highway as well as on ordinary roads. Special suspension systems are used to absorb the shocks transmitted from rough ground, together with knobbly-tread tires.

A modern 46 ft. (14 m) mobile home trailer. Travel trailers are considerably smaller.

Trailer

Travel trailers are designed to be towed by an automobile for touring and vacation use. First built in the 1920s, they have become very popular in Europe and the United States. They are usually made of aluminum or glass reinforced plastic. In the 1960s very large trailers appeared, up to about 50 ft. (15 m) in length, complete with plumbing, electric wiring and central heating. Known as mobile homes, they provide permanent rather than vacation housing, and are not intended to be towed, being transported from factory to site by truck.

Trailer trucks

The chief advantage of trailer trucks is flexibility, an optimum numerical ratio being one tractor to three semi-trailers, so that one semi-trailer will be unloading while a second (loaded) is in transit behind the tractor and the third is being loaded at the tractor's destination. Tractive units may be of two-axle or three-axle types, the latter often having twin steering axles (the second steering

axle may be paired either with the front or the rear axle). Lockable or limited-slip differentials minimize wheel slip on wet roads, while tippers and other types with inherent traction problems are often six-wheelers with drive to both the rear axles.

A tendency to jackknife due to locked wheels can be mitigated by a disk brake on the trailer kingpin, Maxaret units, or a third line braking system. Articulated units pulling trailers (double-bottoms) are used in some countries for long-distance haulage, the trailer being unhitched at an out-of-town depot for local delivery.

Tram

See STREETCAR.

Tramp

A merchant ship which instead of operating a scheduled service on a specific route (see LINER; FREIGHTERS) goes wherever business takes it. The majority of tramps are BULK CARRIERS, and they are normally chartered by the voyage, to carry a specified cargo between two ports.

Trans Alaskan Pipeline Scheme (TAPS)

One of the most ambitious pipeline schemes ever attempted, the TAPS is designed to carry oil 789 mi. (1,285 km) from the oil fields around Prudhoe Bay in northern Alaska to the ice-free port of Valdez in southern Alaska, from where it will be shipped south by tanker to West Coast refineries. The cost of the pipeline is estimated to be some $6 billion, and completion is scheduled for 1977. The first big oil strike on the North Slope of Alaska was made in 1968, and it is now estimated that the region contains a third of American oil reserves and could be producing up to 2 million barrels a day by 1980. A gas pipeline to run alongside is also planned.

The pipeline climbs from sealevel at Prudhoe Bay up to 4,800 ft. (1,460 m) through the Brooks Range and down

again; it then crosses 34 major rivers before passing at 3,500 ft. (1,070 m) through the Alaska Range, and then descends to Valdez. It crosses some of the most inhospitable territory on earth, where winter temperatures plummet to below -50° C. Construction is proceeding simultaneously from 19 points along the route.

Environmentalists caused the pipeline scheme to be held up for several years until it was modified to protect the environment as far as was possible. One of the major objections was that heat from the oil, flowing through the pipeline at about 60° C, would melt the permafrost (permanently frozen ground). This would cause subsidence that could lead to rupture of the pipeline and devastating spillage of oil. Where possible, therefore, the pipeline is carried on supports above ground. Where the pipeline runs through earthquake-prone regions, the pipeline is being raised on special flexible mounts that will permit the welded pipes to move from side-to-side and up-and-down. In regions where the frozen ground is relatively stable the pipeline will be well insulated and buried up to 12 ft. (3.6 m) deep. If rupture of the pipeline does occur, however, electronic sensors will detect the fall in pressure instantly, and the affected segment of the pipeline can then be shut down within minutes.

Trans-Amazonian Highway

The backbone of a new system of highways designed to open up the vast uncharted areas of the Amazon basin in Brazil, it stretches from Recife on the Atlantic coast to the borders of Peru, over 3,200 mi. (5,000 km) to the West. For the most part it is a simple unpaved road of compacted gravelly-clay. Designed initially to carry up to 200 vehicles per day at speeds around 30 mph (50 km/h), it will ultimately be surfaced as settlements develop and traffic builds up. The Highway is the first stage of Brazil's National Integration Program, initiated in 1970 and described as the most important agrarian reform since the historic Homestead Act of 1862. Linking many of the existing river settlements, the road also passes through potentially fertile areas and rich mineral deposits — iron ore, bauxite, diamonds, and gold. Although it was originally planned as an opportunity for the poorer peasants from the drought-ridden Northeast to start a new life clearing and cultivating thousands of 250-acre lots alongside the whole road, the emphasis has now moved to the development of heavily capitalized poles of growth around the mining centers. In other areas, large-scale cattle ranching has developed.

Trans Australian Line

The Trans Australian railroad Line was built to link South and Western Australia across more than 1,100 mi. (1,770 km) of the Nullarbor Plain and the great deserts. The surveyors found their way by compass and took their bearings from the stars. Construction parties began work from Port Augusta in 1912 and from Kalgoorlie in 1913, meeting on October 17, 1917. The first through trains ran five days later. One section of line in the Nullarbor Plain is perfectly straight for 328 mi. (528 km), and is the world's longest straight stretch.

Trans-Canada Highway

The Trans-Canada Highway, completed in 1965, runs for 4,860 mi. (7,820 km) from St. John's, Newfoundland, to Victoria, B.C. Ferries link the Newfoundland section of the highway with Nova Scotia.

Trans-Europe Expresses

The elite of Europe's international express trains, providing high-speed day services between the major cities of nine countries. The T-E-E organization was initially formed in 1957 by the Netherlands and the Swiss Railways. The 28 services now provided are organized jointly by the State railways of Germany, France, Italy, Switzerland, and the Netherlands; with Austria, Belgium, Spain, and Luxembourg also participating. Running under such colorful names as Le Mistral, Rheingold, Saphir, and Edelweiss, these comfortable air-conditioned trains carry over 5 million passengers a year.

The special motive power units and rolling stock are owned and operated by the various railroad administrations forming the group, the T-E-E organization itself being responsible for overall coordination and direction and for the reservation system.

Transmission

A transmission system is used to transmit power from an engine to, for example, an automobile's drive wheels or a ship's propeller. The power is usually transmitted mechanically by means of shafts, chains, or belts, and the system incorporates some form of gearing to adapt engine power and speed to the needs of the drive wheels or propeller. This gearing may be variable, as in road vehicles, and thus able to provide a high torque (turning power) with a low road speed, for starting from rest and hill climbing, or a low torque with a high road speed, for steady cruising on a level road. Variable gearing is unnecessary on a ship, which simply has reduction gearing to lower the necessarily high speed

of the engine shaft to a suitable propeller speed of about 100 rpm.

Unlike steam engines, internal combustion engines develop very little torque when turning over at low speeds, and thus some device is needed to couple the engine to the load gradually when moving off from rest. This may take the form of a mechanical CLUTCH, or an electric or hydraulic system may be used. Both hydraulic and electric transmissions enable very much greater power to be transmitted than is possible with a clutch, and both are widely used on railroad locomotives, while hydraulic transmission is also common on diesel powered ships. In electric transmission an engine (usually diesel) drives an electric generator which in turn powers traction motors, while in hydraulic transmission a centrifugal pump or impeller drives a turbine in an oil-filled chamber.

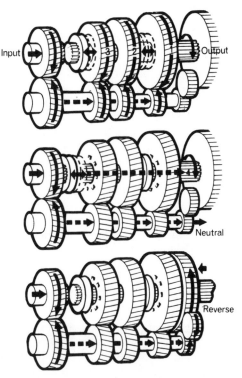

These diagrams show in simplified form the gear train in the gearbox of an automobile transmission system. The top diagram shows which gear wheels are engaged for first, second, and third forward speeds, the middle one shows top, and the bottom one reverse.

One of the simplest common transmission systems is that of the bicycle, in which power is transmitted by roller chain. Reduction gearing is built into the system, the chain wheel on the crank being very much larger than the driving sprocket on the rear wheel. Two forms of variable transmission may be used: the hub gear and the dérailleur (see BICYCLE). In automotive transmission gears may be changed manually or automatically. In a typical manual system drive from the

engine is imparted to the transmission system by the FLYWHEEL. Connecting with the flywheel is a CLUTCH, which provides a means of disconnecting the engine from the rest of the transmission system when changing gear. Drive goes through the clutch to the GEARBOX, which contains a variety of gear wheels in constant mesh. Variation in output-shaft speeds is provided by locking different pairs of gears together. From the gearbox power is transmitted in the conventional front-engine rear-drive arrangement via a PROPELLER SHAFT to the FINAL DRIVE in the rear axle. This incorporates a DIFFERENTIAL, which allows the road wheels to be driven at different speeds when cornering. Front-engine front-wheel drive and rear-engine rear-wheel drive arrangements require no propeller shaft and the transmission unit is more compact. In AUTOMATIC TRANSMISSIONS there is no clutch, but instead a fluid drive called a TORQUE CONVERTER. Different gear ratios are selected automatically at certain engine speeds by means of epicyclic gears.

Transporter bridge

A transporter bridge consists essentially of a movable platform suspended from a lattice girder or suspension bridge. The platform is at road level, and is drawn back and forth to convey vehicles and pedestrians across a waterway. Such a bridge provides an alternative to a ferry or an opening bridge, and is only used where access must be available for tall ships and where the road level is too low for a conventional bridge.

Trans-Siberian Railroad

Crossing the Soviet Union from Chelyabinsk to Vladivostok via Khabarovsk, a distance of 4,607 mi. (7,414 km), the Trans-Siberian Railroad is the longest continuous railroad route in the world. It was begun in 1891 and was built in sections until, using a route partly through Manchuria, through running became possible in 1902. The route has been much improved and largely electrified, and in 1974 the decision was taken to build a new northern Trans-Siberian railroad from Ust Kut near Lake Baikal to Komsomolsk in the east. Some 2,000 mi. (3,219 km) long, crossing mineral-rich virgin territory, and well separated from the Chinese border, the new railroad will need 140 bridges and four tunnels.

Trawler

Type of fishing boat used for towing a trawl (a conical fishing net). They range in size from oceangoing factory ships up to about 380 ft. (115 m) in length down to inshore vessels less than 80 ft. (24 m) long. They are diesel or diesel-electric

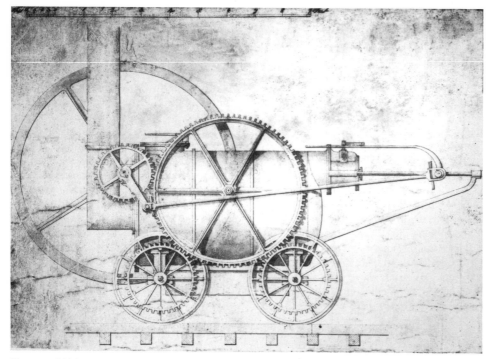

Pioneer of high pressure steam for transportation engines, Richard Trevithick constructed this, the world's first, railroad locomotive in 1804.

Trickle charger

A trickle charger is a device for charging storage batteries. It takes its power from mains electricity, and supplies it to the battery at a low current (three to four amps) and a suitable voltage. It consists essentially of a rectifier to convert alternating to direct current, and a transformer to lower the mains voltage.

Tricycle

A tricycle is a three-wheeled pedal driven vehicle. The first tricycle, invented in England in the 1870s, had two small wheels in line and one large one at the side. The modern tricycle with one wheel in front and two behind evolved in the 1880s. The DIFFERENTIAL gear used in automobiles was originally invented for the tricycle.

Trimaran

A trimaran is a multi-hull boat similar to a CATAMARAN but with three rather than two hulls.

Triplane

Three-winged airplane of the early era which was designed to give extra LIFT. It achieved a good climb rate but at the expense of speed because of DRAG caused by the extra wing and its supports. The Sopwith Triplane proved a successful fighter (1916-17) and Germany in 1917 introduced the Fokker Triplane flown, among others, by the famous Baron von Richthofen. Italy built triplane bombers and America, Britain, France, and Germany all had several triplane prototypes in the main triplane era of 1914-19 (see BIPLANE; WARPLANE).

Trireme

A WARSHIP of the ancient world propelled by three banks of oars placed

powered, and carry advanced SONAR and NAVIGATION equipment.

Modern trawlers tow the net from the stern, although most older vessels are side trawlers, on which the nets are set out and hauled in over the sides. The stern trawler is more highly mechanized, can handle a bigger catch, and requires a smaller crew.

On factory trawlers the catch is prepared and canned or frozen on board. Most of the processes are performed automatically. The largest vessels can remain at sea for nearly six months. Smaller conventional trawlers store the catch in ice, and must return to port or unload onto a factory ship within a few days.

Trevithick, Richard (1771-1833)

Born in Cornwall, England, Trevithick was one of the most important pioneers of steam locomotion. He invented the high-pressure STEAM ENGINE, which was smaller, lighter, and more efficient than James WATT's low pressure engine, and in 1801 he built the world's first practical steam road carriage, known locally as "Captain Dick's Puffer." An improved model was tried out successfully in London in 1803, but aroused little interest. He built the world's first RAILROAD LOCOMOTIVE in 1804 for the 9-mi. (14.5 km) Penydarren Iron Works plateway in South Wales. It hauled five wagons with 10 tons of iron and 70 men the whole length of the plateway, but was too heavy for the track and had to be abandoned. A further locomotive was constructed to his designs by John Steele in 1805 for

Wylam Colliery in Northumberland. His last locomotive was built to run on a circular track in London, hauling one car. He called this CATCH-ME-WHO-CAN, and many Londoners did, becoming the first paying passengers on a locomotive-hauled line. Trevithick was the true Father of the Locomotive, and many of his ideas were later taken up and improved on by others. He was also interested in other aspects of transportation. He attempted to build the first tunnel under the River Thames, and only narrowly failed in the attempt. He was also active in experiments with propeller-driven steam boats, and dredging, and built a steam threshing machine in 1811.

A modern oceangoing Soviet trawler.

one above the other. The trireme had a single mast and square sail (not used during battle), and a pointed ram at the bow.

Troika

A Russian vehicle (often a SLED) drawn by a team of three horses harnessed abreast.

Trolleybus

Passenger-carrying road vehicle for urban transit, similar to a bus except that it has electric traction and obtains its power from overhead cables. It has the advantages of quiet operation, freedom from fumes and rapid acceleration, but lacks the flexibility of a bus as it must follow the cables. In the history of urban transportation the trolleybus occupies a place between the STREETCAR, which in many cities it briefly replaced, and the bus, which in turn has almost universally replaced it. Apart from lack of flexibility, the high cost of electricity and of maintaining substation and overhead cable systems has made trolleybuses expensive to operate.

A Russian troika. The vehicle is so-called because it is drawn by three horses (troika is Russian for three).

Trolleybuses suffer from the same lack of flexibility as streetcars, but they are quiet and pollution-free and are still used in some cities. This one is in Moscow, Soviet Union.

The first trolleybus service began in Germany in 1901, and the idea spread to many countries including Britain, where it achieved its greatest popularity (particularly in London), and the United States. Today trolleybus services continue in Moscow, and in a few other European cities.

Trollhätte Canal

The Trollhätte Canal is part of the Göta Canal connecting the Kattegat and the Baltic Sea, through Sweden. The canal, near Trollhätten, bypasses the falls on the Göta River and has six locks to allow seagoing ships to rise 18 ft. (5.5 m) and enter Lake Vänern. The canal, 47 ft. (14 m) wide and 10 ft. (3 m) deep, was completed in 1800.

Truck

Device for supporting a railroad locomotive or car on a sub-frame free to swivel and move to a limited extent independently of the main vehicle frame. The load that can be applied to the track by one pair of wheels is limited, and so heavy vehicles, such as locomotives, must have several pairs of wheels — in general, the heavier the vehicle, the more wheels. But if all these pairs of flanged wheels were fixed in one rigid line, the vehicle would leave the track on sharp curves. It is usual, therefore, to put two, three, or occasionally four pairs of wheels on a sub-frame which supports the weight through a center pivot. With such a sub-frame at each end, the vehicle can go around curves even if the center section is well out of line with the rails.

A 19th century engraving of an ancient trireme. The artist has given the vessel a rig from a much later period.

Trucks and trucking

The carriage of goods by road has become organized into a highly developed industry since the evolution of the motor truck in the early years of the 20th century and now provides a livelihood for one American in every ten. Transportation companies contribute about 10% of the American national income, and some 10-20% of production cost in the United States is attributable to freight charges.

The trucking industry. In the United States, long-haul trucking has been controlled since 1935 by the Interstate Commerce Commission, which originally acquired its jurisdiction during the depression years to relieve economic distress caused by excessive competition for trade. Carriers may be local operators (within a restricted radius of about 20 mi.; 32 km); private truckers carrying only the goods of the company to which they belong (usually a limited proportion of the concern's total output, since the cost of private transport is only justifiable where there is a regular flow of consignments); contract carriers who operate for hire on a basis of individual contracts with specific firms or individuals (such concerns do not usually have terminal facilities or fixed routes); and common carriers who offer a general service to the public.

There has always been considerable commercial rivalry between the two surface carriers of goods: the railroads and the trucking industry. Ultimately almost all goods are delivered by road, either directly or else after collection from a rail depot by truck, and the road vehicle's facility for providing a door-to-door service has the outstanding advantage of flexibility.

On the other hand, although some modern trucks can accommodate nearly as much as a box car, road restrictions limit the ultimate size of trucks and the railroads are generally able to carry a greater bulk. With the imposition of 55 mph (88 km/h) speed limits on American roads, the railroads have a further advantage of speed.

Ice and heavy snow on mountain routes can delay trucks, but otherwise their reliability compares favorably with that of freight trains, mechanical breakdowns and tire failures being rare. Furthermore, a halted truck will not block a road, but a stalled train will bring all traffic on the line to a halt.

Trucking rates have to be approved by Interstate Commerce Commission and have generally been based on those charged by the railroads, with the continental United States divided up into

Forerunners of the modern truck, small motor vans like this were extensively used for local distribution of goods and as "feeders" for the railroads.

regions and goods grouped into classes for which authorized rates are laid down.

Development. Only just over 6,000 motor trucks were registered in the United States in 1910, but the American trucking industry expanded rapidly during the 1920s — a decade in which the railroads introduced larger and larger box cars at a time when business was tending towards a small inventory policy that required the frequent shipment of small consignments. Furthermore, railroad charges were scaled to give a low rate per ton/mile for long-haul journeys with a relatively high rate for short trips, while a substantial charge was made for the extra care needed to carry high-value finished items (even on long journeys). The trucking industry therefore established itself in the short-haul market, and also penetrated the long-distance haulage business by quoting competitively for the carriage of high-value articles. The 800,000 trucks registered in 1920 had grown to nearly 3.5 million by 1930. Subsequently the trucking industry tended to follow the goods rates set by the railroads when these either rose or were cut, although rises in truck rates were often less than those applied by the railroads in order to maintain a competitive margin.

Economics. In the 1960s, the trucking business was still principally a short-haul operation, with railroads carrying 42.9% of intercity freight (assessed in ton/miles) compared to the 23% that went by road. The average intercity truck journey was 267 mi. (427 km), compared to the 464 mi. (742 km) of the average railroad line-haul, but certain commodities which are particularly vulnerable to deterioration in the event of transit delays (which often occur at railroad depots) were shipped

principally by road. Trucks carry the majority of beverages and tobacco products, clothing, and meat and dairy products. They are somewhat less widely used for canned and frozen foods, or for primary iron and steel products, since road haulage is least competitive on trips exceeding 400 mi. (640 km). The vast majority of agricultural produce travels by road, since trucks can divert off the highway to collect from the fields and then proceed directly to the markets. About 80% of farm livestock arrives at stockyards or packing stations by truck. Rates for agricultural produce are not subject to ICC control.

Other "off-highway" operations for which trucks are indispensable are the shipment of drilling equipment to oil fields and the collection of pulpwood for papermaking factories from forest sites. The return on capital invested in trucking fell as low as 8% during the recession year of 1958, but in 1962 reached almost 12%. Continued regulation of carriage rates is necessary because the trucking industry operates in competition with the railroads, whose freedom to alter goods rates is legally restricted.

In the 1960s there were about 1,100 United States trucking firms with a gross operating revenue of $1 million a year or more, about half of these being general freight haulers. On average these large operators would each have about 60 trucks or tractors and nearly 70 trailers. Most still operate within fairly restricted territorial areas and limit the nature of their operations, but a few cover longer routes, e.g., from the Pacific seaboard to Chicago and St. Louis, where trailers can be exchanged with eastern carriers.

Truck design. The first truck, produced in Germany by Gottlieb DAIMLER in 1896, was powered by a four-horsepower engine with belt drive from a two-speed

This 10-wheel heavy-duty tractor unit has a diesel engine, but increasing use is being made of gas turbines, especially for long-distance trucking operations.

A typical European truck-trailer combination.

and reverse transmission. Two years later the first American-manufactured truck was built by the Winton Company, the power plant consisting of a single-cylinder six-hp unit.

Modern trucks may be either straight (rigid), with all the axles attached to one frame, or articulated (TRAILER TRUCK) with two or more separate frames connected by couplings. Semi-trailers employ a "fifth wheel" coupling, comprising a trunnion plate and latching mechanism on the tractor mating with a kingpin on the semi-trailer. A semi-trailer can be converted into an independent trailer with a converter dolly (an auxiliary axle assembly with the lower half of a fifth wheel, a drawbar, and other special components).

Efforts are being made to standardize fifth wheel couplings so that semi-trailers can be interchanged between different haulage companies, thus increasing the operational flexibility of the trucking industry.

In large modern trucks, the frame is an independent structure (not integrated with either the cab or the body) that is usually built up from two channel sections of alloy steel, the standardized width being 34 in. (86.3 cm). Unitized construction is often employed for semi-trailers and tank trailers, however, and as industrial and consumer goods grow progressively more bulky in relation to their weight the "high cube" trailer has evolved. Constructed of light metal and employing air ride, this type of vehicle complies with state size restrictions but contrives to provide the maximum volume capacity. Special tankers for the chemical industry are manufactured with a variety of linings to accommodate toxic or corrosive substances, and pressure tanks and refrigerated vehicles are commonly used.

For many years front suspension was almost exclusively in the form of a drop-forged single section axle carried by leaf springs with shock absorbers, but during the 1960s various forms of independent front suspension were introduced.

Rear axles are normally suspended on leaf springs, the assembly being fully floating so that in the event of a breakage all of the load will be taken by the axle housing. Single or double reduction gears may be employed, and the driving and braking thrust may either be absorbed by the springs (Hotchkiss-type axle) or transmitted through a series of torque arms. A two-speed axle has a gear change mechanism incorporated in it, which means that every ratio in the gearbox has two alternative final drive ratios.

Tandem drive trucks have two powered axles, sometimes with two drive shafts (one to each axle). Very large intercity tractor/semi-trailer combinations may have as many as 10 wheels and some special units are capable of carrying 30-40 tons.

Steering systems are conventionally of the Ackerman type with a kingpin for each wheel, the maximum cramp angle being about 35°. Two front steering axles are often employed.

Until the 1930s, power units were largely gasoline engines, but extensive development of diesels during World War II led to the widespread adoption of compression-ignition engines in the late 1940s despite their relatively high initial cost. Single-plate dry-disk clutches are commonly used, in conjunction with up to 16 forward speeds — many diesel trucks have a restricted optimum engine-speed range of between 1,500 and 2,200 rpm which necessitates a comprehensive range of ratios. Automatic transmissions have not found widespread favor in heavy trucks.

Solid rubber tires were used until World War I. Cotton was replaced in carcasses by rayon during the 1930s, with wire and nylon coming into use during the ensuing decade. Tubeless truck tires appeared in 1955, and there was subsequently a tendency to replace double wheels with a single wheel carrying a wide tire. For winter conditions, tire chains were introduced in 1904, and snow tires made their appearance in 1936. Steel-belted tires were an innovation of the 1950s. Recapped tires are extensively used by trucking companies, since this process can extend carcass life by 150%.

Braking systems may be operated by means of air exclusively, by a combined air/hydraulic layout, and by electricity. "Full air" is the most widely used method, with an engine-driven compressor delivering compressed air. Methods of avoiding total brake failure in the event of a malfunction include the DD3 parking brake and the spring brake system. Hand brakes usually operate on the drive shafts through the medium of disks.

The Soviet Tupolev Tu-144, the world's first supersonic transport (SST) seen here with its nose in the drooped position. It carries some 120 passengers at a maximum cruising speed of 1,550 mph (2,500 km/h).

Truss Bridge

A truss bridge is a BEAM BRIDGE that has a strengthening steel framework, or truss, above or below its sides. The truss serves to counteract the natural tendency of a beam to bend in the middle under its own weight. The truss usually takes the form of linked triangles; each member is in a state of tension or compression throughout. Many railroad bridges are of trussed design, enabling them to carry heavily loaded trains.

Tsiolkovski, Konstantin Eduardovich (1857-1935)

Russian rocket pioneer. Tsiolkovski has been called the "Father of Astronautics" because he carried out the first really intensive research into the problems of space flight. He examined the problem that any motor used for launching a space vehicle would steadily consume fuel, and would therefore change the weight of the space vehicle. Tsiolkovski decided that a liquid-fueled rocket motor would be more effective than the solid-fueled rockets then generally in use. He put forward the theory that in order to escape from the Earth's gravitational field it would be necessary to have a multi-stage rocket, the basis of all modern space launches.

He also pioneered the use of WIND TUNNELS for aerodynamic research.

Tu-114

Until the Boeing 747 appeared, the Russian Tupolev Tu-114 Rossiya was the largest airliner in service; it first flew in 1957 and some 30 went in service from 1961. Seating 170 passengers, the Tu-114 could fly from Moscow to New York nonstop and from 1967 a Moscow-Tokyo route was flown in conjunction with Japan Air Lines. The Tu-114s were replaced by Ilyushin Il-62s in the early 1970s.

Tu-144

Rissia's first supersonic airliner, similar in conception and size to CONCORDE. The prototype Tu-144 first flew on December 31, 1968, went supersonic from June 1969 and reached Mach 2 in May 1970. It was the first supersonic transport to fly. The second prototype, lengthened and modified, crashed at the 1973 Paris Air Show, but further Tu-144s are scheduled to enter service with Aeroflot, the Russian airlines. The Tu-144's wingspan is 94½ ft. (28.8 m), it is 215 ft. (65.5 m) long and can carry up to 140 passengers.

Tug

A small boat designed to tow or push large ships or trains of BARGES. Tugs have very powerful diesel engines which usually occupy the bulk of the hull, and either twin rudders or variable-thrust propeller arrangements for maximum maneuverability. Pusher tugs have a built-up and strengthened bow, while conventional towing tugs have special towing equipment which compensates for sudden changes in tension.

Tugs are an essential feature of ports and docks, where they maneuver large

Typical harbor tugs taking a large liner to her berth.

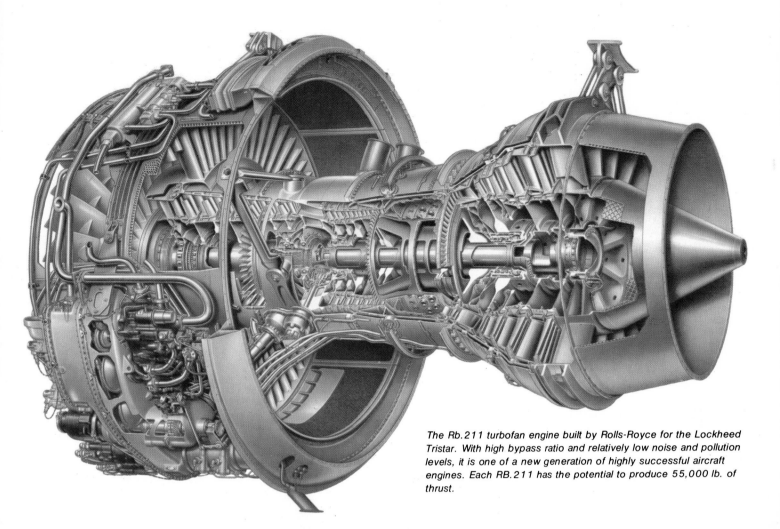

The Rb.211 turbofan engine built by Rolls-Royce for the Lockheed Tristar. With high bypass ratio and relatively low noise and pollution levels, it is one of a new generation of highly successful aircraft engines. Each RB.211 has the potential to produce 55,000 lb. of thrust.

The drive shaft, and part of the triangular rotor and broad figure-of-eight shaped cylinder of the rotary Wankel engine. Each face of the rotor performs the work of a piston in a conventional engine, so there are three power strokes per revolution.

Designed for speed, this 1908 Austin of the veteran era has much cleaner lines than most automobiles of the time.

This 1902 Peugeot is a typical representative of the early automobile era. On their models of the late 1890s Peugeot supplied as a standard accessory a whip for chasing off attacking dogs.

ships onto their berth, and of inland waterways. Large oceangoing tugs are used for SALVAGE work.

Tunnels

The traditional use of tunnels in transportation is to carry highways, railroads, or canals through hills and mountains, and under rivers or other stretches of water. Today tunnels also carry highways under rather than through urban areas, thus preserving the urban environment and allowing the possibility of collecting and processing noxious exhaust fumes before they reach the atmosphere. They can provide a sheltered and extensive underground complex of streets, shops, and so on, linked to subway and railroad systems, an idea that has been developed on a large scale in Montreal, Canada, and one which helps to reduce traffic congestion on the surface.

The Babylonians are reputed to have tunneled under the River Euphrates as long ago as 2100 BC. The Greeks and Romans dug tunnels mainly for drainage and as aqueducts, but a 4,800 ft. (1,463 m) road tunnel was constructed in 36 B.C. linking Naples and Pozzuoli in Italy. There was little development until the increase in trade and the growth of canal networks in the 17th and 18th centuries. The first major canal tunnel, and probably the first in which explosives were used, was the 515 ft. (1,570 m) LANGUEDOC CANAL Tunnel constructed between 1666 and 1681. Britain's first was the 1½-mi. (2.7 km) tunnel on the Grand Trunk Canal, and this was followed by the BRIDGE-WATER CANAL Tunnel of 1761, and by many others in Europe and North America. The canal-builder's techniques were adopted by the railroad pioneers when the railroad age began in the 1820s. Like the canal, the railroad could be built only over relatively level ground, which required extensive tunneling in hilly country. Among outstanding early feats was the driving of a 1,200-ft. (366 m) tunnel under the River Thames by Marc Isambard BRUNEL. He invented the forerunner of the modern tunneling shield in 1824 and used this to bore twin tunnels simultaneously under the river. Opened in 1843 after nine years' actual work, Brunel's tunnel proved the feasibility of subaqueous tunneling and spurred Greathead to develop his improved shield (see GREATHEAD SHIELD). This employed compressed air to keep water out, and made possible the unprecedented feat of building a 7-mi. (11 km) London subway tunnel in 1886 without a single fatality. Another outstanding pioneering feat was the blasting of the 7½-mi. (12 km) MONT CENIS TUNNEL in the Alps, which took from 1857

Work in progress on an underwater tunnel. The large duct at the top draws out stale air, and the rails are needed for transporting excavated "muck" from the tunnel head.

to 1871 to complete and necessitated the development of new surveying techniques as it was driven from both ends simultaneously. Little further progress was made until the introduction in 1861 of the compressed-air drill mounted on a jumbo carriage.

In the United States the first railroad tunnel was built between 1831-33 on the Allegheny Portal Railroad, and was 701 ft. (214 m) long. One of the most notable American achievements was the 4-mi. (6.4 km) Hoosac tunnel which linked Boston to the west under the Berkshire mountains. It took 24 years to build, pioneered (with the Mont Cenis tunnel) modern rock tunneling methods, and was the first in which nitroglycerin was used for blasting work. The construction of the 12-mi. (20 km) SIMPLON TUNNEL between 1898 and 1906 was another epic tunneling feat. Bored 7,000 ft. (2,134 m) below the summit, problems included rock bursts, subterranean hot water, and the construction of a 10 ft. (3 m) thick masonry lining in parts.

The world's first major road tunnel was built under the Hudson River at New York and opened in 1927. Named the Holland Tunnel after its engineer Clifford M. Holland, it is 8,500 ft. (2,590 m) long. Road tunnels are necessarily larger than railroad tunnels, and exhaust fumes pose an additional problems. The Holland Tunnel pioneered the procedure of providing forced-air ventilation through a duct under the roadway, with an exhaust duct overhead. In recent years the driving of the 7-mi. (11 km) long road tunnel

under MONT BLANC by French and Italian engineers was a notable tunneling achievement, and in Japan the ambitious Seikan tunnel project is nearing completion. This 33½-mi. (54 km) undersea rock tunnel beneath Tsugaru strait between the islands of Honshu and Hokkaido will be the world's longest railroad tunnel. 1979 is the estimated date for completion.

Tunnel construction. One of the simplest methods is cut-and-cover construction. Widely used for shallow sub-surface tunnels including the New York subway, it involves excavating a trench, installing tunnel linings, and then covering them over and restoring normal ground level.

Before work begins on any deep-level tunnel detailed geological information about the soil and underlying rock strata must be obtained by, for example, seismic survey and borehole sampling. This can give a good indication of general problems, but for detailed information a pilot tunnel is often driven along the proposed route. Small boreholes drilled through the roof and sides indicate the hardness of the surrounding rock strata and reveal the presence of any faults and weaknesses. Various instruments may be placed in the borehole and tunnel linings. Extensometers measure the strain in the surrounding rock, indicating whether it is in compression or tension and to what degree. Load cells measure the rock pressure on the tunnel lining. Driving a pilot tunnel is expensive, but the detailed information accumulated invariably more than justifies the cost. When full-scale tunneling begins, the pilot tunnel may be simply widened, or it may be used as a service or drainage channel for the main tunnel. All long tunnels present ventilation and drainage problems, and are therefore constructed with ducts in the roof to carry away fumes and under the road to supply fresh air. Huge blowers may be necessary to keep the air circulation. Drainage channels are also required in many tunnels and may need to be pumped out continuously. Electrical conduits may also be installed.

Hard rock tunneling. Most rock tunneling is done with the help of explosives and a rail-mounted jumbo drilling rig. This is a multi-level structure carrying on each level several compressed-air drills which bore a pattern of holes in the rock face. Explosive charges are placed in the holes and fused to fire in a prearranged sequence: the center charges first, those near the edge last. The jumbo rig is then withdrawn, and the charges are fired.

A probe drilling rig for taking samples of the bedrock. Geological survey work is an essential preliminary to undersea tunneling.

Clearing the rockfall, a process known as "mucking," is done with mechanical scraper-loaders which dump the rock in railroad cars for disposal. Other special equipment has been designed to speed up the process. One example is the rail-mounted shuttle car which loads the rock spoil onto an integral conveyor belt. Experimental rock cutting techniques include the use of water or flame jets, electron beams, lasers and ultrasonics. Hard rock tunnels are usually lined with concrete, to knit and bond the rock surface together, and for smoothness. Automatic tunneling machines (moles) have come into use for boring through soft rock such as chalk, sandstone and limestone; and several have been designed for automatic hard rock tunneling. In one ingenious American design the machine drills a small diameter pilot hole, and inserts steel grips to act as an anchor. A rotating cutting head grinds the rock away, driving forward by pulling on the pilot anchor.

Tunneling shields. When tunneling through soft ground, such as soil, sand, and clay, provision must be made to prevent the tunnel from collapsing while digging is in progress. This is done by means of a tunneling shield. The modern shield is a modification of the GREATHEAD SHIELD and is essentially a cylinder with a cutting edge which is driven forward by powerful hydraulic rams. Material is

excavated from the tunnel face from inside the shield and new tunnel linings are put in place behind the shield. The rams then push against the newly fitted lining and drive the cutting edge forward. Cement grout is often injected through holes in the linings to fill any air space. Sometimes excavation is done by hand, but moles with large rotating cutting wheels are being increasingly employed.

Underwater tunnels. When tunneling under water there is always the danger that water may seep through, even in apparently impervious rock. So there must always be provision for pumping. In the traditional method of underwater tunneling the air pressure in the tunnel is increased until it exceeds that of the water. An air lock is provided through which men and materials must pass, and before returning to the surface workmen must be decompressed to avoid danger of caisson disease ("the bends"). After the tunnel linings have been put in place cement grout, gelling solutions, or bituminous emulsions are injected behind them to help prevent subsequent seepage of water.

This pressurized method is expensive and dangerous, and it cannot be used at depths greater than 100 ft. (30 m). Since the 1940s most underwater tunnels have been built on the immersed-tube system pioneered in the early 1900s during construction of the Detroit River Railroad

Tunnel, and the Paris Metro. Large tunnel sections are prefabricated on land, temporarily sealed at each end, floated into position, sunk into a prepared trench in the river bed, and joined together by divers. Often piles are driven into the river bed to provide additional anchorage and support for the tubes, which are usually made of steel and are double skinned. Concrete is poured into the cavity walls to settle the tubes on the river bed. There have been notable recent examples of the immersed-tube system in the United States. The two 1¼-mi. (2 km) tunnel sections of the Chesapeake Bay bridge-tunnel were constructed by this system, as was the major part of the tunnel carrying the San Francisco BAY AREA RAPID TRANSIT (BART) railroad beneath the Bay. To facilitate the trench-digging process, the Japanese have recently developed a remotely-controlled television-monitored underwater bulldozer.

Turbine

A turbine is an engine which is driven by the passage of steam, gas, or oil through the vanes of a wheel on a shaft, causing it to rotate. STEAM TURBINES are used for marine propulsion, and GAS TURBINES or JET ENGINES power most planes. Gas turbines are also used to propel some locomotives, ships, trucks, and even experimental automobiles.

Turbinia

The first practical STEAM TURBINE powered vessel, built in England in 1894 to demonstrate the potential of Charles Parsons' new turbine engine. Some 100 ft. (30 m) long, and powered by three direct-drive steam turbines, she raced among the British fleet during a naval review at the then unprecedented speed of 34.5 knots.

Turbofan

A turbofan is a JET ENGINE in which part of the air drawn into the engine by a huge fan bypasses the combustion chambers and gives additional thrust. It is also called a bypass turbojet, or a fanjet.

Turbojet

A turbojet is a JET ENGINE in which kerosene fuel is burned in compressed air to produce a stream or jet of hot gases. It develops thrust by reaction.

Turboprop

The turboprop engine consists of a propeller coupled to a turbine. There are no reciprocating parts: air passes through a compressor into a combustion chamber; the exhaust gases are then discharged through the turbine.

A small amount of thrust is generated by the exhaust gases, but propulsion is primarily derived from the propeller, which thus limits the speed of turboprop-engined airplanes to the subsonic region (up to about 550 mph). Compared to PISTON ENGINES, turboprops are lighter, have a lower frontal area, are more efficient at the top end of the speed range, and are easier to maintain.

The general layout of a turboprop closely resembles that of a JET ENGINE. Compressors may be either centrifugal (single- or, as in the Rolls-Royce Dart, two-stage), or axial (one- or two-spool), or even a combination of both (the Proteus has a 12-stage axial compressor feeding forwards into a single-stage centrifugal compressor, the overall pressure ratio being 7.2:1).

A free-turbine turboprop has a separate additional turbine to drive the propeller ("free" because it is not mechanically coupled to the compressor). This enables the compressor turbine and the propeller turbine to be operated independently at their most efficient speeds, and permits a wide range of propeller speeds while maintaining a constant compressor speed. Additional power for takeoff can be obtained by methanol-water injection (as on the Dart).

Turboprop engines are now used principally in transport aircraft, particularly those intended for STOL operation. Compared with both jet engines and piston engines, turboprops have the advantage of being notably quiet.

Turbotrain

A gas-turbined, articulated, high-speed, four-car unit being developed by SNCF, the French National Railways. It has two power cars, each with two turbines developing 3,760 kw, and is capable of speeds in excess of 190 mph (300 km/h). SNCF plans to introduce turbotrain passenger services on improved tracks between Paris and Lyons by 1981 (see GAS TURBINE).

Turbulence

When the airflow passes around the WINGS of an airplane, the air accelerates more quickly over the steeply cambered upper surface than it does over the lower surface. As a result the pressure above the wing is less than that below (see LIFT), and air from underneath the wing is constantly trying to force its way into the region of lower pressure above by curling over the trailing edge and around the wing tip. A great deal of the engine's power output is absorbed in overcoming the induced drag caused by turbulence.

Turbulent flow

Turbulent flow is irregular flow in a fluid when its velocity reaches a certain level, determined by the REYNOLDS NUMBER (see FLUID MECHANICS, and contrast LAMINAR FLOW).

Turnpike

A turnpike is a road on which a vehicle must pay to travel. The term originated In England in 1663, and was used for early expressways in the United States, such as the New Jersey Turnpike.

Two-stroke cycle

The two-stroke cycle is an engine-operating cycle in which power is produced every second stroke of the piston. Two-stroke gasoline engines are not common in automobiles, but are widely used for powering motorcycles, lawnmowers and the like. Most large marine diesel engines are of the two-stroke type, some having 12 cylinders and developing more than 20,000 brake horsepower. Many railroad locomotives and heavy road vehicles also have two-stroke diesel engines.

In a two-stroke gasoline engine, for example, the piston moves upward on its compression stroke; as it does so it uncovers the inlet port, allowing fuel mixture to enter the crankcase. At the top of its stroke the mixture is ignited and the piston is driven downward on its power stroke. Near the end of its stroke it uncovers the exhaust port, and the spent gases start to escape. At the same time a transfer port is uncovered on the opposite side of the piston which allows fuel mixture to flow from the crankcase into the cylinder. The top of the piston is so shaped that the fuel mixture is directed to the top of the cylinder and helps to sweep the spent gases through the exhaust port. Inevitably, however, some of the fresh mixture is expelled with the exhaust gases, and some of the spent gases remain in the cylinder. Conventional two-stroke gasoline engines are simpler than engines using the FOUR-STROKE CYCLE, but less economical on fuel. However, experiments with FUEL INJECTION and SUPERCHARGERS may lead to the development of more efficient and widely useful two-stroke gasoline engines

U

Undercarriage

The wheels upon which an airplane maneuvers when it is on the ground. These were originally fixed in position. A practical retractable undercarriage was first used on the Dayton-Wright racer of 1920, and tricycle undercarriages (with a nose wheel instead of a tail wheel) became widely used during the 1940s.

Tail-wheel undercarriages enable power-off three-point landings to be made, but there is a tendency to ground-loop or nose-over. Tricycle undercarriages provide the pilot with better visibility during takeoffs and landings, give a level fuselage position which facilitates loading, and keep jet exhausts from damaging runway surfaces. Aircraft with very low aspect ratio wings cannot be stalled on landing and have short nose wheels to give a negative angle of attack at touchdown so that they are aerodynamically prevented from ballooning.

Bicycle undercarriages have the main-wheels in tandem with outrigger stabilizers. This layout may be used with aircraft that have wings of slender airfoil

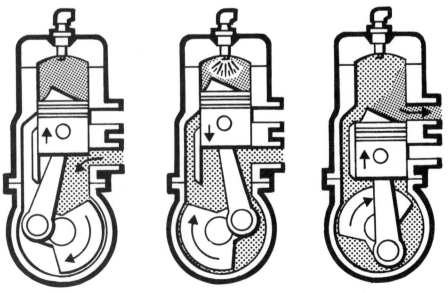

The two stroke cycle. From left to right: 1 compression-induction (as the mixture is compressed above the piston, fresh mixture is drawn in below it). 2 power; 3 exhaust-transfer (exhaust gases escape through the exhaust port and the fresh mixture below the piston moves up into the combustion chamber).

section incapable of accommodating retracted wheels.

The high landing speeds and substantial weight of sophisticated machines require hydraulic systems that often incorporate a long stroke (particularly for aircraft with a high angle of attack at touchdown). Large transports such as the Boeing 747 employ assemblies with a total of perhaps 16 mainwheels.

Underground railroad

See SUBWAYS.

Understeer

Understeer is a condition in which the driver of a vehicle has to turn the steering wheel more than he would expect when cornering. It is caused by differences in the way the front and rear tires behave under the centrifugal stresses of cornering. In understeer the front tires diverge more from the direction in which the wheels are pointing (their slip angle is greater) than the rear tires do. Most vehicles are designed to give a certain amount of understeer in normal driving conditions. But as vehicle speed increases understeer may change to neutral steer and then to OVERSTEER quite quickly, which can be dangerous.

Union Pacific Railroad

The Union Pacific Railroad was one of the two railroads forming the United States' first Transcontinental line. On July 1, 1862, Congress authorized the Union Pacific to build westwards from the Missouri, and the Central Pacific to build eastward from the Pacific coast. Despite the Civil War work began in 1863, and the two lines were linked on May 10, 1869, in a ''golden spike'' ceremony at Promontory, Utah. Today the railroad has 9,700 mi. (15,610 km) of track.

United States

Luxury American passenger liner which on her maiden voyage in July 1952 averaged 35.59 knots on the North Atlantic crossing, a record that has never been beaten. With the most powerful engines ever fitted in a liner, her top speed was 41.75 knots. She carried 1,926 passengers and a crew of 1,000, and could be converted into a troopship for 14,000 men. She was withdrawn from service in 1969 for economic reasons.

Unitized body construction

Also called unitary and integral construction, a form of automobile body construction in which the body shell itself supplies the necessary strength and rigidity. It contrasts with the CHASSIS form of construction, in which the body

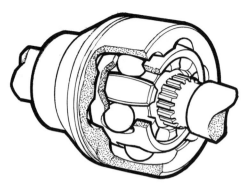

A constant-velocity universal joint. This provides a flexible coupling between two shafts, and is used for example at either end of an automobile's propeller shaft.

is built up from a rigid, heavy chassis. Unitized construction, favored by auto manufacturers in Europe and Japan, is ideally suited to the small autos they produce, since it results in a lighter structure than a separate body and chassis.

A unitized structure is built up by welding together a number of pressed steel panels: roof, fenders (wings), floor, and so on. Some parts, for example the sills beneath the doors, are of box section to provide extra rigidity. The floor panel is also usually ribbed and reinforced for extra strength. Bulkheads fore and aft of the passenger compartment contribute the main torsional stiffness. They are reinforced to form a safety box that helps to resist crushing during impact. Some variations of the unitized design incorporate separate subframes to carry the main mechanical units, such as the engine, gearbox, final drive, and suspension. Others are built with a basic skeletal structure to which unstressed panels, such as fenders, roof, and door panels are then attached.

Unitized construction has several disadvantages. Introduction of a new body design necessitates an extensive and expensive retooling of the production line, while damage to the integral structure often results in large sections having to be repaired or replaced.

Universal joint

A universal joint is a flexible coupling which permits the two shafts it connects to swing at an angle to one another, while still transmitting motion. Several universal joints are used in automobile transmissions, for example, at each end of the PROPELLER SHAFT, which transmits drive between gearbox and rear axle. They permit these two units to move up and down relative to one another and prevent the propeller shaft being subjected to stresses that would distort it. One of the commonest types of universal joints is the Hooke type. This has a center crosspiece, or spider, formed of two pins at right angles to one another. Yokes on

the ends of the shafts to be joined pivot on the arms of the spider. Needle bearings are often incorporated in the joint to reduce friction.

Universal joints are fitted at the ends of the half-shafts of front-wheel drive automobiles. The joint at the road-wheel end of the shaft has to withstand sharp angles because of the steering, and is a specially designed CONSTANT-VELOCITY JOINT.

V

V-1

The pilotless flying bomb powered by a PULSE JET launched from ramps and carrier planes against England and liberated Europe by the Nazis during 1944-45 was officially the Fieseler Fi 103. V-1, meaning *Vergeltungswaffe-1* (vengeance weapon 1), was the name given to it by Goebbels' propaganda ministry. Over 30,000 were produced, including a small number with cockpits that were intended for suicide attacks. The V-1 embodied a 1-ton warhead, its wingspan was 17 ft. (5 m) and length 23 ft. (7 m). Range was 150 mi. (240 km) with a maximum speed of 400 mph (640 km/h).

V-2

During seven months at the end of World War II, the Nazis launched 4,000 V-2 liquid-fueled rockets bearing 2,150-lb. (975 kg) warheads at targets in England, Belgium, the Netherlands, and France. The V-2 (*Vergeltungswaffe-2*, vengeance weapon 2) was the first long-range rocket missile. It measured 46 ft. (14 m) in length and weighed 13 tons; its range was 200 mi. (320 km), and it reached an altitude of 50 mi. (80 km) during its flight, attaining 3,000 mph (4,800 km/h). The V-2 design team was led by Wernher VON BRAUN, who subsequently played a leading part in the American space program.

V-8

A type of GASOLINE ENGINE with two banks of four cylinders arranged in the shape of a V.

Vacuum advance

Vacuum advance is a mechanism attached to the DISTRIBUTOR of a gasoline engine which automatically advances the TIMING of the spark as engine speed increases. It consists of a diaphragm attached to a plate carrying the contact-breaker set. The diaphragm moves according to the extent of partial vacuum in the inlet manifold; the greater the vacuum, the further it moves, advancing arranged so that air is extracted direct from the underside of the piston, but the air from the upper side has to pass through a ball valve.

The brakes are applied by admitting air to the train pipe. The air is free to reach the underside of the pistons, but its own pressure seals the ball valves giving access to the upper side, so that a vacuum is maintained above the piston. Atmospheric pressure then pushes the piston upwards and applies the brakes. Turning on the pump or ejector evacuates the lower part of the cylinder again and the brakes are released.

Should the train pipe break for any reason, air is admitted and the brake is automatically applied. Because of the comparatively low air pressure at which the vacuum brake must operate, the cylinders have to be much larger than with the AIR BRAKE, which uses much higher pressures.

Valve gear:. As the overhead camshaft (top) rotates, it lifts one end of the rocker arm (right). The other end then presses the valve down into the cylinder, thus opening it. When the rocker arm comes off the cam the spring forces the valve shut.

Valve gear

The valve gear in an engine includes the valves and the mechanism which opens and closes them at the correct points in the engine-operating cycle (see TIMING). Each cylinder of a four-stroke gasoline engine has an inlet valve through which the fuel mixture enters the combustion chamber, and an exhaust valve through which the spent gases escape after combustion. Most engines have overhead valves (OHVs), which move in valve guides in the cylinder head. They consist of a flat disk at the end of a long stem, and are known as mushroom or poppet valves. The edge of the disk is beveled and provides a gastight seal on a re-

A German V-2 rocket of World War II being prepared for launching. The V-2 was the forerunner of modern space launch rockets and missiles.

the point at which the cam on the distributor shaft opens the contact points to cause a spark at the plug.

Vacuum brake

A system of train braking in which atmospheric pressure is used to move pistons enclosed in brake cylinders and coupled to the brake blocks. A continuous pipe, with flexible couplings between cars, runs the whole length of the train and is connected to an "ejector" or a pump on the locomotive. In normal running, a partial vacuum is maintained in the train pipe by the pump or ejector and, through it, also in the brake cylinders on both sides of the pistons. The cylinders are mounted vertically and cessed seating in the cylinder head. The inlet valve is somewhat larger than the exhaust valve because fuel intake is slower than the exhaust flow out of the cylinder. The exhaust valve has to be made of heat-resistant steel to withstand the heat of the exhaust gases, and may in time become badly burned.

The valves are actuated by a CAMSHAFT. A side cam (a camshaft located in the cylinder block at the side of the cylinders) operates the valves through tappets, push rods and rocker arms. A projecting cam on the camshaft moves the tappet, which rests on it, upward. This motion is transmitted to a rocker arm on the cylinder head by a long, thin push rod. As the push rod pushes upward on one arm of the centrally pivoted rocker, the other arm presses down on the top of the valve stem opening the valve. When the cam allows the tappet and push rod to fall, the rocker rocks back and a spring snaps the valve shut. To ensure that the valve closes fully, a clearance is left between the top of the valve stem and the rocker, known as the tappet clearance.

The valve-operating gear for overhead-cam (OHC) engines is somewhat simpler, for the cam can bear directly on the valve stem with a simple bucket tappet in between. Alternatively, the cam bears on a lever that pushes against the valve stem.

Vapor lock

Vapor lock can occur in the fuel system of a gasoline engine when the fuel gets overheated. The heat causes bubbles of gasoline vapor to form in the fuel-supply lines; this restricts the passage of gasoline to the carburetor, and causes the engine to falter or stall. In hot weather gasoline suppliers reduce the volatility of their fuel to help avoid this problem.

Variomatic drive

Variomatic drive is a novel form of AUTOMATIC TRANSMISSION used in the DAF automobile which works by means of belts using a centrifugal CLUTCH with limited slip differential.

Venturi

A venturi is a tube with a constriction at one point which is used in CARBURETORS and flow meters. It is named after the Italian physicist Giovanni Venturi (1746-1822). When a fluid flows through a venturi, its velocity increases and its pressure drops (see BERNOULLI'S PRINCIPLE). The acceleration and consequent low pressure of air flowing through a venturi is used to draw the fuel into a carburetor. In a flow meter the pressure drop through the constriction is a measure of the rate of flow.

The Verrazano-Narrows Bridge links Brooklyn and Staten Island across New York Harbor and had until the completion of Britain's Humber Bridge the world's longest span.

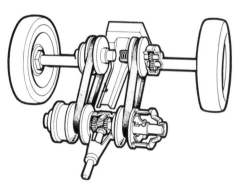

Variomatic drive, an unusual type of infinitely variable automatic transmission with mechanical belt drive. The pulleys move together and apart according to engine speed, thus changing the ratio without the use of gears since the belts are inelastic.

Verrazano-Narrows Bridge

A SUSPENSION BRIDGE with the world's greatest span, the 4,260 ft. (1,298 m) Verrazano-Narrows Bridge was designed by the firm of AMMANN and Whitney, and stands at the entrance to New York Harbor connecting Staten Island and Brooklyn. It carries 12 automobile lanes on two decks and is traversed by some 50 million vehicles per year. Its twin main towers are each 690 ft. (210 m) high, and their tops are 1.6 in. (41 mm) further apart than their bases due to the curvature of the earth. The bridge, which was opened in 1964, pioneered modern high-strength lightweight construction methods.

Vertical-lift bridge

A movable bridge in which the deck can be raised vertically to allow ships to pass beneath it. The ends of the deck are moved up and down vertical towers by means of supporting cables (see ARTHUR KILL BRIDGE).

Viaduct

An elevated structure for lifting a road over the terrain. The word viaduct is sometimes used to describe a long multi-span bridge. The world's longest road viaduct is the 23.87 mi. (38.4 km) second Lake Pontchartrain Causeway linking

Lewisburg and Metairie, Louisiana, while the longest railroad viaduct is the Great Salt Lake Railroad Trestle, which runs for 11.85 mi. (19 km) across Great Salt Lake, Utah (see BRIDGES).

A collector's item of 1903, a Fiat 16/24.

Vintage and veteran cars

Veteran automobiles include those from the beginnings until the end of 1916, with a distinction between pre-1905 (true veterans) and the years 1905-1916 (Edwardians). It has been said with some truth that during the first half of this period designers concentrated on making the new invention run, and during the second on making it run well.

The vintage (or classic) era covers the years 1917 to 1930, while some quality cars of the 1930s are known as "post vintage thoroughbreds" in Great Britain, and "classic cars" in America.

The veteran era was the age when electric and steam cars were at their most popular: they were quieter, more reliable, and easier to start and drive. It was the era of the "car for the day after tomorrow" (the first Mercedes, 1901); the first mass-produced car (the Oldsmobile Curved Dash buggy, 1903); the first "best car in the world" (the Rolls-Royce, 1906); and the first people's car (the Model T Ford, 1909). It was also the era of a vast number of custom-built experimental models produced in back street workshops, and of stately carriages, complete with costly furnishings and a kitchen at the rear.

Driving was for fun, if one can describe crank-starting, frequent roadside repairs, and driving without weather protection, as fun; and it was for the wealthy. Aside from mechanical faults,

there were other hazards including attacks by dogs, potholed and muddy roads, and demands from, for example, the Pennsylvania Farmers' Anti-Motoring Society that one should fire a roman candle every mile and wait ten minutes before continuing (to warn pedestrians and animals).

Technical advances such as electric starters and mechanical windshield wipers, the efforts of Henry Ford, and the widespread use of the automobile in World War I brought new popularity, efficiency, and comfort. During the vintage era the automobile was established as an accepted and essential means of transport for "everyman," and some of the most finely engineered automobiles of all time were built.

Collecting, restoring, driving, and even racing veteran and vintage cars is a very popular pastime. The United States' Antique Automobile Club is probably the largest of its kind in the world with well over 10,000 members; while one of the most famous annual events is the "old crocks" run from London to Brighton (England) for true veterans from all over the world.

Volkswagen

Leading West German automobile manufacturer. In 1934 the designer Ferdinand Porsche, who had been working on the idea of a small utility car for some years, was directed by the Nazi government to develop such an automobile. The new "people's car" (volks-wagen) was on the market in 1939, the rear-engined air-cooled "Beetle."

A simple, robust, and inexpensive

vehicle, the Beetle fulfilled its originators' hopes and became an enormously popular car almost everywhere in the world. In 1962 Volkswagen became the first European firm to produce over 1,000,000 cars in a year, and 10 years later the Beetle passed TIN LIZZIE's total sales figure of 15,007,033 to become the biggest seller of all time.

Over the years many improvements have been made, but the basic design remained essentially the same. Recently Volkswagen has acquired the Audi-NSU group, and has broadened its output with a range of conventional front-engined water-cooled models.

Voltage regulator

A voltage regulator is part of the CONTROL UNIT in an automobile's electrical system.

Von Braun, Wernher (1912-   )

One of the world's leading experts on rockets and space flight. He began working on rocket motors while still a student in Germany, and in the mid-1930s was appointed technical director at Peenemunde, the German army's rocket center on the Baltic Sea. There he designed and produced the V-2 rockets which the Germans used to bombard Britain in the last months of World War II.

Von Braun surrendered to the Americans at the end of the war. He and key members of his team went to the United States to continue their research on military rockets. By 1950 he was director of the army's ballistic weapon center at Huntsville, Alabama. His ambition to build rockets for space flight received official support once the Russians launched Sputnik I in 1957. Under von Braun's direction the first U.S. Earth satellite, Explorer I, was built and launched on January 31, 1958. From 1960 to 1972 von Braun worked under the National Aeronautics and Space Administration (NASA), designing among other rockets the SATURN V used for the APOLLO space flights (see ROCKETS).

VTOL

The HELICOPTER is the most widely used VTOL (Vertical Takeoff and Landing) aircraft, but its limited speed has encouraged research into fixed-wing machines with VTOL capability.

Various methods of achieving VTOL without using rotors have been investigated. The most practical has proved to be vectored thrust — deflecting downwards the exhaust from a jet engine. Other systems include using separate engines to provide lift only, swiveling the engines themselves to provide either vertical or horizontal thrust (Hiller X-18), and designing aircraft to take off and land on their tails (Convair XFY-1).

Considerably more power is required to effect vertical takeoff than is needed to maintain horizontal flight, even at high speed. Consequently, any VTOL aircraft using jet deflection must have an excessively large engine, representing substantial deadweight during normal flight. Separate lift engines have the same drawback, but specially designed power units for this purpose that only operate for a brief period can be built with a very high thrust-to-weight ratio. The use of fans driven off the main power plant to suck air in from above and discharge it vertically downwards has the virtue of a reduced noise level, but the installation is bulky. The Ryan XV-5A of 1963 was powered by such a system, using two J85 turbojets driving lift fans in the wings that were covered during normal flight.

Rotating the engines, either by themselves or in concert with the entire wing, involves substantial mechanical problems and has not been extensively developed. The VJ 101C of 1963 used six Rolls-Royce RB 145 engines, two fixed in the fuselage and two at each wing tip in swiveling pods. Propeller-driven aircraft in this category include the Curtiss-Wright X-19A (with four propellers geared together and located at the ends of two pairs of tandem wings) and the LTV XC 142A of 1964, which had a tilting wing structure (it attained a speed of 380 knots and raised a payload of 8,000 lb., 3,628 kg).

Airplanes that take off from their tails have not proved to be an acceptable proposition because the pilot has great difficulty in seeing the ground as he comes down to land.

The use of several small power units to provide lift was studied on the FLYING BEDSTEAD project, and subsequently the experimental Short SC1 (1961) and Dassault Balzac (1963) both employed the principle. These special lift-producing engines may be installed in a battery within the airframe with doors to seal off the intakes and nozzles during normal flight, or alternatively, they can be housed in special streamlined containers located beneath the wings or at the sides of the fuselage.

The vectored-thrust Hawker Siddeley HARRIER, which flew in 1960, subsequently entered service with the RAF (in 1967) and the U.S. Marine Corps (in 1970) to become the world's first operational VTOL fighter. It has a maximum speed of over 700 mph (1,120 km/h) and will carry bombs and rockets as well as gun pods.

The high noise levels of vectored-thrust VTOL aircraft have so far made them unacceptable for commercial use.

W

Wagons-Lits, Compagnie Internationale des

The Wagons-Lits (sleeping cars) company (CIWL) was founded by a Belgian engineer, Georges Nagelmackers, after seeing sleeping cars in the United States. He first obtained authority to provide a sleeping car service between Ostend, Belgium, and Brindisi, Italy, mainly for British travelers en route to and from India. Then, in 1876, he formed the Wagons-Lits company, which inaugurated the first famous international express train, the Orient Express, in 1883; it ran between Paris, France, and Istanbul, Turkey. CIWL was soon providing luxury sleeping and dining cars on important express trains throughout Europe and even across Asia via Siberia and also in China and North Africa. Today Wagons-Lits sleeping and dining cars run on many famous European expresses.

Wallis, Sir Barnes Neville (1887-   )

A British aeronautical engineer whose long career produced innovation in airplane and airship design. Trained as a marine engineer, Wallis joined the firm of Vickers as an airship designer. In 1929 he designed the R-100, an exceptionally stable airship incorporating many new features, which successfully crossed the Atlantic. Later he headed the firm's research and development team, and during the 1930s he invented the geodetic system of airframe construction in which compression loads in any member of a lattice structure are braced by tension loads in cross members. The famous Wellington bomber of World War II was constructed on these principles. Later Wallis invented variable geometry aircraft, in which the sweep of an airplane's wing can be changed in flight to suit supersonic or low speeds. Wallis is also remembered for designing the "bouncing bomb" used to destroy the Ruhr Dams in Germany. In his later years he continued to work on revolutionary ideas for hypersonic aircraft.

Wankel engine

The most successful rotary internal combustion engine yet developed, the Wankel engine works on a FOUR-STROKE CYCLE and burns gasoline as fuel. It was developed by German engineer Felix Wankel in 1958 and has been fitted to production automobiles since 1964. NSU, Mazda, Mercedes-Benz, and Citroën are among manufacturers who have produced Wankel-powered automobiles.

The Wankel has several advantages over the conventional reciprocating gasoline engine. It has triangular rotors instead of pistons and produces rotary motion directly instead of through a connecting rod and crankshaft. Hence it is smoother and quieter in operation. It is

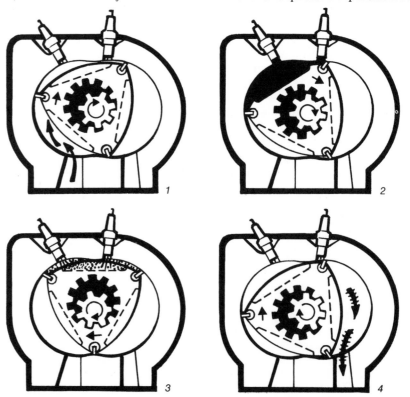

The rotary Wankel engine. Following the face of the rotor opposite the outer arrow, the four diagrams show: induction, compression, power, and exhaust. The other two rotor faces are also following the four-stroke cycle, one rotor thus performing the work of three pistons.

The interceptor and strike Phantom warplane carries a greater armament load than World War II bombers such as the B-29 or the Lancaster.

also much lighter and more compact, and has only two moving parts (the rotor and drive shaft), both of which rotate. However, it has a relatively high fuel consumption and other difficulties relating to the seal between rotor and casing.

The engine consists of a casing of broad figure-of-eight shape, inside which the triangular rotor turns eccentrically so that its tips are always in contact with the casing walls. The space between each side of the rotor and the casing forms a kind of chamber which undergoes a sequence analogous to that of the four-stroke cycle of a piston engine. As one tip of the rotor uncovers the inlet port, mixture rushes into the first chamber, which increases in volume because of the eccentric motion of the rotor. As the rotor continues to turn the mixture becomes trapped between the first and second tips of the rotor, and becomes compressed as the rotor presses close to the casing wall. Then a spark plug ignites the compressed mixture, driving the rotor around. The leading tip of the rotor uncovers the exhaust port, and the spent gases are swept through it by the action of the tip following. The sequence of operations is proceeding simultaneously in each of the three chambers; while one is undergoing induction (intake of fuel), the one before it is undergoing compression, and the one before that is undergoing exhaust. There are thus three power strokes every revolution of the rotor.

Usually Wankel engines for automobiles

have twin rotors driving a common output shaft, which is equivalent to the crankshaft of a conventional piston engine. They invariably have water-cooling systems.

Warplane

At the beginning of World War I the concept of the warplane had hardly been born. Flying machines were envisaged only as a means of reconnaissance, but it was not long before opposing airmen began taking firearms up with them to shoot at each other, and to carry primitive bombs to drop on enemy ground forces.

World War I. Warplanes soon became broadly categorized into small single-seat scouts (later fighters) and larger bomber-reconnaissance machines. BIPLANES predominated, and there were a number of pusher designs (which gave an unrestricted forward field of fire), but the most successful fighter of 1915 was the Fokker MONOPLANE, which had an interrupter gear that enabled its machinegun to fire through the spinning propeller. Russia and Germany developed multi-engined long-range bombers, and SEAPLANES came into widespread use for maritime reconnaissance in support of battle fleets.

Sopwith and Fokker triplane fighters enjoyed a brief success in 1917, but by the end of the war biplane interceptors were capable of climbing to over 20,000 ft. (6,000 m) and attaining 120-150 mph (192-230 km/h) (Fokker D.VII, Sopwith

Camel). The first strategic bombers included the so-called German "Giants," which raided England in company with the smaller twin-engined Gothas, the Handley Page 0/400, and the Handley Page V/1500 (which had a range of 2,500 mi., carrying a 7,500 lb. (3,400 kg) bomb load).

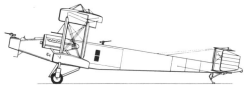

The Handley Page 0/400 World War I bomber.

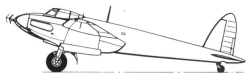

A selection of World War II warplanes: from top to bottom: Spitfire, Mosquito, Me-109, P-38, and Flying Fortress.

World War II. During the 1920s the highly maneuverable biplane remained the basic fighter type, using either a RADIAL ENGINE or an in-line engine and mounting a machinegun. Bombers also continued to adhere to the biplane configuration, but early in the following decade new monoplane types began to supplant traditional designs. Fighters like the Boeing P-26, Messerschmitt 109, and Hurricane appeared, and high-speed bombers were developed, particularly in Germany (Dornier 17, Heinkel 111); the United States evolved high-altitude long-range strategic bombers (Boeing B-17) and FLYING BOATS were still widely used for maritime reconnaissance (Short Sunderland). Piston-engined aircraft reached their ultimate performance during World War II, with fighters capable of nearly 500 mph (800 km/h) (P-51, Spitfire, Focke-Wulf 190) — speeds at which compressibility was beginning to occur. Japanese fighters (Zero) were highly maneuverable but lacked armor protection or self-sealing fuel tanks and readily burst into flames if hit. The traditional machinegun was supplemented by cannon, which was more destructive although slower firing.

The mistaken belief that fast medium bombers could always evade defending fighters led the Germans to neglect the concept of the four-engined bomber, but these long-range warplanes were extensively developed in Britain (Lancaster) and America (B-24, B-29). Luftwaffe fighter defenses made it impossible to operate even the heavily-armed B-17s and B-24s unescorted over Germany, and long-range P-51s and P-47s carrying extra fuel in drop tanks were eventually capable of accompanying them into the heart of the Reich. The twin-engined "heavy fighter" concept was pursued by several countries (P-38, Messerschmitt 110), but lack of maneuverability was an inevitable consequence of increased size and weight. Medium bombers (B-25, B-26) were employed in a largely tactical role, but the British Mosquito, which was made of wood, attained 400 mph (640 km/h) and ranged almost at will over occupied Europe since German fighters could rarely catch it.

The Hawker Siddeley Vulcan bomber is the world's largest delta-wing warplane in service. Introduced in the mid 1950s, it is remarkably maneuverable, and has a top speed of around 620 mph (998 km/h).

The Jet Age. After the war, both the Americans and the Russians made extensive use of German research. The F-86 and the MiG-15 were both supersonic

American battleships steaming in battle line towards the Philippines during World War II. The era of the battleship has passed, the only large surface warships of today being aircraft carriers.

in a dive, and the next generation of jet fighters were capable of Mach 1 in level flight (F-100, MiG-21). The JET ENGINE also replaced the piston engine in long-range bombers (B-47, Tu-16), although the Russian Tu-20 employed turboprops. Fighter aircraft became increasingly complex and costly (Mirage, F-105), and the search for maximum speed, climb and CEILING led to reduced maneuverability (F-104). There was a belief that air-to-air missiles would largely replace cannon in fighters, while the manned bomber would be rendered obsolete by intercontinental ballistic missiles and submarine-launched rockets.

The lessons of air battles in the Middle East and over Vietnam during the late 1960s and early 1970s indicated that the manned combat plane still had an important role: ground-to-air missiles were not infallible (especially in the face of countermeasures), the presence of a crew endowed an airplane with a flexibility no missile could possess, and cannon returned to favor.

At the same time, mounting costs dictated rationalization of design, exemplified by the adoption of SWING-WING DESIGN and the concept of the MRCA (Multi-Role Combat Aircraft), produced by a European consortium in the mid-1970s to serve as a fighter, strike aircraft (nuclear weapons having eliminated the need for large bomb loads), close-support machine, and reconnaissance plane. The twin-engined, two-seat fighter (F-4)

offered the advantage of a second crewman to navigate and to monitor the complex AVIONICS and weapon-aiming equipment, leaving the pilot free to devote his attention entirely to controlling the airplane, but by the mid-1970s the pure fighter was becoming smaller and more maneuverable (F-16). A few military flying boats (Shin Meiwa, Be-12) were still operated for maritime reconnaissance, although this role had largely been taken over by land planes (Neptune, Nimrod, M-4).

For close support in the battle area, VTOL aircraft appeared (see HARRIER; VTOL), together with helicopter gunships, and conflicts involving guerilla warfare led to the development of small aircraft carrying rockets and bombs (Strikemaster, A-37). (See also names of individual airplanes mentioned.)

Warships

The warships of the ancient world were long, fast GALLEYS, armed with a sharp ram at the bow, and with a fighting platform for hand-to-hand fighting. The vessels had a single square sail, but this was lowered during battle since only oars could supply the necessary speed and maneuverability. By Roman times these galleys had become large, fully decked craft with fighting towers or "castles" for archers. Catapults for hurling missiles and, later, "Greek fire," were added.

In the north the Viking LONGSHIP gave way

in the Middle Ages to the much more spacious cog, a merchant ship which, with the addition of large fighting castles at bow and stern, heralded the age of the sailing warship.

The age of the broadside. By the year 1500 warships were normally armed with guns, positioned on deck and in the castles. Then came the invention of the gunport, which enabled ships to carry many more and much heavier guns without sacrificing stability, and the true man of war evolved with up to three tiers of guns along the full length of each "broadside." At the Battle of Lepanto in 1571, the last great sea battle between rowed ships, massive galleasses (crosses between galleys and galleons) with powerful broadsides helped turn the scales against the Turks. And by the time of the Spanish Armada of 1588 the sailing warship had matured in the GALLEON. It reached a peak with the first SHIP O' THE LINE, *Sovereign of the Seas*, built for Charles I of England in 1637, and for the next 200 years warships sailed into battle "in line," relying on their broadsides to smash the enemy's ships.

two years later the more skeptical British navy decided in favor of the screw after its convincing victory in a trial tug-of-war between the screw-propelled *Rattler* and the paddle-driven *Alecto*. The warship had finally freed itself of the wind. With the building of the French *Gloire* (the first IRONCLAD) in 1859 and of the British *Warrior* (the first armored

The U.S. Navy frigate *Ainsworth*. Although by modern standards large warships, frigates displace only about 8,000 tons compared to the 60,000 tons of a typical World War II battleship.

neither ship having powerful enough guns to penetrate the other's armor; but with steam propulsion, all-metal construction, and the revolving gun turret, the stage was set for the warships of World War I.

Largest of these was the dreadnought battleship. Too large and expensive to risk in a sea battle in the traditional ship

An aircraft carrier receiving fuel (through hoses) and supplies and equipment (by helicopter) from the support ship *Sacramento*.

of the line style, they ranged the oceans in small groups. They were assisted by the battle cruisers, equal in gunpower but less heavily armored, and therefore lighter and faster, and by torpedo-carrying destroyers. World War I also saw the development of SUBMARINES and AIRCRAFT CARRIERS. Both were to play a crucial role in World War II, together with the largest and most heavily armored battleships ever built. The Japanese *Yamato* and *Musashi*, the biggest of all, measured 863 ft. (263 m) long and displaced 72,809 tons. With armor plate 8.5 in. (21.6 cm) thick on the deck and 16 in. (40.6 cm) on the sides, it took direct hits by 11 bombs and 16 torpedoes to sink the *Musashi*.

The nuclear age. Today the world's largest and longest warships are the U.S. nuclear-powered aircraft carriers *Nimitz* (displacing 95,100 tons) and *Enterprise* (1,101.5 ft., 335.7 m long). But apart from such giants, large warships are obsolete. The primary weapons of naval warfare are the aircraft, the guided missile, and the submarine, and the main role of surface warships is to combat these, not to fight one another or to bombard shore positions. A few old battleships and CRUISERS have been recommissioned for short periods, and the United States has one nuclear-powered guided-missile cruiser (*Long Beach*). But the modern "big" warships are FRIGATES of around 8,000 tons and DESTROYERS of 4,000 to

Steam, ironclads, and the turret gun. Steam propulsion brought the potential advantages of faster and more maneuverable warships. However, for many years only limited use was made of the new invention in naval ships, because paddlewheels (the then normal method of propulsion) were particularly vulnerable to enemy gunfire. Then, in 1843, the United States launched the world's first screw-propelled warship, *Princeton*, and

all-iron warship) in 1861, it acquired added protection. But it still fired broadsides.

The final revolution came with the launching of the all-iron *Monitor* in 1862, the first warship with a revolving gun turret. This strange craft took part in the first battle between ironclads, which occurred in the American Civil War. Her adversary was the Confederate *Merrimack*. The battle was inconclusive,

A guided-missile destroyer firing a surface to air missile.

7,000 tons. A few are nuclear-powered, and many have gas turbine or combined diesel and gas turbine engines. All are fast, highly maneuverable, and are packed with the latest electronics, missiles, and homing torpedoes to find, identify and destroy enemy submarines, aircraft, and missiles.

Destroyer escorts of 3,000 to 4,000 tons are essentially small-scale destroyers, while smaller ships include CORVETTES and other fast patrol boats with speeds of up to 50 knots, and displacing from 100 to about 1,200 tons. Some are designed specifically as submarine chasers, while others carry surface-to-surface missiles. In addition, many navies have fast HYDROFOIL patrol boats, AIR-CUSHION VEHICLES for amphibious operations, and a wide variety of assault ships, LANDING CRAFT, and amphibians. The largest are 40,000-ton vessels carrying landing craft and helicopters, troops, combat vehicles, and equipment; and 18,000-ton helicopter carriers, which transport some 2,000 troops complete with guns and vehicles. The helicopters' primary duty is to land the troops and their equipment, but they may also have an antisubmarine role.

Water-cooled engine
A water-cooled engine is one which uses a water jacket to remove the heat generated by combustion in the cylinders (see COOLING SYSTEMS).

Water-jet propulsion
A method of driving a vessel through the water by pumping water out through a nozzle at the stern. The American inventor James Rumsey tried the idea with some success in 1787, and it is sometimes used today, particularly on craft which operate in shallow water.

The Kort Nozzle propeller arrangement is an ingenious adaptation of this principle. The screw is shrouded by a cylinder to add a degree of jet propulsion, increasing power by 25%. The bow thruster uses water-jet propulsion as a steering aid for slow speed maneuvers:

the water is thrust out at one side or the other to swing the bow around.

Watertight compartment
The hull of a ship is divided into a number of watertight compartments by internal walls called bulkheads, so that if the ship is holed flooding will not spread throughout the hull. Safety regulations prescribe the degree of subdivision for different types of ships, passenger liners requiring the greatest "unsinkability."

Watt, James (1736-1819)
Scottish engineer and inventor who greatly advanced the steam engine. He became an instrument-maker at Glasgow University, and in 1764 was given a model of a Newcomen steam engine to repair. In this engine the cylinder was alternately heated by the steam, then chilled to condense it. Watt devised an engine with a separate condenser, which was much more efficient. In 1774 he formed a partnership with the manufacturer Matthew Boulton to build steam engines to the new design. In 1781 he invented the sun-and-planet gear for changing reciprocating into rotary motion, and in 1782 he patented an improved double-acting steam engine. Two further inventions followed in 1788 and 1790 (the centrifugal GOVERNOR and the pressure gauge) to complete his famous steam engine. This used only about one quarter of the fuel needed by Newcomen engines, and powered the early steamboats CHARLOTTE DUNDAS and CLERMONT (see STEAM ENGINE).

Weighbridge
A device for weighing laden trucks and railroad cars, the weighbridge consists of a large metal platform which is supported on a series of levers. The levers are connected to a counterbalancing device which effectively reduces the weight so that it can be more easily measured. Further levers connect the system to an indicating mechanism which may also print a ticket showing the weight of the load.

Welland Ship Canal
Linking Lakes Ontario and Erie, and bypassing Niagara Falls, the Welland Ship Canal is 27.6 mi. (44 km) long, and runs from Port Weller, on Lake Ontario, to Port Colborne, on Lake Erie. The eight locks raise ships a total of 326 ft. (100 m) and can accommodate vessels of 730 ft. (222.5 m) length and 75 ft. (22.9 m) beam. The canal has a bottom width of 200 ft. (60 m) and a minimum depth of 30 ft. (9 m). In its present form the canal was completed in 1932 and is an important link in the St. Lawrence Seaway. The first canal, utilizing part of the Niagara River, was opened in 1829, and was extended in 1833 and in the years 1871-87 (see CANALS AND INLAND WATERWAYS).

Westinghouse, George (1846-1914)
An American inventor famous for his railroad airbrake, Westinghouse also experimented with a rotary steam engine, devised a machine for putting derailed cars back on the track, and developed a railroad signal system worked by electricity and compressed air. In the early days brakemen had to move along a train applying each car's brakes by hand. Westinghouse devoted his time to the invention of a brake which would work by compressed air and could be applied by the locomotive crew. He took out a patent in 1869 and a series of tests was begun in 1870. In 1872 Westinghouse patented an improved automatic triple-valve system which ensured that if the compressed air lines along the train were broken (for example, by cars becoming uncoupled) the brakes would be applied automatically. This system was in wide use on passenger trains in the United States by 1886, and was later adopted on freight trains. For many years the British vacuum brake, also an automatically applied system, rivalled the Westinghouse brake in many countries, but the Westinghouse air brake, in its modern form, is now generally accepted as superior.

Whaler

Two types of vessels are employed in whaling: fast, diesel-powered, trawler-like catcher boats, equipped with a harpoon gun and with towing gear for carrying back the day's catch, and "mother" factory ships with a stern slipway through which the dead whales are hauled in for processing. The factory ship may carry a helicopter to help locate the whales, and some are large enough to deal with 4,000 whales and to service and supply a fleet of catcher boats. Originally, the catcher boats were light double-ended rowboats, and the mother ships were broad and deep square-riggers able to carry 2,400 barrels of oil. After the introduction in the late-19th century of powerful harpoon guns and steam-engined catcher boats, whaling eventually became so efficient that today many species are threatened with extinction. The Norwegians, once the principal whaling nation, withdrew, and today the only countries with significant whaling fleets are Japan and the Soviet Union.

Wharf

A raised platform where ships load and discharge, built parallel to the shore, normally at the river's edge outside the main dock area. Wharves are built on concrete piles or on trestles.

Wheel

The wheel is the most important invention in the history of transportation. Nobody knows who made the invention or where, but it seems likely that it took place in Mesopotamia. The ancestor of the wheel was undoubtedly the log, used

Traditional Norwegian whalers, now withdrawn from service as a result of overfishing.

as a roller to facilitate the movement of heavy loads such as blocks of building stone. The earliest known wheels date from around 3500 B.C., and were found in graves at Susa, a city which was to become the capital of the Persian king Darius I. Early wheels were solid and made from three segments of wood held together with copper clamps. Some had metal rims.

The first really significant advance came with the development of the much lighter spoked wheel, which took place about 2000 B.C. in Mesopotamia. By 1600 B.C. spoked wheels were in use in Egypt, and had spread to China 300 years later. The heated metal tire, shrunk on to the wood to fit tightly and provide extra strength, seems to have been invented by the Celts of northern Europe. The Celts used wheels turning on wooden roller bearings, while the Romans evolved bronze

brushes to minimize wear. The dished wheel, shaped like a flattened cone, was introduced in the 1500s to make for easier running over rough, rutted roads. The tensioned, wire-spoked wheel came into use with the bicycle in the late 1800s, and was used in automobiles for many years. In recent times, however, the simple one-piece pressed wheel has largely replaced it on autos.

Although primitive carts and carriages were in use from the earliest days of the wheel, wheeled vehicles remained comparatively rare until medieval times because of the poor state of most roads. The Amerindians of North and South America do not seem to have evolved the wheel independently, and there appear to be no traces of its use before the Spanish invasions of the early 1500s.

Wheel balancing

Wheel balancing involves clipping metal weights onto the rims of road vehicle wheels to counter any unevenness in weight and balance. A special machine which spins the wheel and senses any imbalance is used to determine the positions of the weights. The process is important because at high speed even a slightly unbalanced wheel can set up vibrations which affect the steering and may become dangerous.

Whittle, Sir Frank (1907-   )

British aeronautical engineer, who developed the JET ENGINE. Whittle served in the Royal Air Force from 1923 to 1948, and became a test pilot and instructor. He patented his first jet engine in 1930. In 1937 Whittle joined the British government-backed firm Power Jets Ltd. to develop a jet turbine engine. This powered Britain's first jet plane, a fighter which made its first flight on May 15, 1941. The following year the first American jet plane flew, using engines based on Whittle's design.

Sir Frank Whittle, pioneer of the jet engine, explaining the design of one of his engines (1948).

WIG

Abbreviation of Wing-in-Ground effect machine (see RAM WING).

Windshield

A transparent screen on automobiles, airplanes and boats to protect driver and passengers from wind and rain. On boats plastic may be used, but automobile and aircraft windshields are normally made of laminated glass. This consists of layers of glass and vinyl bonded together, the thicker and the greater the number of layers the stronger the result. Laminated glass is both safer and stronger than the more rigid and brittle tempered safety glass sometimes used for automobile side windows.

Wind tunnel

Wind tunnels are a form of apparatus used to simulate airflow for aerodynamic measurement. They consist essentially of a closed tube through which air is circulated by powerful fans. Depending on the air speed expected to act upon the surfaces being tested, wind tunnels operate at low, high, supersonic, and hypersonic capacity. Wind tunnel trials are an essential part of the design of all high-speed vehicles and for some stationary structures such as bridges and skyscrapers which have to stand up to high winds. Their principal use, however, is for airplane design.

The size of airplanes means that only models are normally installed for testing

A wing model being set up in a low speed wind tunnel for aerodynamic testing.

in wind tunnels. A fan driven by an electric motor forces the air around a gradually widening tunnel fitted with air stream guiding vanes until it passes through a honeycomb and out of a narrowing nozzle into the test chamber. The air is then sucked through the fan again and recycled. Balances to which the model is attached by fine wires or thin rods record the forces generated by the airflow.

Because a model is only a small fraction the size of the actual aircraft, wind tunnel tests have to take into consideration the definitive criteria known as REYNOLDS NUMBER, which measure the character-

istics of fluid flow at the interface with solid surfaces. These mathematically-calculated values are always of substantial numerical magnitude because of the units employed. A low Reynolds number (100,000) will be yielded by a low-speed test in a small wind tunnel; a high Reynolds number indicates that the scale of the test or the speeds simulated in the wind tunnel approach full scale (a large model being tested at very high speed might yield a Reynolds number of 20,000,000).

Apart from overall size differences between a model and the actual aircraft, allowances also have to be made for details (protruding rivet heads, for example) that cannot be reproduced on a model. Furthermore, care must be taken to ensure that the tunnel's walls do not themselves influence the airflow in the proximity of the model to give a false result.

To achieve simulated speeds of above 120 mph (192 km/h), tunnels using compressed air were developed. When it became necessary to test supersonic designs, gas turbines were employed to produce a high pressure at the base of a convergent-divergent nozzle in which the test model is installed. Mach numbers of over 20 have been achieved using helium instead of air to prevent liquefaction as the flow expands down the nozzle. To make the airflow more readily visible, smoke may be introduced and SCHLIEREN PHOTOGRAPHY is used.

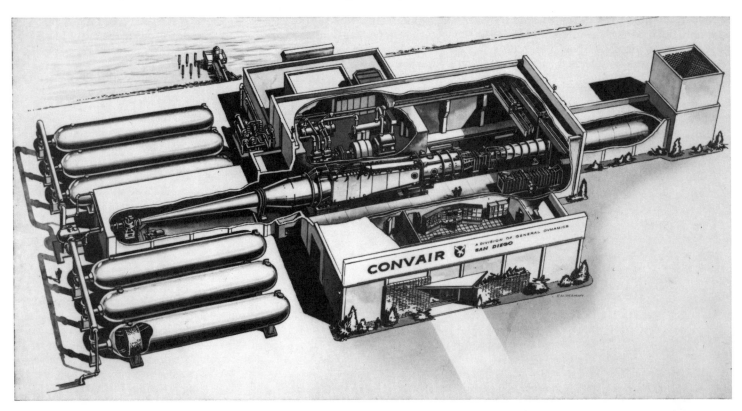

A cutaway view of a wind tunnel. This "straight-through" type can generate a 3,700 mph (5,955 km/h) wind from compressed air stored in the cylinders at the left.

The Wright Brothers' Flyer *making the world's first sustained, controled, powered airplane flight on December 17, 1903.*

Wings

Airplanes derive LIFT from their wings. The front of the wing is known as the leading edge; the back is the trailing edge; the breadth between the leading and trailing edges is known as the chord. Span is measured from wing tip to wing tip.

Wings with a low aspect ratio have a wide chord relative to their span. A high aspect ratio wing, on the other hand, has a wide span and relatively narrow chord. This arrangement is more efficient aerodynamically because the air flowing around the tips from the higher pressure below the wing to the lower pressure above it (causing induced drag) has less influence on the overall airflow. Wide-span wings, however, pose structural problems, add weight, and restrict maneuverability.

A wing's angle of attack is the angle between the direction of the airflow and the chord. If the air strikes the lower surface of the wing, the pressure below the wing is augmented, and there is a greater backward downwash of air, thereby enhancing lift. Increasing the angle of attack up to about 15 or 20° progressively improves the lifting capability of the wing, but above this value the airflow breaks down (see STALLING).

With the cantilever type of wing construction the wing becomes gradually thinner from wing root to tip; this tapering is needed to preserve the proportions of the airfoil section. Braced wings, however, usually have a uniform thickness. Wing sections vary according to the requirements of the aircraft. A thick section with a steep camber will give considerable lift at low speeds and thus reduce the stalling speed. It generates too much drag for high-speed flight, however. This requires a thinner section, but as a result, fast aircraft tend to have high stalling speeds. For SUPERSONIC FLIGHT, symmetrical sections with similar upper and lower profiles are used, and various double-wedge-shaped airfoils are particularly efficient once the speed of sound has been exceeded. (See also AERODYNAMICS.)

Wishbone

Part of the SUSPENSION SYSTEM of some automobiles, so called because of its shape, which is similar to the wishbone of a chicken.

Worm-and-nut

The worm-and-nut is one type of gearing used in automobile steering boxes (see STEERING SYSTEMS).

Wright brothers

The two brothers, Wilbur (1867-1912) and Orville (1871-1948), who made the world's first powered flight near Kitty Hawk, North Carolina, on December 17, 1903. They were also the first men to master gliding and to build and fly a passenger-carrying airplane.

Kites. The brothers had been interested in flying since boyhood, and Wilbur extended his reading in 1899 by approaching the Smithsonian Institution for information on aeronautical books and articles. That same year they built their first aircraft, a BIPLANE kite of 5-ft. (1.5 m) wingspan with a fixed stabilizer and wings that could be staggered. Originally bicycle salesmen at Dayton, Ohio, they expanded eventually to bicycle manufacturing, which provided a workshop. A correspondence with Octave CHANUTE of Chicago, the first aeronautical chronicler, acted as a spur, and their knowledge of AERODYNAMICS was furthered through the works of Otto LILIENTHAL (1848-96).

Gliders. A glider built by the brothers at Dayton in 1900 was taken to the lonely sand dunes near Kitty Hawk where, as Weather Bureau records showed, there were strong and constant winds. This *No. 1* glider, based on the earlier kite, had fixed wings of 17-ft. (5.2 m) span with a warping control. The glider had a prone pilot position, but it was flown mainly as a kite. Unlike other pioneers who strove to find a perfectly stable craft, the Wrights accepted instability and concentrated on control. The Wright *No. 2* glider, also a biplane, but of a 22-ft (6.7 m) span, had drooping wings with warping wires operated by hip movement. This glider, first flown July 27, 1901, made glides as long as 389 ft. (118 m). The following year the brothers made nearly a thousand glides with their third glider, which featured coordinated wing warp and rudder control, the basis of airplane control of the future. That same year of 1902, Wright-type gliders built in Europe started a revival of interest in aviation on that continent.

Powered flight. In 1903, after intense work with gliders, the Wrights built their powered *Flyer*, the first successful airplane. A 12-hp engine drove two pusher propellers by crossed chains so that they counter-rotated. On December 17 they made their epic four flights, the last of which was of 59 seconds' duration. Orville had made the first flight and the brothers alternated. More flights might have been made that day but for damage to an elevator on the fourth flight, which covered about half a mile. The aircraft had a 40 ft. 4 in. (12.2 m) wingspan with a 510 sq. ft. (47 m²) wing area.

The following spring the Wrights flew their *Flyer II* with an engine of increased power, using a site near Dayton which became the world's first airfield. On September 20, 1904, Wilbur flew the first complete circle by an airplane, and followed this on November 9 by the first flight of over five minutes' duration.

In June 1905, with their *Flyer III*, the Wrights had the first fully practical airplane, and with this, on October 4, Orville made the first sustained flight exceeding half an hour. A flight 12 days later was the last the brothers made until 1908; meanwhile the Wright patents were published. Back at Kitty Hawk in the spring of 1908, the Wrights started using upright seating. They were in a position to offer their craft to the American Ordnance Board, but the apparent lack of interest led the brothers to approach the British War Office where there was similar apathy.

During 1908 Wilbur went to France and flew in public there from August 8; a month later Orville was making public flights in the United States, achieving the first flight of an hour's duration on September 9. But eight days later Orville crashed and was injured, and aviation suffered its first fatality when his passenger, Lt. Thomas E. Selfridge, was killed. Wilbur, still in France, continued to set records: the first flight over 1½ hours and first over an hour with a passenger. During 1909 both brothers were feted in Europe and Wright-type biplanes were being built in Britain, France and the United States. The Wrights returned to Kitty Hawk for further experiments, but sadly Wilbur died of typhoid in May 1912. Orville's work was then mainly concerned with legal aspects of the Wright patents.

The Graf Zeppelin, one of the largest airships, named after the pioneer of rigid airships. *Ferdinand von Zeppelin.*

X-1

Rocket-powered research airplane built by the Bell Aircraft Corporation, which in 1947 became the first plane to break the "sound barrier." Piloted by Captain Charles Yeager of the U.S. Air Force, and released at 30,000 ft. (9,000 m) from a mother plane, the X-1 reached 670 mph (1,078 km/h). A later version flew at 1,612 mph (2,594.2 km/h) in 1953.

X-15

Rocket-powered aircraft for research into flight on the border regions between the atmosphere and space. During a series of flights from 1959 to 1968 the X-15, launched like the X-1 from a mother plane, reached an altitude of just over 67 mi. (107 km) and a speed of Mach 6.72 (see MACH NUMBER). This represents 4,534 mph (7,297 km/h), the highest speed reached by any aircraft.

Y

Yacht

A term sometimes used for any pleasure boat, but normally reserved for a cruising or racing boat with a deck and a cabin (or cabins) to provide shelter and accommodation for crew and passengers.

Yachts range from small weekend craft to luxury oceangoing vessels, and include both powered and sailing types. The most common sailing yacht carries a single mast, a Marconi (or Bermuda) mainsail and a Genoa Jib (see SAILBOATS). Most motor yachts are diesel powered, although many smaller craft have gasoline engines.

YF-12A

The Lockheed YF-12A experimental interceptor of 1964 was built largely of titanium alloys to cruise at Mach 3 (see MACH NUMBER). Two J58 turbojets were used, and the configuration was basically that of a delta with a long-nosed, flattened fuselage. The SR71A reconnaissance version flew from New York to London in 1 hour 55 minutes 42 seconds in 1974.

Z

Zambezi Bridge (Victoria Falls Bridge)

Crossing the Zambezi River 1,200 ft. (366 m) below the Victoria Falls, the Zambesi Bridge links the towns of Victoria Falls, Rhodesia, and Livingstone, Zambia. The bridge, a braced arch structure 420 ft. (128 m) above water level, is 657 ft. (200 m) overall, with a span of 500 ft. (150 m). Designed to carry the projected Cape to Cairo railroad, it was completed in 1905 as a railroad bridge, and was adapted to carry a road as well in 1930.

Zeppelin, Count Ferdinand von (1838-1917)

German AIRSHIP pioneer. A career soldier, he fought in the Civil War with the Union forces, where he saw balloons used for reconnaissance. He began designing airships in 1873, and after retiring from the German army in 1891 devoted himself to the work full time.

Zeppelin completed plans for his first airship in 1893. At first the idea was condemned as practically useless, but three years later the Association of German Engineers backed it, and construction of the craft, the LZ1, began. The airship was cigar-shaped, with an aluminum frame 420 ft. (128 m) long and 38 ft. (11.6 m) in diameter, covered with fabric. Lift was provided by rubberized tanks filled with hydrogen. The LZ1 made its first flight in July, 1900. It was wrecked soon after, when landing.

The success of the later model L23 in 1906 won government support for Zeppelin, and his factory began construction of airships on a large scale. During World War I a great many zeppelins were built for the German forces, and carried out air-raids on France and Britain. But the success of antiaircraft fire and fighter airplanes led Germany to abandon zeppelin construction shortly before Zeppelin himself died.

The Lockheed YF-12 A. Holder of the world air speed record (which excludes the rocket powered X-15) since 1965, it reached 2,070.10 mph (3,331.51 km/h).